AF887565

Fort Orange Records

1654–1679

New Netherland Documents Series

View of Fort Orange from Beverwijck's Rutten Kil bridge

Pencil sketch by L. F. Tantillo

Fort Orange Records

1654–1679

Translated and Edited by

CHARLES T. GEHRING

and

JANNY VENEMA

SYRACUSE UNIVERSITY PRESS

Copyright © 2009 by The Holland Society of New York

ALL RIGHTS RESERVED

First Edition, 2009

09 10 11 12 13 14   6 5 4 3 2 1

The paper used in this publication meets the minimum requirements of American National Standard for Information Sciences—Permanence of Paper for Printed Library Materials, ANSI Z 39.48–1984. ∞™

Produced with the support of The Holland Society of New York and the New Netherland Project of the New York State Library.

The preparation of this volume was made possible in part by a grant from the Division of Research Programs of the National Endowment for the Humanities, an independent federal agency.

For a listing of books published and distributed by Syracuse University Press, visit our Web site at SyracuseUniversityPress.syr.edu.

ISBN-13 978-0-8156-3232-0
ISBN-10 0-8156-3232-0

Library of Congress Cataloging-in-Publication Data

Fort Orange (N.Y.)
Fort Orange Records, 1654–1679 / translated and edited by Charles T. Gehring and Janny Venema.
p. cm. — (New Netherland documents series)
Includes index.
ISBN 978-0-8156-3232-0 (hardcover)
1. Albany (N.Y.)—Genealogy. 2. Court records—New York (State)—Albany. 3. Fort Albany (NY)—Registers. 4. Dutch Americans—New York (State)—History—Albany—Genealogy. I. Gehring, Charles T., 1939– II. Venema, Janny. III. Title.
F129.A353A254 2009
929'.34743—dc22

2008061119

MANUFACTURED IN THE UNITED STATES OF AMERICA

This volume is dedicated to

Peck Stacpoole Foundation

for its generous support of the publications
and programs of the New Netherland Project
and the New Netherland Institute

Charles T. Gehring was born in Fort Plain, an old Revolutionary War and Erie Canal village in New York State's Mohawk Valley. After completing his undergraduate and graduate studies at Virginia Military Institute and West Virginia University he continued with post-graduate work at Albert-Ludwigs-Universität in Freiburg, Germany. There he began his study of the Dutch language and first realized that his future research lay much closer to home. He eventually received a Ph.D. in Germanic Linguistics from Indiana University with a concentration in Netherlandic Studies. His dissertation (1973) was a linguistic investigation of the survival of the Dutch language in colonial New York. He is presently director of the New Netherland Project (sponsored by the New York State Library). The Project is responsible for translating the official records of the Dutch colony and promoting awareness of the Dutch role in American history. He has been a fellow of the Holland Society of New York since 1979. In 1994 Her Majesty Queen Beatrix of the Netherlands conferred on him the distinction of Officer in the Order of Orange-Nassau. In 1995 he received the gold medal of the Netherlands Society of Philadelphia. In 2004 he received gold medals from the Holland Society and the St. Nicholas Society of New York.

Janny Venema was born in Nijeveen (Dr.), the Netherlands. After her studies in Groningen she taught Dutch and history at a high school in Haarlem. She has worked in the New Netherland Project since 1985, when she moved to the USA. A short version of her master's thesis from the State University of New York at Albany was published in the Netherlands (Hilversum, 1993) under the title *Kinderen van weelde en armoede. Armoede en liefdadigheid in Beverwijck/Albany, c. 1650–1700*. She has also published two volumes of high school educational materials, a translation of deacons' account books of Albany's First Dutch Church, and various articles on New Netherland, Beverwijck, and Rensselaerswijck. In 2003 she received a Ph.D. from the Vrije Universiteit at Amsterdam, the Netherlands. Her dissertation, *Beverwijck. A Dutch Village on the American Frontier, 1652–1664* (Hilversum/Albany 2003), describes the founding of Albany, NY in 1652, and the city's development during the Dutch period. She became a fellow of the Holland Society of New York in 2005.

Committee on Publication

Ralph L. DeGroff Jr., Chairman
Trustee, Holland Society of New York

John B. VanDerbeek IV
Trustee, Holland Society of New York

Charles W. Wendell
President, New Netherland Institute
Trustee, Holland Society of NewYork

Charles T. Gehring
Director, New Netherland Project
New Yortk State Library

Janny Venema
Assistant Director, New Netherland Project

Martha Dickinson Shattuck
Editor, New Netherland Project

Contents

Acknowledgments

This volume differs from preceding translations in the series *New Netherland Documents*. It is the first time that Gehring and Venema have shared the work of translation. Thus there is graditude to Janny Venema this time not only for her transcriptions but also recognition of her new undertaking as translator. As usual we give special thanks to Martha Dickinson Shattuck for her meticulous editing of the manuscript and careful indexing of the subject index, containing a complex corpus of Dutch names.

Special thanks goes to the Holland Society of New York for its continued support of the translation and publication of records relating to our Dutch heritage; to the New York State Library for treating the New Netherland Project as one of its own programs and to the library staff for its highly professional assistance; to the New York State Archives for ready access to the manuscripts; to the Albany Hall of Records for its patience in allowing long-term access to the "big" and "little" books of Fort Orange records; to the New Netherland Institute for it tireless efforts in promoting the work of the Project and maintaining its financial stability; to the Division of Research Programs of the National Endowment for the Humanities [NEH] whose financial support over the years has given the necessary breath to the Project; to the Peck Stacpoole Foundation for its generous support of the Project's publications and the Institute's programs; to the staff of Syracuse University Press for its expert assitance in the final stages of production; and to all the other contributors both large and small who make it possible for the Project to meet its matching funds obligations with NEH.

Adriaen van der Donck's Map of New Netherland, 1656

Courtesy of the New York State Library; photo by Dietrich C. Gehring

Introduction

The records in this volume represent the next to the oldest surviving archival papers of the Dutch community that eventually became Albany, the capital of New York state. Although the Dutch presence in this area began with the explorations of the East India Company's ship the *Halve Maen* in 1609, local records were first maintained by the officials of the patroonship of Rensselaerswijck.* Surviving records for this quasi-private entity, surrounding the West India Company's trading post of Fort Orange, date from 1648 to 1652. However, the administration of the Company's interests in the area remained in the hands of the council on Manhattan for almost thirty years. Thus records concerning the Company's administration of affairs in this region are found among the minutes of the council on Manhattan or in the registers of the provincial secretary. Local WIC records first appeared in 1652 after the Company established the jurisdiction of Fort Orange and the village of Beverwijck.

Fort Orange/Beverwijck

On April 10, 1652 the West India Company's jurisdiction of Fort Orange/Beverwijck was formed along the banks of the upper Hudson. This act represented the resolution of a four-year dispute over local sovereignty between Petrus Stuyvesant, the director general of New Netherland, and Brant Aertsz van Slichtenhorst, the director of Rensselaerswijck, the patroonship founded by Kiliaen van Rensselaer. On this date Stuyvesant proclaimed a 3000-foot radius around the fort to be within the jurisdiction of the West India Company; an area which incorporated the *bijeenwooningh*, literally "living together," established and promoted by Van Slichtenhorst. No longer were Company

* A.J.F. van Laer (trans. and ed.), *Minutes of the Court of Rensselaersijck 1648–1652*, (Albany, 1922).

affairs on the upper Hudson administered from the council on Manhattan. Overnight a local government was established which not only rivaled the patroon's court in the area but also transformed a considerable number of the patroon's population into inhabitants of Beverwijck.

The new jurisdiction also included the Esopus and Catskill regions south of the patroonship until a court was established at Wiltwijck (Kingston) in 1660. After the English takeover in 1664, the jurisdiction of the court in Albany (formerly Fort Orange/Beverwijck) was expanded to include Rensselaerswijck, as well as Schenectady, which was approved for settlement toward the end of Stuyvesant's administration. During the Dutch restoration of 1673 the name of Albany was changed to Willemstad rather than reverting to the original Beverwijck, while the former Fort Orange, which had become Fort Albany during the English interim period of governors Nicolls and Lovelace, was renamed Fort Nassau. In 1674 New Netherland was returned to English rule as a result of the treaty of Westminster, which ended the third Anglo-Dutch war. During the administration of Governor Edmund Andros, Albany records continued to be kept in Dutch until Governor Dongan granted a charter to the municipality in 1686.

Local Government

The *kleine banck van justitie*, or inferior bench of justice, of Fort Orange/Beverwijck was established to function as the local governing body complete with executive, legislative, and judicial responsibilities. As a local jurisdiction it kept records of its proceedings for future reference. In addition to the minutes of the court, which included ordinary sessions held every Tuesday and frequent extraordinary sessions, records were also kept of various transactions and interactions of members of the community. Such records were cast in the form of a contract requiring the signatures of the parties involved and the attestation of an authorized official. Normally this official would be a notary; however, in the absence of a notary this function was performed by the local secretary. The majority of these records consist of real estate transactions, such as conveyances of property from one individual to another, conditions of sale, conditions of auction, surrenders of claims; they also include acknowledgements of debt, inventories of estates, warrants, powers of attorney, and pledges of security. Such documents carried authentic signatures and could be submitted as legal instruments in court proceedings.

Officials who appear as signatories in this volume are as follows:

Joannes Dijckman who served as vice director and commissary at Fort Orange from 10 April 1652 to June 1655;

Johan de Deckere who served as provisional vice director at Fort Orange from July 1655 to July 1656;

Johannes La Montagne who served as vice director and commissary at Fort Orange from 28 September 1656 to 24 October 1664;

Johannes Provoost who served as clerk under La Montagne, then as secretary of Albany, Colonie, and Rensselaerswijck during the English administration from 12 November 1664 to 8 August 1665;

Dirck van Schelluyne served as notary public in Beverwijck beginning in 1660 and town clerk of Albany from 10 September 1665 to August 9, 1668;

Ludovicus Cobus served as secretary from September 1668 to 24 October 1673, when Provoost was reinstated in the position until 11 August 1675;

Robert Livingston served as secretary of Albany from September 1675 to 1721.

Local Records

The present volume is the second part of the surviving records kept by the Albany municipal archives, known as the Hall of Records. As with other surviving Dutch records in other repositories, they are neither complete nor maintained in their original state. In contrast to the Dutch colonial manuscripts, damaged in the 1911 State Library fire, and now kept in the New York State Archives, they are physically in relatively perfect condition. However, over the years they were subjected to other abuses. Jonathan Pearson described the situation best in the preface to his translation of these same records: "The earliest registers were simply quires stitched together, which at a later date were gathered up by some one ignorant of the language, and bound and labeled regardless of dates or subjects."† Over the years these records were stored, ignored, moved, arranged, and rearranged until they finally were put together in bound

† Jonathan Pearson (trans. and ed.), *Early Records of the City and County of Albany, and Colony of Rensselaerswijck, 1656–1675*, (Albany, 1869). p. iii.

volumes to which labels were attached. As with humpty dumpty, we are no longer able to return them to their original state, but are now compelled to follow arrangements, which at times seem arbitrary or illogical. In some instances groups of documents were bound incorrectly in the 19th century. For example, there are several cases where documents, which end abruptly, have been reunited with their final pages. Unlike volume A this volume has suffered from a lack of attention to chronology when the separate quires and pages were bound.

The first two bound volumes are labeled Deeds A and B respectively. Volume A carries the date 1656–1678 on the lower spine; B is dated 1654–1680. This indicates that there was no overriding concern for chronological order; nor was there an apparent concern for proportion as Volume A contains 431 pages while Volume B weighs in at 869 pages, giving rise to the frequently quoted appelations of "little book" and "big book". The previously translated volume represents Volume A and is subtitled part 1. Volume B was originally planned to be published in two parts because of its size. However, it was decided to maintain the relative size of the bound originals in the published translations, obviating the need for two separate indexes.

Editorial Method

The same editorial principles were followed in this volume as in the Fort Orange Court Minutes and in Volume A. The layout or format of the entries have been adhered to as closely as possible. Proper names have been transcribed rather than translated in order to give researchers every possible onomastic configuration by which an individual or place was identified in its original form. Name variations and translations of Dutch occupations appear in the index and glossary. Damaged portions are indicated by empty brackets which approximate the amount of loss. Actual document page numbers appear in brackets to facilitate access to the original.

Fort Orange Records
1654–1679

[CONVEYANCE OF LOT FROM JAN LABATIE TO PAULUS SCHRICK]

[1] On this nineteenth day of August of the year of the birth of our Lord and Savior Jesus Christ sixteen hundred and fifty-four, in the forenoon, before me, Joannes Dijckman, in the service of the Chartered West India Company, commissary and vice director of Fort Orange, there appeared the honorable Jan Labatie, burgher in Beverwijck who declared that he has ceded, transferred and conveyed to the Hon. *Sr.* Paulo Schrick, merchant, his certain lot, located in the Manathans in New Amsterdam, located between skipper Willem Thomasz and Isaack de Forest, the patent of which is in the custody of the honorable Karel van Brugge; so that he may sell said lot, or cause it to be sold, conveyed and transferred by some other person; also, after the sale to issue a receipt or allow one to be issued, just as if he Labatie were himself in his own person present; to do all such things as pertain to this matter, to collect the purchase money or cause it to be collected demanded and received; also to keep the same together with the former sums; and these receipts and the whole amount which shall come from the sale of the lot shall be used to reduce all such sums of moneys as the aforesaid *Sr.* Paulo Schrick is to receive from said Labatie. In witness whereof this was signed with his own hand in Fort Orange on the aforesaid date.

Jan Labatie

Which I affirm was so executed,
Joannes Dijckman

[in the margin is written:]
Conveyed [ ] August 1654 [ ] April 1655.

[POWER OF ATTORNEY FROM PAULUS SCHRICK TO DOMINE GIDEON SCHAETS AND JAN VERBEECK]

[2] On this the twentieth day of August in the year of our Lord sixteen hundred and fifty-four in the forenoon, before me Joannes Dijckman, in the service of the Hon. Chartered West India Company, commissary

and vice director of Fort Orange, there appeared the honorable Paulus Schrick, merchant, who declared that he has appointed and empowered, as he hereby does appoint and empower, the revered Domine Gidion Schaets and the honorable Jan Verbeeck, magistrate of the court here, in his, the appearer's name and on his behalf, to demand, collect and receive all such sums of money as shall be coming to the aforesaid honorable *Sr.* Schrick upon closing of the accounts of Jan Labatie and He[ndrick] Jansz Westerkamp, for which they have mutually mortgaged their general possessions for the satisfaction of the aforesaid payment, and particularly Jan Labatie's house located in this fort, with the garden belonging thereto, which he, Labatie, will permit to be sold at the time promised, the aforesaid honorable attorneys in this matter taking good and needful care that everything is done which is necessary to be done for the collecting of the moneys, besides making a settlement thereof at the proper time; to do in like manner with the house of Hendrick Jansz Westerkamp, which was also mortgaged for this purpose, and he, appearer, has [ ] a bill of preference on the aforesaid house to have the same the aforesaid house [ ] appraised and as previously sold as satisfaction of the moneys due the appearer from him Westerkamp, promising further [ ] to recognize as good, fast and of value whatever these, his honor's attorneys, shall have done in this matter, provided they make a proper statement of the receipts as before *in forma*, all faithful and true. This signed by the appearer with his own hand [3] in Fort Orange on the aforesaid date in the presence of the honorable Johan de Hulter and *Mr.* Frans Barentsz Pastoor, magistrate of this court, who have signed this as witnesses, being requested hereto for that purpose.

Paulus Schreck
As witnesses,
Johan de Hulter
Frans Barentsen Pastoor
Which I attest,
Joannes Dijckman

I, the undersigned Jan Labatie, promise, in accordance with the above-written power of attorney, to allow my aforesaid house standing in the fort not only first to be appraised, but also in conformity with the aforesaid power of attorney, permit their honors, the substitutes, whenever it is proper and serviceable, to sell, collect, and pay such debts as I owe to *Sr.* Paulus Schrick, provided that after a settlement, what remains over, shall accrue to my benefit. Fort Orange this 20th of August 1654.

Jan Labatie

As Jan Labatie has promised the above written, so also will I, the undersigned, attempt to fulfill the same. Dated as above.

This is the mark of Femmetje  Albertsz in the name of and on behalf of Hendrick Jansz Wester[kamp].

[EXCHANGE OF LOTS BETWEEN WIJNANT GERRITSZ AND ADRIAEN DIRRICKSZ DE VRIES]

[4] On this 21st day of August, 1654, before me, Joannes Dijckman, in the service of the honorable Chartered West India Company, commissary and vice director of Fort Orange, there appeared the honorable Wijnant Gerritsz *kistemaker*, who declared that he has agreed with Adrian Dirricksz de Vries on a certain exchange of their lots, provided that Wijnant Gerritsz, at his own cost, shall take down the shed erected on the lot of the aforesaid Adriaen Dirricksz and move it to his lot, and providing moreover that Adriaen Dirricksz shall receive, and be paid him by Wijnant Gerritsz, four beavers, so that from that time on or at the first opportunity mutual possession shall be had of the aforesaid lots; both parties renouncing completely claim to the others lot, under a pledge of their persons and estates, real and personal, present and future, and further in accordance with the law; and as acknowledgment of the truth, without deceit or guile, the parties sign this with their own hands in Fort Orange, on the aforesaid date.

Wijnant Gerreyts vd Poel
This is the mark of Adriaen  Dirrcksz de Vries,
placed with his own hand.
To which I attest,
Joannes Dijckman

[POWER OF ATTORNEY FROM GYSBERT PHILIPSZ VELTHUYSEN TO PAULUS CORNELISSE VAN APKOUW][*]

[7] On this the twenty-third of August of the year of the birth of our Lord and Savior Jesus Christ 1654, before me, Joannes Dijckman, in the service of the honorable Chartered West India Company, commissary and vice director of Fort Orange, there appeared the honorable Gysbert Philipsz Velthuysen who declared that he has appointed and empowered, as by these presents he does, the honorable Paulus Cornelisse or Schrick van Apkouw,[†] who proposes to depart from this country on the first ship to *patria*, in order in the name of his constituent and on his behalf to collect, demand and receive there in the homeland, coming in Holland, all such sums of moneys as due to the constituent from Cornelis Pietersz, his father–in–law living at Velthuysen, with the aforesaid person to settle, liquidate and balance accounts and to receive the money of the aforesaid constituent upon settlement of the accounts with receipts thereof, and further to execute and do all things therein as if the constituent in his own person were present; indeed, also to do all those things that the matter demands in particular. Thus done without deceit or guile in Fort Orange in the presence of *Mr*. Jacob de Heynsse, *chirurgijn*, and Claes Hendricksz *timmerman*, called and invited as witnesses hereto, and who have also hereby signed.

This is my own hand
Gysbert Phillipsen
As witnesses
De Hinsse
Claes Hendrijckse
To which I attest,
Joannes Dijckman

* Manuscript pages 5 & 6 have been moved to follow Doc. 94; which is where they correctly belong.

† Abcoude (current spelling) is in the province of Utrecht.

[TERMS OF SALE OF GOODS OFFERED BY ROELOFF JANSZ AND LAMMERT CORNELISZ]

[8] Roeloff Jansz and Lammert Cornelisz propose to sell the following itemized goods on these conditions, namely: That the payment for the purchased goods shall be made only in good whole beavers, which payment shall be made within the space of two times twenty-four hours without one hour more delay.

In addition, the sellers offer everything without security for repairs regardless of what the cause may be.

Paulus Martensen *Waerde* for Meus *de Raemaker*, a strong ax and a plane	*f*7:10
Three dishes to Claes Bordingh	*f*2:–
Cornelis Teunise, some finishing planes	*f*2:–
Claes Hendricksen, some chisels	*f1:16*
Meus *de Rademaker*, some chisels	*f*2:9
Gillis Douwesz Fonda, an auger	*f*3:4
Jan Labatie, some augers	*f*4:–
Jan Labatie, some planes	*f*1:–
Gerart Swart, an adze and an auger	*f*4:–
Hendrick Jochems, an ax and an adze	*f*2:14
Claes Hendricksen, some chisels	*f*2:12
The same, some chisels	*f*2:11
Gerart Swart, some chisels	*f*2:10
Claes Bordingh, a pruning knife	*f*4:2
Claes Hendricksen, a hammer	*f*3:11
Claes Hendericksen, an auger	*f*2:11
Jacob Jansz Flodder, a saw	*f*5:12
Claes Jansz van Rotterdam, chisels	*f*1:11
Abraham *Croaet*, a hammer	*f*1:14
Pieter Bronck, some chisels	*f*2: 6:–
Claes Bordingh, some chisels	*f*2:14
Claes Hendricksen, some junk	*f*3:10
	f 63:–

[9] Gillis Douwesz Fonda, some augers	*f*4:12
Jan Roeloff, a set of chisels	*f*5:3

Jacob Jansz Flodder, a chest	*f*2:5
Diirick Bensinck [ ] a chest	*f*3:–
Abraham Crawaat, trousers	*f*4:15
Daniel Rinckhout, a gun	*f*16:10
Hendrick Jochemsz, a gun	*f*21:10
Abraham Crawaat, a sword	*f*13:–
Jacob Jansz Flodder, a barrel of tobacco	*f*6:2
	*f*63:7:–
paid	*f*140:4:-

Lammert Cornelisz, his goods, dated the 23rd of August

Stoffel Jansz, 2 augers	*f*8:9
Claes Hendricksz, 2 slicks	*f*12:4
Claes Hendricksen, some planes	*f*4:18
Jacob Jansz Flodder, some planes	*f*7:–
Claes Hendricksz, some planes	*f*3:5
Claes Bordingh, some planes	*f*2:14
Jan Roeloffsz, some planes	*f*4:9
Jacob Jansz Flodder, some junk	*f*3:–
Claes Hendrickz, some chisels	*f*3:7
Claes Hendricksz, some chisels	*f*3:15
Jacob Jansz Flodder, some carpenter's squares	*f*5:–
Jan Roeloffs, some junk	*f*1:13
Jacob Jansz Flodder, adzes	*f*3:1
Claes Hendricksen, a chest	*f*9:–
Cornelis Theunisz, a garment	*f*38:–
Casper Jacobsz, ax and auger	*f*6:7
Abraham *Crawaet*, some junk	*f*2:10
Juriaen Theunisz, a waistcoat	*f*8:–
Claes Hendricksz, a coat	*f*36:–
Gisbert Gysen, 2 pair stockings	*f*10:10
Jacob Jansz Flodder, some calico	*f*3:10
Cees [?] Houtewael, a hand C	*f*11:5
Harmen *de metselaer*, 2 oars	*f*8:–
Andries Herbertsz, a gun	*f*14:–
Jan Gouw, some knives	*f*12:10
Jan Dijckman, a chest	*f*7: 5:–
	*f*219:12:–

[10] from the other side	*f*219:12:–
Abraham *Crawaet*, a garment	*f*9:–
Jacob Jansz Flodder, a coat	*f*8:–
Jan Roeloffs, some junk	*f*00:12:–
	*f*237: 4:–

Jan Gouw, a gun, an ax, would like cash	*f*181:–

Jan Gouw and Harmen Jansz want to sell a certain case, inlaid with ebony and other woods, on the following conditions, namely: that the payment shall be made in whole, good beavers, which payment shall be made within twice twenty-four hours, without one hour longer delay. Jacob Jansz Flodder became buyer for thirty-two beavers, less two guilders.

In addition, the sellers offer everything without security for repairs regardless of what the cause may be.

Jacob Janssen Flodder

Claes Hendri[cksz] together	93:5:–

[11] Cond[ ] goods or Jacob Thys[sen]
At Jacob Thysz's:

Skipper Frederick, a suit of clothes	*f*24:–
Jan Machielz, a waistcoat	*f*14:6
Jan Dijckman, some stockings	*f*7:10
Claes Hendricksen, some skates	*f*4:5
Andries Herpertsz, some buttons	*f*7:5
Cornelis Theunisz, some bands and ribbon	*f*9:–
Abraham *Crawaet*, for silk	*f*16:–
At Jacob Thysen's, Wijnant Gerritsen, a rope	*f*7:5
Jan Labatie, some cord	*f*12:–
At Jacob [ ] Jacob [ ] some [ ]	*f*16:
Cornelis Theunis, a chest	*f*6:5
Jan Roelofsen, a gun	*f*18:–
Wijnant Gerritse, a coat	*f*17:10
Jacob Jansz Flodder a [ ]	*f*5:1[ ]
At Schermerhoorn's, Willem Jansz Schut, a coat	*f*39:–

paid Jan Roelofs, a sword	*f* 12:–
	f 218:7:–

Harmen *de metselaer*	
Jan Macielsz, a coat	*f*29:–
and Harmen auctioned an andiron	*f* 13:10
Casper Jacobsz, a *snickling* (?)	*f*23:10:–
Some stockings auctioned	*f*21:–
Jacob Theunisz [ ] hat	f12:–
Auctioned a gun	*f*22:10:–
Auctioned [ ]	*f*64:10:–

NB [ ] received and paid as far as [ ]
Machiel *de lamaker*, a suit of clothes paid *f*21:–

Jacob Jansz Flodder	*f*250:–
Claes Hendricksen	*f*275:
Jacob Jansz Flodder	*f*324:-
[ ] the wardrobe auctioned 27 beavers	

[12] [ ] was auctioned a coat	*f*76:–
Claes vanden Hogenbergh, a coat auctioned	*f*22:–
Claes vanden Hogen Bergh sold some clothing and a [ ]	
Willem Janse Schut	*f*25:16:–
a gun, Jan Roeloffse	*f*12:–
paid the 30th of August	*f*37:16:–

[PURCHASE AGREEMENT FOR A HOUSE AND LOT OF FRANCOIS BOON BY JACOB HENDRIXSE MAAT]

[13] On this the twenty-fourth of August sixteen hundred fifty-four in the forenoon, before me Joannes Dijckman, in the service of the honorable Chartered West India Company commissary and vice director of Fort Orange, there appeared the honorable *Sr.* Francois Boon, husband and guardian of Elysabeth Cornelisdr., formerly widow of the late Gisbert Cornelisz, assisted by the honorable Jacob Jansz

Schermerhoren, appointed and chosen guardian of the children left by the aforesaid late Gisbert Cornelisz, and declared that they were well and truly satisfied by Steven Jansz in regard to the purchase of the house bought by him at public auction in the name of Jacob Hendrixse Maat on the [*left blank*] of this month; upon the first payment or installment there shall be a complete delivery of the aforesaid purchased house and lot and on payment of the last installment, they promise to deliver a proper conveyance thereof *in forma*. In acknowledgment of the truth of which he has signed this with his own hand in the presence of the honorable Anthonius de Hooges, and the honorable Jan Verbeeck, magistrate of this honorable court, asked and invited as witnesses hereto, who have co-signed this next to the appearers.

Franscoos Boon
As witnesses:
Antonius de Hooges
Jan Veerbeeck
Which I acknowledge,
Joannes Dijckman

[FARMING OUT OF THE BEER AND WINE EXCISE]

[14] The farming out of the beer and wine excise from now to the coming May of the current date of this within this jurisdiction. Their Honors of the court hereby propose at public sale to farm out to the highest bidder the general and mandated tappers' wine and beer excise, on the following conditions, to wit:

First this farming shall commence and have its beginning on the date hereof.

Payment shall be made on this farming in three installments or payments, the first installment being a third part, shall be paid punctually within the time of two months; the second installment, being also a third part, two months thereafter;

the third installment precisely upon the termination of the farming; provided that the farmer shall be obligated, from the first hour on, to furnish sufficient security to the satisfaction of this court.

And in case he cannot furnish security, the farming shall again be offered at public sale, at his cost and charge.

The payments shall be made in good current sewant, provided that the wine and beer given in up to this day not be included in this farming, the excise thereon already having been paid.

Those of the court further promise proper support to the farmer.

[15] Jacob van Loosdreght became the farmer on the aforementioned conditions for the sum of thirteen hundred guilders.

Jacob Hijndricksz Maat*

We stand as sureties upon the above-stated conditions and in case the principal does not pay, we ourselves will satisfy it in his stead.

Lambert Cornelissen
Claes Jacobse van Rotterdam

Which I acknowledge,
Joannes Dijckman

I the undersigned Steven Jansz offer myself as surety and principal for the person of Lambert Cornelissen, who on the 25th of this [month] stood surety for the farming let out to Jacob Hendrixsz Maat, who has been discharged thereon, and upon the above written conditions, I pledge myself, according to law. Fort Orange this 2nd of September 1654.

* Note that his full name is Jacob Hendricksen Maat van Loosdreght.

[CONDITIONS OF SALE OF VARIOUS GOODS]

[16] Claes Hendricksen desires to sell on the following conditions an inlaid oak cabinet on the following conditions by order of Jacob Jansz Flodder, to wit: that the buyer shall be obligated to make payment tomorrow punctually in good whole beavers. In case he fails to pay or furnish surety, it shall be immediately reauctioned at his cost and charges. The cabinet was bought on the above-stated conditions by the undersigned final bidder for the sum of twenty-two beavers and ten guilders in beavers.

Philip Pieterse
I, the undersigned, stood as surety,
Jan Thomasz

Claes Hendricksen desires to sell on the above-stated conditions some timbers, bought by him yesterday at the house of the Hon. *Hr*. Bronck. *Hr*. Pieter Hartgerts became buyer for the sum of three hundred, one guilders.

Pieter Hartgerts

I acknowledge that I have stood surety for the above-written person.
Frans Barentsen Pastoor

Jacob Jansz Schermerhoren also desires to sell on the above-stated conditions an inlaid ebony and oak cabinet. The above named cabinet was bought by the undersigned final bidder for the sum of eighteen and a half beavers.

Cornelus Thonissen
As surety, Hendrick Jochemsz

[INSTRUCTIONS FOR THE FARMER OF THE WINE AND BEER EXCISE]

[17] Instructions for the farmer Jacob Hendricxsz Maat who yesterday won the bid for the [ ] and tappers' wine and beer excise so that he may regulate himself therein in all faithfulness. First, Jacob Hendricksz, or those whom he shall commission, shall have power to visit the tapsters' cellars, to gauge the wine and beer, and note the gauging accordingly, as is fitting a public officer. The gauging being registered, he may from that time begin the duties of his office. If he finds that anyone has concealed beer or wine, he shall notify the officer thereof, who in such case shall be obligated and pledge himself to offer him a helping hand, whether by night or day.

The fines for smuggling shall be for him, provided that the officer receive a third part thereof. In like manner with those who sell brandy to the Indians, in case they shall be apprehended and convicted.

If any sloop or yacht come up here from Manathans, the manifest shall be immediately examined, and an account taken of the wine and beer which comes up, and he shall address himself to the custom house officer, who receives the permit, and he shall immediately do this and make it known to him, and make a faithful and proper inspection of the sloops, as it is warranted, this 26th of August 1654.

[CONDITIONS FOR THE SALE OF THE HOUSE AND LOT OF ABRAHAM STAETS]

[**18**] *Mr.* Abraham Staets wants to sell at this public auction his house [and] lot standing and located in Fort Orange, bordering to the south the exit out from the gate of the fort, and to the north, the corner of said fort, together with a garden, bounded to the south by the garden of *Mr.* Adriaen Ilpendam, to the north Rem Jansz *smit*, to the east *Heer* Rensselaer, and to the west a common way, all according to the situation and placement of the aforesaid house and garden, upon the following conditions, to wit: that the payment shall be made in whole, good beavers in three installments, the first installment being a just third part within the space of one month from the date of this, precisely, without any exceptions [*word crossed out*]; within which time the aforesaid house and garden shall be able occupied by the buyer on the aforesaid conditions. The second installment within one year from now; and the third and final installment the year thereafter or precisely within two

years; for which payments the buyer shall be obligated according to the terms of auction to furnish sufficient surety to the satisfaction of the seller. Auction fees will be charged to the buyer alone; and in case the winning bidder and buyer as aforesaid is not immediately able to furnish sufficient surety, then the aforesaid house shall be reauctioned at that winning bidder's charges and costs **[19]** and whatever less is comes to be worth, he shall make up the difference and pay himself. Done this 27th of October. As buyer on the announced conditions remained Joannes van Twiller for the sum of twenty-three hundred and twenty-five guilders on the aforesaid date.

J. V. Twiller

I offer myself as aforesaid as surety for Joannes van Twiller for the purchase of the aforesaid house.

J.B. van Rensselaer
Philip Pietersen

[CONDITIONS FOR THE SALE OF THE FARM OF WILLEM BEECKMAN]

[20] *Mr.* Willem Beekman proposes on this date the 27th of August 1654 to sell a certain farm located at the Manathans named the pantile maker's farm, as it presently lies joining on the farm of the honorable lord General Stuyvesant with a dwelling house and barn among others and also a dwelling house standing thereon previously used as a brewery upon the following conditions:

First, the seller shall therewith deliver two cows and two draft oxen. The payment therefor shall be made in three installments or payments, to wit: the first payment, being a just third part, within one month from now; the second payment six months thereafter and the third and last payment six months after that. Payment shall be made in whole, good beavers. The buyer shall have to pay the auction fees. Moreover the winning bidder shall be immediately obligated to furnish sufficient surety to the satisfaction of the seller; and in case not [in case he is not able to do so] it shall be reauctioned at his own charges and costs of the winning bidder. The buyer or buyers hereof let it be known that one can easily produce brick there. [*This sale was not completed*]

[ACKNOWLEDGMENT OF PAYMENT OF DEBT BY JACOB JANSZ FLODDER]

[**21**] On this the twenty-eighth day of August 1654 before me Joannes Dijckman, in the service of the Hon. Chartered West India Company commisary and vice director of Fort Orange, there appeared the honorable Jacob Jansz Flodder and declared before him that he was paid, also completely satisfied, the sum of eighteen beavers and forty-eight guilders in sewant paid to Cornelis Houtewael for Jacob Flodder, which Eldert Gerbertsz had advanced and loaned him, within the space of six weeks to be repaid to him, Eldert Gerritsz [*sic*], by him, Jacob Jansz Flodder, and as long as it has not yet been repaid, the sloop of Jacob Janse Flodder shall remain specially mortgaged without the said yacht neither being sold nor transferred before and until the said eighteen beavers are settled and restored again to Elbert Gerbertsz. Further pledging his person, to wit, Jacob Flodder's, and estate, personal and real, present and future, nothing excepted; also acknowledging that he has accepted Claes Hendricksz van Utreght *timmerman*, [and] Ellert Gerbertsz as partners in the hire of the saw mills of Jacob Jansz Flodder, on the conditions made in this regard by him, Claes Hendricksz, with Jacob Flodder, upon mutual pledge of person and estates and further as according to law. In acknowledgment of the truth, they have subscribed with their own hands, in Fort Orange on the aforesaid date, in the presence of the hon. Jan Thomasz and Pieter Hertgers magistrates of the hon. court here, called as witnesses hereto.

Jacob Jansen Flodder
Claes Hendrijcksen
as witnesses
Jan Thomasz
Pieter Hartgers
To which I attest,
Joannes Dijckman

[ACKNOWLEDGMENT OF PAYMENT OF DEBT
BY PHILIP PIETERSZ SCHUILER]

[22] I the undersigned Juriaen Thysz van Amsterdam acknowledge that I have well and truly received from the Hon. Philip Pietersz Schuiler the sum of twenty-five hundred, sixty-two and a half guilders, to be paid by me or on my behalf in Holland in good, current cash money precisely six weeks after the presenting of this to Mayndert Andryesz, pork buyer or Jacob Jansz Schermerhoren, now ready to depart thither; this growing out of the receipt of well-used goods; promising to make the aforesaid payment punctually, upon pledge of my person and estate, personal and real, present and future, submitting them to the force of all laws and judges. In witness whereof, without craft or guile, two similar instruments have been signed, the one being paid, the other of no value; in Fort Orange the twenty-ninth of August 1654.

Juryan Teyssen

In my presence,
Joannes Dijckman

[POWER OF ATTORNEY FROM JACOB JANSZ SCHERMERHOREN TO
PIETER HERTGERTS AND VOLCKERT JANSZ]

[23] On this the thirtieth of August, sixteen hundred fifty-four, before me Joannes Dijckman, in the service of the Hon. Chartered West India Comp. commissary and vice director of Fort Orange, the afternamed witnesses present, there appeared the Hon. Jacob Jansz Schermerhoren ordinary magistrate of this court here, waiting for his departure for *patria*, and declared that he has appointed and empowered, as he does by these presents, the Hon. Pieter Hertgerts and Volckert Jansz, in his name and on his behalf to act during his absence in Holland, or so long as he may be away, with all the appearer's estate, both houses, gardens and other goods as well as with the merchandise which he is expecting according to letters from his Hon. father in Holland received with the most recently arrived ships, just as if the appearer were present in his own person, indeed, even as if it were herein stipulated and required as a special charge; all to be held good and trustworthy, provided these attorneys upon the appearer's return shall render a proper settlement and report *in forma* of their acts. In acknowledgment of the truth of which, he has with his own hand signed this, in Fort Orange in New Netherland in the presence of *Hr* Francois Boon and Claes Henrixsen van Wtrecht, asked and called as witnesses hereto, and who to that end have also co-signed this paper.

Jacob Schermerhooren
As witnesses,
Franscoos Boon
Claes Hendrijcksen
To which I attest,
Joannes Dijckman

[POWER OF ATTORNEY OF FRANCOIS BOON TO PIETER HERTGERTS AND VOLCKERT JANSZ]

[24] On this the thirtieth of August 1654, before me Joannes Dijckman, in the service of the honorable. Chartered West India Company, commissary and vice director of Fort Orange, there appeared the honorable. *Sr.* Francois Boon, awaiting departure for *patria*, declaring that he has appointed and empowered the honorable. Pieter Hertgerts and Volckert Jansz, in his, the appearer's name and on his behalf to be sent on to his father in *patria,* to demand, collect and receive all lawful obligations, claims, and payments on his sold house; further also to dispose of his goods, expected by the ships from *patria* [and] of the expected ships; provided that on request and demand of the appearer, these attorneys shall be obligated upon his return or demand to render a proper account and statement thereof and generally of all his estate remaining here in this country. In acknowledgment of the truth, of which he has with his own hand signed this in Fort Orange, on the aforesaid date, in the presence of Jan Thomasz and Claes Hendricksz van Wtreght, called and invited as witnesses hereto, who have co-signed this instrument with the appearer.

Franscoos Boon
As witnesses:
Jan Thomasz
Claes Hendrijcksen
To which I attest,
Joannes Dijckman

[ACKNOWLEDGMENT OF DEBT OF JURIAEN THIJSZ TO JAN THOMASZ AND VOLCKERT JANSZ]

[25] I, the undersigned Juriaen Thijsz van Amsterdam, acknowledge and affirm that I am well and truly indebted to, and that I have received here in New Netherland from the honorable Jan Thomasz and Volckert Jansz, the sum of four thousand guilders, to be paid by me or my heirs on my behalf in Holland, in good, current cash money, six weeks after sight or presentation of this there to Jacob Jansz Schermerhoren, standing ready to depart this place, or to his honorable father living in Amsterdam; this debt and payment growing out of good pelts acquired here, promising to make said payment punctually provided that in case I do not, at the appointed and said time, make said payment as is fit and proper, whereby the aforesaid friends would be greatly injured, inasmuch as they have ordered invoices of goods to be bought and the ships generally depart from *patria* to here but once a year, whereby they would be deprived of much interest and the goods for a whole year, to their considerable detriment, I will be bound promptly to make good all such losses and interest, which may arise from delay of payment, and to pay the interest as it is reckoned in this country; all upon pledge of my person and estate, personal and real, present and future, submitting the same to the authority of all courts and judges. In witness whereof, without craft or guile, are made hereof two similar [instruments], the one being paid, the other of no value at Fort Orange in New Netherland this thirty-first of August, sixteen hundred, fifty-four.

Juryan Teyssen
In my presence,
Joannes Dijckman

[POWER OF ATTORNEY OF JAN THOMASZ AND VOLCKERT JANSZ]

[26] On this the thirty-first day of August of the year from the birth of our Lord and Savior Jesus Christ sixteen hundred fifty-four, before me Joannes Dijckman, in the service of the honorable. chartered West India Company, commissary and vice director of Fort Orange, there appeared the honorable Jan Thomasz and Volckert Jansz who declared that they have appointed and empowered, as they hereby do, the honorable Jacob Jansz Schermerhoren, standing ready to depart from here to Holland, or his honorable father living at Amsterdam, in their, the appearers' stead and on their behalf, to demand, collect and receive from Juriaen Thijsz van Amsterdam all such four thousand guilders, which he has received here from the appearers in pelts and therefor is indebted, and according to a signed bill of exchange is to pay upon his arrival in Holland, six weeks after presentation of the same; also to advance the same moneys in order to purchase merchandise for it and to bring the same with [him] or to send it to them at the first opportunity; and in addition to make a proper accounting of the receipts and expenditures and in case the aforesaid Jurian Thijsz should come to default at the precise time of the said payments, they may proceed legally and through these means constrain him to payment and further do everything as if the appearers were themselves there present in their own persons, or if a more particular task were hereby expressly demanded. All justly and in good faith, they sign this with their own hands at Fort Orange on the aforesaid date in the presence of Jacob Steendam and Jacob Tyssen van der Heyden, called as witnesses hereto, who with the principals have hereby co-signed this.

Yan Thomasz
Volckart Jans
As witnesses:
Jacob Steendam
Jacob Teyssen vander Heyden
To which I attest,
Joannes Dijckman

[POWER OF ATTORNEY OF JAN LABATIE]

[27] Being stationed at Fort Orange, located here in New Netherland, Roelant Saverye, in the service of the Hon. Chartered West India Company in the aforesaid fort and during that time boarded ten months at my house, amounting to two hundred guilders, which sum he has accepted upon his pledge at his departure from here to pay upon his return from the Manathans but afterwards having departed to *patria* and has not paid. Therefore, he remains indebted to me for the aforesaid debt. In order to recover said sum, I, Jan Labatie, citizen and inhabitant of New Netherland, to whom the aforesaid moneys are due, have thought it necessary to appoint and empower the honorable Theunis Jansz *seyllemaker* to demand, collect and, receive the aforesaid moneys from the friends and heirs of the aforesaid Rolant Saverij, now deceased; also, in case of refusal to pay according to law; also, further to issue quittance of the receipts and moreover to do all things therein as if the appearer Jan Labatie were there present in his own person, or as if it a special order were hereby expressly demanded. To which end, we, the undersigned Rem Jansen *smit* and Lammert van Valckenborgh, citizens and residents of Fort Orange and Beverwijck, testify that during the aforementioned and said time, the aforesaid Roland Saverij boarded at the house of the aforesaid Jan Labatie or was there as a boarder. All in good faith and without craft or guile, this was signed with my own hand in Fort Orange the 31st of August sixteen hundred fifty-four.

Jan Labatie
As witnesses:
Rem Yansen
the mark + of Lambert van Valckenburgh,
signed with his own hand.
To which I attest,
Joannes Dijckman

[ACKNOWLEDGMENT OF DEBT OF CLAES CORNELISZ TO POULUS CORNELISZ]

[28] I, the undersigned Claes Cornelisz, acknowledge and declare that I am well and truly indebted to Poulus Cornelisz, standing ready to depart

for *patria*, in the sum and number of six beavers, this debt arising from goods and merchandise delivered here in this country, which aforesaid six beavers I promise to pay to the aforesaid Poulis Cornelisz in the coming year after his safe return or if he does not return, this debt shall be null and void. In this regard, I pledge my person and estate, personal and real, present and future, submitting myself to the authority of all courts and judges; in acknowledgment of the truth hereof, two instruments of the same content have been signed, the one having been paid, the other will be of no value, in Fort Orange this first of September 1654.

The mark placed by Claes  Cornelisz
with his own hand.
To which I attest,
Joannes Dijckman

[ORDER TO FARM OUT THE TAPPER'S EXCISE]

[**29**] Their honors of the court of Fort Orange and Beverwijck, having found by experience that their honors' well-intentioned placards and orders, both now and then published and posted at the usual places as appropriate, are not followed and observed; therefore, among other things, the citizens and tappers shall have to get proper permits from the receiver Pieter Rijverding, who by not doing so and not following the aforesaid orders, smuggling has multiplied. Their honors of the court have resolved to farm out the tappers wine and beer excise in this jurisdiction. As the same was also farmed out at public auction on the 25th, Jacob Hendricksz Maat has both remained and become the farmer, who promised the honorable court a proper execution of his office during the time of the farming. Therefore, their honors of the court hereby expressly prohibit and forbid the aforenamed Jacob Hendricksz Maat, his collector, or those he has employed thereto, in words much less in deed to revile, slander and defame and in this his office to place any impediments thereto, upon penalty whoever has done such things shall be punished as the matter demands. And in order to be better able to prevent smuggling, all citizens and residents of this jurisdiction, without regard to person, may not receive and transport any strong

beers, wines or distilled waters, and unload them from incoming ships, before they shall have previously requested and obtained proper permit from the farmer or his collector, who to this end shall hold both before and **[30]** after noon to their set time, in order to provide the community with proper and requested permits; and shall make known the time and place through permits, but the citizenry shall have to pay no excise, except two stuivers for each certificate, upon pain that whoever shall have had any beers and wines delivered in a contrary manner as without having gotten the permit and knowledge of the farmer and to have cellared the same, shall have them confiscated without any contradiction and over and above this forfeit, a sum of three guilders. All brewers living in this jurisdiction are charged that no strong beer is to be permitted to the citizens or tappers, before and unless a permit from the farmer or his collector is presented to them, upon the penalty thereto attached; and further, all boatmen coming from the Manathans are not permitted to unload anything before and unless their passes have been presented and they are properly inspected by the officer here. And also those moneys which shall result from the farming shall be employed solely in the service of the community. And every order cargo is to be regulated hereby precisely and strictly according to the contents of this instrument. Thus done by this honorable court here in Fort Orange the first of September and reconsidered on this the second of September 1654; present the commissary and officer,

Joannes Dijckman
Jan Verbeeck
Jan Thomas
Pieter Hargers
Frans Barentsen Pastoor

[BILL OF SALE OF A HOUSE FROM GOOSEN GERRITSEN TO MARCELIS JANSZ]

[31] On this the second of September of the year from the birth of our Lord and Savior Jesus Christ sixteen hundred fifty-four before me, Joannes Dijckman, in the service of the Hon. Chartered West India

Company Commissary and vice director of Fort Orange, there appeared the honorable Goosen Gerritsen, citizen and resident in the village of Beverwijck and acknowledged that he has contracted and agreed with Marcelis Jansz, also burgher and resident as above, in a certain sale of his house, where presently Goosen Gerritse is living, in order to place said house on his certain lot at the hill, adjacent Pieter Bronck to the north and Jan Roeloffsz to the south; which house he, Goosen Gerritsen, shall be obligated, at his own costs, to break down as well as to set up again, as good and bad as it presently stands on the aforesaid lot, and in case anything happens to be broken in pieces, Goosen Gerritse is obligated to repair it; including glass, side aisle, interior structure, and chimney; and furthermore, just as the aforesaid house is standing there as aforesaid, except what pertains to the cellar, which the buyer Marcelis Jansz shall have to furnish, if he wants to make one there; provided that the buyer also shall be owner of said lot, having obtained a patent thereof, when the house shall be erected upon it. As well as that the house, which there may be erected before or on the first of coming May shall be also complete and finished, according to contract, without fault, in order to be able to move in and live. For which house being erected there on the said lot the buyer Marcelis Jansz shall have to pay the sum of twelve hundred guilders, to be paid in three installments, namely, the first of this coming May upon moving in and taking possession the sum of four hundred guilders; the following year on the first of May four hundred guilders; and [32] the year thereafter on the first of May a like sum of four hundred guilders; to be paid in good current sewant or other current merchandise such as the seller can and ought to be satisfied with, and the other shall be able to pay; provided that the buyer shall have to provide sufficient surety for the aforesaid payments, whereof the seller shall also be satisfied, all upon pledge of their respective persons and estates, personal and real, present and future, submitting themselves to the authority of all courts and judges, in acknowledgment of the truth of this signed with his own hand at the house of the buyer in Beverwijck on the aforesaid date.

Maercelys Jansen
This is the mark 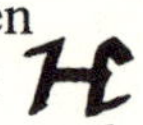 of Goosen Gerritsen,
placed with his own hand.

We, the undersigned Frans Barentsz Pastoor and Arent Andrijsz, acknowledge and declare, as we hereby do that we have offered ourselves as sureties and principals, individually or severally for the purchase money in the stated sum of twelve hundred guilders and in case the buyer shall come to be in default on the set times to make the payments, we or one of us for both will take his place and precisely on the set and promised time pay for the buyer himself, upon pledge of our persons and estates, personal and real, present and future, further as according to law, without craft or guile. Signed on the date and in the place aforesaid with our own hands without craft or guile.

Frans Barentsen Pastoor
Arent Andres
To which I attest,
Joannes Dijckman

[SALE OF RUT ARENTSZ'S HOUSE AND LOT AT AUCTION]

[33] The administrators of the estate of the late Rut Arentsz *kleermaker* propose to sell at public auction to the highest bidder a certain house and lot standing and located at the Manathans behind Fort New Amsterdam, adjacent Hendrick *de Backer* on the east side and Annetge Bogardus on the west side, all being according to the patent thereof, on the following conditions, namely: that the buyer shall have to make the payments in two installments, the first installment, being one half, shall be paid in cash precisely within one month; and the second installment, being the last half, shall be paid six months thereafter, also punctually, which payment shall be made in whole, good beavers, provided that the auction fees shall be charged to the buyer alone. The buyer shall be obligated, shortly after the auction, to provide sufficient surety to the satisfaction of the sellers; and, in case no sufficient sureties are furnished immediately, it shall be immediately re-auctioned at the buyer's own charges and costs. It is further stipulated that the sellers do this without wanting to give any rebate or restitution no matter whatever reason there may be. Willem Fredericksz remained buyer on the aforewritten conditions for the sum of six hundred and twelve guilders

on this 3rd of September 1654. [*In the margin was written*:] 6 pieces of eight drawn.

The mark  placed by Willem Fredricksz
with his own hand.
To which I attest,
Joannes Dijckman

We, the undersigned, offer ourselves as sureties and principals for Willem Fredericksz, according to law.

The mark of  Gysbert [ ],
placed with his own hand.

The mark of  Dirrick Bensinck,
with his own hand.

[SALE OF JACOB JANSZ VAN NORTSTRANT'S
HOUSE AT PUBLIC AUCTION]

[34] Jacob Jansz van Nortstrant intends to sell at public auction his house located in Beverwijck, adjacent Hendrick Gerritsz to the west and the poor house to the east, together with the lot belonging thereto, besides a garden located behind Fort Orange, No. 19, adjacent Domine Schaets to the south and Gisbert Cornelisz to the east, or those who may have the deed thereto; to the west and to the north a road; six and a half rods long, four and a half rods wide, all being according to patent thereof, upon the following conditions, namely: that payment for this house, lot and garden shall be made in two installments or payments, the first payment being half, in cash, within the time of one month precisely, and the second and last payment precisely on the first of this coming May, which payments shall be made in whole, good beavers. Auction fees shall be charged to the buyer alone. In addition the current garden produce which grew there in this year shall remain for the seller alone. The seller further stipulates that he does not want to give any rebate or restitution for whatever reason there should be. In this sale the mill and brewer's tools presently in the aforesaid house are not included. In addition the buyer shall be obligated to furnish sufficient surety to the satisfaction of the seller, and if he cannot, then the lot shall be re-auctioned at his expense. **[35]** The buyer was Rutger Jacobsz upon the preceding conditions for the sum of eight hundred thirty guilders, on this the 3rd of September 1654.

Rutger Jacobsz

We present ourselves as surety for the above standing person and sale, all according to law, this 3rd of September 1654.

Jan Verbeeck
The mark  placed by Goosen Gerritsen with his own hand.

To which I attest,
Joannes Dijckman
The [ ] 32 stivers.

[BILL OF SALE OF LOT OF SIJMON VOLCKERTSZ *BACKER* TO ALBERT GERRITSEN *TIMMERMAN*]

[36] On this the fourth of September sixteen hundred fifty-four in the morning, before me Joannes Dijckman, in the service of the honorable Chartered West India Company, commissary and vice director of Fort Orange, there appeared the honorable Symon Volckertsz *backer,* dwelling in Beverwijck, and acknowledged not only that he had sold to Albert Gerritsen *timmerman* a certain lot located at Manathans next to Adriaen Vincent; width on the west side three rods and one foot, length on the south side five rods and 6 ½ feet, and on the north side five rods, all according to the patent, but also he Symon acknowledged that he has received the sum of thirty beavers for it, being the full sum which he [Albert Gerritsen] had promised to pay for the aforesaid lot. He, Symon Volkertsz herewith giving a perfect conveyance of the aforesaid lot, without his having any action, right or claim on it now, or ever or forever, but putting the aforesaid Albert Gerritsen *timmerman,* in this regard in place of himself, with all such rights as he, the seller and grantor, therein has had, being as aforesaid fully paid for it. In acknowledgment of the truth of which he has signed this instrument with his own hand in Fort Orange, on the aforesaid date, in the presence of Thomas Sanders and Jan van Aecken *smits,* called as witnesses hereto, who have also signed this with the grantor.

The mark placed by Symon Volckertsen,
with his own hand.

Aelbert Gerretsen

As witnesses:
The mark placed by Thomas Sanders
with his own hand.

The mark of Jan van Aecken,
placed with his own hand.
To which I attest,
Joannes Dijckman.

[CONVEYANCE OF HOUSE AND LOT OF THOMAS SANDERSEN TO JAN VAN AECKEN]

[37] On this the fourth of September of the year following the birth of our Lord and Savior Jesus Christ sixteen hundred fifty-four, in the morning, before me Joannes Dijckman in the service of the honorable chartered West India Company commissary and vice director of Fort Orange, there appeared the honorable Thomas Sandersen *smit* who declared that he had sold to Jan van Aecken his certain house and lot standing and located in the village of Beverwijck, adjacent Carsten and Mijndert Fredericksz to the north, and to the south, east and west a road, together with a garden located behind Fort Orange, No. 22 by lottery; width four and a half rods, length seven and a half rods, with the appendages and dependencies thereof; and he, Thomas Sandersz, declares that he is fully satisfied and paid for it, the first penny with the last, giving for it a perfect release for the same from now until all time, without him, Thomas Sandersz, having any longer right or claim to the aforesaid house, lot and garden, and putting in this regard the aforesaid Jan van

Aecken in place of himself in every manner that he Thomas Sandertsen had had therein. Signed in acknowledgment of the truth of this with his own hand in Fort Orange, on the aforesaid date, without craft or guile, in the presence of *Sr.* Joannes van Twiller and Albert Gerritsen *timmerman,* called and requested as witnesses hereto, who have co-signed this together with the grantor.

The mark placed  by Thomas Sandersen
with his own hand.

The mark of  Jan van Aecken,
placed with his own hand.
As witnesses:
J. V. Twiller
Albert Gerretsen
To which I attest,
Joannes Dijckman.

[BILL OF SALE OF HOUSE AND LOT PURCHASED BY ALBERT GERRITSZ]

[38] On this the fourth of September of the year after the birth of our Lord and Savior Jesus Christ sixteen hundred fifty-four, in the morning, before me Joannes Dijckman, in the service of the honorable. chartered West India Company commissary and vice director of Fort Orange, there appeared the honorable Albert Gerritsz *timmerman* who declared that he is well satisfied and paid for a certain forty-five foot lot (namely, board feet), its width in front on the road, running back to the fence sold to him; in addition to the house standing thereon, adjacent Carsten and Mijndert Fredericksz to the south and the seller to the north; for which house and lot, so located and standing, he, Albert Gerritsz, acknowledges that he is fully satisfied and paid, from the first penny to the last, he, Albert Gerritsz, giving for it a perfect release, from now for all time, without his making any claim, demand or pretension to the same, in this regard putting the aforesaid Jan van Aecken thus in place of himself and in every right and ownership, which he the seller and grantor has had therein, promising to free the buyer on this account and to keep it free for a year and a day, as one is bound to do in such a case. In acknowledgment of the truth of this, without craft or guile, signed by the grantor, signed with his own hand, in the presence of the honorable Jan Verbeeck and *Sr.* Joannes van Twiller, called and invited as witnesses hereto, who have also signed this with the grantor.

Albert Gerretsen
The mark placed by Jan van  Aecken
with his own hand.
As witnesses:
Jan Verbeeck
J. V. Twiller
To which I attest,
Joannes Dijckman.

[BILL OF SALE OF HOUSE AND LOT SOLD BY WILLEM JANSZ STOLL TO ARENT VAN DEN BERGH]

[39] On this the fifth of September of the year after the birth of our Lord and Savior Jesus Christ sixteen hundred fifty-four, before me Joannes Dijckman, in the service of the honorable chartered West India Company, commissary and vice director of Fort Orange, there appeared the honorable Willem Jansz Stoll who declared that he was well satisfied and has received from the hands of Arent van den Bergh the sum of five hundred and fifty guilders, being half of the payment for the house, lot and garden located in the fort and behind the same, sold by him Stoll on the 8th of last August at public auction at the house of Hendrick Jochemsz for the sum of eleven hundred guilders, being the house adjacent Hendrick Driesz to the east and Jacob Jansz Stoll to the south and the garden adjacent *Mr.* Abraham Staats's garden to the north and Hendrick Driesz to the south; all according to the conditions of sale; he, Willem Jansz Stoll, giving for it a complete release to the aforesaid buyer for the aforesaid house, lot, and garden, promising upon and with the payment of the last half, to be paid in the month of this coming May precisely, to deliver to the buyer a conveyance of the aforesaid house, lot and garden, as is proper, upon pledge of his person and estate, personal and real, present and future, submitting himself to the authority of all courts and judges, witnessing this with his own hand; signed in Fort Orange, on the date aforesaid, in the presence of Jacob Hendricksz Maat and Lambert van Valckenburgh, called and invited as witnesses hereto.

Willem Jansz Stol
The mark placed by Arent vanden X Bergh

As witnesses:
The mark place by Lambert + van Valckenburgh
Jacob Heyndricksz Maat
To which I attest,
Joannes Dijckman

[POWER OF ATTORNEY OF WILLEM ALBERTSEN VAN MONNICKENDAM]

[40] On this the fifth of September 1654, before me Joannes Dijckman in the service of the honorable chartered West India Company, commissary and vice director of Fort Orange, there appeared Willem Albertsen van Monnickendam who declared that he has appointed and empowered, as he hereby does, the honorable Claes Bordingh, departing for the Manathans, in his, the subscriber's name, and on his behalf, to demand, collect, and receive, first of all such thirty guilders and thirteen stuivers which are owed the subscriber from the aforesaid Terhaer, for funds turned over in sewant, for which the aforesaid Terhaer should have been attached here, however was passed without attachment and also those thirty-six guilders which he, the aforesaid subscriber, is owed by Jan van Leyden, dwelling in Mespachs kil, for delivery of boards, in lieu of which goats were to be delivered, all of which, except for four, he has slaughtered for himself, and the payment which Claes Bording shall endeavor to collect for payment of none of which the subscriber is indebted to Claes Bording; and in case of refusal of the one or the other to pay by law and to act for the subscriber as if he were present in his own person, also to give quittance for the receipts, all without craft or guile; these presents signed with his own hand in Fort

Orange, this aforesaid date, in the presence of Sebastian de Winter and Arent vanden Bergh, called and invited as witnesses hereto.

The mark placed by
Arent  vanden Berg with his own hand.
Willem Albersen
As witnesses:
Basteiaen de Winter
To which I attest,
Joannes Dijckman

[SALE OF GOODS OF GABRIEL LEENDERTSEN
AT PUBLIC AUCTION]

[41] The 5th of September 1654, Gabriel Leendertsen wishes to sell to the highest bidder the goods presented, being specified below, upon the following conditions; namely: that the bidders and buyers shall be obligated to make payment within 24 hours precisely, without delay, so that the seller may depart. The bidders are obligated to furnish sufficient sureties to the satisfaction of the seller. Payments shall be made in whole, good or half beavers, to the greatest extent and the rest in merchantable sewant, and is discounted at...

12 earthenware plates, *dolle* Griet	*f*4:15:
2 platters and six plates, *Mr*. Adriaen	*f*4: 5:
5 pair stockings, *Mr*. Jacob *Barbier*	*f*12:
1 skimmer and a candlestick, Jan Thomasz	*f*6:15
6 pair stockings, *dolle* Griet	*f*26: 5
1 scale and a weight, Goosen Gerritsen	*f*9:
A parcel of cord, Cornelis van Steenwijck the ell, one white	*f*[:]
1 gun, sword and belt, Goosen Gerritse	*f*26:
7 paintings, Jan van Aecken	*f*9:
1 Bible, Cornelis Thunisz	*f*14:
5 bands, Daniel Rinckhout	*f*2:15
1 traveling coat, Barent de Molenaer	*f*f21:
1 book *The Treasury of Health*, *Mr*. Jacob *Barbier*	*f* 8:

2 shirts, carpenter's work bench	*ff* 5:15
1 gun, Daniel Rinckhout	*f*19:10:
4 small drinking pots, Cornelis Thunisz	*f*3: 10
some knives, Volckert Jansz	*f*20: 10
1 cloak, auctioned off in beavers	*f*58:
Carried forward	*f*193:

[42]

6 pewter plates, a sugar bowl and a small drinking pot, Jurriaen Theunisz	*f*10:
10 earthenware plates, Barent *de Molenaer*	*f*3:10
4 bowls, the wife of Abraham Verplanck	*f*4:
1 gun, Barent *de Molenaer*	*f*17:
6 plates of [ ], Michiel *de Laemaker*	*f*2:10
6 pair stockings, Barent *de Molenaer*	*f*18: 10
2 scales and a weight, Willem Bout	*f*12:15
6 weights, Jochem *Backer*	*f*7:
1pair stockings and a bible, Andrys Herpertsen	*f*12:
2 rugs and a carpenter's bench	*f*13:
1 book *Festus Homnius*, Philip Pietersz Scheuler	*f*6:
1 club and balls, Pieter Hartgers Lammert who lives there	*f*6:
a parcel of tobacco, Volckert Jansz	*f*10:
a parcel of snuffers, *dolle* Griet	*f*2:7
3 books, Philip Pietersz	*f*16:
2 planes, Do. Schaets	*f*6:
1 tongs, shovel and chain, Claes Bordingh	*f*9:
1 book, Andryes Herpertsen	*f*5:
1 saw bench, pail, and other junk, Carsten Fredericksz	*f*5:5
2 books, Cornelis Steenwijck	*f*5:
1 book, Jurriaen Theunisz	*f*4:8
1 trunk, Herman de Metselaer	*f*3:5
1 pair of shoes, and slippers and a pair of stockings and a powder flask, Barent de Molenaer	*f*6:15
1 chair and two cushions, Andryes Herpertsen	*f*8:4
	*f*386:9

[POWER OF ATTORNEY OF SYMEN SYMONTSZ GROOT TO ISAACK DE FOREEST]

[43] On this the 9th of August of the year after the birth of our Lord and Savior Jesus Christ 1654, before me Joannes Dijckman, in the service of the honorable chartered West India Company, commissary and vice director of Fort Orange, there appeared the honorable Symen Symontsz Groot who declared that he has appointed and empowered, as he hereby does, *Sr.* Isaack de Foreest, his brother-in-law, living at the Manathans, to sell, convey or verify, as his judgment approves, a certain account, amounting to the sum of 684 guilders earned in the service of the West India Company, and put into the hands of said De Foreest for safe keeping, and also to act in the matter to the best of his, the attorney's judgment, all lawful and without craft or guile, signed by the principal with his own hand on the aforesaid date in the presence of Sebastiaen de Winter and *Mr.* Joannes Megapolensis *chirurghijn*,* called and invited as witnesses hereto, who have also signed this with the appearers.

Symen Symensen de Groot
As witnesses,
Bastiaen de Winter
Mr. Jan Megapolensis

Which I witness,
Joannes Dijckman

[COMPLAINT OF DE VRYES AGAINST SEEGER CORNELISZ AND SCHEELIGHE HERMAN]

[44] De Vryes complains of Seeger Cornelisz on the island and *Scheelighe* Herman for attacking him before his door and before the entire house and complains about the harm they did him in the presence of Jelis Pietersz and the neighbors thereabout.

* Johannes Megapolensis *chirughijn* [barber-surgeon] is the son of Domine Johannes Megapolensis.

[POWER OF ATTORNEY OF RUTGER JACOBSZ *ET AL.*]

On this the 10th of September 1654, before me Joannes Dijckman, in the service of the honorable. chartered West India Company, commissary and vice director of this Fort Orange, there appeared the honorable. Rutger Jacobsz, Cornelis Theunisz van Westbroeck and Goosen Gerritsen, burghers and residents of the village of Beverwijck, who declared that they together had shipped on board the sloop of Cornelis Vos, two chests of beavers containing seven hundred pieces No. 1 and 2; Skipper Reynick No. 1, 200 pieces, No. 2, 500 pieces, to be transshipped with the ships now departing to Holland; if they are not able to be present there, to give hereby to the person of Gerrit Jansz van Swoll, departing down there to the Manathans, full power and authority both to receive said chests as well as to do otherwise, as best he can and judges and as if the principals themselves were present in person. In acknowledgment of the truth of these, signed with their own hands in Fort Orange on the aforesaid date, in the presence of Jochem *Becker Backer* and *Mr.* Joannes Megapolensis *chirurghijn*, called and invited as witnesses hereto.

Rutger Jacobsz
Cornelis Thonisen
The mark placed  by Goosen Gerritsen with his own hand.

As witnesses,
Jochum Backer
Mr. Joannes Megapolensis

Which I witness,
Joannes Dijckman

[LETTER OF RECOMMENDATION FOR COMMISSARY DIJCKMAN AND PIETER HERTGERTS]

[45] Worshipful, valiant, and most noble lord and right honorable gentlemen, Lord General and right honorable gentlemen of the council. In due time the welcomed letter of the right honorable lord general,

dated the 29th of past June, was duly received by us, in which he was pleased to write to us that we, according to our request formerly made in writing to your honors, on or before the arrival of the ships from *patria,* that we dispatch two from our court to make a more detailed request to your honors. Therefore, not being able to omit the execution of your honors' gracious instructions, we have chosen and sent to your honors from among this court, the honorable commissary Joannes Dijckman and Pieter Hertgerts to present to your honors such matters as we have committed unto the same. Our request is that your honors please accept and recognize them as our deputies, also to listen favorably and speedily to come to such resolutions as we trust their honors' wise discretion and judgment may approve. Meanwhile we commit and commend your honors to God's gracious protection and remain, worshipful, valiant and most noble lord and right honorable gentlemen. Your honors humble and faithful servants of the court of Fort Orange and Beverwijck Fort Orange the 11th of September 1654.

[INSTRUCTIONS FOR THE DEPUTIES SENT TO MANHATTAN]

[46] Instructions for the honorable deputation to the Manathans departing on commission according to a letter of the honorable Lord General dated the 29th of last June to Commissary Dijckman and Pieter Hertgerts, appointed by the honorable court of Fort Orange and Beverwijck, so that they may be able to regulate themselves accordingly. First that they shall, with all reverence, solicit of the right honorable lord general and their honors of the high council of this land their honors' resolutions and answer to the propositions both oral as well as written, heretofore made by the aforesaid honorable court, in order that they may hereby be able to regulate themselves. That the said deputation shall also petition for the speedy completion of the new Company house at the Company's expense. Whereas on account of the scarcity of funds and the small income from the excise, which never was resolved to remain for the benefit of the community; that some soldiers may be sent up both to keep watch by night in the fort and because of the insolence of the Indians, who have been plaguing the good community daily; also, that the expense of any guard for this purpose must be paid for in beavers by the court. Moreover for which support it is requested that two stuivers be levied on each beaver coming down from above, as well as for payment of the salaries of the magistrates of this court and also of the commissary; provided that the payers be able to validate such payments and might deduct them in payments of the recognition. They are also to petition for a quantity of gunpowder for the use of this fort, of which this court and the magistrates shall have the supervision, provided [47] that on request made, a proper, though not specific, account be rendered of the same, so that any private person in the future entrusted for cause [ ] that the customary tappers' and beer excise have been necessary to [ ] and that so little [ ] of the daily expenses came into the treasury; and also that places for new lots might be approved in order to give them out because there is trouble daily about lots and there are no more left over. That the necessary instructions for this court, as far as possible, are to be sought (and) may be amplified and further that they, the honorable deputation, whatever might befall them there, to the service of this court and community, here at Fort Orange, this 12th of September 1654. It being deemed necessary that the court messenger, Pieter Ryverding, shall be allotted a reasonable and proper salary and be paid therefrom, their honors of the court here find that notwithstanding [48] the guard and well-conceived order previously made public and posted respecting the citizens as well as the tappers, before being allowed to store their delivered beers and wines, shall have to obtain a proper permit from the import master or farmer of the excises upon punishment assigned thereto, as it can happen that these guards do not properly obey. Thus it is, in order better to prevent all smuggling in the future, all citizens living in this jurisdiction are ordered to store no heavy beers, wines, or distilled spirits, or to allow them to be brought and placed where they are used to place their drinks, upon pain of fifty guilders fine and order the citizenry to regulate themselves in this regard, yet in case someone receives any beers and wines after the office of the impost master might have closed for the evening, such shall be duly reported within twenty-four hours to the impost master for the aforesaid fine. Thus done and ordered by the court of this Fort Orange and Beverwijck, this 12th of September 1654.

[DECLARATION OF JAN THOMASZ AND REYNTGEN PIETERS]

[49] On this, the seventeenth of October sixteen hundred fifty-four, in the morning about nine o'clock, before me Joannes Dijckman, in the service of the honorable Chartered West India Company, commissary and vice director of Fort Orange, there appeared the honorable Jan Thomasz, ordinary magistrate of the honorable court here, and Reyntgen Pieters *Barcquier,* and together declared, as they hereby do declare, at the request of Adriaen Claesz, freeman, how truthful it is that last Wednesday towards evening they were in the house of Abraham Pietersz Vosburgh; and that in the aforesaid person's house there were found and were present among others Jacob Symontsen Clomp *Barcquier* and the aforesaid Ariaen Claesz; which Ariaen Claesz was sent out by the aforesaid Jacob Clomp to fetch a canoe, which lay on the opposite side of the river; which he, Ariaen Claesz, did and, returning with the canoe and having fallen into the water, he Ariaen Claesz came back into the house of Abraham Pietersz Vosburgh [and] he, Ariaen Claesz, had taken his knife in hand to cut loose the lace from one shoe, (and) laying down the knife by his side and having some words with Jacob Clomp respecting Ariaen Claesz's earned wages, Jacob Clomp springing up with the knife in his hand, cut Ariaen Claesz several gashes both in the face as well as on the arm, without these deponents observing that Ariaen Claesz had wanted to place himself to defend against the aforesaid person with the knife nor to fight against him; the deponents ending this their declaration with presentation of need and being asked to confirm the same by oath. Signed by the deponents with their own hands in Fort Orange on the aforesaid date.

Jan Thomas

The mark placed by  Reyntgen Pieters,
with his own hand.

To which I attest,
Joannes Dijckman.

[PLEDGE OF JOCHEM WESSELS]

[50] On this date, the twenty-first of October 1654, I, Jochem *Becker Backer,* citizen in Beverwijck, have offered myself, as I hereby do, as surety and principal for the person of Jacob Sijmonse Clomp *Barcqier,* on account of one hundred seven guilders, which he, Jacob Sijmontsen Clomp, must pay to the commissary and officer within the time of six weeks, according to the tenor of the contract made there between the mutual arbitrators on the 17th of this month, and in case he, Jacob Clomp, fails within said time to pay said sum to said officer, I will immediately take his place and pay the same as my own debt, upon pledge of my person and estate, personal and real, present and future, nothing excepted, without cunning or guile. Signed with my own hand at Fort Orange on the aforesaid date. Jochum Wessels

[POWER OF ATTORNEY OF FRANS BARENTSZ PASTOOR]

[51] On this the twenty-first of October, sixteen hundred fifty-four, before me Joannes Dijckman, in the service of the honorable chartered West India Company, commissary and vice director of Fort Orange, there appeared the honorable. Frans Barentsz Pastoor, magistrate of the honorable court here, and declared that he has appointed and empowered, as he hereby does, the honorable Pieter Cornelisz, living on Long Island at Breuckelen, in his name and on his behalf to demand, collect, and receive all those seventy-six guilders and sixteen stuivers, which Lodewijck Cornelisz, dwelling at Manathans, owes according to a certain obligation of the 28th of August sixteen hundred fifty-one, of which said Lodewijck Cornelisz is indebted to the subscriber both for money lent as well as for duffels, and in case of refusal and longer delay to take the same to court, and proceed accordingly to recover the same, and also to act as may be necessary; and further to do all things therein, as if the constituant in his own person were present, indeed, as though special charge were herein given. In acknowledgment of this, signed with his own hand in Fort Orange on the aforesaid date in the presence of the honorable Jan Verbeeck and Jan Thomasz magistrates of the honorable court here, called and invited as witnesses hereto, who have co-signed the minutes of this case with the principals.

Frans Barentse Pastoor

As witnesses,
Jan Verbeeck
Jan Thomasz

To which I attest,
Joannes Dijckman.

[SURETY OF JACOB HENDRICXS MAAT AND ELDERT GERBERTSEN]

[52] We, the undersigned, Jacob Hendricxs Maat and Eldert Gerbertsen, acknowledge by these our signatures that we have offered ourselves as sureties and principals for Cors Boutsen, presently confined for some offences and are always ready to deliver up again the person of said Cors Boutsen, or to make compensation as for our own indebtedness, all under pledge of our persons and estates, real and personal, present and future, according to law. In acknowledgment of the truth, this is signed with our own hands in Fort Orange this 21st of October 1654.

Jacob Heyndricksz Maet
Ellert Gerbertsz Cruyff

The honorable *Heer* Rensselaer to [ ] concerning the [ ] of Jan Martensen

[CONTRACT OF GOVERT LOKERMANS WITH SAWMILL WORKER ELDERT GERBERTSEN]

[53] In the manner following, the honorable Govert Lokermans, merchant at Manhatans, and Eldert Gerbertsen, sawmill worker, have agreed and contracted, namely: that Eldert Gerbertsen shall be obligated to send all that he shall be able to saw to aforesaid Govert Lokermans, except for what he sells at the mills, to be sold by the same at Manhatans for the profit of Eldert Gerbertse, as best he can; which contract shall begin tomorrow being Monday the twenty-fifth of this month, and continue first one year, but in case, after that, they can come to an agreement, it shall continue from year to year; and for the pains that Govert Lokermans shall have therewith, both with the receipt as well as with the sale, shall he, Lokermans, enjoy five percent of the proceeds over and above all expenses. In acknowledgment of the truth of this, signed with his own hand in the presence of *Monsr*. Joannes van Twiller and Hendrick Jansz, called and invited as witnesses hereto, who have signed this minute with the principals in Fort Orange, this 24th of October 1654.

Govert Loockermans
Ellert Gerbertsz Cruyff

As witnesses,
J.V. Twiller
Hend. J. vande Vin

To which I attest,
Joannes Dijckman.

[REQUEST FOR A SPECIAL ORDER CONCERNING THE WINE AND BEER EXCISE]

[54] Worshipful, valiant and most noble Lord General.
The commissary Dijckman has advised us that he has made known to your honor that we, for a short period, namely: until the first of this coming May, had farmed out the customary tappers' beer and wine excise for the sum of thirteen hundred guilders; it is now such that the aforesaid commissary, being at Catskill, the *Heer* Rensselaer wished to have some wine delivered to those who live in the colony [Rensselaerswijck], without even directing a warrant from the impost master be fetched; also, without directing any impost to be paid. Therefore, we have permitted once again, indeed, for the third time, for though we had a general order, yet there is no special instructions that if wine and strong beer are carried from here out of this jurisdiction into the colony, the excise should be paid, as well as by those who dwell

within it, for reasons previously made known to your honor. It is our request, therefore, that your honor be pleased at the first opportunity to grant us a special order that henceforth, for wine and beer carried out of this jurisdiction, the customs officer issue his permit and seek to prevent evasions of payments. We shall await your honor's speedy order herein; and whether the *Heer* Rensselaer living in this jurisdiction [Beverwijck] having stored some wines may carry some to the colony or someone else may carry some wines or strong beers into the colony before a proper permit from the impost officer is obtained.

Monsr. Johannes van Twiller has remonstrated to us that he had spoken to your honors for permission to have an exit and a cellar door made; **[55]** we refer the matter to your honor; we think, however, that it could be better and more properly done within the fort, still we await the answer which your honor shall be pleased to send. We request, if it please your honor to send an answer and written instructions to the propositions written by the commissary, and according to orders given to your honor, so that we may know how to regulate ourselves. We shall ever remain your honor's true and humble servants of the court of Fort Orange and Beverwijck. Fort Orange this 4th of November 1654.

[CONVEYANCE OF A HOUSE FROM JAN LABATIE TO ADRIAEN JANSZ VAN LEYDEN]

[56] Today the ninth of November 1654 appeared before me, Joannes Dijckman, in the service of the honorable West India Company, commissary and vice director of Fort Orange, the honorable Jan Labatie who declared to have sold, as he hereby does, to Adriaen Jansz van Leyden a certain house standing in Fort Orange, bounded on the south by the south bastion of the aforesaid fort and on the north by the gate of the same, together with a garden located south of the aforesaid fort, bounded on the west by Lambert van Valckenburgh and on the south side by Pieter Jacobsz. [*The following is an exact copy; both of which were canceled and not executed.*]

[CONVEYANCE OF A HOUSE FROM JAN LABATIE TO ADRIAEN JANSZ VAN LEYDEN]

[57] On this the eleventh day of November 1654 in the forenoon appeared before me, Joannes Dijckman, in the service of the honorable chartered West India Company, commissary and vice director of Fort Orange, the honorable Jan Labatie, who declared that he had sold, as he hereby does sell to Adriaen Janse van Leyden, his certain house, standing in Fort Orange, bounden on the south by the south point of said fort and on the north by the gate of the same; with a garden and hog pen included therein, lying to the south of said fort, bounded on the west by Lambert van Valckenborgh, and on the south side by Pieter Jacobsz and on the north by a road, and on the east by the honorable Company's garden; by all appearances the aforesaid house stands constructed there, and the said garden and hog pen, to be delivered free, according to the patent thereof, for which the buyer, Adriaen Jansz van Leyden, must pay for said house, garden, hog pen and appurtenances of the same, the sum of eighteen hundred and twenty-five guilders to the honorable Domine Gideon Schaets and the honorable Jan Verbeeck, as attorneys for *Sr.* Paulus Schrick, in three installments; the first payment, being six hundred guilders, shall be paid on the first of May 1655 in beavers; the second payment, on the first of May 1656, being also six hundred guilders in beavers; and the third and last payment shall be paid on the first of May 1657, being six hundred and twenty-five guilders, in good current sewant; provided that the buyer shall remain in the occupancy thereof until May and during the time of said occupancy and lease, shall pay nothing to the seller; **[58]** for the full payment he shall furnish as sureties *Mr.* Anthonius de Hooges and Pieter Ryverdingh, who, with their signatures, bind themselves, that in case the buyer aforesaid fail to make payment on the set time or times, they will at once step into his place, and themselves the purchase money assume to pay for the buyer, under a pledge of their persons and estates, personal and real, and moreover submitting the same to the force of all laws and judges. In acknowledgment of the same, aforesaid sureties have subscribed these presents with their own hands, with the consent of the honorable attorneys of *Sr.* Paulus Schrick aforesaid; and the seller shall be obligated to warrant and defend aforesaid house, lot, garden and hog pen for a year and a day and in like manner is bound and indebted; all in good faith and without craft and guile. Signed by the buyer, seller, attorneys and sureties in Fort Orange, on the date aforesaid. Jan Labatie Adriaen Jansz van Leyden as attorneys of,

Paulus Schrick
Gideon Schaets, pastor in
Rensselaerswijck
Jan Verbeeck

As sureties:
Antonius de Hooges
Pieter Ryverdinck

Hereby I attest the truth thereof,
Joannes Dijckman.

[*Marginal note*:] The attorneys hereby annul the aforesaid sale and the sureties of the same are discharged; in witness whereof this is subscribed by the attorneys in Fort Orange, this 23nd of April *anno 1655.* Gideon Schaets, pastor in Rensselaerswijck, Jan Verbeeck

[REQUEST TO STUYVESANT FOR GUIDANCE]

[59] Worshipful, valiant and most noble, Lord General.
Our honorable fellow member, Pieter Hertgerts, having come up, has informed us that the papers and resolutions were delivered to your honor, and by word of mouth and by writings has shown the resolutions you directed to be sent up. In all kindness we petition that your honor be pleased to send up speedily, the sooner the better, advice for the regulating of our affairs. How desolate is our condition from the late high water the departing persons will be able to report to your honor verbally. Nevertheless, we cannot refrain from writing that the four points of the fort collapsed because of the great flood or were partly carried away; in addition, scarcely a clapboard remains in the honorable Company's garden; and the damage suffered by the bridges, of which we shall contract to have the one over the Third Kil repaired today. We request that your honor be pleased to advise us concerning means to rebuild the fort among other things. Anticipating expedition thereof, we

commend your honor and family to God's protection and remain your honor's humble and faithful servants of the court of Fort Orange and Beverwijck.

Lord General, your honor's willing and loyal [servants] of the court of Fort Orange and Beverwijck.

[BILL OF SALE OF HOUSE AND LOT OF CLAES HENDRICKSZ VAN WTRECHT TO HENDRICK ANDRYESZ VAN DOESBURG]

[60] On this 16th day of November 1654, appeared before me Joannes Dijckman in the service of chartered West India Company, commissary and vice director of Fort Orange, the honorable Claes Hendricksz van Wtrecht and declared that he had sold to Hendrick Andryesz van Doesburgh his certain house standing in Manathans and the lot thereto belonging, lying on the broad or public road as he the aforesaid Claes Hendricksz bought the same from Jan Peeck, resident of Manathans, which aforesaid house adjoins on the north Evert Pels and on the south Jan *de Metselaer*; by all appearances, the aforesaid house and lot with all appurtenances thereto is located there [*not completed*].

[CONTRACT OF ABRAHAM STAETS WITH BARENT GERRITSZ]

[61] On this 20th day of November, 1654 appeared before me Johannes Dijckman in the service of the honorable chartered West India Company, commissary and vice director of Fort Orange, the honorable Abraham Staets, who declared that he had hired Barent Gerritsz, which Barent Gerritsz himself acknowledges to serve for the time of a whole year commencing on the 7th of October last, and continuing until the 7th of October next, on the conditions that he, Barent Gerritsz, on his honor's land, or wherever he shall have need of him, shall do all the farm labor, during the aforesaid time, upon his bouwery, except the sowing of that portion that cannot be sown, for which service he, Barent Gerritsz, shall receive within the year aforesaid, three hundred and thirty guilders, two hundred in beavers and the rest in current sewant; Barent Gerritsz has also requested in the agreement free washing of two pairs of stockings, and a pair of shoes, upon which conditions the honorable Abraham Staets aforesaid has paid one beaver as a pledge; and for the performance of this contract, they pledge their respective persons and estates, personal and real, present and future, and in acknowledgment of the truth, with their own hands subscribe the same, in the presence of Adriaen Jansz van Leyden and Gillis Douwesse Fonda, as witnesses hereto called and invited who, with the officer aforesaid, and the principals, have also subscribed the same on the date aforesaid in Fort Orange.

Abram Staes
This is the mark set  by Barent Gerritse,
with his own hand.
As witnesses,
Adrian Janse v. Leyden
Jelles Vonda
To which I attest,
Johannes Dijckman.

[CONTRACT OF ANDRYES HERPERTSEN WITH CLAES HENDRICKSE *TIMMERMAN* AND CLAES JANSE VAN ROTTERDAM TO BUILD A HOUSE]

[62] On this 27th of November 1654 appeared before me Joannes Dijckman, in the service of the honorable chartered West India Company, commissary and vice director of Fort Orange, the honorable Andryes Herpertsen who declared that he had contracted and agreed as follows that Claes Hendrixs *timmerman* and Claes Janse van Rotterdam shall for him, Andryes Herpertsen, make, frame and set up a house in Beverwijck upon a lot to be pointed out as great in length and breadth and as good and bad as the house by him at present occupied, for which the contractors shall furnish all the materials in all respects like those in his, the subscriber's house in Beverwijck built structurally of wood both inside and out, nothing excepted; provided also that said house shall be framed and set up by the first of May next, for which when done the contractors shall receive and the subscriber Andryes Herpertsen, shall pay the sum of 1800 guilders in whole beavers. In acknowledgment of the truth of which the parties have subscribed this with their own hands, in presence of Rutger Jacopsen and Hendrick Jochemse, as witnesses hereto called, who also have subscribed this agreement with the contractors.

Andryes Herbertse
Claes Hendrycksen
Claes Jacobse
As witnesses:
Rutger Jacobse
Hendrick Jochemsen

In my presence,
Johannes Dijckman.

[CONTRACT OF JAN LABATIE WITH LABORER EVERT BRANTSE]

[63] Herewith Evert Brantse, soldier, and Jan Labatie agree with each other that the former shall be obliged to labor as a farmer for a whole year, commencing from this date, for which service he shall receive the sum of two hundred guilders, and moreover he promises Jan Labatie, inasmuch as the commissary should need him to apprehend criminals, that he shall be obliged to remain three days to haul wood for the commissary. Fort Orange the 29th of November 1654.

Jan Labatie
The mark set by Evert Brantse  van Amersfoort

To which I attest,
Joannes Dijckman

ACKNOWLEDGMENT OF DEBT OF GIJSBERT EVERTSE]

[64] On this the first day of December 1654 appeared before me, Joannes Dijckman, in the service of the honorable chartered West India Company, commissary and vice director of Fort Orange, the honorable Roeloff Jacopse, as husband and guardian of Griet Jacopsz, which appearers declared to have received a letter from Holland from Gijsbert Evertse, guardian, which the appearer [ ] to the subscriber that his wife or [for] him on her behalf at Bunschoten under Rijck Aelten dwelling there, promising that the money shall be paid and disbursed to *Mr*. Lambert Willemse Munick and Pieter Munick, inhabitants and advocates of the subscribers, who have declared themselves obligated [ ] to acknowledge that the aforesaid appearers' constituant shall hereby have done and have had done [ ] in presence of *Mons*. Robert Vastrick and Pieter Janse as witnesses hereto called and invited, who with the principals, have signed this.

The mark  set by Grietgen Jacobse with her own hand.
Roeloff Jacobsen

As witnesses,
R. Vastrick
Pieter Jansen

To which I attest,
Joannes Dijckman.

[LETTER TO KIT DAVITS FROM THE FORT ORANGE COURT]

[65] Christoffel D:
Kit Davits.
What his honor, the lord general, has written to you can be seen in the enclosed copy, which was sent for this purpose: "That you are to allow his honor De Hulter and his [people] to purchase land and to enjoy free possession thereof and other things, and not to incite the Indians against him or his [people] nor let harm come to his property nor do him the least injury; if you do so, we shall proceed against you according to law.

Let this serve as a final warning to you, according to which to regulate yourself exactly, so that the aforesaid honorable [De Hulter] may enjoy free possession; and in case you act to the contrary, we shall at once proceed against you according to law." [*"Hereby be warned" is crossed out.*]

The court of Fort Orange and Beverwijck, Fort Orange, 3 December 1654.

[CONTRACT OF RUTGER JACOPSEN WITH DIRRICK BENSINCK TO BUILD A HOUSE]

[66] On this the 21st day of December 1654 appeared before me, Joannes Dijckman, in the service of the honorable chartered West India Company, commissary and vice director of Fort Orange, the honorable Rutgert Jacopsen, burgher and inhabitant of Beverwijck, who declared that he had agreed and contracted with Dirrick Bensinck, to frame and make a small house one board in length, to set up and build it behind the house of the said Dirrick Bensinck, now standing and built in Beverwijck, according to the requirements of the work on [ ] to be completed by Dirrick Bensinck at his own expense; further the contractor shall be holden to construct in the house a bedstead and a pantry, also the frame shall have three bents, delivered by the contractor, with braces, floor, a garret door and water tight, all at his own cost; also, the contractor shall make therein a door casement, for which he shall receive five hundred and twelve guilders, 10 stivers to be paid in installments as follows: the first immediately, the second in the month of June, and last [ ]. The ironwork is to be provided by the contractor. All done here in good faith in Beverwijck in the presence of Cornelis Theunisz van Westbroeck and [ ] as witnesses hereto invited.

Rutger Jacobsz
This is the mark set by  Bensinck.
Hendrick Jochemsz
Cornelis Thonisen, as witnesses

To which I attest,
Joannes Dijckman.

[RESOLUTION AGAINST GAMBLING]

[67] With deep regret their honors of the court here having been informed that some fellows [*maats*] have been gambling at the public inns openly and recklessly for great sums of money; therefore, their honors hereby forbid such inordinate [ ] sums of money to proceed according to law; further, in such cases their honors will no longer execute judgment for such winnings and losses [ ] but the officer shall be requested to proceed against and impose the penalty upon, all such unlawful players which are hereby expressly prohibited that the evil consequences which may arise therefrom [ ]

This done in Fort Orange, this 22nd of December 1654. Present in Registro.

[WARNING TO MARIA JANSEN FOR SELLING ALCOHOL TO INDIANS]

[68] Maria Jansen, wife of Steeven Jansz, on the 3rd of November has acknowledged before the court that [ ] was caught by the commissary here selling brandy to the Indians; therefore it is upon her request it be excused because it is the first time, provided that a fine to the clerk and officer shall be paid at once in current sewant for the sum of [ ] under this reservation that in case hereafter she do so anymore, after the full [ ] this serving as a public warning. Fort Orange, this 30 December 1654.

[SALE OF HOUSE OF WILLEM FREDERICSE BOUT AT PUBLIC AUCTION]

[69] Willem Fredericksz Bout proposes to sell at public sale his house and lot at present occupied by himself, adjoining on the south side upon Jan Michielsen on the east side the wagon road; breadth nine rods and ten feet in front, length twelve rods on both sides, breadth in the rear nine rods and five feet, all according to the patent thereof; upon the following conditions: that the payment shall be made in three installments punctually, of which the first being a third part shall be paid in May next, the second six months thereafter, and the last third part, also in the following six months; which payment shall be made in good whole beavers or grain at the choice of the buyer. The auction fees shall be claimed of the buyer alone. The buyer shall be holden to furnish sufficient sureties for the payment. Further, the seller makes the sale on this condition: that no rebate shall be made, whatever may be the occasion. The buyer was Teunis Dirrickse for the sum of nineteen hundred and twenty guilders. We, the undersigned, present ourselves as sureties for the principal for payment for the aforesaid house under obligation according to law, this 11th of January 1655.

The mark  set by Theunis Dirrickse with his own hand.

As sureties:
A. van Curler
Rutger Jacobsz

[PROPOSAL OF WILLEM FREDERICKSE BOUT TO SELL A LOT AND SOME TIMBER FOR A HOUSE]

[70] Willem Fredericksz proposes to sell, on the following conditions, a lot and some timber for a house, adjoining to the north Volckert Janse, and to the south Sander Leendertsen, to the west a wagon road, to the east the path to the river; upon the following conditions: that the payment for the same shall be made in good whole beavers or hard grain. The payments shall be made in three installments: the first, a third part exactly in May; the second, also a third part six months thereafter;

and the final payment, the remaining third part six months thereafter. Payments shall be made in good beavers or hard grain at the choice of the buyer. The buyer shall be responsible for the auction fees. Upon the condition that the buyer shall accordingly provide at once sufficient sureties for payment.
[*Not executed*]

[SALE OF JOCHEM *BECKER'S* WOODLOT
AT PUBLIC AUCTION]

[71] Jochem *Becker* desires to sell at public sale a piece of woodland lying behind Fort Orange, with a house of a board long, just as they lie and stand; the breadth of the land is according to the patent hereof, which shall be delivered to the buyer when the payment is made, reaching south to the Beverkil, west the woodland, north the hill, east the thicket; is in breadth on the south side 50 rods, on the north side 36 rods, length 105 rods, with the fence set round about the same and the house also there built; upon the following conditions, to wit, that the payment shall be made in three installments of a third part each: the first in the month of May next, the second six months after, and the third six months following. The payment must be made in good whole beavers or grain at the choice of the buyer. The auction fees shall be a charge against the buyer; provided that the buyer shall be obligated to furnish sufficient sureties to the satisfaction of the seller for the payment. Philip Pieterse was the buyer on the aforementioned conditions for the sum of four hundred and sixty-eight guilders.

Philip Pietersen
As sureties according to law,
Johan Baptist van Renselaer, A. van Curler
11 January 1655

[REPORT TO STUYVESANT AND COUNCIL CONCERNING REQUEST OF THE MOHAWKS]

[72] Esteemed, valiant, most noble lord and right honorable sirs. Lord general and right honorable sirs: The Mohawks, or some of them, have been here with us, asking us that some Dutchmen might go to the Sinnekens' country to mediate the difficulties which have arisen between them and the Sinnekens; however, because of the difficulties of the times no one has been found; and moreover as one of the leaders of the Sinnekens has been killed by the Mohawks, they are disinclined. Therefore, we have thought it best to write to your honor and the right honorable council, as we judge the same to be a matter of state, for if the Mohawks drive out the Sinnekens, or while war exists, no trade here will yield any returns from that time on. If this war begins we shall expect your honor and the right honorable council in their wise judgment to take this matter into consideration, and our humble petition is that your honor and the right honorable council will please send by the bearer of this, their resolution upon this weighty point; namely, the slaying of the chief of the Sinnekens of Onnedaego, which Indians as aforesaid are threatening seriously to make war upon the Mohawks [ ]. It is a dangerous thing for us to interfere with this tense situation on such an occasion. The Mohawks came to us with a gift, saying that they thought counsel nearly at an end, and therefore sought our intervention with the inflamed parties, and, if possible, to remove the difficulty. We answered them that the time of the year was not propitious for the Dutch to undertake such a journey, even if it were required, and a fit time beforehand were had, so then they ordered what might be fitting therein. [ ] We beg your honor to please send up the accounts of the six soldiers, [73] and other honorable company's servants stationed here, and to order the traders to contribute as much as amounts to a bale of cloth; otherwise, we must at once demand their license. We shall now await your honor's good orders; our power alone avails nothing [ ] that so both the honorable company, and we, may thereby render better service. Wherefore expecting your honor's good orders, lord general and right honorable sirs, we commend your honors to God's protection, and remain, right honorable sirs,

Your humble and trustworthy servants,

The court of Fort Orange and Beverwijck
Fort Orange, 16 January 1654.

[74] [*blank*]

[RESOLUTION CONCERNING THE SALE OF GRAIN]

[75] Honorable Jan Dirrickse van Bremen. Whereas diverse creditors of yours have shared with us in the grain, therefore we have ordered that you sell no grain before the following persons shall have been fully paid: Evert Pells, for the sum of two hundred and seventy; and Pieter Hertgerts, the sum of *f*270; and Willem Fredericksz having satisfied the foregoing [ ] discharged from the arrest [ ] your honor [ ] expressly to [ ] this our given order, on pain of [ ]
[*3 lines illegible*]
13 January 1655. The court of Fort Orange and Beverwijck.

[SALE OF A LOT OF ADRIAEN DIRRIXSZ DE VRIES TO PIETER ADRIAENSEN]

[76] On this the 13th day of January 1655 appeared before me Joannes Dijckman, in the service of the honorable chartered West India Company, commissary and vice director of Fort Orange, Adriaen Dirickse de Vries, who declared that he had sold to Pieter Adriaensen *Soogemacklijck*, a certain lot, lying in Beverwijck, provided that the seller shall [ ] on the first of May have to evacuate the house standing thereupon, bounden on the east and west by Arent de [ ], on the south and north by Stoffel Alberts, provided that the aforesaid seller shall be obligated to pay to the buyer the sum of one hundred and twelve guilders [ ] the remaining eight guilders for payment of the patent is the responsibility of the buyer. The payment must be made [ ]. All in good faith, and under pledge of their persons and estates, personal and real, present and future.

In acknowledgment of the same, signed with their own hands, as well by the buyer as the seller.

The mark of Adrian Dirrickse de Vries,
signed with  by his own hand.

[SALE OF LOT OF FEMMETJE ALBERTSZ TO JAN THOMASZ, PIETER HERTGERTS, AND VOLCKERT JANSZ]

[77] On this the 17th day of January 1655 appeared before me Joannes Dijckman in the service of etc., the honorable Femmetje Albertsz, widow of the late Hendrick Jansz Westerkamp, and declared that she had sold to the honorable Jan Thomasz, Pieter Hertgerts and Volckert Jansz, a certain corner of her lot lying in Beverwijck; in length five rods and six feet, and in breadth six rods and eight feet just as it lies there, for which the seller shall receive in cash the sum of three hundred guilders, to be paid in beavers or hard grain, at the choice of the buyer, whereupon she, the seller of the aforesaid lot, (as well in its length as in its breadth), promises a full release of the same to them and their heirs forever. In acknowledgment of the truth this is signed with their own hands in Fort Orange on the date aforesaid.

The mark set by Femmetje Albertse  with her own hand.
As buyers,
Jan Thomas
Pieter Hertgerts
As witnesses,
Pieter Ryverdingh
To which I attest,
Joannes Dijckman

[RESOLUTION TO SUPRESS SHROVETIDE ACTIVITIES]

[78] Their honors of the court having regretfully learned that certain persons on the solemn festivals of yesterday and Shrovetide evenings, in this jurisdiction, having clothed themselves in strange costumes, and put on women's clothes, therein publicly paraded as harlequins through the city and streets, in the sight of the inhabitants, and besides did other scandalous and unseemly things; moreover, that no one shall pull the goose or shoot the parrot no matter what the pretext may be, for the reason that not only many improprieties thereby take place, but the farm hands and other servants not only cease from their service, but also engage in other insolent activities such as fighting, beating, cursing, and swearing; so is it that their honors of the court hereby expressly forbid such things to be done, on penalty that those who are found doing contrary hereto shall pay to the benefit of the officer here the sum of twenty-five guilders for the first offense, thereafter to arbitrary punishment. Thus done in Fort Orange this 26th of January 1654.

[EXCHANGE OF HOUSES BETWEEN JACOB JANSZ STOLL AND CLAES HENDRIXSZ VAN WTRECHT]

[79] Appeared before me, Joannes Dijckman, in the service of the honorable chartered West India Company, commissary and vice director of Fort Orange, in the presence of the honorable magistrates of the court here, Sander Leendertsz and Pieter Hertgerts, Firstly—Jacob Janse Stoll declared that he has granted, conveyed and transferred for himself and his successors two certain houses standing in Fort Orange with the garden thereto belonging at present, adjoining on the east upon Arent van den Bergh, and to the west on the point of the fort, for which, in exchange, he has agreed with Claas Hendrickse van Wtrecht that in real ownership he [Stoll] shall again receive a certain house standing in Manathans, according to conveyance of date the 17th of May 1654, delivered in the presence of *Messrs*. Nicasius de Sille and La Montagne in New Amsterdam, lying and standing on the island of Manathans in New Amsterdam bounded on the east by the river; in breadth on the road or south side three rods and three and a quarter feet, breadth in the rear, on the north side one rod seven and a half feet, length on the east side ten rods two and half feet, length on the west side twelve rods; and the grantors declare that they confirm both sales, and also for themselves and their heirs will warrant and defend the same forever; promising to hold this conveyance secure, and said grantors acknowledge what has been done above by way of exchange, annulling the former exchange forever, and that what is aforesaid is fast and done in good faith, thus holding this agreement, honestly and in good faith; in the presence of us, signed by both the grantors with their own hands and by the honorable magistrates this twenty-seventh day of January 1655.

Jacob Janse Stoll
Claes Hendryckse
Joannes Dijckman
Saunder Lenrsn
Pieter Hertgerts

[AUCTION OF GOODS OF MARSELIS JANSZ]

[80] 5 February 1655.
At the house of Marselis Jansz.
Cornelis Wouterse desires to sell at this public sale the following goods upon these conditions; namely: the payment shall be made within the period of three weeks, or at the outside one month, in good whole beavers. The buyer shall be obligated to furnish security for the above payment to the satisfaction of the seller, and failing to do so, the articles shall again be auctioned off at his cost and charge. Moreover, the seller rejects any reduction or increase of price for any reason whatever after the sale.

Andries Herpertsz, a bed with 2 pillows and a bolster, for	*f*65.00
Keesie Wouters, a woman's cape	*f*64.00
Ditto, an upper petticoat	*f*36.00
Eldert Gerritse, a little cloak	*f*17.00
Cornelis Theunisz, a ditto, with a stomacher	*f*25.00
Pieter Adriaensz, an upper petticoat	*f*25.00
Barent *de Molenaer*, an upper petticoat	*f*21.00
Cornelis Teunisz, a pair of sleeves	*f*9.00
Barent *de Molenaar*, a Turkish coat	*f*37.00
Lambert Albertsen, a woman's cape	*f*49.00
Andries Herpertsen, two sheets	*f*22.00
Andries Herpertsen, two ditto	*f*25.00

Corn. Bos, two pillow cases	*f*11.00
Grietje Teunisz, two pillow cases	*f*12.00
Lambert Albertsz, three pillow cases	*f*12.00
Janneman, two napkins	*f*8.00
Ditto, five napkins	*f*13.00
	*f*44.7.10
[81] Lambert Albertsz, 2 napkins	*f*10.10
Pieter Meesen, 2 ditto	*f*9.00
Cornelis Theunisz, 2 ditto	*f*8.00
Pieter *So Mackelijck*, 2 ditto	*f*9.00
Pieter Bronck, 2 ditto	*f*9.00
Pieter Bronck, 2 ditto,	*f*10.10
Pr. Bronck, 2 ditto,	*f*9.00
Claes Hendericksz, 2 ditto	*f*8.06
P. Ryverdingh, 2 dittos	*f*8.00
P. Ryverdingh, 6 pewter trenchers	*f*12.00
Hendrick Jochemsz, 6 trenchers for	*f*11.00
Cornelis Teunisz, a chest	*f*21.00
Tgerck, a medal	*f*18.00
	*f*143.18
	*f*447.10
	*f*591.00

Marcelis Jansz sold a cloak exposed for sale a second time, for	*f*40.00
Evert Pels, a gun	6.70
Pieter Ryverdingh sold the following rolls of tobacco:	
Gerrit Seegersz, 8 rolls	*f*31.00
Jan Andriesz de Graff, 4 ditto	*f*10.00
Willem, 3 rolls for	*f*8.10
Cornelis Theunisz, 6 rolls	*f*35.00
Klaas Hendricksz stood security for Gerrit Segerse for 6 rolls for	*f*25.00
Elbert Gerritse stood security for Gerrit Segersz, for 14 rolls of tobacco	*f*[*blank*]

[82] Eldert, 6 rolls	*f*24.10
Gerrit Reyersz, 6 rolls	*f*25.10

[AUCTION OF GOODS OF JOHAN DE HULTER]

[83] *Mr*. Johan de Hulter desires at this sale to sell the following goods, underwritten, upon the following conditions; namely: the payment of the goods sold shall be made punctually, within two months from this day. The payment shall be made in good whole beavers or wheat. Moreover the buyer shall be obligated, at or shortly after the sale, to furnish sufficient sureties to the satisfaction of the seller, if not, the articles shall again be offered at the buyer's expense and charge, and if they sell for less, he shall be obligated to make good the loss.

An iron vise to Cornelis Vos,	*f*36.00
An iron vise to Pieter Hertgerts,	*f*6.17
Three threading dies to Jan van Aecken,	*f*24.00
A drill bit to Mr. Rensselaer,	*f*8.02
A cloak, Pieter Hertgerts,	*f*20.01
A silk camlet robe, Pieter Hertgerts [ ],	*f*30.00
A padded child's coat, Goosen Gerritse,	*f*5.01
A birthing bed, Jan Thomasz,	*f*17.00
An woman's gown, Rutger Jacopsen,	*f*28.00
Two napkins, Mr. Rensselaer,	*f*9.10
Two napkins, Seeger Cornelisz,	*f*9.10
Two napkins, *Mr*. Renselaer,	*f*8.17
Two napkins, Cornelis Vos,	*f*9.13
Mr. Rensselaer, two napkins,	*f*9.00
Giertgen Bouts, two napkins,	*f*9.13
Two napkins, *Jonge* Cees,	*f*9.12
18 Feb. 1655	*f*232.11

[84] Brought from the other side,	*f*241.11
Two napkins, *Jonge* Kees,	*f*9.12
Two napkins, Cornelis Vos,	*f*9.16
Two napkins, Giergen Bouts,	*f*9.10
Two napkins, Cornelis Vos,	*f*9.12

Two napkins, Dicke Cess,	*f*9.14
Six napkins, Giergen Bouts,	*f*31.00
Six napkins, Rutger Jacobsen,	*f*24.00
1 rix-dollar, Claes Janse van Baere,	*f*5.06
1 rix-dollar, Goosen Gerritse,	*f*4.08
1 rix-dollar, Seger Cornelisz,	*f*4.01
1 piece of money, Janneman,	*f*3.16
1 piece of money, Louijs,	*f*15.00
1 piece of money, Thomas Jansz,	*f*4.08
1 piece of money, Segar Cornelis,	*f*4.00
1 piece of money, Dirrick Bensick,	*f*4.80
1 piece of money, Seger Cornelise,	*f*5.15
1 piece of money, *Mr*. Rensselaer,	*f*5.15
1 piece of money, Thomas Jansz,	*f*4.00
1 piece of money, Pieter Meuwse,	*f*4.05
1 piece of money, *Mr*. Rensselaer,	*f*5.11
1 piece of money, Willem Janse Schut,	*f*5.10
1 piece of money, the same,	*f*4.13
1 piece of money, Seger Cornelisz,	*f*5.05
1 piece of money, Cornelis Theunisz,	*f*4.14
1 piece of money, Seger Cornelisz,	*f*4.05
1 piece of money, Janneman,	*f*4.05
1 piece of money, *Mr*. Rensselaer,	*f*4.05
1 piece of money, the same,	*f*5.12
1 piece of money, *Dolle* Griet,	*f*5.10
1 piece of money, ditto, Pieter Meuwse,	*f*4.11
1 piece of money, Arent van Curler,	*f*3.02
1 piece of money, *Mr*. Rensselaer,	*f*3.05
1 piece of money, Keesie Wouterse,	*f*3.02
1 piece of money, Filip Pieters,	*f*3.07
1 piece of money, Jeremias Rensselaer,	*f*3.06
1 piece of money, Kees Wijcoop,	*f*3.06
Carried forward	*f*729.01

[85] Seger Cornelis, a scissor,	*f*2.10
Corler, a scissor,	*f*2.05
A piece of gold, Seger Cornelisz,	*f*12.50
A piece of ditto,	*f*14.15
A piece of ditto,	*f*12.02

Corler, a ring,	*f*39.00
Thomas Jansz, two knife handles,	*f*17.00
Rutger Jacobsen, a ring,	*f*31.10
Cornelis Vos, ditto,	*f*61.10
Corler, two half moons,	*f*24.00
Cornelis Theunis, a gold ring,	*f*92.00
Robbert Engelsz, a piece of gold,	*f*20.13
Robbert Engelsz, a piece of gold,	*f*13.30
Lambert Albertsz, a piece of gold,	*f*11.10
Baerent Pietersz *de molenaer*, two millstones,	*f*26.00
Rut Jacobsz, some felt,	*f*24.00
Rut Jacobsz, a wedding cloak,	*f*148.00
Jan Gowen, a pot [ ],	*f*8.00
Cornelis Vos, two napkins,	*f*9.11
Filip Pietersz, 6 napkins,	*f*29.00
Rem Jansz, 4 napkins,	*f*20.10
	*f*620.04
From the other side	*f*729.01
	*f*1349.0.5

[DEPOSITION CONCERNING AN ALTERCATION AT THE HOUSE OF STEVEN JANSZ]

[86] On this 22nd day of February 1655 appeared before me Joannes Dijckman, in the service of the honorable chartered West India Company, commissary and vice director of Fort Orange, the honorable Jan Labatie and Lambert van Valkenburgh, who hereby declare at the request of Steven Jansz that it is truthful that these deponents yesterday evening were at the house of said Jansz, and among other things, saw, while said deponents were at the house of said Steven Jansz, Jacob Hendricksz Maat come into the house throwing around many abusive words [ ] whereupon he tossed a handkerchief at the petitioner, saying he would shoot him through with a loaded gun; afterwards Jacob Hendrickse Maat, following him outside, drew his knife; then Steven Jansz said, "put up your fists," which these deponents heard, and also declared that Jacob Hendrickse Maat further abused him with many insolent curses, while said Jansz was as far as he could be, patient and remained quietly inside his house. By this deposition enough has been said about what said Jansz was complaining, especially about what was done to him both inside as well as outside his house. This deposition being presented will of necessity and by request be strengthened by oath.

In acknowledgment of the truth this is subscribed by their own hands in Fort Orange on the aforesaid date.

Jan Labatie

The mark set by  Lambert van Valkenborgh
with his own hand.

To which I attest,
Joannes Dijckman

[DEPOSITION CONCERNING THE FOREGOING ALTERCATION]

[87] Appeared before me Pieter Ryverdingh, clerk in the service of the chartered West India Company, the honorable Arent vanden Berch and Hendrick Biermans, who declared, as they hereby do, at the request of Steven Jansz, the truth of the matter that these deponents, yesterday evening, the 20th of this month, were at the house of said Jansz, and among other things, saw and heard Jacob Loserecht utter many abusive words against the aforesaid Jansz and toss a hankerchief at the petitioner, "saying Let's go into the woods and fight it out with guns"; whereupon said Loserecht further invited him, Steven, outside, and Steven answered that he would gladly fight with fists, but not with guns," complaining further of violence done in his, Steven's, house. The foregoing will be strengthened by oath if required. This 22nd of February 1655 in Fort Orange.

The mark of  Arent Vandenberch set with his own hand.

The mark  of Hendrick Bierkmans set with his own hand.

Acknowledged before me,
Pr. Rijverdingh.

[DEPOSITION CONCERNING AN ALTERCATION
AT THE HOUSE STEVEN JANSZ]

[88] Appeared before me Pieter Ryverdingh, clerk, in the service of the honorable chartered West India Company, the honorable Rijck Riddersen, aged about thirty-seven years, and Klaes Andriesz aged about twenty-seven years, who upon the request of Steven Jansz, declared that it is true that they were yesterday evening the 21st of this month at the house of the petitioner, where was present Harmen N., whose surname is unknown; which Harmen uttered many words against the petitioner, without said petitioner's provoking him thereto; and after many words, said Harmen, taking off his jacket, intended to beat up the petitioner in his own house. Steven aforesaid responded, "Go ahead"; thereupon he went immediately to the officer, complaining of the force and violence committed by said Harmen in his, the petitioner's, house. Presentation thereof will of necessity and by request be strengthened by oath. Thus done this 22nd of February 1655 in Fort Orange.

The mark of + Rijck Riddersen
Claes Andriesz

Acknowledged before me,
Pieter Rijverdingh, clerk.

[DEPOSITION CONCERNING ARSON
AT THE HOUSE OF AERT JACOBSZ]

[89] On this third day of February 1654 in the forenoon appeared before me Joannes Dijckman, in the service of the honorable chartered West India Company, commissary and vice director of Fort Orange, the honorable Stoffel Jansz Abeels, aged about thirty-two years, and Jacob Hendricksz Sibinck, aged about twenty-six years, who testified and declared, as they hereby do testify and declare, that Jan Verbeeck had said that the fire at the house of Aert Jacobsz was set by young Paulus, [ ] Cornelis Theunisz on 4 May 1653 in the presence of Oom Dirck, ship's carpenter, [ ] whereupon Cornelis Theunisz answered how is was that the fire was started [ ] another time by Pieter the Fleming and that the said young Paulus had brought some fire by which the fire was kindled.

[NOMINATION OF MAGISTRATES FOR COURT OF FORT ORANGE AND BEVERWIJCK]

[90] Worshipful, valiant, most noble general, and right honorable gentlemen of the high council of New Netherland. As the first of May next will be the time when the terms of office of the three persons now serving as magistrates shall have expired, viz: Jan Verbeeck, Jacob Jansz Schermerhoren, who last year departed for Holland, and Jan Thomasz; therefore, to fill out the bench, according to former custom, a nomination is made of a double number of six persons, viz: Philip Pietersz Schuiler, Derrick Jansz Croon, Volckert Jansz, Rem Jansz, Evert Wendel, and Arent Andriesz, from whom, if it please your honors of the high honorable court, to elect three persons for this bench, to supply the places of the aforesaid retiring officers; and our humble request is that your honor and the court will please make the election at the aforesaid time, otherwise the bench will be deficient, to the great inconvenience of the people here, and also the honorable Company's service; awaiting the same, in the meantime, we pray Almighty God to bless your honor's and the council's government, and that your counsels may long abide. In the meantime, lord general and honorable sirs, we remain your honors' humble and trustworthy servants of the court at Fort Orange and Beverwijck. Fort Orange, 30th of March 1655. [*Canceled*]

[91] [DUPLICATE OF PRECEDING CANCELED DOCUMENT]

[CONDITIONS FOR THE SALE OF GOODS OF STEVEN JANSZ]

[92] The 1st of April 1655. Steven Jansz intends to sell at this sale or auction the following goods on these conditions, to wit: The payments shall be made in good merchantable beavers, without any abatement, in the month of May or by the end of the month at the latest. The buyers shall make said payments at set the time to Pieter Ryverdingh, who shall receive the money for the aforesaid goods:

To Baefjen, a ticktack table,	*f*16.00
Rensselaer, 11 axes with some odds and ends,	*f*9.10
Seger Cornelisz, 36lb. of tobacco,	*f*25.00
Seger Cornelisz, 6 beer glasses,	*f*6.04
Jan *met de baert*, 3 small pictures,	*f*2.00
Henderick Jochemse, a sign,	*f*3.12
Jacob Adriaensz, a gun,	*f*13.00
Pieter Bout, a canoe,	*f*35.00
Jan Thomasz, 3 gutters at 20 guilders a piece,*	*f*60.00
Steven Jansz, a sow,	*f*17.00
Henderick Gerritsz, a hog,	*f*15.00
Huybert *de Guyt,* a cask of no. 1 Holland beer,	*f*41.00
Philip Pietersz, ditto no. 2,†	*f*33.00
	*f*290.6

[93] Willem Pietersz , a barrel of no. 8 Holland beer,	*f*30.00
Willem Pietersz, no. 9, ditto,	*f*24.00
Seger Cornelisz, some tobacco pipes,	*f*2.10
Jan Verbeeck, barrel of no. 4 Holland beer,	*f*24.00
Joan de Hulter, a chest,	*f*9.10

* Marginal note: "Liquidated with the brewery."

† Marginal note: "Paid on 10 June."

Huybert *de Guyt*, a bag of lime,	*f*2.12
Huybert, a trough with a basin,	*f*9.01
Young Kees, 3 benches,	*f*8.10

The 2nd of April.

Joan de Hulter, four hogs at 14 guilders a piece,	*f*54.00
Anthony de Hooges, a barrel of Holland beer,	*f*24.00
Leendert Philipsz, a sleeping bench,	*f*4.00
Dooretge, a billy goat,*	*f*16.00
	*f*208.3

To Jacob van de Vlacte, a dog; however, Andries and Goosen have assumed the debt. Also, to Juryan the glazier, two hogs, for 3½ beavers; however, as Andries Herpertsen and Goosen Gerritse, must also have money for brick, the 3½ beavers go as a deduction.

[AUCTION OF TWO HOUSES BY JAN PEECK]

[94] Jan Peeck desires to sell at this public sale his two houses, standing and lying in Fort Orange with the garden belonging thereto, all according to the patent thereof. The houses adjoin the fort's west point, to the east Arent van den Bergh; to the south of the aforesaid fort lies the garden, adjoining to the north the *Heer* Rensselaer, and to the south a public road. First, the persons who bid off as the buyers, shall be obligated to make the first payment of six hundred guilders in the month of May, or by the end of said month at the latest: half in current sewant, and the other half in good beavers. The second payment, being the last, shall be paid before the following May in the year 1656: half in current sewant, and the other half in beavers as before; on this condition that the person who bids off the same shall be obligated to furnish sufficient sureties; and failing in that, the property shall again be offered for sale at the charge of the buyer, and whatever less it shall bring, the buyer shall

* Marginal note: "Liquidated with the brewery."

make good.† [5] The seller of the aforesaid houses shall be obligated to deliver the garden enclosed in new fencing, together with the sand that may be in the cellar of the one house, which he shall build and complete in a proper manner, after which the buyer must order matters himself. Upon this 14th of April 1655 the honorable Joannes Dijckman remained the highest bidder for the sum of sixteen hundred and twenty-seven Carolus guilders, and on the aforesaid conditions hereunder set his usual signature by hand; pledging the aforesaid houses and his goods, personal and real, all according to law.

Joannes Dijckman

We, the undersigned, as principals, stand sureties for the aforesaid Joannes Dijckman in the purchase of the two houses, according to the conditions, to stand in his stead in case of failure of payment, and to pay the aforesaid money, for which we pledge our goods, personal and real, according to law. Done this 16th of April 1655 in Beverwijck.

As witnesses,
Claes Hendryckse — Pieter Rijverdingh
Willem Pietersen — Evert Pels

[SALE OF A LOT OF JOANNES DIJCKMAN TO CLAES HENDRICKSZ]

On this the 16th day of April *anno* 1655 appeared before me Pieter Ryverdingh, clerk in the service of the chartered West India Company, the honorable Joannes Dijckman, in his capacity as commissary and vice director of Fort Orange, who acknowledged that he had sold to Claes Hendricksz, burgher here, a certain lot adjoining on the south side of Abram Pietersz *timmerman*, and on the north side *Mr.* Jacob [de Hinse] *chirugijn*, on the east side a common cart road; breadth in front and back six rods eight feet, length ten rods, together with a double garden, nos. 1 and 2 [6], lying behind or nearby the aforesaid lot, with

† The following two pages were incorrectly identified as pages 5 and 6 when the account books and loose pages were rebound.

the timber lying there for a house, and the posts for the garden all delivered free, lot, garden and timber; provided that said Claes Hendricksen, shall pay for it the sum of four hundred Carolus guilders, half in good merchantable sewant, and the other half in good whole beavers, with the condition that whenever the said Dijckman delivers the patent for the same, then the promised sum as aforesaid shall be paid without further delay. In acknowledgment of the same they mutually pledge their respective persons and goods, personal and real, present and future, subjecting the same to the authority of all laws and judges. In witness of which, without craft or guile, this is signed with their own hands, on the date aforesaid in Beverwijck.

Johannes Dijckman
Claes Hendryckse

As witnesses,
Andries Herberts
Jan Peeck

Acknowledged before me,
Pieter Ryverdingh, clerk

[POWER OF ATTORNEY OF PIETER GELLISZ TO MARITGEN JACOBSZ]

[95] On this 17th day of April 1655 appeared before me, Joannes Dijckman, commissary and vice director of Fort Orange, in the service of the honorable chartered West India Company, the honorable Pieter Gellisz, at present living at said Fort Orange, who declared that he had appointed and empowered, as he hereby does appoint and empower, the virtuous Maritgen Jacobsz residing on the Prince's canal at Amsterdam, being the subscriber's wife and his bed companion, in her husband's name and for his sake to claim, demand and receive all such sums of money as are due to him for his child's portion, inherited by him from his mother, and further so to do and act as the matter demands, and as the attorney judges wise; the subscriber holding as fixed and irrevocable whatever said attorney, Maritgen Jacobse, has done or shall do herein, as if he were himself present in person. In witness whereof this is signed

with his own hand, with witnesses hereto called and invited. Done as above.

Pieter Jellesse

As witnesses,
Andries Herberts
Pieter Ryverdingh

Acknowledged before me,
Joannes Dijckman

[FARMING OUT OF THE TAPPERS EXCISE]

[96] Their honors of this court desire to farm out at public sale to the highest bidder the tappers' excise of wine and beer for the time of twelve months, beginning on the first of May next, on the following conditions, namely: The collector shall be obligated to pay the promised sum quarterly to the honorable court or to their order. This payment shall be made in good strung sewant. It is a condition that the highest bidder shall be obligated to furnish sufficient security for the payment, failing of which, it shall immediately be offered for sale again, at his cost and charge, without any opposition. On this 23rd of April 1655 at Fort Orange, Marcelis Janse became the buyer for the sum of two thousand and thirteen guilders upon the foregoing conditions, and Claes Janse and Philip Hendricksz became his sureties, to take his place in case of failure of payment, according to the foregoing conditions, pledging mutually their goods, personal and real, present and future, without exception, and subjecting the same to the authority of all laws and judges.In witness whereof this is mutually signed without craft or guile.

As buyer, Marcelis Janse

As sureties,
Flip Hindricksen
Claes Janse

[SALE OF A HOUSE, LOT, AND GARDEN OF ADRIAEN VAN ILPENDAM TO ADRIAEN GERRITSZ]

[97] On the 22nd day of December 1655 Adriaen Gerritsen and Adriaen van Ilpendam, have in friendship assented and agreed in the manner following: The aforenamed Adriaen van Ilpendam has sold his house, lot and garden, with all that is therein fast by earth and nail, standing and lying in Beverwijck, and promises to deliver them on the first day of August 1656 with the patent and a proper conveyance, but expressly on the condition that on the east side about three feet of the lot in front on the street be sold to Rem Jansen *smit*, so that the house of said Rem Jansen may stand on his own ground; for which aforenamed house, lot and garden, Adriaen Gerritsz must pay to Adriaen van Ilpendam eighteen hundred Carolus guilders in good merchantable beaver skins, at eight guilders a beaver, as consideration for the house, lot and garden; on the further condition that Adriaen Gerritse may occupy half of the aforesaid house and cultivate the garden; pledging mutually their persons and estates, personal and real, in subjection to all laws and judges. In witness of which two copies of this agreement are made, and without craft or gule signed. Dated as above.

Adriaen van Ilpendam
Adriaen Gerritsen

Rem Jansen, as witness
Andries Hendrick, as witness

[98] [*blank*]

[SALE OF HOUSE, LOT, AND GARDEN OF JOACHIM *BACKER* TO ADRIAEN VAN ILPENDAM]

[99] On this 28th day of February, 1656 [years] after the birth of our Lord and Savior Jesus Christ, Joachem *Backer* of the one part and Adriaen van Ilpendam of the other side, have in friendship assented and agreed in manner following: Joachim *Backer* aforesaid has sold his house, lot and garden standing and lying in Beverwijck, and promises to deliver the same to said Van Ilpendam with a valid conveyance and the patent as soon as the payment has been made; and he promises also to have a bedstead made at his own expense in the cellar, and to deliver all the shingles needed for the aforesaid house; also some posts as agreed upon to be delivered on the lot, and the buyer may enter into possession of the house, lot and garden next first of May, for which aforesaid house, lot the buyer shall be obligated to pay to the seller, or to his order, thirteen hundred guilders, half in good merchantable beaver skins, at eight guilder a beaver, and the other half in good strung sewant, and the beavers must be paid before the first of August in this year, and the sewant on the first of April 1657; hereby mutually pledging their persons and estates without exception, and subject to all laws and judges. In acknowledgment of the truth, of which they have signed this without craft or guile in Beverwijck. Done as above.

Jochem *Backer*
Adriaen van Ilpendam

T.V. Hamel as witness
Pieter Loockerman as witness

[ACKNOWLEDGMENTS OF PAYMENT TO JOCHEM *BACKER*]

[100] I, the undersigned, acknowledge that I have received upon this contract the first payment, namely: eighty-one beavers, and in confirmation of the same have signed this with my own hand in Beverwijck this 22nd of February 1656.

Jochem *Backer*

I, the undersigned, acknowledge that I have received on this contract two hundred and two guilders in sewant this 27th of April 1657.

Jochem *Backer*

I, the undersigned, Jochem *Backer*, acknowledge that I am paid in full for this contract by him [Adriaen van Ilpendam]; and I thank him for prompt payment and free him from all claims. Done in Beverwijck this last day of April.

Jochem *Backer*

[101] [*blank*]

[102] [*blank*]

[LETTER OF MAGISTRATES OF BEVERWIJCK TO STUYVESANT AND COUNCIL CONCERNING THE TAPPERS EXCISE]

[103] [*several lines lost at top*]...farmed out to the collector, Marcelis Jansz, the wine and strong beer excise at public sale at the house of Henderick Jochemse for the time of a whole year beginning on the first of May next, for the sum of two thousand and thirteen guilders. We cannot conceal from your honor and the council that the report has come to our ears that your honor desires the ordinary excise of wine and beer in the colony not to be paid to us, but rather to establish them [of the colony] in a position against us; in regard to which therefore your honor and the council will please return a very speedy answer, and in the meantime we have sent and delivered to the court of the colony of Rensselaerswijck the following reply: Reply to the written summons and protestation by the court of the colony of Rensselaerswijck, delivered in to our court [of Fort Orange and Beverwijck], on Tuesday last; whereupon the court aforesaid has thought good to return this our reply. Inasmuch as Jan Baptist van Rensselaer, in the capacity of the court of the colony of Rensselaerswijck has been pleased, through the schout of said Rensselaerswijck **[104]** [*several lines lost at top*] ...the farming out of the wine and beer excise;* so it is that until we can show

* Marginal notation: [ ] done at the house of Hendrick Jochumsz.

an order from the right honorable the director general and council of New Netherland† We trust your honor will remain content, for which end your honor's original written summons and protestation have been sent to the right honorable director general and council of New Netherland, who will order, in relation thereto, according to their accustomed resolutions; and if your honor desires to learn them he can address himself to our court as having proper authority. Done in our court of Fort Orange and Beverwijck this 29th of April 1655.

Joannes Dijckman
Jan Verbeeck
Pieter Hertgerts
Franz Barentse Pastoor

[SALE OF HOUSE BY STEVEN JANSZ TO GIJSBERT CORNELISZ]

Upon this the first day of May 1655, Steven Jansz desires to sell at this public sale, the house formerly belonging to the late Gijsbert Cornelisz, as it at presently stands with the cookhouse, in addition to a garden, hogpen and lot of the same, all according to the patent thereof on the following conditions: **[105]** [*Several lines at top lost*]...shall furnish sufficient sureties to the content of the seller, and failing of this, it shall at once be offered for sale again at the expense of the buyer, and whatever less it comes to be worth shall be made good by the buyer. The payment must be made in the three following installments: the first, within fourteen days, or at least by the end of the month of May, the second next Amsterdam fairday, and the third, next 1656, also in May; all to be paid in good whole beavers on the aforesaid conditions without any delay; provided that the buyer or bidder is not to lay claim to the two months rent due from Pieter the Fleming, who at present occupies the

† Marginal notation: Whose order we are obligated by oath to obey with the admonition to your honor that the same [ ] carry out [ ] office and order [ ] impedement [ ] or we shall have to employ other means against it as need and bounden duty demands.

cookhouse, but said cookhouse shall be delivered on the first of July next, after which the buyer is to regulate matters himself.

[106] [*several lines lost at top*]...the person of Theunis Theunisz who shall have to compensate whoever might still be interested in the aforesaid house and from whom the aforesaid house came, and is still unpaid, has remained as surety for the purchase of the aforesaid house.

[TESTIMONY CONCERNING PIETER ADRIAENSZ]

On this the third day of May 1655 I, Joannes Dijckman, in the capacity of clerk and officer, at the earnest petition of Marcelis Jansz, the collector, went to the house of Jacob [*sic*] Adriaens *Soogemackelijck.* There were present sitting before the door the following witnesses, Hendrick Reur and Barent Pieterse, the miller, and the aforesaid *Gemackelijck* himself. It was my initial request that the collector, Marcelis Janse, should gauge his casks according to the farming of the excise, for which reason he had come there. Then I received for an answer from the aforesaid *Soogemackelijck* that there was another gentleman undertaking it and he would not permit it, so then I, Joannes Dijckman, before doing anything else there at the house, made the following protest before the door: since you, Pieter Andriaense *Soogemackelijck*, will not permit us to gauge the wine and beer you have in your cellar, in the name of the right honorable director general and council of New Netherland, I protest that all the damage and expense which the honorable company and collector may suffer shall fall upon your person **[107]** [*several lines lost at top*]...Steven Jansz and also a person whose name I could not tell, from whom, on my friendly request for an answer, I received the same answer as Pieter Adriaensen *Soogemackelijck* gave me; whereupon I departed again with the same protest and went to the house of Adriaen Janse van Leyden, finding him and his wife and the servant girl at home, I received the same answer as the other gentleman gave; he expressly refused to give permission for the gauging, [ ] so I protested against him word for word as I had done against the others. Fort Orange, this 4th of May 1655.

Joannes Dijckman
Marcelys Jansen, collector

[SALE OF LAND OF ANTONIUS DE HOOGES TO VOLCKERT JANSZ]

[108] [*several lines lost at top*]...I, Anthonys de Hooges, acknowledge that I have sold to Volckert Jansz the west portion of my lot extending behind the house of the buyer aforesaid for a certain sum of money to my satisfaction, the length of the aforesaid part, being ten and a half and the breadth four rods, and I therefore so convey and release the same to and for the benefit of Volckert Jansz, with such ownership and possession as were granted to me and others without making any pretension of right, claim, or authority to the same from this time forth. As witness my hand here subscribed in Beverwijck this 5th of May 1655.

Antonius de Hooges

I, Joannes Dijckman, customs officer and vice director in Fort Orange and village of Beverwijck, having seen the above standing conveyance, promise that I will take care that Volkert Jansz shall shortly be furnished with a patent *in debita forma*, for said lot of ground, ten and a half rods in length, and four rods in breadth. Done as above.

Joannes Dijckman

[COMMUNICATION CONCERNING THE TAPPERS EXCISE]

[109] Honorable, valiant, and most noble sir, and right honorable gentlemen of the council of New Netherland. General and right honorable sirs: Our last to your honors was dated the 29th of April last, but to our great surprise, although a continual south wind has been blowing, no answer to the same has been received, notwithstanding the earnest letter that we wrote respecting the farming of the excise, about which the collector, as is proper, at the first opportunity [ ] or otherwise makes thereof heavy claims, of which the honorable president and clerk of this court will give your honors more detailed information by word of mouth, what treatment his honor [the collector] met with from the innkeepers dwelling outside the limits, who would by no means permit the gauging of their spirits, whereupon nothing more has been done than in the presence of the collector, Marcelis Jansz, to protest against the same in the names of your honors, as your honors shall be particularly shown in writing. Now it is so that in case we do not receive the support of your honors in this matter, we shall not only be a mockery, but of little esteem in consequence thereof. We can but hope, therefore, that your honors will, in proper time, put in execution your former resolutions. How needful a secretary is here requires **[110]** [*Several lines at top lost*]...being a serious and capable person to relieve his honor, the clerk, since his honor declines to serve longer here, of which his honor will verbally give your honors an explanation; for his honor confined to his house, is no longer fit to perform the office of secretary in a community so greatly multiplied. Diverse complaints reach us, of those, who, last year furnished your honors with money in a time of need, asking restitution and payment, for examples, Hendrick Jochemsz, Willem Bout, and others; your honors will please, according to promise, make payment thereof, or confirm the writing relating to the same, to which end the original requisition the said honorable custom officer takes with this, and further will so do and act therein as we have given order. Our humble petition is that your honors will give a favorable hearing, and also will please grant it to us speedily; and further referring you to his honor, for a verbal report respecting the condition of things up here; in the meantime, general and right honorable sirs of the council, we pray Almighty God to bless your honors' counsels and prosper more and more, and remain your honors' faithful servants of the court of Fort Orange and Beverwijck. Fort Orange, 10 April 1655.*

* This is the last document recorded by Joannes Dijckman. To replace Dijckman, the council appointed Jan de Deckere as provisional commissary on June 18, 1655. He left in July 1656. Johannes la Montage was then named vice director on September 28, 1656.

[REQUEST OF COURT OF RENSSELAERSWIJCK TO COURT OF BEVERWIJCK CONCERNING AN ALTERCATION]

[111] [*several lines at top lost*]...of the court of Rensselaerswijck, delivered the following petition: The court of the colony of Rensselaerswijck, understanding that from the fight between Steven Jansz and Jacob Hendrixsz Maet, there exists just reasons and motives in the matter of their bounden duty, to be vigilant and watchful in the administration of justice, the offense being such that Steven Jansz was struck in the left side with a knife in the hand of Jacob Jansz [*sic*] aforesaid in such a manner that it has become life-threatening, and that it was committed in the jurisdiction of the aforesaid colony. So it is that they [of the court of Rensselaerswijck] send a friendly request to the honorable court of Fort Orange and Beverwijck, who have proposed the matter that they will please detain the aforesaid Jacob Hendricksz under their honors' jurisdiction, and put him into the hands of our officer, to be disposed of only according to his crime, and to do with his person as shall be found in accordance with the laws; this request of theirs being founded on a reciprocal accommodation and duty in case a like occurrence should happen on their side; their honors also not being ignorant that such is a mutual obligation of all (principally affected) courts, they wait for a speedy resolution and answer to this, inasmuch as danger comes from delay. Done at the session of their honors of the aforesaid colony this 2nd of July 1655. *Presentibus ut in registro.*

Lower stood: By order of the same,
A. de Hooges, schout and secretary.

[REPLY OF COURT OF BEVERWIJCK TO COURT OF RENSSELAERSWIJCK]

[112] [*several lines lost at top*]...reading as follows: the court of Fort Orange and the village of Beverwijck, having seen and examined the request made to them by the court of the colony of Rensselaerswijck, have always shown, and with a like desire for the maintenance of Justice are inspired, and moreover shall not stand idle; on the contrary, their duty indicates that the person of Jacob Hendricksz Maat, in case he shall into the hands of justice, placed and confined in a secure place, until such time as the state and condition of the patient Steven Jansz shall have taken a favorable or unfavorable turn, in order that he may then be dealt with as justice and right may demand. In the meantime their honors [of the Court of Fort Orange] testify their pleasure that the court aforesaid [of Rensselaerswijck] shows itself as a zealous lover of the maintenance of justice. Done at the session of their honors aforesaid on the 7th of July AD 1655. *Presentibus omnibus*.

By order of the same,
J. de Deckere, 1655.

[RESPONSE TO JURISDICTIONAL QUESTION BETWEEN RENSSELAERSWIJCK AND BEVERWIJCK]

[113] [*Several lines at top lost*]...by the schout Swart* made to commissary Johan de Deckere in order that certain persons, dwelling under our jurisdiction may be brought by our court messenger before the tribunal and court of Rensselaerswijck, are answered as follows: Your request sent to me this morning is, I acknowledge, in some cases wholly founded in justice and right, also some cases may occur where the concession sought for with good reason should be withheld, unless the reasons, occasion and question are made known to us, why one dwelling under our jurisdiction should properly appear before your honor's court and there be tried. We request, therefore, that your honors will afford us by the bearer the occasion for this demand of yours that having found reasons for refusal the same may be adhered to, or otherwise renounced, being content under similar circumstances to regulate our conduct in the like manner. *Vale*. Done this 7th of July 1655.

J. de Deckere,
1655.

* Gerrit Swart, schout of Rensselaerswijck.

[REQUEST OF JAN DE DECKERE CONCERNING HIS OFFICE]

[114] Honorable, Valiant, Pious, Prudent, and very Discreet Lords.

Immediately after our arrival here, we composed and promulgated a certain placard, a copy of which accompanies this; the effects we await with more patience than hope, as yet seeing nothing more than a superficial cure, because the disease (in my opinion) has grown old and penetrated to the bone. Concerning the person of Dijckman, we consider him, according to the report of the deputy, to be in a miserable posture, it is doubtful, which is most impeded, his understanding or speech; in any event he is absolutely unfit to attend to civil or judicial matters. As to the salary and hundred guilders for maintenance received by Dijckman, I hope to be allowed the same, and request some evidence or document that I may receive it. Johan de Hulter, on Tuesday last, the 2nd of July, having appeared before the magistrates, asked for a letter of recommendation to your honors, to the end that they would please make and publish the same placard for the prohibition, reformation and checking of the insolence, opposition and disobedience of his servants in particular, and of others in general, complaining and testifying that they are great and intolerable. **[115]** [*several lines at top lost*]...I request that some paper be sent, having up to now used only my own; also, four to five books to replace those advanced by the court messenger. According to order I have boarded at the house of Domine Schaets for six guilders; I request a warrant by which the same may be paid. Herewith, honorable sir, I commend you to the protection of the Almighty. Fort Orange the [ ] of July 1655.

[TESTIMONY CONCERNING RESISTENCE TO THE GAUGING OF BEER]

On the 23rd of July 1655, I, Johan de Deckere, in the capacity of commissary and officer, at the request of Marcelis Jansz, collector, assisted by our court messenger, went to the house of Jacob Adriaensen *Soogemackelijck*, and requested him to please let the collector make a proper gauging of the wine and beer he has in his possession.

Whereupon the aforesaid *Soogemackelijck* gave me as an answer that he could not serve two masters, and also that it was forbidden him. Since nothing else can be done at this time, I, Johan de Deckere, have made the following protest. As you, Pr. Adriaensz *Soogemackelijck*, will not permit us to gauge the wine and beer in your cellar **[116]** [*several lines at top lost*]...in the name and on behalf of the honorable the director general and high council in New Netherland for all the expense, damage and interest which the honorable company and the collector have been put to and suffered through your refusal, and by your persistence therein shall cause them to suffer that upon your person and those who may have ordered the same, such a punishment may be rendered as shall be proper. And in the act of making this protest there appeared the person of Jan Baptist van Rensselaer accompanied by his brother [Jeremias] and Brant van Slechtenhorst, who having been informed of the reasons of my coming there, said that I ought not to appear there without proper credentials, demanded the same of me, and declared that unless the same were shown he would never permit the gauging, on the other hand, if the same were shown, the gauging should immediately be ordered; also that it was not according to the rules of war or the custom of soldiers, without previously notifying the person, as if boarding a vessel that before they were brought to the knowledge thereof, they might have armed themselves against the same. So, in like manner, on this occasion, I have protested against the same as before. As before, I went to the house of Maria Goosens, and made the aforementioned demand of her; she made the same kind of answer as *Soogemackelijck* did before. Accordingly I protested against her as before. **[117]** [*several lines lost at top*]...at the house of Arien Appel, and to him made the same demand. He gave for an answer that he dare not take it upon himself. Therefore I protested against him also as before. Done on the 23rd of July.

Marcelys Janse J. de Deckere 1655

[COMMUNICATION TO STUYVESANT AND THE COUNCIL ON MANHATTAN]

Honorable, valiant and most noble lord general, and right honorable gentlemen of the council etc. My lords:

Herewith is sent a copy of a placard, which was referred to in a former letter but inadvertently not sent; there goes also with this a copy of certain questions and answers, and the protest made thereto, from which the condition of things may easily be judged and considered and that without your honors, nothing more can be done by us for the maintenance of order. Therefore we shall await, with regard to this matter, for advice or the pleasure of your arrival. In the meantime, lord general and right honorable gentlemen, may Almighty God grant his favor and blessing upon your honors' government. We remain your honors' humble servants.

[SUBMISSION OF DOUBLE LIST OF CANDIDATES TO FILL MAGISTRATE VACANCIES]

[118] [*Several lines at top lost*]...Most noble *heer* general and right honorable gentlemen of the council of New Netherland. My lords:

With the expiration of the service of magistrates Jan Verbeeck and Jan Tomasz, according to old custom and use, we think it proper to propose to your honors herewith a double number of persons, namely: Rut Jacobsz, Andries Herpertsz, Dirck Jansz Croon, and Dirck Teljer. We request that you will please, out of the said proposed number, or otherwise out of the body of the burghers, two such persons to elect in place of the aforenamed, according to your honors' accustomed wisdom, for the service of the aforesaid office of commissaries, as you shall judge fit and capable. Lord general, we cannot neglect this opportunity to congratulate your honor on your safe and happy voyage and return;* we proclaim that the report and news of them were very pleasant for us to hear; it gave us occasion to thank Almighty God for it, and to pray that He would please more and more be present by His grace in your honors' government, and bless your honors' weighty affairs.

* In December of 1654 Stuyvesant set sail with three ships for Barbados. His mission was to test English enforcement of the navigation acts following the conclusion of the first Anglo–Dutch war. He returned to New Netherland in June of 1655 via Curaçao.

Your honors' willing and trusty servants of the court of Fort Orange and Beverwijck, the 30th of July 1655.

[LETTER FROM PROVISIONAL PRESIDENT DE DECKERE TO DIRECTOR GENERAL STUYVESANT]

[119] [*several lines at top lost*]...nevertheless afterwards being in discourse with Domine Schaets, and from him understanding that the poor's purse was richly garnished, I particularly requested him in your honors' name for the remission of some alms with the recommendation that the church consistory should propose the same, it being a point that the power only depends on them, wherein he was wholly agreed and consented that it was in the highest degree proper and Christian that to the poor without distinction, the helping hand should be stretched out; accepting his authority to be used therein with the consistory, and having delivered over to him an extract out of the letter relating to this point, it was allowed by the consistory, and a sum of 200 guilders was sent to the deacons of the city of New Amsterdam. The last matter to dispatch about the disobedient tappers, is the most scandalous; some being willing rather to fight to the last drop of blood, and another to turn his Gelderland back on us than bear to have those persons sent away. In the meantime with this explanation (since winter is upon us), we shall wait till the next year. *Mons.* Rensselaer desires to send a pleasant greeting; he has as yet threshed no grain, on the contrary appears not inclined to do so. Tomas Chambers alias Clabbort (so it was reported), has indeed several hundred schepels of wheat; but on account of his absence at the Esopus he cannot be spoken to. Whereof, on his return the business can be arranged and a vessel dispatched also. Your honor may look for the grain ordered, or at least a part of it. **[120]** In place of the 4000 ordered not more than 2050 pantiles were sent, there being no more at present to be had; these were all sold to a third person, who not being able to get them off, threw up the purchase. The matters entrusted to Sander Leendertse should have been dispatched by this time, except that in respect to the contemplated blockhouse of necessity to be set up and used, those of the respective courts ordered that it should be delivered again by Sander Leendertse to your honor next spring (God willing), or a contract and agreement be made with him on account thereof. Yesterday the six soldiers sent here arrived. I wish your honor had given orders for more provisions, indeed I see not how a barrel of meat can help us (for all have been called upon), and from what magazine to draw rations for them; and though I well remember that your honor has given some serious recommendation in this regard to the magistrates, and letters have been received by them, and quick promises made; nevertheless, I also observe that they are ostensibly inclined and indicate a superficial acceptance of short duration; and at once the major part as soon as your honor is lost sight of, will artfully get rid of their [ ] and thrust the weight upon my neck (who have no remedy for it or any means in hand); although it is just what commonly happens with such shady magistrates, having been too long in the world, your honor, not to have experienced the proof thereof at some time; nevertheless, I shall do whatever is granted me within my short reach, and whatever shall fall within my capacity. Also, there came here about 300 Mohawks, proposing to go to fight against the French Indians; in the meantime we shall keep an eye open and double the watch. What conversation was had with them today, your honor can see from the annexed document. **[121]** [*several lines at top lost*]...the magistrates must allow (although contra [ ]), and thought highly needful to make a demand on the farmer of the excise for one or two hundred guilders to be used for the purchase of wood and light for use by the guardhouse, together with some food for the soldiers as necessity shall demand. The aforesaid Clabbort is here also today. On his arrival, I spoke to him and asked for the aforesaid wheat; Clabbort said, (although I don't believe it) that he had none to spare. I see no chance elsewhere for doing anything. Herewith, your esteemed honor, I commend myself to your honor's favor and yourself to that of Almighty God, concluding in my capacity, my lord, on this 19th of November 1655.

[PROPOSITIONS MADE BY THE MOHAWKS]

Present:
J. de Decker
Rutger Jacobse
Andries Herperts
Volckert Jansz
J. Bpt. van Rensselaer

A. van Curler
J. van Twiller
J. Hap
H. Jochemse
Philip Pr. etc.

Propositions made by certain sachems of the Mohawks before the commies and those of the respective courts of Fort Orange and the colony of Rensselaerswijck, together with some burghers on the 19th of November 1655.

The first proposition was a remembrance of the late affairs and a renewal of harmony and peace, including the French nation, together with the river Indians down to the Esopus. Also they said they would go to war with the French Indians, and feared that the French were opposed to their treaty, and their promises of being mingled with many lies; hence their request was that, in that case, we would keep ourselves quiet and show neutrality. Thereupon they laid down a belt of sewant. The second and third proposals were in the form of a complaint that we did not entertain them in such a manner as they entertained us when visiting their land. **[122]** [*several lines lost at top*]...that we did not provide the least thing for them and repair their guns or other things, except that they asked for payment in sewant for it; with other trifles of like kind. They considered it not altogether brotherly. Whereupon they gave us two bundles or belts of sewant.

Answer to the aforesaid propositions, namely:
To the first that we were inclined as yet and at all times to maintain with their chiefs a renewal of peace, faithfully and without breach, that we could do nothing having an opposite appearance and recommended that they on their side should remain faithful, suggesting that with their fights and wars we should not meddle or concern ourselves as being external to, and not concerning us. Hereupon were given them fifteen bars of lead.

On the second complaint that we did not entertain and satisfy them as fully as they did us [we answered] that if one, two, or three of them came as we did they should be properly lodged and accommodated, but that justice and law provided in this respect that none should be compelled to do so, since every person being free must earn his own maintenance, and that no one was obliged to be another's servant for nothing, that such being the custom among us, no more complaints were to be made about it, as our other brothers did. Whereupon there was laid down and presented to them 25 pounds of gunpowder. All of which they received and accepted with their customary barbarian applause. Done *ut supra*.

J. de Deckere,
Anno 1655

[REQUEST OF DE DECKERE TO STUYVESANT
CONCERNING THE TAPPERS' EXCISE]

[123] Most noble, worshipful, valiant and right honorable lord general: Since my last intelligence delivered orally by Andries Herpertse, touching the offenses of the tappers, to me recommended and given in charge, that your honor [it being your purpose to come hither] should think it useless to begin the execution of my order and commission; the written countermand thereof has been received, causing me to doubt and stand in suspense till such time as your honor, in answer to this, shall have further declared his meaning and wishes. In the meantime inasmuch as your honor's written order continues in existence, I request more detailed commissions, or at least instructions how to conduct myself in case of certain opposition, resistance, or affront, which I suspect will happen. Provided your honor will appear with the first open water, you shall not for the present be troubled with any particular complaints, but they shall be postponed till then. I have been accosted and asked several times by various people and recently by the housewife of Dijckman for some aid in her distress for settling with certain traders for provisions. I protest that I have no opportunity or means at hand from which to help her. But if your honor forbids any money to be levied from the farmer of the excise, we ourselves shall suffer from the same. Your honor will first make known the same, and give an order to levy fifty, sixty or an hundred guilders out of the farmer's money, for this purpose, or inform me what is to be done. I desire also that an authentic copy of the instructions for the subaltern bench of justice be made and sent to me. Herewith most noble, etc. lord general, kissing your hand, I remain your highly esteemed honor's humble servant. 10 January 1656.

[MAGISTRATES OF FORT ORANGE/BEVERWIJCK TO STUYVESANT WITH NEWS AND NEW YEAR'S GREETINGS]

[124] Most honorable, noble, valiant, wise and highly esteemed lord general and the right honorable gentlemen of the council:

All is well here, God be praised. The thirty Dutchmen, who, as rumor had it at Manhatans, were killed, we expect to be still alive, and the report of the same post or messenger, of the infraction of the peace and the commencement of war between the two nations is false. Lord general and right honorable council, as nothing of material has occurred just now, I shall make no further complaints, especially as your honor proposes to arrive by the first open water. Everyone concerned is very desirous to understand the condition of things there, the news about which, by the bearer, we shall anxiously await. In the meantime we wish your honor and the right honorable council a happy and more prosperous new year. We hope on the one hand that with the old year shall cease all sad rumors, adversities and calamities, and on the other hand that with the new year the rod of God's wrath shall also be cast into the fire, and at once with general tranquility, prosperity and wealth be renewed. To this end we supplicate the court of heaven that the divine majesty will please to preside as well in the assemblies of the burgomasters, as of your honor and right honorable council, and that He will inspire the spirit of prudence, wisdom and manly valor, and also bless their designs and expeditions with the desired outcome for the glory, especially of His holy name, and the welfare of this province and the inhabitants of the same. Herewith lord general and honorable gentlemen, we remain you honors' faithful servants of the court of Fort Orange and Beverwijck. 16 January 1656.

[MAGISTRATES OF FORT ORANGE/BEVERWIJCK TO STUYVESANT CONCERNING LOCAL MATTERS]

[125] Worshipful, valiant and honorable Heer General and right honorable gentlemen of the council:
On the ninth of September last, your honors' letters with the accompanying placards came to hand, which, having examined, it was

thought proper to publish two of them, *viz*: those for the combination of separate dwellings, and the farming out of the duties on peltries; the third, relating to the duties, or payment of the twentieth penny on slaughtered animals, hogs, etc., we have for pregnant reasons withheld, judging it to be unreasonable to publish or post the same, it being apparent at this juncture of time, and on the occasion of excessive expense which the community has incurred or shall hereafter incur by reason of the building of the fort, blockhouse and other works connected with the same, together with the ransoming of prisoners; that nothing less than murmurs, opposition, and resistance would arise; which we trust will be considered and examined by your honors with due deliberation. For the purpose of meeting the aforesaid expense, we convened the community, causing them to stand within, one by one, and inciting them to a free contribution, which ended to our reasonable contentment; upon the unwilling we imposed a certain tax. **[126]** We have built a blockhouse according to resolution, 50 feet square and a man's height high; receiving a communication from four qualified supervisors that they desired to have it pulled down, and in place of it, contracted for a house with bays, the size of which and reasons for it, the bearers of this, Sander Leendertse, and Dirck Janse Croon, our assistants and fellow magistrates, will inform your honors and what is pertinent thereto; further recital is therefore unnecessary. Wherefore we are necessitated and forced to find some new source of taxation; though to make the best of it, together with the first [tax] it cannot reach farther than a bare subsistence. We would petition your honors therefore to solicit and dispose the inhabitants of the city of New Amsterdam to a liberal contribution for the completion of the church begun by us here, and truly will they less doubt and mistrust this, inasmuch as on similar and other occasions, and especially in regard to the church there, we and our citizens gave and contributed according to our ability. From your communication can easily be perceived the uncertainty of your honor's coming up, which we earnestly request, and esteem the presence of your honor's person and the influence of greater authority highly needful, and especially is it demanded for the introduction of new imposts, and chiefly in reference to opposing factions whose shoulders are unaccustomed to such burdens. **[127]** Herewith goes a copy of a certain placard against the congregation of certain persons of the Lutheran sect, published and executed by us against the transgressors and disobedient; we will await your earliest approbation, and otherwise request your honor's wise advice, how we must conduct ourselves on such an occasion. Herewith, lord general and right honorable gentlemen, we pray God to enrich and bless your honors' government, and remain your honors' trusty and faithful court of Fort Orange and Beverwijck. Done at Fort Orange, the 10th of March 1656.

[MAGISTRATES OF FORT ORANGE/BEVERWIJCK TO STUYVESANT CONCERNING NOMINATIONS AND OTHER LOCAL MATTERS]

Worshipful, valiant and honorable *Heer* General and right honorable gentlemen of the council:
The time having come again that three of the existing magistrates, S. Leendertse, Frans Barentse Pastoor, and Volckert Janse , according to custom ought to be dismissed from their office; therefore, in accordance with the same custom, we desire to nominate and propose to your honors a double number, *viz*: Abram Staets, Jacob Janse Schermerhoorn, Goosen Gerritse, Philip Prse. Schuyler, Cornelis Teunise Bos, and Evert Wendel, to the end of that your honors will choose from the same two others as ordinary and one as extraordinary magistrates, as may be deemed fittest according to your usual wise discretion and judgment. We are much surprised that no answer to our last letter, at least none on the subject of our expected collection there, has been received by us, indicating good success for it; with respect to the contracting for the blockhouse church, and the excessive **[128]** expenses for the same, [ ] our expectation and hope in the commencement having been very greatly set thereon, in case of a failure of the same, we should be very much confounded and distressed; even if everything should turn out for the best, it would be very difficult to collect the remainder from the church here. Will your honors please recollect the next article of our instructions; and if ever orders ought to be carried into effect, these certainly, on this occasion, would bring forth good results, and be accomplished in the right time. Your honors cannot be ignorant of the fact that the consumption of wine and beer here ought immediately be farmed out, without any communication respecting the same having hitherto been received; in consequence of this we are uncertain how to regulate ourselves. It is true that the commissary, Johan de Deckere, by a special mandate given to him by

the lord general, has reported to us that the payment of the excise should not be suspended, but continued until further orders of the collector thereon; likewise, that no new farming out of the excise was to be made before the arrival of the lord general or committee, with a recommendation, besides, to the collector, to keep a record of the wine and beer consumed both in the colony and in our jurisdiction; to which, your honors, we would object that it is uncertain whether the collector will accept of, or acquiesce in, the aforesaid continuation; and if he would, it must be done on the foregoing conditions and extension, which has not been done by him hitherto, and would require no little knowledge and exertion to carry out. Moreover, about three hundred guilders, not to be retained, have been paid by him on the promised excise money to relieve him from the promised conditions. **[129]** [ ] At present, and before the close of the term [of the excise], it is impossible for any more money to be paid (so he says), arising from a registering of the beer, etc., consumed by the three public tappers, *Soogemackelijck*, Mary Goosens and Arien Jans van Leyden, but is more reduced than the remainder of the excise money would amount to, wherefore, according to what he says, no money should come into his hands, so that the aforesaid continuation in the future would cause and bring forth nothing but a mere pretense. If, on the contrary, the collector shall decline or refuse the aforesaid registry, and further, if the honorable commissary, De Deckere, be impracticable, then your honors' orders, highly necessary in respect to that, or what is much better, your honor's immediate arrival in person will be awaited and expected. Herewith, etc., your honors' obedient and faithful servants of the court of Fort Orange and Beverwijck. Sent the 8th of April 1656.

[DE DECKERE TO STUYVESANT AND COUNCILORS CONCERNING LOCAL MATTERS]

Highly esteemed, valiant, wise and right honorable gentlemen. Gentlemen: In accordance with your honors' order to apprehend and securely send away the public tappers Pr. Ariensen, alias *Soogemackelijck*, and Arien Janse van Leyden, the business was so directed by me that the aforesaid Pr. Ariensen had notice to come to my house, and was consequently detained; I guarded him with some soldiers till evening, when Jan Baptist van Rensselaer, with the schout of the colony, appeared before me, requesting that the prisoner might be set free, on representation that he, Rensselaer, was ready to interpose and answer for him; which by me, being declined, I was asked if he (the intervenient) was not considered sufficient; my answer was that his sufficiency or insufficiency was not disputed, **[130]** but that my order was simply to send the prisoner away, and that if he wished to answer for him he could do so; finally he requested *ilico en stante pede* a copy of my order and commission, but this was denied him; whereupon threatening me with various mischief, etc., he delivered a protest and therewith departed. This day being Wednesday, I sent the yacht to the other side of the river, and with Rutger Jacobsen, having examined the boards, I was with the yacht's boat, for some tools for the vessel and for my own service, having likewise two soldiers to keep up a constant watch; rowed to the fort again to catch in the trap the rat who had as yet not been taken; in the meantime, let the men on the yacht busy themselves loading the boards; the plan, hitherto so successful, was, by the disobedience and carelessness of those clowns, the boatmen and soldiers, to my extreme distress and vexation, shamefully spoiled. Firstly. By the boatmen who came to me in the evening insisting on the boat, saying that it was necessary for getting in the rest of the boards in proper manner at night, so I crediting them, yielded with the express and reiterated order nevertheless that the boat before the next morning, at least by daybreak, should be brought to the fort, my intention being to carry the prisoner then immediately to the yacht; **[131]** in the meantime, that he might be well watched and securely kept, I made him sleep in my bed by my side; but inquiring in the morning, I could hear of neither boat nor boatmen, without which I could not get to the yacht unless some other vessel was at hand. Owing to the carelessness of the three soldiers and my Negro, to whom the keeping and watch were interested, he was suffered in their presence to run away. I was made aware of his escape and speedily was at the heels of the fugitive, and it would not have been in vain, except that he retired and took refuge in the house of the aforesaid Rensselaer. Nevertheless, I addressed him there, and admonished him to go back with me, otherwise it would go hard on him; yet he refused, but said if I took the other tappers, then he would willingly go with me; on the other hand, came Johannes van Twiller, also Rensselaer not being at home, but with some of his companions last night at the house of Arian Janse had watched with their guns and awaited my coming there), and asked what I wanted there; my answer was that I wished to bring the prisoner away from there; he replied that that should by no means be; being alone and having no help nor soldiers there present and not seeing how I could conveniently succeed, I returned again to my house. I judge it to be in the highest degree absurd that there should be an asylum in the midst of our jurisdiction for fugitives, and a free place for other abuses and usurpations, as have now lately existed in regard to De Hulter's widow, who while dwelling in our fort, would hold a public sale of some wood without consulting me therein, and regardless of my rights with respect to the payment of the auction fees, whereupon a registry and interdict being made to her, to hold no public sale in our jurisdiction without consulting me, or **[132]** having paid my just dues, yet said widow, notwithstanding, held the aforesaid sale without consulting me in the church or at the house of the aforesaid Rensselaer, which and other impertinences and violences will the more exist in the future, not so much through the impulse of the people themselves, as indeed through the inducements and persuasions of certain bullies and boasters who have the management of the colony [Rensselaerswijck], unless a fitting and timely order be made for it by your honors, according to your wise discretion. I would have gone to the house of Arien Janse van Leyden today with proper assistance, except that the aforesaid Rensselaer (fearing the same, so it seems) came to my house yesterday evening, saying that if I would keep quiet, he would be answerable for the aforesaid persons, and, would go with the first yacht to Manhatans; considering that there was not much danger in this, and moreover that the one had escaped, I acquiesced to the proposal, leaving the disputes with the other people to your honors. If the leaders are there, your honors will be able to judge and understand that the tappers in question and others still at large, must appear there. Please send up more soldiers, among whom are one or two who are not too delicate to take hold of someone, so that the people may be intimidated by numbers and all bloodshed and trouble may be prevented. I have spoken to Dijkman's wife, and requested to have her husband sent to Manhatans, to go to Holland on the warship, about which she could hardly make up her mind. She is more inclined to speak about the matter herself with **[133]** your honor, perceiving which, I advised her that the sooner she does it the better, and to take her husband with her, where she will learn the time thereof [departure]. In the meantime having commended your honor to the protection and defense of the Almighty, with my respects, I conclude, as your honor's humble servant. Sent the 26th of May 1656.

[DE DECKERE TO STUYVESANT CONCERNING TAPPERS]

In accordance with the command and order, dated 13 May last, to me, the subscriber, given and granted by the director general, Petrus Stuyvesant, to apprehend and securely to send away the persons of Pieter Adriaensen alias *Soogemackelijck* and Arien Janse van Leyden, both tappers, I, Johan de Deckere, commissary at Fort Orange, on the 24th following, brought the person of said *Soogemackelijck* to my house and detained him there; through the carelessness of certain soldiers, in whose care he was entrusted, he escaped the following day and fled. In the meantime, watching for an opportunity to apprehend in like manner the aforesaid Arien Janse, this evening *Mr*. Jan Baptist van Rensselaer came to my house and posed the question, whether I would keep quiet and not send away said tappers? If yes, he promised, in such case, personally to go to the Manhatans by the first yacht, declaring that the aforesaid persons were guiltless, as it was through his persuasion; and moreover that he would be responsible for them, **[134]** to which I acquiesced for the following reasons: First. Because the aforesaid *Soogemackelijck* having fled, would perhaps remain away for some time. Second. From fear of shedding blood, because as was reported, the aforesaid Rensselaer, with some of his colleagues, passing the night watching at the house of said Arien Janse, waited and watched for my coming there, from which it is easy to see what might follow. And, finally. In consequence of the aforesaid free proposal, considering that the commotion while they were in durance, the outworkings also of their desires, would indeed be put to rest and subjection. Notwithstanding this, on the 29th of this month, having received a certain letter from the said director general of the date 23rd of May past, containing a renewal of my aforesaid order to send away also besides the aforesaid two persons, Mary Goossens; so I, Johan de Deckere aforesaid, in conformity with the aforesaid reiterated order and commission, followed by three soldiers and the aforenamed witnesses, found myself before the house of Mary Goossens, but the door not being opened, I went from there to the houses of Pieter Ariensen and Arien Janse van Leyden, and there finding the secretary of the colony

[Rensselaerswijck], and in the presence of them all, in the name and on behalf of the director general and council of New Netherland, I warned, admonished and commanded the aforesaid tappers, immediately to go with me and commit themselves into my hands and keeping; whereupon they separately answered as before, "There sits my lord," pointing to the aforesaid Rensselaer, "who will answer for me"; and said Rensselaer, in like manner acquiesced the same, not allowing the tappers to go with me. **[135]** Whereupon, I, the commissary aforesaid, as well against the aforesaid Rensselaer and colleagues, as against said tappers, respectively, in the name, etc,. as before, protested in respect to all costs, damage and interests, which the honorable company, through their opposition, disobedience and non-compliance with the excise, have suffered, and may hereafter suffer, to be reclaimed and recovered, as shall be found reasonable. Done and protested on the 31st day of May 1656, in the presence of Rutger Jocobsen, Andries Herpertsen, and Jacob Schermerhooren, as witnesses hereto invited.

J. de Deckere, 1656.

[DE DECKERE'S ACCOUNT OF A CONFRONTATION WITH JAN BAPTIST VAN RENSSELAER]

According to the order and mandates of the director general and council of New Netherland dated 28 June 1656 to *Mr*. Rensselaer and those of the court of the colony [of Rensselaerswijck], to request that the placard, regarding the tenths, may be published in the colony, I, Johan de Deckere, chief commissary at Fort Orange, went with the aforenamed witnesses, to the session and meeting of the court aforesaid, and said order introduced in the name, etc., as before, and requested that they would please cause said placard to be published among them, as was done by us. Whereupon *Mr*. Rensselaer answered: "We are not bound to do so, and we do not intend to do it." Thus done, introduced and answer received on the 6th of July 1656, in the presence of Rutger Jacobsen and Dirk Janse Croon as witnesses requested hereto. J. de Deckere, 1656

[*This concludes De Deckere's records*.]

[**136-138**] [*blank*]

[ACCOUNT KEPT BY FORMER COMMISSARY DIJCKMAN]

[139] Namely 500 B[eavers]		1657
The 20th of June, J. *de Kaper* with beavers sent down from here.	2,000	
The 25th, Klaes This, with about	1,500	
The 28th, Pieter Jacobse with	1,500	
2nd of July, Lucas Andriese, with	1,500	
Ditto, Klaas Borden,	1,400	
10th, de Fries,	300	
The 10th, Johannes Verbruggen,	3,000	
Ditto,	300 otters	8,400
12th, ditto	1,800	7,400
Ditto, Jan *de Kaper*,	300	3,000
	1,000	300
18th, with Abraham Staas,	1,900	1,800
Lucas Anderiessen,	3,000	300
Remke [?],	1,000	12,800
Ditto, Aryaen Klaes,	70	2,000
27 Ditto, Derick Bensick,	5,000	
First of Aug. Michiel *de Karreman*,	1,000	14,070
2 Aug. Eevert Pels,	2,000	7,400
3 Aug. Claes Thys	1,800	3,000
6 ditto, Klaes Bordingh,	200	300
Ditto, Hans Karel	2,300	1,800
Ditto, Lucas Andriesse	250	300
10 ditto, with Abraham Staes,	2,000	2,000
14 ditto, Abraham de Triu,	120	14,300
25 ditto, Abraham Staes,	300	9,670
Ditto, Evert Pels,	100	
Ultimo, Michel *de Karreman*,	400	
Ditto, De Fries,	300	19,370
First of Sept., Hans Kaerle,	100	
13 Sept., Jan *de Kaper*,	400	
Ditto, Pieter Jacobsz,	300	
8 ditto, Jan van Bremen,	300	
27 ditto, Jan Jostensz,	400	8,400
Ditto, Jan van St Aubin	100	14,070

9,670
32,140
1,800
33,940

[140] NB: A worker of Ellert *de Goyer* [ ] has settled with me on their behalf for ƒ60 for which Willhem Fredericksz Bout is security.

Claes *de Goyer* has been fined the sum of ƒ200 for which Willhem Fredericksz Bout is security.

[141] Memorandum
Jan *de Bock* has complained to me that Jacob Arentsz, being his servant, has hired himself to Jan Heelmersz for a year, who has paid to said Jacob, in hand, a half barrel of beer and three guilders, as earnest money, but this same Jacob Arentsz has again hired himself out to Hans de Vos at Katskiel.

On the 8th of March 1657 Jan Andriesse complained to me on behalf of Willem Fredericksz Bout, collector of the excise at Fort Orange, village of Beverwijck, about Hans de Vos for selling brandy and spirits to the Indians; he submitted an affidavit of the same to me, signed L. A. with his own hand.

On the 3rd of March Pieter Stevensz declared to the magistrates that some improprieties had been committed at the house of Albert de *timmerman* on last Shrovetide; that some had walked about in women's clothing.

On the 8th of March [*names canceled*] to me that at Albert *de timmerman's*, when they were erecting his house, Thomas Paulus, and Marcelis Jansz, had [*text canceled*] in the presence of many people, namely:
Claes Hendricks with his servant,
Kip Haecker
Jan Vinhagel

Jan Roeloffsz
Jacob Lokerman
Pieter *Laedemaeker*, deceased.

On Sunday the 25th of Feb. I found at Albert *de timmerman's*, during the morning service, Cornelis Theunisse, alias *Schornsteen*[*veger*] and Jan Gou.

Tuesday, 13th Feb. 1656. Pieter Timensz at Harme *de timmerman's* put on woman's clothes; present: Volcker Jansz.

Saturday, the 7th of April, Claes Ripsz, injured Harmen *de metselaer* with a tankard. [ ] for 2 beavers; paid.

The 10th ditto. Hans de Vos has been apprehended.

Ditto. Harmen Jacobsz, alias Bambus, sailed with his yacht from here for Manhatans loaded with three hundred planks.

The 13th Jan van St. Aubin sailed from here loaded with [*left blank*].

Ditto, Frederick Hendricksz [*left blank*]

Thursday, the 18th of April. Pieter Bronck fought with the wheelwright of Madam van Thulert [de Hulter]; and afterwards aforesaid Pieter Bronck had a dispute with Harmen, the servant of Jan Thomas, and drew his knife; present: Martin *de metselaer*, Gerard Slichtenhorst, and Jacob, the servant of Frans Barentsz; [ ] happened at Bambus's; [ ] fined ƒ200.

[142] Monday, the 23rd of April. Frans Barense Pastoor, with a bare knife in his hand at his place, chased Jacobus Teunisse, alias *de Looper*, to his own fence, who leaped over it with curses in order to escape his grasp; in the presence of the honorable Gerard Sward, schout of Rensselaerswijck, Jacob Schermerhooren, Jan Verbeek, and Pieter Arentsz, and sentenced by me to pay a fine of ƒ100.

The 19th of April. Steven *timmerman* drew his knife at Maerten *de brouwer's* inn and wounded Seeger Wyp in two places, in the presence of Ariaen Appel and Jan This de Baerth, Gerber *de Goyer*, wounded Hendrick the former cowherder at Jan *de wever's*, on the 27th of April.

NB. To submit a request to ask the merchants to supply sail rigging;
An increase of 10 or 12 soldiers;
For 200 lbs of gunpowder;
2 light cannons.
Of the barrels, those of oak need to be weighed.

Sunday evening, the 4th of June. Marten *de metselaer*, in the guard room of the burgherguard, slashed and wounded Pieter Bosboom in the head with his dagger, for which action I had him hauled out of his bed early on Thursday, the 7th of June, and placed in irons.

The 21st of July. Jacobus Teunisse, alias *de Looper*, fought with Hendrick, alias *Kint met sijn moeder* [Child with his mother].

The 22nd ditto. Jacob Lookerman drew his knife and with it wounded Mewus Hoogboom, servant of Claes Hendricksz, for which he was sentenced in a bond of ƒ350, of which I have acquitted him my third part, and he has paid the two thirds to the court and the deacons.

[143] The 23rd of July, Fob Barentsz complained that Elbert de Goyer called him a thief and beat him in the presence of Jacob Schermerhoorn and Simon Janssen.

The 19th of August, Thomas Koning insulted the court, calling the magistrates unjust, maliciously, upon the blessing of Dijckman who had sung the 82nd psalm, calling the high council scoundrels and informers, in the presence of Evert Pels and Aert Jacobsz and Gillis Fonda.

The 29th of August, Harmen Bastiaensz complained to me that Meynert Fredericksz had called him a hay thief in the presence of Tierck and Spietsberg at Meynert's house.

Saturday, the 26th of August, Henderick *Klootdraeyer* drew his sword on the street, and threatened to hack Montagne's door to pieces with the same; present, Jan Hendricksz Snyder, Abraham Steinwijck's servant Remsen, and many others.

Gerbert Gisberd arrested on behalf of Ellert Gerbertsz.

The 19th of November Pieter Stevensz, alias the Godless Domine, filed a complaint against Pieter Bronck who was indebted to him for work during harvest at the Flats [   ] with Pieter *Laedemaker* and Jan Roelofsen.

November 22nd. Evert Knool complained of violence done in his house by Jan Gou on the 20th about 10 o'clock in the evening, in the presence of the honorable Jan Thomas, Willhem Bout, Ale Klaes, Claes Jansz and others; and he was condemned to pay a fine of 12 stivers.

The 13th of May 1658. Ruth Jacobse is to pay three whole beavers, *f*30, for his servant named Hendrick *de Brower*.

[144] The 21st of November. Klaes *de Goyer* drew his knife At the Trumpet* against Pieter Stevensz, alias the Godless Domine, and was condemned by the court, upon which sat J. Schermerhoorn, Philip Pietersz, and Jan Thomas, to pay a fine of *f*100 for which sum Willhem Fredericksz Bout is security.

The 2nd of December Jan Roeloffs cracked the skull of J. Evaerdsz, soldier, with a tankard "At the Trumpet," for which offence he must pay *f*50, according to the statutes of Amsterdam.

The 10th of December. Cornelis Teunisz, alias Keys Koeste has settled with me over the offence he and his wife committed in the house of Gossen Gerritsen, in the presence of Rutger Jacobsz and Jan Verbeeck (who witnessed that he had settled with Gossen Gerritsz) for a beaver coat for me and two beavers for the poor.

The 14th of December. Henderick *de Backer* has settled with me regarding the injuries that he and his wife had done to Andries Herpertsz, in the presence of the same Andries Herpertsz, Jan Verbeeck and the magistrate Philip Pietersz, for two beavers to Harmen.

* At the Trumpet [*Tot de Trompet*] is the name of a tavern.

[145] The 9th of December. Derick Klaes, skipper of the *Eendracht*, came here from Klaveracht [Claverack] with Lambert Matroos.

The 12th ditto. They brought me for the account of H. Jacobsz, *f*23, 12 stivers for consumed vituals.

The 25th ditto. The skipper came here from Klaeverraecht with Lambert.

The 11th of Jan., 1658. Willhem Fredericksz complained to me about Marcelis Jansz who reviled him as a thief on the 9th of Jan., in the presence of Philip Pietersz, Dirick Jansz Croon, Ruth Jacobsz, and H. Jocemsz.

The 25th of January. Cornelis Woutersz and Pieter Messen pledged security for the offense of Jan Andries and Pieter Jacobsz Voosborch and Kip Haecker, in the presence of Gisbert van Imbroeck and Johannes Provost.

The 27th of January. Jacob Haep has arrived, bringing in the servant of Ariaen *de Boer* who escaped from the Indians.

Friday the 22nd of Feb. Jacob Theunisz, alias *de Looper*, drew his knife on the *Mael Boer* and after that on Jan Roeloffs, wounding the same at or before the door of Jan *de wever*.

The 25th of Feb. Jan Gou drew his knife and wounded the *Scheel* Harmen, whom *Mr*. Jacobsz visited and attended to.

The 9th of March is Haermen, commonly called the *Scheel* Haermen, [fined] the sum of *f*60, for which sum Willhem Fredericksz Bout is surety.

The 21st of June Jacobus Theunisz, night watch officer, saw an Indian go in and out at Thomas Paulus's; he said that he, the same Thomas, is giving out wine, beer or brandy; in the presence of Wynter, Jan Theunisz, and Bastiaen Pietersz.

The 27th of April Pieter Jansz *Laemacker* complained to me that Evert Nolding had assaulted him at his place and drew his knife on him and

after that fetched his sword and [ ] in the presence of Lowys Kobes, Arnoud Cornelisz, Jan Mangelssen.
Piter Jansen

[*The following pages were kept by Johannes Provoost.*]

[146] On this 27th day of April 1659 appeared before the honorable commissary Johan de la Montagne, Cornelis Theunisz van Breuckelen and Evert Pels who offered surety, according to the judgment of the court, for the fine of Evert Nolden who was indicted by Pieter Jansz as appears in his own hand, dated as above. Acknowledged by his own signature at Fort Orange.
Corn. Th. [*faded or incomplete*]
Evert Pels

Before me as witnesses,
Ludovicus Cobes, court messenger.

[*In the hand of De la Montagne*:] On the 5th of May Matheus Jansen complained to me about Jacobus Theunisz who struck him without cause in the garden of Jeoryaen *Glasemaeker*, in the presence of the aforesaid Juriaen Jacob vanden Linden, Juryaen *de Cupper* [*Cuyper*], Arnaud and many others.

[147–154] [*blank*]

[CONDITIONS FOR THE SALE OF HENDERICK JOCHIMSEN'S HOUSE AT OPEN AUCTION]

[155] Conditions and terms upon which Henderick Jochimsen intends to sell at public sale to the highest bidder his house and lot, lying near Fort Orange or to the north of the same in which lives Johannes Dijckman who has rented the aforesaid house and lot until the first of May *anno* 1660 for the sum of *f* 140. The buyer shall have the benefit of the full rent from the first of May *anno* 1659 until the first of May 1660.

First. The aforesaid house shall be delivered to the buyer, also the lot as it lies enclosed by fence with all that is earth and nailed fast, from this 16th day of July. Payment shall be made in two installments; the first, on the first day of September 1659, half in good merchantable beavers, and the other half in good marketable sewant. The buyer shall be obliged to furnish two suitable sureties, each for the whole, immediately, to the satisfaction of the seller, and if the buyer cannot furnish said sureties in said time, then it shall be offered for sale again at his expense and cost, and whatever less it comes to be worth, he shall be obliged to make good, and whatever more it comes to be worth, he shall derive no benefit from. The auction fees accrue to the expenses of the buyer.

After bidding closed Roeloff Swartwout remained the last bidder for the sum of five hundred and seven guilders, according to the aforesaid conditions. [*This paragraph was canceled in the original.*]

After much bidding Cornelis Cornelissen Sterrenvelt remained the last bidder for the sum of five hundred and seven guilders, according to the aforesaid conditions and offers as securities and principals Cornelis Teunissen Bosch and Cornelis Theunissen van Slijck for payment of the aforesaid sum, for which they bind their persons and estates, real and personal, present and future, submitting the same to all laws and judges. Done in the village of Beverwijck, the 16th of July 1659.

Cornelis Cornelissen Sterrenvelt
Cornelis Theunisen Bos
This is the mark of 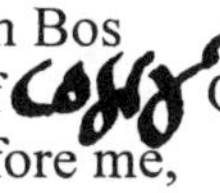 Cornelis Teunissen made with own hand.
Acknowledged before me,
La Montagne, commissary at Fort Orange.

[CONDITIONS FOR THE SALE OF HENDERICK JOCHIMSEN'S HOUSE AND LOT AT PUBLIC AUCTION]

[157] Conditions according to which Henderick Jochimsen intends to sell at public sale to the highest bidder his house and lot where he presently lives, situated near Fort Orange.

First. The aforesaid house and lot shall be delivered to the buyer, as it stands enclosed by fence, with all that is earth and nail fast, just as the seller possessed it.

Delivery shall be made on the first of September *anno* 1659.

The payment shall be made in three installments and that each installment shall be half in merchantable beavers and the other half in good, marketable sewant; namely, the first installment upon delivery of the house and lot, the second installment on the first of July *anno* 1660 and the third installment on the first of July *anno* 1661.

The buyer shall be obliged to offer two suitable sureties immediately, both as principals to the satisfaction of the seller.

If the buyer is unable to offer the aforesaid suitable sureties in the appointed time, then it shall be auctioned again at his own cost and expense, and whatever less it comes to be worth, he shall be obliged to make good, and whatever more it comes to be worth, he shall derive no benefit from. The auction fees accrue to the expenses of the buyer.

[*not completed*]

[158] [*blank*]

[CONDITIONS FOR THE SALE OF ARENT VANDEN BERGH'S HOUSE AT PUBLIC AUCTION]

[159] Conditions and terms upon which Arent vanden Bergh intends to sell at public sale to the highest bidder his house lying in Fort Orange bounded on the east by Henderick Andriessen, on the west by Michiel Janssen.

First. The aforesaid house shall be delivered to the buyer, as it stands, with all that is earth and nail fast, just as the seller possessed and owned it with a garden located behind Fort Orange together with the garden produce.

Delivery shall be made on this coming first of August.

Payment shall be in two installments: half of each installment in good merchantable beavers, the other half in good marketable sewant; namely, the first installment with the delivery and the second installment on the first of September of this year *anno* 1659.

The buyer shall be obliged to provide two suitable sureties immediately, both as principals to the satisfaction of the seller.

If the buyer is unable to offer the aforesaid suitable sureties in the appointed time, then it shall be auctioned again at his own cost and expense, and whatever less it comes to be worth, he shall be obliged to make good, and whatever more it comes to be worth, he shall derive no benefit from. The auction fees shall accrue to the expenses of the buyer.

[*not completed*]

[160] [*left blank*]

[CONDITIONS FOR THE SALE OF PIETER BRONCK'S HOUSE AND LOT AT PUBLIC AUCTION]

[161] Conditions and terms upon which Pieter Bronck intends to sell to the highest bidder at open auction his house and lot, located in the village of Beverwijck at the hill where Jacob Teunissen presently lives.

First. The aforesaid house, one board long, shall be delivered to the buyer with an Indian house next to it, except for a little shed belonging to Jacob Teunissen which he shall tear down immediately, otherwise resign it to the seller, provided that the aforesaid Jacob Teunissen receive proper satisfaction for it, if they can come to an agreement with a piece of land next to it, twenty rods in length and five rods wide, according to the patent thereof.

Delivery shall be made on this coming first of August.

Payment shall be in two installments in good merchantable beavers, the first installment with the delivery and the second installment on the first of July of this year *anno* 1659.

The buyer shall be obliged to provide two suitable sureties immediately, both as principals to the satisfaction of the seller.

If the buyer is unable to offer the aforesaid suitable sureties in the appointed time, then it shall be auctioned again at his own cost and expense, and whatever less it comes to be worth, he shall be obliged to make good, and whatever more it comes to be worth, he shall derive no benefit from. The auction fees shall accrue to the expenses of the buyer.

[*not completed*]

[ACCOUNT OF GOODS SOLD BY PIETER CLAERBOUT]

[162] Goods sold by Pieter Claerbout for beavers in the period of eight days; what is otherwise not paid in beavers is to be reckoned in sewant at *f*12 guilders the beaver. This 16th of July 1659.

Geurt Gerritsen, one painting,	*f*9.0.0
Abraham Staets, one ditto,	*f*8.0.0
The Lord Rencelaer, one ditto,	*f*8.5.0
Cornelis Teunissen Bosch, one ditto,	*f*14.10.0
Adriaen Gerritsen, two candlesticks,	*f*9.0.0
Cornelis Teunissen Bosch, a flat iron with a lamp,	*f*10.5.0
Jan *de Kuyper*, 3 porcelain cups,	*f*5.5.0
Willem Janssen Schut, 3 ditto,	*f*4.4.0
Roeloff Willemsz, 2 porcelain bowls,	*f*6.16.0
Pieter Jacobsen, 6 ditto trenchers,	*f*5.5.0
Loewies Cobussen, 7 ditto,	*f*6.13.0
J. Lamontagne, 3 ditto dishes,	*f*5.10.0

Fredrick Harmsen, 3 ditto,	*f*5.0.0
Geurt Gerritsen, 3 ditto,	*f*7.0.0
Jan Tomassen, 4 ditto,	*f*9.0.0
Adriaen Gerritsen, 2 valances with 2 curtains,	*f*24.0.0
Arent Isaacksz, a black apron,	*f*21.5.0
Abraham Staets, a black jacket,	*f*35.0.0
Withdrawn, a child's apron with a waist coat,	*f*17.0.0
Gerrit Gerritsen, a red coat,	*f*44.0.0
Aernout Cornelissen, a Leiden cloth coat,	*f*48.0.0
Henderick Jochimsen, a blue coat,	*f*42.0.0
Woutert *de backer*, a black coat,	*f*52.0.0
Arent vanden Bergh, a child's garment,	*f*14.4.0
and Lord Lamontagne, a black linen apron,	*f*13.0.0
	*f*414.02.0
[163] Eldert Gerbertsen, a small bible,	*f*14.15.0
Barent Pietersen, 2 children's caps,	*f*8.16.0
Abraham, a child's apron,	*f*5.5.0
Withdrawn, a silver belt,	*f*20.0.0
Withdrawn, two gold rings; the one for *f*20,	
the other for *f*16, together,	*f*36.0.0
Harmen Vedder, a diaper basket,	*f*2.0.0
	86.6.0
	414.2.0
	500.8.0
	73.0.0
	427.8.0

[ACKNOWLEDGMENT OF DEBT]

Appeared before me, Johannes Lamontagne, commissary of Fort Orange and the village of Beverwijck, Evert Pels, who openly declared his indebtedness to the honorable Henderick van Dijck for fifteen whole and merchantable beavers, as the balance of an obligatory note. Done at Fort Orange, the 16th of July *anno* 1659.

Lamontagne, commissary at Fort Orange.

[CONVEYANCE OF HALF A HOUSE AND LOT FROM BARENT MEYDERSEN TO BARENT REYNDERSEN]

[164] Appeared before me, Johannes Lamontagne, on behalf of the general chartered West India Company, commissary of Fort Orange and the village of Beverwijck, in the presence of the honorable Francoys Boon and Anderies Herbertsen, magistrates of the same court, Barent Meyndersen who declared to have conveyed, as he hereby does cede and convey in real and actual possession, to the benefit of Barent Reyndersen, his heirs or those who shall receive title from him, the just half of his house and lot, lying in the village of Beverwijck to west of Gerrit Bancken and to the east of Rutger Jacobsen, with all the right and title, which the conveyance has had therein, which title the aforesaid conveyor has received from Jan Vinhagel, dated the 12th of July *anno* 1658, and releases furthermore the grantee from all claims, demands or pretensions, which may hereafter arise; pledging therefor his person and estate, real and personal, present and future, submitting the same to all laws and judges. Done at Fort Orange, the 17th of July, *anno* 1659.

Barent Meynders
Andries Herberts
Francoys Boon

[CONVEYANCE OF HOUSE AND LOT FROM CORNELIS SEGERSEN TO GERRIT SLICHTENHORST]

[165] Appeared before me, Johannes Lamontagne, on behalf of the general chartered West India Company, commissary at Fort Orange and the village of Beverwijck, in the presence of the honorable Jan Verbeeck and Sander Leendersen Glen, magistrates of the same court, Cornelis Segersen, burgher and inhabitant of Colonie Rencelaerswijck, who declares to have ceded and conveyed, as he hereby cedes and conveys in real and actual possession to the benefit of Gerrit Slichtenhorst, burgher and inhabitant here, his heirs or those who have title from him, a house and lot, lying in the aforesaid village near the hill along the road; in length nine rods, west of the hill six rods and three feet wide, to the east five rods and one to two feet (not understood), to the north nine rods; which title the conveyor has received from Jan Roeloffsen, on 10 December *anno* 1657, and furthermore releases the conveyor of all claims, demands and pretensions, which hereafter many come against it; pledging his person and estate, real and personal, present and future, making the same subject to all laws and judges. Done at Fort Orange, the 18th of July *anno* 1659.

Wtnesses:
Corneliys Zeegerszoon
Jan Verbeeck
Sander Lenrsen Glen.

[CONVEYANCE OF A GARDEN FROM JAN ROELOFFSEN TO HENDERICK JOCHIMSEN]

[166] Appeared before me, Johannes Lamontagne, on behalf of the general chartered West India Company, in the presence of Sander Leendersen and Jan Verbeeck, magistrates of the same court, Jan Roeloffsen who declares to have conveyed, as he hereby cedes and conveys in real and actual possession to the benefit of Henderick Jochimsen, his heirs or those who shall have title from him, a garden, lying in the village of Beverwijck behind Fort Orange bounded on the east by the garden of Pieter Loockermans, to the north by the garden of Rem Jansen, on the west and south by the road; on the north side, three rods and one foot in length, on the south three rods and 8 feet in length, on the east side, five rods and four feet in width, on the west, five rods and seven feet; which aforesaid garden the aforesaid Jan Roelofsen was granted by the honorable director general and council of New Netherland, dated 24 March *anno* 1654, promising to release the grantee from all claims, demands, and pretensions, which hereafter many come against it; pledging his person and estate, real and personal, present and future, making the same subject to all laws and judges. Done at Fort Orange, the 18th of July *anno* 1659.

Witnesses:
Jan Roelofsen

Sander Lenresen
Jan Verbeeck

[SALE OF TOMAS JANSSEN MINGAEL'S HOUSE AND LOT AT PUBLIC AUCTION]

[167] Conditions and terms upon which Tomas Janssen Mingael intends to sell at public auction to the highest bidder his house and lot, lying in the village of Beverwijck, to the north Henderick *de backer,* to the south Pieter Loockermans.

The same house shall be delivered as it stands today met all that is earth and nail fast, together with the lot as it stands within the fence. The transfer shall take place on Monday, being the next 4th of August.

Payment shall be made in two installments, two-thirds in good whole merchantable beavers and one-third in good marketable sewant, and that in two installments, the first upon transfer, the second on the last day of September of this year *anno* 1659.

The buyer shall be obliged to provide two suitable sureties immediately, both as principals to the satisfaction of the seller.

If the buyer is unable to offer the aforesaid suitable sureties in the appointed time, then it shall be auctioned again at his own cost and expense, and whatever less it comes to be worth, he shall be obliged to make good, and whatever more it comes to be worth, he shall derive no benefit from. The auction fees shall accrue to the expenses of the buyer.

[*not completed*]

[TERMS FOR SALE OF CHRISTOFFEL DAVIDS' GOODS]

[168] Goods of Christoffel Davids to be paid in beavers within the period of three weeks from this date the 29th of July.

Willem Brouwer, 6 pewter trenchers and 7 napkins,	*f*21.0.0
Andries Herbertsen, dito,	*f*20.10.0

[CONDITIONS FOR SALE OF A HORSE BY *MR*. SCHRICK]

Conditions upon which *Mr*. Schrick intends to sell a horse to the highest bidder, which will be delivered immediately to the buyer; to be paid in beavers, half in cash and the other half over two months, or otherwise to pay in sewant at *f*12 the beaver, beginning on this date, provided that the buyer shall provide a suitable surety. The fees shall accrue to the expenses of the buyer.

[ACKNOWLEDGMENT OF DEBT OF CLAES RIPSEN]

[169] Appeared before me, Johannes La Montagne, on behalf of the general chartered West India Company, commissary at Fort Orange and the village of Beverwijck, in the presence of the honorable Sander Leendersen Glen and Jan Verbeeck, magistrates of the same court, Claes Ripsen who openly declared his indebtedness to Henderick Anderiessen and Cornelis Wijncoop thirty-nine good whole beavers and promises to pay the aforesaid beavers in the month of June *anno* 1660; which debt stems from the purchase of a house and lot that the aforesaid Claes Ripsen bought at public auction from the aforesaid Henderick Anderiessen and Cornelis Wijncoop; which aforesaid house and lot the buyer places in mortgage and as a special pledge for payment of the aforesaid thiry-nine beavers. Whereupon he further pledges his person and estate, moveable and immoveable, now and in the future, subjecting the same to all judges and courts. Done at Fort Orange, the 18th of August *anno* 1659.

Witnesses:
Claes Ripsen van Dam
Sander Lenrsen
Jan Verbeeck

Acknowledged by me,
La Montagne, commissary at Fort Orange.

[POWER OF ATTORNEY FOR JAN COSTER VAN AECKEN]

[170] Appeared before me, Johannes La Montagne, on behalf of the general chartered West India Company, commissary at Fort Orange and the village of Beverwijck, subscribed below on this date in the presence of the witnesses named below, Jan Coster van Aecken who declares to constitute and empower as proxy, as he hereby does, the honorable Stoffel Janssen and Pieter *de Maecker*, to act in the constituent's name and on his behalf, and to receive in Hollad from the honorable Jan Dareth, presently ready to depart for *patria*, the sum of three hundred twelve guilders and ten stivers in Holland money, stemming from fifty beavers, which the aforesaid Jan Daret bought from the aforesaid Jan Koster van Aecken at six guilders, five stivers a piece, issuing upon receipt thereof an acquittance; in case of his refusal, to employ every legal means thereto and to act in the same matter as if the constituent himself was present, promising to remain good and true to all that the attorneys shall have done in this matter, pledging his person and estate, moveable and immoveable, now and in the future, submitting the same to all laws and judges. Done in Fort Orange in New Netherland, in the presence of Harmen Albertse Vedder and Johannes Provoost, witnesses called thereto on this 18th of August *anno* 1659.

This is the mark  of Jan Coster van Aecken
made with his own hand.
Harman Albertse Vedder
Johannes Provoost, as witnesses

Acknowledged by me,
La Montagne, commissary at Fort Orange.

[ACKNOWLEDGMENT OF DEBT OF JACOB LOOCKERMANS]

[171] Appeared before me, Johannes La Montagne, on behalf of the general chartered West India Company, commissary at Fort Orange and the village of Beverwijck, in the presence of the honorable Francoys Boon and Anderies Herbertsen, magistrates of the same court, Jacob Loockermans, burgher and inhabitant of the aforesaid village, who acknowledges openly that he is indebted to the honorable Johannis Withart, merchant here, the sum of four hundred forty guilders in good whole merchantable beavers, for merchandise received to his satisfaction; and promises to pay the aforesaid sum of four hundred forty guilders the first of July 1660, specifically pledging for it his house and lot, lying in the village of Beverwijck, and that as a binding mortgage and security for payment of the aforesaid sum as well as his person and estate, moveable and immoveable, now and in the future, making the same subject to all laws and judges. Done at Fort Orange, the 18th of August *anno* 1659.

Jacob Lokermans

[POWER OF ATTORNEY OF JACOB ADRIAENSEN]

[172] Appeared before me, Johannes Provoost, clerk of the court of Fort Orange and the village of Beverwijck, subscribed on this date, in the presence of the witnesses named below, Jacob Adriaensen, who declares to constitute and empower, as he hereby does, the honorable Eldert Gerbertsen to act and receive in the constituent's name and on his behalf all the outstanding debts that the constituent is due here in New Netherland, according to bonds and other proofs relating thereto, as well as to pay all the constituent's debts, which shall be submitted to the proxy with good proof; in particular, in case of refusal to pay, to sell the house of Paulus Martensen, promising to consider as good and just all that the proxy shall have done in the same matter, pledging his person and goods, moveable and immoveable, now and in the future, making the same subject to all laws and judges. Done at Fort Orange in the presence of Sacharias Sickels and Jan Eerraerts called hereto as witnesses on this 20th of August *anno* 1659.

Jacob Adryaens
Sachariyas Syckelsz
Johannes Eerraertsz

Acknowledged before me,
Johannes Provoost, clerk.

[POWER OF ATTORNEY OF JAN DARETH]

[173] Appeared before me, Johannes Provoost, clerk of the court of Fort Orange and the village of Beverwijck, subscribed on this date in the presence of the witnesses named below, Jan Dareth, presently about to depart for *patria*, who declares that he has constituted and empowered, as he hereby does, the honorable Gerrit Swart, schout of the colony of Rensselaerswijck, to act and receive in the constituent's name and on his behalf from Reynier Wisselpenningh such monies as are due the constituent according to his obligation, issuing upon receipt thereof an acquittance; in case of his refusal, to employ every legal means for a definitive judgment and final execution, including also, to proceed, if required, with the attachment of persons and goods, and furthermore to do and to act as if the constituent was present himself, promising to consider as good and just all that the proxy shall have done in the same matter, provided that the proxy shall be obliged to render a proper account and return. Thus done and approved at Fort Orange in the presence of Arent Janssen and Jan Barensen, as witnesses sought hereto on the 20th of August *anno* 1659.

Jan Dareth
Arent Janse
Jan Barentsen

Acknowledged by me,
Johannes Provoost, clerk.

[POWER OF ATTORNEY OF JAN FRANCEN VAN HOESEM]

[174] Appeared before me, Johannes Lamontagne, on behalf of the general chartered West India Company, commissary at Fort Orange and the village of Beverwijck, subscribed on this date in the presence of the witnesses named below, Jan Francen van Hoesem, who declares that he has constituted and empowered, as he hereby does, Tieleman van Vleck, notary public, residing at Amsterdam in New Netherland, specifically, in the subscriber's name, to demand and receive from Gysbert van Loenen the sum of one hundred eleven guilders, arising from food and drink together with related expenses, issuing upon receipt thereof an acquittance; in case of his refusal, to employ every legal means for a definitive judgment and final execution, including also, to proceed, if required, with the attachment of persons and goods, and furthermore to do and to act as if the constituent was present himself, promising to consider as good and just all that the proxy shall have done in the same matter, provided that the proxy shall be obliged to render a proper account and return. Thus done and confirmed at Fort Orange in the presence of Jan Barentsen and Arent Janssen, as witnesses called hereto on this 20th of August *anno* 1659.

This is the mark  of Jan Fransen van Hoesem, made himself.
Arent Janse
Jan Barentsen
Acknowledged by me,
La Montagne, commissary at Fort Orange.

[POWER OF ATTORNEY OF HENDERICK MARTENSE VAN COPPENHAGEN]

[175] Appeared before me, Johannes La Montagne Senior, licensed by the lord director general and council of New Netherland as clerk and vice director of Fort Orange and the village of Beverwijck, residing in the aforesaid Fort Orange, Henderick Martensen van Coppenhaegen, who in the presence of the subscribed witnesses, declared that he had granted, transferred, and assigned to and for the benefit of Lucas Dircksen for merchandise enjoyed to his contentment and satisfaction before the execution of this, the sum of fifty guilders to be received in the fatherland for his monthly wages and subsistence owed him; furthermore, the aforesaid Henderick Martensen van Coopenhagen hereby appoints and empowers the lawful holder of this paper to solicit, demand, and receive the said sum of fifty guilders in the fatherland from the highly esteemed directors of the chartered West India Company, the chamber at Amsterdam, issuing upon receipt thereof an acquittance, which shall be valid as if granted by the subscriber himself, also to do and perform all things relating to the receipt of the aforesaid sum, were the subscriber himself present, could or might have done; **[176]** in addition, wherever the matter demands greater and more special authority than appears expressed herein, promising always to hold as good and true whatever shall be done by virtue of this instrument, pledging his person and estate thereto. Thus done at Fort Orange in the presence of Gerrit Slichtenhorst and Sacharias Sickels as witnesses called hereto on this 21st of August *anno* 1659, at Fort Orange in New Netherland.

This is the mark of **X** Henerick Martensen,
made with his own hand.
Gerrit Slichtenhorst
Sacharyas Seeckelsz

Acknowledged by me,
Lamontagne, commissary at Fort Orange.

[POWER OF ATTORNEY OF PIETER CORNELISSEN DE JONGH AND CORNELIS JACOBSEN]

[177] Appeared before me, Johannes La Montagne, licensed by the lord director general and council of New Netherland as clerk and vice director of Fort Orange and the village of Beverwijck, residing in the aforesaid Fort Orange, Pieter Cornelissen *de Jongh* and Cornelis Jacobsen, both merchants here and also about to depart together for the fatherland, who declare that they have appointed and empowered, as they hereby do, the honorable Evert Wendel to collect, demand, and receive here in New Netherland in the constituents' names and on their behalf such outstanding debts as are owed the subscribers, according to bonds and other instruments, which serve the same purpose, issuing upon receipt thereof an acquittance; in case of refusal, to employ every legal means for a definitive judgment and final execution, including also, if required, to proceed with the attachment of persons and goods, and furthermore to do and to act as if the constituent was present himself, promising to consider as good and just all that the proxy shall have done in the same matter, provided that the proxy shall be obliged to **[178]** render a proper account and return, pledging his person and estate thereto. Thus done and confirmed at Fort Orange in New Netherland in the presence of Claes Pietersen and Johannes Provoost, called as witnesses hereto on this 22nd of August *anno* 1659.

Pieter Cornelis *de Jonge*
Cornelis Jacobsz
Clas Pytersen
Johannes Provoost, witnesses

Acknowledged by me,
La Montagne, commissary at Fort Orange.

[POWER OF ATTORNEY OF ZACHARIAS SICKELS VAN *WEENEN*]

[179] Appeared before me, Johannes La Montagne, licensed by the lord director general and council of New Netherland as clerk and vice director of Fort Orange and the village of Beverwijck, residing in the aforesaid Fort Orange, Zacharias Sickles van *Weenen* [Vienna], who, in the presence of the witnesses named below, declares to have granted, transferred, and assigned to and for the benefit of Reindert Janssen Hoorn for goods received to his contentment and satisfaction, the sum of thirty-six guilders and ten stivers, to be received in the fatherland from his credited monthly wages and subsistence, which he earned on the island of Curaçao at Fort Amsterdam in the service of the honorable directors of the chartered West India Company as a naval cadet, according to the account thereof signed by Rodenborgh and Verellen; in addition, the aforesaid Zacharias Sickels van Weenen hereby appoints and empowers the lawful holder of this [document] to request, demand,

and receive the aforesaid sum of thirty-six guilders and ten stivers in the fatherland from the right honorable directors of the chartered West India Company in the chamber of Amsterdam, and having received it to issue a receipt thereon, **[180]** which shall be valid as though it were given by the subscriber himself, moreover to do and perform all things in order to obtain the aforesaid sum, which the subscriber himself being present could or might do; also, if the matter demands more special authority than is expressed herein, promising at all times to hold good and true whatever by virtue hereof shall be done, pledging his person and estate. Thus done at Fort Orange in the presence of Lowies Cobussen and Johannes Provoost as witnesses sought hereto on this 28th of August *anno* 1659.

Sacharyas Seeckelsz
Ludovicus Cobes
Johannes Provoost, witnesses

Acknowledged by me,
La Montagne, commissary at Fort Orange.

[POWER OF ATTORNEY OF DIRCK DIRRICKSEN KEYSER AND WALRAEFF PIETERSEN CLAERHOUT]

[181] Appeared before me, Johannes La Montagne, licensed by the lord director general and council of New Netherland as clerk and vice director of Fort Orange and the village of Beverwijck, residing in the aforesaid Fort Orange, on the date written below and in the presence of the subscribed witnesses, the honorable Dirck Dirricksen Keyser and Walraeff Pietersen Claerhout, who hereby declare to have constituted and empowered the honorable Philip Pietersen Schuyler to demand and receive in the constituents'name and on his behalf all such outstanding debts as are owed to these constituents here at Fort Orange in New Netherland, according to bonds and other instruments, which serve similar purpose, to issue a quittance upon receipt thereof, and in case of refusal to exact the payment with the right and rigor of the law until final judgment and execution; in addition to this, also to proceed to attach persons and estates, and furthermore to do and perform everything which the constituent deems and proper, promising to hold good and **[182]** true all that the constituent shall have done in the matter, provided that he shall be obliged, upon request, to make a proper statement and return of his transactions and returns, pledging their persons and estates. Thus done and issued at the fort in the presence of Zacharias Sickels and Johannes Provoost as witnesses sought hereto, on this 28th of August *anno* 1659.

Dirck Dircksz Keyser
Walrave Pietersz Claerhout
Zacharyas Seeckels
Johannes Provoost, witnesses.
Acknowledged by me,
La Montagne, commissary at Fort Orange.

[ACKNOWLEDGMENT OF RECEIPT OF BONDS BY PHILIP PIETERSEN SCHUYLER]

[183] Appeared before me, Johannes La Montagne, licensed by the lord director general and council of New Netherland as commissary of Fort Orange and the village of Beverwijck, residing in the aforesaid Fort Orange, on the date written below and in the presence of the subscribed witnesses, Philip Pietersen Schuyler, who declares to have received from Dirck Dircksz Keyser and taken for safekeeping the following bonds for which he is attorney: Rutger Jacobsz, one of thirty-eight and another of thirty-two beavers; Jurriaen Teunissen, a bond of 22 beavers; Jan Verbeeck, one ditto of 27 beavers; Pieter Adriaensen *Soogemackelijck*, one ditto amounting to 7 beavers; Anderies Herbertsen, one bond of 28 beavers; Jacob Tyssen vander Heyden, one ditto $16\frac{3}{8}$ beavers; *Broer* Cornelis, one ditto of $33\frac{1}{2}$ beavers; Henderick *Bierman*, one of 12 beavers; Geurt Hendericksen, one of ditto of 3 beavers.

Which foregoing bonds the aforesaid Philip Pietersen or the appearer promises to bring back to the aforesaid Kirrick Dirricksen Keyser or to make an account thereof as soon as **[184]** he returns from the fatherland, pledging his person and goods, moveable and immoveable, for now and the future, subjecting the same to all laws and judges. Done at Fort Orange, the 29th of August *anno* 1659, in the presence of Jan Barensz and Johannes Provoost as witnesses sought hereto on this 29th of August *anno* 1659.

Philip Pieterse Schyler
Jan Barentsen
Johannes Provoost, as witnesses
Acknowledged by me,
Lamontagne, commissary at Fort Orange.

[POWER OF ATTORNEY OF JOANNES DIJCKMAN]

[185] Appeared before me, Johannes La Montagne, licensed by the lord director general and council of New Netherland as vice director and commissary of Fort Orange and the village of Beverwijck, residing in the aforesaid Fort Orange, on the date written below and in the presence of the subscribed witnesses, the honorable Joannes Dijckman, assisted by his wife Maria Bosijns, who declares to have constituted and empowered the honorable Crijn Pietersen van Seventer, bookkeeper of the general chartered West India Company, chamber at Amsterdam, to request and demand in the constituent's name and on their behalf, all such claims as owed to them by way of the estate left by Aeltien Poulus Root, widow of Joris Dijckman, father and mother of the subscriber, and in the same inquiries and requests to act as if the constituents were present, promising to hold good and true all that the attorney in aforesaid matter shall do, pledging his person and estate, moveable and immoveable. Thus done at Fort Orange in New Netherland in the presence of Adriaen Janssen van Leyden and Arent Janssen, as witnesses sought hereto, on this 3rd of September *anno* 1659.

Joannes Dijckman
Maria Bosijns
A. Jans van Leyden
Arent Jansen
Acknowledged by me,
Lamontagne, commissary at Fort Orange.

[POWER OF ATTORNEY OF VOLCKERT JANSSEN DOUW]

[186] Appeared before me, Johannes La Montagne, licensed by the lord director general and council of New Netherland as vice director and commissary of Fort Orange and the village of Beverwijck, residing in the aforesaid Fort Orange, on the date written below and in the presence of the subscribed witnesses, the honorable Volckert Janssen, burgher of the aforenamed village of Beverwijck [and] landlord of a farm located in the colony of Rencelaerswijck, who declares to have constituted and empowered, as he hereby does, the honorable Poulus Schrick, merchant at Herfort [Hartford] in New England, to make inquiries in the constituent's name and on his behalf in New England or elsewhere concerning Pieter Pietersen Lassen and Willem Symonsen, both servants of the appearer, as can be seen by the contracts thereof, which aforesaid servants have runaway from here; having found the aforesaid servants to bring them to their master, the appearer, with all due force and rigor of justice, or to deliver them into his hands; and if necessity should demand it, the attorney is authorized to constitute in his place one or more [persons] in order legally to recover the aforesaid servant, and to act in the same matter as though the **[187]** subscriber himself was present, promising, in addition, to hold good and true all that the attorney shall do in the matter, pledging his person and estate. Thus done in Fort Orange in the presence of Master Jacob de Hince and Johannes Provoost, called as witnesses hereto on this 21st of September *anno* 1659.

Volckertt Jansz
De Hinsse
Johannes Provoost, witnesses

Acknowledged by me,
Lamontagne, commissary at Fort Orange.

[CONDITIONS FOR FARMING OUT THE SLAUGHTER EXCISE]

[188] Conditions upon which the honorable lord commissary and the honorable lords magistrates of Fort Orange and the village of Beverwijck intend to farm out to the highest bidder the slaughter excise for the period of one year.

The farmer of the aforesaid slaughter excise shall commence the first of October of this year *anno* 1659 and cease the end of September *anno* 1660.

The farmer shall receive for the slaughtered animals, whether ox, cow, calf, bull, pig, goat or sheep, one stiver from each guilder of the value of the same,* disputes to be settled by impartial persons.

The farmer is obligated to furnish two sufficient sureties to the satisfaction of the honorable contractors for the excise money, a just fourth part of the same to be paid every quarter year in good currant zewant; and, if the farmer cannot furnish sufficient sureties, it shall be auctioned off again at his own cost and expense, and whatever less it comes to be worth, he shall be obligated to make good, and whatever more it comes to be worth, he shall gain no profit from it.†

Upon auctioning of the preceding conditions of the slaughter excise, it was closed at six hundred and forty guilders; the honorable contractors having consulted together again and with Marcelis Janssen thereon, came to an agreement, which the aforesaid Marcelis Janssen has accepted from the aforesaid lords contractors according to the aforesaid conditions for the sum of seven hundred guilders; and furnished as sureties and principals for the aforesaid sum Rutger Jacobsen and Henderick Anderiessen to the satisfaction of **[189]** the honorable lords contractors, pledging their persons and estates, moveable and

* The following maginal note intended for insertion here has been canceled: "from everyone except for the minister and lord Renselaer"

† A line following this paragraph, which has been canceled, reads as follows: "The final bid for the above-standing contract was Marcelis Janssen for the sum of seven hundred guilders."

immoveable, now and in the future, subjecting the same to all laws and judges. Done in the village of Beverwijck, the first of October *anno* 1659.

Marcelis Jansen
Ruger Jacobsz
Henderick Andryssen
Acknowledged by me,
Johannes Provoost , clerk.

[POWER OF ATTORNEY OF RIJCK RIDDERSEN]

[190] Appeared before me, Johannes La Montagne, licensed by the lord director general and council of New Netherland as vice director and commissary of Fort Orange and the village of Beverwijck, residing in the aforesaid Fort Orange, on the date written below and in the presence of the subscribed witnesses, Rijck Riddersen, former soldier, who declares to have ceded, conveyed, and assigned to and for the benefit of the honorable Elmerhuysen Cleyn for goods received to his contentment and satisfaction the sum of one hundred and forty-one guilders and nineteen stivers, to be received for his monthly wages and subsistence, which he has earned as a soldier at Fort Orange in New Netherland in the service of the chartered West India Company; in addition, the aforesaid Rijck Riddersen, or the lawful holder of this document, hereby authorizes the aforesaid sum of one hundred and forty-one guilders and nineteen stivers, to be requested, demanded, and received at Amsterdam in New Netherland at the treasury of the same, and upon receipt to issue an acquittance for it, which shall be valid as though it was granted by the subscriber himself; furthermore, to do and perform all things for receiving the aforesaid sum, which the subscriber himself being present might or could do, and if the matter should demand **[191]** greater and more special authority than is expressed herein, promising to hold the same as good and true at all times, whatever shall be done by virtue of this document, pledging his person and goods. Thus done in Fort Orange in the presence of Sacharias Sickels and Johannes Provoost called hereto as witnesses on the 4th of October *anno* 1659.

This is the mark + of Rijck Riddersen
made with his own hand.
Sacharyas Seeckelsz
Johannes Provoost, witnesses
Acknowledged by me,
La Montagne, commissary at Fort Orange.

[POWER OF ATTORNEY OF ZACHARIAS SICKELS VAN WEENEN]

[192] Appeared before me, Johannes La Montagne, appointed by the lord director general and council of New Netherland as vice director and commissary of Fort Orange and the village of Beverwijck, residing in the aforesaid Fort Orange, on the date written below and in the presence of the subscribed witnesses, Zacharias Sickels van Weenen,† corporal of the honorable company, who declares to have ceded, conveyed, and assigned to and for the benefit of the honorable Goossen Gerritsen for goods received to his contentment and satisfaction the sum of forty-eight guilders, to be received for his monthly wages and subsistence, which he has earned as a corporal at Fort Orange in New Netherland in the service of the chartered West India Company; in addition, the aforesaid Sacharias Sickels, or the lawful holder of this document, hereby authorizes the aforesaid sum of forty-eight guilders, to be requested, demanded, and received at Amsterdam in New Netherland at the treasury of the same, and upon receipt to issue an acquittance for it, which shall be valid as though it was granted by the subscriber himself; furthermore, to do and perform all things for receiving the aforesaid sum, which the subscriber **[193]** himself being present might or could do, and if the matter should demand greater and more special authority than is expressed herein, promising to hold the same as good and true at all times, whatever shall be done by virtue of this document, pledging his person and goods. Done at Fort Orange in the presence of Dirrick Janssen Croon and Gysbert van Imborgh, as witnesses called hereto on this 10th of October *anno* 1659.

---

† *Weenen* is the Dutch rendering of Vienna.

Sacharias Sijckelsz
Dirck Jansen Croon
Gijsbert van Imbroch
Acknowledged by me,
La Montagne, commissary at Fort Orange.

[CONVEYANCE OF A HOUSE AND LOT FROM TOMAS JANSEN MINGAEL TO TEUNIS TEUNISSEN *METSELAER*]

[194] Appeared before me Johannes Lamontagne in the service of the general chartered West India Company, vice director and commissary at Fort Orange and the village of Beverwijck, in the presence of Francoys Boon and Jan Verbeeck, magistrates of the same court, Tomas Janssen Mingael, who declares to have ceded and conveyed, as he hereby cedes and conveys, in real and actual possession, for the benefit of Teunis Teunissen *Metselaer*, his heirs or assigns, a house and lot lying in the aforesaid village, bounded on the north by Matthewes Abrahamsen, on the south by Wouter de *Ramaecker*, east and west the street; in breadth on the south as well as the north side, four rods long from one street to the other, which aforesaid lot was granted by patent to Hage Bruynsen and by him conveyed to Gillis Pietersen, from whom it was received by conveyance, and acknowledges that he has received satisfaction for the aforesaid house and lot from the grantee, wherefore he frees it from all claims and pretensions which may hereafter arise, pledging his person and estate, moveable and immoveable, now and in the future, subjecting the same to all laws and judges. Done at Fort Orange the 2nd of November 1659.

Tomas Jansen Mingael
Francoys Boon
Jan Verbeeck
Acknowledged by me,
Lamontagne, commissary at Fort Orange.

[CONVEYANCE OF A LOT FROM MEYNDERT AND CARSTEN FREDERICKSEN]

[195] Appeared before me Johannes Lamontagne in the service of the general chartered West India Company, commissary at Fort Orange and the village of Beverwijck, Meyndert Fredericksen and Carsten Fredericksz, burghers and inhabitants who declare to have ceded and conveyed, as they hereby cede and convey in real and actual possession, for the benefit of the honorable lords magistrates of the Fort Orange and the village of Beverwijck, a lot for a house lying in the aforesaid village, to the west Rem Janssen, in length six rods four feet and four inches, to the north Jan Daret, in the rear two rods, to the east Jan Harmsen, in length six rods eleven feet three inches, on the street, in breadth two rods six feet eight inches, which lot's breadth extends as far as the present house, with all the title which the grantors have had and could claim in the aforesaid place, promising to free said lot from all claims or pretensions, which may hereafter arise, pledging their persons and estates, moveable and immoveable, now and in the future, subject the same to all laws and judges. On this same date the aforesaid magistrates conveyed the aforesaid lot again, just as they were granted it, to Jan Costersen van Aeckens with all the title and pretensions, which they have in the same, **[196]** promising to free the same from all claims, pledging as before. Done at Fort Orange on the 10th of December *anno* 1659 in the presence of Johannes Provoost and Lowies Cobussen, as witnesses called hereto.

Karsten Fredericksen
This is the mark  of Meyndert Fredericksen
made himself.
Francoys Boon
Andries Herbertsen
Sander Lenrsen
Johannes Provoost, witness
Acknowledged by me,
Lamontagne, commissary at Fort Orange.

[CONVEYANCE OF A HOUSE AND LOT FROM MARCELIS JANSSEN TO CORNELIS WIJNKOOP]

[197] Appeared before me Johannes Lamontagne in the service of the general chartered West India Company, commissary at Fort Orange and the village of Beverwijck, in the presence of the honorable Sander Leendersen and Jan Verbeeck, magistrates of the same court, Marcelis Janssen, who declares to have ceded and conveyed, as he hereby cedes and conveys, in real and actual possession, for the benefit of Cornelis Wijnkoop his heirs or assigns, a house and lot lying in the village of Beverwijck, to the south the grantor, to the north Pieter Bronck, to the west the hill, to the east the street; the lot is in breadth, thirty wood feet, and in length according to the patent, except what was taken for a street, which lot the grantor received by conveyance from Goossen Gerritsen and Goossen Gerritsen as a patent from the honorable lord director general and council of New Netherland, dated the 25th of October *anno* 1653, for which house and lot the grantor acknowledges to have received satisfaction, and promises to free the same from all claims, demands and pretensions, which may arise hereafter, pledging his person and estate, moveable and immoveable, now and in the future, subjecting the same to all laws and judges. Done at Fort Orange on the 11th of December *anno* 1659.

Marcelys Jansen
Sander Lenrsen
Jan Verbeeck
Acknowledged by me,
La Montagne, commissary at Fort Orange.

[BILL OF SALE OF HOUSE AND LOT FROM COBUS JANSSEN TO FRANS BARENTSEN PASTOOR]

[198] Appeared before me Johannes Provoost, clerk of the court of Fort Orange and the village of Beverwijck, Cobus Janssen and the honorable Frans Barentsen Pastoor, burgher and inhabitant of the aforesaid village, who declare, in the presence of the subscribed witnesses that they have agreed in all friendship and amity about the purchase of a house; namely, that Cobus Janssen sells his house and lot lying in the village of Beverwijck to Frans Barentsen Pastoor with everything that is earth and nail fast, adjoining to the south Jacob Tijssen van der Heyden and to the north Lambert Albertsen van Neck, east and west the street; the lot is as long and wide as it is enclosed in its fence, and that for the sum of nine hundred guilders in beavers, which sum the aforesaid Frans Barentsen promises to pay in three installments; the first on the first of the next July, forty beavers; the second installment on the first of July 1661, half of the remainder; and the remainder on the first of July 1662. The first of next May the seller grants delivery as also the conveyance with all the right, title, and ownership, which the aforesaid seller has had therein. Thus done in the presence of Arent van den Bergh and Jan Cloet, as witnesses called hereto on this 10th of January *anno* 1660 at Fort Orange.

This is the mark X of Cobus Janssen,
made himself
Frans Barents Pastoor
This the mark AB of Arent van den Bergh,
made himself.
Johan Clute, as witnesses
Acknowledged by me,
Johannes Provoost, clerk.

[CONVEYANCE OF HOUSE AND LOT FROM WOUTERT ALBERTSEN TO JURRIAEN TEUNISSEN]

[199] Appeared before me Johannes Lamontagne in the service of the general chartered West India Company, commissary at Fort Orange and the village of Beverwijck, in the presence of Anderies Herbertsen and Jan Verbeeck, magistrates of the same court, Woutert Albertsen, burgher and inhabitant in the aforesaid village, who declares to have ceded and conveyed, as he hereby cedes and conveys, for the benefit of Jurriaen Teunissen, his heirs or assigns, a house and lot, lying in the aforesaid village; the lot is in length to the south of the street, eighteen rods and six feet; to the east, breadth five rods; to the north [of] the kil, length eighteen rods seven feet; to the west Jochem *de Backer*, four rods and eight feet, which aforesaid house and lot the grantor received by conveyance from Jochem Wesselse, dated the 16th of July 1658, and Jochem Wesselse by patent from the honorable lord director general and council of New Netherland, dated the 25th of October 1653; promising the aforesaid house and lot to be free from all claims, demands, and pretensions, which may arise hereafter, pledging his person and estate, moveable and immoveable, now and in the future, subjecting the same to all laws and judges. Done at Fort Orange the 2nd of February 1660.

Wouter Albertsen
Jan Verbeeck
Andries Herberts
Acknowledged by me,
La Montagne, commissary at Fort Orange.

[CONVEYANCE OF HOUSE AND LOT FROM TEUNIS TEUNISSEN METSELAER TO ANDERIES HERBERTSEN AND PHILIP HENDERICKSZ]

[200] Appeared before me Johannes Lamontagne in the service of the general chartered West India Company, commissary at Fort Orange and the village of Beverwijck, in the presence of Sander Leendersen and Jan Verbeeck, magistrates of the same court, Teunis Teunissen *Metselaer* who declares to have ceded and conveyed, as he hereby cedes and conveys, in real and actual possession, for the benefit of the honorable Anderies Herbertsen and Philip Hendericksz, their heirs or assigns, a house and lot, lying in the village of Beverwijck, adjoining to the north Pieter Adriaensen, and to the south Adriaen Janssen van Leyden, east and west a street, length and breadth according to the patent, which Carsten Janssen was granted by the lord director general and council of New Netherland, dated the 25th of October *anno* 1653, for which house and lot the grantor acknowledges satisfaction and promises to free the same from all claims, demands or pretensions, which may arise hereafter, pledging his person and estate, moveable and immoveable, now and in the future, subjecting the same to all laws and judges. Done at Fort Orange the 29th of February *anno* 1660.

Teunis Teunisz *Metselaer*
Jan Verbeeck
Sander Lenresen
Acknowledged by me,
La Montagne, commissary at Fort Orange.

[CONVEYANCE OF HOUSE, LOT, AND GARDEN FROM ANDERIES HERBERTSEN TO LEENDERT PHILIPSEN]

[201] Appeared before me Johannes Lamontagne in the service of the general chartered West India Company, vice director and commissary at Fort Orange and the village of Beverwijck, in the presence of Sander Leendersen and Jan Verbeeck, magistrates of the same court, the honorable Anderies Herbertsen, who declares to have ceded and conveyed, as he hereby cedes and conveys, in real and actual possession, for the benefit of Leendert Philipsen, burgher and inhabitant of the aforesaid village, his heirs or assigns, a house, lot, and garden in the aforesaid village of Beverwijck, adjoining to the north Pieter Bronck, to the south Jan Verbeeck, length and breadth according to the specifications of the patent granted to the grantor by the lord director general and council of New Netherland in the year *anno* 1652; for which house, lot, and garden the grantor acknowledges satisfaction, promising to free the same from all claims, demands and pretensions, which may arise hereafter, pledging his person and estate, moveable and immoveable, now and in the future, subjecting the same to all laws and judges. Done in Fort Orange the 19th of February *anno* 1660.

Andries Herberts
Jan Verbeeck
Sander Lenrsen
Acknowledged by me,
La Montagne, commissary at Fort Orange.

[CONVEYANCE OF HOUSE AND LOT FROM JURRIAEN TEUNISSEN TO ANDERIES HERBERTSEN]

[202] Appeared before me Johannes Lamontagne in the service of the general chartered West India Company, commissary at Fort Orange and the village of Beverwijck, in the presence of the honorable Francoys Boon and Jan Verbeeck, magistrates of the same court, Jurriaen Teunissen, burgher and inhabitant of the aforesaid village, who declares to have ceded and conveyed, in real and actual possession, for the benefit of Anderies Herbertsen, also burgher and inhabitant of the aforesaid village of Beverwijck, his heirs or assigns, a house and lot, lying in the village of Beverwijck, adjoining to the south the street, to the east and west a road; length and breadth ten rods, with another piece of a lot south of the house about twenty-three feet, which lot the grantor received by patent from the lord director general and council of New Netherland. At the same time the aforesaid Anderies Herbertsen conveyed the aforesaid house lot as well as the piece of lot, lying at the side of the house, to Jan Martensen or those who may hereafter receive his title hereof, and that in real and actual possession and ownership; whereas the aforesaid grantors acknowledge to have had satisfaction and consequently promise to free the same from all claims or pretensions, which may arise thereafter **[203]**, thereupon pledging their persons and estates, moveable and immoveable, now and in the future, subjecting the same to all laws and judges. Done at Fort Orange the 24th of February 1660.

Jurejan Tunsen
Andries Herberts
Francoys Boon
Jan Verbeeck
Acknowledged by me,
La Montagne, commissary at Fort Orange.

[POWER OF ATTORNEY OF CORNELIS WOUTERSEN]

[204] Appeared before me Johannes Provoost, clerk of the court of Fort Orange and the village of Beverwijck, in the presence of the subscribed witnesses, Cornelis Woutersen who declares to have constituted and empowered, as he hereby does, Jan Anderiessen to demand, collect, and receive in the subscriber's name and on his behalf from Cornelis Pietersen Hoogenboom, presently residing in Amsterdam in New Netherland, the sum of ten and a half beavers and one hundred and fourty guilders in sewant, stemming from disbursed monies; the quittance issued upon receipt thereof shall be valid as if given by the subscriber himself; furthermore, to do and perform anything to obtain the aforesaid sum, as were the subscriber himself present, could do or be capable of doing; and if the matter requires more special authority than expressed in this document, promising at all times to hold good and true whatever shall be done by virtue hereof, pledging his person and estate. Thus done at Fort Orange in the presence of Daniel Verveelen and Jan Pietersen Muller, as witnesses called hereto on the 30th of April *anno* 1660.

Cornelis Woutersen
Jan Pieters Mulder
Daniel Verveelen.

[ACKNOWLEDGMENT OF DEBT OF JACQUES TIJSSEN]

[205] Appeared before me Johannes Lamontagne in the service of the general chartered West India Company, commissary at Fort Orange and the village of Beverwijck, in the presence of Sander Leendersen and Jan Verbeeck, magistrates of the same court, Jacques Tijssen, who acknowledges to be honestly and truly indebted to Teunis Spitsbergen and Barent Pietersen for the sum of one hundred twenty-seven guilders for planks, which the aforesaid Jacques Tijssen has received, and promises to pay the aforesaid sum from the first rent of his house, lying in the village of Beverwijck, where Nicolaes Marrechael resides; furthermore, the aforesaid Jacques Tijssen puts up his aforesaid house as mortgage and special pledge for satisfaction and payment of the aforesaid sum, for which he pledges his person and estate, moveable and immoveable, now and in the future, subjecting the same to all laws and judges. Done at Fort Orange the 9th of June *anno* 1660.

Jaques Teissen
Jan Verbeeck
Sander Lenrsen
Acknowledged by me,
La Montagne, commissary at Fort Orange.

[POWER OF ATTORNEY OF HENDERICK VAN DIJCK]

[206] Appeared before me Johannes Lamontagne, commissary at Fort Orange and the village of Beverwijck, the honorable Henderick van Dijck, who declares, in the presence of the subscribed witnesses, to have constituted and empowered, as he hereby does, Johannes Provoost to demand, collect, and receive in the subscriber's name here at Fort Orange in New Netherland such monies as are owed to him according to the bonds and other documents serving thereto; upon receipt thereof to issue a quittance, and in case of unwillingness, to demand the payment with law and rigor of justice, carrying judicial proceedings to final execution, including attachment of persons and goods, and in addition to do everything that the attorney shall deem necessary and appropriate, promising to hold as good and true all that the attorney shall have done, provided that the attorney render a proper statement and return as requested thereto. Thus done and issued at Fort Orange in the presence [*left blank*] as witnesses called hereto on this 8th of July *anno* 1660.

H. van Dijck.

[ACKNOWLEDGMENT OF DEBT OF JAN MICHIELSEN]

[207] Appeared before me Johannes La Montagne in the service of the general chartered West India Company, commissary at Fort Orange and the village of Beverwijck, in the presence of the honorable Frans Barentsen Pastoor and Jan Verbeeck, magistrates of the same court, Jan Michielsen, inhabitant of the aforesaid place, who declares to be honestly and truly indebted to *Mr*. Paulus Schrick for the sum of eighty guilders in good whole merchantable beavers for goods received to his satisfaction; which aforesaid sum he promises to pay to the aforesaid Schrick or his attorney in the coming spring *anno* 1661 with the interest accruing from this date; for which aforesaid sum of eighty guilders with the aforesaid interest Jan Michielsen pledges his house and lot, lying in the village of Beverwijck, putting up as mortgage and special pledge for payment of the aforesaid sum, pledging his person and goods, moveable and immoveable thereto, now and in the future, subjecting the same to all laws and judges. Done at Fort Orange on the 28th of July *anno* 1660.

Jan Mychgijelsen
Frans Barentsen Pastoor
Jan Verbeeck
Acknowledged by me,
La Montagne, commissary at Fort Orange.

[ACKNOWLEDGMENT OF DEBT OF JAN MICHIELSEN][†]

[208] Appeared before me Johannes La Montagne in the service of the general chartered West India Company, commissary at Fort Orange and the village of Beverwijck, in the presence of Frans Barentsen Pastoor and Jan Verbeeck,[‡] magistrates of the same court, Jan Michielsen, who declares that he is honestly and truly indebted to *Sr.* Asser Levy van Swellem[§] for the sum of one hundred eighty-four guilders in good whole merchantable beavers for goods received to his satisfaction, and promised to pay the aforesaid sum of one hundred eighty-four guilders in beavers in the coming spring *anno* 1661, about June, for which aforesaid sum the aforesaid Jan Michielsen puts up as mortgage and special pledge his house and lot in the village of Beverwijck where he

† A marginal note states: "The second mortgage on the house of Jan Michielsen."

‡ Evert Janssen Wendel's name has been replaced by Jan Verbeeck.

§ Schwelm is in the German state of North Rhine–Westphalia.

himself resides as payment and satisfaction of the aforesaid sum, pledging his person and goods, moveable and immoveable thereto, now and in the future, subjecting the same to all laws and judges. Done at Fort Orange the 28th of July *anno* 1660.

Jan Mychgyelsoon
Frans Barentsen Pastoor
Jan Verbeeck
Acknowledged by me,
La Montagne, commissary at Fort Orange.

[209] [*blank*]

[CONDITIONS FOR THE SALE OF PIETER BRONCK'S BREWERY]†

> **[210]** Conditions and terms upon which Pieter Bronck intends to offer at public auction to the highest bidder his brewery or brew house presently located in the village of Beverwijck.

First. The brewery or brew house shall be delivered to the buyer with all that is earth and nail fast; furthermore, all the brewing equipment, such as it exists and has been used by the seller, whereby there is one kettle of 11 half barrels liquid measure, a fermentation tub with a wort tub and cooler, a filling tub, the buyer shall receive as many of the half barrels as can be found in the brewery or elsewhere with the seller's mark thereon, a drying cloth, and he shall deliver the bricks of an old malt kiln, which are in the mill house, in order to make a new one; together with the lot, in breadth to the east, forty-six wood feet, to the west, thirty-eight wood feet, in length to the south, one hundred twelve wood feet, to the north, one hundred fourteen wood feet. Transfer shall take place upon payment in good whole merchantable beavers in three installments: the first installment at the end of this coming September, and the same to be

† Entry canceled.

paid to the honorable Jeremias van Rencelaer; the second at the end of June *anno* 1661; the third at the end of June *anno* 1662.

[211] The buyer shall be obligated to appoint two suitable sureties each as principals to the satisfaction of the seller and that within the period of 24 hours. If the buyer is unable to appoint two sureties in the prescribed time, then it shall be auctioned off again at his expense and cost; and whatever it falls short, the buyer shall be obligated to make good, and if it brings greater value, he shall derive no profit from it. Auction fees will be charged to the buyer.

[CONDITIONS FOR THE SALE OF PIETER BRONCK'S HOUSE AND LOT]†

[212] Conditions and terms upon which Pieter Bronck will auction off to the highest bidder his house and lot in the village of Beverwijck at the hill in which Jan van Breemen presently dwells.

First. The aforesaid house shall be transferred to the buyer with everything that is earth and nail fast, with the lot of 5 rods width and twenty rods length, according to the patent thereof, together with a *hansjoos* house‡ next to it.

Transfer shall take place in a month from today's date. Payment shall be made in two installments in good whole merchantable beavers: the first with the transfer of the aforesaid house, the second installment at the end of June *anno* 1661. The buyer shall be obligated to appoint two suitable sureties each as principals to the satisfaction of the seller and that within the period of 24 hours. If the buyer is unable to appoint two sureties in the prescribed time, then it shall be auctioned off again at his expense and cost; and whatever it falls short, the buyer shall be

---

† Entry canceled.

‡ *Hansjoos* is a term associated with items designated for the Indian trade or with the trading houses west of Beverwijck's stockade.

obligated to make good, and if it brings greater value, he shall derive no profit from it. Auction fees will be charged to the buyer.

[CONDITIONS FOR THE SALE OF TOMAS JANSSEN MINGAEL'S LOT IN NEW AMSTERDAM]†

[213] Conditions and terms upon which Tomas Janssen Mingael will auction off to the highest bidder his lot located in Amsterdam in New Netherland, south of Reynout *de Schoemaecker*. First. The buyer shall receive the aforesaid lot, which is twenty-five feet wide and about sixty feet long to the rear fence. The transfer shall take place on this coming 4th of August, and upon delivery payment of half in good whole beaver and the other half in good merchantable sewant. The buyer shall be obligated to appoint two suitable sureties each as principals to the satisfaction of the seller and that immediately. If the buyer is unable to appoint two sureties in the prescribed time, then it shall be auctioned off again at his expense and cost; and whatever it falls short, the buyer shall be obligated to make good, and if it brings greater value, he shall derive no profit from it. Auction fees will be charged to the buyer.

[CONDITIONS FOR THE SALE OF A HORSE BY *MR*. SCHRICK]

[214] Conditions upon which *Mr*. Schrick will auction off to the highest bidder a horse, which will be delivered to the buyer at once, and to be paid for in beavers, half in cash and the half over two months or else in sewant for *f*12 the beaver; the buyer shall be obliged to provide two sufficient sureties at once to the satisfaction of the seller. Auction fees will be charged to the buyer.

The last bidder for the horse was Eldert Gerbertsen for the sum of one hundred and fifty-four guilders, and provides Capt. Jan Jacobsen as

---

† Incomplete.

surety pursuant to the conditions. Done in the village of Beverwijck the 30th of July *anno* 1659.

Elbert Gerbertsen
Jan Jacobs

[CONDITIONS FOR THE SALE OF A HOUSE BY PIETER HARTGER AND JAN ROELOFFSEN]†

[215] Conditions and terms upon which Pieter Hartger and Jan Roeloffsen will auction off to the highest bidder their house in the village of Beverwijck.

First. The buyer shall receive the aforesaid house with everything that is earth and nail fast, located on the Third Kil, in which the aforesaid Jan Roeloffsen lives; with a lot along the road nine rods in length, in width thirteen rods at the one end at Jan Martensen's lot [and] seven rods at the river's edge.

Transfer shall take place on the first of May *anno* 1660. Payment shall be made in two installments in good whole merchantable beavers: the first on the 14th of this coming August, the second installment on the first of August *anno* 1660. The buyer shall be obligated to provide two suitable sureties each as principals to the satisfaction of the seller and that done immediately. If the buyer is unable to provide suitable sureties in the prescribed time, then it shall be auctioned off again at his expense and cost; and whatever it falls short, the buyer shall be obligated to make good, and if it brings greater value, he shall derive no profit from it. Auction fees will be charged to the buyer.

† Incomplete.

[CONDITIONS FOR THE SALE OF A LOT BY DOMINE GIDEON SCHAETS]†

[216] Conditions, as follows, upon which Do. Gideon Schaets intends to sell at public auction to the highest bidder a lot lying in the Colonie Rencelaerswijck, to the north Henderick Reur, to the south Roelof Swartwout; in length until the thicket and 80 feet wide; and to make payment in two installments, half in good whole merchantable beavers and the other half in good current sewant; the first installment on the first of this coming September, the second payment on the first of September *anno* 1660. The buyer shall be obliged to provide two suitable sureties immediately to the satisfaction of the seller. Transfer shall take place at once. Auction fees are charged to the buyer.

[BILL OF SALE FOR A HOUSE OF MICHIEL JANSSEN TO LOWIES COBUS]

[217] Appeared before me Johannes Provoost, clerk of the court of Fort Orange and the village of Beverwijck, Michiel Janssen and Lowies Cobus, who declare, in the presence of the subscribed witnesses that they have agreed in all friendship and amity about the purchase of a house; namely, that the aforesaid Michiel Janssen has sold to the aforesaid Lowies Cobussen his house, lying in Fort Orange to the east Arent van den Bergh, to the west Teunis Spitsbergen; and that in such ownership as the seller possesses the same according to the conveyance, which the seller shall deliver with the first payment; for which Lowies Cobus promises to pay the sum of five hundred and fifty guilders, which payment the aforesaid seller shall receive at Manhattan or in the office of the honorable chartered West India Company as a deduction from his salary or stipend, in such payment as the honorable Company has been giving to their employees with the special condition that the aforesaid house be held as collateral until payment is complete from the buyer; namely, in four installments: the first this coming May *anno* 1660 being *f*150, the second installment the first of May *anno* 1661 also *f*150, the

† Incomplete.

third installment shall be the first of May *anno* 1662 in the same amount, the fourth and last on the first of May *anno* 1663 one hundred guilders. All on the pledge of his person and estate, moveable and immoveable, now and in the future, subjecting the same to all laws and judges. In the presence **[218]** of Jan Pietersen and Arent van den Bergh as witnesses. Done at Fort Orange, at the end of July *anno* 1659. Done by me Machgghiel Jansen.

Ludovicus Cobes
Jan Pieters
This is the mark of  Arent van den Bergh.
Acknowledged by me,
Johannes Provoost, clerk.

[CONVEYANCE OF A GARDEN LOT BY ULDERICK KLEYN]

[219] Appeared before me Johannes la Montagne in the service of the general chartered West India Company, commissary at Fort Orange and the village of Beverwijck, in the presence of the honorable Sander Leendersen and Jan Verbeeck, magistrates of the same court, Ulderick Kleyn, burgher and inhabitant of the aforesaid place, who declares to have conveyed, as he hereby cedes and conveys, in real and actual possession, to the benefit of Jan Tomassen, also burgher and inhabitant here, his heirs or assigns, a lot for a garden, lying near Fort Orange, to the south Luycas Pietersen, to the north a plain, to the east the wagon road, to the west the plain; in breadth it is five rods and in length seven rods, which aforesaid lot was granted a patent by the honorable director general and council of New Netherland dated the first of November *anno* 1653, and which he accordingly promises to free from all claims, demands, or pretensions, which may arise hereafter, pledging his person and estate, moveable and immoveable, now and in the future, subjecting the same to all courts and judges. Done at Fort Orange, the first of August *anno* 1659.

Ulderijck Klein
Jan Verbeeck
Sander Lenrsen

Acknowledged by me,
La Montagne, commissary at Fort Orange.

[CONVEYANCE OF A HOUSE AND LOT BY ULDERICK KLEYN]

[220] Appeared before me Johannes la Montagne in the service of the general chartered West India Company, commissary at Fort Orange and the village of Beverwijck, in the presence of the honorable Francoys Boon and Anderies Herbertsen, magistrates of the same court, Ulderick Kleyn, burgher and inhabitant of the aforesaid place, who declares to have conveyed, as he hereby cedes and conveys, in real and actual possession, to the benefit of Jan Henderickse van Bael, also a burgher and inhabitant of the aforesaid village, his heirs or assigns, a house and lot, lying in the village of Beverwijck bounded on the south by Symon Groot, on the north Reyer Elbertsen, east and west the wagon road; in width four rods and in length eight rods, according to the patent granted to him by the honorable director general and council of New Netherland, dated the 25th of October *anno* 1653, which he accordingly promises to free from all claims, demands, or pretensions, which may arise hereafter, pledging his person and estate, moveable and immoveable, now and in the future, subjecting the same to all courts and judges. Done at Fort Orange on the 2nd of August *anno* 1659.

Ulderyck Klein
Francoys Boon
Andries Herbertsen

Acknowledged by me,
La Montagne, commissary at Fort Orange.

[CONVEYANCE OF CORNELIS VOSCH]*

[221] Appeared before me Johannes La Montagne in the service of the general chartered West India Company, commissary at Fort Orange and the village of Beverwijck, in the presence of the honorable Anderies Herbertsen and Jan Verbeeck, magistrates of the same court, Cornelis Vosch, who declares to have ceded and conveyed, as he hereby cedes and conveys in real and actual…

[222] [*blank*]

[CONVEYANCE OF A HOUSE AND LOT BY PIETER *DE MAECKER* TO CORNELIS CORNELISSEN *DE BOER* AND DANIEL VERVEELEN]

[223] Appeared before me Johannes La Montagne in the service of the general chartered West India Company, commissary at Fort Orange and the village of Beverwijck, in the presence of the honorable Anderies Herbertsen and Jan Verbeeck, magistrates of the same court, Jan Coster van Aecken and Stoffel Janssen, attorneys of Pieter *de Maecker*, who declare to have ceded and conveyed, as they hereby cede and convey, to Cornelis Cornelissen *de Boer* and Daniel Verveelen, their heirs or assigns, a house and lot, lying in the village of Beverwijck. The house is as wide as it stands under its roof, in length twenty-five feet; and the lot behind it stretches to the kil, the breadth at the house or north end the same as the gable of the aforesaid house, in length from the rear gable until the kil, sixty-five feet to the kil from the common fence of Dirck Janssen Croon until the end of a straight line drawn from the first post set on the east side to the rear breadth of the same place, which place has a rear breadth of eighteen feet; on the condition that whenever the old house of Cornelis Vosch is torn down, a proper drip must be furnished or exacted from the aforesaid Vosch; also, that the grantee shall receive the water that comes from the gutter; furthermore with all the right and title, which the grantor has had therein, for which aforesaid house and lot the grantor acknowledges that he has received satisfactory payment,

* Canceled.

promising to free the same from all demands and pretensions, which may hereafter arise, **[224]** pledging his person and estate, personal and real, now and in the future, submitting the same to all laws and judges. Done at Fort Orange the 8th of August *anno* 1659.

This is the mark of  Jan Coster van Aecken,
made with his own hand.
Stoffel Jansz
Acknowledged by me,
La Montagne, commissary at Fort Orange.

[CONVEYANCE OF A HOUSE AND LOT BY JAN ROELOFFSEN]

[225] Appeared before me Johannes la Montagne in the service of the general chartered West India Company, commissary at Fort Orange and the village of Beverwijck, in the presence of the honorable Francoys Boon and Jan Verbeeck, magistrates of the same court, Jan Roeloffsen, burgher and inhabitant of the aforesaid village, who declares to have ceded and conveyed, as he hereby cedes and conveys, in real and actual possession, for the benefit of the honorable Pieter Hartgers, also burgher and inhabitant here, his heirs or assigns, a house and lot, lying in the village of Beverwijck aforesaid; to the south the Third Kil, to the east Jan Martensen, to the north the road; which aforesaid lot is nine rods long along the wagon road, and thirteen rods wide at the end of Jan Martensen's lot, seven rods wide at the river's edge; and that with all the rights and privileges, which the aforesaid Jan Roelofsen possessed, as well as promising to free the same from all claims or pretensions, which may arise thereon, pledging his person and estate, moveable and immoveable, now and in the future, subjecting the same to all laws and judges. Done at Fort Orange on the 12th of August *anno* 1659.

Jan Roelofsen
Francoys Boon
Jan Verbeeck
Acknowledged by me,
La Montagne, commissary at Fort Orange.

[ACKNOWLEDGMENT OF DEBT OF SANDER LEENDERTSEN GLEN TO DIRCK JANSSEN CROON]

[226] Appeared before me Johannes Lamontagne in the service of the general chartered West India Company, commissary at Fort Orange and the village of Beverwijck, in the presence of the honorable Francoys Boon and Anderies Herbertsen, magistrates of the same court, Sander Leendertsen Glen, who declares himself to be truly and honestly indebted to the honorable Dirck Janssen Croon for the amount of one hundred forty-five good whole beavers, which he promises to pay to the aforesaid Dirck Janssen Croon or his attorney on the first of June *anno* 1659, whereupon he pledges his person and estate, moveable and immoveable, now and in the future; in particular he pledges his house and lot, located in the village of Beverwijck in which Jan Vinhagel resides as mortgage and special collateral for payment of the aforesaid number of beavers. Done at Fort Orange the 14th of August *anno* 1659.

[CONVEYANCE FOR A HOUSE AND LOT OF JURRIAEN TEUNISSEN]

[227] Appeared before me Johannes La Montagne in the service of the general chartered West India Company, commissary at Fort Orange and the village of Beverwijck, in the presence of the honorable Anderies Herbertsen and Jan Verbeeck, magistrates of the same court, Jurriaen Teunissen, who declares to have hereby ceded and conveyed in real and actual possession to the benefit of Jan Roeloffsen, his heirs or assigns, a house and lot located in the village of Beverwijck; to the south the Third Kil, to the east Jan Martensen, to the north the road; which aforesaid lot is nine rods long along the road, thirteen rods wideat the end of Jan Martensen's lot and seven rods wide at the river's edge, which aforesaid lot the was granted to the conveyor by the lord director general and council of New Netherland, dated the 25th of October *anno* 1653; furthermore with all the right and title, which the conveyor has had therein, promising to free the grantee from all demands and pretensions, which may hereafter arise, pledging his person and estate, personal and real, now and in the future, submitting the same to all laws and judges. Done at Fort Orange the 14th of August *anno* 1659.

Jurreyaen Herberts
Jan Verbeek

Acknowledged by me,
La Montagne, commissary at Fort Orange.

[CONVEYANCE OF A HOUSE OF MICHIEL JANSSEN TO LOWIES COBUSSEN]

[228] Appeared before me Johannes La Montagne in the service of the general chartered West India Company, commissary at Fort Orange and the village of Beverwijck, in the presence of the honorable Sander Leendersen and Jan Verbeeck, magistrates of the same court, the honorable Michiel Janssen, burgher and inhabitant here, who declares to have ceded and conveyed, as he hereby cedes and conveys, in real and actual possession, to the benefit of Lowies Cobussen, his heirs or assigns, a house located in Fort Orange, which aforesaid house the grantor received by conveyance from Frans Barentsen Pastoor, dated the 20th of November *anno* 1656, and the aforesaid Frans Barentsen from Jacob Jansen Hap, who was granted the patent by the lord director general and council of New Netherland, dated the 3rd of July *anno* 1649; furthermore, with all the right and title, which the conveyor has had therein, promising to free the house from all demands and pretensions, which may hereafter arise, pledging his person and estate, personal and real, now and in the future, submitting the same to all laws and judges. Done at Fort Orange the 14th of August *anno* 1659.

Machghyel Yansen

[CONVEYANCE OF A GARDEN BY ROELOFF SWARTWOUT TO PHILIP PIETERSEN SCHUYLER]

[229] Appeared before me Johannes La Montagne in the service of the general chartered West India Company, commissary at Fort Orange and the village of Beverwijck, in the presence of the honorable Francoys Boon and Anderies Herbertsen, magistrates of the same court, Roeloff Swartwout, who declares to have ceded and conveyed, as he hereby cedes and conveys, in real and actual possession, to the benefit of Philip Pietersen Schuyler, his heirs or assigns, a garden located in the village of Beverwijck; to the east the road, to the west Domine Schaets, to the south Annetie Bogardus, which aforesaid garden the lord director general and council granted to Antoni de Hoges, deceased, the former husband of the wife of the aforenamed Roelof Swartwout. The length and breadth, according to the patent received by the grantee, shall be with all the right and title, which the conveyor has had therein, promising to free the house from all demands and pretensions, which may hereafter arise, pledging his person and estate, personal and real, now and in the future, submitting the same to all laws and judges. Done at Fort Orange, the 15th of August *anno* 1659.

Roeloff Swartwout
Francoys Boon
Andries Herberts
Acknowledged by me,
La Montagne, commissary at Fort Orange.

[CONVEYANCE OF A HOUSE AND LOT OF STOFFEL JANSSEN TO FRANCOYS BOON]

[230] Appeared before me Johannes La Montagne in the service of the general chartered West India Company, commissary at Fort Orange and the village of Beverwijck, in the presence of the honorable Sander Leendersen and Jan Verbeeck, magistrates of the same court, Stoffel Janssen, who declares who declares to have ceded and conveyed, as he hereby cedes and conveys, in real and actual possession, to the benefit of the honorable Francoys Boon, his heirs or assigns, a house and lot located in the village of Beverwijck; east, west and north a street, to the south Gillis Pietersen; length and breadth according to the patent or as it stands enclosed by his fence, which patent the conveyor was granted by the lord director general and council of New Netherland, dated the 25th of October *anno* 1653; furthermore, with all the right and title, which the aforenamed Stoffel Janssen has had, acknowledging to have had satisfaction therein and promising to free the house and lot from all demands and pretensions, which may hereafter arise, pledging his person and estate, personal and real, now and in the future, submitting the same to all laws and judges. Done at Fort Orange the 15th of August *anno* 1659.

Stoffel Jansz Abeel
Sander Lenrsen
Jan Verbeeck
Acknowledged by me,
Lamontange, commissary at Fort Orange.

[CONVEYANCE OF A HOUSE AND LOT OF TEUNIS CORNELISSEN SLINGERLANT TO JOHAN DARETH]

[231] Appeared before me Johannes La Montagne in the service of the general chartered West India Company, commissary at Fort Orange and the village of Beverwijck, in the presence of the honorable Francoys Boon and Anderies Herbertsen, magistrates of the same court, Teunis Cornelissen Slingerlant, who declares to have ceded and conveyed, as he hereby cedes and conveys, in real and actual possession, to the benefit of the honorable Johan Dareth, burgher and inhabitant of the aforesaid village, his heirs or assigns, a house and lot located in the village of Beverwijck; to the north the grantor, to the south Henderick Gerritsen, to the east the street, to the west Jacob *de Brouwer*; in length thirty feet and in breadth twenty-eight wood feet, which the conveyor was granted from the patent of Jacob *de Brouwer*, by whom the aforesaid patent is held. Furthermore, with all the right and title, which the aforenamed Slingerlant has had, acknowledging to have had satisfaction therein, and promising to free the house and lot from all demands and pretensions, which may hereafter arise, pledging his person and estate, personal and real, now and in the future, submitting the same to all laws and judges. Done at Fort Orange the 15th of August *anno* 1659.

Teunys Cornelis Slyngherlant
Francoys Boon
Andries Herberts
Acknowledged by me,
Lamontagne, commissary at Fort Orange.

[CONVEYANCE OF A HOUSE AND LOT OF LEENDERT PHILIPSEN TO HENDERICK HENDERICKSE]

[232] Appeared before me Johannes La Montagne in the service of the general chartered West India Company, commissary at Fort Orange and the village of Beverwijck, in the presence of the honorable Sander Leendersen Glen and Jan Verbeeck, magistrates of the same court, Leendert Philipsen, burgher and inhabitant of the aforesaid village, who declares to have ceded and conveyed, as he hereby cedes and conveys, in real and actual possession, to the benefit of Henderick Henderickse, his heirs or assigns, a house and lot located in the village of Beverwijck; to the south Claes Janssen, to the north the grantor, to the east the river's edge, to the west the public road; in length nine rods and in breadth thirty-six wood feet; which lot is a portion of the patent of Anderies Herbertsen, granted to him by the lord director general and council of New Netherland dated the 23rd of April *anno* 1652, for which house the grantor acknowledges to have had satisfaction and promises to free the same from all demands and pretensions, which may hereafter arise, pledging his person and estate, personal and real, now and in the future, submitting the same to all laws and judges. Done at Fort Orange the 15th of August *anno* 1659.

Leendert Phijles
Sander Lenrsen
Jan Verbeeck
Acknowledged by me,
Lamontagne, commissary at Fort Orange.

[CONVEYANCE OF A HOUSE AND LOT OF HENDERICK HENDERICKSE TO STOFFEL JANSSEN]

[233] Appeared before me Johannes La Montagne in the service of the general chartered West India Company, commissary at Fort Orange and the village of Beverwijck, in the presence of the honorable Sander Leendertsen Glen and Jan Verbeeck, magistrates of the same court, Henderick Henderickse, who declares to have ceded and conveyed, as he hereby cedes and conveys, in real and actual possession, to the benefit of Stoffel Janssen, his heirs or assigns, a house and lot located in the village of Beverwijck; to the south Claes Janssen, to the north Leendert Philipsen, to the east the river's edge, to the west the public road; in length nine rods and in breadth thirty-six wood rods, which lot is a portion of the patent of Anderies Herbertsen, granted to him by the lord director general and council of New Netherland dated the 23rd of April *anno* 1652, for which aforesaid house and lot the grantor acknowledges to have had satisfaction and promises to free the same from all demands and pretensions, which may hereafter arise, pledging his person and estate, personal and real, now and in the future, submitting the same to all laws and judges. Done at Fort Orange the 15th of August *anno* 1659.

Hendrick Hendricksen
Sander Lenrsen
Jan Verbeeck
Acknowledged by me,
Lamontagne, commissary at Fort Orange.

[CONDITIONS FOR THE SALE OF SOME GOODS BY PIETERTIE JANS]

[234] Conditions upon which Pietertie Jans intends to sell to the highest bidder at public auction some household goods; to be paid for on this date within twenty-four hours in good whole merchantable beavers. Done in Beverwijck the 15th of August 1659.

Aernout Cornelisse	2 pewter plates	*f*8:-
Antony Janssen	3 ditto trenchers and one ditto plate	*f*6:-

Cornelis Teunissen	a silk coverlet	*f* 14:-
Idem	a black coat	*f* 32
		f 60

[ACKNOWLEDGMENT OF DEBT OF ROELOFF SWARTWOUT]

[235] Appeared before me Johannes La Montagne in the service of the general chartered West India Company, commissary at Fort Orange and the village of Beverwijck, in the presence of the honorable Sander Leendertsen and Jan Verbeeck, magistrates of the same court, Roeloff Swartwout, who declares himself to be honestly and truly indebted to the honorable Jan Bastiaensen van Gudsenhoven for the sum of one hundred forty-seven guilders in good whole merchantable beavers, and promises to pay the same on the first of July of the coming year 1660; for the payment of said sum he, the aforenamed Roeloff Swartwout, puts up as mortgage and special pledge his house and lot located in the village of Beverwijck where he presently resides, as well as the patent that will be held by the aforesaid Gudsenhoven until the time of full payment; pledging his person and estate, moveable and immoveable, now and in the future, subjecting the same to all laws and judges. Done at Fort Orange the 16th of August *anno* 1659.

Roelof Swartwout

[POWER OF ATTORNEY OF ARIAENTIE LEENDERS]

[236] Appeared before me Johannes Lamontagne in the service of the general chartered West India Company, commissary at Fort Orange and the village of Beverwijck, on this date in the presence of the subscribed witnesses, Claes Cornelissen, husband and guardian of Ariaentie Leenders, widow of the deceased Sijmon Tijssen, who declares to have constituted and empowered, as he hereby does constitute and empower, the honorable Stoffel Janssen to demand in the constituant's name and on his behalf, and to receive from the honorable lords orphan masters of

the orphanage of Amsterdam, such monies owed to the aforesaid Ariaentie Leenders from her deceased uncle, Dirck Janssen, and to issue quittance upon receipt thereof, acting in the matter as if the subscriber were himself present; provided that the attorney shall be obliged to provide a proper statement and return of his transactions and receipts, promising to hold the same as good and true at all times everything that the attorney shall have done in this matter, pledging his person and goods, moveable and immoveable, subjecting the same to all laws and judges. Done at Fort Orange the 16th of August *anno* 1659.

In the presence of:
Sacharias Sickels and Johannes Provoost
Claes Cornelis
This is the mark of X Ariaentie Leenders
made with her own hand.
Sacharyas Syckels
Johannes Provoost
Acknowledged by me,
La Montagne, commissary at Fort Orange.

[CONDITIONS FOR SALE OF HOUSE AND LOT BY SIJMON SIJMONSEN GROOT]†

[237] Conditions and terms upon which Sijmon Sijmonsen Groot intends to offer at public auction to the highest bidder his house and lot located in the village of Beverwijck.

First. The buyer shall be delivered the house with everything that is earth and nail fast, except for a horse stall. The house is twenty feet square with a lot four rods in breadth and seven and half rods in length.

The seller shall deliver the aforesaid house and lot at the end of August. The payment shall be made in two installments, the first upon delivery of the aforesaid house and lot in good whole merchantable beavers; the

† Incomplete.

second on the first of June anno 1661 in good current sewant at *f* 12 for a beaver.

The buyer shall be obligated to appoint two suitable sureties each as principals to the satisfaction of the seller and that within the period of 24 hours. If the buyer is unable to appoint two sureties in the prescribed time, then it shall be auctioned off again at his expense and cost; and whatever it falls short, the buyer shall be obligated to make good, and if it brings greater value, he shall derive no profit from it. Auction fees will be charged to the buyer.

[ACKNOWLEDGMENT OF DEBT OF JAN MARTENSEN TO NICOLAES MEYER]

[238] Appeared before me Johannes La Montagne in the service of the general chartered West India Company, commissary at Fort Orange and the village of Beverwijck, in the presence of the honorable Frans Barentsen Pastoor and Jan Verbeeck, magistrates of the same court, Jan Martense, burgher and inhabitant of the aforesaid village, who declares to be honestly and truly indebted to the honorable Nicolaes Meyer, merchant at Amsterdam in New Netherland, for the sum of five hundred seventy-six guilders in good whole merchantable beaver skins received as merchandise to his satisfaction, and promises to pay the aforesaid sum of five hundred seventy-six guilders in the coming spring, being on the first of May *anno* 1661; in particular he pledges his house, lot, and garden located in the village of Beverwijck, which he presently occupies, as a firm mortgage and collateral for payment of the aforesaid sum, so that, if need be the same may be recovered without loss or damage; also, pledging his person and goods, moveable and immoveable thereto, now and in the future, subjecting the same to all laws and judges. Done at Fort Orange the second of August *anno* 1660.

This is the mark + of Jan Martensen
made with his own hand.
Jan Verbeeck
Frans Barens Pastoor

Acknowledged by me,
La Montagne, commissary at Fort Orange.

[CONVEYANCE OF A HOUSE AND LOT FROM PIETER LOOCKERMANS TO JAN COSTERSEN VAN AKEN]

[239] Appeared before me Johannes La Montagne in the service of the general chartered West India Company, vice director and commissary at Fort Orange and the village of Beverwijck, in the presence of the honorable Sander Leendersen and Rutger Jacobsen, magistrates of the same court, Pieter Loockermans, senior, burgher and inhabitant of the aforesaid village, who declares to have ceded and conveyed, as he hereby cedes and conveys, in real and actual possession, to the benefit of Jan Costersen van Aken, his heirs or assigns, his house and lot located in the village of Beverwijck, adjoining to the south Henderick *de Backer,* to the north the grantor; the lot is with the house on the street front one rod eleven feet and nine inches, in length north and south five rods, less three inches; to the west one rod and eleven feet wide, which lot is a portion of a patent granted to the conveyor by the lord director general and council of New Netherland dated the 7th of July *anno* 1653; for which house and lot the aforesaid grantor acknowledges to have made full payment, promising to free the same from all demands, claims, and pretensions which may hereafter arise against the same, pledging his person and estate, moveable and immoveable, now and in the future, subjecting the same to all laws and judges. Done at Fort Orange the 2nd of August 1660.

Pieter Loockermans
Sander Lenrsen
Rutger Jacobsz
Acknowledged by me,
La Montagne, commissary at Fort Orange.

[POWER OF ATTORNEY OF NICOLAES MEYER]

[240] Appeared before me Johannes Provoost, clerk of the court of Fort Orange and the village of Beverwijck, Nicolaes Meyer, merchant at Amsterdam in New Netherland, who declares, in the presence of the subscribed witnesses, to have constituted and empowered, as he hereby constitutes and empowers, Jan Costersen van Aken, burgher and inhabitant of the aforesaid village of Beverwijck, to appear before the court in his absence and there to defend his action for injuries done against the subscriber by Pieter Adriaensen *Soogemackelijck*, and further the same by process of law, producing the affidavits and other evidences for the advantage of the subscriber; to proceed against the aforesaid Pieter Adriaense and to do and perform anything, which, were the subscriber himself present, could do or be capable of doing; and if the matter requires more special authority than expressed in this document, promising at all times to hold good and true whatever shall be done by virtue hereof, pledging his person and estate, moveable and immoveable. Done at Fort Orange on the 3rd of August *anno* 1660, in the presence of Reyndert Pietersen and Pieter Bronck as witnesses invited hereto.

Nicolaes Meyer
This is the mark RP of Reyndert Pietersen
made with his own hand.
Pyeter Bronck

[ACKNOWLEDGMENT OF DEBT OF PIETER BRONCK
TO REYNDERT PIETERSEN]

[241] Appeared before me, Johannes La Montagne, admitted by the lord director general and council of New Netherland as vice director and commissary of Fort Orange and the village of Beverwijck, residing in the aforesaid Fort Orange, in the presence of the subscribed witnesses the honorable Rutger Jacobsen and Evert Janssen Wendel, magistrates of the same court, Pieter Bronck, burgher and inhabitant of the aforesaid village, who declares to be honestly and truly indebted to Reyndert Pietersen for the sum of eight hundred and thirty-two guilders in good whole merchantable beaver skins for goods received to his satisfaction, with the interest thereof; which aforesaid sum of eight hundred and thirty-two guilders with interest he promises to pay on the first of July 1661, pledging in particular his brewery and lot located in the village of Beverwijck as a mortgage and collateral toward payment of the aforesaid sum, as well as his person and estate, moveable and immoveable, now and in the future, subjecting the same to all laws and judges. Done at Fort Orange on the 4th of August *anno* 1660.

Pyeter Bronck
Rutger Jacobsen
Evert Jansz Wendel
Acknowledged by me,
La Montagne, commissary at Fort Orange.

I, the subscribed Reyndert Pietersen, acknowledge that the above mortgage standing as a charge against Pieter Bronck has been paid in full. Done at Fort Orange the 5th of August *anno* 1662.

This is the mark of RP Reyndert Pietersen
made with his own hand.
J. Provoost, clerk

[BILL OF SALE OF A LOT FROM JOHANNA EBBINGHS TO AERT PIETERS AND JAN WILLEMSEN]

[242] Appeared before me, Johannes Provoost, in the service of the general chartered West India Company, clerk at Fort Orange, madam Johanna Ebbinghs, wife of Jeronimus Ebbingh, who declares, in the presence of the subscribed witnesses, on the one side to have sold and Aert Pieters and Jan Willemsen on the other side who have bought a piece of land located in the Esopus in New Netherland, adjoining on the north and west the seller, to the south the thicket, to the east the hill; in size forty-eight morgens and seventy-two rods, and that for the sum of six hundred and fifty guilder to be paid in three installments, the first installment on the first of June *anno* 1661, two hundred guilder in good whole beavers, the second on the first of June *anno* 1662, half in grain at market price, and the third installment on the first of June *anno* 1663, two hundred and fifty guilders, in grain and whole beavers as specified above. Thus done and agreed upon in all friendship and amity in the presence of Arent vanden Bergh and Gillis den Necker as witness sought hereto on this the 5th of August *anno* 1660 at Fort Orange.

Johanna Ebbinck

This is the  mark of Aert Pietersen
made with his own hand.

This is the  mark of Jan Willemsen
made with is own hand.

This is the  mark of Arent vanden Bergh
made with is own hand.

This is the  mark of Gillis den Necker
made with is own hand.

[ACKNOWLEDGMENT OF DEBT OF SANDER LEEDERSEN GLEN TO DIRRICK JANSSEN CROON]

[243] Appeared before me, Johannes La Montagne, admitted by the lord director general and council of New Netherland as vice director and commissary of Fort Orange and the village of Beverwijck, residing in the aforesaid Fort Orange, in the presence of the subscribed witnesses the honorable Jan Verbeeck and Frans Barentsen Pastoor, magistrates of the same court, acknowledges that he is honestly and truly indebted to Dirrick Janssen Croon for the sum of five hundred and seventy-six guilders with interest on the same at 10 percent, beginning on this date to be paid in good whole merchantable beaver skins, at eight guilders a piece, which aforesaid sum of five hundred and seventy-five guilders Sander Leenderse aforesaid promises to pay to the aforesaid Dirrick Janssen Croon or his attorney, in the month of June 1661, pledging in particular his house and lot located in the village of Beverwijck, adjoining to the east Jan Tomassen, to the west Annetie Bogardus, and which Jan Vinhagel at present occupies, as a firm pledge and mortgage for the payment of the aforesaid sum, and pledging his person and estate, moveable and immoveable, now and in the future, subjecting the same to all laws and judges. Done at Fort Orange the 13th of August *anno* 1660.

Sander Lenrsen
Jan Verbeeck
Frans Barentsen Pastoor
La Montagne, commissary at Fort Orange.

[POWER OF ATTORNEY OF ADRIAEN JANSSEN CROON]

[244] Appeared before me, Johannes La Montagne, admitted by the lord director general and council of New Netherland as vice director and commissary of Fort Orange and the village of Beverwijck, residing in the aforesaid Fort Orange, Adriaen Janssen Croon, presently ready to depart for *patria*, who declares, in the presence of the subscribed witnesses, to have constituted and empowered, as he hereby does, the honorable Adriaen Gerritsen to demand, collect, and receive here at Fort Orange in New Netherland, or elsewhere at Manhattan, such debts and monies as are due him, according to the evidences thereof, and to issue quittance upon receipt thereof, and in case of unwillingness, to demand the payment with law and rigor of justice, carrying judicial proceedings to final execution, including attachment of persons and goods, and in addition to do everything that shall be deemed necessary and appropriate, promising to hold as good and true all that shall have been done, as prescribed by law. Thus done at Fort Orange on the 20th of August *anno* 1660 in the presence of Johannes Provoost and Nataniel Pieterse as witnesses.

Adryaen Jansz Croon
Johannes Provoost, secretary
Nattanyel Pieterdse
Acknowldeged by me,
La Montagne, commissary at Fort Orange.

[CONVEYANCE OF A LOT FROM ANDERIES HERBERTSEN AND RUTGER JACOBSZ TO ADRIAEN JANSSEN VAN ILPENDAM AND CATALIJN BERCX]

[245] Appeared before me, Johannes La Montagne, admitted by the lord director general and council of New Netherland as vice director and commissary of Fort Orange and the village of Beverwijck, residing in the aforesaid Fort Orange, the honorable magistrates of this court in the persons of Anderies Herbertsz and Rugter Jacobsz, who declare to have ceded and conveyed, as they hereby cede and convey, in real and actual possession, to the benefit of Adriaen Janssen van Ilpendam and Catalijn Bercx, widow of the deceased Dirrick Bensinck and their heir or assigns, a certain lot located in the village of Beverwijck, to the south Dirrick Bensinck, deceased, and to the north Adriaen Janssen van Ilpendam, east and west to the street; in breadth twenty-eight feet and four inches, in length from one street to the other, namely, east and west; which lot the aforesaid conveyers promise in their aforesaid capacities to free from all claims or pretensions that could arise hereafter from the interest of the commonalty of this place or the village of Beverwijck. Done at Fort Orange on the 23rd of August *anno* 1660.

Andris Herberts
Acknowledged by me,
La Montagne, commissary at Fort Orange.

[CONVEYANCE OF A HOUSE AND LOT FROM CATALIJN BERCX TO JACOB TYSSEN VAN DER HEYDEN]

[246] Appeared before me, Johannes La Montagne, admitted by the lord director general and council of New Netherland as vice director and commissary of Fort Orange and the village of Beverwijck, residing in the aforesaid Fort Orange, in the presence of the honorable Johan Verbeeck and Evert Janssen Wendel, magistrates of the same court, Catalijn Bercx, widow of the deceased Dirrick Bensing, who declares to have ceded and conveyed, in real and actual possession, to the benefit of Jacob Tyssen van der Heyden, his heirs or assigns, a certain house and lot to the south of Adriaen Janssen van Ilpendam and north of the grantee; the lot is at the north ten rods in length, and at the south the same, to the east and west one rod, eleven feet, and 6 inches in breadth; which lot is a portion of the patent granted to Daniel Rinckhout by the lord director general and council of New Netherland dated the 25th of October *anno* 1653, of which the conveyer received from him by conveyance, as well as a part of the lot granted to her by the honorable magistrates of this court, for which the conveyer acknowledges to have fully paid and **[247]** subsequently promises to free the same from all complaints, claims, or pretensions that may hereafter arise, pledging her person and estate, moveable and immoveable, now and in the future, subjecting the same to all courts and judges. Done at Fort Orange the 23rd of August *anno* 1660.

This is the mark X of Catalijn Bercx
made with her own hand.
Jan Verbeeck
Evert Jansz Wendel
Acknowledged by me,
La Montagne, commissary at Fort Orange.

[ACKNOWLEDGMENT OF DEBT OF TRIJNTIE JANS]

Copy. Appeared before us the undersigned *schepenen* of the city of Amsterdam in New Netherland, Trijntie Jans, the housewife of Rut Jacobsen, living at Fort Orange in the village of Beverwijck who acknowledges to be truly and honestly indebted to the lord Cornelis Steenwijck, *schepen* of the aforenamed city for the sum of five thousand four hundred eighty-two guilders and two stivers, stemming from a matter of obligation dated 24 November 1657 issued by her husband to him, lord Steenwijck; which aforesaid five thousand four hundred eighty-two guilders and two stivers she, the appearer, has by virtue of a power of attorney dated 27 August 1658 of her husband, Rut Jacobsz, in which it was approved what she shall do herein, promising to assume it fully and pay in the coming May 1659 with interest at one percent per month, beginning the first of last May *anno* 1658 and ending in May 1659, and that in good whole beavers at eight guilders a piece, pledging in particular her house and lots located here on Manhattan northward the

High Street, westward the house and lot of Willem Herck, as well as a **[248]** house and lots of the appearer, standing and located at Fort Orange; furthermore, her person and estate, moveable and immoveable, nothing excepted, subject to all courts and judges. In witness of the truth, this is subscribed by her as well as by the lord schepenen, Johannes de Peyster and Isaac de Foreest. Signed in the protocol on the 4th of September 1658 in Amsterdam in New Netherland and confirmed by the lord president, the city's seal being affixed thereon.

Below stood: Agrees with the aforesaid protocol.
Was signed: Johannes Nevis, secretary.

[ORDER TO INSERT PRECEDING MORTGAGE INTO PROTOCOL]

Appeared before me, Johannes La Montagne, admitted by the lord director general and council of New Netherland as vice director and commissary of Fort Orange and the village of Beverwijck, the honorable Rutger Jacobsen, magistrate of the same court, who has requested that the preceding mortgage be inserted in the protocol of this court, which took place in the presence of Anderies Herberts and Evert Janssen Wendel, magistrates of the same court, to serve in time and place accordingly. Done at Fort Orange on this 24th of August *anno* 1660.

Rutger Jacobsz
Evert Wendel

[ACKNOWLEDGMENT OF DEBT OF JAN MARTENSEN]

[249] Appeared before me, Johannes La Montagne, admitted by the lord director general and council of New Netherland as vice director and commissary of Fort Orange and the village of Beverwijck, in the presence of the honorable Anderies Herbertsz and Frans Barentsen Pastoor, magistrates of the same court, Jan Martensen, who acknowledges to be honestly and truly indebted to *Sr.* Jan Bastiaensen van Gudshoven for the sum of one thousand forty-two guilders, two stivers and eight pennies, in payment of good whole merchantable beaver skins at eight guilder a piece, stemming from receipt of goods and merchandise, which aforesaid sum of one thousand forty-two guilders, two stivers and eight pennies, the aforesaid Jan Martensen promises to pay to the aforesaid Jan Bastiaensen van Gudshoven or his attorney on the first of July *anno* 1661; for which the aforesaid Jan Martensen pledges and places his house, lot, and garden as a special mortgage and collateral, located in the village of Beverwijck and presently still occupied by him, securing the payment if need be of the aforesaid sum without cost and loss; also his person and estate, moveable and immoveable, now and in the future, nothing excepted, subjecting the same to all courts and judges. Done at Fort Orange on the 24th of August *anno* 1660.

This the mark + of Jan Martensen
made with his own hand.
Andries Herbertsen
Frans Barents Pastoors
Acknowledged by me,
La Montagne, commissary at Fort Orange.

[POWER OF ATTORNEY OF DANIEL RINCKHOUT]

[250] Appeared before me, Johannes La Montagne, admitted by the lord director general and council of New Netherland as vice director and commissary of Fort Orange and the village of Beverwijck, Daniel Rinckhout, inhabitant of Beverwijck, who declares in the presence of the subscribed witnesses that the has appointed and empowered, as he hereby appoints and empowers, Sacharius Janssen, living in Munnekendam in Holland, in the subscriber's name and for his sake to demand of Nicolaes Broeck, living in Amsterdam, one of the guardians of the subscriber, a statement and return of the administration of the guardianship, which he has exercised over the effects belonging to the subscriber by way of the estate of Johannes Rickhout, deceased, the subscriber's uncle, and upon receipt of the aforesaid account and return to issue a quittance of the same, acting in the matter as the constituent could do or be capable of were he himself present, without exception; and in case of refusal, to sue the aforesaid Nicolaes Broeck, and to pursue the matter before a competent judge to a definitive sentence, and from aforesaid sentence to appeal or accept the same accordingly as he shall deem proper, with power, in case of need for furthering the same matter, to substitute one or more person in his place; promising to **[251]** hold good and true all that the attorney in the matter shall do, renouncing all regulations and laws that might militate against his good intensions (provided that the attorney shall make a statement and return to the subscriber of his activities), pledging his person and estate, moveable and immoveable, now and in the future, submitting the same to all laws and judges. Done at Fort Orange in New Netherland the 25th of August *anno* 1660, in the presence of Johannes Provoost and Zacharias Sickels as witnesses invited hereto.

Daniel Rinckhaut
Zacharias Syckels
Johannes Provoost, witness
La Montagne, vd and commissary of Fort Orange.

[POWER OF ATTORNEY OF CAREL JANSSEN]

[252] Appeared before me Johannes Provoost in the service of the general chartered West India Company, clerk of the court of Fort Orange and the village of Beverwijck, Carel Janssen, presently about to depart for *patria*, who declares in the presence of the subscribed witnesses that he has appointed and empowered, as he hereby does appoint and empower, Pieter Gillissen, living in the aforesaid village of Beverwijck, in the subscriber's name and for his sake, to demand, collect, and receive here at Fort Orange in New Netherland, or elsewhere at Manhattan, such out standing debts and monies as are owed him, the subscriber, according to the evidences and instruments serving thereto, issuing quittance upon receipt thereof, and in case of unwillingness, to demand payment with law and rigor of justice, carrying judicial proceedings to final execution, including attachment of persons and goods, and in addition to do everything that the subscriber himself being present could and might do, provided that the attorney be obliged to render a proper statement and return as requested thereto, pledging his person and estate, moveable and immoveable.

Carel Janse
This the mark of **SH** Dirrick Hendirick

This the mark of  Anderies Hanssen
Acknowledged by me,
Johannes Provoost, clerk.

[POWER OF ATTORNEY OF TEUNIS PIETERSZ TEMPEL]

[253] Appeared before me Johannes Provoost in the service of the general chartered West India Company, clerk of the court of Fort Orange and the village of Beverwijck, Teunis Pietersz Tempel, presently about to depart for *patria*, who declare in the presence of the subscribed witnesses to have constituted and empowered, as he hereby does, Pieter Gillissen and Dirrick Carstensen, presently living in the aforesaid village, in the subscriber's name and for his sake, to demand, collect, and receive here at Fort Orange in New Netherland, or elsewhere at Manhattan, such out standing debts and monies as are owed him, the subscriber, according to the evidences and instruments serving thereto, issuing quittance upon receipt thereof, and in case of unwillingness, to demand payment with law and rigor of justice, carrying judicial proceedings to final execution, including attachment of persons and goods, and in addition to do everything that the subscriber himself being present could and might do, provided that the attorney be obliged to render a proper statement and return as requested thereto, pledging his person and estate, moveable and immoveable. Thus done at Fort Orange in the presence of Dirrick Hendericksz and Anderies Janssen as witnesses invited hereto on this 27th of August *anno* 1660.

Thuenes Pietersen Tempel

This the mark of **SH** Dirrick Hendericksz

This the mark of  Anderies Janssen

Acknowledged by me,
Johannes Provoost, clerk.

[ACKNOWLEDGMENT OF DEBT OF MARRETIE PIETERS]

[254] Appeared before me, Johannes La Montagne, in the service of the general chartered West India Company, admitted vice director and commissary at Fort Orange and the village of Beverwijck by the lord director general and council of New Netherland, in the presence of Anderies Herbertsz and Evert Wendel, magistrates of the same court, Marretie Pieters, widow of Anderies van der Sluys, deceased, who acknowledges to be honestly and truly indebted to the honorable Gerrit Bancker and Harmen Albertsen Vedder for the sum of five hundred Carolus guilders in payment of good whole merchantable beaver skins at eight guilders a piece, which aforesaid sum of five hundred guilders she promises to pay to the aforesaid Bancker and Harmen Vedder or to their attorney, as soon as possible, pledging in particular her house, lot, and garden located in the Esopus next to Tomas Chambert, for the payment and satisfaction of the aforesaid sum, on a pledge of her person and estate, moveable and immoveable, now and in the future, nothing excepted, submitting the same to all courts and judges. Done at Fort Orange on the 28th of August *anno* 1660.

This is the mark  of Marretien Pietersen
made with her own hand.
Andris Herberts
Evert Jansz Wendel

Acknowledged by me,
La Montagne, commissary at Fort Orange.

[CONVEYANCE OF A HOUSE AND LOT FROM PIETER MEESSEN VROOMAN TO CORNELIS CORNELISSEN STERREVELT]

[255] Appeared before me, Johannes La Montagne, in the service of the general chartered West India Company, admitted vice director and commissary at Fort Orange and the village of Beverwijck by the lord director general and council of New Netherland, in the presence of the honorable Frans Barentsen Pastoor and Evert Wendel, magistrates of the same court, Pieter Meessen Vrooman, who declares to have ceded and conveyed, as he hereby cedes and conveys, to the benefit of Cornelis Cornelissen Sterrevelt, his heirs or assigns, a house and lot located in the village of Beverwijck, together with a garden located on the Third Kil, to the east Albert *de Ramaker*; in length 9 rods, to the north Anderies de Vosch, in breadth five rods seven feet six inches; to the east an empty lot, in legth seven rods; to the south a wagon road, in breadth five rods seven feet six inches; to the south Symon Groot, in length seven rods four feet, to the east a road, in breadth four rods, to the north Eldert *de Gojer*, in length seven rods and four feet, to the west a road, in breadth four rods; which lot the conveyer was granted by a patent dated 17 August *anno* 1660, for which aforesaid house and lot the conveyer acknowledges to have had payment and consequently promises to fee the same from all demands, claims, and pretension, which may arise hereafter, pledging his person and estate, moveable and immoveable, now and in the future, submitting the same to all courts and judges. Done at Fort Orange the first of September *anno* 1660.

Pieter Meesz Vrooman
Frans Barentsen Pastoor
Evert Jansz Wendel

Acknowledged by me,
La Montagne, commissary at Fort Orange.

[CONVEYANCE OF A HOUSE AND LOT FROM CORNELIS CORNELISSEN STERRENVELT TO CORNELIS TEUNISSEN BOSCH]

[256] Appeared before me, Johannes La Montagne, in the service of the general chartered West India Company, vice director and commissary at Fort Orange and the village of Beverwijck, in the presence of the honorable Anderies Herbertsen and Jan Verbeeck, magistrates of the same court, Cornelis Cornelissen Sterrenvelt, who declares to have ceded and conveyed, as he hereby cedes and conveys, in real and actual possession, to the benefit of Cornelis Teunissen Bosch, his heirs or assigns, a house and lot located in the village of Beverwijck; to the south Sijmon Groot, in length seven rods four feet, to the east a road, in breadth four rods, to the north Eldert *de Gojer*, in length seven rods four feet, to the west a road, in breadth four rods, together with a a lot for a garden located on the Third Kil, to the east Albert *de Rademaker*, in length nine rods, to the north Anderies de Vosch, in breadth five rods seven feet six inches, to the west one empty lot, in length 7 rods, to the south a wagon road, in breadth 5 rods 7 feet 6 inches, which lot and garden was granted to Pieter Meessen Vrooman by patent of the lord director general and council dated 17 August *anno* 1660, from whom the grantor received the same by conveyance and promises to free the same from all demands, claims or pretensions, which may hereafter arise, pledging his person and estate, moveable and immoveable, submitting the same to all courts and judges. Done at Fort Orange the first of September 1660.

Cornelis Cornelissen Sterrenvelt
Andris Herberts
Jan Verbeeck

Acknowledged by me,
La Montagne, commissary at Fort Orange.

[CONVEYANCE OF A HOUSE AND LOT FROM REM JANSSEN *SMIT* TO CORNELIS TEUNISSEN BOSCH]

[257] Appeared before me, Johannes La Montagne, in the service of the general chartered West India Company, vice director and commissary at Fort Orange and the village of Beverwijck, in the presence of the honorable Anderies Herbertsen and Jan Verbeeck, magistrates of the same court, Rem Janssen *smit*, burgher of the aforesaid village of Beverwijck, who declares to have ceded and conveyed, as he hereby cedes and conveys, in real and actual possession, to the benefit of Cornelis Teunissen Bosch, his heirs or assigns, a house and lot located in the village of Beverwijck, adjoining to the east Adriaen Gerritsen, to the west Jan Tomassen, is two rods and two feet wide in front on the road, to the west and east six rods three feet in length, to the north two rods and eight feet in breadth, which lot was granted to Rut Adriaensen by the lord director general and council of New Netherland dated the 23rd of April 1652, and by him conveyed to Henderick Gerritsen, from whom the grantor received it by conveyance, for which aforesaid house and lot the grantor acknowledges that he has had payment and promises to free the same from all demands, claims or pretensions, which may hereafter arise, pledging his person and estate, moveable and immoveable, now and in the future, submitting the same to all courts and judges. Done in Fort Orange on the 3rd of September *anno* 1660.

Rem Jansen
Andris Herbertsen
Jan Verbeeck
Acknowledged by me,
La Montagne, commissary at Fort Orange.

[CONVEYANCE OF A HOUSE AND LOT FROM REM JANSSEN *SMIT* TO JAN TOMASSEN]

[258] Appeared before me, Johannes La Montagne, in the service of the general chartered West India Company, vice director and commissary at Fort Orange and the village of Beverwijck, in the presence of the honorable Jan Verbeeck and Evert Wendel, magistrates of the same court, Rem Janssen *smit*, burgher and inhabitant of the aforesaid village, who declares to have ceded and conveyed, as he hereby cedes and conveys, in real and actual possession, to the benefit of Jan Tomassen, also burgher and inhabitant here, his heirs or assigns, a house and lot located in the aforesaid village of Beverwijck, adjoining to the west Jan van Aecken and to the east Cornelis Teunissen Bosch; the lot is in breadth on the street side two rods one foot and six inches, to the east in length six rods and three feet, to the north in breadth one rod six feet, to the west in length six rods and three feet; which lot the lord director general and council of New Netherland granted to Rut Adriaensen by patent dated the 23rd of April *anno* 1652 and conveyed by him to Henderick Gerritsen, from whom the grantor received it by conveyance, and promises to free the house and lot from all demands, claims or pretensions, which may hereafter arise, pledging his person and estate, moveable and immoveable, now and in the future, submitting the same to all courts and judges. Done in Fort Orange the 3rd of August *anno* 1660.

Rem Janssen
Jan Verbeeck
Evert Jansz Wendel
Acknowledged by me,
La Montagne, commissary at Fort Orange.

[ACKNOWLEDGMENT OF DEBT OF PHILIP HENDRICKSZ]

[259] Appeared before me, Johannes La Montagne, in the service of the general chartered West India Company, vice director and commissary at Fort Orange and the village of Beverwijck, in the presence of the honorable Frans Barensen Pastoor and Evert Janssen Wendel, magistrates of the same court, Philip Hendricksz, who acknowledges to be honestly and truly indebted to Henderick Anderiesse for the sum of three thousand one hundred and forty-four guilders in payment of good whole merchantable beaver skins at eight guilders a piece, stemming from the purchase of a house and brewery; which aforesaid sum of three thousand one hundred and forty-four guilders the aforesaid Philip Hendericksen promises to pay on the first of July *anno* 1661, pledging in particular his aforesaid house and brewery and lot as a firm mortgage and special collateral for payment of the aforesaid sum, so that, if it is necessary, the aforesaid sum can be recovered without loss or damage, pledging also his person and estate, moveable and immoveable, now and in the future, nothing excepted, submitting the same to all courts and judges. Done at Fort Orange on the 2nd of September *anno* 1660.

Flip Henricksen
Frans Barentsz Pastoor
Evert Jansz Wendel
Acknowledged by me,
La Montagne, commissary at Fort Orange.

[POWER OF ATTORNEY OF WOUTER AERTSEN VAN NIEUKERCK]

[260] Appeared before me, Johannes La Montagne, in the service of the general chartered West India Company, admitted vice director and commissary at Fort Orange and the village of Beverwijck by the lord director general and council of New Netherland, Wouter Aertsen van Nieukerck, who declares, in the presence of the subscribed witnesses, that he has appointed and empowered, as he hereby appoints and empowers, the honorable Harmen Albertsen Vedder, in the subscriber's name and on his behalf, to request, demand, and receive in the fatherland from the honorable lords directors of the chartered West India Company at the chamber of Amsterdam, a certain one hundred nine guilders, fourteen stivers and two pennies, due to him, the subscriber, for his monthly wages and subsistence earned in their service as a soldier, according to the account signed Willem Kieft; to receive the aforesaid sum of one hundred nine guilders, fourteen stivers and two pennies, and being received to issue a quittance thereof, which shall be valid as if the same was given by the subscriber; furthermore, to do and perform all things, which he, the subscriber, being present, might or could do even if the matter requires greater and more special authority than stands expressed herein; promising to hold good and true all that shall be done by virtue of this instrument, pledging his person and estate, moveable and immoveable. Thus done at Fort Orange the 3rd of September *anno* 1660 in the presence of J. Provoost and Jan Pietersen Muller.

This is the mark  of Wouter Aertsz
made with his own hand.
Johannes Provoost, witness
Jan Pietersz Mulder
Acknowledged by me,
La Montagne, commissary at Fort Orange.

[POWER OF ATTORNEY OF HENDERICK ANDERIESSEN]

[261] Appeared before me, Johannes La Montagne, in the service of the general chartered West India Company, admitted by the lord director general and council of New Netherland vice director and commissary at Fort Orange and the village of Beverwijck, residing in the aforesaid fortress, Henderick Anderiessen, living in the aforesaid village, who declares, in the presence of the subscribed witnesses, to have appointed and empowered, as he hereby appoints and empowers, *Sr.* Abel de Wolff, residing in Amsterdam to collect, pursue, and receive from *Sr.* Gerrit Barentsen Koers, also residing in Amsterdam, a certain five thousand six hundred ninety one guilders and fifteen stivers owed to the subscriber according to the instruments and proofs hereto affixed, issuing a quittance upon receipt hereof; and upon refusal to compel payment by legal means and rigor of justice unto sentence and extreme execution; also, to proceed by attachment against persons and estates; furthermore, to do and perform all that he shall deem proper, with authority, if needs be, to further the business, to substitute one or more persons in **[262]** his place, promising to hold good and true all that the attorney in aforesaid business shall do, renouncing all statutes and laws, which might militate against his good intentions, provided that the attorney be obligated to make a proper statement and return, pledging his person and estate, moveable and immoveable, now and in the future, submitting the same to all courts and judges. Done at Fort Orange in New Netherland the 2nd of September *anno* 1669, in the presence of Gysbert van Imborgh and Johannes Provoost as witnesses invited hereto on this 10th of September *anno* 1660.

Hendryck Andriesen
Gysbert van Imborgh
Acknowledged by me,
La Montagne, commissary at Fort Orange.

[BILL OF SALE FOR LAND FROM JOHANNA DE LAET
TO TJERCK CLAESSEN]

[263] Appeared before me, Johannes La Montagne, in the service of the general chartered West India Company, admitted by the lord director general and council of New Netherland vice director and commissary at Fort Orange and the village of Beverwijck, Madam Johana de Laedt, assisted by the honorable Jeronimus Ebbinck as husband and guardian of the same on the one side, and Tjerck Claessen, inhabitant of the colony of Rensselaerswijck on the other side, who have agreed and contracted with each other as follows: namely, that the aforesaid Madam Johanna de Laet *per forma* of exchange two pieces of land lying in the Esoopus west by north of the *Binne Kil* of Esoopes and lying on the other side of the same; the north field comprises thirty-five morgens and one hundred and fifty-five rods, and the other, adjoining the west side consists of thirty-five morgens and one hundred ten rods; in exchange for which the aforesaid Tierck Claesen gives his house twenty feet long and with the side aisle thirty feet wide; the lot is ten rods long and twenty-nine feet or more, lying in the village of Beverwijck, adjoining on the east side the street, on the west side the garden of Henderick Anderiesen and Lambert van Neck, on the north side the house of Lambert van Neck, and on the south side the house of Hendrick de Backer; with the condition that the respective parties shall deliver proper contracts and instruments securing complete possession on the first of May in the year 1661, without craft or guile, pledging their persons and estates, moveable and immoveable, now and in the future, submitting the same to all courts and judges. Done at Fort Orange the 11th of September 1660 in the presence of Jan Pietersen Mulder and Arent Jansen.

Johanna de Laet
Jeronimus Ebbinck

Tierck Claessen de Witt
Acknowledged by me,
La Montagne, commissary at Fort Orange.

[POWER OF ATTORNEY OF DANIEL VERVEELEN]

[264] Appeared before me, Johannes La Montagne, in the service of the general chartered West India Company, admitted by the lord director general and council of New Netherland vice director and commissary at Fort Orange and the village of Beverwijck, *Sr.* Daniel Verveelen, merchant here, who declares to have constituted, as he hereby does constitute and empower Wouter Albers, burgher and inhabitant of the village of Beverwijck, in his name and on his behalf, to request and demand payment of such monies and of such persons as the accounts and other instruments, which the subscriber has given into the hands of the attorney, shall indicate, to proceed against aforesaid persons by process of law to final sentence, to appeal from aforesaid or acquiesce therein, as he shall deem proper, to issue acquittance for monies received, and to act in the aforesaid matter as if the subscriber were himself present, provided that the attorney shall be obligated to submit an account of his activities to the subscriber, promising to hold good and true all that the attorney shall do in this matter, pledging his person and estate, moveable and immoveable, now and in the future, submitting the same to all courts and judges. Done the 18th of September 1660 in the presence of Jan Pietersen and Geurt Hendricksen.

Daniel Vervelen
Jan Pieters
Geurt Heyndrycksen

La Montagne, commissary at Fort Orange.

[BILL OF SALE FOR LAND FROM JOHANNA DE LAET TO AERT JACOBSEN]

[265] Appeared before me, Johannes La Montagne, in the service of the general chartered West India Company, admitted by the lord director general and council of New Netherland vice director and commissary at Fort Orange and the village of Beverwijck, Madam Johanna de Laet, wife of Jeronimus Ebbingh, who declares, in the presence of the subscribed witnesses, on the one side, that she has sold, and Aert Jacobsen, on the other side, that he has bought a certain piece of land lying in the Esoopus in New Netherland, adjoining on the northeast side the land of Jan Schoon and Aert Pietersen Tack, on the northwest side Tierck Claesen, on the southwest the hill, containing forty-seven morgens and two hundred fifteen rods, for the sum of six hundred guilders, half in beavers and half in wheat at market price, in three installments, namely: in June *anno* 1661, the third part of the aforesaid sum, in June *anno* 1662, another third part, and the remaining third part in June *anno* 1663; the aforesaid Madam promising to clear the aforesaid lot from all demands and pretensions, which may arise against aforesaid land, the respective parties pledging their persons and estates, moveable and immoveable, now and in the future, for the maintenance of the aforesaid contract, submitting the same to all courts and judges, as the acceptant also does his person. Done at Fort Orange the 17th of September 1660, in the presence of Jan Pietersen Muller and Geurt Hendricksen, witnesses.

Johanna de Laet
Aert Jacobsen
Jan Pieters Mulder
Geurt Heyndrycksen
Acknowledged by me,
La Montagne, commissary at Fort Orange.

[AWARD OF THE SLAUGHTER EXCISE TO MARCELIS JANSEN]

[266] On the last day of September *anno* 1660 the slaughter excise was offered at public auction by the honorable commissary and magistrates of Fort Orange, according to the conditions of the year 1659, and Marcelis Jansen remained the last bidder for the sum of seven hundred twenty guilder, for which sum his sureties were Cornelis Teunissen Bosch and Gerrit Slechtenhorst, each for all, as principals, pledging their persons and estates, moveable and immoveable, now and in the future, submitting the same to all courts and judges. Done as above.

Marelys Jansen
Cornelis Thonisen Bosch
Gerrit Slichtenhorst
Acknowledged by me,
La Montagne, commissary at Fort Orange.

[POWER OF ATTORNEY OF REM JANSSEN *SMIT*]

[267] Appeared before me, Johannes La Montagne, in the service of the general chartered West India Company, admitted by the lord director general and council of New Netherland vice director and commissary at Fort Orange and the village of Beverwijck, Rem Jansen *smit*, who declares to have constituted and empowered, as he hereby does constitute and empower, Daniel Rinckhout, burgher and inhabitant of the aforesaid village, in his name and on his behalf, to collect, demand, and receive here at Fort Orange in New Netherland, first, from Jan Helmsen the sum of sixty-five guilders in beavers or wheat; from Eldert Gerbertsen forty-one gulders payable as before; from Evert Pels forty-two guilders; Jan Tijssen thirty-six guilders; and from Gijsbert van den Bergh 32 guilders; and in case of unwillingness to compel payment by law and rigor of justice to final sentence and execution; also, to proceed by attachment against persons and estates; furthermore, to do and perform all things, which he, the subscriber, being present himself, could or might do, although the matter may require greater and more special authority than is expressed in this instrument, provided the attorney be obliged to submit a proper account **[268]** and return to the subscriber, pledging his person and estate, moveable and immoveable. thus done at Fort Orange in New Netherland on this 3rd of October *anno* 1660.

Rem Yansen
Johannes Clute
Johannes Provoost, witnesses
Acknowledged by me,
La Montagne, commissary at Fort Orange.

[CONVEYANCE OF A HOUSE AND LOT FROM CORNELIS SEGERSEN TO GERRIT SLICHTENHORST]

Appeared before me, Johannes La Montagne, in the service of the general chartered West India Company, admitted by the lord director general and council of New Netherland vice director and commissary at Fort Orange and the village of Beverwijck, in the presence of the honorable Frans Barensen Pastoor and Evert Janssen Wendel, magistrates of the same court, Cornelis Segersen, who declares to have ceded and conveyed, as he hereby cedes and conveys, in actual and real possession, to and for the benefit of Gerrit Slichtenhorst, his heirs or assigns, a house and lot, lying in the village of Beverwijck at the hill, adjoining on the south Marcelis Janssen, on **[269]** the north, east and west the street; the lot is in length twenty rods, in width five rods, one foot or 2 (indeterminate), to the west the hill, breadth seven rods and a half, which lot before this was granted by patent from the lord director general and council of New Netherland to Jan Roeloffse, from whom the grantor received it by conveyance, and promises to clear the same from all demands, claims, and pretensions, which may arise hereafter against the same, pledging his person and estate, moveable and immoveable, now and in the future, submitting the same to all courts and judges. Done at Fort Orange the 10th of December *anno* 1660.

Cornelis Seegerszoon
Frans Barentsen Pastoor
Evert Jansen Wendel
Acknowledged by me,
La Montagne, commissary at Fort Orange.

[CONVEYANCE OF A LOT FROM CORNELIS TEUNISSEN BOSCH TO THE MAGISTRATES]

[270] Appeared before me, Johannes La Montagne, in the service of the general chartered West India Company, admitted by the lord director general and council of New Netherland vice director and commissary at Fort Orange and the village of Beverwijck, in the presence of the honorable magistrates of the same court, Cornelis Teunissen Bosch, who declares to have ceded and conveyed as he hereby cedes and conveys, in real and actual possession, to and for the benefit of the aforesaid magistrates, a certain lot, being cleared by their honors as a street for the common good, adjoining to the south of the house of Jan Teunissen alias *de Paep*; in length thirteen rods and in width two rods; which lot is a portion of the patent granted to him, the grantor, by the lord director general and council of New Netherland on the 23rd of April *anno* 1652; for which lot the aforesaid grantor acknowledges to have been paid and promises to clear the aforesaid lot from all demands, claims or pretensions, which may hereafter arise, pledging his person and estate, moveable and immoveable, now and in the future, submitting the same to all courts and judges. Done at Fort Orange on the 10th of December *anno* 1660.

Cornelis Thonisen Bos
Anderies Herberts
Jan Verbeeck
Acknowledged by me,
La Montagne, commissary at Fort Orange.

[CONVEYANCE OF A PORTION OF A LOT FROM ANNETIEN BOGARDUS TO DAVIDT PIETERSEN SCHUYLER]

[271] Appeared before me, Johannes La Montagne, in the service of the general chartered West India Company, admitted by the lord director general and council of New Netherland vice director and commissary at Fort Orange and the village of Beverwijck, in the presence of the honorable [magistrates] Frans Barensen Pastoor and Evert Janssen Wendel, Annetien Bogardus, who declares to have ceded and conveyed, as she hereby does cede and convey, in real and actual possession, to and for the benefit of Davidt Pietersen Schuyler, his heirs or assigns, a portion of a lot lying in the village of Beverwijck, adjoining on the west the conveyer, on the south and east Sander Leendersen, on the north the street; the aforesaid lot is six rods and three feet long to the west at the conveyer's, in front on the street one rod six feet and eight inches wide, to the east on Sander Leendersen six rods three feet, to the west one rod seven feet and eight inches wide, which aforesaid lot is a portion of the patent granted to the conveyer by the lord director general and council of New Netherland on the 23rd of April *anno* 1652; for which the aforesaid conveyer acknowledges that she has had satisfaction and promises to clear the same from all demands, claims or pretensions, which may hereafter arise, pledging her person and estate, moveable and **[272]** immoveable, now and in the future, submitting the same to all courts and judges. Done at Fort Orange the 22nd of December *anno* 1660.

This is the mark  of Annetien Bogardus
made with her own hand.
Frans Barentsen Pastoor
Evert Jansz Wendel

Acknowledged by me,
La Montagne, commissary at Fort Orange.

[ACKNOWLEDGMENT OF DEBT OF PIETER ADRIAENSEN *SOOGEMACKELIJCK* TO GERRIT SLICHTENHORST]

Appeared before me, Johannes La Montagne, in the service of the general chartered West India Company, admitted by the lord director general and council of New Netherland vice director and commissary at Fort Orange and the village of Beverwijck, Pieter Adriaensen *Soogemackelijck*, inhabitant of the colony of Rensselaerswijck, who acknowledges, in the presence of the aforesaid witnesses, that he is truly and honestly indebted to the honorable Gerrit Slichtenhorst as bookkeeper of the deaconry, in the amount of thirty-three and a half pieces of good whole merchantable beaver skins at eight guilder a piece, stemming from a purchase of sewant, which he received at fifteen guilders the beaver to his satisfaction; therefore, the **[273]** aforesaid Pieter Adriaensen promises to pay the aforesaid amount of thirty-three and half beavers in the year 1661, half in June, pledging his person and estate, moveable and immoveable, now and in the future, with no exceptions, subjecting himself to all courts and judges. Done at Fort Orange the 2nd of February *anno* 1661 in the presence of... [*incomplete; not executed*].

[ACKNOWLEDGMENT OF DEBT BY ADRIAENSEN *SOOGEMACKELIJCK*]

Appeared before me, Johannes La Montagne, in the service of the general chartered West India Company, admitted by the lord director general and council of New Netherland vice director and commissary at Fort Orange and the village of Beverwijck, Pieter Adriaensen *Soogemackelijck*, inhabitant of the colony of Rensselaerswijck, who declares, in the presence of the subscribed witnesses, to have received from the hand of Gerrit Slichtenhorst, bookkeeper of the deaconry, the sum of five hundred guilders in sewant for his use for one year from this date **[274]** and no longer, for which use, the aforesaid Pieter Adriaensen promises to interest at ten percent, and at the end of the aforesaid year to return the principal sum, for which he pledges his person and estate, moveable and immoveable, now and in the future, nothing excepted, submitting the same to all courts and judges. Done at Fort Orange the 2nd of February *anno* 1661 in the presence of...[*incomplete*]

[275/276][†]

---

† This page has been incorrectly bound in the volume. Document 275 correctly represents the final paragraph of a document, beginning on document page 304. The reverse side or page 276 is blank.

[CONVEYANCE OF A HOUSE LOT AND GARDEN FROM JAN DARETH TO JACOB JOOSTEN VAN CORVELENS]

[277] Appeared before me, Johannes La Montagne, in the service of the general chartered West India Company, admitted by the lord director general and council of New Netherland vice director and commissary at Fort Orange and the village of Beverwijck, in the presence of the honorable Philip Pietersen Schuyler and Adriaen Gerritsen, magistrates of the same court, the honorable Jan Dareth, inhabitant of the aforesaid place, who declares to have ceded and conveyed, as he hereby does cede and convey, in real and actual possession, to and for the benefit of Jacob Joosten van Corvelens, his heirs and assigns, a lot for a house and a garden located in the village of Beverwijck; to the east of the road six rods in length, to the north the road three rods in width, to the west Tomas Pouwel six rods in length, to the south the plain three rods in width, according to the patent granted to him, the conveyer, by the lord director general and council of New Netherland on the 5th of February *anno* 1660; and the conveyer promises to clear the aforesaid lot from all charges, claims, or pretensions, which may arise hereafter, **[278]** pledging his person and estate, moveable and immoveable, now and in the future, submitting the same to the authority of all courts and judges. Done at Fort Orange the 2nd of February 1662.

Jan Dareth
Philip Pietersen
Adriaen Gerritsen
Acknowledged by me,
La Montagne, commissary at Fort Orange.

[CONVEYANCE OF A HOUSE FROM JAN LABATIE TO EVERT PELS]

[279] Appeared before me, Johannes La Montagne, in the service of the general chartered West India Company, admitted by the lord director general and council of New Netherland vice director and commissary at Fort Orange and the village of Beverwijck, in the presence of the honorable Anderies Herbertsen and Evert Janssen Wendel, magistrates of the same court, Jan Labite, inhabitant of the colony of

Rensselaerswijck, who declares to have ceded and conveyed, as he hereby does cede and convey, in real and actual possession, to and for the benefit of Evert Pels, also inhabitant of the colony of Rensselaerswijck, his heirs or assigns, a house located in Fort Orange, forming the curtain on the east side and adjoining on the south side the gate; in length forty-six feet and in width twenty two feet, with a garden outside the aforesaid fort , according to the patent granted by the lord director general and council of New Netherland on the 12th of April *anno* 1650; and he promises to clear it of all charges, demands or pretensions, which might arise hereafter, pledging his person and estate, moveable and immoveable, now and in the future, subjecting the same to the authority of all courts and judges. Done at Fort Orange on the 4th of February *anno* 1661.

Jan Labatie
Andries Herberts
Evert Jansz Wendel
Acknowledged by me,
La Montagne, commissary at Fort Orange.

[CONVEYANCE OF A HOUSE FROM EVERT PELS TO JAN BARENTSEN WEMP]

[280] Appeared before me, Johannes La Montagne, in the service of the general chartered West India Company, admitted by the lord director general and council of New Netherland vice director and commissary at Fort Orange and the village of Beverwijck, in the presence of the honorable Andries Herbertsen and Evert Janssen Wendel, magistrates of the same court, Evert Pels, inhabitant of the colony of Rensselaerswijck, who declares to have ceded and conveyed, as he hereby does cede and convey, to and for the benefit of Jan Barentsen Wemp, his heirs or assigns, a house standing in Fort Orange, forming a section of the east curtain, to the south the gate, with a garden outside the aforesaid fort, all according to the patent granted to Jan Labite by the lord director general and council of New Netherland on the 12th of April *anno* 1650, and conveyed to him by the aforesaid Jan Labite, for which house and garden the conveyer acknowledges that he has had satisfaction, promising to clear the same from charges, demands or pretensions, which may arise hereafter, pledging his person and estate, moveable and immoveable, now and in the future, submitting the same to all courts and judges. Done at Fort Orange the 4th of February *anno* 1661.

Evert Pels
Andries Herberts
Evert Jansz Wendel
Acknowledged by me,
La Montagne, commissary at Fort Orange.

[281–284] [*blank*]

[CONVEYANCE OF AN ISLAND FROM ITS INDIAN OWNERS TO ANDERIES HERBERTSEN AND RUTGER JACOBSEN]

[285] Appeared before me, Johannes La Montagne, in the service of the general chartered West India Company, admitted by the lord director general and council of New Netherland vice director and commissary at Fort Orange and the village of Beverwijck, two Indians named Maghsapeet alias Machackniemanauw, the other names Sansewaneuwe; also, an Indian named Paneenseen, and an Indian woman named Nipapoa, being joint owners of the island named Pachonakellick, in the presence of Aepjen and Nietamorit, being with the chiefs of the Mahicanders, who declare to have ceded and conveyed, as they hereby do cede and convey, to and for the benefit of Anderies Herbertsen and Rutger Jacobsen, inhabitants of this village of Beverwijck, a certain island named Pachonakellick, located in this river obliquely across from Betlehem, called Long or Mahikanders Island by the Dutch, together with complete ownership rights that they therein possess, for a certain sum in goods paid to them for which the grantors acknowledge having received satisfaction. Thus done at the village of Beverwijck in the presence of Gerrit Bancker and Johannes Provoost as witnesses invited hereto on this 8th of February *anno* 1661.

This is the mark of  Sansewanouwe
made with his own hand.

This is the mark of  the Indian woman Nipapoa
made with her own hand.

This is the mark of  Machackeniemanqauw
made with his own hand.

This is the mark of  Jan Symon
made with his own hand.

This is the mark of  Aepjen.
This is the mark of  Nitamorit.

Gerret Bancken
Johannes Provoost
Acknowledged by me,
La Montagne, v. d. and commissary at Fort Orange.

[CONVEYANCE OF A HOUSE, LOT, AND GARDEN FROM ALBERT GISBERT *RAEDEMAEKER* TO ARENT VAN CURLAER]

[**287**] Appeared before me, Johannes La Montagne, in the service of the general chartered West India Company, admitted by the lord director general and council of New Netherland v. dr. and commissary at Fort Orange and the village of Beverwijck, Albert Gisbert *Raedemaeker*, inhabitant of the village of Beverwijck and the honorable Arent van Curlaer, councilor of the colony of Rensselaerswijck, who declare to have contracted with one another respectively in the manner as follows, namely: that the aforesaid Albert Gisbert grants and conveys, as he hereby does grant and convey, in real and actual possession, to the aforesaid lord Arent van Curlaer, his heirs or assigns, his house, house lot, and garden located in the village of Beverwijck, adjoining on the east side Jan Barentsen Wemp, and the south Wouter *de Raedemaeker*, on the west the public road, on the north the defensive [wall] of the village of Beverwijck; the garden is located on the Third Kil between

Andries de Vos's land, for which house, lot, and garden the aforesaid Arent van Curlaer has given in payment two full-grown horses and cow of three years, which horses and cow the aforesaid Albert Gisbert acknowledges to have received to his satisfaction, and promises the to clear the conveyed house, lot, and garden from all claims and demands, and to deliver a proper patent of the same into the hands of the aforesaid lord Arent van Curlaer, pledging his person and estate, moveable and immoveable, now and in the future, submitting the same to all courts and judges. Done at Fort Orange the first of March 1661 in the presence of Jan Mayndertsz and Dirck Andriessen, witnesses invited hereto.

This is the mark of  Albert Gisbert
made with his own hand.
A.van Curler
Jan Meinersen
This is the mark of  Dirck Andriesse.

Acknowledged by me,
La Montagne, commissary at Fort Orange.

[CONVEYANCE OF A HOUSE AND LOT FROM EVERT PELS TO JEREMIAS VAN RENSSELAER]

[288] Appeared before me, Johannes La Montagne, in the service of the general chartered West India Company, admitted by the lord director general and council of New Netherland vice director and commissary at Fort Orange and the village of Beverwijck, in the presence of the honorable Frans Barensen Pastoor and Evert Janssen Wendel, magistrates of the same court, Evert Pels who declares to have ceded and conveyed, as he hereby does cede and convey, in real and actual possession, to and for the benefit of the lord Jeremias van Rensselaer, director of the colony of Rensselaerswijck, and for the account of the lords patroons of the aforesaid colony, their heirs, or assigns, a house and lot, located in the village of Beverwijck, adjoining to the east the river, to the south the adjoining garden of Sander Leendersen, to the west the street, and to the north Volckert Janssen; in length eleven rods, in breadth four rods and two feet, according to the patent granted by the lord director general and council of New Netherland to Willem Frederickse Bout dated [*blank*] *anno* [*blank*], from whom the conveyer has received by conveyance; in addtition, he, the conveyer, conveys to the aforesaid lords a garden located in the aforesaid village, adjoining to the south Willem Teljer, to the north Willem Bout, extending from the street to the river; in length ten rods and in breadth seven rods, granted by patent to Sander Leendersen dated the 23rd of April *anno* 1652, for which house, lot, and garden the conveyer acknowledges to have had satisfaction, and promise to clear the same from **[289]** all demands, claims or pretension, which may arise hereafter, pledging his person and estate, moveable and immoveable, now and in the future, submitting the same to all courts and judges. Done at Fort Orange the 14th of March *anno* 1661.

Evert Pels
Frans Barentsz Pastoor
Evert Jansz Wendel
Acknowledged by me,
La Montagne, commissary at Fort Orange.

[CONVEYANCE OF A HOUSE AND LOT FROM WILLEM JANSSEN STOL TO JOHAN VERBEECK]

[290] Appeared before me, Johannes La Montagne, in the service of the general chartered West India Company, vice director and commissary at Fort Orange and the village of Beverwijck, in the presence of the honorable Evert Janssen Wendel and Frans Barensen Pastoor, magistrates of the same court, Willem Janssen Stol, husband and guardian of the widow of Claes Hendericksz, deceased, who declares to have ceded and conveyed, as he hereby does cede and convey, in real and actual possession, to and for the benefit of the honorable Johan Verbeeck, magistrate of the aforesaid place, his heirs or assigns, a house and lot located in the aforesaid village of Beverwijck, adjoining to the south and west the public road, to the north Claes Janssen and to the east also a public road; in width on the west side fifty seven wooden feet, and to the east in breadth forty seven wood feet, which lot is a part of the patent granted by the lord director general and council of New

Netherland dated the 23rd of April *anno* 1652 to Jan Tomassen, from whom the conveyer received the same by conveyance; for which aforesaid house and lot the conveyer acknowledges to have had satisfaction, and promises to clear the same from all demands, claims or pretension, which may arise hereafter, pledging his person and estate, moveable and immoveable, now and in the future, submitting the same to all courts and judges. Done at Fort Orange the 15th of March *anno* 1661.

Willem Jansz
Frans Barentsz Pastoor
Evert Jansz Wendel

Acknowledged by me,
La Montagne, commissary at Fort Orange.

[CONVEYANCE FROM WILLEM JANSSEN STOL
TO ADRIAEN SYMONSEN]

[291] Appeared before me, Johannes La Montagne, in the service of the general chartered West India Company, vice director and commissary at Fort Orange and the village of Beverwijck, in the presence of the honorable Rutger Jacobsen and Johan Verbeeck, magistrates of the same court, Willem Janssen Stol, husband and guardian of the widow of Claes Hendericksz, deceased, who declares to have ceded and conveyed, as he hereby does cede and convey, in real and actual possession, to and for the benefit of Adriaen Symonsen, his heirs or assigns... [*Incomplete*]

[292] [*blank*]

[CONVEYANCE OF A LOT FROM WILLEM JANSSEN STOL TO JAN BARENTSEN]

[293] Appeared before me, Johannes La Montagne, in the service of the general chartered West India Company, vice director and commissary at Fort Orange and the village of Beverwijck, in the presence of the honorable Johan Verbeeck and Anderies Herbertsen, magistrates of the same court, Willem Janssen Stol, husband and guardian of the widow of Claes Hendericksz, deceased, who declares to have ceded and conveyed, as he hereby does cede and convey, in real and actual possession, to and for the benefit of Jan Barentsen, burgher and inhabitant of the village of Beverwijck, his heirs or assigns, a piece of land in the village of Beverwijck, adjoining to the east the road, to the south Abraham Staets, to the west the plain, to the north Claes van Rotterdam; in length twelve rods and two feet, and in breadth two rods, eight and half feet, which lot is the true half of the patent granted to the conveyer by the lord director general and council of New Netherland dated the 15th of September *anno* 1657, and promises to clear the aforesaid lot from all demands, claims or pretensions, which may arise hereafter, submitting the same to all courts and judges. Done at Fort Orange the 15th of March *anno* 1661.

Willem Jansz
Jan Verbeeck
Andries Herbertsz
Acknowledged by me,
La Montagne, commissary at Fort Orange.

[CONVEYANCE OF A LOT FROM WILLEM JANSSEN STOLL TO CLAES JACOBSEN VAN ROTTERDAM]

[294] Appeared before me, Johannes La Montagne, in the service of the general chartered West India Company, vice director and commissary at Fort Orange and the village of Beverwijck, in the presence of the honorable Jan Verbeeck and Evert Janssen Wendel, magistrates of the same court, Willem Janssen Stol, husband and guardian of the widow of Claes Hendericksz, deceased, who declares to have ceded and

conveyed, as he hereby does cede and convey, in real and actual possession, to and for the benefit of Claes Jacobsen van Rotterdam, his heirs or assigns, a piece of land located in the village of Beverwijck, adjoining on the east side the street, on the south side Jan Barentsen, on the west the plain, and on the north side Teunis Dirricksz; in length twelve rods and two feet, and in breadth two rods, eight and a half feet, which lot is the true half of the patent granted to Claes Hendricksen, deceased, by the lord director general and council of New Netherland dated the 15th of September *anno* 1657; and promises to clear the aforesaid lot of all demands, claims or pretensions, which may arise hereafter, pledging his person and estate, moveable and immoveable, submitting the same to all courts and judges. Done at Fort Orange the 15th of March *anno* 1661.

Willem Jansz
Jan Verbeeck
Evert Jansz Wendel
Acknowledged by me,
La Montagne, commissary at Fort Orange.

[Document pages 517–594 follow, which were displaced in the 19th-century bound volume.]

[DECLARATION OF WILLEM JANSSEN SCHUT AS SURETY FOR LUYCAS ELDERSEN]

[517] Appeared before me, Johannes La Montagne, in the service of the general chartered West India Company, commissary at Fort Orange and the village of Beverwijck, Willem Janssen Schut, who declares himself surety for the person of Luycas Eldersen regarding the use of a canoe, which is in dispute with Cornelis Cornelissen and Jan Hendericksz Bruyn. Acknowledged by signature with his own hand. Done at Fort Orange at the end of March *anno* 1661. In the presence of J. Provoost.

Willem Janssen

[POWER OF ATTORNEY OF WILLEM JANSSEN STOLL]

[518] Appeared before me, Johannes La Montagne, in the service of the general chartered West India Company, vice director and commissary of Fort Orange and the village of Beverwijck, Willem Janssen Stoll, presently about to depart for the Esopus, who declares in the presence of the subscribed witnesses that he has appointed and empowered, as he hereby does appoint and empower, *Sr.* Evert Janssen Wendel, burgher and inhabitant of the village of Beverwijck in order to collect, request, and receive on behalf of the constituent thirty and a half beavers from Claes Janssen *timmerman*, which are owed the constituent from the sale of a lot, among which number of thirty and a half beavers there are twenty-four for which the attorney is to request ten percent interest for the period of three years; and in case of **[519]** unwillingness, to demand payment with law and rigor of justice, carrying judicial proceedings to final execution, including attachment of persons and goods, and in addition to do everything that the subscriber himself being present could and might do, provided that the attorney be obliged to render a proper statement and return as requested thereto, pledging his person and estate, moveable and immoveable. Thus done at Fort Orange on the 20th of April *anno* 1661, in the presence of Eldert Gerbertsen and J. Provoost.

Willem Jansz Stol
Ellert Gerbertsz Cruyf
Johannes Provoost, witnesses
Acknowledged by me,
La Montagne, commissary at Fort Orange.

[CONTRACT BETWEEN ELDERT GERBERTSEN KRUYFF AND WILLEM JANSSEN STOLL]

[520] Appeared before me, Johannes Lamontagne, in the service of the general chartered West India Company, vice director and commissary at Fort Orange and the village of Beverwijck, Eldert Gerbertsen Kruyff, who declare to have agreed with one another that Eldert Gerbertsen agrees to complete the contract made between him and Claes

Hendericksz for repairs or completion of the house, which the aforesaid Kruyff bought from the aforesaid Claes Hendericksz; and to keep an account of the expenses that shall be paid according to the liquidation of the parties, namely, in case he expends more money that he has at hand, then Willem Janssen Stoll shall pay for the excess, and should he expend less, then he shall return it to the aforesaid Willem Janssen Stoll. Thus done the 20th of April *anno* 1661, in the presence of Evert Wendel and J. Provoost.

Elbert Gerbertsz Cruyf
Willem Jansz Stoll
Eevert Jansz Wendel
J. Provoost Clercq
Acknowledged by me,
La Montagne, commissary at Fort Orange.

[CONVEYANCE OF A PIECE OF LAND TO JURRIAEN TEUNISSEN]

[521] Appeared before me, Johannes La Montagne, in the service of the general chartered West India Company, vice director and commissary at Fort Orange and the village of Beverwijck, the honorable magistrates of the aforesaid place, who declare to have ceded and conveyed, as they hereby do in real and actual possession, for the benefit of Jurriaen Teunissen, his heirs or assigns, a place lying in the middle of his lot previously surveyed for use as a road. It is in length from the road to the kil and in width three rods and four feet; therefore, their honors promise to free him of any actions, claims or pretensions, which may arise hereafter. Thus done at Fort Orange on the first of May *anno* 1661.

Andris Herberts
Jan Verbeeck
Frans Barentsz Pastoor
Evert Jansz Wendel
Acknowledged by me,
La Montagne, commissary at Fort Orange.

[CONVEYANCE OF A GARDEN LOT FROM HENDERICK GERRITSEN TO ARENT VANDEN BERGH]

[522] Appeared before me, Johannes La Montagne, in the service of the general chartered West India Company, admitted by the lord director general and councilors of New Netherland vice director and commissary at Fort Orange and the village of Beverwijck, in the presence of the honorable Philip Pietersen Schuyler and Adriaen Gerritsen, magistrates of the same court, Henderick Gerritsen, inhabitant of the aforesaid village, who declares to have ceded and conveyed, as he hereby does cede and convey, in real and actual possession, to and for the benefit of Arent vanden Bergh, cadet here of the honorable Company, his heirs or assigns, a lot for a garden located near or behind the aforesaid fortress; in breadth in front along the road four rods two and a half feet, to the south the grantor eight rods, to the west Jeremias van Rencelaer in breadth four rods, to the north Gerrit Bancker in length eight rods; everything in such possession and ownership as the grantor has possessed, promising the grantee to free it from all actions, claims, or pretensions, which may arise hereafter, pledging his person and estate, real and personal, now and in the future, subjecting the same to the authority of all courts and judges.

Done at Fort Orange, the 10th of May *anno* 1661.

Hindrick Gritsen
Philip Pietersz
Adriaen Gerretsen
La Montagne, commissary at Fort Orange.

[523] Appeared... [*remainder of page left blank*]

[ACKNOWLEDGMENT OF DEBT OF ALEXANDER LEENDERSEN]

[524] Appeared before me, Mattheus de Vosch, notary public, admitted by the honorable esteemed lords director general and councilors of New Netherland in residence, and the subscribed witnesses, the honorable

Alexander Leendersen, living in the town of Beverwijck at Fort Orange, and acknowledged for himself and his heirs to be truly and honestly indebted to the honorable *Sr.* Jan Sebastiaensen van Gutsenhoven, also residing in the aforesaid town of Beverwijck, for the sum of nine thousand seven hundred fifty-three guilders, twelve stivers, eight pennies, stemming from delivered goods and merchandise, according to the account thereof in the subscriber's hands, who declares that he has received all that is listed in the aforesaid account to his satisfaction, which aforesaid sum of 9753 guilders, 12 stivers, 8 pennies, he, the subscriber, promises and agrees to pay of have paid to *Sr.* Jan Sebastiaensen van Gudsenhoven or on his properly authenticated order at the latest in the upcoming month of September of 1661 in good merchantable beaver skins a eight guilder a piece; and for the punctual execution of the same, the subscriber pledges his person and his entire estate, moveable and immoveable, now and in the future, nothing excepted no matter where it may be found in the world, submitting the same to all courts and judges, promising hereby to grant a mortgage thereon or to have it done in his name upon his, the subscriber's, estate, nothing excepted until the **[525]** claims of the aforesaid *Sr.* Jan Sebastiaensen are paid in full, submitting as before. Done in good faith at Amsterdam in New Netherland; present: Jacques Carteljou and Harmanus Letschoo, inhabitants of this city, witnesses, and have signed this instrument together with the subscriber on the seventh of May 1661. Was subscribed: This agrees with the original instrument, *quod attestor* Mattheus de Vos, notary public.

The above-written copy was inserted in this protocol by me, J. La Montagne, commissary of Fort Orange and the village of Beverwijck at the request of *Sr.* Jan Sebastiaensen van Gudsenhoven, to serve him in time and place as needed.

Done at Fort Orange the 2nd of June *anno* 1661.

Quod attestor,
La Montagne, commissary at Fort Orange.

[CONDITIONS FOR THE SALE OF A HOUSE, LOT, AND GARDEN OF JURRIAEN TEUNISSEN AT PUBLIC AUCTION]

[526] Conditions and terms upon which Jurriaen Teunissen intends to sell at public auction his house, lot, and garden located in the village of Beverwijck bounded by Jochim *de Backer* on the east and presently occupied by the seller.

First. The aforesaid house, lot, and garden and shall be handed over to the buyer with everything that is earth and nail fast.

Transfer shall take place eight days after the upcoming old Amsterdam fair.

Payment shall be made in two installments of good whole merchantable beavers: the first installment on the 20th of this coming July and the second or last on the 20th of July *anno* 1662.

The buyer shall be obligated to appoint two suitable sureties each as principals to the satisfaction of the seller and that within the period of 24 hours. If the buyer is unable to appoint two sureties in the prescribed time, then it shall be auctioned off again at his expense and cost; and whatever it falls short, the buyer shall be obligated to make good, and if it brings greater value, he shall derive no profit from it. Auction fees will be charged to the buyer.

[POWER OF ATTORNEY OF JACOB VAN DER COELEN]

[527] Appeared before me, Johannes La Montagne, admitted by the lord director general and council of New Netherland as vice director and commissary of Fort Orange and the village of Beverwijck, Jacob van der Coelen, residing in the fortress, who declares in the presence of the subscribed witnesses that he has conveyed, ceded, and transferred, as he hereby does, for and to the benefit of Marcelus Janssen, inhabitant of the aforesaid village, his entire credit due him from monthly wages and subsistence earned from the honorable West India Company for his service as a private soldier; in addition, the aforesaid Jacob van der

Coelen, or the legal holder hereof, hereby constitutes and empowers [him] to request, demand, and receive the aforesaid money at Amsterdam in New Netherland from the lord treasurer of the honorable West India Company at his office there, and having received the same to issue a receipt thereof, which shall be as valid as if done by the subscriber himself; and furthermore, to do and perform everything to receive the aforesaid monthly salary and subsistence as if he, the subscriber, himself being present, could or might do even if the matter were to demand greater or more particular authority than is expressed herein; promising to consider valid at all times everything that shall be done by virtue of this authority, pledging his **[528]** person and estate, moveable and immoveable.

Thus done at fort Orange in the presence of Nataniel Pietersen and Wallerom du Mon, as witnesses requested hereto on this 29th of June *anno* 1661.

Jacop vander Coulen
Nattaneiel Pettersa
Woallerand du Mont
Acknowledged by me,
La Montagne, commissary at Fort Orange.

[CONDITIONS FOR THE SALE OF HOUSE AND LOT OF PIETER ADRIAENSEN]

[529] Conditions upon which Pieter Adriaensen intends to sell to the highest bidder at public auction his house and lot standing and lying in the village of Beverwijck, to the north Adriaen Janssen van Leyden and to the south Jan Barentsen.

First. The aforesaid house and lot shall be handed over at once with everything that is earth and nail fast; which house is thirty-seven and a half feet long and twenty-six feet wide, and properly run up with brick all around, with the accompanying lot being ten rods in length and four rods in width, whereof the buyer shall receive the patent and proper conveyance with the final payment.

Payment shall be made in three installments: the first installment six weeks from today's date in good whole merchantable beavers at eight guilder a piece; the second installment in the month of May *anno* 1662 to be paid in good trade sewant at sixteen guilders the beaver; and the third or final installment on the first of August *anno* 1662 in good whole merchantable beavers as above.

The buyer shall be obligated at once to appoint two suitable sureties each as principals to the **[530]** satisfaction of the seller. If the buyer is unable to appoint two sureties in the prescribed time, then it shall be auctioned off again at his expense and cost; and whatever it falls short, the buyer shall be obligated to make good, and if it brings greater value, he shall derive no profit from it. Auction fees will be charged to the buyer.

After many offers Philip Pietersen Schuyler remained the final bidder for the sum of one thousand three hundred and six guilders, according to the aforesaid conditions for which the honorable Adriaen Gerritse and Harmen Vedder offered themselves as sureties and principals for the payment of the aforesaid sum, pledging their persons and estates, moveable and immoveable, now and in the future, subjecting themselves to the authority of all courts and judges.

Done in Beverwijck this 15th of July *anno* 1661.

Philip Pietersen Schuyler
Adriaen Gerretsen
Harmen Vedderen
Acknowledged by me,
La Montagne, commissary at Fort Orange.

[CONDITIONS FOR THE SALE OF HOUSE, LOT, AND GARDEN OF PIETER ADRIAENSEN]

[531] Conditions and terms upon which Pieter Adriaensen intends to sell to the highest bidder at public auction his house, lot, and garden located in the Colonie Rencelaerswijck and presently occupied by him.

First. The aforesaid house, lot, and garden shall be transferred to the buyer just as it stands and lies within its fence with everything that is earth and nail fast, except for the fruit trees therein; and that [all] free and unencumbered without any claims thereon, except for the lord's right.

Transfer shall take place on the first of May *anno* 1662.

Payment shall be made in three installments: the first installment six weeks from today's date in good whole merchantable beavers at eight guilder a piece; the second installment in the month of May *anno* 1662 to be paid in good trade sewant at sixteen guilders the beaver; and the third or final installment on the first of August *anno* 1662 in good whole merchantable beavers as above.

The buyer shall be obligated at once to appoint two suitable sureties each as principals to the **[532]** satisfaction of the seller. If the buyer is unable to appoint two sureties in the prescribed time, then the aforesaid house, lot, and garden shall be auctioned off again at his expense and cost; and whatever it falls short, the buyer shall be obligated to make good, and if it brings greater value, he shall derive no profit from it. Auction fees will be charged to the buyer. [*not executed*]

[CONDITIONS FOR THE SALE OF HOUSE AND LOT OF MARCELIUS JANSSEN]

[533] Conditions upon which Marcelius Janssen intends to sell to the highest bidder at public auction his house and lot, in which the seller presently is living, with all in the enclosure that is earth and nail fast.

First. The house and lot shall be transferred to the buyer just as it is occupied by him and stands within the fence according to the patent thereof.

Transfer of the aforesaid house and lot shall take place on the first of May *anno* 1662 together with the conveyance of the same.

Payment shall occur in three installments in good whole merchantable beaver skins: the first installment on the first of June, and the third installment one year after the second, being on the first of June *anno* 1664.

The patent shall be handed over with the final installment.

The buyer shall be obligated at once to appoint two suitable sureties each as principals to the satisfaction of the seller. If the buyer is unable to appoint two sureties in the prescribed time, then the **[534]** aforesaid house and lot shall be auctioned off again at his expense and cost; and whatever it falls short, the buyer shall be obligated to make good, and if it brings greater value, he shall derive no profit from it. Auction fees will be charged to the buyer.

Upon the aforesaid conditions Asser Levy remained the final bidder for the sum of one thousand seven hundred and nine guilders, for which the honorable Johan Verbeeck and Jochim Wesselsen offered themselves as sureties and principals for the payment of the aforesaid sum, pledging their persons and estates, moveable and immoveable, now and in the future, subjecting themselves to the authority of all courts and judges.

Done at Fort Orange this 15th of July *anno* 1661.

Asser Leevi
Jan Verbeeck
Jochem *Backer*
Acknowledged by me,
La Montagne, commissary at Fort Orange.

[CONVEYANCE FRAGMENT]

[535] Appeared before me, Johannes La Montagne, admitted by the lord director general and councilors of New Netherland as vice director and commissary of Fort Orange and the village of Beverwijck, residing in the aforesaid fort, in the presence of the honorable Rutger Jacobsen and Evert Wendel, magistrates of the same court...[*incomplete*]

[536] [*left blank*]

[CONVEYANCE FOR HOUSE AND LOT OF HENDERICK JOCHEMSEM TO ABRAHAM STAETS]

[537] Appeared before me, Johannes La Montagne, admitted by the lord director general and council of New Netherland as vice director and commissary of Fort Orange and the village of Beverwijck, in the service of the general chartered West India Company, Henderick Jochemsen, burgher and inhabitant of the village of Beverwijck, who declares in the presence of the honorable Frans Barentsen Pastoor and Adriaen Gerritsen, magistrates of the same court, to have hereby ceded and conveyed in real and actual possession to the benefit of Captain Abraham Staets, also a burgher and inhabitant of the same place, his heirs or assigns, his house and lot lying outside Fort Orange according to the patent, and instrument of concession for a certain parcel annexed to the lot, for a certain sum, for which he, grantor, acknowledges to have received payment and satisfaction, promising to free the aforesaid house and lots from all actions and claims, pledging his person and estate, moveable and immoveable, now and in the future, submitting the same to all courts and judges.

Thus done at Fort Orange the 20th of July *anno* 1661.

Hendrick Jochemsz
Frans Berentsen Pastoor
Adriaen Gerretsen

Acknowledged by me,
La Montagne, commissary at Fort Orange.

[CONDITIONS FOR THE SALE OF HOUSE AND LOT OF CORNELIS VOSCH]

[538] Conditions and terms upon which Cornelis Vosch intends to sell to the highest bidder at public auction his house and lot, standing and lying in the village of Beverwijck to the east Daniel Verveelen.

First. The aforesaid house shall be transferred to the buyer with all that is earth and nail fast, (except for the little lean-to at the east side of the aforesaid house with the chimney and oven belonging thereto); the house is in length twenty-five feet and in breadth eighteen feet; and should it happen that the buyer repair or tear down or put up another in its place, then he, the buyer, will be obligated to allow for a suitable drip for this and Daniel Verveelen's house. The lot that will be transferred to the buyer is with the house nine rods in length; behind at the kil it is seventeen and a half feet in breadth; at the front it is as wide as the aforesaid house and an alleyway of three and half feet.

Transfer shall occur on the first of May *anno* 1662.

Payment shall be made in good whole merchantable beavers, and that in two installments: the first in eight days from today's date and the last installment on the first of July *anno* 1662.

The buyer shall be obligated at once to appoint two suitable sureties each as principals to the **[539]** satisfaction of the seller. If the buyer is unable to appoint two sureties in the prescribed time, then the aforesaid house and lot shall be auctioned off again at his expense and cost; and whatever it falls short, the buyer shall be obligated to make good, and if it brings greater value, he shall derive no profit from it. Auction fees will be charged to the buyer. [*not executed*]

[CONDITIONS FOR THE SALE OF A LOT OF CORNELIS VOSCH]

[540] Conditions and terms upon which Cornelis Vosch intends to sell to the highest bidder at public auction his lot located in the village of Beverwijck next to his house.

First. The aforesaid lot shall be transferred to the buyer in length nine rods, in width at the road twenty-three feet and thirty-six feet in width behind at the kil. The lot shall be transferred to the buyer on the first of May *anno* 1662.

The buyer shall be obligated at once to appoint two suitable sureties each as principals to the satisfaction of the seller. If the buyer is unable to appoint two sureties in the prescribed time, then the aforesaid house and lot shall be auctioned off again at his expense and cost; and whatever it falls short, the buyer shall be obligated to make good, and if it brings greater value, he shall derive no profit from it. Auction fees will be charged to the buyer.

[541] [*left blank*]

[CONDITIONS FOR THE SALE OF A HOUSE AND LOT OF HENDERICK JOCHIMSEN]

[542] Conditions and terms upon which Henderick Jochimsen intends to sell to the highest bidder at public auction his house and lot located in the colony of Rencelaerswijck.

First. The aforesaid house and lot shall be transferred to the buyer with all that is earth and nail fast, and the lot as enclosed by the fence...[*remainder of page blank*]

[GRANT OF LAND ON THE MOHAWK RIVER TO ARENT VAN CORLAER]

[543] Appeared before me, Johannes La Montagne, in the service of the general chartered West India Company, admitted by the lord director general and council of New Netherland as vice director and commissary of Fort Orange and the village of Beverwijck, some chiefs of the

Mohawk country named Cantuquo, Sonareetse, Aiadane, Sodacherasse, owners of a certain piece of land named in Dutch the Great Flats, lying behind Fort Orange, between the same and the Mohawk country, which they declare to have ceded and conveyed, as they hereby do cede and convey, in real and actual possession and ownership, to the benefit of *Sr.* Arent van Corlaer; the aforesaid piece of land or Great Flats, called in Indian Schonowe, including in the circumference its woods and kils, for a certain amount of merchandise, for which the grantors acknowledge satisfaction, renouncing henceforth and forever all ownership and claims, which they have heretofore had to the aforesaid pieces of land, promising to free it of all claims, which other Indians might have. Done at Fort Orange, the 27th of July *anno* 1661, in the presence of Marten Mouris and Willem Montagne, requested thereto.

This is the mark  of Cantuquo

This is the mark  of Aiadane

This is the mark  of Sonareetsie

Acknowledged by me,
La Montagne, vice director and commissary at Fort Orange.

[544] [*blank*]

[BILL OF SALE FOR BRICK KILN FROM PIETER JACOBSEN BOSBOOM TO ABRAHAM STAETS]

[545] Today, date underwritten, in the presence of the subscribed witnesses, Abraham Staets purchased at public auction from Pieter Jacobsen Bosboom a brick kiln, except for the bricks presently contained therein, together with the lot, in size as described in the patent; and that for the sum of three hundred and fifty guilders in good merchantable sewant, to be paid in two installments, the first installment within the period if one month from today's date and the other installment on the first of May *anno* 1662. In the meantime, the buyer is obligated to provide for the auction fees and pay the auction master one stiver for every guilder, pledging his person and estate, moveable and immoveable, now and in the future, subjecting the same to all courts and judges. Done in Beverwijck, this 28th of July *anno* 1662.

Abram Staas
Ludovicus Cobes, witnesses
Johannes Provoost, witness
La Montagne, commissary at Fort Orange

[ACKNOWLEDGMENT OF DEBT OF JAN VERBEECK TO JAN BASTIAENSEN VAN GUDSENHOVEN]

[546] Appeared before me, Johannes La Montagne, in the service of the general chartered West India Company, vice director and commissary at Fort Orange and the village of Beverwijck, in the presence of the honorable Abraham Staets and Adriaen Gerritsen, magistrates of the same court, *Sr.* Jan Verbeeck, former magistrate, who acknowledges to be honestly and truly indebted to *Sr.* Jan Bastiaensen van Gudsenhoven for the sum of four hundred sixty two guilders and seven stivers, stemming from merchandise and goods, which he has had for his satisfaction for a period of three to four years; which aforesaid sum of four hundred and sixty two guilders and seven stivers, he, the appearer, promises to pay to the aforesaid Jan Bastiaensen or his attorney in good whole merchantable beaver skins at eight guilder a piece, at the latest within the period of one year from today punctually without further delay, pledging thereby his person and estate, moveable and immoveable, now and in the future, nothing excepted; in particular he places his new house and the lot thereto standing and lying in the village of Beverwijck and occupied by **[547]** him, the appearer, as a mortgage and firm collateral to secure the payment, if needs be, of the aforesaid sum of four hundred and sixty two guilders and seven stivers, without cost or loss, submitting himself, as before, to all courts and judges. Done at Fort Orange, this 30th of July *anno* 1661.

Jan Verbeeck
Abram Staas
Adriaen Gerretsen

Acknowledged by me,
La Montagne, commissary at Fort Orange.

[ACKNOWLEDGMENT OF DEBT OF LEENDERT PHILIPSEN TO JAN BASTIAENSEN VAN GUDSENHOVEN]

[548] Appeared before me, Johannes La Montagne, admitted by the lord director general and council of New Netherland as vice director and commissary of Fort Orange and the village of Beverwijck, in the presence of the honorable Rutger Jacobsen and Evert Janssen Wendel, magistrates of the same court, the honorable Leendert Philipsen, inhabitant of the aforesaid village, who acknowledges to be honestly and truly indebted to *Sr.* Jan Bastiaensen van Gudsenhoven for the sum of one thousand one hundred and thirty seven guilders and eight stivers, stemming from merchandise and goods, which he has received to his satisfaction; which aforesaid sum of one thousand one hundred and thirty seven guilders and eight stivers with interest on the same at ten percent annually, beginning from this date and running until full payment, he the subscriber, promises to pay to Jan Bastiaensen, or his attorney, in good whole merchantable beaver skins at eight guilder a piece, the latest in the period of one year from this date, without further delay, pledging thereby his person and estate, moveable and immoveable, now and in the future, nothing excepted; in particular he places **[549]** his house and the lot lying in the village of Beverwijck and presently occupied by him as a mortgage and firm collateral to secure the payment, if needs be, of the aforesaid sum of one thousand one hundred and thirty seven guilders and eight stivers, with the interest thereon, without cost or loss, submitting everthing, as before, to all courts and judges. Done at Fort Orange, this 30th of July *anno* 1661.

Leendert Phyles
Rutger Jacobsz
Evert Wendel
Acknowledged by me,
La Montagne, commissary at Fort Orange.

[CONDITION FOR THE SALE OF A HOUSE AND LOT
BY CORNELIS VOS]

[550] Conditions and terms upon which Cornelis Vos intends to sell to the highest bidder at public auction his house and lot lying in the village of Beverwijck, to the east Daniel Verveelen.

First. The buyer shall receive the house just as it stands: the fore-house is 25 feet long and 18 feet wide, excluding the secondary roof on the east side of the same; the aforesaid lot with the house is nine rods long, in breadth seventeen and a half feet in the rear along the kil, in the front along the road it is as wide as the house, with a passageway on the east side of the house of three and a half feet. If the buyer should he come to remove the house and build another in its place, the buyer is then obligated to leave a proper drip for both his and Daniel Verveelen's house.

Transfer shall be made on the first of May *anno* 1662. The payment shall be made in good whole merchantable beaver skins at eight guilder a piece, in two installments: the first upon transfer, the second on the first of July *anno* 1663. The buyer shall be obligated to appoint two suitable sureties each as principals to the satisfaction of the seller immediately. If the buyer is unable to appoint two sureties in the prescribed time, then it shall be auctioned off again at his expense and **[551]** cost; and whatever it falls short, the buyer shall be obligated to make good, and if it brings greater value, he shall derive no profit from it. Auction fees will be charged to the buyer.

Upon gavel blow Barent van Marle remained the highest bidder for the sum of one thousand and twenty guilders, for which the honorable Jan Verbeeck and Anderies Herbertsen offered themselves as sureties and principals for the payment of the aforesaid sum, pledging their persons and estates, moveable and immoveable, now and in the future, subjecting themselves to all courts and judges. Done in the village of Beverwijck, this 30th of July *anno* 1661.

Barent van Marle
Jan Verbeeck

Andris Herbertsen
Acknowledged by me,
La Montagne, commissary at Fort Orange.

[POWER OF ATTORNEY OF SOPHIA VAN WIJCKERSLOOT TO ASSER LEVY]

[552] Appeared before me, Johannes La Montagne, admitted by the lord director general and council of New Netherland as vice director and commissary of Fort Orange and the village of Beverwijck, Madam Sophia van Wijckersloot, assisted by her husband *Sr.* Toinel, who declares, in the presence of the subscribed witnesses, to have sold and conveyed to *Sr.* Asser Levy all the goods and merchandise that they expect with the ship the *Bever* from *patria*, consigned to her by her father, for which the aforesaid Asser Levy is obligated to pay to the skipper seventy-five percent advance on its cost in Holland, in addition to the freight of the aforesaid goods, hereby appoint and empower the aforesaid Asser Levy to receive the aforesaid goods from the Company's warehouse and to open and inspect the aforesaid goods, and to demand compensation for damage (if there be any); furthermore, to act in the matter as she, the subscriber, might or could if she were present herself, promising to maintain as good and true all that the attorney shall have done by virtue of this [instrument], provided that he be obligated to render to the subscriber a statement and return of his actions and receipts, pledging his person and estate, **[553]** moveable and immoveable, now and in the future, submitting the same to all laws and judges. Done at Fort Orange in the presence of Johannes Provoost and Jan Pietersen as witnesses, requested hereto on this first of August *anno* 1661.

Sophia van Wijckersloot
Anthony Toinel
Jan Pietersen Mulder
Johannes Provoost, witnesses
Acknowledged by me,
La Montagne, v. d. and commissary at Fort Orange.

[ACKNOWLEDGMENT OF DEBT OF JAN VERBEECK
TO BARENT VAN MARLE]

[554] Appeared before me, Johannes La Montagne, in the service of the general chartered West India Company, admitted vice director and commissary at Fort Orange and the village of Beverwijck by the lord director general and council of New Netherland, in the presence of the honorable Rutger Jacobsen and Frans Barentsen Pastoor, magistrates of the same court, *Sr.* Jan Verbeeck, former magistrate, who declares and acknowledges to be honestly and truly indebted to *Sr.* Barent van Marle for the sum of two hundred and sixty-six guilders and ten stivers, stemming from goods and merchandise that he has received to his satisfaction, for which he promised to pay the sum of two hundred and sixty-six guilders and ten stivers. [*three lines crossed out*] He, appearer, promises to pay the aforesaid Barent van Marle, or his attorney, in good whole merchantable beaver skins at eight guilders a peice, and that within the period of one year exactly from this date, pledging his person and estate, moveable and immoveable, now and in the future, nothing exempt; in particular, his new house and lot standing and lying in the **[555]** village of Beverwijck and presently occupied by him, as a firm mortgage and special collateral to be able to secure, if need be, the payment of the sum without cost or loss thereon. Done at Fort Orange, this 2nd of August *anno* 1661.

Jan Verbeeck

[*canceled*]

[ACKNOWLEDGMENT OF DEBT OF JAN LAMBERTSEN VAN BREEMEN
TO JAN BASTIAENSE VAN GUDSENHOOVEN]

[556] Appeared before me, Johannes La Montagne, in the service of the general chartered West India Company, admitted vice director and commissary at Fort Orange and the village of Beverwijck by the lord director general and council of New Netherland, in the presence of the honorable Frans Barentsen Pastoor and Evert Wendel, magistrates of the same court, Jan Lambertsen van Breemen, who acknowledges and declares to be honestly and truly indebted to *Sr.* Jan Bastiaensen van

Gudsenhoven for the sum of sixty-five guilders and fifteen stivers, stemming from goods and merchandise that he received to his satisfaction in the year anno 1656, which sum of sixty-five guilders and fifteen stivers, he, appearer, promised to pay the aforesaid Jan Bastiaensen van Gudsenhoven, or his attorney, in good whole merchantable beaver skins at eight guilder a piece, at the latest within the period of one year from now and not longer; whereby he, the aforesaid appearer, places in mortgage and as special collateral his house and lot standing and lying in the village of Beverwijck, and the same which he presently occupies, to be able to secure, if need be, the payment of the aforesaid sum of sixty-five guilders and fifteen [557] stivers with interest thereon, without cost or loss, pledging his person and estate, moveable and immoveable, now and in the future, submitting the same to all courts and judges. Done at Fort Orange, this 11th of August *anno* 1661.

This is the mark of + Jan Lambertsen van Breemen,
made with his own hand.
Frans Barentsen Pastoor
Evert Wendel
Acknowledged by me,
La Montagne, commissary at Fort Orange.

[CONVEYANCE OF LAND FROM CHRISTOFFEL DAVIDS TO GEERTRUY ANDERIESEN]

[558] Appeared before me, Johannes La Montagne, in the service of the general chartered West India Company, admitted vice director and commissary at Fort Orange and the village of Beverwijck by the lord director general and council of New Netherland, in the presence of the honorable Frans Barentsen Pastoor and Evert Janssen Wendel, magistrates of the same court, Christoffel Davids, who declares to convey and cede as he hereby cedes and conveys in real and actual possession to and for the benefit of Geertruy Anderiesen, widow of Jancob Janssen Stoll, deceased, her heirs or assigns, a piece of cleared cultivatable land, lying in the Esopus bounded to the north Madam Ebbinghs and to the south Jurriaen Westvael, lying in two parcels

together about thirty-six morgens in size with a piece of pasture also about twenty morgens, extending from the woods; for the sum fourteen hundred guilders, of which aforesaid sum he, grantor, acknowledges to have had satisfaction, except for six hundred guilders in sewant that he conveys and assigns to the honorable Jeremias van Rencelaer by agreement of the aforesaid Geertuy Anderiessen according to the conveyance of the aforesaid Jacob Janssen Stoll, deceased, dated the 13th of July *anno* 1657, which aforesaid sum of six hundred guilders, she, the grantee, agrees to pay to the aforesaid Rencelaer within one year from next November, in good winter wheat calculated at four guilders the skipple, and other grains in proportion. He, conveyor, **[559]** promises to free the aforesaid land of all claims, actions or pretensions that may hereafter arise, pledging his person and estate, moveable and immoveable, now and in the future, submitting himself to all courts and judges. Done at Fort Orange, the 15th of August *anno* 1661.

This is the mark  of Christoffel Davids,
made with his own hand.
This is the mark  of Geertruy Anderiessen,
made with her own hand.
Frans Barentsen Pastoor
Evert Wendel
Acknowledged by me,
La Montagne, commissary at Fort Orange.

[ACKNOWLEDGMENT OF DEBT OF JAN VERBEECK TO BARENT VAN MARLE]

Appeared before me, Johannes La Montagne, in the service of the general chartered West India Company, admitted vice director and commissary at Fort Orange and the village of Beverwijck by the lord director general and council of New Netherland, in the presence of the honorable Rutger Jacobsen and Adriaen Gerritsen, magistrates of the same court, the honorable Jan Verbeeck, who acknowledges and declares to be indebted to *Sr.* Barent van Marle for the sum of **[560]** two hundred sixty-six guilders and ten stivers, arising from goods and merchandise that he received to his satisfaction, which aforesaid sum of two hundred sixty-six guilders and ten stivers he promised to pay to the aforesaid Marle or his attorney on the first of June *anno* 1662, and that in good whole merchantable beaver skins at eight guilders a piece; for which he, aforesaid appearer, offers as a firm mortgage and special collateral his old house and the lot in back of the same, which he presently occupies, to be able to secure, if need be, the payment of the aforesaid sum without cost or loss, pledging his person and estate, moveable and immoveable, now and in the future, submitting the same to all courts and judges. Done at Fort Orange, this 16th of August *anno* 1661.

Jan Verbeeck
Rutger Jacobsz
Adriaen Gerretsen
Acknowledged by me,
La Montagne, commissary at Fort Orange.

[ACKNOWLEDGMENT OF DEBT OF JAN MICHIELSEN TO NICOLAES MEYER]

[561] Appeared before me, Johannes La Montagne, in the service of the general chartered West India Company, admitted vice director and commissary at Fort Orange and the village of Beverwijck by the lord director general and council of New Netherland, in the presence of the honorable Rut Jacobsen and Adriaen Gerritsen, magistrates of the same court, Jan Michielsen, inhabitant here, who hereby acknowledges and declares to be truly and honestly indebted to *Sr.* Nicolaes Meyer for the sum of sixty-four guilders for goods that he has received to his satisfaction, which aforesaid sum of sixty-four guilders he promises to pay to the aforesaid Meyer or his attorney on the first of June *anno* 1662 in good whole merchantable beaver skins at eight guilders a piece; for which he, appearer, offers as a firm mortgage and special collateral his old house and the lot in back of the same, which he presently occupies, to be able to secure, if need be, the payment of the aforesaid sum without cost or loss, pledging his person and estate, moveable and immoveable, now and in the future, submitting the same to all courts and judges. Done at Fort Orange, this 18th of August *anno* 1661.

Jan Mijchgyelsoon
Rutger Jacobs
Adriaen Gerretsen
Acknowledged by me,
La Montagne, commissary at Fort Orange.

[ACKNOWLEDGMENT OF DEBT OF HENDERICK GERRITSEN TO NICOLAES MEYER]

[562] Appeared before me, Johannes La Montagne, in the service of the general chartered West India Company, admitted vice director and commissary at Fort Orange and the village of Beverwijck by the lord director general and council of New Netherland, in the presence of the honorable Evert Wendel and Adriaen Gerritsen, magistrates of the same court, Henderick Gerritsen, inhabitant of the aforesaid place, who hereby acknowledges and declares to be truly and honestly indebted to *Sr.* Nicolaes Meyer for the sum of fifty-six guilders for goods that he has received to his satisfaction, which aforesaid sum of fifty-six guilders he promises to pay to the aforesaid Meyer or his attorney on the first of May *anno* 1662 in good whole merchantable beaver skins at eight guilders a piece; for which he, appearer, offers as a firm mortgage and special collateral his two houses and lots, one in which he and the other in which Jan *de Kuyper* lives, together with his garden lying behind Fort Orange, as well as the rent of the house in which Jan *de Kuyper* has been living for the period of one year, amounting to the sum of one hundred fifteen guilders in sewant, to be able to secure, if need be, the payment of the aforesaid sum of **[563]** fifty-six guilders without cost or loss, pledging his person and estate, moveable and immoveable, now and in the future, submitting the same to all courts and judges. Done at Fort Orange, this 18th of August *anno* 1661.

Hyndrich Gerisen
Evert Wendel
Adriaen Gerretsen
Acknowledged by me,
La Montagne, commissary at Fort Orange.

[CONVEYANCE OF HOUSE AND LOT OF DANIEL VERVEELEN TO CORNELIS CORNELISSEN DE BOER]

Appeared before me, Johannes La Montagne, in the service of the general chartered West India Company, admitted vice director and commissary at Fort Orange and the village of Beverwijck by the lord director general and council of New Netherland, in the presence of the honorable Evert Wendel and Adriaen Gerritsen, magistrates of the same court, *Sr.* Daniel Verveelen, merchant, who declares to have ceded and conveyed, as he hereby does cede and convey, in real and actual possession to the and for the benefit of Cornelis Cornelissen *de Boer*, his heirs or assigns, his true half of the house and lot that he and the grantee bought together through the **[564]** power of attorney of Pieter *de Maker*, in such form, regarding extent and size, as the conveyance that they both received from the attorney, to wit: Stoffel Janssen and Jan Costersen van Aken, for which half and part of the aforesaid house and lot he, grantor, acknowledges to have had satisfaction and promises to free the same of all actions, claims, and pretensions, which may arise hereafter, pledging his person and estate, moveable and immoveable, now and in the future, nothing excepted, submitting himself to all courts and judges. Done at Fort Orange, this 25th of August *anno* 1661.

Daniel Verveelen
Evert Wendel
Adriaen Gerretsen
Acknowledged by me,
La Montagne, commissary at Fort Orange.

[ACKNOWLEDGMENT OF DEBT OF JAN MANGELSEN TO PIETER ADRIAENSEN]

[565] Appeared before me, Johannes La Montagne, in the service of the general chartered West India Company, admitted vice director and commissary at Fort Orange and the village of Beverwijck by the lord director general and council of New Netherland, in the presence of the honorable Rutger Jacobsen and Frans Barentsen Pastoor, magistrates of the same court, the honorable Jan Mangelsen, burgher of the aforesaid place, who hereby declares and acknowledges to be honestly and truly indebted to his father-in-law Pieter Adriaensen, living in the Colonie Renselaerswijck, for the sum of six hundred guilders in sewant and a total of ten good whole beaver skins for sewant and other merchandise that he received to his satisfaction; which sum he, appearer, promises to pay within the period of ten days, pledging his person and estate, moveable and immoveable, now and in the future, nothing excepted, subjecting himself for payment of the aforesaid sum to all courts and judges. Done at Fort Orange, the 25th of August *anno* 1661.

Jan Mangelsz

The honorable court does not deem it proper that the above-standing committee sign this promissory note of Jan Mangelsen before and until the foregoing judgment both of Jan Claessen Back and others has been satisfied and paid. Done in session at Fort Orange, the 30th of August *anno* 1661. By order of the honorable court, Johannes Provoost, clerk.

[CONVEYANCE OF LOT OF PIETER JACOBSEN BOSBOOM TO ABRAHAM STAETS AND GOOSSEN GERRITSE VAN SCHAICK]

[566] Appeared before me, Johannes La Montagne, in the service of the general chartered West India Company, admitted vice director and commissary at Fort Orange and the village of Beverwijck by the lord director general and council of New Netherland, in the presence of the honorable Rutger Jacobsen and Frans Barentsen Pastoor, magistrates of the same court, Pieter Jacobsen Bosboom, who declares to have ceded and conveyed, as he hereby does cede and convey, in real and actual possession, to and for the benefit of Capt. Abraham Staets and the honorable Goossen, their heirs or assigns, a lot lying along the First Kil, to the north the hill in width five rods, to the east in length twenty three rods, to the south the road in width sixteen rods, to the west in length seventeen rods, according to the patent granted to him by the lord director general and councilors of New Netherland, dated the 23rd of February *anno* 1660, for which lot the grantor acknowledges to have had satisfaction, promising to free the same of all actions, claims or pretensions, which may arise hereafter, pledging his person and estate, moveable and immoveable, now and in the future, submitting himself to all courts and judges. Done at Fort Orange, the 29th of August *anno* 1661.

Pieter Jacopsen Borsboom
Rutger Jacobsz
Frans Barentsz
Acknowledged by me,
La Montagne, commissary at Fort Orange.

[ACKNOWLEDGMENT OF DEBT OF MARCELUS JANSSEN TO CORNELIS JACOBSEN]

[567] Appeared before me, Johannes La Montagne, in the service of the general chartered West India Company, admitted vice director and commissary at Fort Orange and the village of Beverwijck by the lord director general and council of New Netherland, in the presence of the honorable Rutger Jacobsen and Frans Barentsen Pastoor, magistrates of the same court, to Marcelus Janssen, burgher of the aforesaid place, who hereby declares and acknowledges to be honestly and truly indebted to Cornelis Jacobsen for the sum of two hundred and two guilders and sixteen stivers in good whole merchantable beaver skins at eight guilders a piece; which aforesaid sum he, appearer, promises to pay together with the interest thereof at ten percent on the first of June *anno* 1662, as the first installment on his house, which Asser Levy bought at public auction and remains as a firm mortgage and special collateral for the payment of the aforesaid sum, pledging his person and estate, moveable and immoveable, now and in the future, nothing excepted, submitting the same to all courts and judges. Done at Fort Orange, the 30th of August *anno* 1661.

Maercelijs Janssen
Rutger Jacobsen
Frans Barents Pastoor

Acknowledged by me,
La Montagne, commissary at Fort Orange.

[MARGINAL NOTATION FOR PRECEDING DOCUMENT]

Today, the 4th of June 1663, appeared before me, J. Lamontagne, commissary of Fort Orange and the village of Beverwijck, Pieter Claessen Kay, attorney for Cornelis Jacobsen, who acknowledges and declares that the above-standing mortgage for the benefit of the aforesaid Cornelis Jacobsen and standing as a charge against Marcelis Janssen to be fully paid and satisfied without having any further claim against the aforesaid Marcelis Janssen. Dated as above.

Pieter Claesse Kay
Acknowledged by me,
La Montagne.

[ACKNOWLEDGMENT OF DEBT OF RUTGER JACOBSEN
TO TEUNIS CORNELISSEN VANDER POEL]

[568] Appeared before me, Johannes La Montagne, in the service of the general chartered West India Company, admitted vice director and commissary at Fort Orange and the village of Beverwijck by the lord director general and council of New Netherland, in the presence of the honorable Frans Barentsen Pastoor and Evert Janssen Wendel, magistrates of the same court, the honorable Rutger Jacobsen, who hereby declares and acknowledges to be truly and honestly indebted to Teunis Cornelissen vander Poel for the sum of three hundred fifty-two guilders in good whole beaver skins at eight guilder a piece, in addition to two beavers and two otters; he, appearer, promises to pay the aforesaid sum of three hundred fifty-two guilders in good whole beaver skins at eight guilder a piece, with an additional two beavers and two otters on the first of June *anno* 1662 and upon lapse of the aforesaid promised period to pay, he, appearer, shall be obligated to pay the interest of the aforesaid sum from this date, and as security for the aforesaid payment, both for the principal as well as the interest, the aforesaid appearer places as firm mortgage and special collateral his part of the island, lying diagonally opposite Betlehem, which he and Andries Herbertsen have together in mutual ownership, in order to secure, if need be, the payment of the aforesaid sum for the two beavers and two otters, without cost or loss, pledging his person and estate, moveable and immoveable, now and in the future, submitting the same to all courts and judges. Done at Fort Orange, the end of August *anno* 1661.

Rutger Jacobsz
Frans Barentsz Pastoor
Evert Janssen Wendel
Acknowledged by me,
La Montagne, commissary at Fort Orange.

[RECEIPT OF INSTALLMENT ON DEBT FROM MARCELUS JANSSEN TO CORNELIS CORNELISSEN DE BOER]

[569] Appeared before me, Johannes Provoost, in the service of the general chartered West India Company, admitted clerk at Fort Orange and the village of Beverwijck by the lord director general and council of New Netherland, Marcelus Janssen, burgher of the aforesaid village, who declares in the presence of the subscribed witnesses to have ceded and conveyed to Cornelis Cornelissen *de Boer* a total of ten and a half good whole merchantable beaver skins at eight guilders a piece as first installment of the conveyor's house that Asser Levy bought in public auction, and from whom the acceptant has to receive it, and *De Boer* has the preference from Seger Cornelissen, which debt stems from the deed of Adriaen Symonsen that has been thus accepted by the conveyor and conveyed to the aforesaid installment of his house; whereupon he pledges for payment thereof his person and estate, moveable and immoveable, now and in the future, nothing excepted, under submission to all courts and judges. Done at Fort Orange, the 31st of August *anno* 1661, in the presence of J. Verbeeck and Segger Cornelissen.

Maercelijs Jansen
Jan Verbeeck
This is the mark  of Segger Cornelissen,
made with his own hand.
Acknowledged by me,
J. Provoost, clerk.

[RECEIPT OF INSTALLMENT ON DEBT FROM MARCELUS JANSSEN TO SEGER CORNELISSEN]

[570] Appeared before me, Johannes Provoost, clerk of the court of Fort Orange and the village of Beverwijck, Marcelus Janssen, burgher of the aforesaid place, who declares to have ceded and conveyed to Seger Cornelissen a total of thirty-four good whole merchantable beaver skins as first installment of his house that Asser Levy bought in public auction, from whom the acceptant has to receive it, which debt stems from the deed of Adriaen Sijmonsen that has been thus accepted by the conveyor and conveyed to the aforesaid installment of his house; whereupon he pledges for payment thereof his person and estate, moveable and immoveable, now and in the future, nothing excepted, under submission to all courts and judges. Done at Fort Orange, the 31st of August *anno* 1661, in the presence of the honorable Jan Verbeeck and Cornelis Cornelissen *de Boer*.

Maercelijs Jansen
Jan Verbeeck
Cornelis Cornelissen *de Boer*
Acknowledged by me,
Johannes Provoost, clerk.

[CONVEYANCE OF LAND FROM RUTGER JACOBSEN TO GERRIT BANCKER]

[571] Appeared before me, Johannes La Montagne, in the service of the general chartered West India Company, admitted vice director and commissary at Fort Orange and the village of Beverwijck by the lord director general and council of New Netherland, in the presence of the honorable Evert Wendel and Philip Pietersen Schuyler, magistrates of the same court, the honorable Rutger Jacobsen, inhabitant in the aforesaid village, who declares to have ceded and conveyed, in real and actual possession, to and for the benefit of *Sr.* Gerrit Bancker, merchant here, his heirs or assigns, a piece of a lot lying in the aforesaid village of Beverwijck bounded on the east by Goossen Gerritsen, on the west by Barent Reyndersen, on the south by the kil and on the north by the acceptant; the length extends to the kil, on the south it is three rods and ten inches in width and, on the north it is of the same width; aforesaid lot is a parcel of the patent granted to him, conveyor, by the lord director general and councilors of New Netherland, dated the 23rd of April *anno* 1652, and promises therefore to free the aforesaid lot from all actions, claims or pretensions, which might arise, pledging his person and estate, moveable and immoveable, now and in the future, submitting the same to all courts and judges. Done at Fort Orange, this 2nd of September *anno* 1661.

Rutger Jacobsz
Evert Jansz Wendel
Philip Pietersen
Acknowledged by me,
La Montagne, commissary at Fort Orange.

[POWER OF ATTORNEY OF REYNIER WISSELPENNINGH TO LOWIES COBUSSEN]

[572] Appeared before me, Johannes Provoost, in the service of the general chartered West India Company, admitted clerk at Fort Orange and the village of Beverwijck by the lord director general and council of New Netherland, Reynier Wisselpenningh, presently awaiting departure for the Manhatans, who declares, in the presence of the subscribed witnesses to have appointed and empowered as he hereby does appoint and empower, Lowies Cobussen, court messenger here, to act in his, the constituent's, name and on his behalf before the aforesaid court of Fort Orange, and to plead in the dispute that they have with one another regarding the outfitting of their yacht that they have begun to construct together; and to proceed against the aforesaid Tomas Lodewijcksz in a legal manner until reaching definitive sentence and final execution; and furthermore, to do and perform all things that he, the attorney, deem proper, promising to hold good and just all that the aforesaid attorney shall do in aforesaid matter, provided that he make a proper return of this transactions. Thus done on this 5th of September *anno* 1661, in the presence of Harmen Hendericksz van Barnevelt.

Reynier Wysselpengh
Heremen Hendrick
Acknowledged by me,
J. Provoost, clerk.

[ACKNOWLEDGMENT OF DEBT OF CORNELIS VOSCH
TO GERRIT BANCKER]

[573] Appeared before me, Johannes La Montagne, in the service of the general chartered West India Company, admitted vice director and commissary at Fort Orange and the village of Beverwijck by the lord director general and council of New Netherland, in the presence of the honorable Philip Pietersen Schuyler and Adriaen Gerritsen, magistrates of the same court, Cornelis Vosch, who hereby declares and acknowledges to be truly and honestly indebted to *Sr.* Gerrit Bancker for the sum of three hundred guilders in good whole merchantable beaver skins at eight guilder a piece, for goods received to his satisfaction; and promised to pay the aforesaid sum of three hundred guilders in the coming year *anno* 1662 during the trading season, and failing that, in the year *anno* 1663; for which payment he places in mortgage and as collateral his lot lying in the village of Beverwijck bounded on the east by Barent van Marle, on the west by the street, on the south by the First Kil and on the north by the road, in order to secure, if need be, the payment of the aforesaid sum of three hundred guilders without cost or loss, pledging his person and estate, moveable and immoveable, now and in the future, submitting the same to all courts and judges. Done at Fort Orange, this 9th of September *anno* 1661.

Cornelis Vos
Philip Pietersen
Adriaen Gerretsen
Acknowledged by me,
La Montagne, commissary at Fort Orange.

[CONVEYANCE OF A LOT FROM RUTGER JACOBSEN
TO BARENT REYNDERSEN]

[574] Appeared before me, Johannes La Montagne, in the service of the general chartered West India Company, admitted vice director and commissary at Fort Orange and the village of Beverwijck by the lord director general and council of New Netherland, in the presence of the honorable Frans Barentsen Pastoor and Evert Janssen Wendel, magistrates of the same court, the honorable Rutger Jacobsen, who declares to have ceded and conveyed, as he hereby does cede and convey, in real and actual possession, to and for the benefit of Barent Reyndersen, his heirs or assigns, a lot lying in the village of Beverwijck bounded on the west by Gerrit Bancker, to the east the conveyor, to the south the street, to the north the kil; in length from the front on the street to the back on the kil, and in breadth along the aforesaid kil twenty-seven feet; which lot is a portion of a patent granted to the conveyor by the lord director general and councilors of New Netherland, dated the 23rd of April *anno* 1652, and he promises to free the aforesaid lot of all actions, claims or pretensions, which might hereafter arise, pledging his person and goods, moveable and immoveable, now and in the future, submitting the same to all courts and judges.

Done at Fort Orange, the 9th of September *anno* 1661.

Rutger Jacobsen
Frans Barensz Pastoor
Evert Jansz Wendel
Acknowledged by me,
La Montagne, commissary at Fort Orange.

[ACKNOWLEDGMENT OF DEBT OF RUTGER JACOBSEN
TO PIETER SIJMONSEN]

[575] Appeared before me, Johannes La Montagne, in the service of the general chartered West India Company, admitted vice director and commissary at Fort Orange and the village of Beverwijck by the lord

director general and council of New Netherland, in the presence of the honorable Frans Barentsen Pastoor and Evert Wendel, magistrates of the same court, the honorable Rutger Jacobsen, who adcknowledges to be honestly and truly indebted to Pieter Sijmonsen for the sum of one thousand and thirty-two guilders for goods received to his satisfaction; which aforesaid sum of one thousand and thirty-two guilders he, appearer, promises to pay to the aforesaid Pieter Sijmonsen or his attorney on the first of June *anno* 1662, and that in good whole merchantable beaver skins at eight guilders a piece, for which he, appearer, places in mortgage and as special collateral his yacht, upon which Abraham de Truwe is skipper, in order to secure, if need be, the payment of the aforesaid sum of one thousand and thirty-two guilders in beavers without cost or loss, pledging his person and estate, moveable and immoveable, now and in the future, submitting the same to all courts and judges.

Done at Fort Orange, this 10th of September *anno* 1661.

Rutger Jacobsz
Frans Barensz Pastoor
Evert Jansz Wendel
Acknowledged by me,
La Montagne, commissary at Fort Orange.

[POWER OF ATTORNEY OF HENDERICK ANDERIESSEN TO FRANS BARENTSEN PASTOOR]

[576] Appeared before me, Johannes La Montagne, in the service of the general chartered West India Company, admitted vice director and commissary at Fort Orange and the village of Beverwijck by the lord director general and council of New Netherland, in the presence of the subscribe witnesses and dated as below, the honorable Henderick Anderiessen presently awaiting departure for *patria*, who declares to have constituted and empowered, as he hereby so does, the honorable Frans Barentsen Pastoor, magistrate of the court of the aforesaid place, to collect, request, and receive, in his name as much as is possible, from Philip Hendericksen *Brouwer*, here at this place, three thousand one hundred and ninety-four guilders in beavers, which are owed to him, stemming from the purchase of a brewery as it stands with all its equipment, and, if the aforesaid Philip Hendericksz should come to sell the aforesaid brewery, to lay hands on the money and if the aforesaid brewery should come to be worth less than the aforesaid sum of three thousand one hundred and ninety-four guilders in beavers, he shall seek to exact the further payment by law and rigor of justice; to which end to observe all extents of the law for a **[577]** definitive judgment and final execution thereof; also, if need be, to proceed with attachment on persons and goods, and to issue a quittance of the receipts thereof; furthermore, to do and perform all things, which he, the attorney shall judge proper, promising at all times to hold as true all that the aforesaid attorney shall perform in the aforesaid matter, provided that the attorney shall be obliged, when asked, to make a proper return of his accounts.

Thus done and confirmed in the presence of Johannes Provoost and Walleran Dumont, requested as witnesses hereto, on this 13th of September *anno* 1661 at Fort Orange.

Hendrick Aendriesen
Johannes Provoost, witnesses
Wallerand Du Mont
Acknowledged by me,
La Montagne, commissary at Fort Orange.

[ACKNOWLEDGMENT OF DEBT OF ANDERIES HERBERTSEN TO GOOSSEN GERRITSEN]

[578] Appeared before me, Johannes La Montagne, in the service of the general chartered West India Company, admitted vice director and commissary at Fort Orange and the village of Beverwijck by the lord director general and council of New Netherland, in the presence of the honorable Evert Wendel and Philip Pietersen Schuyler, magistrates of the same court, the honorable Anderies Herbertsen, who hereby acknowledges and declares to be honestly and truly indebted to the honorable Goossen Gerritsen for the sum of one thousand and fifteen guilders, fourteen stivers, and eight pennies for goods that he received since the year *anno* 1657 to his satisfaction; which aforesaid sum of one thousand and fifteen guilders, fourteen stivers, and eight pennies he, appearer, promises to pay to the aforesaid Goossen Gerritsen or his attorney on the first of June *anno* 1662, and that in good whole merchantable beaver skins at eight guilders a piece and for all the time beyond the aforesaid date, the subscriber shall be obliged to pay proper interest; for compliance thereof he binds and places in mortgage and as special collateral his house and lot lying in the village of Beverwijck, in which he presently resides, in order to secure, if need be, the payment of the aforesaid sum without cost or loss, pledging his person and estate, moveable and immoveable, now and in the future, submitting the same to all courts and judges. Done at Fort Orange, this 13th of September *anno* 1661.

Andris Herbertsen
Evert Jansz Wendel
Philip Pieterse
Acknowledged by me,
La Montagne, commissary at Fort Orange.

[POWER OF ATTORNEY OF DANIEL RINCKHOUT
TO PIETER *DE MAKER*]

[579] Appeared before me, Johannes La Montagne, in the service of the general chartered West India Company, admitted vice director and commissary at Fort Orange and the village of Beverwijck by the lord director general and council of New Netherland, dated as below in the presence of the subscribed witnesses, Daniel Rinckhout, residing in the aforesaid village, who declares to have constituted and empowered, as he hereby does, the honorable Pieter *de Maker*, house carpenter, residing in Amsterdam, to collect and request in his, the constituent's, name from Sacharias Kreleman, residing in Rotterdam, being the guardian of the constituent, accounts and returns of monies due to him, constituent, from the inheritance of Johannes Rinckhout, deceased, the constituent's uncle, to issue a quittance of the receipts; and upon unwillingness to seek to demand the aforesaid inheritance with the right and rigor of justice, to which end to observe all extents of the law for a definitive judgment and final execution thereof; also, if need be, to proceed with attachment on persons and goods; furthermore, to do and perform all things, which he, the appearer, being present could or might do, provided that the attorney shall be obliged, when asked, to make a proper return of his accounts, promising at all times to hold as **[580]** good and worthwhile all that the aforesaid attorney shall have done in the aforesaid matter.

Thus done and confirmed on this 14th of September *anno* 1661 at Fort Orange in New Netherland, in the presence of Arent vanden Bergh and Johannes Provoost as witnesses requested hereto.

Daniel Ringhout
This is the mark AB of Arent vanden Bergh,
made with his own hand.
J. Provoost, witness
Acknowledged by me,
La Montagne, commissary at Fort Orange.

[POWER OF ATTORNEY OF JAN VAN AKEN
TO GOOSSEN GERRITSEN]

Appeared before me, Johannes La Montagne, in the service of the general chartered West India Company, admitted vice director and commissary at Fort Orange and the village of Beverwijck by the lord director general and council of New Netherland, Jan van Aken, who declares, in the presence of the subscribed witnesses, to have constituted and empowered, as he hereby so does, the honorable Goossen Gerritsen, in his name and on his behalf at Amsterdam in New **[581]** Netherland, to request, collect, and receive at the office of the lord treasurer of the general chartered West India Company three hundred guilders in beavers, which are owed him through Jan Cloet as appears by an instrument signed by C. V. Ruyven [provincial secretary]; to issue a quittance of the receipts, which shall be as valid as if it was granted to the constituent himself; furthermore, to do and transact everything to obtain the aforesaid sum of three hundred guilders, which he, the appearer, being present could or might do, even though the matter might demand greater and more special authority than is expressed herein, promising at all times to hold as good and worthwhile all that shall be done by virtue of this instrument. [*Five lines crossed out.*] Thus done at Fort Orange in the presence of Sacharias Sickels and Johannes Provoost as witnesses requested hereto, on this the 14th of September *anno* 1661.

This is the mark  of Jan van Aken,
made with his own hand.
Zacharias Seckelsz
Johannes Provoost, witnesses
Acknowledged by me,
La Montagne, commissary at Fort Orange.

[POWER OF ATTORNEY OF GOOSSEN GERRITSEN
TO JAN SIBINCK]

[582] Appeared before me, Johannes La Montagne, in the service of the general chartered West India Company, admitted vice director and commissary at Fort Orange and the village of Beverwijck by the lord director general and council of New Netherland, Goossen Gerritsen, residing in the aforesaid village, who declares, in the presence of the subscribed witnesses, to have constituted and empowered, as he hereby so does, *Sr.* Jan Sibinck, residing at Amsterdam, to agree and settle with Gillis Verbruggen, also residing at Amsterdam, regarding goods and merchandise, likewise regarding outstanding debts, which the constituent has on his account (being in partnership with the aforesaid *Sr.* Verbrugge) and to make thereof an equitable division, assessing the same, whether more or less, with authority to substitute one or more in his place, if need be, promising to hold good and true all that the attorney or his substitute shall have done in this aforesaid matter, provided that he shall make a proper account and return thereof, pledging his person and estate. Thus done at Fort Orange in New Netherland in the presence of Jan van Aken and Johannes Provoost requested hereto as witnesses, on this 14th of September *anno* 1661.

This is the mark  of Goossen Gerritsen,
made with his own hand.

[POWER OF ATTORNEY OF JAN CLAESSEN BACKER AND LAMBERT JANSSEN VANDER LANGE TO FRANCOYS BOON]

[583] Appeared before me, Johannes La Montagne, in the service of the general chartered West India Company, admitted vice director and commissary at Fort Orange and the village of Beverwijck by the lord director general and council of New Netherland, the honorable Jan Claessen Backer and Lambert Janssen van der Lange, both presently awaiting departure for *patria*, who together declare, in the presence of the aforesaid witnesses, to have constituted and empowered, as they hereby so do, *Sr.* Francoys Boon to collect, demand and receive in the constituents' name all monies and debts that are outstanding to the constituents, each in particular, here at Fort Orange in New Netherland and owed them according to the receipts and instruments serving thereto, and to issue a quittance of the receipts; and upon unwillingness to demand the payment with the right and rigor of justice, to which end to observe all extents of the law for a definitive judgment and final execution thereof; (also, if need be), to proceed with attachment on persons and goods; furthermore, to do and perform all things, which he, the attorney, shall deem good and advisable, provided that he keep a record of his **[584]** transactions and produce a proper account and return thereof, if requested, pledging his person and estate, moveable and immoveable, now and in the future, nothing excepted. Thus done at Fort Orange in the presence of Sacharias Sickels and Arent vanden Bergh, as witnesses requested hereto, on this 15th of September *anno* 1661.

Jan Claesz Backer
Lammert Jansse vande Laen
Zachariasz Sickelsz
This is the mark  of Arent vanden Bergh, as witnesses.

[POWER OF ATTORNEY OF CORNELIS JACOBSEN TO EVERT WENDEL]

[585] Appeared before me, Johannes La Montagne, in the service of the general chartered West India Company, admitted vice director and commissary at Fort Orange and the village of Beverwijck by the lord director general and council of New Netherland, Cornelis Jacobsen, merchant, presently awaiting departure for *patria*, who declares, in the presence of the subscribed witnesses, to have constituted and empowered the honorable Evert Wendel, magistrate of the aforesaid place, to collect, demand, and receive in the constituent's name and on his behalf, here at Fort Orange in New Netherland, such outstanding debts and monies owed to him, constituent, as appear in receipts and instruments thereof, and to issue a quittance of the receipts; and upon unwillingness to demand the payment of the aforesaid outstanding debts with the right and rigor of justice, to which end to observe all extents of the law for a definitive judgment and final execution thereof; (also, if need be), to proceed with attachment on persons and goods; furthermore, to do and perform all things, which he, the appearer, being present could **[586]** or might do, provided that the attorney shall be obliged, when asked, to make a proper return of his accounts, promising at all times to hold as good and worthwhile all that the aforesaid attorney shall have done in the aforesaid matter, provided that he keep a record of his transactions and produce a proper account and return thereof, if requested, pledging his person and estate, moveable and immoveable, now and in the future.

Thus done and confirmed at Fort Orange in the presence of Sacharias Sickels and Johannes Provoost, as witnesses requested hereto, on this 15th of September *anno* 1661.

Cornelis Jacobsz
Zacharias Seckelsz
Johannes Provoost, witnesses.
Acknowledged by me,
La Montagne, commissary at Fort Orange.

[CONVEYANCE OF A HOUSE, LOT, AND GARDEN OF ADRIAEN SIMONSZ BET TO BARENT PIETERSZ]

[587] Appeared before me, Johannes La Montagne, in the service of the general chartered West India Company, admitted vice director and commissary at Fort Orange and the village of Beverwijck by the lord director general and council of New Netherland, in the presence of Philip Pietersz Schuller and Ariaen Gerritsz, magistrates of the same court, Adriaen Simonsz Bet, merchant presently residing in the village of Beverwijck, who declares to have ceded and conveyed, as he hereby cedes and conveys to the benefit of Barent Pietersz, his heirs or assigns, his house and lot, garden everything belonging thereto, according to the patent of the same house etc. to possess in real and actual possession, renouncing all claims and pretensions that he, conveyor, could have on the aforesaid house, freeing the same of all actions and claims, pledging his person and estate, moveable and immoveable, now and in the future, submitting the same to all courts and judges. Thus done at Fort Orange on the 22nd of September *anno* 1661.

Aryan Sijmense
Philip Pietersen
Adriaen Gerretsen
Acknowledged by me,
La Montagne, commissary at Fort Orange.

[CONVEYANCE OF BEAVER PELTS FROM SEGER CORNELISSEN TO CORNELIS CORNELISSEN]

[588] Appeared before me, Johannes La Montagne, in the service of the general chartered West India Company, admitted vice director and commissary at Fort Orange and the village of Beverwijck by the lord director general and council of New Netherland, Seger Cornelissen, who declares to have ceded and conveyed, as he hereby so does, to Cornelis Cornelissen *de Boer* some thirty-four good whole merchantable beaver skins, that are owed to him, conveyor, for the first installment on the house of Marcelis Janssen bought by Asser Levy in public auction; which aforesaid thirty-four good beavers the conveyor acquired by conveyance from Marcelis Janssen in order to receive the aforesaid beavers for the installment from Asser Levy, from whom the aforesaid Cornelis Cornelissen *de Boer* shall have to demand and receive it in place of the conveyor, and use them in full ownership as the goods belonging to him, without expecting any claims or demands from the conveyor, pledging his person and estate, moveable and immoveable, submitting the same to the authority of all courts and judges.

Done at Fort Orange, on the 27th of September *anno* 1661, in the presence of Johannes Provoost.

This is the mark  of Seger Cornelissen,
made with his own hand.
Johannes Provoost, witness
Acknowledged by me,
La Montagne.

[CONDITIONS FOR FARMING OF THE SLAUGHTER EXCISE AT PUBLIC AUCTION]

[589] Conditions upon which the honorable lords commissary and magistrates of Fort Orange and the village of Beverwijck intend to farm out at public auction to the highest bidder the slaughter excise for the period of one year. The farming of the aforesaid slaughter excise shall begin the first of October of this year *anno* 1661 and end on the last day of September *anno* 1662. The farmer shall receive for the slaughtered beasts, whether ox, cow, bull, calf, hog, goat or sheep, one stiver for every guilder in value of the same, and in case of dispute to be decided by impartial parties. The farmer shall be obliged to furnish two sufficient sureties to the satisfaction of the lords farming contractors for the excise money, and to pay every quarter a just fourth part in good current sewant; and if the farmer cannot furnish sufficient sureties, it shall be offered for sale again at his cost and charge, and whatever less it comes to be worth he shall be obliged to make good, and whatever more it becomes worth he shall enjoy no benefit therefrom. Marcelis Janssen remained the last bidder for the above farming for the sum of six **[590]** hundred and eight guilders, for which the aforesaid sum Cornelis Teunissen Bosch and Gerrit Slichtenhorst offered themselves as sureties and principals for the payment of the same, pledging their persons and estates, moveable and immoveable, now and in the future, submitting themselves to the authority of all courts and judges. Done in the village of Beverwijck, the end of September *anno* 1661.

Marcelijs Jansen
Cornelus Thonisen Bos
Gerrit Slichtenhorst

Acknowledged by me,
La Montagne, commissary at Fort Orange.

[CONDITIONS FOR THE SALE OF HOUSE, LOT, AND GARDEN OF REYNIER WISSELPENNINGH]

[591] Conditions and terms upon which Reynier Wisselpenningh intends to sell at public auction to the highest bidder his house, lot , and garden, lying in the village of Beverwijck and in which he presently resides.

First. The buyer shall receive the aforesaid house with everything that is earth and nail fast, as well as the lot, just as it stands; in lengththirty-two wood feet, and in breadth forty-eight wood feet, together with the garden as it stands enclosed in his fence; bounded at the south by the garden of Gerrit Bancken and at the north by the garden of Henderick Gerritsen, except for the garden produce; transfer shall take place on the 20th of this coming month of October of this year 1661. Payment shall take place in three installments: the first installment upon transfer, a just fourth part of the total sum in good merchantable sewant to be paid against beavers at sixteen guilders a beaver; the second installment on the first of May *anno* 1662, also a just fourth part, paid as above; and the thirds or final installment on the 20th of July *anno* 1662 in good whole merchantable beaver skins at eight guilders a piece.

The buyer shall be obligated to appoint two suitable sureties each as principals to the satisfaction of the seller and that within the period of 24 hours. If the buyer is unable to appoint two sureties in the prescribed time, then it shall be auctioned off again at his **[592]** expense and cost; and whatever it falls short, the buyer shall be obligated to make good, and if it brings greater value, he shall derive no profit from it. Auction fees will be charged to the buyer. [*not executed*]

[CONDITIONS FOR FARMING THE STRONG DRINK EXCISE]

[593] Conditions and terms upon which the commissary and magistrates, in the name and on behalf of the honorable lords director general and councilors of New Netherland, intend to farm out at public auction to the highest bidder the excise on all wines, beers, and distilled spirits dispensed by the innkeepers, tappers, and retailers in and about Fort Orange, the village of Beverwijck, and Colonie Renselaerswijck.

The farming out as well as the farming shall be done in accordance with the laudable regulations of our fatherland and in accordance with the printed ordinances and placards of the high and mighty lords States General coming from the department of finance.

The farming shall begin on the first of November and terminate on the end of October *anno* 1661, being a period of twelve months, during which time the farmer shall be allowed to collect and receive from all wines, beers or distilled spirits consumed and dispensed by the tappers and innkeepers in or around Fort Orange, the village of Beverwijck or Colonie Rensselaerswijck, as follows:

For a tun of domestically brewed beer,	*f*4:
For a tun of overseas beer,	*f*6:
For a hogshead of French wine,	*f*20:
For an ancker, ditto,	*f*4:
For an ancker of Spanish wine, brandy-wine, mead, or distilled spirits,	*f*7:
For an ancker of cider,	*f*2:
More or less measurements in proportion.	

[594] And that in beavers or otherwise in sewant at 12 white or six black for one stiver at the choice of the payer. The farmer or highest bidder shall be obliged to furnish sufficient sureties to the satisfaction the lords farming contractors for the excise money, [and] to pay every three months in beavers of otherwise in sewant at 12 white or six black for one stiver, a just fourth part of the promised excise money.

In order to prevent misunderstandings and frauds it is stipulated and agreed upon that at the expiration of this farming, when the new farming shall be made again, the new farmer shall have liberty on the day of the new farming, or the following day, or at the latest within three days after the farming is made, to gauge, in the presence of the past farmer, if he wants to be present, the remaining wines, beers, or distilled spirits, held over by the tappers and innkeepers, two-thirds parts of the receipts, or excise due from the old or foregoing farmer is to be returned and made due to his successor, or the following farmer. The lords farming contractors reserve to themselves the interpretation and amplification hereof and promise the farmer all appropriate maintenance and assistance.

[295] The final bidder of the above stated lease was Jan Gerritsen van Marcken for the sum of three thousand eight hundred and sixty seven guilders, according to the aforesaid conditions, pledging his person and estate, moveable and immoveable, now and in the future, nothing excepted, subjecting himself to the authority of all courts and judges. Done in the village of Beverwijck, the 18th of November *anno* 1661.

J. G. van Marcken. †

[CONFIRMATION OF SURETIES FOR THE FARMER OF THE EXCISE]

On this day, the 19th of November *anno* 1661, appeared for the honorable farmers of the excise, Jurriaen Teunissen, Pieter Adriaensen, and Arent van den Bergh, who offered themselves as sureties, each as principal, for the payment of the sum of three thousand eight hundred and sixty-seven guilders, for which Jan Gerritsen van Marcken became the farmer of the excise, according to the above conditions, for the payment of which, pledging their persons and estates, moveable and immoveable, now and in the future, nothing excepted, submitting the same to the authority of all courts and judges. Done in Beverwijck, dated as above.

---

† This final paragraph represents the continuation of the 1661 records which were displaced in the 19th-century bound volume as 517–594.

Jure Jan Tunsen
Pieter Adriaen
This is the mark  of Arent van den Bergh,
made with his own hand.

[296] The above farming took place in the presence of the honorable commissary and magistrates, who bear witness:
La Montagne, commissary at Fort Orange
Rutger Jacobsz
Frans Barensen Pastoor
Evert Janssen Wendel
Adriaen Gerritsen.

[CONVEYANCE OF TWO BONDS FROM ADRIAEN SYMONSEN BOER TO JAN FRANSEN VAN HOESEM]

[297] Appeared before me, Johannes Provoost, clerk of the court of Fort Orange and village of Beverwijck, Adriaen Sijmonsen *Boer*, who declares, in the presence of the subscribed witnesses, to have ceded and conveyed, as he hereby does cede and convey, to Jan Fransen van Hoesem, two certain bonds: the one of Ulderick Kleyn for the sum of one hundred and sixteen guilder in beavers, with interest thereto; the other of Dirckjen Martensen, amounting to two hundred guilders in beavers, also with appropriate interest, the same to be received in real ownership for the securing of payment for board and other things, for which the assignor is indebted to the aforesaid Jan Fransen van Hoesem, pledging his person and estate, moveable and immoveable, now and in the future, subjecting the same to all courts and judges. Done in Beverwijck at the end of October *anno* 1661, in the presence of Jurriaen Teunissen and Aernout Cornelissen.

Aryaen Symense
Jurejan Tunsen, witnesses
Aernout Cornelisz Veilen
Acknowledged by me,
Johannes Provoost, clerk.

[CONDITIONS FOR FARMING OUT THE BURGHER WINE AND BEER EXCISE]

[298] Conditions on which the commissary and magistrates of Fort Orange and the village of Beverwijck propose to farm out to the highest bidder the burgher wine and beer excise for the period of one year. The lease as well as the farming shall begin on the first of November of this year *anno* 1661 and end at the end of October *anno* 1662, according to the ordinances of our fatherland. The farmer shall receive for a barrel of good beer, one daelder, for a barrel of small beer, ten stivers, for an ancker of brandy, Spanish wine, or spirits, two guilders, figuring 12 white and six black sewant for a stiver; and the farmer shall refuse no certificates to any burghers who have been granted the burgher excise. The farmer shall be obliged to furnish two sufficient sureties, each for all and as principals, to the satisfaction of the honorable farmers of the excise, to pay the aforesaid burgher's excise every quarter year a true fourth part of the whole sum in good, strung sewant at twelve white and six black sewant a stiver; and should the farmer fail in the aforesaid surety, then the farming shall be auctioned again at his expense, and whatever **[299]** amount it decreases, he shall be obliged to make good and whatever it increases, he shall make no profit from. Marcelis Janssen remained the last bidder by gavel stroke for the sum of two thousand two hundred and eight guilders, the same to be paid at twelve white and six black sewants the stiver, according to the above conditions, for the payment of which *Sr.* Gysbert van Imborgh and Jan Labite offer themselves as sureties and principals to the satisfaction of the honorable farmers of the excise, pledging their persons and estates, moveable and immoveable, now and in the future, nothing excepted, subjecting the same to all courts and judges.

Done in Beverwijck the first of November *anno* 1661.

Marcelys Jansen
Jan Labatie
Gysbert van Imbroch

[CONVEYANCE OF THE BURGHER EXCISE FROM MARCELIS JANSZ TO JAN GERRITSZ]

Appeared before me, J. La Montagne, on behalf of the honorable lords directors of the general chartered West India Company, for the honorable lords director general and councilors of New Netherland, vice director and commissary of Fort Orange and the village of Beverwijck, in the presence of Philip Pieterse Schueller and Ariaen Gerritsz, magistrates of the same court, Marcelis Jansz, inhabitant of this village of Beverwijck, who declared to have ceded and conveyed to Jan Gerritsz, also presently an inhabitant of this place, the burgher's excise of wine and beer here consumable, according to the above conditions, for which Juriaen Theunissen, Pieter Adriaensz, and Arend van den Bergh, serve as sureties, each as principal, for which they pledge their persons and estates, moveable and immoveable, now and in the future, submitting the same to all courts and judges. Done in Beverwijck the 25th of November *anno* 1661.

J. G. Marcken
Marcelijs Jansen
Philip Pietersen
Adriaen Gerritsen
This is the mark  of Arent van den Bergh
Acknowledged before me,
La Montagne, commissary at Fort Orange.

[CONVEYANCE OF MORTGAGE PAYMENTS FROM MARCELIS JANSSEN TO GYSBERT VAN IMBORGH AND JAN LABITE]

[300] Appeared before me, Johannes La Montagne, in the service of the general chartered West India Company, admitted by the lord director general and council of New Netherland vice director and commissary at Fort Orange and the village of Beverwijck, in the presence of the honorable Evert Wendel and Adriaen Gerritsen, magistrates of the same court, Marcelis Janssen who hereby declares to have conveyed and pledged to Master Gysbert van Imborgh and Jan Labite the two final payments on his house, which Asser Levy has bought at public auction;

furthermore, his entire estate, moveable and immoveable, now and in the future, nothing excepted; all of which stems from surety concerning the burgher's excise, being public money, which above written is to last until the final payment of the aforesaid excise. Thus done in Beverwijck the first of November *anno* 1661.

Marcelys Jansen
Evert Jansz Wendel
Adriaen Gerretsen
Acknowledged by me,
Lan Montagne, commissary at Fort Orange.

[ACKNOWLEDGMENT OF DEBT OF PIETER BRONCK]

[301] Appeared before me, Johannes La Montagne, in the service of the general chartered West India Company, admitted by the lord director general and council of New Netherland vice director and commissary at Fort Orange and the village of Beverwijck, in the presence of the honorable Philip Pietersen Schuyler and Adriaen Gerritsen, magistrates of the same court, Pieter Bronck who acknowledges to be honestly and truly indebted to Jacob Geveck for the sum of two thousand two hundred and seventy-two Carolus guilders in payment of good whole merchantable beaver skins at eight guilder a piece, for which I, Bronck, promise to pay annually in interest one guilder for each beaver, until completion of the principal sum; for which I pledge my person and estate, moveable and immoveable, now and in the future, nothing excepted; in particular, pledging my brew house and millhouse as a mortgage and collateral, together with the lots belonging thereto, as compensation for the aforesaid sum of two thousand tow hundred and **[302]** seventy-two guilders with the interest thereon, if it be necessary, without cost or loss. Done at Fort Orange the 17th of November *anno* 1661.

Pieter Bronck
Philip Pietersen
Adriaen Gerretsen

Acknowledged by me,
La Montagne, commissary at Fort Orange.

I, the undersigned Jacob Gevick, acknowledge that the above mortgage (in force against Pieter Bronck) has been fully paid and satisfied. Done at Fort Orange on the 5th of August *anno* 1662.

This is the mark of Jacob Gevick,
made with his own hand.

In my presence,
J. Provoost, clerk.

[CONDITIONS FOR AUCTION OF HOUSE AND LOT OF FRANCOYS BOON]

Conditions and terms upon which *Sr.* Francoys Boon intends to sell at public auction to the highest bidder his house and lot, located in the village of Beverwijck.

First. The buyer shall receive the aforesaid house, cookhouse, and lot, as enclosed in its fence, with all that is attached to earth and nail. Delivery shall take place on the first of May *anno* 1662 **[303]** on the express condition that the seller shall occupy the aforesaid house and lot after expiration of the aforesaid delivery as a renter until the first of November, for payment of which the buyer shall deduct thirteen beavers from the final installment. Payment shall take place in two installments and that in good merchantable beaver skins at eight guilders a piece, whereof the first half shall be in June *anno* 1662 and the second installment also in June *anno* 1663. The buyer shall receive the patent with the final payment. The buyer shall be obliged to furnish two sufficient sureties at once, each for all as principals, to the satisfaction of the seller. If the buyer cannot furnish the aforesaid sureties within the prescribed time, then the aforesaid house and lot shall be auctioned again at his charge and expense, and whatever less it comes to be worth, he shall make good, and whatever more it comes to be worth, he shall derive no profit. The auction fees become a charge to the buyer.

[304] Upon the above conditions Jochim Wesselsen *Backer* was the high bidder for the sum of one thousand five hundred and two guilders, pledging his person and estate, moveable and immoveable, now and in the future, nothing excepted, subjecting the same to all courts and judges. Done in Beverwijck the 18th of November *anno* 1661.

This is the mark  of Jochim Wessel *Backer*,
made with his own hand.
Acknowledged by me,
La Montagne, commissary at Fort Orange.

[ACKNOWLEDGMENT OF DEBT OF JOCHIM WESSELSEN *BACKER* TO FRANCOYS BOON]

Appeared before me, Johannes La Montagne, in the service of the general chartered West India Company, admitted by the lord director general and council of New Netherland vice director and commissary at Fort Orange and the village of Beverwijck, in the presence of the honorable Frans Barensen Pastoor and Evert Janssen Wendel, magistrates of the same court, Jochim Wesselsen *Backer*, who hereby acknowledges to be truly and honestly indebted to *Sr*. Francoys Boon for the sum of one thousand five hundred and two Carolus guilders in payment of good whole merchantable beaver skins at eight guilders a piece, stemming from the purchase of a house and lot, which he the subscriber bought at public auction from the aforesaid Francoys Boon; and as he failed in providing the two sufficient sureties, which the conditions, required, he, Jochim Wesselsen *Backer* mortgages, and in particular pledges the aforesaid house and lot, together with the house and lot, which are at present occupied by him, to be collected without cost or loss after the expiration of the stipulated term stated in the conditions of sale. Done at Fort Orange on the first of December *anno* 1661.

Jochem *Backer*
Frans Barensen Pastoor
Evert Jansz Wendel

Acknowledged by me,
La Montagne, commissary at Fort Orange.

[INDIAN PATENT FOR LAND TO PIETER BRONCK]

[305] Appeared before me, Johannes La Montagne, in the service of the general chartered West India Company, [admitted] by the lord director general and councilors of New Netherland vice director and commissary at Fort Orange and the village of Beverwijck, two Indians, the one named Sioketas and the other Sachemoes, the son of Keesjen Wey, both owners, and in addition having authority from the co-owners of the land located along the North River on the west bank between Marten Gerritsen's island and the Neutenhoeck, called Koxhackien in the Indian language. The cleared land is a short distance in the woods with the kil, extending from the aforesaid kil, which is opposite Marten Gerritsen's island, westward into the woods until the Katskil path; from there southward along the path until the Stony Kil; from there eastward until opposite the Notenhoeck; from there northward along the river until the aforesaid kil opposite Marten Gerritsen's island; which land and kil they, the grantors, declare to have sold, ceded, and conveyed, as they hereby do, to Pieter Bronck, inhabitant of the village of Beverwijck, and that with all the right and title, which they, the grantors, have therein, for a certain sum in goods, to be paid to them, amounting to about one hundred and fifty guilders in beavers, of which sum the buyer promises to pay half next May, when he shall come to live there, and the other half on the first of May *anno* 1663. Thus done at Fort Orange **[306]** the 13th of January *anno* 1662 in the presence of Jan Verbeeck, Frans Barentsen, and Jan Daret as witnesses invited hereto.

This is the mark of  Sioketas made with his own hand.

This is the mark of  Siachemoes made with his own hand.

This is the mark of  Pawanoos, as witness.

Pyeter Bronck
Jan Verbeeck

Frans Barensen Pastoor
Jan Dareth
Acknowledged by me,
La Montagne, commissary at Fort Orange.

[CONDITIONS FOR AUCTION OF A HOUSE AND LOT BY THE WIDOW OF HENDERICK *DE BACKER*]

[**307**] Conditions upon which the widow of Henderick *de Backer*, deceased, intends to sell at public auction to the highest bidder her house and lot located in the village of Beverwijck; namely, the same which she presently occupies.

First. The house shall be delivered to the buyer, as stated, with everything that is attached by earth and nail, together with the lot in the size as enclosed in its fence. Delivery shall take place on the first of May of this year *anno* 1662. Payment shall be in two installments and that in good whole merchantable beaver skins; namely, the first installment in June *anno* 1662 and the second in June *anno* 1663. The buyer shall be obligated to furnish two sufficient sureties at once, each for all as principals, to the satisfaction of the seller. If the buyer is unable to furnish the aforesaid sureties in the aforesaid time, then the aforesaid house and lot shall [**308**] be auctioned again at his expense and cost; and whatever less it comes to be worth, he shall make good, and whatever more it comes to be worth, he shall derive no profit. The auction fees become a charge to the buyer. [*not executed*]

[CONDITIONS FOR THE AUCTION OF HOUSE AND LOT BY JAN LAMBERTSEN]

[**309**] Conditions upon which Jan Lambertsen intends to sell at public auction to the highest bidder his house and lot located in the village of Beverwijck, which Marten Hoffman, *saelmaker*, occupies. The house and lot shall be delivered to the buyer on the coming Amsterdam fair

day, with everything that is attached by earth and nail; the lot is six rods long and three rods wide, the patent of which the buyer shall receive with the final installment, together with the appropriate conveyance. Payment shall take place in two installments in good whole merchantable beaver skins: the first upon delivery of the aforesaid house and lot, and the second on the first of June *anno* 1663. The buyer shall be obliged to furnish at once two sufficient sureties, each for all as principals, to the satisfaction of the seller. If the buyer cannot furnish the aforesaid sureties in the aforesaid time, then the aforesaid house and lot **[310]** shall be auctioned again at his cost and charge, and whatever less it comes to be worth, he shall be obliged to make good, and whatever more it becomes worth, he shall derive no profit from it. The auction fees shall become a charge to the buyer.

[308b] Upon the above stated conditions Cobus Janssen remained the buyer of the house of Jan Lambertsen for the sum of four hundred Carolus guilders, according to the aforesaid conditions; for which Frans Barentsen Pastoor and Seeger Cornelissen presented themselves as sureties and each as principals, to pay the aforesaid sum, if necessary, pledging their persons and estates, moveable and immoveable, now and in the future, submitting the same to the authority of all courts and judges.

Done at Beverwijck the 19th of January *anno* 1662.†

This is the mark of + Cobus Janssen made with his own hand.
Frans Barentsen Pastoor
This is the mark of Seger Cornelissen made with his own hand.

Acknowledged by me,
La Montagne, commissary at Fort Orange.

† The paragraph ending this document that begins on **[309]** was recorded in the empty space below **[308a]**, which is the final paragraph of a canceled document.

[CONDITIONS FOR THE AUCTION OF BREW HOUSE AND MILLHOUSE OF PHILIP HENDERICKSZ]

[311] Conditions and terms upon which Philip Hendericksz intends to sell at public auction to the highest bidder his brew house and mill house with the lot belonging thereto, except for the mill therein, located in the village of Beverwijck and presently occupied by him, the seller.

First. The buyer shall receive the aforesaid brew house, as it stands with everything attached by earth and nail, except for the furniture and household utensils being therein, together with the lot as large as it lies within the fence. To be delivered with the brewery: one kettle, two tubs, one cooler, 25 half barrels, six beer tubs, one funnel, one scoop, and one malt cloth.

Delivery shall take place on the first of May of this year *anno* 1662; the buyer is granted from the date of purchase to brew once every week, as he pleases. Payment shall take place in good whole merchantable beavers in three payments. The first shall be on the first of July of this year *anno* 1662, the second installment on the first of July 1663, the third or final installment on the first of July *anno* 1664. The buyer shall receive the patent with the final installment. **[312]** The buyer shall be obliged to furnish at once two sufficient sureties, each for all as principals, to the satisfaction of the seller. If the buyer cannot furnish the aforesaid sureties in the aforesaid time, then the aforesaid house and lot shall be auctioned again at his cost and charge, and whatever less it comes to be worth, he shall be obliged to make good, and whatever more it becomes worth, he shall derive no profit from it. The auction fees shall become a charge to the buyer. [*not executed*]

[ACKNOWLEDGMENT OF DEBT OF RUTGER JACOBSEN]

[313] Appeared before me, Johannes La Montagne, in the service of the general chartered West India Company, [admitted by] the lord director general and councilors of New Netherland vice director and commissary at Fort Orange and the village of Beverwijck, in the presence of the honorable Frans Barentsen and Evert Janssen Wendel, magistrates of the same court, the honorable Rutger Jacobsen, who hereby declares and acknowledges to be honestly and truly indebted to Jacob Gevick for the sum of one thousand two hundred guilders with interest thereon at twelve percent, beginning on the 23rd of June *anno* 1661, payment in good whole beaver skins, which aforesaid sum with the stated interest he promises to pay in two installments, the first in the course of this year and the second installment in the year *anno* 1663, and that in grain, beavers, or other merchandise at beaver's value; for which he, the appearer, for satisfaction thereof, places as mortgage and special collateral his part of the island called Mahicanders island located opposite Betlehem, which he equally shares with Anderies Herbertsen, in order, if need be, to recover the payment of the aforesaid sum of one thousand two hundred guilders together with the interest **[314]** without damage or cost. Done at Fort Orange the 3rd of March *anno* 1662.

Rutger Jacobsen
Frans Barensen Pastoor
Evert Janssen Wendel
Acknowledged by me,
La Montagne, commissary at Fort Orange.

[CONVEYANCE OF LOT FROM SANDER LEENDERSEN GLEN TO JAN TOMASSEN]

Appeared before me, Johannes La Montagne, in the service of the general chartered West India Company, admitted by the lord director general and councilors of New Netherland vice director and commissary at Fort Orange and the village of Beverwijck, in the presence of the honorable Philip Pietersen Schuyler and Adriaen Gerritsen, magistrates of the same court, the honorable Sander Leendersen Glen, who declares hereby to have ceded and conveyed, in real and actual possession, to and for the benefit of Jan Tomassen, inhabitant of the **[315]** aforesaid village, his heirs or assigns, a piece of land located in the aforesaid village up against the hill, to the east the grantor, six rods, to the west the grantor also six rods in length, in breadth in front on the street one rod, four feet and six inches, to the north also in width one rod, four feet and six inches; which piece of land is a portion of the patent granted to him, grantor, on date of the 23rd of April *anno* 1652, and he acknowledges to have been satisfied by the grantee, and therefore he promises to free the same from all demands, claims or pretensions, which may arise hereafter upon pledge of his person and estate, moveable and immoveable, submitting himself to all courts and judges. Done at Fort Orange the 17th of April *anno* 1662.

Sander Lenrsen Glen
Philip Pietersz
Adriaen Gerretsen
Acknowledged by me,
La Montagne, commissary at Fort Orange.

[CONVEYANCE OF A GARDEN LOT FROM CORNELIS VOSCH TO ABRAHAM STAETS]

[316] Appeared before me, Johannes La Montagne, in the service of the general chartered West India Company, admitted by the lord director general and councilors of New Netherland vice director and commissary at Fort Orange and the village of Beverwijck, in the presence of the honorable Philip Pietersen Schuyler and Adriaen Gerritsen, magistrates of the same court, Cornelis Vosch, who declares to have granted and conveyed, as he hereby does grant and convey, in real and actual possession, to and for the benefit of Capt. Abraham Staets, his heirs or assigns, a lot for a garden located in the village of Beverwijck, adjoining to the north Van Slichtenhorst's gate and on the west side Dirrick Janssen; in length seven rods and in breadth five rods, according to a patent granted to him, grantor, by the lord director general and councilors of New Netherland on 23 April *anno* 1652, for which garden the grantor acknowledges to have **[317]** had satisfaction and promises to clear the same from all demands, claims or pretensions, which may arise hereafter, pledging his person and estate, moveable and immoveable, submitting himself to all courts and judges. Done at Fort Orange the 5th of May *anno* 1662.

Cornelis Vos
Philip Pietersen

Adriaen Gerretsen
Acknowledged by me,
La Montagne, commissary at Fort Orange.

[ACKNOWLEDGMENT OF PAYMENT OF DEBT
BY PHILIP HENDERICKSZ]

Appeared before me, Johannes La Montagne, in the service of the general chartered West India Company, vice director and commissary at Fort Orange and the village of Beverwijck, in the presence of the honorable Francoys Boon and Jan Tomassen, magistrates of the same court, Philip Hendericksz, who has declared, as he hereby declares, payment of the sum of three thousand one hundred and forty four guilders in beavers, stemming from the purchase of a brewery; which brewery already was mortgaged on the 2nd of September *anno* 1660 for the aforesaid sum to the benefit of Henderick Anderiessen for the aforesaid sum by virtue of a mortgage, which aforesaid sum was paid in the year 1661 by various assigns for the sum of six hundred and seventy two guilders in beavers; so that he, the appearer, for the further payment **[318]** of the aforesaid sum mortgages all his estate, real and personal, now and in the future, nothing excepted, in particular his farm at the Great Flats, of which he intends to take possession this summer, including horses and livestock, in order to recover the payment if necessary of the aforesaid sum without cost and loss.

Done at Fort Orange, the 10th of May *anno* 1662.

Pflip Henricxsen
Francoys Boon
Jan Thomasz
Acknowledged by me,
La Montagne, commissary at Fort Orange.

[CONVEYANCE OF LAND BY THE INDIANS PAMITEPIET AND
TATANKENAT TO FRANS JANSEN VAN HOESEM]

[319] Appeared before me, Johannes Provoost, clerk at the court of Fort Orange and the village of Beverwijck, two Indians; the one named Pamitepiet, or in Dutch Kesjen Wey, and the other Hans Vos, or in Indian Tatankenat, both owners, and in addition having authority from the co-owners of the land located in the Klaverrack on the east bank, who declare in the presence of the afternamed witnesses that they have sold, ceded and conveyed, as they hereby do, to and for the benefit of Jan Fransen van Hoesem, a piece of land located in the aforesaid Claverrack extending from the little kil of Jan Hendericksz, alias *Roothaer* to the land of Slichtenhorst. In which piece of land are included three of the clover [fields] on the south side of the said *Roothaer*; extending into the woods for about an hour's walk until across a large kil; further, the circumference is of such magnitude as the grantors have staked it out by the trees and kils, and this for a certain sum paid to them, grantors, in goods, amounting to about *f*500: in beavers, for which they also promise to free the aforesaid land from further claims or demands of other Indians, who may sinisterly lay claim thereto. Thus done at Fort Orange the 5th of June *anno* 1662 in the presence of Gerrit Fisbeeck [*sic*] and Carsten Claessen as **[320]** witnesses invited hereto.

This is the mark  of Pamitepiet made with his own hand.

This is the mark of  Tatankenat made with his own hand.

Gerret Visbeeck

This is the mark of  Carsten Claessen made with his own hand.

Acknowledged by me,
La Montagne, commissary at Fort Orange.

Today, the 11th of June *anno* 1664, there appeared before me, as above, an Indian named Sickaneeck or by the Dutch named Teunis, co-owner of the land described above, who acknowledges and declares that on the 5th of June 1662 together with Pamitepiet *alias* Keesie Weij, he has sold the land described above to Jań Francen van Hoesen and that he was fully satisfied and paid therefor, freeing him from all claims of other Indians. Done as above.

This is the mark  of Sickaneeck, also known as Teunis, made with is own hand.

[ACKNOWLEDGMENT OF DEBT BY WIJNANT GERRITSEN VAN DER POEL]*

[321] Appeared before me, Johannes La Montagne, in the service of the general chartered West India Company, vice director and commissary at Fort Orange and the village of Beverwijck, in the presence of the honorable Philip Pietersen and Adriaen Gerritsen, magistrates of the same court, Wijnant Gerritsen van der Poel, who hereby acknowledges and declares to be honestly and truly indebted to *Meester* Jacob Hendericksz Vervanger *chirurgijn* for the number of sixteen hundred good merchantable boards, stemming from an agreement regarding twelve hundred and sixty-one guilders, nineteen stuivers and four pennies Holland money, which he promises to deliver here within the time of six consecutive years, each year one just sixth part of the entire number, of which one installment for this current year already has expired. For the satisfaction of the said boards the appearer places as a mortgage and special collateral his house and lot located in the village of Beverwijck, and which presently is occupied by him, to recover, if necessary, the aforesaid number or quantity of sixteen hundred good merchantable boards without cost or damage. Thus done at Fort Orange the 22nd of June *anno* 1662.

Wijnandt Gerrreijdts van der Poel
Philip Pietersz Schuijler
Adriaen Gerretsen
Acknowledged by me,
La Montagne, commissary at Fort Orange.

* In the margin was written: This was canceled and dispatched; the bill of which, passed by Gerrit Jansz Stavast, was seen by me on this 19th of June 1671. Ludovicus Cobes, secretary.

[ACKNOWLEDGMENT OF DEBT BY THEUNIS CORNELISZ SLINGERLANDT]

[322] Appeared before me, Johannes de la Montagne, in the service of the general chartered West India Company, admitted by the honorable lord director general and councilors of New Netherland vice director and commissary at Fort Orange and the village of Beverwijck, in the presence of the honorable Abraham Staats and Philip Pietersz Schuller, magistrates of the same court, Theunis Slingerlandt, inhabitant of the village of Beverwijck, who declares to be honestly indebted to the honorable Ariaen Gerritsz, magistrate at the said court, for the number of twenty-seven merchantable beavers at eight florins apiece, which he promises to pay within a year from this date at an interest of ten percent, pledging his person and estate, personal and real, present and future, and for the full satisfaction of the said beavers and interest on the same he places as mortgage and special collateral his house and the lot, which lies behind it, located in the village of Beverwijck, and which he occupies at present, renouncing all exceptions which might be brought against the same. Done at Fort Orange, the 22nd of July *anno* 1662.

Tuenyes Corneles Slyngerlant
Abram Staas
Philip Pietersz
Acknowledged before me,
La Montagne, commissary at Fort Orange.

[323 and **324]** [*blank*]

[CONDITIONS FOR THE AUCTION OF A HOUSE AND LOT BY GIJSBERT JANSZ]

[325] Condition and terms upon which Gijsbert Jansz intends to sell at public auction to the highest bidder his house and lot with everything that is attached by earth and nail, located in this village of Beverwijck, and where at present he dwells. It is long 30 feet Rhineland measure, and wide 22 feet and 4 inches. The aforesaid house will be delivered to the buyer 14 days after today. Payment shall take place in three installments in good whole and merchantable beaver skins at eight guilders apiece. The first upon delivery 14 days from now, the second the next year, and the third a year later again; each time a just third part of the promised purchase money. A proper conveyance and patent shall be delivered to the buyer upon the final payment, and he shall be obliged to furnish two sufficient sureties at once, one for all and each as principal, to the satisfaction of the seller. If the buyer cannot furnish the sufficient sureties within the aforesaid time, the aforesaid auctioned [house and lot] shall be reauctioned, and whatever less it comes to be worth he shall be obliged to make good, and whatever more it becomes worth, he shall derive no profit from it. **[326]** The auction fees shall become a charge to the buyer in payment as above. Dated this 24th of July *anno* 1662. [*not executed*]

[CONDITIONS FOR THE AUCTION OF A HOUSE AND LOT BY VOLCKERT JANSZ FOR JAN BARENTSZ KUNST]

[327] Conditions and terms upon which Volckert Jansz, attorney for Jan Barentsz Kunst, intends to sell at public auction to the highest bidder the house and lot of Jan Barentsz Kunst with everything that is attached by earth and nail, standing and located in this village of Beverwijck, adjoining to the south of the house of *Mr*. Abraham Staats, to the north of the house of Claes van Rotterdam, as it stands within its fence. The house shall be delivered to the buyer at once. Payment shall take place in two installments; the first installment in beavers at *f*8 apiece upon delivery, and the second on the first of May *anno* 1663, one half in sewant, and the other half in beavers, provided that the sewant is worth *f*20 in sewant a beaver. The buyer shall receive a proper conveyance upon the final payment, and he shall be obliged to furnish two sufficient sureties, one for all and each as principal, to the satisfaction of the seller, and to do so at once. **[328]** If the buyer cannot furnish the sureties within the aforesaid time, the aforesaid auctioned [house and lot] shall be reauctioned, and whatever less it comes to be worth, he shall be obliged to make good, and whatever more it becomes worth, he shall derive no

profit from it. The auction fees shall become a charge to the buyer. In payment as above, this 24th of July *anno* 1662.
[*not executed*]

[CONDITIONS FOR THE AUCTION OF TWO HOUSES AND A LOT BY THEUNIS CORNELISZ SLINGERLANT]

[329] Conditions and terms upon which Theunis Cornelis Slingerlant intends to sell at public auction to the highest bidder his two houses adjacent to each other with the lot belonging thereto, with everything that is attached by earth and nail. The largest house is 30 wood feet long, and 22 wood feet wide. The small house is 15 feet square. The lot is as it stands within its fence. The aforesaid two houses shall be delivered to the buyer on the first of May *anno* 1663. Payment shall take place in two installments in good whole merchantable beaver skins at *f*8 apiece; the first in the month of July of this year 1662, and the second a year later. With the final payment the buyer shall receive a proper conveyance and patent, and he remains obliged to furnish two sufficient sureties, one for all and each as principal, to the satisfaction of the seller, and to do so at once. If the buyer cannot furnish the sureties within the aforesaid time, the aforesaid auctioned [houses] shall be re-auctioned, **[330]** and whatever less it comes to be worth, he shall be obliged to make good, and whatever more it becomes worth, he shall derive no profit from it. The auction fees shall become a charge to the buyer. In payment as above. Dated the 24th of July *anno* 1662.
[*not executed*]

[CONDITIONS FOR THE AUCTION OF THE BREWERY, MILLHOUSE, STABLE AND HAYHOUSE BY PIETER BRONCK]

[331] Conditions and terms upon which Pieter Bronck intends to sell at public auction to the highest bidder his brewery with millhouse, a stable and hayhouse as it is operating, with everything that is attached by earth and nail; situated in this village of Beverwijck as it stands in fence, which the prospective buyers will be able to see, and the half barrels, malt cloth, kettle, and other tools that are there will be delivered to the buyer along with it.

The aforesaid brewery with millhouse, hay house, and stable shall be delivered to the buyer on the first of November of this year 1662. Payment shall be made in 3 installments; the first upon delivery in good whole and merchantable beaver skins at *f*8 apiece; the second on the last of June 1663, in payment as before, and the third a year later, in kind as above. With the last installment an appropriate conveyance shall be delivered to the buyer and he shall be obliged to furnish two sufficient sureties, each as principals, to the satisfaction of the seller and to do so immediately. **[332]** If the buyer cannot furnish sufficient sureties in the aforesaid time, the auctioned [buildings] will be reauctioned, and whatever it comes to be worth less he shall make good, and from whatever it comes to be worth more, he shall derive no profit. The auction fees shall become a charge to the buyer, in payment as above. To prevent all quibbling and misunderstandings, it is announced to the public that the aforesaid brewhouse, millhouse and lot are burdened with two mortgages, to wit, the first to Rhijndert Pitersz, amounting to *f*832: in beavers with the interest thereof, and the second to Jacob Gevick, amounting to *f*2272 in beavers with the interest thereof, according to promissory note and mortgage for each beaver one guilder annually, starting on the 17th of November 1661 until the date of the full satisfaction. These mortgages were read to the public and shall be taken on by the buyer. [*not executed*]

[333 and 334] [*blank*]

[CONDITIONS FOR THE AUCTION OF PIETER BRONCK'S LOG HOUSE, LOT, AND BARRACK BARN]

[335] Conditions and terms upon which Pieter Bronck intends to sell at public auction to the highest bidder his log house with the lot and a barrack barn† with everything that is attached by earth and nail; located in this village of Beverwijck, as it was measured out, which the

† *schuerberch*

prospective buyers will be able to see. The aforesaid log house with the aforesaid will be delivered free and unencumbered to the buyer on the coming first of May 1663. Payment will be made in three installments; the first upon delivery in good whole and merchantable beaver skins at *f*8 apiece; the second, a year later, *in specie* as above, and the third a year after that *in specie* as before. With the last payment an appropriate conveyance and patent shall be delivered to the buyer, who remains obliged to furnish two sufficient sureties, each as principals, one for all and each as principal, to the satisfaction of the seller and to do so immediately. If the buyer cannot furnish sufficient sureties in the aforesaid time, the auctioned [log house, lot and barn] will be reauctioned, and whatever it becomes worth less, he shall make good, and from whatever it comes to be worth more, he will derive no profit. [336] The auction fees shall become a charge to the buyer, in payment as above. Dated this 2nd of August 1662. [*not executed*]

[CONDITIONS FOR THE AUCTION OF A SMALL HOUSE AND LOT BY PIETER BRONCK]

[337] Conditions and terms upon which Pieter Bronck intends to sell at public auction to the highest bidder his little house adjacent to the log house with the lot as it stands fenced in, located in this village of Beverwijck, which the prospective buyers will be able to see. The aforesaid little house will be delivered to the buyer on the first of May *anno* 1663. Payment shall take place in two installments in good whole and merchantable beaver skins at *f*8 apiece; the first on the first of June *anno* 1663, and the second a year later. With the final payment a proper conveyance shall be delivered to the buyer, and he remains obliged to furnish two sufficient sureties, one for all and each as principal, to the satisfaction of the seller and to do so immediately. If the buyer cannot furnish sufficient sureties in the aforesaid time, the auctioned [house and lot] will be reauctioned, and whatever less it comes to be worth, he shall be obliged to make good, and from whatever more it becomes worth, he will derive no profit. [*not executed*]

[338] [*blank*]

[CONDITIONS FOR THE AUCTION OF A HOUSE AND LOT BY PIETER BRONCK]

[339] Conditions and terms upon which Pieter Bronck intends to sell at public auction to the highest bidder his house and lot, located at the hill in this village of Beverwijck. The lot is 20 rods long and 5 wide, according to the patent thereof. The aforesaid house and lot will be delivered to the buyer on the first of May of this year 1663. Payment shall occur in two installments in good whole merchantable beaver skins at *f*8 apiece; the first installment on the first of June *anno* 1663, and the second on the first of June *anno* 1664. A proper conveyance and patent will be delivered to the buyer upon the last installment, and the buyer shall be obliged to furnish two sufficient sureties, one for all and each as principal, to the satisfaction of the seller, and to do so immediately. If the buyer cannot furnish sufficient sureties in the aforesaid time, the auctioned [house and lot] shall be reauctioned, and whatever less it comes to be worth, he shall be obliged to make good, and whatever more it comes to be worth, he shall derive no profit from it. **[340]** The auction fees shall become a charge to the buyer, in payment as above. [*not executed*]

[CONVEYANCE OF A HOUSE *ET AL*. BY PIETER BRONCK TO JACOB GEVICK AND REYNDER PIETERSEN]

[341] Appeared before me, Johannes La Montagne, in the service of the general chartered West India Company, admitted by the lord director general and councilors of New Netherland vice director and commissary at Fort Orange and the village of Beverwijck, in the presence of the honorable Francoijs Boon and Jan Tomassen magistrates of the same court, Pieter Bronck, inhabitant of the aforesaid village of Beverwijck, who declares to have granted and transferred, as he hereby does grant and transfer in real and actual possession, to and for the benefit of Jacob Gevick and Reijndert Pietersen, their heirs or assigns, his brew house and dwelling in front, with the mill house and horse stable, together with the well and the lot thereto belonging, located in the said village of Beverwijck; wide in front on the street, three rods, one foot, and six inches, to the south the log house, long eleven rods, eight feet; to the east wide three rods 6 feet, to the north of Leendert Philipsen long eleven rods eight feet;* which is a part of the patent [**342**] granted to him, grantor, by the lord director general and councilors of N: Netherland, dated the 25th of October *anno* 1653. Likewise said Bronck conveys another house and lot located at the hill in the aforementioned village of Beverwijck, wide five rods and long twenty rods, lying in its square, according to the patent granted to him, grantor, by the said lord director general and councilors of New Netherland on the 25th of October *anno* 1653. Which the aforesaid grantor promises to free from all actions, claims and demands which hereafter may arise, pledging his person and estate, moveable and immoveable, present and future, submitting himself to all laws and judges. Done in Fort Orange, the 5th of August *anno* 1662.

Pijeter Bronck
Francoijs Boon
Jan Thomasz
Acknowledged by me,
La Montagne, commissary at Fort Orange.

[CONVEYANCE OF A HOUSE AND LOT BY RUTGER JACOBSEN TO CORNELIS STEENWIJCK]

[**343**] Appeared before me, Johannes La Montagne, in the service of the general chartered West India Company, admitted by the lord director general and councilors of New Netherland vice director and commissary at Fort Orange and the village of Beverwijck, in the presence of the honorable Abraham Staets and Jan Tomassen,

* The original text reads: ... *breet voor aen de straet drie roeden een voet en ses duijm, ten suijden het blockhuijs lanck elff roeden acht voeten, ten oosten breet drie roeden 6 voeten, ten noorden van L eendert Philipsen lanck elff roeden acht voeten.* This literally means that both the *blockhuijs* and Leendert Philipsen are on the south of this lot. The *blockhuijs* [block house] may be the same as the *balckenhuijs* [log house] mentioned in document [**335**].

magistrates of the same court, the honorable Rutger Jacobsen, who declares to have granted and transferred, as he hereby does grant and transfer, in real and actual possession, to and for the benefit of *Sr.* Cornelis Steenwijck, merchant at Amsterdam in New Netherland, his heirs or assigns, a house and lot located in the village of Beverwijck at the hill; adjoins to the south the street, to the north the kil, to the west Barent Reijndersen, and to the east Gijsbert Janssen, where a common alley runs between both. Wide in front on the road forty-seven wood feet, in the rear on the kil wide thirty-six feet, long to the east one hundred and thirty-five feet, on the west side as long as before. Which lot is a part of the patent granted to him, grantor, by the lord director general and councilors **[344]** of New Netherland, and he promises to free the same from all demands, claims or pretensions, which may arise hereafter, pledging his person and estate, moveable and immoveable, present and future, with no exception, submitting himself to all laws and judges. Done at Fort Orange the 7th of August *anno* 1662.

Rutger Jacobsen
Abram Staas
Jan Thomasz
Acknowledged by me,
La Montagne, commissary at Fort Orange.

[CONVEYANCE OF A HOUSE AND LOT FROM GIJSBERT JANSSEN TO HARMEN ALBERTSEN VEDDER]

[345] Appeared before me Johannes Provoost, clerk of the court of Fort Orange and the village of Beverwijck, Gijsbert Janssen at one side, and Harmen Albertsen Vedder at the other side, who declare in the presence of the afternamed witnesses that in all friendship and amity they have contracted and agreed with each other, namely, that the said Gijsbert Janssen sells to the aforesaid Harmen Vedder his house and lot located in this said village of Beverwijck; adjoining immediately next to Philip Pietersen Schuijler. The house is 30 feet long and twenty-two feet wide; similarly, the lot is 11 rods long and 22 Rhineland feet wide. Likewise, does the said Harmen Albertsen Vedder accept the aforesaid purchase for the sum of one thousand and six hundred Carolus guilders in good whole merchantable beaver skins at eight guilders apiece and that in three installments; the first upon delivery, which will be in the time of 3 or 4 days after today; the second a year later, and the third on the first of August *anno* 1664. Hereby is also especially stipulated that, as the buyer has rented the house from Pieter Hartgers for the period of two years, **[346]** the seller will have to move into the house and pay the rent of five quarter years as is stated in the buyer's tenancy agreement. Thus done and passed, without any craft or guile, both parties submitting themselves to all laws and judges, in the presence of *Mr.* Antonij van Aelst and Bastiaen de Winter, as witnesses requested hereto on this 10th of August *anno* 1662 in Beverwijck.

Geijsbert Yanssen
Harmen Vedderen
Anthonij van Aelst
Basteyaen de Winter

Acknowledged by me,
Johannes Provoost, clerk.

[CONVEYANCE OF A HOUSE AND LOT FROM HARMEN BASTIAENSEN TO CARSTEN CLAESSEN]

[347] Appeared before me, Johannes La Montagne, in the service of the general chartered West India Company, admitted by the lord director general and councilors of New Netherland vice director and commissary at Fort Orange and the village of Beverwijck, in the presence of the honorable Philip Pietersen Schuijler and Francoijs Boon, magistrates of the same court, Harmen Bastiaensen, who hereby declares to have granted and transferred, as he hereby does grant and transfer in real and actual possession to and for the benefit of Carsten Claessen, his heirs or assigns, a house together with a lot belonging thereto, located in the village of Beverwijck; adjoins to the north the grantor, and to the south Jan Henderickse van Bael. In front on the street it is wide twenty-seven wood feet and nine inches; long on the north side 73 wood feet, wide on the south 62 wood feet and two inches; in the rear on the river wide eight feet and 8 inches; which lot is a part of the patent granted to him, grantor, by the lord director general and councilors of New Netherland, of date the 23rd of April *anno* 1652. And he promises to free the same from all actions, claims or demands **[348]** which may arise hereafter, pledging his person and estate, moveable and immoveable, present and future, submitting himself to all laws and judges. Done at Fort Orange the 12th of August *anno* 1662.

Harmen Bastiaens
Philip Pietersz Schuijler
Francoijs Boon
Acknowledged by me,
La Montagne, commissary at Fort Orange.

[ACKNOWLEDGMENT OF DEBT BY JAN VERBEECK TO DIRCK DIRCKSZ KEYSER]

Appeared before me, Johannes La Montagne, in the service of the general chartered West India Company, admitted by the lord director general and councilors of New Netherland vice director and commissary at Fort Orange and the village of Beverwijck, in the presence of the honorable Francoijs Boon and Jan Tomassen, magistrates of the same court, the honorable Jan Verbeeck, who acknowledges and declares to be well, honestly and truly indebted to Dirrick Dirricksz Keyser, merchant, for the sum of two hundred and fifty-five guilders to be paid in good whole merchantable beaver skins at eight guilders apiece, which aforesaid sum **[349]** he promises to pay during this current year, and in case of failure, he, appointer, shall be obliged from year to year to pay an interest of ten percent to make full payment. For satisfaction thereof, said Jan Verbeeck places as mortgage and special collateral his old house together with the lot belonging thereto,* which he occupies at present, in order to recover, if necessary, the payment of the said sum of two hundred and fifty-five guilders or the

* Marked for insertion at this point is: " and also a little house standing on the said lot on the waterside," making it unclear which of the two houses is occupied by Jan Verbeeck.

quantity of thirty-eight and seven-eighth beavers, without cost and damage. Done in Fort Orange, the 15th of August *anno* 1662.

Jan Verbeeck
Francoijs Boon
Jan Thomasz
Acknowledged by me,
La Montagne, commissary at Fort Orange.

[POWER OF ATTORNEY FROM JAN BARENTSEN DULLEMAN TO GERRIT JANSSEN KUIJPER]

[350] Appeared before me, Johannes La Montagne, in the service of the general chartered West India Company, admitted by the lord director general and councilors of New Netherland vice director and commissary at Fort Orange and the village of Beverwijck, in the presence of the witnesses mentioned hereafter, on the date subscribed, Jan Barentsen Dulleman, *backer* in the aforesaid village, who declares that he has appointed and empowered as he hereby does appoint and empower the honorable Gerrit Janssen Kuijper dwelling at Amsterdam, to collect, demand, and receive in his, appointer's name, and on his behalf, from the honorable Luijcas Aertsen and Mattijs Harmsen dwelling at Swoll, uncles and guardians of the appointer, such five hundred Carolus guilders, together with a larger sum, due to him on account of the inheritance of his deceased father and mother; to issue quittance for the receipts, and in case of unwillingness, to demand payment by law and rigor of justice, observing all terms of the law thereto. Further, to do and perform everything that he, the appointer, could or might do if he were present, on condition that the attorney shall be obliged to render proper accounts of his transactions and receipts upon pledge of his person and estate, personal and real. Thus done in Fort Orange in New Netherland in the presence of Harmen Albertsen Vedder and David Provoost, as witnesses invited hereto on this 16th of August *anno* 1662.

Jan Barentsen Dulleman
Harmen Vedderen

David Provoost
Acknowledged by me,
La Montagne, commissary at Fort Orange.

[PAYMENT OF BEAVERS BY MARCELIS JANSSEN TO JAN VAN AKEN]

[351] Appeared before me Johannes Provoost, clerk of the court of Fort Orange and the village of Beverwijck, Marcelis Janssen, who declares in the presence of the witnesses named hereafter, that he has granted and fully conveyed, as he hereby does, to and for the benefit of Jan van Aken the number of sixty-six and a half good whole merchantable beavers, to be received out of the second payment for his house through the hands of Asser Levij, who has bought the aforesaid house at public auction; and this in true ownership, to do and transact with it as he can do with his other own estates in such manner that nobody will be able to make any claims or institute any overreaching demands, but that the grantee will be able to dispose of, use, or alienate the aforesaid number of sixty-six and a half beavers in the same way as he can do this with his other own estate. Under pledge according to law. Thus done in Fort Orange, the 18th of August *anno* 1662 in the presence of Arent vanden Bergh and Harmen Vedder, as witnesses invited hereto.

Marcelijs Jansen
Harmen Vedderen
This is the mark  of Arent vanden Bergh.
Acknowledged by me,
Johannes Provoost, clerk.

[CONVEYANCE OF A HOUSE AND LOT BY JAN LABATIE TO JACOB DE HINSSE]

[352] Appeared before me, Johannes La Montagne, in the service of the general chartered West India Company, admitted by the lord director general and councilors of New Netherland vice director and commissary at Fort Orange and the village of Beverwijck, in the presence of the honorable Philip Pietersen Schuijler and Francoijs Boon, magistrates of the same court, the honorable Johan Labate, who declares that he has granted and transferred, as he hereby grants and transfers in real and actual possession to and for the benefit of *Sr.* Jacob de Hinse *chirurgijn* a house and lot located in the village of Beverwijck, adjoins to the north the First Kil and Jochim Wessels, west on the street, to the south the grantor, and to the east the riverside. In front on the street it is nine rods wide, long on the south side thirteen rods, in the rear on the east side wide four rods and nine feet, long on the north side seventeen rods. Of which lot a width of forty feet is taken off in front on the street, and a width of twenty feet in the back; together with a garden behind Fort Orange, which the grantor keeps for himself. Thus the patent hereof shall be delivered into the hands of the grantee, which patent was granted to the grantor by the lord director general and councilors of New Netherland on October 25th *anno* 1653; **[353]** and he promises to free the same from all actions, demands or claims which may arise hereafter, pledging his person and estate, moveable and immoveable, nothing excepted, submitting himself to all laws and judges. Done at Fort Orange the 20th of August *anno* 1662.

Jan Labatie
Philip Pietersz Schuijler
Francoijs Boon
Acknowledged by me,
La Montagne, commissary at Fort Orange.

[CONVEYANCE OF A HOUSE AND LOT BY ASSER LEVI TO ROBBERT SANDERS]

[354] Today, the 7th of September *anno* 1662 appeared before me Johannes Provoost, clerk of the court of Fort Orange and the village of Beverwijck *Sr.* Asser Levij, merchant at Amsterdam in New Netherland on one side, and Robbert Sandersz, inhabitant of Beverwijck on the other side, who in the presence of the afternamed witnesses declare that they, in all friendship and amity, have contracted and agreed with each other, to wit, that the aforenamed Asser Levij has sold to the said Robbert Sandersz his house and lot, located in the village of Beverwijck at the hill; the same [house] that he, grantor, has bid on and bought at public auction from Marcelis Janssen, and all of this as it stands and lies within its fence, with everything that is attached by earth and nail, with another little house on the side of the large house, that the seller had built after his purchase. Further, its size according to the patent thereof, as also the said Robbert Sandertsen acknowledges to have bought the same, and promises to pay therefore the sum of one thousand nine hundred and twenty guilders payable in good whole merchantable beaver skins at *f*8 apiece, along with three beavers for a hat for the seller. It is stipulated and negotiated that, as the aforesaid house is leased for the time of two years, the buyer, according to the agreement, is obligated to buy out the tenant and pay him. The delivery shall take place on the first of May *anno* 1663. **[355]** Payment shall occur in five installments. The first installment on the first of July *anno* 1663, which will be the number of fifty beavers; the following installments from year to year, each time a just fifth part. Further, the aforesaid house and lot will remain a special security to guarantee complete payment, for which the buyer pledges his person and estate, moveable and immoveable, present and future without exception, submitting himself to all the lords laws and judges. Thus done in the village of Beverwijck in the presence of the honorable Frans Barentsen Pastoor and Jacob Tijssen van der Heijden, as witnesses invited hereto on the date as above. Done as above.

Asser Leevi
Robbert Sandersz
Frans Barents Pastoor
Jacob Theijsen
Acknowledged by me,
Johannes Provoost, clerk.

[CONVEYANCE OF A HOUSE AND LOT BY REYNDERT PIETERSEN AND JACOB HEVICK TO HENDERICK ROOSEBOOM]

[356] Appeared before me Johannes Provoost, clerk of the court of Fort Orange and the village of Beverwijck, Reijndert Pietersen and Jacob Hevick on the one side and Henderick Roosenboom on the other side, who declare who in the presence of the witnesses mentioned hereafter, that they, in all friendship and amity, have agreed with each other, namely that the said Reijndert Pietersen and Jacob Hevick declare that they have sold to said Henderick Rosenboom their house and lot located at the hill in the village of Beverwijck, which they have bought from Pieter Bronck, and this, as it stands with everything that is attached by earth and nail, as large as is stated in its patent. Likewise, said Henderick Roosenboom accepts the aforesaid, and acknowledges to have bought it for the sum of five hundred and fifty guilders in payment of good whole merchantable beavers at *f*8 apiece, and this in two installments; the first on the first of July *anno* 1663, the just half, and the second installment on the first of July *anno* 1664. The delivery shall take place on this date, and stands at the buyer's risk; for which the respective parties pledge their persons and estates. Thus done in Beverwijck in the presence of Frans Barentsen Pastoor and Marcelis Janssen, as witnesses requested hereto on this 13th of September *anno* 1662.

Frans Barents Pastoor
This is the mark of RP Reyndert Pietersen,
placed with his own hand.
This is the mark of  Jacob Hevick,
placed with his own hand.
Henderijck Yansen Rooseboom
Acknowledged by me,
J. Provoost, clerk.

[PLEDGE OF SECURITY BY WOUTER ALBERTSEN FOR HENDERICK ROOSENBOOM]

[357] On the date written below appeared before me, Johannes Provoost, clerk of this court of Fort Orange and the village of Beverwijck, Wouter Albertsen, who presents himself as surety and principal for the person of Henderick Rosenboom for the satisfaction of the sum of five hundred and fifty guilders in beavers, stemming from of the purchase of a house and lot, which the said Rosenboom has bought from Reyndert Pietersen and Jacob Gevick; for this he, appearer, pledges himself, if necessary, to the said sellers for the payment of the same sum, under the pledge of his person and estate, moveable and immoveable, present and future, submitting himself to all laws and judges. Done in Beverwijck, the 13th of September *anno* 1662 in the presence of Frans Barentsen Pastoor and Marcelus Janssen, as witnesses requested hereto.

Frans Barentsen Pastoor
WouterAlbers
Marcelijs Jansen

Acknowledged before me,
J. Provoost, clerk.

[AGREEMENT BETWEEN REYNDERT PIETERSEN AND JACOB HEVICK]

[358] Today, the 13th of September *anno* 1662 appeared before me, Johannes Provoost, clerk of the court of Fort Orange and the village of Beverwijck, Reijndert Pietersen and Jacob Gevick who declare in presence of the afternamed witnesses, that they have settled with each other everything they have jointly participated in, such as the house, brewhouse, accrued interest, and other issues; that for that purpose it has been found that Reyndert Pietersen still participates for the sum of fourteen hundred and fifty-six guilders in the said brewery and the house at the hill, which they bought from Pieter Bronck, and that two thousand five hundred and fifty-six guilders comes to Jacob Gevick, the portions of each as they have settled at this date. Thus done in presence of Frans Barentsen Pastoor and Adriaen Janssen van Leijden, as witnesses requested hereto on the date as above. Done as above.

This is the mark of **RP** Reijndert Pietersen,
placed with his own hand.
This is the mark of Jacob Gevick
placed with his own hand.

Frans Barentsen Pastoor
Arien Jansz van Leijden

Acknowledged by me,
J. Provoost, clerk.

[PRENUPTIAL AGREEMENT BETWEEN JACOB GEVICK AND GEERTRUIJ BARENTS]

[359] In the name of the Lord Amen. Be it known by the contents of this present instrument, that in the year of our Lord Jesu Christy 1662, on the 23rd day of September, there appeared before me Johannes La Montagne, in the service of the general chartered West India Company, admitted by the lord director general and councilors of New Netherland vice director and commissary at Fort Orange and the village of Beverwijck, Jacob Gevick, born at Meckelenborgh, on the one side, and Geertruij Barents from Dwingeloo, widow of Henderick Hendericksz van Harstenhorst, deceased, on the other side, who, in the presence of the afternamed witnesses, declare that, for the honor of God, they have resolved upon a future marriage, and before the bands of the same, they have consented to the following conditions: First. That the aforesaid married people for the support of this marriage mutually shall bestow and bring together all present and such goods and effects, of whatever nature, in whatever place, and with whatever persons the same may lie outstanding and remaining; none of those effects excepted, which they each at present possess, or to which they each are entitled, and which is equitable to be possessed by them in common, according to the law of our fatherland; except that from the bride's goods, **[360]** to wit, of the estate left [by her late husband], half shall be reserved for the two children left by the late Henderick Hendericksz van Harstenhorst; the one named Lysbet Henderickse, about six years old, and the other, Judick Henderickse, three years old; which, with the agreement of the bride, by the orphan masters and said witnesses was assessed to be worth about one hundred good whole merchantable beaver skins at *f*8 apiece. Furthermore, that, in case the bridegroom comes to die before the bride without children procreated by the two of them, the bride will remain in full possession of the entire estate, as his only heir, without recognizing any other heirs. And if the bride comes to die before the bridegroom, also without children procreated by the two of them, the bridegroom shall be obliged to pay to her children half of the remaining estate, and, in addition, to pay to he same one hundred beavers, as before. Therefore he shall remain in full possession of the entire estate, on condition that also after the decease of the aforesaid bride the children will be entitled to inherit all of their mother's clothes, including gold rings and silverware, belonging to her person. Likewise, that the aforesaid married couple will bring up the aforesaid children in the fear of the Lord, and provide for them with food and clothing until their majority and married state, without diminishing their patrimonial and inherited estate. Which marriage conditions the said bridegroom and bride promise **[361]** to keep without craft or guile, pledging their persons and estates, moveable and immoveable, present and future without any exception, submitting themselves to all laws and judges. Thus done in the presence of the honorable Frans Barentsen Pastoor and Adries de Vos, as witnesses requested hereto on date as above. Done in Beverwijck.

This is the mark  of Jacob Gevick,
placed with his own hand.
This is the mark  of Geertruij Barents van Dwingeloo, placed with her own hand.
Frans Barentsen Pastoor
By me Andrys de Vos
Evert Jansz Wendel as orphan master.
Acknowledged by me,
La Montagne, commissary at Fort Orange.

[CONDITIONS FOR FARMING OUT THE SLAUGHTER EXCISE]

[362] Conditions and terms upon which the lord commissary and magistrates of Fort Orange and the village of Beverwijck intend to farm out at public auction to the highest bidder the slaughter excise for the period of one year.

The farming of the aforesaid slaughter excise shall begin on the first of October of this year and end on the last of September *anno* 1663. The farmer shall receive for the slaughtered animals, whether it will be an ox, cow, calf, bull, hog, goat or sheep, one stuiver for each guilder of the value of the same, to wit, whatever has been bought for beavers will bring 20 stuivers in sewant for one beaver, and in case of dispute, to be valued by impartial persons. The farmer is obligated to furnish, to the satisfaction of the lords farming supervisors, two sufficient sureties for the excise money, and every quarter year to pay a just fourth part of the excise in good merchantable sewant; and if the farmer cannot provide sufficient sureties, it shall be reauctioned at his costs and charges; and all that it falls short, he shall be obligated to make good, and whatever it brings more, he shall derive no profit therefrom.

After offering the above farming for sale, which brought the lords lessors *f*750, there appeared before their honors Jan Gerritsen van Marcken, who accepted the said farming **[363]** and who took the job of farmer for the sum of seven hundred and eighty guilders according to the aforesaid conditions. And on account of his being released from furnishing sureties, he promises to pay half of the promised purchase money in the time of fourteen days or three weeks, for which he pledges his person and estate, moveable and immoveable, present and future, without exception, submitting himself to all laws and judges. Done in Beverwijck the 30th September *anno* 1662.

J G V Marcken

[SALE OF THE SLAUGHTER EXCISE BY JAN GERRITSEN VAN MARCKEN TO HENDERICK JANSSEN ROOSEBOOM]

Appeared before me Johannes Provoost in the service of the general chartered West India Company, clerk of the court of Fort Orange and the village of Beverwijck, in the presence of the honorable Adriaen Gerritsen and Goossen Gerritsen magistrates of the same court, Jan Gerritsen van Marken on one side, who declares to have granted and transferred as he hereby does, to Hendrick Janssen Rosenboom on the other side, the farming of the slaughter excise, consumable in Fort Orange and the village of Beverwijck, and this, according to the above conditions, just as the grantor has leased the same. Likewise, does the said Henderick Janssen Rosenboom declare himself **[364]** farmer of the aforesaid slaughter excise, for the satisfaction of which Wouter Albertsen and Gerrit Slichtenhorst stand sureties and each as principals, to pay the sum of seven hundred and eighty guilders, pledging their persons and estates, moveable and immoveable, present and future without exception, submitting themselves to all laws and judges. Done at Beverwijck the 5th of October *anno* 1662.

Wouter Albers
JGV Marcken
Henderijck Yansen Rooseboom
Gerrit van Slichtenhorst
Adriaen Gerretsen
Goossen Gerritsen

[CONVEYANCE OF A HOUSE AND LOT BY POULUS MARTENSEN TO CLAES CORNELISSEN VAN DEN BERGH]

[365] Appeared before me, Johannes La Montagne, in the service of the general chartered West India Company, admitted by the lord director general and council of New Netherland vice director and commissary at Fort Orange and the village of Beverwijck, in the presence of the honorable Philip Pietersen Schuijler and Adriaen Gerritsen, magistrates of the same court, Poulus Martensen, who declares to cede and convey, as he hereby does, in real and actual possession, to and for the benefit of Claes Cornelissen van den Bergh, his heirs or assigns, a house and lot, situated in the village of Beverwijck near Fort Orange, adjoins to the north Captain Abraham Staets, to the south the said fort; as large as at present it lies within its fence, according to the patent thereof granted by the lord director general and councilors of New Netherland to Jacob Luijersen, deceased, on date of the 25th of October *anno* 1653. And he, grantor, acknowledges to be paid and satisfied therefor, and promises to free the same from all actions, demands or claims which may arise hereafter, under pledge of his person and estate, moveable and immoveable, present and future, submitting himself to all laws and judges. Done at Fort Orange the 12th of October *anno* 1662.

Poulis Marten
Philip Pietersen Schuijler
Adriaen Gerretsen
Acknowledged by me,
La Montagne, commissary at Fort Orange.

[ACKNOWLEDGMENT OF DEBT BY ADRIAEN JANSSEN VAN LEIJDEN TO JOHANNES BAPTIST VAN RENSSELAER]

[366] Appeared before me, Johannes La Montagne, in the service of the general chartered West India Company, admitted by the lord director general and councilors of New Netherland vice director and commissary at Fort Orange and the village of Beverwijck, in the presence of the honorable Adriaen Gerritsen and Goossen Gerritsen, magistrates of the same court, the honorable Adriaen Janssen van Leijden, surnamed Appel, who hereby acknowledges and declares that he is honestly and truly indebted to the lord Johannes Baptist van Renselaer for the sum of six hundred and forty-three guilders and six stuivers to be paid in good whole merchantable beaver skins at *f*8 apiece, stemming from goods and merchandise received to his content; which aforesaid sum he, appearer, promises to pay to the aforesaid Johannes Baptist van Renselaer or his attorney, Jeremias van Renselaer, on the 12th of July *anno* 1663 with proper interest thereon, beginning on the 12th of July *anno* 1662. To recover, if necessary, the payment of the aforesaid sum of six hundred and forty-three guilders and six stuivers in beavers with its interest without cost or damage, he places his house and lot, located in the village of Beverwijck, as a mortgage and special collateral. Done in Fort Orange the 15th of October *anno* 1662.

Adriaen Jansz van Leijden
Adriaen Gerretsen
Goosen Gerretsen
Acknowledged by me,
La Montagne, commissary at Fort Orange.

[CONVEYANCE OF A HOUSE AND LOT BY SANDER LEENDERTSEN GLEN TO JAN BASTIAENSEN VAN GUDTSENHOVEN]

[367] Appeared before me, Johannes La Montagne, in the service of the general chartered West India Company, admitted by the lord director general and councilors of New Netherland vice director and commissary at Fort Orange and the village of Beverwijck, in the presence of the honorable Philip Pietersen Schuijler and Adriaen

Gerritsen, magistrates of the same court, the honorable Sander Leendersen Glen, who declares to have ceded and conveyed, as he hereby cedes and conveys in real and actual possession, to and for the benefit of Jan Bastiaensen van Gudtsenhoven, his heirs or assigns, his house with the stone gable, which he at present occupies; together with the lot and garden and another little house standing behind the large house; everything in size as it lies within its fence at present, with another barn and lot and another garden behind the said barn, situated on the west side of the street, opposite the said large house; all as it stands within its fence, with everything that is attached by earth and nail, with another two gardens behind Fort Orange, according to the patents thereof, and this for the sum of three thousand two hundred guilders, **[368]** and this to be paid in beavers as a deduction of a promissory note passed by the same Sander Leendersen on the 7th of May *anno* 1661; in such manner, that he, seller of the said sold goods acknowledges to be paid and completely satisfied by the buyer. Further, the seller keeps for himself the small house that is standing opposite the large house, as it was lying in its fence before. The said seller also promises to tear down within the time of a year the small house standing to the north of the large house, and which he keeps for himself, and not to build anything closer to the large house than within the space of nine feet, but that the same can be used as an alley for the convenience of the seller. Further, the grantor promises to free everything from all actions, demands or claims, which may arise hereafter, under pledge of his person and estate, moveable and immoveable, present and future without exception, submitting the same to all laws and judges. Done at Fort Orange the 25th of October *anno* 1662.

Sander Lenrsen Glen
Philip Pietersz Schuijler
Adriaen Gerretsen

Acknowledged by me,
La Montagne, commissary at Fort Orange.

[CONVEYANCE OF A HOUSE AND LOT BY SANDER LEENDERTSEN GLEN TO TOMAS POULUSSEN]

[369] Appeared before me, Johannes La Montagne, in the service of the general chartered West India Company, admitted by the lord director general and councilors of New Netherland vice director and commissary at Fort Orange and the village of Beverwijck, in the presence of the honorable Goossen Gerritsen and Jan Tomassen, magistrates of the same court, the honorable Sander Leendertsen Glen, who declares to have ceded and conveyed, as he hereby cedes and conveys in real and actual possession to and for the benefit of Tomas Poulussen his heirs or assigns, a house and lot located in the village immediately next to *Dom*: Schaets. Adjoins to the south and to the west the street, to the north Jan Bastiaensen. Long to the north ten rods; in front on the road wide two rods and ten feet; to the south long ten rods and eight and a half feet; to the west, along Jan Bastiaensen's fence, wide 5 rods and 3 feet; which lot is a part of the patent granted to him, grantor by the lord director general and councilors of New Netherland on the date the 23rd of April *anno* 1652. And he acknowledges that he has been satisfied and paid for the aforesaid, and therefore he promises to free the same house and lot from all actions, demands, or claims, **[370]** which may arise hereafter, under pledge of his person and estate, moveable and immoveable, present and future without any exception, submitting the same to all lords and judges. Done at Fort Orange the 26th of October *anno* 1662.

Sander Lenrsen Glen
Goosen Gerretsen
Jan Thomas
Acknowledged by me,
La Montagne, commissary at Fort Orange.

Settled with the lords magistrates all conveyances and mortgages that were due to them until this date.

[CONDITIONS FOR FARMING OUT THE BEER, WINE, AND SPIRITS EXCISE]

[371] Conditions and terms upon which the lords commissary and magistrates intend to farm out at public auction, in the name of and on behalf of the honorable director general and councilors of New Netherland, to the highest bidder the excise of all wines, beers, and spirits consumable and to be drawn by the innkeepers, tappers, and retailers in and around Fort Orange, the village of Beverwijck, and the colony of Renselaerswijck.

The farming out as well as the collection of duties shall be done according to the laudable custom of our fatherland, and in accordance with the printed ordinances and placards of the High and Mighty Lords States General, required for the matter of finances.

The farming of the excise shall begin on the first of November, and end on the last of October *anno* 1663, being the time of twelve months, during which time the farmer may collect and receive for all wines, beers, or distilled waters by the tappers and innkeepers to be drawn or consumed in or around Fort Orange, the village of Beverwijck, as follows:

For a barrel of domestic brewed beer	*f*4
For a barrel of overseas beer	*f*6
For a hogshead of French wine	*f*20
For an anker of the same	*f*4
For an anker of Spanish wine, brandy, mead, or distilled waters	*f*7
For an anker of cider	*f*2

[372] larger and smaller containers in proportion, and this in beavers or else in sewant, 12 white or 6 black for one stuiver to the payer's choice. The farmer or bidder shall be obliged to furnish, to the satisfaction of the lords contractors, sufficient sureties for the excise moneys, and every three months to pay a just fourth part of the purchase money in beavers, or else, in sewant at 12 white or 6 black a stuiver.

In order to prevent any quibbling, misunderstanding, and fraud, it is stipulated and agreed that after the expiration of this contract, whenever the farming out shall be renewed, it shall be permitted to the new farmer, on the day of the new farming out, or on the following day, or definitely within the time of three days after the farming has been let, in the presence of the former farmer, if he wishes to be present, to gauge the remainder of the wines, beers or distilled waters kept by the tappers and innkeepers, and two-third of the excise received or due, shall be returned and restored by the former or previous farmer to his successor or old farmer.†

[373] The lords farming supervisors reserve to themselves the interpretation and amplification of this and promise the farmer all proper protection and assistance.

For the above farming Jan Gerritsen van Marcken remained the final bidder for the sum of four thousand guilders according to the aforesaid conditions, for the payment of which Jurriaen Teunissen and Jochim Wessels stood sureties and principals, respectively pledging their persons and estates, moveable and immoveable, present and future without any exception, submitting themselves to all laws and judges. Done in the village of Beverwijck, the last of October *anno* 1662.

J. G. V Marcken
Jure Jan Tunsen
Jochem *Backer*

Today, the last day of October, the above farming was made in our presence according to the aforesaid conditions, which we attest,

La Montagne, commissary
Philip Pietersz Schuijler
Adriaen Gerretsen
Goosen Gerretsen

---

† Original says "old," but it should be "new" — see *FOR* 1: 94.

Acknowledged by me,
Johannes Provoost, clerk.

[374] [*blank*]

[CONDITIONS FOR FARMING OUT THE BURGHER BEER, WINE, AND SPIRITS EXCISE]

[375] Conditions and terms on which the lords commissary and magistrates of Fort Orange and the village of Beverwijck intend to farm out to the highest bidder the burgher wine and beer excise for the time of one year. The farming as well as the collection of duties shall begin on the first of November of this year *anno* 1662, and end on the last of October *anno* 1663, according to the ordinance of our fatherland. The farmer shall receive for a barrel of good beer a daelder, for a barrel of small beer ten stuivers, for a hogshead of French wine six guilders, for an anker of brandy, Spanish wine, or [distilled] waters two guilders at twelve white and six black a stuiver. And the aforesaid farmer shall not deny any certificate to any burgher, indicated on the burgher excise.

The farmer is obliged to furnish two sufficient sureties one for all and each as principals to the satisfaction of those who farm out the excise, in order to pay for the same burgher excise, each quarter year a just quarter part of the entire sum in good strung sewant at 12 white and six [376] black sewant a stuiver. And if the aforesaid farmer fails to furnish the said sureties, the aforesaid farming shall be reauctioned at his cost and charge, and whatever less it comes to be worth, he shall be obliged to make good, and whatever more it comes to be worth, he shall derive no profit from it. Jan Gerritsen van Marcken remained the last bidder and farmer for the above for the sum of two thousand two hundred and twenty guilders, according to the aforesaid condition, and for the payment of the aforesaid sum Jurriaen Teunissen and Jochim Wessels presented themselves as sureties, pledging their persons and estates, moveable and immoveable, present and future without any exception, making themselves subject to all laws and judges. Done in the village of Beverwijck on the last of October *anno* 1662.

J. G.V. Marcken
Jure Jan Tun[sen
Jochem *Backer*

Today, the 31st of October *anno* 1662, the above farming was done in our presence, according to the aforesaid conditions, which we, the undersigned, attest,
La Montagne, commissary
Philip Pietersz Schuijler
Adriaen Gerretsen
Goosen Gerretsen
Acknowledged by me,
Johannes Provoost, clerk.

[SALE OF A HOUSE, LOT AND BARN BY THE ADMINISTRATORS OF THE ESTATE OF ANDRIES HERBERTSEN TO JURRIAEN JANSSEN]

[377] Conditions and terms upon which the administrators of the estate Anderies Herbertsen, together with said Anderies Herbertsen's wife, intend to sell at public auction to the highest bidder the house and lot of the aforesaid A: Herbertsen, with a barn on the same lot, located in the village of Beverwijck, together with all that appertains thereto, as it is occupied by the said wife. First, the aforesaid house and lot, barn, and all that appertains thereto shall be delivered to the buyer as it is fenced in, with everything that is attached by earth and nail, on the first of May *anno* 1663. Payment will take place in two installments in good whole merchantable beaver skins; the first installment on the first of July *anno* 1663, and the second installment on the first of July *anno* 1664. The buyer shall be obliged to furnish two sufficient sureties, one for all and each as principals, to the satisfaction of the sellers, and to do so immediately. If the buyer cannot furnish the aforesaid sureties in the aforesaid time, then the aforesaid house and lot with everything that appertains thereto shall be reauctioned at his cost and charge, and whatever less they come to be worth, he shall be obliged to make good, and whatever more they become worth, he shall derive no profit from it. **[378]** The auction fees shall become a charge to the buyer in payment as before. After offering the property for sale Jurriaen Janssen remained the final bidder for the sum of one thousand three hundred and fifty guilders, for the satisfaction of which Jacob Schermerhoorn and Henderick Janssen Rosenboom stood sureties and principals according to the said conditions (provided that the aforesaid house, lot and barn remain a mortgage and collateral for the relief of said sureties), pledging their persons and estates, moveable and immoveable, making themselves subject to all laws and judges. Done in Beverwijck the 16th of November *anno* 1662.

This is the mark  of Jurriaen Janssen,
made with his own hand
Jacob Jansen Schermerhooren
Henderijck Yansen Rooseboom

Acknowledged by me,
La Montagne, commissary at Fort Orange.

[SALE OF THE TILE WORKS AND LOT BY THE ADMINISTRATORS OF THE ESTATE OF ANDRIES HERBERTSEN TO GERRIT SLICHTENHORST]

[379] Conditions and terms upon which the administrators of the estate Andries Herbertsen, together with the wife of the same, intend to sell at public auction to the highest bidder the tile works and lot of the aforesaid A: Herbertsen located in the colony of Rensselaerswijck. First, the tile works with the lot and all the fixtures will be delivered to the buyer with everything that is attached by earth and nail according to the conveyance and bill of sale thereof, except for a small corner, one board wide, and long to the corner at the south side of Pieter Bont's brick yard, which was sold to the aforesaid Pieter Bont. In addition, Kees Pott, *pannebacker* [tile baker], shall remain contracted for a year to work therein, according to the contract made between him and Anderies Herbertsen, provided that the buyer will annually pay two guilders to the patroon as an ACKNOWLEDGMENT. Delivery shall take place in this current year *anno* 1662, as soon as the goods have been finished off. Payment shall take place in three installments in good whole merchantable beaver skins or half of each installment in sewant at twenty guilders a beaver, of which the first will be on the first of July *anno* 1663; the second on the first of July *anno* 1664, and the third installment on the first of July *anno* 1665.

The buyer shall be obliged to furnish two **[380]** sufficient sureties at once, one for all and each as principals, to the satisfaction of the seller. If the buyer cannot furnish the aforesaid sureties in the aforesaid time, then the aforesaid tile works shall be reauctioned at his cost and charge, and whatever less it comes to be worth, he shall be obliged to make good, and whatever more it becomes worth, he shall derive no profit from it. The auction fees shall become a charge to the buyer. After the auction on the above conditions Gerrit Slichtenhorst remained the final bidder for the sum of one thousand nine hundred guilders, for the satisfaction of which Wouter Albertsen and David Schuijler stood sureties and principals according to the aforesaid conditions, provided that the tile works remain a mortgage and special collateral for the relief of said sureties, pledging their persons and estates, moveable and immoveable, making themselves subject to all laws and judges. Done in Beverwijck the 16th of November *anno* 1662.

Gerrit van Slichtenhorst
Wolter Albers
Davijdt Schuijler
Acknowledged by me,
La Montagne, commissary at Fort Orange.

[SALE OF HALF ISLAND BY THE ADMINISTRATORS OF THE ESTATE OF ANDRIES HERBERTSEN TO JEREMIAS VAN RENSSELAER]

[381] Conditions and terms upon which the administrators of the estate Anderies Herbertsen, together with the wife of the same, intend to sell at public auction to the highest bidder half the island that belongs to him and Rut Jacobsen, located diagonally opposite from Bethlehem. The half island will be delivered to the buyer according to patent with half of the house, barn and two hayricks; the island is sown with 53 *schepels* of winter grain, half of which is the buyer's portion.

Delivery shall occur at once, but the sellers will have the freedom to thresh the wheat there, which at present is in straw. Payment shall take place in two installments in grain at beaver's price, the first installment on the last of November *anno* 1663; the second installment on the last of November *anno* 1664.

The buyer shall be obliged to furnish two sufficient sureties at once, one for all and each as principals, to the satisfaction of the sellers. If the buyer cannot furnish the aforesaid sureties in the aforesaid time, then the aforesaid half island shall be reauctioned at his cost and charge, and whatever less it **[382]** comes to be worth, he shall be obliged to make good, and whatever more it becomes worth, he shall derive no profit from it. The auction fees shall become a charge to the buyer. After the auction of the above the lord Jeremijas van Renselaer remained the final bidder for the sum of one thousand three hundred and eighty-five guilders, for the payment of which *Mr*. Gerrit Swart and Dirrick van Schelluijne stood sureties and principals according to the aforesaid conditions, pledging their persons and estates, moveable and immoveable, making themselves subject to all laws and judges. Done in Beverwijck the 16th of November *anno* 1662.

Jeremias van Rensselaer
G. Swart
D. V. Schelluijne
1662
Acknowledged by me,
La Montagne, commissary at Fort Orange.

[SALE OF A HOUSE AND LOT BY JOCHUM WESSELSZ
TO DAVID SCHUYLER]

[383] Conditions and terms upon which Jochum Wessels intends to sell at public auction to the highest bidder his house and lot located in this village of Beverwijck, formerly belonging to *Monsr*. Boon. First, the aforesaid house and lot will be delivered to the buyer at once, with everything that is attached by earth and nail. The payment will occur in three installments, and this half in sewant, and half in beavers, the sewant figured at twenty guilders a beaver. The first installment shall take place on the first of June *anno* 1663, the second installment a year later, and the third, likewise. With the payment of the last installment a proper conveyance and patent shall be delivered to the buyer. The buyer shall be obliged to furnish two sufficient sureties at once, one for all and each as principals, to the satisfaction of the seller. If the buyer cannot furnish sufficient sureties, then the aforesaid house and lot will be reauctioned at his cost and charge, and whatever less it comes to be worth, he shall be obliged to make good, and whatever more it becomes worth, he shall derive no profit from it. **[384]** The auction fees shall become a charge to the buyer in payment as above. On these above conditions David Schuijler remained the final bidder for the sum of one thousand and seven guilders, for the satisfaction of which Philip Pietersen Schuijler and Gerrit Slichtenhorst stood sureties and principals according to the aforesaid conditions, pledging their persons and estates, moveable and immoveable, submitting themselves to all laws and judges. Done in Beverwijck the 16th of November *anno* 1662.

Davijdt Schuijler
Gerrit Slichtenhorst
Acknowledged by me,
La Montagne, commissary at Fort Orange.

[CONDITIONS FOR THE AUCTION OF A HOUSE IN FORT ORANGE BY JAN BASTIAENSEN]

[385] Conditions and terms upon which Jan Bastiaensen, attorney for the masters of Johannes van Twillert, in the presence of the lord Jeremijas van Rensselaer, intends to sell at public auction to the highest bidder a house located in Fort Orange named the house of Johannes van Twillert, according to the patent thereof, together with a garden behind the said Fort Orange.

The aforesaid house and garden shall be delivered to the buyer at once, as it stands, with everything that is attached by earth and nail.

The payment shall take place in three installments in good whole merchantable beaver skins, of which the first shall be on the first of July *anno* 1663, the second the first of July *anno* 1664, and the third or last installment *anno* 1665.

The buyer shall be obliged to furnish two sufficient sureties one for all and each as principals, to the satisfaction of the seller. If the buyer can [not] furnish sureties, then the aforesaid house and garden shall be reauctioned at his cost and charge, and whatever less it comes to be worth, he shall be obliged to make good, and whatever more it becomes worth, he shall derive no profit from it. The auction fees shall become a charge to the buyer in payment as above. [*not executed*]

[CONDITIONS FOR THE AUCTION OF A HOUSE AND LOT BY DAVID PIETERSEN SCHUYLER]

[386] Conditions and terms upon which David Pietersen Schuijler intends to sell at public auction to the highest bidder his house and lot located in the village of Beverwijck at the hill to the west of Annetien Bogardus.

The aforesaid house and lot shall be delivered to the buyer at once, with everything that is attached by earth and nail, long six rods and three feet; in front on the street wide one rod, and six feet, and eight inches, to the east Sander Leendersen, long six rods and three feet, to the north wide one rod, seven feet and eight inches, according to conveyance, with behind it still a little *hansioos* house, in which are a chimney and baking oven.

The payment shall take place in two installments, and this in good whole merchantable beavers, the first on the first of June of this year *anno* 1663, and the second installment on the first of June *anno* 1664.

The buyer shall be obliged to furnish two sufficient sureties one for all and each as principals, to the satisfaction of the seller. If the buyer cannot furnish the aforesaid sureties, then the aforesaid house and lot will be reauctioned at his cost and charge, and whatever less it comes to be worth, he shall be obliged to make good, and whatever more it becomes worth, he shall derive no profit from it. The auction fees shall become a charge to the buyer in payment as before.
[*not executed*]

[**387**] [*blank*]

[CONDITIONS FOR THE AUCTION OF A HOUSE, LOT, AND TWO GARDENS BY HANS CARELSEN]

[**388**] Conditions and terms upon which Hans Carelsen intends to sell at public auction to the highest bidder his house and lot located in the village of Beverwijck at the bend of the hill on the plain, which he occupies at present. First, the aforesaid house and lot shall be delivered to the buyer, with everything that is attached by earth and nail, on the next first of May, with two gardens with the aforesaid house, of such size as the seller has possessed them. The payment shall take place in two installments, the first installment on the next first of May upon delivery in good whole merchantable sewant at beavers' price, and the second on the first of May *anno* 1664 in good whole merchantable beavers at *f*8 apiece. The buyer shall be obliged to furnish two sufficient sureties at once, one for all and each as principals, to the satisfaction of the seller. If the buyer cannot furnish the aforesaid sureties, then the aforesaid house, lot and two gardens will be reauctioned, and whatever less it comes to be worth, he shall be obliged to make good, and whatever more it becomes worth, he shall derive no profit from it. The auction fees shall become a charge to the buyer in payment as before.
[*not executed*]

[SALE OF COWS BY JAN MARTENSEN
TO GOOSSEN GERRITSEN]

[389] Appeared before me, Johannes La Montagne, in the service of the general chartered West India Company, [admitted] by the lord director general and councilors of New Netherland vice director and commissary at Fort Orange and the village of Beverwijck, Jan Martensen, inhabitant of said village, who declares to have sold to the honorable Goossen Gerrit, magistrate of the aforesaid place, the number of seven head of cattle, large as well as small, for the sum of five hundred and eighty guilders in beavers' payment, for which sum the aforesaid Jan Martensen acknowledges to be fully satisfied and paid. In witness of the truth he, appearer, has signed this with his own hand. Done at Fort Orange on the 15th of March *anno* 1663 in presence of J. Provoost and David Provoost.

This is the mark + of Jan Martensen,
made with his own hand.

Johannes Provoost, witness
David Provoost

Acknowledged by me,
La Montagne, commissary at Fort Orange.

[CONVEYANCE OF A HOUSE AND LOT BY JAN COSTERSEN VAN
AECKEN TO AERNOUT CORNELISSEN]

[390] Appeared before me, Johannes La Montagne, in the service of the general chartered West India Company, admitted by the lord director general and councilors of New Netherland vice director and commissary at Fort Orange and the village of Beverwijck, in the presence of the honorable Goossen Gerritsen and Jan Tomassen, magistrates of the court of the same, the honorable Jan Costersen van Aecken, who declares that he has ceded and conveyed, as he hereby does cede and convey in real and actual possession, to and for the benefit of Aernout Cornelissen, his heirs or assigns, a house and lot located in the village of Beverwijck, to the south Jochim Kettelheijm, long eight rods six feet and three inches, on the road wide two rods and ten feet, to the north, Wijnandt Gerritsen, long six rods, eleven feet, in the back wide three rods ten feet, according to the patent, granted to him, grantor, by the lord director general and councilors of New Netherland, on date of the 7th of March, *anno* 1661, for which **[391]** aforesaid house and lot the grantor acknowledges to have been satisfied and paid. Therefore, he promises to free the same from all actions, claims or demands, which may arise hereafter, pledging his person and estate, moveable and immoveable, present and future without exception, submitting himself to all courts and judges. Done at Fort Orange the 17th of March *anno* 1663.

Jan Koster van Aacken
Goosen Gerretsen
Jan Thomas

[CONVEYANCE OF A CELLAR AND LOT BY ROELOF WILLEMSEN TO GEURT HENDRICKSEN]

[392] Appeared before me Johannes Provoost, clerk of the court of Fort Orange and the village of Beverwijck Roelof Willemsen and Geurt Hendericksen, who in the presence of the witnesses named hereafter, declare that in all friendship and amity, they have agreed, to wit, that the aforesaid Roelof Willemsen hereby acknowledges to have sold to said Geurt Hendericksz his certain cellar with over it a leanto and the lot with it; in size as long and as wide as is stated in the patent thereof; likewise, the aforesaid Geurt Hendericksen accepts, and acknowledges to have bought the same cellar with the lot from the said Roelof Willemsz, for which he promises to pay the sum of two hundred and seventy-five guilders in good strung sewant. Delivery of the aforesaid cellar will take place today at the buyer's risk. Thus done without craft or guile in the presence of Jacob Janssen and David Provoost, as witnesses invited hereto on this 23rd of March *anno* 1663 in Fort Orange.

Roelef Willemsen
Geurt Hendrycksen
Jacob Jansen Floder
David Provoost
Acknowledged by me,
J. Provoost, clerk.

[MARRIAGE AGREEMENT BETWEEN MEYNDERT FREDERICKSZ AND PIETERTIEN TEUNIS]

[393] In the name of the Lord Amen. Be it known by the contents of this present instrument, that in the year sixteen hundred sixty-three, on the 18th day of May, there appeared before me Johannes La Montagne, in the service of the general chartered West India Company, admitted by the lord director general and councilors of New Netherland vice director and commissary at Fort Orange and the village of Beverwijck, Meijndert Fredericksz, widower of the late Catarijna burgher, who, in the presence of the afternamed witnesses, declares that, for the honor of God, he has resolved upon a future marriage with Pietertien Teunis, spinster, and before the bands of the same, he, appearer, has consented to the following conditions: First, that the aforesaid spouses, for the support of this marriage, mutually will bring together all present and such estates and effects, of whatever nature, at whatever place, and with whatever persons the same may lie outstanding and remaining; none of those effects excepted, which they each at present possess, or to which they are each entitled, and which is equitable to be possessed by them in common, according to the law of our fatherland. With the exception that out of the appearer's estate, to wit, of the estate left by Catarijna Burger, deceased, the sum of eight hundred guilders in beaver's payment shall be reserved for the children left by her, **[394]** to wit, Fredrick Meijndersen, six years old, and Burgert Meijndersen, three years old, being their matrimonial inheritance. The aforesaid spouses, however, remain obliged to bring up the aforesaid children in the fear of the Lord, to have them learn reading and writing in the schools, and moreover, to provide for them with food and clothing until their majority or married state, without reduction of their matrimonial and inherited estates. Which aforesaid [marriage conditions] the appearer promises to keep without craft or guile, pledging his person and estate, moveable and immoveable, present and future without exception, subject to all laws and judges. Thus done in presence of the lord Arent van Curler and Jan Dareth and Pieter Bronck, guardians of the aforesaid children, in addition to Jan Verbeeck and Evert Wendel, orphan masters. Dated as above.

This is the mark of  Meijndert Fredericksz,
made with his own hand.
A. van Curler
Jan Dareth
Jan Verbeeck
Evert Janssen Wendel
As orphan masters
Pijeter Bronck
Acknowledged by me,
La Montagne, commissary at Fort Orange.

[SALE OF A LOT BY HARMEN THOMASSEN
TO TJERCK CLAESSEN DE WITT]

[395] Appeared before me, Johannes La Montagne, in the service of the general chartered West India Company, admitted by the lord director general and councilors of New Netherland vice director and commissary at Fort Orange and the village of Beverwijck, in the presence of the honorable Goossen Gerritsen and Jan Thomassen, magistrates of the same court, Harmen Tomassen, husband and guardian of Catarina Bercx, widow of Dirrick Bensingh, deceased, who declares that he has ceded and conveyed, as he hereby does cede and convey to Tjerck Claessen de Wit, his heirs or assigns, a lot located in the village of Beverwijck; adjoins to the south Lambert van Neck, to the north Hans Coenraets, and to the west the street; long ten rods, and wide two rods, three feet; which aforesaid lot the appearer's predecessor received by conveyance from Michiel Rijckertsen on the 29th of April *anno* 1656. And the grantor acknowledges that has been fully satisfied and paid for the purchase and transfer of the same, and therefore he promises to free the same from all actions, demands or claims which may arise hereafter, pledging his person and estate, moveable and immoveable, present and future, submitting himself to all laws and judges. Done at Fort Orange the 28th of May, 1663.

Harman Thomasz
Goosen Gerretsen
Jan Thomasz
Acknowledged by me,
La Montagne, commissary at Fort Orange.

[SALE OF A HOUSE AND LOT BY HARMEN THOMASSEN TO LAMBERT ALBERTSEN VAN NECK]

[396] Appeared before me, Johannes La Montagne, in the service of the general chartered West India Company, admitted by the lord director general and councilors of New Netherland vice director and commissary at Fort Orange and the village of Beverwijck, in the presence of the honorable Goossen Gerritsen and Jan Tomassen, magistrates of the same court, Harmen Tomassen, being husband and guardian of Catarijna Bercx, widow of the late Dirck Bensingh, who declares that he has ceded and conveyed, as he hereby does cede and convey in real and actual possession to and for the benefit of Lambert Albertsen van Neck, his heirs or assigns, a house and lot located in the village of Beverwijck; adjoins to the north Tjerck Claessen, to the south Frans Barentsen; long ten rods, and wide twenty-five or twenty-six feet; which lot is a portion of the patent granted by the lord director general and councilors of New Netherland to Daniel Rinchout on the date of the 25th of October, 1653; he, grantor, acknowledging that he has been fully satisfied and paid for the said house and lot, promising therefore to free the same from all actions, demands or claims which may arise hereafter, pledging his person and estate, moveable and immoveable, present and future, making himself subject to all laws and judges. Done at Fort Orange the 28th of May, 1663.

Harman Thomasz
Goosen Gerretsen
Jan Thomasz

Acknowledged by me,
La Montagne, commissary at Fort Orange.

[SALE OF A LOT BY GILLIS PIETERSEN TO HARMEN TOMASSEN]

[397] Appeared before me, Johannes La Montagne, in the service of the general chartered West India Company, admitted by the lord director general and councilors of New Netherland vice director and commissary at Fort Orange and the village of Beverwijck, in the presence of the honorable Jan Thomassen and Johan Verbeeck, magistrates of the same court, Gillis Pietersen, who declares that he has ceded and conveyed, as he hereby cedes and conveys in real and actual possession to and for the benefit of Harmen Tomassen, husband and guardian of Catarijna Bercx, widow of the late Dirck Bensingh, his heirs or assigns, a lot, located in the village of Beverwijck; adjoins to the south of Evert Janssen Wendel, north and west the street; long on the south side nine and a half rods, and on the north side five rods; wide on the west side seven and a half rods, on the east side eight rods, which lot the grantor received by patent from the lord director general and councilors of New Netherland on date the 14th of April *anno* 1654. And he, appearer, acknowledges that he has been fully satisfied and paid for the purchase of the same, and therefore promises to free the same lot from all actions, demands or claims which may arise hereafter, pledging thereto his person and estate, moveable and immoveable, present and future without exception, making himself subject to all laws and judges. Done at Fort Orange the 28th of May, *anno* 1663.

Jelis Pietersz
Jan Thomasz
Jan Verbeeck
Acknowledged by me,
La Montagne, commissary at Fort Orange.

[SALE OF A LOT BY HARMEN THOMASSEN
TO MARRIETIEN DAMENS]

[398] Appeared before me, Johannes La Montagne, in the service of the general chartered West India Company, admitted by the lord director general and councilors of New Netherland vice director and commissary at Fort Orange and the village of Beverwijck, in the presence of the honorable Jan Verbeeck and Gerrit Slichtenhorst, magistrates of the same court, Harmen Tomassen, husband and guardian of Catarina Bercx, widow of Dirrick Bensingh, deceased, who declares that he has ceded and conveyed, as he hereby cedes and conveys in real and actual possession, to and for the benefit of Maritien Damens, widow of the late Henderick Anderiessen, her heirs or assigns a lot located in the village of Beverwijck; in length south of the lots, nine rods, nine feet six inches, to the north the grantor, long seven rods, eight feet, to the east Tjerck Claessen wide three rods, to the west the road, wide three rods; which lot is a portion of the patent by the lord director general and councilors of New Netherland granted to Gillis Pietersen on date the 14th of April *anno* 1654. And he, grantor, acknowledges that he has been fully paid and satisfied for the purchase of the said lot, and therefore he promises to free the aforesaid lot from all actions, demands or claims which may arise hereafter, pledging there for his person and estate, moveable and immoveable, present and future, submitting himself to all laws and judges. Done at Fort Orange the 29th of May, *anno* 1663.

Harman Thomasz
Jan Verbeeck
Gerrit Slichtenhorst

Acknowledged by me,
La Montagne, commissary at Fort Orange.

[CONDITIONS FOR THE AUCTION OF A HOUSE AND LOT BY THE HEIRS OF ANNETIEN BOGARDUS, DECEASED]

[399] Conditions and terms upon which the heirs of Annetien Bogardus, deceased, intend to sell at public auction to the highest bidder her house and lot located in the village of Beverwijck at the hill.

First, the aforesaid house, with a side aisle on the east side and a chicken coop on the place, and the lot belonging thereto shall be delivered to the buyer with the first payment. To the west [the lot] with the house is long five rods, nine feet, and to the east 5 rods, 8½ feet, wide to the north, 2 rods, 8½ feet, and to the south wide 2 rods, 7 feet, with everything that is attached by earth and nail, with the exception of the little lean-to that is standing on the west side of the aforesaid house, and the little Indian house to the east, which will remain with the little Indian house, for the benefit of Jonas and Pieter Bogardus. Payment shall take place in good whole merchantable beaver skins at *f*8 apiece, and this in three installments; the first installment on the first of August of this year *anno* 1663, the second on first of July *anno* 1664, and the third or final installment on the first of July *anno* 1665, each time a just third part of the entire sum, provided that the aforesaid house and lot will remain a mortgage and collateral to recover the full payment. **[400]** The buyer shall be obliged to furnish two sufficient sureties at once, one for all and each as principals, at most within the time of 24 hours to the satisfaction of the sellers. If the buyer cannot furnish the aforesaid sureties within the aforesaid time, then the aforesaid house and lot will be reauctioned at his cost and charge, and whatever less it comes to be worth, he shall be obliged to make good, and whatever more it becomes worth, he shall derive no profit from it. The auction fees shall become a charge to the buyer, the kind of payment as before. [*not executed*]

[CONVEYANCE OF A HOUSE AND LOT BY THE HEIRS OF ANNETIEN BOGARDUS TO DIRCK WESSELSZ TEN BROECK]

[401] Appeared before me, Johannes Provoost, clerk of the court of Fort Orange and the village of Beverwijck, the heirs of the late Annetien Bogardus, on the one side and Dirrick Wesselsen on the other side, who in the presence of the afternamed witnesses declare that in all friendship and amity they have contracted and agreed with each other, namely, that the aforesaid heirs (being the children left by the aforesaid Annetien Bogardus, deceased) have sold to said Dirrick Wesselsen, as they hereby do, their late mother's house and lot located in the village of Beverwijck; adjoins to the east Jonas and Pieter Bogardus, and to the west Evert Janssen Wendel, [being] the same [house and lot] that she has occupied until the day of her death. Long to the west, together with the house, five rods, nine feet, and to the east 5 rods and 8½ feet, wide to the north two rods 8½ feet, and to the south wide 2 rods 7 feet; with still a leanto on the east of the same house, which has been rented out for about three months until the date of this purchase, which rent shall be to the benefit of the buyer. For which house and lot said Dirrick Wesselsen as buyer promises to pay the sum of one thousand guilders, to be paid in good whole merchantable beaver skins at *f*8 apiece, and this in three installments; the first installment at once, the second installment on the first of July *anno* 1664, and the third or final payment on the first of July *anno* 1665, each time a just third part of the entire sum. The aforesaid house and lot shall be delivered to the buyer upon the first payment, **[402]** and meanwhile the aforesaid house shall be occupied at his risk. With the final payment the buyer will be given a proper conveyance, as well. The parties promise to mutually hold the above for good and true, under pledge according to law. Done in Beverwijck in the presence of Wouter Albertsen and David Provoost as witnesses requested hereto on this 21st of June *anno* 1663.

P. Bogardus
Jan Roeloffs
Cornelis Bogardus, by order of the other heirs
Dirck Wesselsz ten Broeck
Wouter Alberts
David Provoost

Acknowledged by me,
Johannes Provoost, clerk.

[CONDITIONS FOR THE SALE OF WHEAT BY THE ADMINISTRATORS OF THE ESTATE OF ANDRIES HERBERTSEN AND RUT JACOBSEN]

[403] Conditions and terms upon which the administrators of the estate of Anderies Herbertsen together with Rut Jacobsen intend to sell at public auction to the highest bidder all the grain that is standing and that has been sown on their island (located diagonally opposite from Bethlehem). The aforesaid grain will be delivered to the buyer at once, [the island] being completely seeded with 53 schepels of winter grain, 8 schepels of which is rye, the remainder all wheat, which the buyer will be allowed to harvest and gather in the barn and hay barrack presently standing there. The buyer shall also allow (at the end of the harvest) that two men, who will plow and sow the land again, lodge there in the house with their luggage. Payment shall occur on the 15th of January *anno* 1664 in beavers or grain at beaver's price, within which time he, buyer will be obliged to clear [the land], and depart with his purchased grain, whether threshed out or not.

The buyer shall be obliged to furnish two sufficient sureties at once, one for all and each as principals, to the satisfaction of the sellers. If the buyer cannot furnish the aforesaid sureties in the aforesaid time, then the aforesaid grain will be reauctioned at his cost and charge, and whatever less it comes to be worth, he shall be obliged to make good, and whatever more it becomes worth, he shall derive no profit from it. [*not executed*]

[404] [*blank*]

[SALE OF THE HALF ISLAND OF ANDRIES HERBERTSEN AND RUTGER JACOBSEN TO VOLCKERT JANSSEN]

[405] Conditions and terms upon which the administrators of the estate of Anderies Herbertsen intend to sell at public auction to the highest bidder the half island belonging to him, Herbertsen and Rutger Jacobsen in partnership except for the grain presently standing there. The aforesaid half island will be delivered to the buyer as soon as the grain, presently standing there, has been harvested, in order to then plow it properly, and this in such ownership, right and title as the said Anderies Herbertsen has therein, according to the purport and contents of the patent granted to him by the lord director general and councilors of New Netherland. The seller shall allow the buyers of the grain that presently is standing on the island, to store and keep their grain in the barn and hay barrack there at their convenience, and to thresh it out according to their contract, and this until the 15th of January *anno* 1664. The buyer shall be obliged to pay his promised purchase money in good whole merchantable beavers or grain at beaver's price, and this in two installments; the first installment on the first of July *anno* 1664, and the second installment on the first of July *anno* 1665. The buyer shall be obliged to furnish two sufficient sureties within the time of 24 hours, one for all and each as principals, to the satisfaction of the seller. **[406]** If the buyer cannot furnish the aforesaid sureties in the aforesaid time, then the aforesaid half island will be reauctioned at his cost and charge, and whatever less it comes to be worth, he shall be obliged to make good, and whatever more it becomes worth, he shall derive no profit from it. The auction fees shall become a charge to the buyer in payment as before.

After the auctioning of the above Volckert Janssen remained the final bidder for the sum of six hundred and twenty guilders, for the payment of which Adriaen Gerritsen and Jan Thomassen stood sureties and principals, pledging their persons and estates, moveable and immoveable, present and future, making themselves subject to all laws and judges. Done in Beverwijck, the 26th of June *anno* 1663.

Volckart Jansz
Adriaen Gerretsen
Jan Thomasz

La Montagne, commissary at Fort Orange.

[AUCTION OF WHEAT BY THE ADMINSTRATORS OF ANDRIES HERBERTSEN'S ESTATE AND RUTGER JACOBSEN]

[407] Conditions and terms upon which the administrators of Anderies Herbertsen's estate together with Rutger Jacobsen intend to sell at public auction to the highest bidder all the grain standing and sown on their island, located diagonally opposite Bethlehem. The aforesaid grain will be delivered to the buyer at once, [the island] being completely seeded with 53 schepels of winter grain, to wit, 45 schepels of wheat and 8 schepels of rye, which the buyer will be allowed to harvest and gather in the barn and hay barrack presently standing there. The buyer shall be obliged to pay the promised purchase money on the 15th of January *anno* 1664, and this in payment of good whole merchantable beaver skins or wheat at beaver's price. The buyer shall also be obliged to furnish two sufficient sureties at once, one for all and each as principals, to the satisfaction of the sellers. If the buyer cannot furnish the said sureties within the said time, then the aforesaid grain will be reauctioned at his cost and charge, and whatever less it comes to be worth, he shall be obliged to make good, and whatever more it becomes worth, he shall derive no profit from it. The auction fees shall become a charge to the buyer in payment as before. **[408]** After the auctioning of the above Rutger Jacobsen remained the last bidder and buyer for the sum of five hundred and ninety guilders, pledging his person and estate, moveable and immoveable, making himself subject to all laws and judges. Done in Beverwijck, the 26th of June *anno* 1663.

Rutger Jacobsz

Today, the 28th of July 1663 there appeared before me, Johannes La Montagne, in the service of the general chartered West India Company, vice director and commissary at Fort Orange, Jan Anderiesz and Anderies Hanssen van Sweeden, who stood sureties and principals for the person of Rutger Jacobsen for the payment of half of the above mentioned sum of five hundred and ninety guilders on account of the purchase of the said grain of Anderies Herbertsen, said half being two hundred and ninety-five guilders, which they, sureties, accept and promise to pay to the administrators of said Anderies Herbertsen's estate mentioned above, in grain from the crop presently standing thereupon; and they are not allowed to remove any grain from there before the said administrators have been fully paid therefor, pledging their persons and estates, moveable [and immoveable], present and future, submitting themselves to all laws and judges. Done in Fort Orange, as above.

This is the mark of  Jan Anderiessen,
made with his own hand
This is the mark  of Anderies Hanssen,
made with his own hand
J. Provoost, witness

[SALE OF A HOUSE AND LOT BY JAN LAMBERTSEN VAN BREEMEN TO PIETER JANSSEN *DE BOER*]

[409] Appeared before me, Johannes La Montagne, in the service of the general chartered West India Company, admitted by the lord director general and councilors of New Netherland vice director and commissary at Fort Orange and the village of Beverwijck, in the presence of the honorable Francoijs Boon, Jan Tomassen, Stoffel Janssen, magistrates of the same court, Jan Lambertsen van Breemen, who declares to have ceded and conveyed, as he hereby does, in real and actual possession to and for the benefit of Pieter Janssen *de Boer*, his heirs or assigns, a house and a lot, located in the village of Beverwijck; adjoins, according to the patent, to the east *Meester* Jacob, long six rods, to the west Jan van Breemen, long six rods, and to the north the road, wide three rods, to the south, the plain, wide three rods, which patent was granted to him, grantor, by the lord director general and councilors of New Netherland on the last of April *anno* 1663. For which house and lot he, grantor, acknowledges to have had satisfaction, and therefore he promises to free it from all demands, claims or pretensions, which may arise hereafter, pledging thereto his person and estate, moveable and immoveable, making himself subject to all laws and judges. Done at Fort Orange the 29th of June *anno* 1663.

This is the mark of Jan Lambertsen van Breemen,
made with his own hand.
Jan Thomasz

Stoffel Jansz

Acknowledged by me,
La Montagne, commissary at Fort Orange.

[410] [*blank*]

[MARRIAGE AGREEMENT BETWEEN EVERT JANSSEN WENDEL AND MARIA ABRAHAMS]

[411] In the name of the Lord Amen. Be it known by the contents of this present instrument, that in the year sixteen hundred sixty-three, on the xxxth of June, appeared before me Johannes La Montagne, in the service of the general chartered West India Company, admitted by the lord director general and councilors of New Netherland vice director and commissary at Fort Orange and the village of Beverwijck, the honorable Evert Janssen Wendel, former magistrate of this place, widower of the late Susanna de Truwe, who, in the presence of the afternamed witnesses and the honorable Jan Verbeeck, magistrate and orphan master, declares that, for the honor of God, he has resolved upon a future marriage with Maria Abrahams, widow of the late Tomas Janssen Mingael, and before the bands of the same, he, appearer, has consented to the following conditions: First, that the aforesaid spouses, for the support of this marriage, mutually shall collect and bring together all present and such estates and effects, of whatever nature, at whatever place, and with whatever persons the same may lie outstanding and remaining; none of those effects excepted, which they each possess, or to which they are each entitled, and which is equitable to be possessed by them in common, according to the law of our fatherland. With the exception that from the appearer's estate, to wit, from the estate left by Susanna de Truwe, deceased, the sum of a thousand guilders at beaver's price shall be reserved for the six children left by her, namely: Elsien Wendels 16 years old, Johannes Wendel 14 years old, Diewer Wendel 10 years old, Jeronimus Wendel 8 years old, Philip Wendel five years old, and Evert Wendel 3 years old, being their matrimonial **[412]** inheritance. For this purpose he, appearer, for the satisfaction of the same not only assigns the aforesaid sum upon his house and lot, but he pledges the same as a special mortgage and collateral, in order to recover, if necessary, satisfaction of said sum. For this purpose the said appearer appoints as guardians the honorable Isaack Foreest and Symon Symonsen Groot, uncles of the aforesaid children on their late mother's side. Meanwhile, the aforesaid spouses, however, shall be obliged to bring up the aforesaid children in the fear of the Lord, to have them learn reading and writing in the school, and moreover, to provide for them with food and clothing until their majority and married state, without reduction of their matrimonial and inherited estate. Which marriage conditions the aforesaid appearer promises to keep without craft or guile, pledging his person and estate, moveable and immoveable, present and future without exception, subjecting himself to all laws and judges. Thus done in presence of Adriaen Gerritsen, former magistrate and Johannes Provoost, as witnesses requested hereto, on date as above.

Evert Jansz Wendel
Jan Verbeeck
Adriaen Gerretsen
Johannes Provoost, witness
Acknowledged before me,
La Montagne, commissary at Fort Orange.

[ACKNOWLEDGMENT OF DEBT BY ARENT ISAACKSZ VAN HOECK TO PHILIP HENDERICKSZ]

[413] Appeared before me, Johannes la Montagne, in the service of the general chartered West India Company, admitted by the lord director general and councilors of New Netherland vice director and commissary at Fort Orange and the village of Beverwijck, in the presence of the honorable Jan Verbeeck and Stoffel Janssen, magistrates of the same court, Arent Isaacksz van Hoeck, burgher of the aforesaid village, who hereby acknowledges and declares to be honestly and truly indebted to Philip Hendericksz, inhabitant of Schanhechtade, for the sum of four hundred guilders, which aforesaid sum he, appearer, promises to pay in good whole merchantable beaver skins in the month of July *anno* 1664, with its interest of ten percent, beginning on this date. For which he, appearer, pledges his person and goods, moveable and immoveable, present and future, especially his, appearer's, house and lot, situated in the village of Beverwijck, immediately next to Philip

Pietersen's house, being the same house that the appearer bought from said Philip Hendericksz, and which he pledges as a mortgage and special collateral, in order, if necessary, to recover the payment of the aforesaid four hundred guilders without damage or cost. Done at Fort Orange the 6th of July *anno* 1663.

Arent Isacks van Hoeck

[ACKNOWLEDGMENT OF DEBT BY TEUNIS CORNELISSEN SLINGERLANDT TO JERONIMUS EBBINCK]

[414] Appeared before me, Johannes Provoost, clerk of the court of Fort Orange and village of Beverwijck, Teunis Cornelissen Slingerlandt, inhabitant of said village, who acknowledges and declares in the presence of the afternamed witnesses, to be honestly and truly indebted to *Sr.* Jeronimus Ebbinck, merchant at Amsterdam in New Netherland, for the sum of one hundred and seventy guilders and twelve stuivers in payment of good whole merchantable beaver skins; which aforesaid sum he, appearer, not only assigns, but fully cedes and conveys over upon the second payment for his house, bought by Antony den Milt, also dwelling at Amsterdam in New Netherland in the same house, and from whom the subscriber should receive it in June *anno* 1664, when the time of payment will expire; for which the said Milt will make correct payment, which he, above anyone else, is preferred to receive. Whereto he pledges his person and estate, moveable and immoveable, present and future without exception, making himself subject to all laws and judges. Done at Fort Orange the 21st of July *anno* 1663.

Tuenyes Cornelis Slyenghe[rlant]
This is the mark of  Arent vanden Bergh,
made with his own hand.
This is the mark  of Rijck Rutgersen,
made with his own hand.

Acknowledged by me,
J. Provoost, clerk.

[ACKNOWLEDGMENT OF DEBT BY LEENDERT PHILIPSEN TO JOHANNES VAN DER MEULEN]

[415] Appeared before me, Johannes La Montagne, in the service of the general chartered West India Company, admitted by the lord director general and councilors of New Netherland vice director and commissary at Fort Orange and the village of Beverwijck, in the presence of the honorable Jan Verbeeck and Gerrit Slichtenhorst, magistrates of the same court, Leendert Philipsen, inhabitant of the said village, who acknowledges and declares to be honestly and truly indebted to *Sr.* Johannes van der Meulen, merchant at Amsterdam in New Netherland, for the sum of twelve hundred and two guilders in good whole merchantable beaver skins at *f*8 apiece, stemming from goods and merchandise delivered, which he has received to his content out of the hands of Isaack de Haen; which aforesaid sum he promises to pay in this trading season *anno* 1663. For the satisfaction of which he, appearer, pledges as a mortgage and special collateral his house and lot, located in the village of Beverwijck, which he presently occupies. Moreover, to secure the payment of the aforesaid sum of one thousand two hundred guilders in beavers without cost of damage, [he pledges] his person and estate, moveable and immoveable, present and future without exception. Thus done at Fort Orange, the 27th of July *anno* 1663.

Leendert Pylypse
Jan Verbeeck
Gerrit van Slichtenhorst
Acknowledged by me,
La Montagne, commissary at Fort Orange.

[POWER OF ATTORNEY FROM GEERTRUY BARENTS VAN DWINGELOO TO PIETER CLAERBOUT AND WOUTER ALBERTSEN]

[416] Appeared before me, Johannes Provoost, clerk of the court of Fort Orange and village of Beverwijck, Geertruij Barents van Dwingeloo, at present being about to depart for *patria*, who in the presence of the afternamed witnesses declares to appoint and empower, as she hereby does, Pieter Claerbout and Wouter Albertsen, burghers here, in her, appearer's name and on her behalf, to collect, demand and receive here in Fort Orange in New Netherland such outstanding debts as are due to her according to the existing writings and evidences thereof, to issue quittance of the receipts, and in case of unwillingness, to demand payment by law and rigor of justice, observing all terms of the law thereto, including, if necessary, sentence and extreme execution. In case of arrest, to proceed against persons and estates, and moreover, to do everything that her attorneys will judge advisable; promising to accept everything that the attorneys shall have done in the aforesaid matter, provided that the attorneys shall be obliged to render proper accounts of their transactions and receipts. Thus done in Fort Orange in the presence of Willem de La Montagne and Carsten Carstensz, as witnesses requested hereto on this 4th of August *anno* 1663.

This is the mark  of Geertruij Barents,
made with her own hand.

Willem de La Montagne

This is the mark  of Carsten Carstensen.
Acknowledged by me,
Johannes Provoost, clerk.

[MORTGAGE OF A HOUSE AND LOT BY GEERTRUY BARENTS AND JACOB HEVICK]

[417] Appeared before me, Johannes La Montagne, in the service of the general chartered West India Company, admitted by the lord director general and councilors of New Netherland vice director and commissary at Fort Orange and the village of Beverwijck, in the presence of the honorable Goossen Gerritsen and Jan Tomassen, magistrates of the same court, Geertruij Barents van Dwingeloo, assisted by Jacob Hevick, her husband and guardian, presently being about to depart for *patria*, who declares, as she hereby does, that she mortgages and pledges her house and lot located in the village of

Beverwijck, to secure payment stemming from a certain hundred good whole merchantable beaver skins at *f*8 apiece, which she has assigned to the two children left by Henderick Hendericksz van Harstenhorst, her husband, deceased, 6 weeks after her said late husband's death. She, appearer, does this at the desire of Pieter Claerbout and Wouter Albertsen, being guardians of the said children, and no less persuaded thereto by the orphan master; and therefore she, appearer, promises to secure the said hundred beavers in the fatherland, and, as a discharge hereof, to bring or send proper evidence of where, and in which security the aforesaid number of beavers or the value of the same, are secured, pledging, in her capacity, **[418]** her estate, moveable and immoveable, present and future, with no exception, making herself subject to all laws and judges. Thus done in Fort Orange in New Netherland, the 4th of August *anno* 1663.

This is the mark of  Jacob Hevick,
made with his own hand.
Pieter Claerboudt Gerttruet Barens
as guardian
Wouter Albers

[CONVEYANCE OF A HOUSE AND LOT BY CORNELIS CORNELISZ DE BOER TO JAN HENDERICKSZ DE BRUYN]

[419] Appeared before me Johannes Provoost, clerk of the court of Fort Orange and the village of Beverwijck, and in the presence of the afternamed witnesses, Cornelis Cornelissen *de boer* and Jan Hendericksz Bruijn, who declare that they have, in all friendship and amity, contracted and agreed with each other, to wit, that the aforesaid Cornelis Cornelissen *de boer* sells to said Jan Hendericksz Bruijn, as he hereby does, his house and lot located in the village of Beverwijck, adjoining to the west Barent van Marle and to the east Dirrick Janssen Kroon in such possession, magnitude and boundaries as he has received it from Pieter *de Maker*, according to the tenor of the conveyance received from him, for which the said Jan Hendericksz Bruijn promises to pay the sum of one thousand two hundred and twenty-four guilders to be paid in good whole merchantable beaver skins, and this in two installments. The first, on the last of July *anno* 1664, and the second installment on the last of July *anno* 1665, for the performance of which the parties pledge their persons and estates, moveable and immoveable. Thus done without craft or guile in the presence of Pieter van Alen and Lowies Cobussen as witnesses requested hereto on this 9th of August *anno* 1663 in Fort Orange.

Cornelis Cornelisse de boer
Jan Henderick Bruyns
Pieter van Alen
Ludovicus Cobes
Acknowledged by me,
Johannes Provoost, clerk.

[POWER OF ATTORNEY FROM CORNELIS CORNELISSEN *DE BOER* TO HANS HENDERICKSZ AND PIETER VAN ALEN]

[420] Appeared before me Johannes Provoost, clerk of the court of Fort Orange and the village of Beverwijck, and in the presence of the afternamed witnesses, Cornelis Cornelissen *de boer*, who declares to appoint and empower as he hereby does appoint and empower Hans Hendericksz and Pieter van Alen, in his name and for his benefit to collect, demand, and receive such outstanding debts and moneys as are due to him, appointer, here at Fort Orange in New Netherland, according to the writings and evidences serving thereto; to issue quittance of the receipts, and in case of unwillingness, to demand payment by law and rigor of justice, observing all terms of the law for final sentence and extreme execution thereto, including, in case of arrest, to proceed against persons and estates, and moreover, to do everything that they, attorneys, will judge advisable and reasonable, provided that the attorneys shall be obliged to bring proper statement and account of their transactions and receipts, he, appointer, promising to accept everything that they shall have done in his case. Thus done in Fort Orange in the presence of Captain Abraham Staets and Arent van den Bergh, as witnesses requested hereto on this 16th of August *anno* 1663.

Cornelis Cornelisse de boer
Abram Staas
This is the mark  of Arent van den Bergh,
made with his own hand.
Acknowledged by me,
J. Provoost, clerk.

[ACKNOWLEDGMENT OF DEBT BY TEUNIS CORNELISSEN SLINGERLANDT]

[421] Appeared before me, Johannes La Montagne, in the service of the general chartered West India Company, admitted by the lord director general and councilors of New Netherland vice director and commissary at Fort Orange and the village of Beverwijck, in the presence of the honorable Francoijs Boon and Goossen Gerritsz, magistrates of the same court, Teunis Cornelissen Slingerlandt, who hereby acknowledges and declares to be honestly and truly indebted to the honorable Pieter Dirricksz, merchant, dwelling at Amsterdam, for the sum of five hundred and sixty-one guilders and fourteen stuivers for goods and merchandise received to his content, which aforesaid sum he, appearer, promises to pay to the aforesaid Pieter Dirricksz or to his attorney, *Sr.* Nicolaes Meijer, merchant as well, and this in good whole merchantable beaver skins in two installments; the first in the month of July *anno* 1664, the just half, and the second installment in the month of July, *anno* 1665, for the satisfaction of the aforesaid sum he, the appearer, places as fixed mortgage and special collateral his house and lot together with a small house next to the same house, located in the village of Beverwijck, which he presently occupies, in order, if necessary, to recover the payment of the aforesaid sum of five hundred and sixty-one guilders and fourteen stuivers without damage or cost. Done at Fort Orange the 27th of August *anno* 1663.

Tuenijes Cornelis Slyengherlant
Francoijs Boon
Goosen Gerretsen
Acknowledged by me,
La Montagne, commissary at Fort Orange.

[SALE OF A GARDEN BY LEENDERT PHILIPSEN TO NICOLAES MEYER]

[422] Appeared before me, Johannes La Montagne, in the service of the general chartered West India Company, admitted by the lord director general and councilors of New Netherland vice director and commissary at Fort Orange and the village of Beverwijck, in the presence of the honorable Jan Verbeeck and Gerrit Slichtenhorst, magistrates of the same court, Leendert Philipsen, inhabitant of the aforesaid village, who declares to have ceded and conveyed, as he hereby cedes and conveys in real and actual possession to and for the benefit of *Sr.* Nicolaes Meijer, merchant at Amsterdam in New Netherland, his heirs or assigns, a garden located in the aforesaid village; to the west the basin of the river, to the east the street, to the south Pieter Bronck, to the north of the street, as well.† [It is] of such magnitude as it presently lies in its fence, and within a short time it shall be measured by the surveyor, as the garden has been reduced, which garden was acquired by the grantor by conveyance from Anderies Herbertsen, who was granted the same by virtue of a patent from the lord director general and councilors of New Netherland on date 23 April, *anno* 1652. He, appearer, acknowledges to have been fully satisfied and paid for the garden with the number of fifteen beaver skins, and thus he promises to free the same from all demands, or claims which may arise hereafter, **[423]** pledging therefor his person and estate, moveable and immoveable, present and future, submitting himself to all laws and judges. Done at Fort Orange the 27th of August *anno* 1663.

Leendert Phyles
Jan Verbeeck
Gerrit Slichtenhorst

Acknowledged by me,
La Montagne, commissary at Fort Orange

---

† As the river would have been to the east side of the garden, it is possible that upon recording the information all directions were reversed. Accordingly, it would have been as follows: "to the west of the basin of the river, to the east of the street, to the south of Pieter Bronck, and to the north of the street, as well."

[ACKNOWLEDGMENT OF DEBT BY TEUNIS CORNELISSEN SLINGERLANDT TO PIETER RENS KRAMER]

Appeared before me Johannes Provoost, clerk of the court of Fort Orange and the village of Beverwijck, and in the presence of the afternamed witnesses, Teunis Cornelissen Slingerlandt, inhabitant of the said village, who acknowledges and declares to be honestly and truly indebted to Pieter Rens, peddler, dwelling at Amsterdam, for the sum of two hundred and eighty Carolus guilders, according to agreement made between the appearer and *Sr.* Nicolaes Meijer, merchant at Amsterdam in New Netherland, attorney for the said Rens, stemming from goods and merchandise brought by him, appearer, from him, Rens, on bottomry from Holland, of which the main sum is *f*330, the bottomry, *f*78, and its interest *f*48; which aforesaid sum of two hundred and eighty guilders, to which they agreed, he, appearer, promises to pay to the aforesaid Rens or his attorney in good whole merchantable beaver skins, and this in two installments; the first in the month of July *anno* 1665, **[424]** and the second installment in the month of July *anno* 1666, for which he pledges his person and estate, moveable and immoveable, present and future without exception, making himself subject to all laws and judges. Thus done and passed at Fort Orange in New Netherland in the presence of...[*not executed*]

[POWER OF ATTORNEY BY JAN CORNELISSEN VAN DER HEIJDEN TO CORNELIS JACOBSEN VAN DER HEIJDEN]

[425] Appeared before me, Johannes La Montagne, in the service of the general chartered West India Company, admitted by the lord director general and councilors of New Netherland vice director and commissary at Fort Orange and the village of Beverwijck in New Netherland, and in the presence of the honorable lords Francoijs Boon and Jan Verbeeck, magistrates of the same court, the honorable Jan Cornelissen van der Heijden, inhabitant here, who declares to have appointed and empowered, as he hereby does empower and appoint, his father Cornelis Jacobsen van der Heijden, dwelling at Sevenbergen in Brabant, especially to collect, demand, and receive out of the hands of the heirs of his uncle and guardian, the late Jacob van Duren, such goods, inheritance and estate as is coming to him on account of the death of his grandmother, deceased, Neeltien Block, from his mother Sara Janssen van Duren, and his brother deceased, Jacob Cornelissen van der Heijden, whether by virtue of will or *ab in testato;* for this purpose, to demand condition and inventory of the estate, to approve of the same, or, if necessary, to verify it; and to give quittance for the receipt of his rightful and hereditary portion; and in case of unwillingness (which is not hoped for), to demand the same by means and ways of justice; for this purpose, to observe all terms of justice to reach sentence and extreme execution, including powers to agree, compromise and **[426]** compound; also, if necessary, to have one or more persons substitute for him; and moreover, to do, perform and execute everything necessary and that he thinks advisable, promising at all times to accept everything that his father as his attorney, or his substitute, shall have done or performed in this matter, without any opposition, under pledge according to law thereto provided. Done in Fort Orange in New Netherland, the 3rd of September *anno* 1663.

Jan Cornelisz van der Heijden
Francoijs Boon
Acknowledged by me,
La Montagne, commissary at Fort Orange.

[CONVEYANCE OF A HOUSE AND LOT BY WILLEM JANSSEN SCHUT TO CORNELIS BOGARDUS]

[427] Appeared before me, Johannes La Montagne, in the service of the general chartered West India Company, [admitted] by the lord director general and councilors of New Netherland vice director and commissary at Fort Orange and the village of Beverwijck, in the presence of the honorable Jan Tomassen and Jan Verbeeck, magistrates of the same court, Willem Janssen Schut, who declares that he has ceded and conveyed, as he hereby cedes and conveys in real and actual possession to and for the benefit of Cornelis Bogardus, his heirs or assigns, a house and lot located in the village of Beverwijck; adjoins on the westerly side the house and lot of Anderies Herbertsen, present owner Jurriaen Janssen, on the northerly side the public road, on the easterly side Jacob Loockerman, and on the southerly side the garden of said Jurriaen Janssen. The lot is of such size as at present it is lying in its fence, according to the aforesaid boundaries; which said house is standing on the lot, bought by the seller from the said Anderies Herbertsen, being a portion of the patent granted to him, Herbertsen, by the lord director general and councilors of New Netherland on date [blank], for which house and lot the grantor acknowledges to be fully satisfied and paid with the sum of eighty good whole merchantable beaver skins at eight guilders apiece, and that by a draft as a part payment of what he, grantor, owes Johannes Withart; therefore he **[428]** promises to free the same from all actions, claims and demands which hereafter may arise, pledging thereto his person and estate, moveable and immoveable, present and future, submitting himself to all laws and judges. Done in Beverwijck, the 11th of September *anno* 1663.

Willem Janssen Schut

As besides the aforesaid sum of eighty beavers there are still differences about other outstanding accounts between them, to wit, between J. Withart and Willem Janssen Schut, these remain the way they are. Dated the 11th of September *anno* 1663, in Beverwijck.

Willem Janssen Schuet
Jan Jansen, attorney for Joan Withart.

[POWER OF ATTORNEY FROM RUTGER JACOBSEN TO TEUNIS CORNELISSEN SPITSBERGEN AND JACOB HEVICK]

[429] Appeared before me Johannes Provoost, clerk of the court of Fort Orange and the village of Beverwijck and in the presence of the afternamed witnesses, Rutger Jacobsen, at present being about to depart for the Manhatans, who declares that he has appointed and empowered, as he hereby does, Teunis Cornelissen Spitsbergen and Jacob Hevick, in his, appointer's name and on his behalf, to sell to the highest bidder at public auction his, appointer's, half island, named Constapel's island; thus to do and act in this matter as he, appointer, being present, could or might do, he, appointer, promising to accept everything that the attorneys will do and perform in the matter of the aforesaid sale, provided that they render proper statement and evidence of their transactions. Thus done in Fort Orange in the presence of Rijck Rutgersen as witness requested hereto on this 12th of September *anno* 1663.

Rutger Jacobsz
This is the mark of + Rijck Rutgersen made with his own hand.
Acknowledged by me,
J. Provoost, clerk.

[430] [*blank*]

[CONDITIONS FOR THE SALE OF THE SLAUGHTER EXCISE]

[431] Conditions and terms upon which the lord commissary and magistrates of Fort Orange and the village of Beverwijck intend to farm out at public auction to the highest bidder the slaughter excise for the period of one year.

The farming of the aforesaid slaughter excise shall begin on the first of October of this year and end on the last of September *anno* 1664. The farmer shall receive for the slaughtered animals, whether it will be an ox, cow, calf, bull, hog, goat or sheep, a stuiver for each guilder of the value of the same, to wit, whatever has been bought for beavers will bring 20 stuivers in sewant for one beaver, and in case of dispute, to be valued by impartial persons. The farmer is obligated to furnish, to the satisfaction of the lords farming supervisors, two sufficient sureties for the excise money, and within the time of six weeks to pay the just half of the promised excise money, and the other half with the two last quarter years, each quarter year one fourth portion of the entire sum, and that in good merchantable sewant. If the farmer cannot provide sufficient sureties, it shall be reauctioned at his costs and charges; and all that it falls short, he shall be obligated to make good, and whatever it brings more, he shall derive no profit therefrom.

[432] On the above conditions Henderick Roosenboom remained the final bidder and farmer for the sum of seven hundred and ninety guilders according to the aforesaid condition, for the payment of which sum

Philip Pietersen Schuijler and Wouter Albertsen stand as sureties and principals, pledging their persons and estates, moveable and immoveable, present and future, without exception, submitting themselves to all laws and judges. Done at Beverwijck the 29th September *anno* 1663.

Henderick Jansen Rooseboom
Philip Pietersz Schuijler
Wouter Albersen
Acknowledged by me,
La Montagne, commissary at Fort Orange.

[CONVEYANCE OF A PIECE OF LAND BY WATTAWIT AND PEPEWITSIE TO VOLCKERT JANSSEN AND JAN TOMASSEN]

Appeared before me, Johannes La Montagne, in the service of the general chartered West India Company, admitted by the lord director general and councilors of New Netherland vice director and commissary at Fort Orange and the village of Beverwijck, in the presence of the afternamed witnesses an Indian named Wattawit with his mother named Pepewitsie, who declare to have sold, ceded and conveyed, as they hereby sell, cede and convey in real and actual possession to and for the benefit of Volckert Janssen and Jan Tomassen their certain land **[433]** situated on the Goojer's kil on Apjen's island, or else by the Indians named Schotack—their portion of the said Apjens Island—which the buyers accept for the sum mentioned hereafter. The north end extending from the said northern end until straight across the south end of the green flat, cutting right across Apjen's island until the kil that separates or creates the island; together with a piece of land on the east bank of the kil, being the mainland where the house of Machacknotaes stood, and this, extending into the woods; for the sum of *f*442 in beavers guilders, paid in merchandise, which they, grantors, acknowledge to have received and been paid for, promising therefore to free the aforesaid piece of land, both on the mainland and on the island, from all further demands, claims, or pretensions of other Indians, who may sinisterly lay claim to something. Thus done in the village of

Beverwijck in the presence of Tomas Chambert and Johannes Provoost as witnesses requested hereto on this 4th of October *anno* 1663.

This is the mark of  Wattawit made with his own hand.

This is the mark of the  mother of Wattawit,
made with her own hand.
Thomas Chambers
Johannes Provoost, clerk
Acknowledged by me,
La Montagne, commissary at Fort Orange.

[CONVEYANCE OF A PIECE OF LAND BY NASPAHAN AND PASIES TO VOLCKERT JANSSEN AND JAN TOMASSEN]

[**434**] At the same time, on the date as before, there appeared before me, Johannes La Montagne, commissary, in the aforesaid capacity, an Indian and an Indian woman, the Indian named Naspaliasn, or else, Pofponick, and the Indian woman named Pasies, owners of the south end of Aepiens island named Schotack, who declare to have sold, ceded and conveyed, as they hereby cede and convey in real and actual possession to and for the benefit of Volckert Janssen and Jan Tomassen, their heirs or assigns, the said south end of the aforesaid island, being the largest half, beginning [at a point] across from the south end of the green flat, and extending to the south end of said Aepjen's island, so that the entire island of said Aepjen belongs to them, grantees, for the sum of *f*500 in beavers, paid to them in merchandise, which they, grantors, acknowledge to have received, and promising therefore to free the same from any demands or claims of other Indians, who may lay claim to something. Thus done in Beverwijck in the presence of Tomas Chambert and Johannes Provoost as witnesses requested hereto on this 4th of October *anno* 1663.

This is the mark of  Naspahan made with his own hand.

This is the mark of the Indian woman Pasies  made with her own hand.

Thomas Chambers
Johannes Provoost,
Acknowledged by me,
La Montagne, commissary at Fort Orange.

[POWER OF ATTORNEY FROM STOFFEL JANSSEN ABEEL TO PIETER JACOBSEN]

[435] Appeared before me, Johannes Provoost, clerk of the court of Fort Orange and the village of Beverwijck, and in the presence of the afternamed witnesses, Stoffel Janssen Abeel, magistrate of the same court, who declares to have appointed and empowered, as he hereby does, the honorable Pieter Jacobsen, merchant, dwelling at Amsterdam in New Netherland, in his, appointer's name and on his behalf in all humility especially to request of the lord director general and councilors of New Netherland restitution of his, appearer's, certain goods and merchandise, which were retained by the lord fiscal because, by a mistake of the clerk Liefferingh at Amsterdam in Holland they had not been entered in the invoice, about which error said Liefferingh has written and provided an explanation. [If he is] unable to receive the said merchandise in kind, then only to request that the same may be validated and serve as payment of the recognition fee. For this purpose to use all proper means, which he, the appearer, could or might use if he were present, although the case requires more, and more specialized authority than hereby is expressed. He, appearer, promising to accept everything that the attorney shall have done in this matter, **[436]** provided that the attorney shall remain obliged to render proper accounts of his transactions and receipts, upon pledge of his person and estate. Thus done in Fort Orange in the presence of Jan Harmsen and Harmen Tomassen, as witnesses invited hereto on this 6th of October *anno* 1663.

Stoffel Janssen Abeel
Jan Harmensen Weendorp
Harman Thomasz
Acknowledged by me,
J. Provoost, clerk.

[CONVEYANCE OF A HOUSE AND LOT BY SANDER LEENDERTSEN GLEN TO JAN CLUTE]

[437] Conditions and terms upon which the honorable Sander Leendersen Glen intends to sell at public auction to the highest bidder his house and lot located in the village of Beverwijck at the hill, adjoining on the east side Wouter Albertsen and on the west side Jan Tomassen.

The aforesaid house and lot shall be delivered to the buyer as it is situated within its fence, with everything that is attached by earth and nail, an appropriate conveyance of which shall be delivered to him upon payment of the final installment.

The payment shall take place in two installments, the first on the first of June *anno* 1664, and the second on the first of June *anno* 1665, and this in good whole merchantable beaver skins. The buyer shall be obliged to furnish two sufficient sureties at once, one for all and each as principals, to the satisfaction of the seller. If the buyer cannot furnish the aforesaid sureties within the aforesaid time, then the aforesaid house and lot shall be reauctioned at his cost and charge, and whatever less it comes to be worth, he shall be obliged to make good, and whatever more it becomes worth, he shall derive no profit from it. The auction fees shall become a charge to the buyer in payment as before.

[438] Upon the above stated conditions Jan Cloet remained the final bidder for the sum of six hundred and thirty guilders, for which Jacob Tijssen vander Heijden and Barent Reijndersen presented themselves as sureties and principals, pledging their persons and estates, moveable and immoveable, making themselves subject to all laws and judges. Dated the 17th of October *anno* 1663 in Beverwijck.

Johannes Clute
Jacob Theijsen
Barent Reijnderts

[CONDITIONS FOR FARMING OUT THE BEER, WINE, AND SPIRITS EXCISE]

[439] Conditions and terms on which the lords commissary and magistrates of Fort Orange and the village of Beverwijck, in the name and on behalf of the honorable lord director general and councilors of New Netherland, intend to farm out to the highest bidder the excise of all wines, beers, and spirits consumable and to be drawn by the innkeepers, tappers, and retailers in and around Fort Orange, the village of Beverwijck, and the colony of Rensselaerswijck.

The farming out as well as the collection of duties be done according to the laudable custom of our fatherland, and this in accordance with the printed ordinances and placards of the High and Mighty Lords States General, issued on the matter of finances. The farming shall begin on the first of November, and end on the last of October *anno* 1664, being the time of twelve months, during which time the farmer may collect and receive for all wines, beers, or distilled waters to be consumed and drawn by the tappers and innkeepers in or around Fort Orange, the village of Beverwijck, as follows:

For a barrel of domestic brewed beer	*f*4
For a barrel of overseas beer	*f*6
For a hogshead of French wine	*f*20
For an anker of the same	*f*4
For an anker of Spanish wine, brandy, mead, or distilled waters	*f*7
For an anker of cider	*f*2

larger and smaller containers in proportion, and this in beaver's price, or else, 12 white or [440] six black at the payer's choice. The farmer or bidder shall be obliged to furnish two sufficient sureties for the excise moneys to the satisfaction of the lords contractors, and every three months to pay a just fourth part of the promised excise money in beavers, or else, in sewant at 12 white or six black a stuiver. To prevent any quibbling, misunderstanding, and frauds, it is stipulated and agreed that after the expiration of this contract, whenever the farming out shall be renewed, the new farmer shall be permitted immediately on the day of the new contract, or on the following day, or always within the time of three days after the new farming, in the presence of the former farmer, if he wishes to be present, to gauge the remainder of the wines, beers or distilled waters kept by the tappers and innkeepers, and two-third of the excise received or still due, shall be returned and restored by the former or previous farmer to his successor or the next farmer.

The honorable farming supervisors reserve to themselves the interpretation and amplification of this, and promise the farmer all proper protection and assistance.

At the auction Willem Fredricksz Bout remained the final bidder for the above farming for the sum [441] of three thousand eight hundred guilders according to the aforesaid conditions, for the payment of which Harmen Bastiaensen and Jan Vinhagen stood sureties and principals according to the aforesaid conditions, pledging therefor their persons and estates, moveable and immoveable, present and future without exception. Thus done in Beverwijck, the last of October *anno* 1663.

This is the mark  of Willem Fredricksz Bout,
made with his own hand.
Harmen Bastiaens
Jan Dircksen Vinhaeghen
Acknowledged by me,
La Montagne, commissary at Fort Orange.
By order of the lords magistrates,
J. Provoost, clerk.

[CONDITIONS FOR FARMING OUT THE BURGHER BEER, WINE, AND SPIRITS EXCISE]

[442] Conditions and terms on which the lords commissary and magistrates of Fort Orange and the village of Beverwijck intend to farm out to the highest bidder the burgher wine and beer excise for the time of one year.

The farming out, as well as the collection of duties, shall begin on the first of November of this year *anno* 1663, and end on the last of October *anno* 1664, according to the ordinance of our fatherland. The farmer shall receive for a barrel of good beer one daelder, for a barrel of small beer ten stuivers, for a hogshead of French wine six guilders, for an anker of brandy, Spanish wine, or [distilled] waters two guilders at twelve white and six black beads of sewant a stuiver. And the aforesaid farmer shall shall not deny any burgher indicated on the burgher excise any certificate.

The farmer is obliged to furnish two sufficient sureties, one for all and each as principals to the satisfaction of the honorable contractors, and each quarter year to pay for the said burgher's excise a just quarter part of the entire sum in good strung sewant at 12 white and 6 black sewant a stuiver. And if the aforesaid farmer fails to furnish the said sureties, the **[443]** aforesaid farming shall be reauctioned at his cost and charge, and whatever less it comes to be worth, he shall be obliged to make good, and whatever more it comes to be worth, he shall derive no profit from it. The honorable farming supervisors reserve to themselves the interpretation and amplification of this and promise the farmer all proper protection and assistance.

Willem Fredericksz Bout remained the final bidder and farmer of the above farming for the sum of two thousand five hundred guilders, for the satisfaction of which Harmen Bastiaensen and Jan Dirricksz Vinhagen stand as sureties and principals according to the aforesaid condition, pledging thereto their persons and estates, moveable and immoveable, present and future without exception. Thus done in Beverwijck on the last of October *anno* 1663.

This is the mark of  Willem Fredricksen Bout,
made with his own hand.
Harmen Bastiaens
Jan Dircksen Vinhaeghen
Acknowledged by me,
La Montagne, commissary at Fort Orange.
By order of the lords magistrates,
J. Provoost, clerk.

[ACKNOWLEDGMENT OF DEBT BY CLAES JANSSEN VAN BAREN TO ANDERIES JOCHIMSEN]

[444] Appeared before me, Johannes La Montagne, in the service of the general chartered West India Company, admitted by the lord director general and councilors of New Netherland vice director and commissary at Fort Orange, in the presence of the honorable Jan Verbeeck and Goossen Gerritsen, magistrates of the same court, Claes Janssen van Baren, who acknowledges and declares that he is honestly and truly indebted to Anderies Jochimsen for the sum of two hundred and forty-four guilders in beavers, stemming from the purchase of a lot; which aforesaid sum of two hundred and forty-four guilders in beavers, together with its interest at ten percent, which began four years ago and runs until the effectual payment, he, appearer, promises to pay to the aforesaid Anderies Jochimsen or his attorney on the first of June *anno* 1664, pledging thereto his person and goods, moveable and immoveable, present and future, with no exception, especially his house and lot located in the village of Beverwijck; adjoins to the south Stoffel Janssen, and to the north the aforesaid magistrate Jan Verbeeck, as a mortgage and special collateral, in order, if necessary, to recoup the payment of the aforesaid sum with its interest without cost or damage. Submitting him self for this purpose to all laws and judges. Done at Fort Orange the 14th of November *anno* 1663.

Claes Jansen
Goosen Gerretsen
Jan Verbeeck
Acknowledged by me,
La Montagne, commissary at Fort Orange.

[*In the margin was written*:]

With the transfer of the house of Claes Janssen that she took in possession, Celetie Fredericx, as attorney for her husband Anderies Jochimsz, acknowledges that she is fully satisfied and paid for the claimed sum of two hundred and forty-four guilders in beavers with its interest, without claiming anything else in the world anymore from Claes Janssen. Done in Albany, 3 August 1665 old style.

Selytien Fredericksz
Acknowledged by me,
Johannes Provoost, clerk.

[POWER OF ATTORNEY BY WOUTER ALBERTSEN
TO JAN PIETERSEN MULLER *SOLDAET*]

[445] Appeared before me, Johannes Provoost, clerk of the court of Fort Orange and village of Beverwijck, and in the presence of the afternamed witnesses, the honorable Wouter Albertsen, inhabitant of the said village, who declares to have appointed and empowered, as he hereby does appoint and empower, Jan Pietersen Muller *soldaet* in the service of the honorable Company—in garrison at the Esopus in the village of Wildwijck. This, to collect, demand, and receive in his, appointer's name, such debts and outstanding moneys as are due to him, appointer, in the aforesaid Esopus, according to writings and evidences thereto serving; to issue quittance of the receipts, and in case of unwillingness, to demand payment by law and rigor of justice, thereto observing all terms of the law for final sentence and extreme execution, including, in case of arrest, to proceed against persons and estates; moreover, to do everything that he, the appearer, could or might do if he were present, even if the case would require more, and more specialized authority than hereby is expressed, provided that, if requested, the attorney shall be obligated to render a proper statement and account of his transactions and receipts, upon pledge of his person **[446]** and estate, moveable and immoveable. Thus done in Fort Orange in the presence of Arent van den Bergh and Jochim Lambertsen as witnesses requested hereto on this 23rd of November *anno* 1663.

Wouter Albertsen
This is the mark of  Arent vanden Bergh,
made with his own hand.
Jochem Lambersen
Acknowledged by me,
Johannes Provoost, clerk.

[INVENTORY OF JAN GERRITSEN VAN MARCKEN]†

[447] Found in the kitchen:
5 small earthenware pots;
another 7 ditto, small and large;
10 pewter table plates;
1 pewter bowl;
4 pewter saucers;
11 pewter spoons;
1 copper frying pan;
1 iron pot hanger;
2 iron pots and 1 copper ditto;
1 copper kettle;
2 small wooden pails;
1 lantern;
1 small ash pail;
1 skimmer;
2 wooden bins;

[448] [*blank*]

[INVENTORY OF JAN GERRITSEN VAN MARCKEN]

[449] Inventory of the goods of Jan Gerritsen van Marcken, farmer [of the excise], taken on the 11th of December 1663.

Found in a clothing press [*kleerkas*]:
A small bundle of black sewant;
4 blue aprons [*schortekleden*];
an ivory tabocco box;

---

† Doc. [**477**] has been incorrectly placed in the bound volume. It should be associated with the inventory starting with doc. [**449**].

8 men's and women's shirts;
another 2 shirts;
5 sleeping sheets;
another 2 ditto;
2 white jerkins;
1 white coarse bed cloth;
18 pillow cases, both large and small;
another one ditto;
15 napkins;
3 table cloths;
5 hand towels;
a towel full with children's stuff;
a white woman's waistcoat/undervest;
1 pair of white underpants/drawers;
2 white aprons;
4 red towels;
1 small piece of tick;
a small baby-linen basket;
2 small red flowered curtains;
2 pairs of gloves;
3 black hoods;
a red woman's bodice;
a small piece of cloth;
4 black small woman's coats 2 missing;
1 red man's waistcoat missing;
1 piece of red cloth;
1 pair of woman's shoes;
3 woman's stomachers missing;
2 black aprons one missing;
1 green garment;
1 blue coat missing;
1 red coat and 2 black coats missing;
[450] a *vlieger*†, the coat missing;
1 pair of man's and 1 pair of woman's stockings, the woman's are missing;
1 brown cloth man's garment;

† A long woman's gown with a standing collar and wide sleeves.

1 serge man's outfit missing;
1 pair of underpants;
1 black man's coat missing;
3 children's blankets;
2 diapers;
2 green valances missing;
2 green curtains missing;
1 bed spread;

Goods hanging loose around the house:
2 guns;
2 pocket pistols;
1 mirror;
1 [*istickaet*?] in a cane;
2 books, both small and large;
3 paintings;
1 gridiron;
1 flat iron;
1 iron pot hanger;
1 pair of tongs;
3 earthenware saucers;
1 slate almanac;

Found in the attic:
15 small white earthenware bowls/pitchers;
12 white ditto table plates;
a bunch of wine glasses;
3 earthenware salt cellars;
4 white ditto bowls;
3 earthenware saucers;
3 wooden women's foot stoves;
a bunch of locks and pot hangers;
bed and bolster;

[DECLARATION BY JAN CLAESSEN CONCERNING THE ESTATE OF PIETER JACOBSEN VAN RINSBORGH, DECEASED]

[451] Appeared before me, Johannes Provoost, clerk of the court of Fort Orange and the village of Beverwijck, and in the presence of the afternamed witnesses, Jan Claessen, husband and guardian of Lijsbet Donneur, widow of Pieter Jacobsen van Rinsborgh, deceased, who acknowledges and declares, as he hereby declares that he has agreed with the administrators of the estate of the aforesaid Pieter Jacobsen van Rinsborgh, that he, appearer, absolutely disassociates and renounces the said estate by receiving the sum of three hundred guilders in heavy money, which he, appearer, shall receive in merchandise from *Sr.* Johannes Withart; but the sum of one hundred guilders light money shall be subtracted from the aforesaid sum for commissary Johannes La Montagne for the benefit of the honorable Company, which was furnished to the aforesaid Pieter Jacobsen van Rinsborgh, deceased, on his sickbed. Therefore he, appearer, acquits the aforesaid estate of any further claims or pretensions, pledging thereto his person and estate, moveable and immoveable. Thus done in Fort Orange, the 23rd of November *anno* 1663, in the presence of Wouter Albertsen and Arent vanden Bergh, as witnesses invited hereto.

Jan Klassen
Wouter Albersen
Jan Verbeeck, administrator
Evert Wendel, administrator

This is the mark of  Arent vanden Bergh,
made with his own hand.
Acknowledged before me. [*unsigned*]

[CONVEYANCE OF TWO GARDENS BY SANDER LEENDERTSEN GLEN TO JURRIAEN TEUNISSEN]

[452] Appeared before me, Johannes La Montagne, in the service of the general chartered West India Company, admitted by the lord director general and councilors of New Netherland vice director and commissary at Fort Orange and the village of Beverwijck, in the presence of the honorable Goossen Gerritsen and Jan Tomassen, magistrates of the same court, the honorable Sander Leendersen Glen, who declares to have ceded and conveyed, as he hereby cedes and conveys in real and actual possession to and for the benefit of Jurriaen Teunissen, his heirs or assigns, two gardens lying next to each other, located near the aforesaid village of Beverwijck behind the lord Renselaer's house in the second street toward the hill; adjoins on the south Jan Bastiaensen van Gudsenhoven and on the north Goossen Gerritsen, each in such size as they were distributed before by the drawing of lots. For which aforesaid two gardens said Jurriaen Teunissen promises to pay the sum of one hundred and seventy-five guilders in sewant, for which **[453]** the grantor promises to free the said two gardens from all actions, claims and demands of someone else who may lay claim to it, pledging therefor his person and estate, moveable and immoveable, present and future, without exception, submitting himself to all laws and judges. Done in Fort Orange, the 28th of December *anno* 1663.

Sander Lenrsen Glen
Jurejan Tunsen
Goosen Gerretsen
Jan Thomasz

Acknowledged by me,
La Montagne, commissary at Fort Orange.

[CONVEYANCE OF A LOT AND GARDEN BY SANDER LEENDERSEN GLEN TO CASPAER JACOBSEN]

Appeared before me, Johannes La Montagne, in the service of the general chartered West India Company, admitted by the lord director general and council of New Netherland vice director and commissary at Fort Orange and the village of Beverwijck, in the presence of the honorable Gerrit Slichtenhorst and Stoffel Janssen, magistrates of the same court, the honorable Sander Leendersen Glen, who declares to have ceded and conveyed, as he hereby **[454]** cedes and conveys in real and actual possession to and for the benefit of Caspaer Jacobsen, his heirs or assigns, a lot for a garden lying next to the said Fort Orange; adjoins to the west the lot of Jeremias van Renselaer, to the north of the lot of the grantee; long sixteen and a half rods, and wide three rods eight and a half feet; which lot was granted to the to the grantor by patent of the lord director general and councilors of New Netherland on date of the 13th of July *anno* 1658, and therefore the grantor promises to free the same from all actions, claims and demands which hereafter may arise, pledging thereto his person and estate, moveable and immoveable, present and future, submitting himself to all laws and judges. Done in Fort Orange, the 29th of December *anno* 1663.

Sander Lenrsen Glen
Gerrit Slichtenhorst
Stoffel Jansz

Acknowledged by me,
La Montagne, commissary at Fort Orange.

[CONVEYANCE OF A PIECE OF LAND BY PANASIT AND WAPTO TO JAN TOMASSEN AND VOLCKERT JANSSEN]

[455] Appeared before me, Johannes Provoost, clerk of the honorable court of Fort Orange and the village of Beverwijck, in the presence of the afternamed witnesses two Mahican Indians, one named Panasit and the other Wapto, brothers and owners of the mainland on the east side of Aepjens Island, extending from one end of the aforesaid island to the other end, who declare to have sold, ceded, and conveyed as they hereby do, in real and actual possession to and for the benefit of the honorable Jan Tomassen and Volckert Janssen, their heirs or assigns, the aforesaid land extending along the east side as [mentioned] before, and further, running into the woods, for a certain sum paid to them in merchandise, which they, grantors, acknowledge to have received; and having been fully satisfied and paid for said land, they therefore renounce and part with the same land on the said east side, and promise to free the same from any claims or demands of other Indians, who may sinisterly lay claim to something. Thus done in the village of Beverwijck in the presence of Rutger Jacobsen and *Meester* Jacob de Hince as witnesses requested hereto on this 17th of January *anno* 1664.

This is the mark of  Paensit made with his own hand.

This is the mark of  Wapto, made with his own hand.

Rutger Jacobsen
J de Hinsse

Acknowledged by me,
J. Provoost, clerk.

[AGREEMENT BETWEEN GOOSEN GERRITSEN AND GERRIT REIJERSEN]

[456] Today, the 21st of February *anno* 1664 there appeared before me, Johannes Provoost, clerk of the court of Fort Orange and the village of Beverwijck, and in the presence of the afternamed witnesses the honorable Goossen Gerritsen, magistrate of the said place, on the one side, and Gerrit Reijersen his half brother, for his share on the other side, who hereby declare that they have made with each other a separation and buying out of a certain contract between them and Henderick Coster and Gerrit Reijersen in partnership, commenced on the 11th of August 1662, concerning a certain six thousand guilders, which they have borrowed from Goosen Gerritsen and at their expense invested in order to use the same for the period of two years, provided that they will pay the interest thereon at ten percent. The division of which [will be] as follows: Gerrit Reijersen shall deliver by inventory all such goods as he has on hand, moveable and merchandise, and likewise, he hereby transfers, in addition to the ledger, all debts outstanding as a result of and inherited from the above mentioned sum. But he shall collect the outstanding debts, or else, on departure to *patria*, he shall obtain from the debtors proper promissory notes and acknowledgment of debt, and as also some beavers of the main sum are held as a return to Holland, and some money is due there, Goosen Gerritsen shall have the benefit of the surplus that will return from Holland in merchandise and take it; upon which said Goossen Gerritsen, for the buying out [457] promises to pay to said Gerrit Reijerse the number of thirty good whole beaver skins, and in addition ninety-nine guilders in beavers, which Gerrit Reijersen personally owes to the capital, without further claims there for; together with one hundred and twelve guilders in sewant and two beavers for moneys advanced, which Goossen Gerritsen shall also pay to him and commpensate for; both parties pledging hereto their respective persons and estates, moveable and immoveable. Thus done without craft or guile in the presence of Dirck van Schelluijne and Pieter van Alen as witnesses invited hereto on date as above.

Goosen Gerretsen
Gerrit Reijersen
DV Schelluijne
1664
Pieter van Alen

Acknowledged by me,
Johannes Provoost, clerk.

[SECOND INVENTORY OF JAN GERRITSEN VAN MARCKEN'S ESTATE]

[458] Date 25 March 1664.
Inventory of the goods of Jan Gerritsz van Marcken taken for the second time, as he has broken the seal and opened the clothes press [*kas*], and taken out of it some goods; which press, containing some goods to be inventoried later, has again been brought to the house of Jochim Wessels for safe keeping.

Loose goods:
3 earthenware saucers, with two small ditto and a small porcelain cup;
7 pewter saucers, 1 pewter bowl, and ditto small cup;
8 pewter spoons and 2 copper ditto;
5 earthenware table plates;
1 white earthenware colender, 2 small red earthenware, and ditto small white cup;
1 copper smoothing iron;

1 copper skimmer;
1 iron trivet;
1 iron chopping knife;
1 iron pot hanger and a ditto hook;
a small wooden spoon rack;
1 copper lamp
1 scrubber;
1 shot pouch
1 small tin drawer;
1 small copper kettle
1 iron pot
2 small pewter wine pints
A full chest with pipes and a clothing press which were left standing in the house.†
1 pewter mustard pot;
1 candle drawer
an earthenware oil pot white
a small ditto white pitcher
A clothing chest but not knowing what it contains.
a gridiron and a pan;
a colander, red;
a red earthenware saucer;
3 small earthenware pots;
1 red wooden bin;
a ticktack board;
1 painting;
1 pitcher rack;
1 round table;
1 gun;
1 (more of less decorated) chest with 6 bottles;
1 small wooden arm bucket, 3 dusters;
[459] a mangling board and the stick/rolling pin;
1 kolf stick;
1 wood ax;
1 water pail;
a bed with bolster and 2 pillows and 3 ship blankets which were left in the house of Jan Gerritsen for his convenience;
2 green curtains;
2 pairs of iron fire tongs;
15 pewter table plates;
1 small screened cupboard for keeping edibles;

---

† Notation has been canceled in the original.

Secured from the attic:
4 white earthenware table plates;
1 red earthenware stew pan;
5 small earthenware saucers;
10 small white earthenware pitchers, and one blue ditto;
5 small white earthenware mustard pots;
1 small ditto white oil pot;
3 white earthenware salt cellars;
4 white ditto bowls;
4 small earthenware pots with;
3 small white saucers;
1 earthenware pot with 8 small trinkets in it;
7 earthenware pots, small and large;
a lantern;
2 market pails;
1 duster;
1 iron pot cover;
1 iron pot hanger;
8 iron door locks;
13 iron scissors;
4 pairs of iron pot hangers;
1 church foot-warmer;
2 latches;
2 iron hammers with some small rings;
8 large wine glasses;
21 bundles of straw with wine glasses;
1 hat press;
1 small basket;
1 iron weight of ten pounds;
a bunch of pipes lying loose in the attic;

[460] Today, this first of March 1664, the press of Jan Gerritsen van Marcken was opened and found in it were:
3 pieces of fake lace;
3 bunches of *piet* ?;
2 small square paintings;
8 pocket handkerchiefs;
4 tin telescopes;
3 scrubbers and a rubbing brush;

2 pocket pistols;
3 small copper rods;
1 wreath;
1 pair of little children's stockings;
1 small knit children's waistcoat;
1 old green valance;
1 travelling bag;
3 small children's blankets, 1 green and two white;
1 pair of gray patched man's stockings;
1 green valance;
1 red diaper;
1 man's under pants, half red and half white;
1 brown man's garment;
2 silk damast valances;
1 green diaper;
1 small piece of apple blossom cloth;
1 small black cloak or coat without sleeves;
1 black grogram apron;
1 silk grogram hood;
1 bundle or a small roll of very coarse linen;
1 tabard bodice in a piece of white cloth;
1 beads' basket;
2 pairs of knit gloves, 1 black and one pair of gray;
1 ivory tobacco box;
1 pair of woman's shoes;
1 silver head brooch;
2 white linen aprons;
2 small white man's coats;
5 pillow cases, another 3 pillow cases;
1 small linen bag;
1 small piece of bombazine and 1 ditto white woolen;
1 man's and 1 woman's shirt;
1 blue checked valance;
1 black woman's apron;
[461] 1 pair of white bombazine under pants;
5 pillow cases, another 2 small ones;
1 white woman's undershirt;
1 small red garment;
1 woman's shirt;

1 small black old borate coat;

A piece of cloth full with children's stuff, in which was found:
a piece of cloth with a bunch of sewant;
2 old silk hoods;
2 chair cushions;
5 blue aprons;
a small woman's arm-basket;
16 books large and small;
a white small fine basket in which were some odds and ends;
2 books with maps;
a hat rack;
3 small paintings;
1 large mirror;
a perpetual almanac;
a green coverlet;
a piece of tick;
3 tablecloths;
18 napkins both small and large;
6 hand towels and a piece of cloth to keep warm in a red diaper;
a small and a large brush;

a wooden bin in which were 11 coifs and hats and 4 night neckerchiefs, 3 fine neckerchiefs, and three small pieces of cloth, and 3 tuckers and 3 *santees*
1 cane with a rapier blade therein [cf. **450**];
5 handkerchiefs tied together;
15 tuckers;
2 *santeen*;
2 woman's neckerchiefs;
2 white aprons;
8 coifs;
1 woman's stitched hat;
5 pocket handkerchiefs
a seal;
a white apron holding odds and ends;

[462] A chest in which was found:
20 children's hats, both girls' and boys' hats;

some *hansioos* jewelry;
10 wooden recorders;
1 pair of yellow children's stockings;
a pair of leather man's stockings;
3 chair cushions;
one pair of blue linen underpants;
1 old woman's waistcoat;
1 cloth pair of pants;
1 scarlet waistcoat with silver buttons;
1 serge man's suit;
1 black hat;
a cloth with starch;
a pilot's bow with 2 compasses.

[LEASE OF A FARM AT KLAVERRACK BY ABRAHAM STAETS TO JAN ANDERIESSEN]

[463] Today, the 12th of March *anno* 1664, the honorable Abraham Staets on the one side and Jan Anderiessen *de Iersman* on the other side have hereby contracted and agreed as follows: namely, that the aforesaid Abraham Staets leases to said Jan Anderiessen his farm located in the Klaverrack, with the land, house, barn, and hay barrack as it stands at present for the time of four and a half successive years, beginning on the first of April of this year, and ending on the first of September *anno* 1669. To that end he delivers six milk cows, two horses, and a mare with a stallion and six sows, for which Jan Anderiessen promises to pay for rent as follows: for the first half year he shall, at the end of the lease, deliver in the ground for the benefit of the lessor, three mudde of wheat, and a tight fence; the following year one hundred guilders, the next three years each time one hundred and fifty guilders in beavers or grain at beaver's price. And further, he promises to keep the buildings in good repair; also, the increase of the said animals shall be shared half and half by lessee and lessor, and annually of each of the six sows' increase a slaughter hog. Also, at the end of the lease the lessor shall be obliged to deliver the full number of animals. Concerning the orchard, both parties shall enjoy half of the fruits, provided that they also will jointly defray and take care of the costs of the fence, but the lessee shall take all possible care **[464]** that the fruits will not decrease in quality.

Thus done in Beverwijck in amity and friendship, and in the presence of me, J: Provoost clerk, dated as above.

Abram Staas
This is the mark  of Jan Anderiessen *de Iersman*,
made with is own hand.
Acknowledged by me,
J. Provoost, clerk.

[ACKNOWLEDGMENT OF DEBT BY ANTHONY TOINEL TO PHILIP PIETERSEN SCHUIJLER]

Copy.

I, the undersigned, acknowledge to be indebted to Philip Pietersen Schuijler for the sum of 50 [guilders] Holland money for my fare [to be paid to] skipper Pieter, for which he has stood security, as I had not paid for it myself in Holland; and furthermore, two beavers, one lent to me formerly, and one at present, with 10 guilders silver money, which sum I promise to pay back to him to his content when next year, God willing, I may return from Holland. In acknowledgment of the truth I have subscribed here with my own hand.

Anthonij Toinel
*f*60 Holland money and two beavers
Dated 12 August 1662 in Fort Orange in N: Netherland.

[465] [*blank*]

[MARRIAGE AGREEMENT BETWEEN WILLEM TELLER AND MARIJA VERLET]

[466] In the name of the Lord, Amen. Let it be known that in the year of our Lord Jesu Christy sixteen hundred sixty-four, the xixth day of April, there appeared before me Johannes La Montagne, in the service of the general chartered West India Company, admitted by the lord director general and councilors of New Netherland vice director and commissary at Fort Orange and the village of Beverwijck, the honorable Willem Teller, widower of the late Margariet Donckesen, who, in the presence of the after named witnesses, declares that, for the honor of God, he has resolved upon a future marriage with Marija Verlet, widow of the late Poulus Schrick, and before the bands of the same, he, appearer, has made up and exhibited for the seven children left by Margriet Donckesen (his, appearer's, wife, deceased) the sum of three thousand five hundred Carolus guilders at beaver's price, exclusive of all debts made hitherto, which he, appearer, accepts to pay, to be divided by the following, namely: Anderies Teller 22 years old, Helena Teller 19 years old, Martjen 16 years, Elijsabeth Teller 12 years, Jacob Teller 9 years, Willem Teller 7 years, and Johannes Teller 5 years, being their matrimonial inheritance. And for the payment of the aforesaid sum he, appearer, pledges his entire estate, moveable and immoveable, as a mortgage and collateral, to which end said appearer appoints as guardians the honorable Sander Leendersen Glen and Pieter Loockermans, uncles of the said children. In the meantime, the appearer **[467]** shall be obligated to bring up the said children, to wit, the minors, in the fear of the Lord, to have them learn reading and writing in the school, and moreover, to provide for them with food and clothing until their majority and married state, without reduction of their matrimonial and appropriate inheritance. All of the above the appearer promises to maintain without craft or guile, pledging therefor his person and estate, moveable and immoveable, present and future. Thus done in the village of Beverwijck in the presence of the honorable Evert Wendel and Johannes Provoost, as witnesses invited hereto on date as above.

Willem Teller
Evert Jansz Wendel, as witness.
Johannes Provoost, witness.

Acknowledged by me,
La Montagne, commissary at Fort Orange.

[AUCTION OF A HOUSE AND BREWERY BY ADMINISTRATORS OF PHILIP HENDERICKSZ'S ESTATE]

[468] Conditions and terms upon which the administrators of the estate of Philip Hendericksz intend to sell at public auction to the highest bidder the house, brewery, and mill house of the aforesaid Philip Hendericksz.

First, the said house and brewery shall immediately be delivered to the buyer with one kettle, two tubs and a cooler, and the mill house except for the mill, together with the lot and garden in such magnitude as it lies in its fence.

Payment shall occur in good whole merchantable beaver skins in three installments. The first installment on the 15th of July of this year 1664, the second installment a year later, and the third installment also on the 15th of July *anno* 1666.

The buyer shall be obliged to furnish two sufficient sureties at once, one for all and each as principals, to the satisfaction of the sellers. If the buyer cannot furnish the aforesaid sureties in the aforesaid time, then the aforesaid house, brewery, millhouse, lot and garden shall be reauctioned at his cost and charge, and whatever less it comes to be worth, he shall be obliged to make good, and whatever more it becomes worth, he shall derive no profit from it. The auction fees shall become a charge to the buyer in payment as before. After offering the above condition for sale, Jan Dircks van Eps remained the final bidder for the brewery for the sum of one thousand **[469]** one hundred and fifty guilders on the above conditions, for the payment of which Cornelis van Nes and Pieter van Alen stood sureties and principals. Thus done in the village of Beverwijck the 29th of April *anno* 1664.

Jan Dircksz van Eps
Pieter van Alen

Cornelis van Nes
La Montagne, commissary at Fort Orange.

[CONDITIONS FOR THE SALE OF THE FARM, HOUSE, LOT AND GARDEN BY THE ADMINISTRATORS OF THE ESTATE OF PHILIP HENDERICKSZ]

Conditions and terms upon which the administrators of the estate of Philip Hendericksz intend to sell at public auction to the highest bidder the farm, house, lot and garden of the aforesaid Philip Hendericksz at Schaenhechtade, existing of a lot of about 25 morgens, or as much as other inhabitants of each lot will receive.

First, the aforesaid lot, or farm of Philip Hendericksz shall be delivered to the buyer, and this in such magnitude as told above, all broken land, of which a portion is sown with 9½ schepels of winter wheat, 2½ schepels of summer wheat; further, the house and lot, 200 square feet in size with the garden as it lies within its fence, along with a barn, two hay barracks, the one a 4- and the other a 5-post hay barrack, two draught-horses and a one-year old filly foal, two milk cows and a two-year old heifer, and a one-year old heifer, and a young calf, 5 sows, 3 of which are bearing piglets, a passable wagon and a span of ropes, a rear plow.

[470] Payment shall occur in good whole merchantable beaver skins, and this in three installments or payments. The first installment on the 15th of July of this year *anno* 1664, the second on the 15th of July *anno* 1665, and the third installment *anno* 1666, also on the 15th of July. The buyer shall be obliged to furnish two sufficient sureties, one for all and each as principals, at once, to the satisfaction of the sellers. If the buyer cannot furnish the aforesaid sureties in the aforesaid time, then the aforesaid farm shall be reauctioned at his cost and charge, and whatever less it comes to be worth, he shall be obliged to make good, and whatever more it becomes worth, he shall derive no profit from it. The auction fees shall become a charge to the buyer in payment as before. [*not executed*]

[SALE OF TWO DISTILLER'S KETTLES BY HESTER DOUWES TO JAN COSTERSEN VAN AKEN]

[471] Today the 29th of April *anno* 1664 appeared before me, Johannes Provoost, clerk of the court of Fort Orange and the village of Beverwijck, Hester Douwes, assisted by her son Douwe Gillis and her daughter Geertien Gillis, on the one side and Jan Costersen van Aken on the other side, who declare to have made a sale as follows, to wit, that Hester Douwes hereby sells to the aforesaid Jan van Aken two distiller's kettles, to be delivered in May, or else, to pay interest on the money, which Jan van Aken accepts, and promises to pay the sum of four hundred guilders in good strung sewant for it in the next month of May, which sale the parties promise to maintain for fixed and indissoluble. Thus done without craft or guile. Done in Beverwijck in the presence of Jan Schekel. Dated as above.

Hester Douwes
Douwe Jellisz
Jan Koster
Jan Scheckel
Johannes Provoost, clerk.

[SALE OF A FARM, HOUSE, LOT AND GARDEN BY THE ADMINISTRATORS OF THE ESTATE OF PHILIP HENDERICKSZ TO CORNELIS VAN NES]

[472] Conditions and terms upon which the administrators of the estate of Philip Hendericksen intend to sell at public auction to the highest bidder the farm, house, lot and garden of the aforesaid Philip Hendericksz *brouwer*, at Schaenhechtade, consisting of a lot of about 25 morgens, or as much as shall be allotted to the other inhabitants of each lot.

First, the aforesaid farm or lot shall be delivered to the buyer at once, and that in such magnitude as told above, all plowed land, of which a portion was seeded with 9½ schepels of winter wheat, 3½ schepels of summer wheat; further, the house and lot, 200 feet square in size with the garden as it lies within its fence, together with a barn, long 30 feet and wide 24 feet, except for the side aisle, two hay barracks, the one a 4 and the other a 5–post haybarrack, a passable wagon and a span of ropes with a rear plow.

Payment shall occur in good whole merchantable beaver skins, and this in three installments. The first installment on the 15th of July of this year *anno* 1664, the second on the 15th of July *anno* 1665, and the third or final installment the 15th of July *anno* 1666. The buyer shall be obliged to furnish two sufficient sureties at once, one for all and each as principals, to the satisfaction of the sellers. If the buyer cannot furnish the aforesaid sureties in the aforesaid time, then the aforesaid shall be reauctioned at his cost and charge, and whatever less it comes to be worth, he shall be obliged to make good, and whatever more it becomes worth, he shall derive no profit from it. The auction fees shall become a charge to the buyer in payment as before.

[473] After auctioning Cornelis van Nes remained the final bidder for the farm for the sum of one thousand two hundred and eighty-seven guilders according to the above condition; for which said sum Volckert Janssen and Jan Dircksen van Eps stand as sureties and principals according to the aforesaid condition. Done in the village of Beverwijck the 29th of April *anno* 1664.

Cornelis van Nes
Volckart Jansz
Jan Diercksz van Eps
Acknowledged by me, [*unsigned*]

[SALE OF A HOUSE AND LOT BY THE ADMINISTRATORS OF THE ESTATE OF ANDERIES HERBERTSEN TO CORNELIS VAN NES]

Conditions and terms upon which the administrators of the estate of Anderies Herbertsen, together with Cornelis van Nes, husband and guardian of Marritje Damen, each participating for one half, intend to sell at public auction to the highest bidder a house and lot located in the village of Beverwijck; adjoins to the north of David Schuijler and to the south of Wouter *de Rademaker* according to the patent thereof. First, the aforesaid house and lot, according to the patent being four rods wide and eight rods long, will be delivered to the buyer at once. Payment shall occur in good whole merchantable beaver skins, or else sewant at *f*20 a beaver, and this in two installments, the first installment on the first of July of this year *anno* 1664, and the second installment on the first of July *anno* 1665.

[474] The buyer shall be obliged to furnish two sufficient sureties, one for all and each as principals, to the satisfaction of the seller, and to do so at once. If the buyer cannot furnish the aforesaid sureties in the aforesaid time, then the aforesaid house and lot shall be reauctioned at his cost and charge, and whatever less it comes to be worth, he shall be obliged to make good, and whatever more it becomes worth, he shall derive no profit from it. The auction fees shall become a charge to the buyer in payment as before.

After auctioning it on the above conditions Cornelis van Nes remained the final bidder for the sum of two hundred and seventy-two guilders, for whom Jan Dircksz van Eps and Pieter van Alen stand as sureties and principals. Done in the village of Beverwijck the 29th of April *anno* 1664.

Cornelis van Nes
Jan Dircksz van Eps
Pieter van Alen
Acknowledged by me, [*unsigned*]

[SALE OF SOME HORSES, COWS AND A HORSE MILL BY THE ADMINISTRATORS OF THE ESTATE OF PHILIP HENDERICKSZ]

[475] Conditions and terms upon which the administrators of the estate of Philip Hendericksz intend to sell some horses and cows, together with a horse mill as it stands. Payment should occur on the 15th of July of this year *anno* 1664, and that in good whole merchantable beaver skins. The auction fees become a charge to the buyer in payment as above. Dated the 29th of April *anno* 1664, Beverwijck.

Jan van Eps a mare named *Snel* for	*f*175:–
Idem, another horse, being a gelding for	*f*160:–
Idem, another one-year-old filly foal for	*f*119:–
Idem, another cow with a heifer calf	*f*119:–
Matteuwes Abrahamsen, a cow for	*f*118:–
Jan van Eps, a two-year-old heifer *f*84	*f* 84:–
Jacob Tijssen, a one-year-old heifer	*f* 40:–
Jan Eps, 5 sows for	*f* 77:–
Cornelis Teunisse Bos, the running works of a horse mill for	*f*112:–
	*f*1004:–

I, Harmen Harmensen van Gansevoort, stand surety for the person of Jacob Tijssen for the payment of *f*40:– on account of the purchase of a calf.

Harmen van Gansevoort

[*In the margin stood*:] Jacob Tijssen has paid *f*40: for the calf.

Cornelis Teunissen Bos hereby stands surety and principal for the person of Teuwes Abrahamsen for the payment of the sum of *f*118:– in beavers for the purchase of a cow. Done in Beverwijck, the 29th of April 1664.

Cornellis Tonisen Bos.

Similarly, Mateuwes Abrahamsen stands surety for Cornelis Bos for the payment of *f*112: on account of the purchase of a horse mill.

This is the **M** mark of Mateuwes Abrahamsen,
made with his own hand.

[476] We, the undersigned Cornelis van Nes and Pieter van Alen, stand sureties and principals for the person of Jan Dircksen van Eps for the payment of the above horses and cows, which he has bought at public auction, amounting to the sum of [*blank*] which, in case of failure of payment, they accept to take on and satisfy. Done in Beverwijck, the 29th of April *anno* 1664. [*not executed*]

I, the undersigned Jan Dircksz van Eps, remain the buyer and bidder of 3 horses, a cow with a calf, and a 2-year old heifer, and 5 hogs, amounting to the sum of seven hundred and thirty-four [guilders], for which we, Cornelis van Nes and Pieter van Alen, stand sureties and principals in order to pay and satisfy, in case of failure of the buyer, the aforesaid sum. Done in Beverwijck the 29th of April *anno* 1664.

Jan Diercksz van Eps
Cornelis van Nes
Pieter van Alen

[SALE OF A HORSE MILL BY CORNELIS VAN NES TO JAN DIRCKSZ VAN EPS]

[477] Appeared before me, Johannes Provoost, clerk of the court of Fort Orange and the village of Beverwijck, Cornelis Teunissen Bos, who in the presence of the afternamed witnesses declares to convey, as he hereby does, to Jan Dircksz van Eps, the horse mill which he has bought at public auction from the administrators of the estate of Philip Hendericksz; which the grantee accepts, and this for the same price as he has bought the same, amounting to one hundred and twelve guilders, to be paid in beavers, according to the conditions. Renouncing, moreover, all claims and demands he has therein. Thus done in Fort Orange, the first of May *anno* 1664.

Cornelus Thonisen Bos
Jan Diercksz van Eps
Acknowledged by me,
J. Provoost, clerk.

[ACKNOWLEDGMENT OF DEBT BY JAN MARTENSEN
TO HARMEN VEDDER]

[**478**] Appeared before me, Johannes Provoost, clerk of the court of Fort Orange and the village of Beverwijck, and in the presence of the afternamed witnesses, Jan Martensen, who hereby declares to be honestly and truly indebted to Harmen Vedder for the sum of two hundred and eighty-six guilders and eleven stuivers in beavers and thirty-one guilders and five stuivers in sewant for goods and merchandise received to his content, which aforesaid sums he, appearer, promises to pay on the first of May *anno* 1665, pledging herefor his person and estate, moveable and immoveable, present and future, especially seventeen hogs which he has on his farm, and which, in case of failure of payment, shall be paid according to value to said Harmen Vedder in preference of any one else, as a deduction of the aforesaid sums. Thus done in the village of Beverwijck, the first of May *anno* 1664, in the presence of Barent Reijndersen and Jan Bijvangh as witnesses.

This is the mark + of Jan Martensen,
made with his own hand.
Barent Reijndersen
Jan Bijvanck

Acknowledged by me,
Johannes Provoost, clerk.

[POWER OF ATTORNEY BY JAN MARTENSEN
TO HARMEN VEDDER]

[**479**] Appeared before me, Johannes Provoost, clerk of the court of Fort Orange and the village of Beverwijck, and in the presence of the afternamed witnesses, Jan Martensen, who hereby declares to appoint and empower, as he hereby does, Harmen Vedder, in his, appointer's name and on his behalf, to collect, demand and receive from various persons, both in the village of Wildwijck and here in Beverwijck, the following moneys due to him, appointer, namely, from Jan van

Aemsfort six schepels of wheat, *f*18:–; from Cornelis Slecht in wheat *f*51; from Geertruij Haps *f*40:4 in wheat; Henderick Janssen alias Ribbide *f*61 in beavers; Aert Otterspoor *f*45:– in beavers; Poulus *de Noorman* *f*28:–; from Jurrian Westvael, according to promissory note *f*141:– in wheat; to issue quittance of the receipts, and in case of unwillingness to demand payment by law and rigor of justice, observing all terms of the law for final sentence and extreme execution, including to proceed against persons and estates in case of arrest and furthermore, to do everything that he, appearer, if present, could or might do, provided that the attorney shall be obligated to render proper accounts of his transactions and receipts. But the attorney shall keep for himself and receive in advance the sum of two hundred and eighty-six guilders and eleven stuivers in beavers and thirty-one guilders and five stuivers in sewant as payment of a promissory note made on date of today. Thus done in Beverwijck the first of May *anno* 1664, in the presence of Jan Hendericksz, and Jan Janssen Bleecker as witnesses.

This is the mark of + Jan Martensen,
made with his own hand.
This is the mark IH of Jan Hendericksz,
made with his own hand.
Jan Jansen Bleecker
Acknowledged by me,
J. Provoost, clerk.

[CONDITIONS FOR THE SALE OF SOME FURNITURE AND HOUSEHOLD EFFECTS BY THE ATTORNEY OF DIRCK JANSSEN KROON]

[480] Conditions and terms upon which Adriaen Gerritsen, attorney for Dirck Janssen Kroon, intends to sell at public auction to the highest bidder some furniture and household goods belonging to said Kroon, for which payment shall occur in good whole merchantable beaver skins within the time of one month after today; everything that is less than a beaver the buyer shall pay for at *f*22:– a beaver. For whoever buys more than one item, the sums will be added together, and reduced to whole beavers. The buyer shall also be obligated to furnish sufficient sureties for the purchase money at once. The auction fees shall become a charge to the buyer in payment as before.

[*In the margin was written*:] One bed retained for *f*140.

Slichtenhorst a lantern	*f*3: 5
Jochum Wessels a tin colender	*f*4:
Philip Pietersen a large tin bucket	*f*5:
Mr. Jan Leck [Beck?] a pewter bowl and 1 ditto salt cellar	*f*7: 5
Mr. Jacob a pewter lidded tankard	*f*4: 5
Adriaen Gerritsen a pewter chamber pot	*f*5:
Jurriaen Teunisse 1 tin sugar canister	*f*3:
Idem a pewter colender	*f*5: 5
Philip Pietersen a copper mortar	*f*8:15
Adriaen Gerritsen 2 pewter saucers	*f*7:15
Idem a copper shafing dish	*f*7:10
J. Provoost 2 pewter saucers	*f*7:
Adriaen Gerritsen a small pewter oil pitcher	*f*3:5
Philip Pietersen 1 funnel, one large copper spoon	*f*5:
J: Provoost 2 copper candlesticks	*f*8
Stoffel Janssen 2 pairs of copper snuffers	*f*2:
Adriaen Gerrit a pewter saucer	*f*4:10
Henderick Rosenboom a copper stewpan	*f*15:15
Jan van Aken an iron candlestick	*f*2:5
Gijsbert *de snijder* a sconce	*f*1:10
	*f*110: 5

[481] Stoffel Janssen an iron candlestick	*f*1:
Isaack de Haen pewter beaker, gilt	*f*2:5
Philip Pietersen one ditto	*f*2:15
Isaack de Haen a sconce	*f*1:
Jan Cloet an iron pepper mill	*f*3:
Henderick Rosenboom an iron shafing dish	*f*3:
Jan Vinhagel 2 small pewter saucers	*f*2:
Philip Pietersen a pewter pitcher	*f*3:10
Willem Brouwer a pewter beaker	*f*2:15
Volcker Janssen a small pewter pint	*f*2:10
Idem 2 small pewter saucers	*f*2:10
Philip Pietersen 2 small pewter cups	*f*2:

Adriaen Gerritsen a small pewter pint	*f*2:10
Gerrit Slichtenhorst a skimmer	*f*3:15
Adriaen Gerritsen a mustard pot	*f*1:10
Idem a small copper pan	*f*5:
Jan Cloet a pewter bowl	*f*5:
Slichtenhorst a small pewter beaker	*f*1:
Volckert Janssen one ditto	*f*1:
J: Provoost a pewter salt cellar	*f*1:15
Adriaen Gerritsen 6 pewter table plates	*f*7:
Johannes Provoost a pewter saucer	*f*5:10
Idem 2 andirons	*f*7:10
Jan Hendericksen Bruijn 6 pewter spoons	*f*2:5
Isaack de Haen a tin powder box	*f*2:10
Gijsbert *de snijder* a chopping knife	*f*2:10
C: Bogardus a lamp and a sconce	*f*3:
Henderick Rosenboom a chain pot hanger	*f*4:5
Volckert Janssen an iron tongs	*f*2:5
Adriaen Gerritsen a frying pan	*f*2:15
Jan van Aken an iron ditto	*f*1:10
Adriaen Gerritsen a pot hanger	*f*6:
Jan van Aken a mirror	*f*10:
Barent *de smit* 2 copper taps	*f*2: 5
Meester Jacob 4 paintings	*f*31:
Robbert 2 small paintings	*f*8:5
Jurriaen Teunissen 2 ditto	*f*6:5
Cor. Bogardus a slate almanac	*f*3:10
Rosenboom one ditto	*f*2:
Jan Bastiaensen 3 small paintings	*f*3:
Meester Adriaen 3 ditto	*f*4: 5
	*f*277:10

[482] *Meester* Adriaen another 3 small paintings	*f*4:
Wouter *de ramaker* 3 ditto	*f*3:10
Meester Adriaen 3 ditto	*f*2: 5
Rosenboom 3 ditto	*f*2: 5
Idem 3 ditto	*f*1:15
Robbert Sandersen three ditto	*f*1:5
J: Provoost 2 curtains and a valance	*f*20:10
Gerrit Lansingh 2 curtains	*f*11:5

Adriaen Gerritsen a coverlet	*f*13:5
Jan Bastiaensen 3 small earthenware saucers	*f*3:
Jurriaen Teunissen 3 ditto	*f*1:10
Rosenboom 3 ditto	*f*1:10
C. Bogardus three ditto	*f*1:15
Jurriaen Teunissen 2 ditto	*f*2:5
Roosenboom 2 ditto	*f*2:
Dirck Wesselsz 2 small paintings	*f*5:
Rosenboom 2 dito	*f*3:10
Poulus Martensz 2 ditto	*f*3:15
Adriaen Gerritsen a brush	*f*2:5
Jacob Schermerhoorn 2 chair cushions	*f*6:
Adriaen Gerritsen 2 sheets	*f*14:
Antony Janssen 2 ditto	f8:
Jan Hendr. Bruijn 2 ditto	f8:
Rosenboom 2 whole and one old pillow case	*f*5:
Volckert Janssen 1 wooden bin and 7 or 8 ditto table plates	*f*1:
Goossen Gerritsen a duster	*f*1:10
Paulus Martensen 3 paintings	*f*2:10
Barent *de smit* 3 ditto	*f*2:5
Goossen Gerritsen 1 large chest	*f*11:
Jan Janssen Ouderkerck 3 chairs	*f*4:
	*f*427: 5

[DECLARATION ABOUT LAND AT THE GOJER'S KIL BY QUESKIMIET, AEPIE, WICKEPE, KLEIJN DAVIDTIE]

[483] Today, the 14th of May *anno* 1664 appeared before me, Johannes La Montagne, in the service of the general chartered West India Company, admitted by the lord director general and councilors of New Netherland vice director and commissary at Fort Orange and the village of Beverwijck, in the presence of the honorable Jan Hendericksz van Bael and Jan Costersen van Aken, magistrates of the same court, these Indians mentioned below named Queskimiet, son of Pacies, Aepie, Wickepe, *Kleijn* Davidtie, who, at the request of Jan Tomassen and Volckert Janssen, and translated by Jan Dareth, testify and declare as follows:

First, they say that it is eighteen years ago that Jacob Janssen Flodder bought the Gojers kil, but no land with it, only a small piece to the north of the aforesaid kil, which was allowed to him to make a garden, for which they, witnesses owners have received only one piece of cloth for rent. The witnesses being asked whether Jacob Janssen Flodder has bought any land at Schotack, unanimously declare no, but that he only has had a small piece of land that they had consented to him for one year to sow oats upon; furthermore, that he has had a hay barrack there, which was to store his grain for the winter, but that he never has had any property there. The witnesses asked again, who are the right owners of Schotack and the mainland as far as the island extends, they declare Jan Tomassen and Volckert Janssen to be the true owners **[484]**, who have bought the same and paid for it, and nobody else. They also declare that, according to the bill of sale of Wattawit, dated the 4th of October *anno* 1663, that Wattawit has been the true owner of the land on the mainland where Machack Notas' house has stood. They say that yesterday, the 13th of this month, they also have declared all of the above at the house of Mr. Renselaert, in the presence of the translator Jan Daret and Marten Gerritsen. Thus done in Fort Orange, the 14th of May *anno* 1664.

This is the mark of  Queskimiet made with his own hand.

This is the mark of  Aepje made with his own hand.

This is the mark of  Wickepe made with his own hand.

This is the mark of  Davidie made with his own hand.

In acknowledgment of the truth this has been signed by us, magistrates mentioned above,
J.H. van Bael
Jan Koster
Jan Dareth
La Montagne, commissary at Fort Orange.

[COMPLAINT BY VOLCKERT JANSEN AND JAN TOMASSEN]

[485] Appeared before me, Johannes La Montagne, in the service of the general chartered West India Company, admitted by the lord director general and councilors of New Netherland vice director and commissary at Fort Orange and the village of Beverwijck, Volckert Janssen and Jan Tomassen, who by way of complaint declare that on the 12th of this month the lord Renselaer, together with *Schout* Swart and the secretary Schelluijn have been on the island of Schotack and there have forbidden Jan Martensen, tenant of the appearers, to continue the tillage of plowing and sowing, upon which prohibition the tenant was afraid to continue the tillage. Therefore, the appearers freed said tenant, Jan Martensen, from all damage concerning the cultivation of the land that may come upon him on account of the said prohibition; which is done without physical offense, and only intended to complain to the officer and the appearers about the violence that may be done to them. Done in Fort Orange 15 May *anno* 1664.

Volckart Jansz
Jan Thomas
La Montagne, commissary at Fort Orange.

[ACKNOWLEDGMENT OF DEBT BY PIETER JANSSEN *DE BOER* TO PIETER RIJVERDINGH]

[486] Appeared before me, Johannes La Montagne, in the service of the general chartered West India Company, admitted by the lord director general and councilors of New Netherland vice director and commissary at Fort Orange and the village of Beverwijck, in the presence of the honorable Jan Verbeeck and Gerrit Slichtenhorst, magistrates of the same court, Pieter Janssen *de boer* who hereby acknowledges and declares to be well, honestly and truly indebted to *Sr.* Pieter Rijverdingh for the sum of eighty guilders Holland money stemming from goods and merchandise received to his content; which aforesaid sum of eighty guilders Holland money the appearer promises to pay to said Rijverdinck or his attorney Adriaen Janssen van Leijden on the first of July *anno* 1665. In case said appearer, Pieter Janssen, fails, he promises to pay interest on the same at 12 percent, which shall commence on this date, pledging therefor his person and estate, moveable and immoveable, present and future, and as a mortgage and special collateral he pledges his house and lot, located in the village of Beverwijck; adjoins immediately next to Claes Uijlspiegel and Lambert van Valckenborgh, in order, if necessary, to recover the payment of the aforesaid sum without damage or cost. Done at Fort Orange the 10th of June *anno* 1664.

This is the mark  of Pieter Janssen *de boer*,
made with his own hand.
Gerrit Slichtenhorst
Jan Verbeeck

Acknowledged by me,
La Montagne, commissary at Fort Orange.

[ACKNOWLEDGMENT OF DEBT BY JACKES CORNELIS TO SWEERUS TEUNESEN]

[487] Appeared before me, Johannes La Montagne, in the service of the general chartered West India Company, admitted by the lord director general and councilors of New Netherland vice director and commissary at Fort Orange and the village of Beverwijck, in the presence of the honorable Jan Hendricksen van Baelen and Jan van Aken, magistrates of the same court, Jacus Cornelis, dwelling at Schonhechtede, who hereby acknowledges and declares to be honestly and truly indebted to Sweerus Teunesen for the sum of six hundred and ninety-three guilders in beavers for goods and advance received to his full content; which said sum he, Jacus Cornelissen, promises to pay in the year of our Lord *anno* 1668 in the month of May. For the payment of said sum he pledges his person and estate, moveable and immoveable, but mainly, he mortgages the island located at Schonhechtede, named Marten's island, renouncing all exceptions, which might militate against the mortgage. Done at Fort Orange, 3 July *anno* 1664.

The mark of Jacus
 Corneelissen

[ACKNOWLEDGMENT OF DEBT BY JAN VAN EECKELEN TO CORNELIS TEUNISSEN BOS, ADMINISTRATOR OF THE ESTATE OF CORNELIS MAERSEN]

[488] Appeared before me, Johannes La Montagne, in the service of the general chartered West India Company, admitted by the lord director general and councilors of New Netherland vice director and commissary at Fort Orange and the village of Beverwijck, in the presence of the honorable Jan Verbeeck and Jacob Schermerhoorn, magistrates of the same court, Jan van Eeckelen, who hereby acknowledges and declares to be well, honestly and truly indebted to Cornelis Teunissen Bos, administrator of the estate of Cornelis Maersen, for the sum of thirty-two beavers and a half, stemming from a draft by Albert Gerritsen due to the said estate, which aforesaid number of thirty-two and a half beavers he, appearer, by agreement made with said administrator, promises to pay within the time of three years from this date, or sooner, but with interest at 10 percent, commencing on next 6th of August, the appearer pledging therefore his person and estate, moveable and immoveable, present and future; he especially pledges his house and lot, situated in the village of Beverwijck; adjoins to the north of Jan Dareth, and to the south of Pieter Loockemans, as a mortgage and special collateral, in order, if necessary, to recover the payment of the aforesaid number of thirty-two and a half beavers without cost or damage. Done at Fort Orange the 7th of July *anno* 1664.

Ian Iansen van Eeckel
Jan Verbeeck
Jacob Schermerhoorn

Acknowledged by me,
La Montagne, commissary at Fort Orange.

[SALE OF A HOUSE AND LOT BY FRANCOYS BOON TO JOCHIM WESSELSZ *BACKER*]

[489] Appeared before me, Johannes La Montagne, in the service of the general chartered West India Company, admitted by the lord director general and councilors of New Netherland vice director and commissary at Fort Orange and the village of Beverwijck, in the presence of the honorable Gerrit Slichtenhorst and Stoffel Janssen, magistrates of the same court, the honorable Francoijs Boon, former magistrate of the said place, who declares to have ceded and conveyed, as he hereby does cede and convey in real and actual possession to and for the benefit of Jochim Wesselsz *backer*, his heirs or assigns, a house and lot located in the village of Beverwijck; adjoins east and west and to the south of the public road, to the north of the house of Gillis Pietersz, and that in such magnitude as it lies enclosed in its fence, with all the right and title that he, grantor has had therein by virtue of a conveyance granted to him by Stoffel Janssen Abeel of date August 15 *anno* 1659. The grantor acknowledges to have been fully satisfied and paid for the sale, and therefore he promises to free the said house and lot from all actions, claims or demands, which may arise hereafter, excepting the Lord's right, pledging his person and estate, moveable and immoveable, present and future, submitting himself to all laws and judges. Done at Fort Orange the 17th of July *anno* 1664.

Francoijs Boon
Gerrit Slichtenhorst
Stoffel Jansz Abeel

Acknowledged by me,
La Montagne, commissary at Fort Orange.

SALE OF GRAIN BY RUTGER JACOBSEN TO JACOB HEVICK]

[490] Appeared before me Johannes Provoost clerk of the court of Fort Orange and the village of Beverwijck in the presence of the afternamed witnesses Rutger Jacobsen, who hereby declares to have sold, ceded and conveyed to Jacob Hevick, his share of the grain that is standing on the seller's island, being a fourth portion of what is standing there upon, for the number of thirty-five good whole merchantable beaver skins, which said Jacob Hevick promises to pay to said Rut Jacobsen by an abatement on the mortgage which the said Hevick has upon the seller's island; moreover, the seller renounces said grain and hereby empowers the buyer to harvest the same without any hindrance or obstacle by anyone, from which he also promises to free him. Thus done without craft or guile in Fort Orange in the presence of Claes Jacobsen and Sacharias Sickels as witnesses invited hereto on this 16th of July *anno* 1664.

Rutger Jacobsz
This is the mark of  Jacob Hevick,
made with his own hand.
Claes Jacobse
Sacharias Seckelsz

[SALE OF A GARDEN BY FRANCOYS BOON
TO JURRIAEN TEUNISSEN]

[491] Appeared before me, Johannes La Montagne, in the service of the general chartered West India Company, admitted by the lord director general and councilors of New Netherland vice director and commissary at Fort Orange and the village of Beverwijck, in the presence of the honorable Jan Verbeeck and Gerrit Slichtenhorst magistrates of the same court, the honorable Francoijs Boon, former magistrate of the said place, who declares to have ceded and conveyed, as he hereby does cede and convey in real and actual possession, to and for the benefit of Jurriaen Teunissen, his heirs or assigns, a garden located in the village of Beverwijck behind Fort Orange; adjoins on the west and on the north the public road, and this in such magnitude as it is lying within its fence, with all the right and title that he, grantor has had therein, and the grantor acknowledges to have been fully satisfied and paid for the sale [*three lines crossed out*], pledging therefor his person and estate, moveable [and immoveable], present and future, submitting himself to all laws and judges. Done at Fort Orange the 16th of July *anno* 1664.

Francoijs Boon
Gerrit Slichtenhorst
Jan Verbeeck

Acknowledged by me,
La Montagne, commissary at Fort Orange.

[SALE OF A GARDEN BY JAN ROELOFFSEN
TO WILLEM BROUWER]

[492] Appeared before me, Johannes La Montagne, in the service of the general chartered West India Company, admitted by the lord director general and councilors of New Netherland vice director and commissary at Fort Orange and the village of Beverwijck, in the presence of the honorable Jan Hendericksz van Bael and Jan Coster van Aken, magistrates of the same court, Jan Roeloffsen, inhabitant of the said village, who declares that he has ceded and conveyed, as he hereby does cede and convey in real and actual possession to and for the benefit of Willem Brouwer, his heirs or assigns, a garden located in the village of Beverwijck near Fort Orange; adjoins in the back Lord Renselaer, to the south of Annetje Bogardus' heirs, to the east of the road, and to the north of Abraham Staets, long seven rods and wide five rods; which garden on the 25th of October 1653 was by the lord director general and councilors of New Netherland granted by patent to Albert Gerritsen, from whom the grantor has received it by conveyance on date the 4th of July *anno* 1658. The grantor acknowledges to have been fully satisfied and paid for the sale, promising to free the said garden from all actions, claims or demands, which may arise hereafter, pledging thereto his person and estate, moveable and immoveable, present and future, submitting himself to all laws and judges. Done at Fort Orange the 24th of July *anno* 1664.

Jan Roeloffs
Jan Koster
Acknowledged by me,
La Montagne, commissary at Fort Orange.

[SALE OF A GARDEN BY WILLEM BROUWER TO ABRAHAM STAETS]

[**493**] Appeared before me, Johannes La Montagne, in the service of the general chartered West India Company, admitted by the lord director general and councilors of New Netherland vice director and commissary at Fort Orange and the village of Beverwijck, in the presence of the honorable Jan Verbeeck and Stoffel Janssen Abeel, magistrates of said village, Willem Brouwer, inhabitant of said village, who, by virtue of conveyance of this date granted to him, grantor, by Jan Roeloffsen, declares that he has again ceded, conveyed and transported, as he hereby does cede and transport in real and actual possession, to and for the benefit of Capt. Abraham Staets, former magistrate of this place, his heirs or assigns, a garden located in the village of Beverwijck near Fort Orange; adjoins in the back lord Renselaer, to the south of Annetie Bogardus's heirs, to the east of the road, and to the north the grantee, long seven rods and wide five rods; which garden was granted to Albert Gerritsen by patent on the 25th of October 1653 by the lord director general and councilors of New Netherland; the grantor acknowledges to have been satisfied and paid for the sale and delivery, for which he promises to free the said garden from all actions, claims or demands, which may arise hereafter, pledging thereto his person and estate, moveable and immoveable, present and future, submitting himself to all laws and judges.

Done at Fort Orange the 24th of July *anno* 1664.

Willem Brouwer
Jan Verbeeck
Stoffel Jansz

Acknowledged by me,
La Montagne, commissary at Fort Orange.

[SALE OF A HOUSE AND LOT BY NICOLAES GOUVERNEUR TO JAN HENDERICKSZ BRUYN]

[**494**] Appeared before me Johannes Provoost clerk of the court of Fort Orange and the village of Beverwijck the honorable Nicolaes Gouverneur, substitute for the honorable Cornelis Steenwijck, attorney for Barent van Marle on the one side, and Jan Hendericksz Bruijn on the other side, who in presence of the afternamed witnesses declare that they have agreed about the purchase of the house and lot of Barent van Marle, deceased, located in the village of Beverwijck, in the following manner: first, said Claes Gouverneur, by virtue of a power of attorney sells to said Jan Hendericksz Bruijn the house and lot of the aforesaid van Marle, deceased, in such size and boundaries as the said Barent van Marle has purchased it from Cornelis Vos, according to bill of sale of date the 30th of July *anno* 1661, and he shall deliver the aforesaid house fourteen days after this date, free and unencumbered, except for the lord's right; for which Jan Hendericksz Bruijn promises to pay immediately upon delivery the number of sixty good whole merchantable beaver skins and fourteen half beavers in one sum, and moreover, an appropriate conveyance will be delivered to the buyer upon payment. Thus done in the presence of the honorable Gerrit Swart and Jacob de Hince, without craft or guile, in Fort Orange on the 14th of August *anno* 1664.

Claes Gouverneur
Jan Hendrick Bruijn
G. Swart
De Hinsse

Acknowledged by me,
J: Provoost, secretary.

[SALE OF A HOUSE AND LOT BY SANDER LEENDERSEN GLEN TO JAN HENDERICKSZ VAN BAEL]

[**495**] Appeared before me, Johannes La Montagne, in the service of the general chartered West India Company, admitted by the lord director

general and councilors of New Netherland vice director and commissary at Fort Orange and the village of Beverwijck, in the presence of the honorable Jan Verbeeck and Stoffel Janssen, magistrates of said village, the honorable Sander Leendersen Glen, (former magistrate), who declares that he has sold, ceded, and conveyed, as he hereby does in real and actual possession to and for the benefit of the honorable Jan Hendericksz van Bael, magistrate of the said place, his heirs or assigns, a house and lot, situated in the village of Beverwijck at the hill; adjoins to the north Jan Tomassen, to the south Henderick Kuijler, east and west the street, in such magnitude as it lies enclosed in its fence. Which lot the grantor has bought at public auction from the lords magistrates under an execution order on the person of Marten Herbertsen; and he, grantor, acknowledges to have been fully satisfied and paid for the sale and delivery hereof with the sum of eight hundred seventy-six guilders in beavers, for which he promises to free the said house and lot from all actions, claims or demands, which may arise hereafter, except for the lord's right, pledging his person and estate, moveable and immoveable, present and future, submitting himself to all laws and judges. Done at Fort Orange the 18th of August *anno* 1664.

Sander Lenrsen Glen
Stoffel Jansz Abeel
Jan Verbeeck

Acknowledged by me,
La Montagne, commissary at Fort Orange.

[ACKNOWLEDGMENT OF DEBT BY JAN FRANCEN VAN HOESEM TO NICOLAES MEIJER]

[**496**] Appeared before me, Johannes La Montagne, in the service of the general chartered West India Company, admitted by the lord director general and councilors of New Netherland vice director and commissary at Fort Orange and the village of Beverwijck, in the presence of the honorable Gerrit Slichtenhorst and Jan Hendericksz van Bael, magistrates of the same court, Jan Francen van Hoesem,

inhabitant of the said village, who hereby acknowledges and declares to be well, honestly and truly indebted to *Sr.* Nicolaes Meijer *schepen* and merchant at Amsterdam in New Netherland, for the sum of one thousand three hundred and forty-six Carolus guilders and eleven stuivers in good whole merchantable beaver skins, stemming from goods and merchandise delivered, as well as monies provided, according to an honest account thereof received; which aforesaid sum of one thousand three hundred and forty-six guilders and eleven stuivers the appearer promises to pay in two installments, of which the first will be on the first of August *anno* 1665, the just half; and the other half on the first of July *anno* 1666, and that with its interest at ten percent, commencing on this date and lasting until the full payment, but the interest shall not continue longer than that it will please the acceptor, for which said Jan Francen van Hoesem pledges his person and goods, moveable and **[497]** immoveable, present and future, he especially pledges both his houses with the lot and garden behind the same, everything as it stands, situated in the village of Beverwijck; adjoins to the north of Jochim Wessels, and said Meijer shall also draw and receive the rent of his, appearer's, house which is occupied by Cornelis van Dijck, and similarly his, appearer's farm and lands located in the Claverrack, to recover, if necessary, with all of this the payment of the aforesaid sum without cost or damage. Thus done at Fort Orange on date of the 26th of August *anno* 1664.

This is the mark of  Jan Francen van Hoesem,
made with his own hand.
Gerrit Slichtenhorst
J. H. van Bael

Acknowledged by me,
La Montagne, commissary at Fort Orange.

[SALE OF A HOUSE AND LOT BY CLAES GOUVERNEUR TO JAN HENDERICKSZ BRUIJN]

[**498**] Appeared before me, Johannes La Montagne, in the service of the general chartered West India Company, admitted by the lord director general and councilors of New Netherland vice director and commissary at Fort Orange and the village of Beverwijck, in the presence of the honorable Stoffel Janssen Abeel and Jan Hendericksz van Bael, magistrates of the same court, *Sr.* Claes Gouverneur, administrator of the estate of Barent van Marle, who declares that he has granted and conveyed, as he hereby does grant and convey, in real and actual possession to and for the benefit of Jan Hendericksz Bruijn, his heirs or assigns, a house and lot located in the village of Beverwijck; adjoins to the south the street, to the north the kil, to the east the grantee, and to the west Jurriaen Teunissen; entire length nine rods, wide in the rear on the kil seventeen and a half feet, in front as wide as the house, with a three and a half feet-wide alley on the entire length of the east side of the house; which lot is a portion of the patent granted by director general and councilors to Cornelis Vos, and the grantor acknowledges to have been fully satisfied and paid for the sale and delivery of the same, of which the lord Jeremias van Renselaer has received the sum of three hundred and ninety-six guilders in beavers, which was due to him by virtue of a mortgage on the aforesaid house and lot; and the appearer promises to free the said house and lot from all demands, claims or pretensions, which [**499**] may arise hereafter, pledging his person and estate, moveable and immoveable, present and future without exception, submitting himself to all laws and judges. Thus done at Fort Orange the 28th of August *anno* 1664.

Claes Gouverneur
Stoffel Jansz Abeel
J. H. van Bael

Acknowledged by me,
La Montagne, commissary at Fort Orange.

[ACKNOWLEDGMENT BY JEREMIAS VAN RENSSELAER OF PAYMENT FROM CLAES GOUVERNEUR]

Appeared before me, Johannes Provoost, clerk of the court of Fort Orange and the village of Beverwijck, in the presence of the honorable Stoffel Janssen and Jan Hendericksz van Bael, magistrates of the same court, the lord Jeremias van Renselaer, who hereby acknowledges to have received from *Sr.* Claes Gouverneur, attorney for Barent van Marle, deceased, the sum of three hundred and ninety-six guilders in beavers as satisfaction of a portion of a mortgage which he has on the second payment for Cornelis Vos' house, which the aforesaid Barent van Marle had bought, and the said Renselaer promises to free the said Gouverneur in his said capacity, or his successor after him, from all demands or claims, which may arise hereafter. Done in Fort Orange the 28th of August *anno* 1664.

Stoffel Jansz Abeel
Jeremias van Rensselaer
J. H. van Bael

[SALE OF A HOUSE AND LOT BY PIETER ADRIAENSZ TO PHILIP PIETERSEN SCHUIJLER]

[500] Appeared before me, Johannes La Montagne, in the service of the general chartered West India Company, admitted by the lord director general and councilors of New Netherland vice director and commissary at Fort Orange and the village of Beverwijck, in the presence of the honorable Jan Hendericksz van Bael and Jan Coster van Aken, magistrates of the same court, Pieter Adriaensz, inhabitant of Schanhechtade, who declares that he has ceded and conveyed, as he hereby does cede and convey in real and actual possession to and for the benefit of the honorable Philip Pietersen Schuijler, his heirs or assigns, a house and lot located in the village of Beverwijck; adjoins to the north Adriaen Appel, and to the south Jan Barentsen Poest, deceased, to the west the street; long ten rods, and wide four rods; which lot was by the director general and councilors of New Netherland granted to the said grantor by patent on date [*blank*] *anno* 16 [*blank*]; and he, grantor, acknowledges to have been fully satisfied and paid for the sale and delivery hereof, promising to free the same from all actions, claims or demands, which may arise hereafter, pledging therefor his person and estate, moveable and immoveable, present and future, submitting himself to all laws and judges. Done at Fort Orange the 11th of September *anno* 1664.

Pieter Adriaensz
J. H. van Bael
Jan Koster

Acknowledged by me,
La Montagne, commissary at Fort Orange.

[ACKNOWLEDGMENT OF DEBT BY TOMAS POULUS TO JAN KOSTER VAN AKEN]

[501] Appeared before me, Johannes La Montagne, in the service of the general chartered West India Company, admitted by the lord director general and councilors of New Netherland vice director and commissary at Fort Orange and the village of Beverwijck, in the presence of the honorable Jan Verbeeck and Stoffel Janssen, magistrates of the same court, Tomas Poulus, inhabitant of the said village, who hereby acknowledges and declares to be well, honestly and truly indebted to the honorable Jan Koster van Aken for the number of twelve good whole merchantable beaver skins, for goods and merchandise received to his content, and he promises to pay the aforesaid twelve beavers on the first of May *anno* 1665; and by failure of payment he shall be obliged to pay appropriate interest; for which he, appearer, pledges his person and estate, moveable and immoveable, present and future, and he especially pledges as a mortgage and special collateral his house and lot, located in the village of Beverwijck on the west side of the street right opposite Jan Labate, to, if necessary, recover the payment of the said twelve beavers without loss or damage. Done in Fort Orange, the 15th of September *anno* 1664.

Thomas Powell
Jan Verbeeck
Stoffel Jansz Abeel
Acknowledged by me,
La Montagne, commissary at Fort Orange.

[SALE OF A HOUSE AND LOT BY REYER ALBERTSEN TO JOHANNES BAPTIST VAN RENSSELAER AND GOOSSEN GERRITSEN]

[**502**] Appeared before me, Johannes La Montagne, in the service of the general chartered West India Company, admitted by the lord director general and councilors of New Netherland vice director and commissary at Fort Orange and the village of Beverwijck, in the presence of the honorable Jan Hendericksz van Bael and Jan Koster van Aken, magistrates of the same court, Reijer Albert, inhabitant of said village, who declares that he has ceded and conveyed, as he hereby does cede and convey in real and actual possession to and for the benefit of the lord Johannes Baptist van Renselaer and Goossen Gerritsen, former magistrate of this place, their heirs or assigns, a house and lot located in the said village of Beverwijck on the Third Kil; adjoins to the north and to the west the grantor, and to the south and east the public road; long six rods and wide four rods, which lot is a portion of the patent granted to him, grantor by the lord director general and councilors of New Netherland on the 25th of October *anno* 1653; and the grantor acknowledges to have been fully satisfied and paid for the sale and delivery hereof, and therefore promises to free the said house and lot from all actions, demands, claims or demands which may arise hereafter, pledging thereto his person and estate, moveable and immoveable, present and future, making himself subject to all laws and judges. Done at Fort Orange the 15th of September *anno* 1664.

This is the mark of  Reijer Albertsen.
Jan Koster
J.H. van Bael
Acknowledged by me,
La Montagne, commissary at Fort Orange.

[SALE OF A HOUSE AND LOT BY JEREMIAS VAN RENSSELAER TO GOOSSEN GERRITSEN]

[503] Appeared before me, Johannes La Montagne, in the service of the general chartered West India Company, admitted by the lord director general and councilors of New Netherland vice director and commissary at Fort Orange and the village of Beverwijck, in the presence of the honorable Jan Verbeeck and Jan Koster van Aken, magistrates of the same court, the lord Jeremias van Renselaer, attorney for his brother Johan Baptist van Renselaer, who, by virtue of a conveyance given to him, grantor, and Goossen Gerritsen on date of today, declares to have ceded and conveyed again, as he hereby does cede and convey in real and actual possession to and for the benefit of the said Goossen Gerritsen, his heirs or assigns, his portion of the house and lot (being one half) that he and the grantee have bought in company, situated in the village of Beverwijck on the third kil; adjoins to the north and west the said Reijer Elbertsen, to the south and east the public road; in total long six rods and wide four rods; and the grantor acknowledges to have been fully satisfied and paid for the sale and delivery hereof, and therefore promises to free the same from all actions, demands, claims or demands which may arise hereafter, except for the lord's right, pledging thereto his person and estate, moveable and immoveable, present and future, making himself subject to all laws and judges. Done at Fort Orange the 15th of September *anno* 1664.

Jeremias van Rensselaer
Jan Koster
Jan Verbeeck
Acknowledged before me,
La Montagne, commissary at Fort Orange.

[SALE OF A HOUSE AND LOT BY GOOSSEN GERRITSEN TO HENDERICK KOSTER]

[504] Appeared before me, Johannes La Montagne, in the service of the general chartered West India Company, admitted by the lord director general and councilors of New Netherland vice director and commissary at Fort Orange and the village of Beverwijck, in the presence of the honorable Jan Verbeeck and Jan Koster van Aecken, magistrates of the same court, the honorable Goossen Gerritsen, former magistrate, who declares to have ceded and conveyed, as he hereby does cede and convey in real and actual possession to and for the benefit of Henderick Koster, his heirs or assigns, a house and lot situated in the village of Beverwijck at the hill; adjoins to the north of Henderick Rosenboom, to the south of Henderick Anderissen's widow, east and west the public road; [it] is wide five rods and long twenty rods, according to the patent thereof, by the lord director general and councilors of New Netherland granted to Lourens Lourensen, on the 25th of October *anno* 1653; and the grantor acknowledges to have been fully satisfied and paid for the sale and delivery hereof, and therefore promises to free the said house and lot from all actions, demands, claims or demands which may arise hereafter (except for only the lord's right), pledging his person and estate, moveable and immoveable, present and future, submitting himself to all laws and judges. Done at Fort Orange the 15th of September *anno* 1664.

Goossen Gerritsen
Jan Verbeeck
Jan Koster
Acknowledged by me,
La Montagne, commissary at Fort Orange.

[SALE OF A HOUSE AND LOT BY MARCELUS JANSSEN TO ASSER LEVIJ]

[505] Appeared before me, Johannes La Montagne, in the service of the general chartered West India Company, admitted by the lord director general and councilors of New Netherland vice director and commissary at Fort Orange and the village of Beverwijck, in the presence of the honorable Jan Verbeeck and Jan Coster van Aken, magistrates of the same court, Marcelus Janssen, inhabitant of the colony of Rensselaerswijck, who declares to have ceded and conveyed, as he hereby does cede and convey in real and actual possession to and for the benefit of Asser Levij, merchant at Amsterdam in New

Netherland, his heirs or assigns, a house and lot located in the said village of Beverwijck at the hill; adjoins to the north Gerrit Slichtenhorst, to the south the lot of Claes Ripsen, east and west the public road; long according to the patent, twenty-one and a half rods, and wide six rods, specifically that thirty feet of the entire width shall be taken off for the benefit of said Claes Ripsen; which patent was granted to Goossen Gerritsen by the lord director general and councilors of New Netherland on date the 25th of October *anno* 1653, from whom the grantor has received it by conveyance; and the grantor acknowledges to have been fully satisfied and paid for the sale and delivery hereof, and therefore he promises to free the said house and lot from all actions, claims or demands which may arise hereafter (except for the lord's right), pledging thereto his person and estate, moveable and immoveable, making himself subject to all laws and judges. Done at Fort Orange the 15th of September *anno* 1664.

Maercelijs Janssen
Jan Verbeeck
Jan Koster
Acknowledged by me,
La Montagne, commissary at Fort Orange.

[SALE OF A HOUSE AND LOT BY PHILIP PIETERSEN SCHUIJLER TO GOOSSEN GERRITSZ]

[506] Appeared before me, Johannes La Montagne, in the service of the general chartered West India Company, admitted by the lord director general and councilors of New Netherland vice director and commissary at Fort Orange and the village of Beverwijck, in the presence of the honorable Jan Verbeeck and Jan Koster van Aken, magistrates of the same court, the honorable Philip Pietersen Schuijler, former magistrate of this place, who declares that he has ceded and conveyed, as he hereby does cede and convey in real and actual possession to and for the benefit of Goossen Gerritsz, his heirs or assigns, his portion of the house and lot (being one half) that he owns together with the grantee in company; located in the said village of Beverwijck at the hill; adjoins to the north of Henderick Roosenboom and to the south of the widow of Henderick Anderiessen, east and west the public road; in its entirety twenty rods long, and wide five rods according to the patent thereof, which was granted to Lourens Lourensz by the lord director general and councilors of New Netherland on date the 25th of October *anno* 1653. And the grantor acknowledges to have been fully satisfied and paid for the sale and delivery hereof, and therefore promises to free the same from all actions, claims or demands which may arise hereafter, pledging thereto his person and estate, moveable and immoveable, present and future, submitting himself to all laws and judges. Done at Fort Orange the 15th of September *anno* 1664.

Philip Pietersz Schuijler
Jan Verbeeck
Jan Koster
Acknowledged by me,
La Montagne, commissary at Fort Orange.

[SALE OF A LOT BY ABRAHAM STAETS TO PHILIP PIETERSEN SCHUIJLER]

[507] Appeared before me, Johannes La Montagne, in the service of the general chartered West India Company, admitted by the lord director general and councilors of New Netherland vice director and commissary at Fort Orange and the village of Beverwijck, in the presence of the honorable Jan Verbeeck and Jan Koster van Aken, magistrates of the same court, the honorable Abraham Staets, former magistrate of this place, who declares to have ceded and conveyed, as he hereby does cede and convey to and for the benefit of the honorable Philip Pietersen Schuijler, also former magistrate, his heirs or assigns, a lot located in the village of Beverwijck; adjoins to the east the hill, to the west a common alley, to the south the street, to the north the kil; wide from the common alley toward the west six rods two feet, long from the street in front until on the kil in the back, which lot is a portion of the patent granted to him, grantor, by the lord director general and councilors of New Netherland on the 25th of October *anno* 1653. And the grantor acknowledges to have been fully satisfied and paid for the sale and delivery hereof, and therefore promises to free the same lot from all actions, claims or demands which may arise hereafter, pledging thereto his person and estate, moveable and immoveable, present and future, submitting himself to all laws and judges. Done at Fort Orange the 15th of September *anno* 1664.

Abram Staes
Jan Verbeeck
Jan Koster
Acknowledged by me,
La Montagne, commissary at Fort Orange.

[SALE OF A LOT BY PHILIP PIETERSEN SCHUIJLER
TO GIJSBERT JANSSEN

[**508**] Appeared before me, Johannes La Montagne, in the service of the general chartered West India Company, admitted by the lord director general and councilors of New Netherland vice director and commissary at Fort Orange and the village of Beverwijck, in the presence of the honorable Stoffel Janssen and Jan Coster van Aken, magistrates of the same court, the honorable Philip Pietersen Schuijler, who declares to have ceded and conveyed, as he hereby does cede and convey to and for the benefit of Gijsbert Janssen, his heirs or assigns, a lot situated in the village of Beverwijck at the hill; adjoins to the east the grantor, to the west a common alley or the domicile of Cornelis Steenwijck, to the south the street, to the north the kil; is wide one rod ten feet minus 2½ inches, long from the street in front until the kil in the back, which lot is a portion of the patent granted to the honorable Abraham Staets of date 25th of October *anno* 1653, from whom the grantor has received it by conveyance; and he, grantor, acknowledges to have been fully satisfied and paid for the sale and delivery hereof, and therefore promises to free the said lot from all actions, claims or demands which may arise hereafter, pledging thereto his person and estate, moveable and immoveable, present and future, making himself subject to all laws and judges. Done at Fort Orange the 15th of September *anno* 1664.

Philip Pietersen Schuijler
Stoffel Jansz Abeel
Jan Koster
Acknowledged by me,
La Montagne, commissary at Fort Orange.

[CONVEYANCE OF A HOUSE AND LOT BY GIJSBERT JANSSEN TO HARMEN ALBERTSEN VEDDER]

[**509**] Appeared before me, Johannes La Montagne, in the service of the general chartered West India Company, admitted by the lord director general and councilors of New Netherland vice director and commissary at Fort Orange and the village of Beverwijck, in the presence of the honorable Gerrit Slichtenhorst and Stoffel Janssen, magistrates of the same court, Gijsbert Janssen, who declares to have ceded and conveyed, as he hereby does cede and convey in real and actual possession to and for the benefit of Harmen Albertsen Vedder, his heirs or assigns, a house and lot located near Fort Orange in the village of Beverwijck at the hill; adjoins to the east Philip Pietersz Schuijler, to the west a common alley or the domicile of *Sr.* Cornelis Steenwijck, to the south the street, to the north the kil; is wide one rod ten feet minus 2½ inches, long from the street in front until the kil in the back, which lot the grantor has acquired by conveyance from the said Philip Pietersen Schuijler, by virtue of a patent granted to the honorable Abraham Staets of date 25th of October *anno* 1653, of which this lot is a portion; and the grantor acknowledges to have been fully satisfied and paid for the sale and delivery hereof, and therefore he promises to free the said house and lot from all actions, claims or demands which may arise hereafter, pledging thereto his person and estate, moveable and immoveable, present and future, submitting himself to all laws and judges. Done at Fort Orange the 15th of September *anno* 1664.

Gijsebert Yansen
Stoffel Jansz Abeel
Acknowledged by me,
La Montagne, commissary at Fort Orange.

[CONDITIONS FOR THE SALE OF THE SLAUGHTER EXCISE]

[**510**] Conditions and terms upon which the lords magistrates of Albany† intend to farm out at public auction to the highest bidder the slaughter excise for the period of one year.

The farming of the slaughter excise shall begin on the first of October of this year and end on the last of September *anno* 1665, old style. The farmer shall receive for the slaughtered animals, whether it will be an ox, cow, calf, bull, hog, goat or sheep, a stuiver of each guilder of the value of the same, to wit, whatever has been bought for beavers will bring 20 stuivers in sewant for one beaver, and in case of dispute, to be valued by impartial persons. The farmer remains obligated to furnish, to the satisfaction of the honorable farming supervisors, two sufficient sureties for the excise money each as principal, at the choice of the honorable farming supervisors, and within the time of six weeks after this date to pay the just half of the promised purchase money, the other half on New Year's day, being the first of January *anno* 1665, old style, in good merchantable sewant; and if the farmer cannot provide sufficient sureties, it shall be re-auctioned at his costs and charges; and all that it falls short, he shall be obligated to make good, and whatever it brings more, he shall derive no profit there from. The farmer shall receive of the slaughtered animals what has been declared since the first of October, new style.

After offering it for sale Henderick Roosenboom remained the final bidder and farmer for the sum of seven hundred and eighty guilders according to the aforesaid conditions, [**511**] for which Jan Tomassen and Evert Janssen Wendel stand sureties and principals, pledging their persons and estates, moveable and immoveable. Done at Albany, the 27th of September *anno* 1664, old style.

---

† The reference to Albany instead of Fort Orange and Beverwijck reflects the English takeover of New Netherland. The articles of transfer were agreed to on 27 August 1664, old style, as the English used the Julian calendar, which was ten days behind the modern Gregorian calendar used by the Dutch.

Henderijck Rooseboom
Jan Tomasz
Evert Jansz Wendel

[SALE OF A HOUSE AND LOT BY THE ADMINISTRATORS OF THE ESTATE OF ANDERIES HERBERTSEN TO JURRIAEN JANSSEN]

[**511**] Appeared before me Johannes Provoost, by the lords magistrates of Albany admitted clerk of its honorable court, and in the presence of the honorable Gerrit Slichtenhorst and Jan Koster van Aken, chosen witnesses out of their honorable board, Volckert Janssen and Adriaen van Ilpendam, the administrators of the estate of Anderies Herbertsen, who declare that they have ceded and conveyed, as they hereby do cede and convey in real and actual possession to and for the benefit of Jurriaen Janssen, his heirs or assigns, a house and lot located in the village of Albany at the hill, adjoining to the south of Jacob Schermerhoorn, to the north and east of the road, to the west of the hill;[†] it is wide five rods and long twenty rods according to the patent thereof granted to Gijsbert Cornelis[sen] van Wesop on the 25th of October 1653, which the said Andries Herbertsen had by transport acquired from Francoijs Boon, for which house and lot the grantors acknowledge to have been fully satisfied and paid, and therefore promise to free the same from all actions, claims or demands which may arise thereafter, pledging thereto their persons and estates, moveable and immoveable, present and future, making themselves subject to all laws and judges. Done at Albany, the first of October 1664, old style.

Volckart Jansz
Adriaen van Ilpendam
Gerrit Slichtenhorst
Jan Koster.

---

† The text reads: *palende besuyden Jacob Schermerhoorn, benoorden ende beoosten de wegh bewesten het geberchte*. As this would place the lot west of the hill instead of east of it, these directions should be reversed and read: "adjoining to the south Jacob Schermerhoorn, to the north and east the road, to the west the hill."

[CONDITIONS FOR FARMING OUT THE BEER, WINE, AND SPIRITS EXCISE]

[**513**] Conditions and terms on which the highest officer and the lords magistrates of Albany intend to farm out, in the name of and on behalf of the lord governor of New York, to the highest bidder the excise of all wines, beers, and spirits consumable and to be drawn by the innkeepers, tappers, and retailers in and around Albany and the colony of Rensselaerswijck.

The farming of the excise shall begin on the 22nd of October, old style, and the first of November, new style, and end on the 22nd of October, old style, *anno* 1665, being the time of twelve months, during which time the farmer may collect and receive for all wines, beers, or distilled waters by any tappers and innkeepers to be consumed or drawn, as follows:

For a barrel of domestic brewed beer	*f*4,
For a barrel of overseas beer	*f*6,
For a hogshead of French wine	*f*20,
For an anker of the same	*f*4,
For an anker of Spanish wine, brandy, mead, or distilled waters	*f*7,
For an anker of cider	*f*2,

Larger and smaller containers in proportion, and this in beavers' price or else 16 white or 8 black [sewant] for a stuiver, at the payer's choice. The farmer or bidder remains obliged to furnish, to the satisfaction of the lords farming supervisors, two sufficient sureties for the excise moneys, one for all and each as principal, and every three months to pay in beavers, or else in sewant at 16 white or 8 black for a stuiver, a just fourth part of the promised excise money.

[**514**] In order to prevent any quibbling, misunderstanding, and frauds, it is stipulated and agreed that after the expiration of this contract, whenever the farming out shall be renewed, it shall be permitted to the new farmer, immediately on the day of the new farming out, or on the following day, or absolutely within the time of three days after the farming is let, to gauge in the presence of the former farmer if he wishes

to be present, the remainder of the wines, beers and distilled waters held over by the tappers and innkeepers, and two-third of the excise received or due, shall be returned and restored by the former or previous farmer to his successor or the next farmer.

The lords farming supervisors reserve to themselves the interpretation and amplification of this and promise the farmer all proper protection and assistance.

On the above date the aforesaid farming was posted, but no more than *f* 1000 was offered; thus, on the 22nd of October Willem Bout appeared before the highest officer and lords magistrates of Albany at the house of Anthonie Jansz *herbergier*, and promised to pay twenty-nine hundred guilders for the tappers' excise on the said conditions, and next Monday to furnish sufficient sureties according to these contents. To satisfy what is written above, Herman Bastiaensen and Jan Vinhaegen stand sureties and principals, respectively pledging their persons and estates, moveable and immoveable, present and future without exception. Done in Albany, the 24th of October 1664.

The mark of Willem  Frederixsz,
made with his own hand.
Harmen Bastiaens
Jan Vinhaeghen

Passed in the presence of the highest officer and lords magistrates,
Ludovicus Cobes, court messenger.

[CONDITIONS FOR FARMING OUT THE BURGHER BEER, WINE, AND SPIRITS EXCISE]

[515] Conditions and terms on which the lords magistrates of Albany intend to farm out to the highest bidder the burgher excise of wine and beer for the time of one year. The farming as well as the collection of duties shall begin on the 22nd of October, old style, and the first of November, new style, of this year 1664, and end on the 22nd of October, old style, *anno* 1665. The farmer shall receive for a barrel of good beer, a daelder, for a barrel of small beer, ten stuivers, for a hogshead of French wine, six guilders, for an anker of brandy, Spanish wine, or [distilled] waters, two guilders at twelve white and six black beads of sewant a stuiver. And the aforesaid farmer shall deny no certificate to any burghers, entered on the burgher excise. The Captain shall be free from this burgher excise, and the soldiers shall be free from the excise on small beer; the minister shall also be free from this excise.

The farmer shall be obliged to furnish two sufficient sureties, one for all and each as principals to the satisfaction of the lords contractors, and each quarter year to pay a just quarter part of the entire sum in good strung sewant at 12 white and 6 black sewant for a stuiver. And if the aforesaid farmer fails to furnish the said sureties, the aforesaid farming shall be reauctioned at his cost and charge, and whatever less it comes to be worth, he shall be obliged to make good, and whatever more it comes to be worth, he shall derive no profit from it.

[516] The lords farming supervisors reserve to themselves the interpretation and amplification of this and promise the farmer all proper protection and assistance.
[*incomplete*].

[517–594]†

[DECLARATION BY VARIOUS SHOEMAKERS ABOUT THE QUALITY OF LEATHER]

[595] On this 10/18th of November *anno* 1664 Jan Evertsen, Barent Meijndersen and Rut Arentsen, shoemakers by trade, attest and declare that they were sent for at the request of Willem Brouwer on account of

---

† This range of document pages has been moved to its proper location, beginning on page 185, where it completes the records for 1661.

dissatisfaction with some leather, which he, Brouwer, says to have received from Abel Harden[bergh]; therefore, we, deponents, have looked at the leather and, checking the weight, found that there is fourteen pounds of sole leather and inner sole leather, and another two small Spanish leather skins, weighing one pound and one and a half quarter, another dressed calf skin estimated at two guilders, which, as Willem Brouwer says, should be the payment for six ox hides, which he is not satisfied with, because he has too little for his six hides, which aforesaid facts we, deponents, if necessary, are willing to attest by solemn oath.

Done at Albany as above.

This is the mark  of Jan Evertsz,
made with his own hand.
Barent Meijndersz
Rut Arentsen

[CONVEYANCE OF A HOUSE AND LOT BY THE MAGISTRATES TO SANDER LEENDERSEN GLEN]

[596] We, magistrates of Fort Orange and the village of Beverwijck hereby declare to have ceded and conveyed as we hereby do, to Sander Leendersen Glen a house and lot located in the village of Beverwijck at the hill, long and wide as it lies enclosed in its fence, which we do by virtue of a court order issued on Marten Herbertsen dated [*blank*], which lot he has acquired by patent from the lord director general and councilors of New Netherland, dated 23 April *anno* 1652, and as the said Sander Leendersen has paid the promised moneys to said Martens Herbertsen's creditors, he is freed from all actions, claims or demands which may arise hereafter. [*not executed*]

[PRENUPTUAL DECLARATION BY CATARIJN ANDRIESSEN DE VOS]

[597] In the name of the Lord, Amen. Be it known by the contents of this present instrument that in the year of our Lord Jesu Christij sixteen hundred and sixty-four, the 12/22nd of November, there appeared before me Johannes Provoost,[†] clerk of the court of Albany, in the presence of the officer Johannes La Montagne, and the honorable Jan Verbeeck and Evert Janssen Wendel, orphan masters, Catarijn Andriesen de Vos, widow of the late Arent Anderiessen, who declares that, for the honor of God, she has resolved upon a future marriage, and before the banns of the same, she, appearer, has consented to the following conditions, namely, that she assigns to the six children left by said Arent Anderiessen, deceased, named Jesie, 15 years old, Ariaentie thirteen years old, Anderies, 11 years old, Corneli[ ] nine years old, Samuel five years old, and Dirck Anderiessen three years old, and promises to pay to them jointly the sum of a thousand guilders in beaver's value without further ado, which they shall together receive as their patrimonial inheritance; each his portion at his majority, for the security of which she, appearer, pledges her house and farm located at Schanhechtade, as a special mortgage and collateral, for which, by request, Andries de Vos, because of defect or refusal of [Albert] Anderiessen, uncle of the said children of their [ ] and Jurriaen Teunissen consent to act as guardians and overseers of said children, moreover, said appearer promises to bring up the aforesaid children in the fear of the Lord, to have them taught reading and writing, and to provide for them with food and clothing until their majority or married state, without reduction of their patrimonial and appropriate inherited estate. Which said conditions she, appearer, promises to maintain without craft or guile, pledging her person and estate, moveable and immoveable. Thus done in N: Albany, dated as above.

This is the mark K of Catarijn Anderiessen de Vos,
made with her own hand.
Andryes de Vos
Jurejan Tunsen
Jan Verbeeck as [orphan] master

† In the margin is written, "Provoost's book of conveyances." The book begins on 12 November 1664 and ends on 15 March 1667.

Evert Jansz Wendel, as orphan master
Acknowledged by me, [J. Provoost].

[SALE OF A HOUSE AND LOT BY SANDER LEENDERSEN GLEN TO ADRIAEN GERRITSZ AS ATTORNEY FOR DIRCK JANSZ CROON]

[598] Appeared before me Johannes Provoost, clerk of the court of Albany and in the presence of the honorable Jan Verbeeck and Jacob Schermerhoorn, magistrates of the same court, the honorable Sander Leendersz Glen, who declares to have ceded and conveyed, as he hereby does cede and convey, in real and actual possession, to and for the benefit of Adriaen Gerritsz, attorney for Dirck Janssen Croon, his heirs or assigns, a house and lot located in the village of Beverwijck at the hill; adjoins to the north the street, to the south Jan Hendericksz van Bael, to the east Jan Tomassen, to the west Wouter Albertsz, in such size as it lies enclosed in its fence; which he does by virtue of a conveyance granted to him by the lords magistrates of Fort Orange and the village of Beverwijck, and he, grantor, acknowledges to have been fully satisfied and paid for the sale and delivery hereof by a deduction of an account, consisting of a mortgage of five hundred and seventy-six guilders with its interest of three years at 10 percent, and in addition, another hundred guilders in sewant, received in hand; therefore he, grantor, promises to free the said house and lot from all actions, claims or demands which may arise hereafter, pledging there for his person and estate, moveable and immoveable, present and future, submitting himself to all laws and judges.

Done at Albany, the 12/22nd of November 1664.

Sander Lenrsen Glen
Jan Verbeeck
Jacob Schermerhooren.

[CONVEYANCE OF A HOUSE AND LOT BY THE MAGISTRATES TO SANDER LEENDERSEN GLEN]

[**599**] We, magistrates of the court of Fort Orange and the village of Beverwijck, hereby declare to have ceded and conveyed, as we hereby do cede and convey, to Sander Leendersen Glen, his heirs or assigns, a house and lot located in the village of Beverwijck at the hill; adjoining to the north the street, to the south Jan Hendericksz van Bael, to the east Jan Tomassen, and to the west Wouter Albertsz, in such size as it lies enclosed in its fence; which we do by virtue of a court order issued on the person of Marten Herbertsen,* which lot was granted to him by patent of the lord director general and councilors of New Netherland on the 23rd of April *anno* 1652, and as the said Sander Leendersen has paid the purchase money to said Marten Herbertsen's creditors, he is freed from all actions or demands which may arise hereafter, upon pledge according to law. Done in Albany on date 12/22 November *anno* 166[4].

Jan Verbeeck
as [ ] for Glen
Jacob Schermerhooren

[**600**] [*blank*]

[SALE OF A HOUSE AND LOT BY DAVID PIETERSZ SCHUIJLER TO WOUTER ALBERTSZ VAN DEN UIJTHOFF]

[**601**] We, the undersigned Cornelis van Nes and Jan van Bael, magistrates of Albany, Colony of Rensselaerswijck and Schanechtede hereby testify and declare that before us have appeared the honorable David Pietersz Schuijler and Wouter Albertsz van den Uijthoff, burghers and inhabitants in Albany, he, David Pietersz Schuijler acknowledging and declaring that he hereby cedes, conveys and transports in true and honest ownership to and for the benefit of said

* In the margin was written: "Sold by public auction."

Wouter Albertsz van den Uijthoff (who hereby accepts) a certain piece of lot situated in Albany, formerly named Beverwijck, with the domicile and other buildings, built by the grantor, standing thereupon; adjoins to the south and east Sander Leendertsen, to the north the street, and to the west the grantor; the lot being long on the east six rods three feet, in front on the street wide one rod six feet eight inches, to the east of Sander Leendertsen long six rods three feet, and to the west wide one rod seven feet eight inches, and this by virtue of a patent for a larger lot, by the lord director general and councilors of New Netherland granted to Annetie Bogardus, deceased, on the 23rd of April 1652; also by virtue of a deed of conveyance by Annetie Bogardus passed to him on the 22nd of December 1660; everything free and unencumbered, without any claims standing or issuing against the same except for the lord's right, without him, grantor, having, keeping, or reserving any further right of ownership, claim, or demand in it, acknowledging to have been fully satisfied and paid for it, the last penny with the first, out of the hands of the grantee; giving therefore *plenam actionem cessam* and full authority to the grantee, his heirs, or those who may receive title from him to dispose of, do and transact with **[602]** said lot, domicile, and buildings standing thereupon, as he might do with his own patrimonial estate, with promises never to do or to have anything done against this with or without law in any way, but to free the same from all actions or claims of each and every person, pledging his person and estate, moveable and immoveable, present and future without exception, subject to all laws and judges. Done in Albany the first day of September *anno* 1665, old style.

Davyd Schuiler
Wouter Albertsen
Cornelis van Nes
Jan van Bael
Acknowledged by me,
D. V. Schelluyne, secretary 1665.

[SALE OF A HOUSE AND LOT BY JURRIAEN TEUNISSEN TO ANTHONIJ JANSZ]

We, the undersigned, Cornelis van Nes and Jacob Schermerhoorn, magistrates of Albany, Colony of Rensselaerswijck and Schanechtede, hereby attest and declare that before us appeared Jurriaen Theunisz and Anthony Jansz, burghers and inhabitants here; he, Jurriaen Theunisz acknowledging that he has ceded, conveyed and granted in true, honest, and free ownership, and he, Anthonij Jansz, that he has accepted a certain, the grantor's domicile, lot and garden, as the same is built upon, fenced in, and enclosed, standing and located in Albanij (formerly named Beverwijck), at present being occupied by the grantee, as he has acquired the same by conveyance from Wouter Albertsz vanden Uijthoff on date the second of February 1660, including a small portion of a lot, purchased from the lords magistrates *anno* 1659 or 1660, according to the declaration of the lords Jan Verbeeck and Evert **[603]** Jansz Wendel of date 26 September/6 October 1665. The aforesaid house, lot and garden are in length, width, and boundaries according to the purport and contents of the aforesaid deed of conveyance and declaration to which here is referred, and which are hereby delivered to the grantee; everything free and unencumbered without any claim standing or issuing against the same except for the lord's right, without he, grantor, having, keeping, or reserving any further right or claim of ownership upon the same, acknowledging, according to bill of sale of date the 14th of January 1662 to be fully satisfied, contented and paid for the same, the last penny with the first; therefore giving to the grantor, his heirs and descendants, or his assigns, *plenam actionem cessam*, and complete authority to dispose of, to do and trade transact with the aforesaid premises, lot and garden as he might do with his own patrimonial estate, promising nevermore, either with or without law in any manner, to do nor to let anything be done against the same, but to protect and free the said premises, lot and garden from all actions, trouble, or demands against everyone, pledging his person and estate, moveable and immoveable, without exception, subject to all laws and judges. Done in Albany the 26th of September/6th of October 1665.

Jure Jan Tunsen
Anthonij Jansz
Cornelis van Nes

Jacob Schermerhooren
Acknowledged by me,
D. V. Schelluijne, Secretary, 1665.

[SALE OF A HOUSE AND LOT BY HARMEN THOMASZ TO COBUS JANSZ]

[604] We, the undersigned Gerard Swart, officer, and Jan van Bael, magistrate of Albany, colony of Rensselaerswijck and Schanechtede attest and declare that on the date underwritten there appeared before us Harmen Thomasz van Amersfort, having married the widow of the late Dirck Bensingh, and Cobus Jansz, he, Herman Thomasz, hereby acknowledging and declaring that by virtue of a patent for a larger lot granted to him by the lord director general and councilors of New Nederland of date the 25th of October 1653, he has ceded, conveyed and made over in true and honest ownership to him, Cobus Jansz, who accepts the conveyance, a certain house and lot with everything that is attached by earth and nail, and moreover, as the same stand within its fence and boundaries in Albanij, and built upon by the said Dirck Bensingh, deceased, together with a small strip of the lot included within the said fence, which the grantor acquired from Jillis Pietersz; adjoins to the east the public road, to the south Lambert van Neck, to the west also the public road, and to the north Jacob Tijssen vander Heijde; and all of this free and unencumbered without any claims standing or issuing against the same, except for the lord's right, without he, grantor, having any claim upon the same anymore, acknowledging to be fully satisfied, contented and paid for the same, the last penny with the first, by the hands of him, Cobus Jansz; therefore giving to him, Cobus Jansz, his heirs and descendants, or his assigns, *plenam actionem cessam*, and complete authority to dispose of the same and to do with it as he might do with his own patrimonial estate. **[605]** Promising therefore to protect and free the said house and lot from all actions, trouble or demands against every person as is right, and nevermore to do or to let anything be done against the same, either with or without law in any manner, pledging his person and estate, moveable and immoveable, without exception, subject to all laws and judges. Done in Albany the 9/19th of October 1665.

This mark was made by + said Cobus Jansz
Harman Thomasz
As witness, G. Swart J. v. Bael
Acknowledged by me,
D.V. Schelluijne, secretary 1665.

[SALE OF A HOUSE AND LOT BY COBUS JANSZ TO JAN VERBEECK, ATTORNEY FOR FRANS BARENTSZ PASTOOR]

We, the undersigned Gerard Swart and Jan van Bael, magistrate of Albany, colony of Rensselaerswijck and Schanechtede attest and declare that on the date underwritten, there appeared before us Cobus Jansz and *Sr.* Jan Verbeeck, he, Cobus Jansz, acknowledging and declaring that he has ceded, conveyed and made over in true, honest and free ownership, and he, Jan Verbeeck, as attorney for Frans Barentsen Pastoor, that he has accepted a certain, the grantor's domicile and lot with everything that is attached by earth and nail, and moreover, as it stands within its fence and boundaries in said Albanij as the grantor acquired it by the purchase from Dirck Bensingh, deceased, and by deed of conveyance today passed by Hermen Thomasz van Amersfort, presently husband and guardian of the widow of said Dirck **[606]** Bensingh; adjoins on the east the public road, on the south Lambert van Neck, on the west also the public road, and on the north Jacob Tijsz vander Heijde; and all of this free and unencumbered without any claim standing or issuing against the same, except for the lord's right, without he, grantor, having any further claim upon the same anymore, acknowledging to be fully satisfied and paid for the same, the last penny with the first; giving therefor to him, the aforesaid Jan Verbeeck in capacity as mentioned, his heirs and descendants or his assigns, *plenam actionem cessam*, and complete authority to dispose of the same, and to do with it as he might do with his own patrimonial estate. Promising therefore to free the said house and lot from all trouble, actions or demands against every person as is right, and nevermore to do or to let anything be done against the same, in any manner either with or without law, upon pledge of his person and estate, moveable and immoveable, present and future without exception, subject to all laws and judges. Done in Albany the 9/19th of October 1665.

This mark + was made by said Cobus Jansz.
Jan Verbeeck
As witness G. Swart
J. v. Bael
Acknowledged by me,
D. V. Schelluijne, secretary 1665.

[SALE OF A HOUSE AND LOT BY JAN VERBEECK AS ATTORNEY FOR FRANS BARENTSEN PASTOOR TO JACOB TIJSSEN VAN DER HEIJDE]

We, the undersigned Cornelis van Nes, and Jan van Bael, magistrates of Albany, colony of Rensselaerswijck and Schanechtede hereby attest and declare that today, on the date underwritten, there appeared before us *Sr.* Jan Verbeeck, in capacity of attorney for Frans Barentsz Pastoor, and Jacob Tijssen vander Heijde, the said Verbeeck **[607]** in his said capacity, acknowledging that he has ceded, conveyed and made over in true, honest and free ownership, and he, Jacob Tijsz vander Heijde, that he has accepted a certain house and lot with everything that is attached by earth and nail, and moreover as the same stands within its fence and boundaries in said Albanij, in the past built by Dirck Bensingh, deceased, and as he has acquired it by conveyance from Cobus Jansz; adjoins to the east the public road, to the south Lambert van Neck, to the west also the public road, and to the north said Vander Heijde; and this all free and unencumbered without any claims standing or issuing against the same, except for the lord's right, without he, grantor, having the least claim upon the same anymore, acknowledging to be fully satisfied and paid for the same, the last penny with the first; giving therefor to Jacob Tijssen vander Heijde, his heirs and descendants, or his assigns *plenam actionem cessam*, and complete authority to dispose of, and do with the same as he might do with his own patrimonial effects; promising therefore to free the said house and lot from all trouble and demands against every person as is right, and nevermore to do nor to let anything be done against the same in any manner, either with or without law, upon pledge of his person and estate, moveable and immoveable, present and future without exception, subject to all laws and judges. Done in Albany the10/20th of October 1665.

Jan Verbeeck
Jacob Teijsen vander Heijden
Cornelis van Nes
J. v. Bael
Acknowledged by me,
D. V. Schelluijne, secretary 1665.

[SALE OF HALF OF A HOUSE AND LOT BY VOLCKERT JANSZ AND ADRIAEN VAN ILPENDAM, ADMINISTRATORS OF THE ESTATE OF ANDRIES HERBERTSZ, TO CORNELIS VAN NES]

[**608**] We, the undersigned Arent van Curlar and Jacob Schermerhoorn, magistrates of Albany, Rensselaerswijck and Schanechtade, attest and declare that before us have appeared Volckert Jansz and *Mr.* Arien van Ilpendam, in capacity of administrators of the estate of Andries Herbertsz, and Cornelis van Nes, husband and guardian of Maritie Damen, last widow of the late Hendrick Andriesz, the said administrators acknowledging to have ceded, conveyed and made over in true honest and free ownership, and he, Van Nes, that he has accepted, the just half of a domicile and lot standing and located in the village of Beverwijck, now named Albany, the other half of which is owned by said Maritie Damen, by virtue of a conveyance by Theunis Theunisz *metselaer* for the benefit of said Andries Herbertsz, passed on date of the 19th of February 1660, and this with everything that is attached by earth and nail, and as the same is standing within its fence and boundaries; adjoins to the north Pieter Adriaensz, now Philip Pietersz Schuijler, to the south Adriaen Jansz van Leijden, and east and west the public street, as the same was bid on and purchased by Van Nes at public auction on the 29th of April 1664; everything free and unencumbered without any claims standing or issuing against the same except for the lord's right, without they, grantors, having, maintaining or reserving any claim or demand thereon, acknowledging to have been fully satisfied and paid for it through the hands of him, Van Nes, the last penny with the first; giving therefore *plenam actionem cessam* to the said Van Nes, his heirs and descendants, or his assigns, and complete authority to dispose of, and to do and transact with the said just half of the domicile and lot as he might do with his own patrimonial estate;

promising therefore to free and protect the said half house and lot from all trouble and demands against every person as is right, and nevermore in any manner, either with or without law, to do nor to let anything be done against the same, upon pledge of their persons and estates, moveable and immoveable, present and future without exception, subject to all laws and judges. Done in Albany the 11th/21st of November 1665.

Volckart Jansz
Adriaen van Ilpendam
Cornelis van Nes
A van Curler
Jacob Schermerhoorn
Acknowledged by me,
D. V. Schelluijne Secretary.

[SALE OF HALF AN ISLAND BY ADRIAEN VAN ILPENDAM AS ADMINISTRATOR OF ANDRIES HERBERTSEN'S ESTATE TO VOLCKERT JANSZ]

[609] We, the undersigned Arent van Curlar and Cornelis van Nes, magistrates of Albany, the colony of Rensselaerswijck and Schanechtade, attest and declare that before us have appeared *Mr*. Arien van Ilpendam, in capacity as administrator of the estate of Andries Herbertsz, and Volckert Jansz; the said *Mr*. Arien van Ilpendam in his said capacity acknowledging to have ceded, conveyed and made over, and he, Volckert Jansz that he has accepted the half island that belongs to him, Andries Herbertsz and Rutger Jacobsz, deceased, together in company, according to patent granted by the lord director general and councilors of New Netherland dated the 19th of March 1661, and as he, Volckert Jansz, has bid on and bought the same at public auction on the 26th of June1663; and this free and unencumbered without any claims standing or issuing against the same except for the lord's right, in such a way as the aforesaid island is situated in the North River in the said colony below Fort Albany; without the grantor having, maintaining or reserving any claim or demand thereon anymore, acknowledging to have been satisfied and paid for it through the hands of the said Volckert

Jansz to his content, the last penny with the first; giving therefore *plenam actionem cessam* to the said Volckert Jansz, his heirs and descendants, and complete authority to dispose of, to do and transact with the said half island as he might do with his own patrimonial estate; promising therefore to protect and free the said half island from all trouble and demands of every person as is right, and nevermore in any manner either with or without law, to do or to let anything be done against the same, upon pledge of his person and estate, moveable and immoveable, present and future without exception, subject to all laws and judges. Done in Albany the 11th/21st of November 1665.

Adriaen van Ilpendam
Volckart Jansz
A. van Curler
Cornelis van Nes
Acknowledged by me,
D. V. Schelluijne Secretary, 1665.

[SALE OF A LOT FOR A GARDEN BY VOLCKERT JANSZ AND ADRIAEN VAN ILPENDAM, ADMINISTRATORS OF ANDRIES HERBERTSEN'S ESTATE, TO ANTHONIJ JANSZ]

[**610**] We, the undersigned Arent van Curlar and Cornelis van Nes, magistrates of Albany, the colony of Rensselaerswijck and Schanechtade, hereby attest and declare that on this date appeared before us Volckert Jansz and *Mr.* Adriaen van Ilpendam, in capacity of administrators of the estate of Andries Herbertsz *Constapel,* who acknowledge to have ceded, conveyed and made over in true, honest and free ownership to and for the benefit of Anthonij Jansz, who accepts this conveyance of a certain lot for a garden, by drawing of lots no. 18, adjoining to the south of Pieter Hartgers, to the north and east of the public road, and to the west of Jacob *de brouwer,* wide 4½ rods and long seven rods, as the same is fenced in and located in the village of Beverwijck, now named Albany, and this by virtue of a patent for a larger lot by the lord director general and councilors of New Netherland granted to said Andries Herbertsz, on date the 25th of October 1653. Everything free and unencumbered without any claims standing or

issuing against the same except for the lord's right; without they, grantors, having, maintaining or reserving any claim or demand thereupon anymore, acknowledging to have been fully satisfied and paid for it, the last penny with the first; giving therefore *plenam actionem cessam* to the said Anthonij Jansz, his heirs and descendants, or his assigns, and complete authority to dispose of, and to do with it as he might do with his own patrimonial estate; promising therefore to protect and free the said lot from all trouble and demands of every person, as is right, and moreover, promising nevermore to do nor to let anything be done against the same, in any manner either with law or without, upon pledge of their respective persons and estates, without exception, subject to all laws and judges. Done in Albany the $11^{th}/21^{st}$ of November 1665.

Volckart Jansz
Adriaen van Ilpendam
Anthonij Jansz
A. van Curler
Cornelis van Nes
Acknowledged by me,
D. V. Schelluijne, secretary, 1665.

[SALE OF A HOUSE AND LOT BY WILLEM JANSZ SCHUT TO CORNELIS BOGARDUS]

[611] We, the undersigned Cornelis van Nes and Jan van Bael, magistrates of Albany, the colony of Rensselaerswijck and Schanechtade, attest and declare that on the date underwritten appeared before us Willem Jansz Schut, dwelling in the said colony, who declares to hereby cede, convey and make over in true, honest and free ownership to and for the benefit of Cornelis Bogaerdus a certain domicile and lot of the grantor, as he has acquired the same from Andries Herbertsen *Constapel* (being the house on the lot that the grantor himself had had built), standing and located here in Albany, extending from the said Constapel's gate to the fence of Trijn Claes, and moreover, as the same is enclosed and fenced according to the bill of sale dated the 4th of August 1662, and other evidences thereof; without he, grantor, having, maintaining or reserving any claim or demand upon it anymore, acknowledging to have been fully satisfied and paid for it, the last penny with the first, by the hands of Johannes Withart, namely with the sum of eighty-five whole merchantable beaver skins; giving therefore *plenam actionem cessam* and complete authority to the said Bogaerdus, his heirs and descendants or said Witthart, who, by virtue of the said payment has claim and right thereto, to dispose of and to do with the said domicile and lot as he might do with his own patrimonial estate and effects; promising nevermore in any manner either with or without law, to do or to let anything be done against the same, on pledge of his person and estate, moveable and immoveable, present and future, without exception, subject to all laws and judges. Done in Albany the 6/16th of May 1666.

Willem Jansen Schuet
Cornelis van Nes
Jan van Bael
Acknowledged by me,
D. V. Schelluijne, secretary 1666.

[SALE OF A HOUSE AND LOT BY JOCHEM WESSELSZ *BACKER*, ATTORNEY FOR PIETER JANSZ *DE BOER*, TO HENDRICK BRIES]

[**612**] We, the undersigned Arent van Curlar and Cornelis van Nes, magistrates of Albany, the colony of Rensselaerswijck and Schanechtade, hereby attest and declare that on date underwritten appeared before us Jochem Wessels *Backer*, attorney for Pieter Jansz *de Boer*, dwelling in the aforesaid colony, who declares to hereby cede, convey and make over in true, rightful and free ownership to and for the benefit of Hendrick Bries *schoenmaecker* here in Albany a certain house and lot that he, Bries, has bought from him, Pieter Jansz, and which he, Bries, presently occupies; and this by virtue of a patent and a conveyance thereof, dated the 29th of June 1663, as he acquired it from Jan Lambertsen van Bremen, everything according to purport and contents of the said deed of conveyance, to which here reference is made, and which hereby will be delivered to him, Bries, giving therefore to him, Bries, his heirs and descendants, complete power to do

with it as he might do with his own patrimonial estate and effects, without he, grantor, in his said capacity, having any claim thereto anymore, acknowledging to have been fully satisfied and paid, the last penny with the first, promising therefore to protect and free the said house and lot from all trouble and claims against every person as is right, especially from the mortgage that Pieter Riuerdingh has upon the said house and lot, dated the 10th of June 1664, for which said Jochem Wesselsz *backer* hereby privately stands surety and principal for this pledge, he, grantor, and the surety promising, moreover, nevermore to do nor to let anything be done against the same, in any manner, either with or without law, upon pledge according to law, everything sincere and in good faith. Done in Albany the 8/18th of June 1666.

Jochem *Backer*
A. van Curler
Cornelis van Nes
Acknowledged by me,
D. V. Schelluijne.

[SALE OF A PORTION OF A LOT BY VOLCKERT JANSZ, ATTORNEY FOR HENDRICK JOCHEMSZ TO PHILIP PIETERSZ SCHUIJLER]

[613] We, the undersigned Arent van Curlar and Richard van Renselaer, magistrates of Albany, the colony of Rensselaerswijck and Schanechtade, hereby attest and declare that on date underwritten appeared before us Volckert Jansz, attorney for Hendrick Jochemsz, who, by virtue of a patent and conveyance dated the 23rd of April 1652 and the 16th of April of this year 1666 respectively thereof, as well as a bill of sale dated the 10/20th of February also of this year 1666, declared that he has ceded and conveyed in true, rightful and free ownership to and for the benefit of Philip Pietersen Schuijler a portion of the lot of the aforesaid Hendrick Jochemsz and the garden across the back street, the lot extending in front along the street wide thirty feet, in length until behind the fence of Harmen Rutgers's brewery, where it has the same width, including the small alley that runs to the garden, in such a way as the aforesaid portion of the lot and garden is located here in Albany; adjoins according to the purport and contents of the said bill of sale, to which reference is made here, as can also be seen in the aforesaid conveyance in the Esopus passed by Femmetie Alberts, widow of Hendrick Jansz Westerkamp, deceased, to the said Hendrick Jochemsz; without he, grantor in his said capacity having any claim thereto anymore, acknowledging to have been fully satisfied and paid, the last penny with the first, by hand of said Schuijler, giving therefor complete authority to the said Schuijler, his heirs and descendants, or his assigns, to do with and dispose of the same, as he might do with his patrimonial effects and estate; promising to protect and free the said lot from all trouble, demands and objections of every person as is right, and moreover, **[614]** nevermore to do nor to let anything be done against the same in any manner either with or without law, upon pledge according to law. Done in Albany the 9/19th of June 1666.

Volckart Jansz
A. van Curler
R. V. Rensselaer
Acknowledged by me,
D. V. Schelluijne, secretary, 1666.

[SALE OF A LOT BY JURRIAEN JANSZ GROENEWOUT TO POULUS MARTENSZ VAN BENTHUIJSEN]

We, the undersigned Jacob Schermerhoorn and Jan van Bael, magistrates of Albany, the colony of Rensselaerswijck and Schanechtade, hereby attest and declare that on date underwritten appeared before us Jurriaen Jansz Groenewout, husband and guardian of Maritie Thomas Mingael, last widow of the late Cornelis Theunisz van Westbroeck, assisted by *Sr.* Johan Verbeeck and Stoffel Jansz Abeel, as invited co-guardians of Weijntie Cornelis, minor daughter of the said Cornelis Theunisz and Maritie Thomas, and Poulus Martens van Benthuijsen, he, Jurriaen Jansz acknowledging and declaring that he has conveyed in true, rightful and free ownership to and for the benefit of him, Poulus Martensz, a certain lot upon which he, Poulus has built a house, as the aforesaid lot within its fence, enclosure and boundaries is located here in Albany, and as the same is now occupied by Poulus Martensz; **[615]** and this by virtue of a bill of sale dated the

24th of April 1660, and by virtue of a patent thereof for a larger lot dated the 23rd of April *anno* 1652; also according to further evidence derived from a right of way cut off by the lot, and released from the said Poulus Martensz; moreover on condition that the fence on the south side (which Marij Dijckman now has in use, or dwells next to it) neither on the one side or the other shall be built against without the consent and permission of both parties; without he, grantor, having any claim thereto anymore, acknowledging to have been fully satisfied and paid therefor, the last penny with the first, giving therefor complete power and authority to said Poulus Martensz and his assigns, to dispose of the said lot as he might do with his own patrimonial estate; promising at any time to protect and free the said lot from all trouble and demands against every person as is right, and moreover, nevermore to do or to let anything be done against the same in any manner, either with or without law, upon pledge of his person and estate, moveable and immoveable **[616]** without any exception, subject to all laws and justices. Done in Albany the 26th June/6th of July 1666.

This  is the mark made by said Jurriaen Jansz.
Poulus Marten
Jacob Schermerhooren
Jan van Bael
Jan Verbeeck as guardian
Stoffel Jansz Abeel as guardian
Acknowledged by me,
D. V. Schelluijne, secretary 1666.

[SALE OF A HOUSE AND LOT BY TJERCK CLAESZ DE WITH TO JERONIMUS EBBINGH]

[617] We, the undersigned Arent van Curlar and Abraham Staets, magistrates of Albany, the colony of Rensselaerswijck and Schanechtade, hereby attest and declare that on date underwritten appeared before us Tjarck Claesz de With, farmer, dwelling at the Esopus, who declares that hereby he has ceded, conveyed and made over in true, rightful and free ownership to and for the benefit of *Sr.* Jeronimus Ebbingh, merchant at New York, his certain domicile and lot standing and located here in Albany; adjoins on the east side the public road, on the south side the house of Hendrick *de backer*, on the west side the garden of Hendrick Andriesz and Lambert van Neck, and on the north side the house of Lambert van Neck; the lot in front on the street wide thirty-two wood feet and four inches, and long ten rods, as he has acquired the said lot by sale and delivery from the late Dirck Bensingh according to the deed of conveyance thereof, and the premises that the grantor has built upon it, and this with everything attached by earth and nail, free and unencumbered, without any claims issuing against the same except for the lord's right, he, grantor, acknowledging to have been fully satisfied and paid for it with some lands in the Esopus, accepted by way of exchange from him, Ebbingh, and his wife *joffr.* Johanna de Laet, according to the deed thereof dated the 11th of September 1660, without the grantor having, maintaining or reserving any claim or demand thereon anymore, but hereby renouncing and giving up the same for the benefit of said Ebbingh, his heirs and descendants or his assigns, promising to protect and free the said house and lot from all trouble, actions and objections against every person as is right, and moreover, nevermore to do nor to let anything be done against the same in any manner, either with or without law, **[618]** upon pledge of his person and estate, moveable and immoveable, present and future without exception, subject to all laws and judges. Done in Albany the 14th/24th of July 1666.

Tierck Clasen de Witt
A. van Curler
Abram Staas
Acknowledged by me,
D. V. Schelluijne, Secretary 1666.

[POWER OF ATTORNEY FROM BASTIAEN DE WINTER TO DANIEL JANSZ VAN ANTWERPEN]

[619] We, the undersigned Jan van Bael and Abram Staes, magistrates of Albany, the colony of Rensselaerswijck and Schanechtade, hereby declare that on date underwritten appeared before us Bastiaen de Winter, dwelling at said Schanechtade, who declares that he hereby appoints and empowers Daniel Jansz van Antwerpen, the bearer of this, intending to depart for Holland, especially to collect, demand and receive from *Sr.* Anthonij More, merchant, presently staying at Amsterdam or wherever else he might be and reside, such a sum of one hundred seventy-seven guilders at 20 stuivers apiece as, according to promissory note dated the 15th of May 1655, the same owes to *Sr.* Mathijs Oosterman, dwelling at Meuwes [Nevis] in the Caribbean islands, whose right and action the appearer has according to a draft of date the 26th of June 1658 in the English language, of which translation and authentic copy of the promissory note have been placed into the hands of the attorney; to issue quittance for the receipts, and if necessary and demanded, to clear of all claims, and in case of unwillingness (which is not hoped for), with law and rigor of justice to constrain him to the payment of the aforesaid sum with its costs, damage and interest, **[620]** to which end to observe after the custom of the place, all terms of justice until sentence, including extreme execution, together with power to substitute one or more persons *ad lites tantum* in his place, also to compromise, agree and arrange a compromise, and moreover, to do, transact and conduct whatever he thinks necessary and advisable, promising without any gainsaying, at all times to accept everything that the attorney and his substitute will have done in this matter, provided that the attorney, if requested, shall be obliged to properly justify his transactions and receipts. For the confirmation of which the appearer, in our presence has signed this with his own hand. In Albany, the 15th/25th of July 1666.

Basteiaen de Winter
Jan van Bael
Abram Staas

Acknowledged before me,
D. V. Schelluijne, secretary 1666.

[POWER OF ATTORNEY FROM THEUNIS WILLEMSZ
TO HIS SISTER EVERTIE WILLEMSDR.]

[**621**] We, the undersigned Jacob Schermerhoorn and Cornelis van Nes, magistrates of Albany, the colony of Rensselaerswijck and Schanechtade, attest and declare that on date underwritten appeared before us Theunis Willemsz, farmer, young man born at Heijvelt in the diocese of Utrecht, who declares that he hereby has appointed and empowered his sister Evertie Willemsdr., dwelling at Uytrecht aforesaid at the honorable Lord van Wulven's, especially to collect, demand and receive from the heirs of the late Willem Theunisz, his deceased uncle, or at the appropriate place, payment and satisfaction of a sentence, as it is held by his said sister, (and which is) chargeable to the said heirs and others, for what he inherited from his father, deceased, Willem Theunisz, and uncle Barent Theunisz, deceased. Everything according to purport and contents of the said sentence of the same; to issue quittance for the receipts, and in case of unwillingness, to bring the same sentence to execution and observe all terms of justice according to the custom of the place; to which end, if necessary, to substitute one or more persons or attorneys in her place *ad lites*; also to compromise, agree and arrange a compromise, and moreover, to do, transact and conduct everything that may be necessary, and which she thinks advisable; promising, at all times without any gainsaying to accept everything that shall be done and performed by his [**622**] appointed sister and her substitute in this said matter, provided that the attorney shall, if requested, be obligated to properly justify her transactions and receipts. Done in Albany, the 17th/27th of July 1666.

This mark is  made by said Theunis Willemsz
Jacob Schermerhooren
Cornelis van Nes

Acknowledged by me,
D. V. Schelluijne, secretary 1666.

[SALE OF A GARDEN BY NICOLAES MEYER TO DANIEL RINCHOUT]

[**623**] We, the undersigned Cornelis van Nes and Rijchard van Rensselaer, magistrates of Albany, the colony of Rensselaerswijck and Schanechtade, attest and declare that on date underwritten appeared before us *Sr.* Nicolaes Meijer, merchant at New York, at present here in Albany, who declared that he hereby has ceded, conveyed and made over in true, rightful, and free ownership to and for the benefit of Daniel Rinchout dwelling at Albany a certain garden located in said Albany, in size according to the survey bill thereof, and adjoins according to the purport and contents of the deed of conveyance passed by Leendert Philipsz for the benefit of the grantor on 23rd of August 1663 in Fort Orange; and this by virtue of the same deed of conveyance, and in accordance with the bill of sale dated the first of July 1665, and a later deed of confirmation, written on the back of the bill of sale, and signed by him, Rinchout, dated the 20th/30th of April 1666; also pursuant to a sentence of the honorable court here, dated the 5th/15th of this month of July, to all of which is referred here, without he, grantor, having, keeping, or reserving the least claim or demand on said garden anymore, acknowledging to have been fully satisfied and paid for it through the hands of the said Rinchout, the last penny with the first, giving; therefore *plenam actionem cessam*, and full power and authority to said Rinchout, his heirs and descendants, or those who may receive title from him, to dispose of said garden, and to transact and do with the same as he might do with his own patrimonial lands and estate. Promising to protect and free the same from all trouble, actions or claims of each and every person, and moreover, [**624**] never to do or to let anything be done against the same, either with or without law in any way, upon pledge of his person and estate, moveable and immoveable, without exception, subject to all laws and judges. Done in Albany the 19th/29th of July 1666.

Nicolaes d Meijer
Cornelis van Nes
Richard van Rensselaer

Acknowledged by me,
D. V. Schelluijne, secretary 1666.

[ACKNOWLEDGMENT OF DEBT BY ANTHONIJ JANSZ
TO JAN VAN AECKEN AND GOOSSEN GERRITSEN]

[**625**] We, the undersigned Jan van Baele and Jacob Schermerhoorn, magistrates of Albany, the colony of Rensselaerswijck and Schanechtade, attest and declare that on date underwritten appeared before us Anthonij Jansz, *herbergier* here in Albany, who acknowledged to be well and honestly indebted to Jan van Aecken for the quantity of seventy-five good merchantable beavers, and to Goossen Gerritsz for twenty-five beavers as before, growing out of a matter of money lent, received by him to his satisfaction on the *2*nd of September *anno* 1662, and used for the payment of the first installment of the house and lot which he presently occupies, and which was conveyed to him by Jurriaen Theunisz. Which said respective sums of seventy-five and twenty-five beavers with their appropriate interest commencing on said date of the 2nd of September *anno* 1662, and running until their full and complete payment, he, the appearer, promises to pay exactly within the time of a year from date at the most, without any further delay, pledging thereto his person and estate, moveable and immoveable, present and future without any exception, especially the said house and lot, in order to recover the payment thereof without any cost and damage; everything subject to all laws and judges. Done in Albany, the 9th/19th of August 1666.

Anthonij Jansz
Jan van Bael
Jacob Schermerhooren
Acknowledged by me,
D. V. Schelluijne, secretary 1666.

[**626**] [*blank*]

[SALE OF A HOUSE AND LOT BY CORNELIS WIJNCOOP
TO CLAES RIPSEN]

[**627**] We, the undersigned Abraham Staes and Cornelis van Nes, magistrates of Albany, attest and declare that before us appeared Cornelis Wijncoop, who declared that he hereby has ceded, conveyed and made over in true, rightful and free ownership to Claes Ripsen his

certain domicile and lot as he has acquired it by conveyance from Marcelis Jansz according to the conditions thereof at the public sale on the 10th and 17th of January 1658, with everything that is attached by earth and nail, in length and width according to the purport and contents of the aforesaid deed of conveyance and conditions to which here is referred, as the aforesaid house and lot is standing and located here in Albany at the hill without he, grantor, having the least claim or demand upon it anymore, acknowledging to have been fully satisfied and paid for it through the hands of him, Claes Ripsen, the last penny with the first; giving therefore *plenam actionem cessam*, and full authority to said Ripsen, his heirs and descendants or those who may receive title from him, to do and transact with said house and lot as he might do with his own patrimonial estate, promising to protect and free the said domicile and lot from all actions, trouble and claims of each and every person, as is right, and moreover, never to do nor to let anything be done against the same, either with or without law in any way, under pledge of his person and estate, moveable and immoveable, without exception, subject to all laws and judges. Done in Albany the 15th/25th of August 1666.

Cornelis Wijnckoop
Abram Staas
Cornelis van Nes
In my presence,
D.V. Schelluijne, secretary.

[**628**][*blank*]

[SALE OF A LOT BY JAN VERBEECK, ATTORNEY FOR THEUNIS CORNELISZ TO WILLEM BOUT]

[**629**] We, the undersigned Cornelis van Nes and Jacob Schermerhoorn, magistrates of Albany, colony of Rensselaerswijck and Schanechtade, attest and declare that on date underwritten appeared before us *Sr.* Jan Verbeeck, attorney for his brother-in-law Theunis Cornelisz, who, by virtue of a patent for a larger lot dated the 23rd of April 1652, declared

that he hereby has ceded, conveyed and made over in true, rightful and free ownership to and for the benefit of Willem Bout a certain lot, belonging to him, Theunis Cornelisz, located here in Albany, adjoins to the north Jaques Thijsen, to the east and south the said Theunis Cornelisz, and to the west the public road; the lot in front and rear being wide three rods Rhineland measure, and in length like the lot of said Jaques Thijsen, without Theunis Cornelisz having the least claim on said lot anymore, acknowledging to have been fully satisfied and paid for it through the hands of said Willem Bout, the last penny with the first; giving therefore *plenam actionem cessam*, and full power and authority to said Willem Bout, his heirs and descendants, to do with it as he might do with his own patrimonial effects, promising to protect and free the said lot from all trouble, actions and claims of each and every person as is right, and moreover, never **[630]** to do or to let anything be done against the same either with or without law in any way, under pledge of his person and estate, without exception, subject to all laws and judges. Done in Albany the 27th of August/8th of September 1666.

Jan Verbeeck
Cornelis van Nes
Jacob Schermerhooren
In my presence,
D. V. Schelluijne, secretary 1666.

[SALE OF A HOUSE AND LOT BY CLAES RIPSEN TO OMIJ LAGRAND]

[631] We, the undersigned Jan van Bael and Abraham Staes, magistrates of Albany, colony of Rensselaerswijck and Schanechtade, attest and declare that on date underwritten appeared before us Claes Ripsen, master carpenter, here in Albany, who declared that he has hereby ceded, conveyed and made over in true, rightful and free ownership to and for the benefit of Omij Lagrand, master tailor, a certain domicile and lot together with the just lower half of the lot lying thereby, to be measured from top to bottom, as the entire lot is enclosed and fenced, standing and located here in Albany, and presently occupied by him, Lagrand. And this, according to a bill of sale dated the 16th/26th of January past, and by virtue of a conveyance of a larger lot by Cornelis

Wijncoop, passed to him on the 15th/25th of this month of August, to which here is referred, without the grantor having the least claim on said domicile and lot and just half of the lot anymore, acknowledging to have been fully satisfied and paid for it through the hands of him, Lagrand, the last penny with the first; giving therefore *plenam actionem cessam*, and full power and authority to said Lagrand, his heirs and descendants, to do and transact with it as he might do with his own patrimonial effects, promising therefore to free and protect the said domicile, lot and just half lot of all actions, trouble, and claims of each and every person as is right, and moreover, never to do or to let anything be done against the same, either with or without law in any way, **[632]** under pledge of his person and estate, without exception, subject to all laws and judges. Done in Albany the 21st /31st of August 1666.

Claes Ripsen van Dam
Jan van Bael
Abram Staas
In my presence,
D. V. Schelluijne, secretary 1666.

[SALE OF A HOUSE AND LOT BY WILLEM BOUT TO JAN CLUTE]

[633] We, the undersigned Abraham Staets and Jan van Bael, magistrates of Albany, colony of Rensselaerswijck and Schanechtade, hereby attest and declare that on date underwritten appeared before us Willem Bout, who hereby declares that he has ceded, conveyed and made over in true, rightful and free ownership to and for the benefit of Jan Clute a certain domicile and lot, standing and located in Albany; adjoins to the north Jaques Thijsen, to the east the lot upon which the lord Rensselaer's mill has stood, and to the south Theunis Cornelisz, and to the west the public street; and this by virtue of a conveyance passed today, the 27th of August/8th of September 1666; width in front on the street thirty wood feet, and length to the said lot of lord Rensselaer, without the grantor having the least claim on it anymore, acknowledging to have been satisfied and paid for it to his content through the hands of him, Jan Cloet, the last penny with the first; giving therefore *plenam actionem cessam* and full power and authority to said

Jan Cloet, his heirs and descendants to do with it as he might do with his own patrimonial effects. Promising therefore to protect and free the said domicile and lot from all actions, trouble, and claims of each and every person as is, and moreover, nevermore to do or to let anything be done against the same, either with or without law, in any way, [**634**] under pledge of his person and estate, without exception, subject to all laws and judges. Done in Albany the 27th of August/8th of September 1666.

This mark  is made by said Willem Bout.
Abram Staas
Jan van Bael
Acknowledged by me,
D. V. Schelluijne, secretary 1666.

[AGREEMENT BETWEEN THE MAGISTRATES AND JAN VAN AECKEN]

[**635**] In Beverwijck *anno* 1656, the 13th of May. We, the undersigned magistrates acknowledge that we have agreed and contracted with Jan van Aecken that we can build the church as far on his smithy as the door is wide, and this, on condition that we shall be obliged to move his house upon the building line of Rem Jansse, and that we shall deliver a lot fitting for the bakery; the large house we have to move at our own expense. Was signed Rutger Jacobsz, Andries Herbertsz, Jacob Jansz Schermerhoorn, Phillip Pietersen,  this is the mark of Goossen Gerritsz, Dirck Janssen Croon,  this is the mark of Jan van Aecken.

After collation with the original, dated and signed as above, this copy is found to agree with the same. In Albany the 16th /26th of March 1667.

By me, D.V. Schelluijne, Secretary 1667.

[SALE OF A HOUSE AND LOT BY JAN KOSTER VAN AECKEN TO JAN CLUTE]

We, the undersigned Arent van Curler and Richard van Rensselaer, magistrates of Albany, colony of Rensselaerswijck and Schanechtade, hereby attest and declare that on date underwritten appeared before us Jan Koster van Aecken, dwelling here in Albany, who hereby acknowledges that, according to agreement with the lords magistrates made on the 13th of May 1656, and by virtue of a patent for a larger lot dated the 25th of October 1653, committed to the care of Carsten Fredericksz smith, and according to a bill of sale dated the 19th /29th of December 1665, he has hereby ceded, conveyed and made over in true, rightful and free ownership to and for [**636**] the benefit of Jan Clute a certain domicile and lot, in length and width as the same is standing within its fence and enclosure here in Albany; adjoins according to the purport of the said bill of sale, without him, grantor, having the least claim upon it anymore, acknowledging to have been fully satisfied and paid for it by Jan Clute, namely, with the sum of sixty beavers received by him, and a mortgage for the amount of four hundred and fifty guilders in beavers to be passed by Jan Clute for his benefit; giving therefore *plenam actionem cessam* and full power to said Jan Clute, his heirs and descendants, or his assigns to do with it as he might do with his patrimonial effects, promising, according to the said bill of sale, to protect and free the said domicile and lot from all trouble, actions, and claims of each and every person as is right, and moreover, nevermore to do or to let anything be done against the same, either with or without law, in any way, under pledge of his person and estate, without exception, subject to all laws and judges. Done in Albany the 16th/26th of March 1667.

Jan Koster
A. van Curler
R. van Rensselaer
In my presence,
D. V. Schelluijne, secretary 1667.

[SALE OF A HOUSE AND LOT BY JAN COSTER VAN AECKEN TO GERRIT BANCKERT]

[637] We, the undersigned Richard van Rensselaer and Philip Pietersz Schuijler, magistrates of Albany, colony of Rensselaerswijck and Schanechtade, attest and declare that on date underwritten appeared before us Jan Coster van Aecken, who, by virtue of a patent for a larger lot granted by director general and councilors of New Netherland to Albert Gerritsz on the 23rd of April 1652, held by *Mr*. Adriaen van Ilpendam, declares that he has ceded, conveyed and made over in true, rightful and free ownership to and for the benefit of Gerrit Banckert a certain domicile and lot of the grantor standing and located here in Albany, at present occupied by Jan Dareth; adjoins to the north Jan van Eeckelen, and to the south Mijndert Fredericksz, as the same stands within its enclosure and fence. Wide in front on the street three rods and four feet, in the rear ten and a half feet Rhineland measure according to the survey bill thereof by the surveyor Harmen Bastiaensz dated the 12th/22nd of March 1667, without him, grantor, making any further claim upon it anymore, acknowledging to have been satisfied and paid for it to his content, the last penny with the first; giving therefore *plenam actionem cessam* and full power to said Banckert, or his assigns, to dispose of the same as he might do with his patrimonial effects, promising on his behalf to protect and free the said domicile and lot from all actions, trouble, and claims of each and every person as is right, and moreover, nevermore to do or to let anything be done against the same, either with or without law in any way, under pledge of his person and estate, without exception, subject to all laws and judges. Done in Albany the 8th/18th of April 1667.

Jan Koster
Richard van Rensselaer
Philip Pietersz Schuijler

In my presence,
D. V. Schelluijne, secretary 1667.

[CONVEYANCE OF A HOUSE AND LOT BY HARMEN ALBERTSEN VEDDER TO GERRIT BANCKERT]

[**638**] Copy.

Harmen Albertsz Vedder hereby declares that he hereby transfers and makes over to Gerrit Banckert in true free ownership the house and lot mentioned on the other side of this [page], without him, in the world having any claim to it anymore, acknowledging to have been fully satisfied and paid for it, the last penny with the first; promising to protect and free the same from all trouble and actions of each and every person as is right, with promises nevermore to do or to let anything be done against the same, either with or without law, in any way, under pledge of his person and estate, without exception, subject to all laws and judges. Done in Albany the 8th/18th of April 1667 in the presence of the lords magistrates Phillip Pietersz Schuijler and Richard van Rensselaer.

Was signed:
Harmen Vedder together with
Philip Pietersz Schuijler
Richard van Rensselaer
And in presence of me,
D. V. Schelluijne, secretary.

Note: The original of this paper is the conveyance issued and approved by the lord vice director and commissary La Montagne, dated the 14th of September 1658.

[SALE OF A LOT BY JURRIAEN JANSZ GROENEWOUT TO SYMON VOLCKERTSZ]

[**639**] We, the undersigned Philip Pietersz Schuijler and Goossen Gerritsz, magistrates of Albany, colony of Rensselaerswijck and Schanechtade, attest and declare that on date underwritten appeared before us Jurriaen Jansz Groenewout, husband and guardian of Maritie Thomas, last widow of the late Cornelis Theunisz Bos, assisted by *Sr.*

Jan Verbeeck and Stoffel Jansz Abeel as invited co-guardians of Weijntie Cornelis, minor daughter of the aforesaid Cornelis Theunisz and Maritie Thomas, who declared that they have hereby ceded, conveyed and made over in true, rightful and free ownership to and for the benefit of Sijmon Volckertsz *backer*, presently dwelling at Schanechtade, a lot located here in Albany upon which said Sijmon Volckertsz has had a house built, the lot being long to the south a common road twenty rods nine feet, to the west the street, wide four rods, to the north the said Theunis Cornelisz, long twenty rods nine feet, to the east the river, wide nine feet, according to the survey bill thereof of the surveyor Jan Roeloffs dated the 1st of April 1661, and by virtue of a patent for a larger lot granted by the lord director general and councilors of New Netherland to him, the late Bos, dated the 23rd of April 1652, without he, grantor in his aforesaid capacity, or in any manner, having the least claim upon it anymore, as his aforesaid wife [acknowledges] to have been fully satisfied and paid for it, the last penny with the first, already before the date of her marriage with the grantor, her present husband, giving therefore **[640]** *plenam actionem cessam*, authority and full power to the aforesaid Sijmon Volckertsz, his heirs and descendants, or those who hereafter may acquire his title, to, by virtue as before, dispose of the same lot and domicile built thereupon, and to do with it as he might do with his own patrimonial lands and effects, promising to protect and free the aforesaid lot from all trouble, action and objections of each and every person as is right, and moreover, nevermore to do nor to let anything be done against the same, either with or without law, in any way, under pledge of his person and estate, moveable and immoveable without exception, subject to all laws and judges. Done in Albany the 9th/19th of April 1667.

This  mark is made by said Jurriaen Jansz Groenewout.
Philip Schuijler
Jan Verbeeck
Stoffel Jansz Abeel
Goosen Gerretsen
In my presence,
D. V. Schelluijne, secretary 1667.

[SALE OF A LOT AND A GARDEN BY JURRAEN JANSZ GROENEWOUT TO HUIJBERT JANSZ]

We, the undersigned magistrates of Albany, colony of Rensselaerswijck and Schanechtade declare that on date underwritten appeared before us Jurriaen Jansz Groenewout, husband and guardian of Maritie Thomasdr., last widow of the late Cornelis Theunisz Bos, assisted [**641**] by *Sr.* Jan Verbeeck and Stoffel Jansz Abeel as requested co-guardians of Weijntie Cornelis, minor daughter of the aforesaid Cornelis Theunisz and Maritie Thomasdr., who declared that hereby they have ceded, conveyed and made over in rightful, true and free ownership to and for the benefit of Huijbert Jansz a certain lot, long on the north side seven rods and nine feet, on the south side eight rods and ten feet, on the east side two rods and six feet, and on the west side two rods; also a garden across the public road, located on the riverside, long on the north and south side four rods, on the west side two rods seven feet wide, on the east side wide three rods. Both lot and garden are located in Albany and adjoin on the south side the grantor, on the west and north side the public streets, and on the east side the river. And this by virtue of a patent for a larger lot dated the 23rd of April 1652, granted to said Cornelis Theunisz by director general and councilors of New Netherland, without they, grantors, having the least claim upon the aforesaid anymore, as he, Huijbert Jansz having fully satisfied and paid for the same, the last penny with the first; therefore giving *plenam actionem cessam*, and full power to said Huybert Jansz, his heirs and descendants or those, who hereafter may acquire his title, to dispose of the same as he might do with his own patrimonial effects, promising, moreover, to protect and free the said lot and garden from all trouble, actions, and claims of each and every person as is right, and moreover, nevermore to do or to let anything be done against the same, either with or [**642**] without law, in any way, under pledge of their persons and estates, without exception, subject to all laws and judges. Done in Albany the $9^{th}/19^{th}$ of April 1667.

This mark  is made by said Jurriaen Jansz Groenewout.
Jan Verbeeck
Stoffel Jansz Abeel
Philip Pietersz Schuijler
Goosen Gerretsen

In my presence,
D. V. Schelluijne, secretary 1667.

[SALE OF HALF A LOT AND A HOUSE BY JURRIAEN JANSZ GROENEWOUT TO GEERTRUIJT BARENTS]

We, the undersigned magistrates of Albany, colony of Rensselaerswijck and Schanechtade declare that on date underwritten appeared before us Jurriaen Jansz Groenewout, burgher and inhabitant here in Albany, husband and guardian of Maritie Thomas Mingael, late widow of the deceased Cornelis Theunisz van Westbroeck, who declared to hereby have ceded, conveyed and made over in true, rightful and free ownership to and for the benefit of Geertruijt Barents, late widow of the deceased Hendrick Hendricksz, presently wife of Jacob Hevingh the half of a lot with the domicile standing thereon, in length, width and enclosure according to conveyance thereof, dated the 4th of June 1658, to which hereby is referred, without him, grantor, having the least claim upon the aforesaid anymore, acknowledging that he has been fully satisfied and paid for it, the last penny with the first, promising nevermore to do or to let anything be done against the same, in any way, under pledge of his person and estate, without exception, subject to all laws and judges. Done in Albany the $9^{th}/19^{th}$ of April 1667.

This mark is made by said Jurriaen Jansz Groenewout
This mark is made by Huijbert Jansz
Philip Pietersz
Goosen Gerritsen

In my presence,
D. V. Schelluijne, secretary 1667.

[SALE OF A HOUSE AND LOT BY HANS HENDRICKSZ AND PIETER VAN AELEN, ATTORNEYS FOR CORNELIS CORNELISSEN *DE BOER* TO JAN HENDRICKSZ BRUIJN]

[643] We, the undersigned magistrates of Albany, colony of Rensselaerswijck and Schanechtade attest and declare that on date underwritten appeared before us Hans Hendricksz and Pieter van Aelen, attorneys for Cornelis Cornelissen *de Boer,* who declared to hereby have ceded, conveyed and made over in true, rightful and free ownership to and for the benefit of Jan Hendricksz Bruijns a certain domicile and lot, standing and located here in Albany, in length and width and with such duties and rights as said *De Boer* has acquired the same by conveyance from Jan Coster van Aecken and Stoffel Jansz, attorneys for Pieter *de Maecker*, passed to the benefit of him, *De Boer* and Daniel Vervelen on the 8th of August 1659. Together with a certificate of conveyance passed by the same Vervelen for the benefit of the said *De Boer* on the 25th of August 1661. Also according to a bill of sale made between him, *De Boer*, and said Bruijns on the 9th of August 1663, to all of which has been referred here, without the grantors having the least claim on it anymore, acknowledging to have been fully satisfied and paid for it by said Jan Hendricksz Bruijns, the last penny with the first; giving therefore *plenam actionem cessam*, and full power to said Bruijns, his heirs and descendants, or those who hereafter may acquire his title, to dispose of the same as he might do with his patrimonial effects, promising on behalf of said *De Boer*, to protect and free the said lot and garden from all actions, trouble, and charges of each and every person as is right, and moreover, **[644]** nevermore to do or to let anything be done against the same, either with or without law, in any way, under pledge of his person and estate, without exception, subject to all laws and judges. Done in Albany the 12th/22nd of April 1667.

Hans Heindricksz
Pieter van Alen
Philip Pietersz
Richard van Rensselaer
In my presence,
D. V. Schelluijne, secretary 1667.

[SALE OF A HOUSE AND LOT BY HENDRICK MARCELIS TO ROBBERT SANDERSEN SMITH]

We, the undersigned magistrates of Albany, colony of Rensselaerswijck and Schanechtade hereby attest and declare that on date underwritten appeared before us Hendrick Marcelis, who hereby declares to cede, convey and make over in true, rightful and free ownership to and for the benefit of Robbert Sandertsz *smith* his house and lot standing and located here in Albany; adjoins to the south and east the public street, to the north Harmen Jansz Rijckmans, and to the west Volckie Jurriaense, widow of the late Jan van Hoesem; wide to the east 5 rods and eight feet, long to the south 9 rods and 11 feet, to the west 4 rods 11 feet, and to the north 9 rods 8 feet 8 inches, and this by virtue of a patent for a larger lot granted to him, grantor, by the lord director general and councilors of New Netherland dated the 24th of March 1654, **[645]** for which said domicile and lot the grantor acknowledges to have been fully satisfied and paid the last penny with the first, giving therefore *plenam actionem cessam* and complete power to said Robbert Sandertsz his heirs and descendants, or those who hereafter may acquire his title to dispose of the same as he might do with his patrimonial effects, promising to protect and free said domicile and lot of all actions and claims of each and every person as is right, and moreover, nevermore to do or to let anything be done against the same, either with or without law, in any way, under pledge of his person and estate, without exception, subject to all laws and judges. Done in Albany the 13th /23rd of April 1667.

This mark  was made by said Hendrick Marcelis.
Philip Pietersz
Richard van Rensselaer
In my presence,
D. V. Schelluijne, secretary 1667.

[SALE OF A LOT BY HENDRICK MARCELIS TO VOLCKIE JURRIAENS]

[646] We, the undersigned magistrates of Albany, colony of Rensselaerswijck and Schanechtade hereby attest and declare that on date underwritten appeared before us Hendrick Marcelis, who declares to hereby cede, convey and make over in true, rightful and free ownership to and for the benefit of Volckie Jurriaense, widow of Jan van Hoesem, a lot located here in Albany; adjoins to the east Robbert Sandertsz, to the south the public street, to the west Andries de Vos, and to the north Harmen Jansz Rijckman, long ten rods, wide on the east 4 rods 8 feet, and to the west 4 rods 4 feet, and this by virtue of a patent for a larger lot dated the 24th of March 1654, for which he, grantor, acknowledges to have been fully satisfied and paid, the last penny with the first, giving therefore *plenam actionem cessam* and complete power to said Volckie Jurriaense, her heirs and descendants or those, who may receive title from her, to do with it as she might do with her patrimonial effects, promising to protect and free said lot from all actions, trouble and claims as is right, and moreover, nevermore to do or to let anything be done against the same, either with or without law, in any way, under pledge of his person and estate, without exception, subject to all laws and judges. Done in Albany the $13^{th}/23^{rd}$ of April 1667.

This mark  is made by said Hendrick Marcelis.
Abram Staas
Richard van Rensselaer
In my presence,
D. V. Schelluijne, secretary 1667.

[SALE OF A LOT BY VOLCKIE JURRIAENSZ TO ANDRIES DE VOS]

[**647**] There appeared before us, the undersigned magistrates, Volckie Jurriaens, widow of the late Jan Franssen van Hoesem, who, by virtue and as a consequence of the above standing conveyance passed by Hendrick Marcelis to her benefit, declares to hereby cede, convey and make over in true, rightful and free ownership to and for the benefit of Andries de Vos, the lot mentioned in the said conveyance, in length and width and boundaries here in Albany as is expressed and stated in the same, and to which here is referred, without she, grantor having the least claim upon it anymore, acknowledging to have been fully satisfied and paid for it through the hands of him, De Vos, the last penny with the first, giving therefore to him, De Vos, his heirs and descendants or those, who may receive title from him such right and power as she has

acquired the same from said Hendrick Marcelis, with promise on her behalf to protect and free the same from all actions, trouble and claims as is right, and moreover, nevermore to do or to let anything be done against the same, either with or without law, in any way, under pledge of her person and estate, without exception, subject to all laws and judges.

Done in Albany the 13th/23rd of April 1667.

This mark  is made by said Volckie Jurriaens.
Richard van Rensselaer
Abram Staas

In my presence,
D. V. Schelluijne, secretary 1667.

[SALE OF A FARM AT SCHANECHTADE BY CORNELIS VAN NES TO JAN VAN EPS

[648] We, the undersigned magistrates of Albany, colony of Rensselaerswijck and Schanechtade attest and declare that on date underwritten appeared before us *Sr.* Cornelis van Nes, former magistrate of this court, who declares to hereby cede, convey and make over in true, rightful and free ownership to and for the benefit of Jan van Eps, son of his present wife Maritie Dames, a farm consisting of two parcels of land, together 21 morgens and 570 rods, located at Schanechtade, according to patent of the lord director general and councilors of New Netherland dated the 16th of June 1664, together with a house, lot and another lot for a garden located in the *bijeenwooninge* at said Schanechtade; both being bounded, and in length and width according to the contents of the certificate thereof of said director general to the benefit of him, Van Nes, dated the 20th of April 1665 *stilo novo,* to which said patent and certificate here is referred; without he, grantor, having the least claim upon it anymore, acknowledging to have been fully satisfied and paid for it through the hands of him, Jan Eps, the last penny with the first, giving therefore *plenam actionem cessam* and full power to the said Jan Eps, his heirs and descendants or those, who thereafter may receive title from him to dispose of the said farm, house, lot and garden as he might do with his own patrimonial lands and effects with promise [**649**] to protect and free the same from all actions, trouble and claims of each and every person as is right, and moreover, nevermore to do or to let anything be done against the same, either with or without law, in any way, under pledge of his person and estate, without exception, subject to all laws and judges. Done in Albany the 15th/25th of April 1667.

Cornelis van Nes
Richard van Rensselaer
Abram Staas
In my presence,
D. V. Schelluijne, secretary 1667.

[SALE OF A HOUSE AND LOT BY WILLEM JANSZ SCHUT TO JACOB LOOCKERMANS]

We, the undersigned magistrates of Albany, colony of Rensselaerswijck and Schanechtade attest and declare that on date underwritten appeared before us Willem Jansz Schut, farmer, who declares to hereby cede, convey and make over in true, rightful and free ownership to and for the benefit of Jacob Loockermans, all his title and right that he has had to the house and lot here in Albany, presently occupied by him, Loockermans; and this by virtue of a patent for a larger lot dated the 25th of October 1653, granted by the lord director general and councilors of New Netherland to the widow of the late Gijsbert Cornelisz van Wesop, presently wife of *Sr.* Francois Boon, who had conveyed his right to the same to Andries Herbertsz *Constapel* on the 22nd of August 1654; from which [**650**] Andries Herbertsz he, grantor, by sale and delivery had acquired a portion of the lot mentioned in the said patent, and by the regulation of the public road a portion was taken from the one side of his, Loockerman's lot, which was added again on the other side by the said lord director general and magistrates on the 6th of October 1656, which is annotated on the back of the patent, so that the aforesaid domicile and lot is standing free within its enclosure and fence; below the road two rods eight feet and a half, to the east of the road three rods, south one rod eleven feet, and west two rods seven feet, according to the survey bill of surveyor Harmen Bastiaensen thereof, dated the 13th/23rd of this month of April, without him, grantor, having the least claim upon the said domicile and lot anymore, acknowledging to have been fully satisfied and paid for it by him, Jacob Loockermans, giving therefore *plenam actionem cessam* and full power to the said Loockermans or those, who hereafter may acquire his title to dispose of the same as he might do with his own patrimonial effects, promising to protect and free the same from all actions, trouble and claims on his behalf of each and every person as is right, and moreover, nevermore to do or to let anything be done against the same, either with or without law, in any way, under pledge of his person and estate, without exception, subject to all laws and judges. Done in Albany the 15th/25th of April 1667.

Willem Jansen Schudt
Abram Staas
Richard van Rensselaer
In my presence,
D. V. Schelluijne, secretary 1667.

[SALE OF A HOUSE AND LOT BY JAN HENDRICXSZ VAN BAEL TO GERRIT LANSINGH]

[**651**] We, the undersigned magistrates of Albany, colony of Rensselaerswijck and Schanechtade, attest and declare that on date underwritten appeared before us *Sr.* Jan Hendricxsz van Bael, former magistrate of this court, who declared to hereby cede, convey and make over in true, rightful and free ownership to and for the benefit of Gerrit Lansingh a certain domicile and lot as he acquired it by purchase at public auction from Ulderick Cleijn on date the 22nd of July, 1658, and by virtue of a patent for a larger lot granted to the said Ulderick Cleijn by director general and councilors of New Netherland on date the 25th of October 1653, and the first of November of the same year; standing and located here in Albany, adjoining to the south on Sijmon Groot, to the north the road across from which is Rijer Elbertsz, east and west the wagon road, but presently in its enclosure and fence according to the survey bill thereof, as the same was surveyed to his, Lansingh's, content by the surveyor Harmen Bastiaensz on the 13th/23rd of this month of

April; without him, grantor, having the least claim upon the same anymore, acknowledging to have been fully satisfied and paid for it, the last penny with the first: namely, with the sum of 273 guilders in beavers and a mortgage of which still the sum of 260 guilders 13 in beavers remains to be paid in the coming trading season;† **[652]** giving therefore *plenam actionem cessam* and full power to the said Gerrit Lansingh, his heirs and descendants, or those who hereafter may acquire his title to dispose of the said domicile and lot as he might do with his own patrimonial lands and effects, promising on his behalf to protect and free the same from all actions, trouble and claims of each and every person as is right, and moreover, nevermore to do or to let anything be done against the same, either with or without law, in any way, under pledge of his person and estate, without exception, subject to all laws and judges. Done in Albany the 15th/25th of April 1667.

Jan H. van Bael
Richard van Rensselaer
Abram Staas
In my presence,
D. V. Schelluijne, secretary 1667.

Notwithstanding Van Bael acknowledges, according to the above conveyance to have been fully satisfied and paid, the said Lansingh remains indebted for the house and lot for sixty-two guilders and 13 stuivers in beavers, which he promises to pay in the coming trading season, pledging therefor his person and estate, and especially the said domicile and lot to recover the payment thereof if necessary. Done in Albany, dated as above.

Gerrit Lansinck
Jan van Bael
In my presence,
D. V. Schelluijne, secretary 1667.
[*The above paragraph was crossed out in the original.*]

---

† The amount beginning with "namely" has been crossed out in the original.

[*In the margin is written*:] Jan van Bael acknowledges to have been fully satisfied and paid for these contents, and therefore, the same contract is canceled and annuled. Done in Albany the 29th of August/8th of September 1667.

[SALE OF A LOT FOR A HOUSE AND GARDEN BY WOUTER AERTSZ *RADEMAKER* TO GEURT HENDRICXSZ]

[653] We, the undersigned magistrates of Albany, colony of Rensselaerswijck and Schanechtade attest and declare that on date underwritten appeared before us Wouter Aertsz, *rademaker* here, as holding the title and right of Pieter Meusz Vroman, according to patent granted to him, Pieter Meusz, by director general and councilors of New Netherland on the 31st of October 1658, who declared to hereby cede, convey and make over in true, rightful and free ownership to and for the benefit of Geurt Hendricxsz, master carpenter here, a lot for a house and garden, located here in Albany, presently occupied and possessed by the said Geurt Hendricxsz; in length, width and boundaries according to purport and contents of the said patent, without the grantor having the least claim upon the same anymore, acknowledging to have been fully satisfied and paid for it, the last penny with the first, through the hands of said Geurt Hendricxsz, giving therefor to the same Geurt Hendricxsz, his heirs and descendants, or those who hereafter may acquire his title, *plenam actionem cessam* and full power to dispose of the said lot and garden and the buildings standing thereupon, as he might do with his own patrimonial lands and effects, promising to protect and free the same from all actions, trouble and claims of each and every person as is right, and moreover, nevermore to do or to let anything be done against the same, either with or without law, in any way, under pledge of his person and estate, without exception, subject to all laws and judges. Done in Albany the 16th/26th of April 1667.

Pieter Meesz Vrooman
This mark  was made by said Wouter Aertsz.
Richard van Rensselaer
Philip Pietersz

In my presence,
D. V. Schelluijne, secretary 1667.

[SALE OF A LOT BY ABRAHAM STAES
TO PHILIP PIETERSZ SCHUIJLER]

[654] We, the undersigned magistrates of Albany, colony of Rensselaerswijck and Schanechtade attest and declare that on date underwritten appeared before us Capt. Abraham Staes, fellow magistrate, who, by virtue of a patent granted to him by director general and councilors of New Netherland on date the 25th of October 1653, declared to hereby cede, convey and make over over in true, rightful and free ownership to *Sr.* Phillip Pietersz Schuijler, also magistrate of the said court, a certain lot here in Albany upon which he, Schuijler, has built his houses, extending to the west of the lot of Ruth Jacobsen, deceased, between which two [lots] is a path of five feet wide; from the path westward six rods and two feet, and southward twelve rods. (In addition, he, Schuijler, in the year 1659 was granted by the magistrates eight feet of ground westward, upon which his Indian hut is now standing); without him, grantor having the least claim upon the same anymore, acknowledging to have been fully satisfied and paid for it through the hands of said Schuijler, the last penny with the first, giving therefore *plenam actionem cessam* and full power to the said Schuijler, his heirs and descendants, or those, who hereafter may acquire his title, to dispose of the same as he might do with his own patrimonial lands and effects, promising to protect and free the same lot from all actions, trouble and claims of each and every person as is right, and moreover, nevermore to do or to let anything be done against the same, either with or without law, in any way, under pledge of his person and estate, without exception, subject to all laws and judges. Done in Albany the 17th/27th of April 1667.

Abram Staas
Goosen Gerretsen
R. van Rensselaer
In my presence,
D. V. Schelluijne, secretary 1667.

[SALE OF A LOT BY GIDEON SCHAETS TO PHILLIP PIETERSZ SCHUIJLER]

[655] We, the undersigned magistrates of Albany, colony of Rensselaerswijck and Schanechtade attest and declare that on date underwritten appeared before us Do. Gideon Schaets, minister of God's Holy Word in this place, who declared to hereby cede, convey and make over in true, rightful and free ownership to and for the benefit of *Sr.* Phillip Pietersz Schuijler, fellow magistrate of this court, a lot located between the lord Rensselaer's garden, and beginning at the clapboards of Abraham Pietersz; adjoins to the east a wagon road, south also a road, and west an empty lot; south wide four rods and long ten rods, according to the patent granted to him by director general and councilors of New Netherland dated the 22nd of September 1653; without the grantor having the least claim upon the same anymore, acknowledging to have been fully satisfied and paid for it through the hands of said Schuijler, the last penny with the first, giving therefore to the said Schuijler, his heirs and descendants, or those who hereafter may acquire his title *plenam actionem cessam* and full power to dispose of it as he might do with his own patrimonial lands and effects, promising on his behalf to protect and free the same lot from all actions, trouble and claims of each and every person as is right, and moreover, nevermore to do or to let anything be done against the same, either with or without law, in any way, under pledge of his person and estate, without exception, subject to all laws and judges. Done in Albany the 17th/27th of April 1667.

Gideon Schaets
Abram Staas
Goosen Gerretsen
In my presence,
D. V. Schelluijne, secretary 1667.

[SALE OF A LOT BY ANDRIES DE VOS TO JURRIAEN THEUNISZ *GLAESEMAECKER*]

[656] We, the undersigned magistrates of Albany, colony of Rensselaerswijck and Schanechtade attest and declare that on date underwritten appeared before us Andries de Vos, father-in-law of Cornelis Vos, who declared to hereby cede, convey and make over in true, rightful and free ownership to and for the benefit of Jurriaen Theunisz *glaesemaecker* a lot located here in Albany, at present built upon and occupied by Jurriaen Theunisz, adjoins to the east of Barent van Marle, is seven rods long, and with the lords' consent, one rod at the kil; wide along the kil two rods and five feet, long along the street eight rods, width in front as the house is standing according to the survey bill thereof by surveyor Jan Roeloffs, and this also by virtue of a patent for a larger lot granted to said Cornelis Vos by director general and councilors of New Netherland of the 23rd of April 1652, also according to the bill of sale signed by said Cornelis Vos and him, Jurriaen Theunisz dated the 10th of August 1662; without the said Cornelis Vos, or him, grantor, having the least claim upon the same anymore, as he, grantor, is aware that he, Cornelis Vos, before his departure from here for Holland has, as stated before, been satisfied and paid for it by the aforesaid Jurriaen Theunisz, promising therefore, on behalf of Cornelis Vos, to protect and free the said lot from all claims and trouble of each and every person for the benefit of Jurriaen Theunisz, his heirs and descendants or those who hereafter may acquire his title, and moreover, **[657]** nevermore to do or to let anything be done against the same, either with or without law, in any way, under pledge of his person and estate, without exception, subject to all laws and judges. Done in Albany the 18th/28th of April 1667.

Andrijes de Vos
Abram Staas
Philip Pietersz Schuijler
In my presence,
D.V. Schelluijne, secretary 1667.

[SALE OF A LOT BY PHILIP PIETERSZ SCHUIJLER
TO JAN *DE NOORMAN*]

We, the undersigned magistrates of Albany, colony of Rensselaerswijck and Schanechtade attest and declare that on date underwritten appeared before us *Sr.* Philip Pietersz Schuijler, fellow magistrate of the same court, who declared to hereby cede, convey and make over in true, rightful and free ownership to and for the benefit of Jan *de Noorman* a lot upon which his house has stood, which house he has moved, and this by virtue of a conveyance dated the 11th of September 1664 by Pieter Adriaensz passed for the benefit of him, Schuijler; adjoins to the north Adriaen Appel and to the south Jan Barentsz Poest, deceased, here in Albany, the aforesaid lot being long ten rods, and wide four rods, without he, grantor, having the least claim upon the same anymore, acknowledging **[658]** to have been fully satisfied and paid for it through the hands of said Jan *de Noorman*, the last penny with the first, giving therefore *plenam actionem cessam* and full power to the said Jan *de Noorman*, his heirs and descendants, or those who hereafter may acquire his title, to dispose of the same as he might do with his own patrimonial effects, promising on his behalf to protect and free the same lot from all actions, trouble and claims of each and every person as is right, and moreover, nevermore to do or to let anything be done against the same, either with or without law, in any way, under pledge of his person and estate, without exception, subject to all laws and judges. Done in Albany the 18th/28th of April 1667.

Philip Pietersen Schuijler
Goosen Gerretsen
Abram Staas
In my presence,
D. V. Schelluijne, secretary 1667.

[SALE OF A HOUSE AND LOT BY FEMMETIE ALBERTS TO DANIEL RINCHOUT *BACKER*]

We, the undersigned magistrates of Albany, colony of Rensselaerswijck and Schanechtade attest and declare that on date underwritten appeared before us Femmetie Alberts, widow of Hendrick Jansz Westercamp, at present dwelling in the Esopus, now being here in this place, who declared to hereby cede, convey and make over in true, rightful and free ownership to and for the benefit of **[659]** Daniel Rinchout *backer* her certain domicile and lot standing and situated here in Albany, presently occupied by said Rinchout, being the same domicile and lot, in boundaries, length and breadth according to purport and contents of the survey bill by the surveyor thereof, and by virtue of a patent for a larger lot granted by the lord director general and councilors of New Netherland on the 23rd of April 1652, to which hereby reference is made; without the grantor making the least claim upon the same anymore, acknowledging to have been fully satisfied and paid for it by the hands of him, Rinchout, the last penny with the first, and according to the bill of sale passed before the secretary Dirck van Hamel, deceased, on the 8th of March 1660; giving therefor full right and power to the said Rinchout, his heirs and descendants, to dispose of the said house and lot as he might do with his patrimonial lands and effects, promising on her behalf to protect and free the said house and lot from all actions, trouble and claims of each and every person as is right, and moreover, nevermore to do or to let anything be done against the same, either with or without law, in any way, under pledge of her person and estate, without exception, subject to all laws and judges. Done in Albany the $19^{th}/29^{th}$ of April 1667.

This + mark was made by said Femmetie Alberts.
Philip Pietersz
R. V. Rensselaer
In my presence,
D. V. Schelluijne, secretary 1667.

[660][*blank*]

[SALE OF A HOUSE AND LOT BY ADRIAEN VAN ILPENDAM,
ATTORNEY FOR ALBERT GERRITSZ, TO
JAN JANSZ VAN EECKELEN]

[661] We, the undersigned magistrates of Albany, colony of Rensselaerswijck and Schanechtade attest and declare that on date underwritten appeared before us *Mr*. Adriaen van Ilpendam, attorney for Albert Gerritsz, dwelling in the Esopus, who in his said capacity declared to hereby cede, convey and make over in true, rightful and free ownership to and for the benefit of Jan Jansz van Eeckelen a certain domicile and lot standing and located here in Albany, and this by virtue of a patent granted by the lord director general and councilors of New Netherland to said Albert Gerritsz on the 23rd of April 1652, of which a portion was conveyed to Jan van Aecken, and by him, Van Aecken, to Gerrit Bancker, with whom remains the surveyor's survey bill; also according to a bill of sale dated the 3rd of March 1660, passed between said Albert Gerritsz and Jan van Eeckelen; without he, grantor, in his said capacity, making the least claim upon the said house and lot anymore, acknowledging to have been fully satisfied and paid for it through the hands of him, Van Eeckelen, the last penny with the first; giving therefore *plenam actionem cessam* and complete power to the said Jan van Eeckelen, his heirs and descendants, or those who hereafter may acquire his title, to dispose of the same as he might do with his own patrimonial lands and effects, promising, in his said capacity, to protect and free the said house and lot from all actions, trouble and claims as is right, and moreover, [**662**] nevermore to do or to let anything be done against the same, either with or without law, in any way, under pledge of his person, in his said capacity, and estate, without exception, subject to all laws and judges. Done in Albany the 20th/30th of April 1667.

Adriaen van Ilpendam
R. V. Rensselaer
Philip Pietersz Schuijler
In my presence,
D. V. Schelluijne, secretary 1667.

Notwithstanding the said conveyance passed as before, Jan Jansz van Eeckelen acknowledges that according to settlement made with *Mr*. Adriaen van Ilpendam he still owes *per resto* on said house and lot the sum or quantity of thirty good whole merchantable beaver skins figured at eight guilders apiece, to be paid in the month of July next coming punctually, without further delay, pledging therefore his person and estate, moveable and immoveable without exception, and especially the aforesaid house and lot, to recover payment, if necessary, without costs and damage. Done in Albany, dated as above.

Ian Iansen van Eeckel
In my presence,
D. V. Schelluijne, secretary 1667.

[SALE OF A LOT BY HUIJBERT JANSZ TO CORNELIS VAN NES]

[663] We, the undersigned magistrates of Albany, colony of Rensselaerswijck and Schanechtade attest and declare that on date underwritten appeared before us Huijbert Jansz, dwelling here in Albany, who declared to hereby cede, convey and make over in true, rightful and free ownership to and for the benefit of Cornelis van Nes, husband and guardian of Maritie Dames, last widow of Hendrick Andriesz, as holding the right and title of Phillip Hendricxsz *brouwer*, his certain lot situated here in Albany, long seventy-three wood feet, wide on the east side thirty feet, and on the westward side wide between twenty-six and twenty-seven feet, as it is standing within its fence, according to the bill of sale dated the 6th of March 1659; together with a deed of conveyance from him, grantor, on the 9th/19th of April of this year passed for his benefit by Jurriaen Jansz Groenewout, husband and guardian of Maritie Thomas, last widow of the late Cornelis Theunisz Bos; to all of which is referred here, without him, grantor, having the least claim upon it anymore, acknowledging to have been fully satisfied and paid for it through the hands of the said Phillip Hendricxsz, the last penny with the first; giving therefore such right and power to the said Van Nes, his heirs and descendants or those who hereafter may acquire his title, to dispose of it as he might do with his patrimonial effects, promising, on his behalf, to protect and free the said house and lot from all actions, trouble and claims of each and every person as is right, and moreover, nevermore to do or to let anything be done against the same, either with or without law, in any way, under pledge of his person and estate, without exception, subject to all laws and judges. Done in Albany the 23rd of April/3rd of May 1667.

This mark  is made by said Huijbert Jansz.
R. V. Rensselaer
Teunis Cornelisz

In my presence,
D. V. Schelluijne, secretary 1667.

[SALE OF THE ABOVE LOT BY CORNELIS VAN NES
TO HENDRICK GERRITSZ VERMEULEN]

[**664**] Appeared likewise said Cornelis van Nes, who in his aforesaid capacity declared to cede and convey in true, rightful and free ownership to and for the benefit of Hendrick Gerritsz Vermeulen, master tailor, the lot mentioned above with such right and title as the aforesaid Huijbert Jansz has conveyed the same to him, acknowledging to have been fully satisfied and paid for it, and promising moreover, nevermore to do or to let anything be done against the same, under the same pledge and subjection as above. Done in Albany, dated as above.

Cornelis van Nes
R. V. Rensselaer
Teunis Cornelisz
In my presence,
D. V. Schelluijne, secretary 1667.

[SALE OF THE ABOVE LOT BY HENDRICK GERRITSZ VERMEULEN
TO ARENT JANSZ *TIMMERMAN*]

Hendrick Gerritsz Vermeulen, by virtue of the above conveyances, hereby declares to cede and make over to and for the benefit of Arent Jansz *timmerman* here in Albany, his heirs and descendants, or his those, who may receive title from him, the aforesaid lot with such right and title as the same was conveyed by Huybert Jansz to Cornelis van Nes in the above mentioned conveyance, and by him, Van Nes, as having the right and title of Philip Hendricxsz *brouwer*, to him, the grantor; without he, grantor, having the least claim upon it anymore, acknowledging to likewise have been fully satisfied for it; also promising nevermore to do or to let anything be done against the same, also under the same pledge and subjection as mentioned in the aforesaid conveyance. Done in Albany, dated as above.

Hindrick Gerritsen
R. V. Rensselaer
Teunis Cornelisz

[ACKNOWLEDGMENT OF DEBT BY HENDRICK GERRITSZ TO CORNELIS VAN NES AND FINANCIAL ARRANGEMENT BETWEEN HENDRICK GERRITSEN AND ARENT JANSZ]

[665] Although the aforesaid conveyances were passed as before, Hendrick Gerritsz Vermeulen, nevertheless acknowledges that concerning the remaining purchase money of the aforesaid lot and garden, he is still indebted to the aforesaid Phillip Hendricxsz, or now to the said Van Nes, for the sum of one hundred and nine guilders in beavers, and, likewise, Arent Jansz *timmerman* to Hendrick Gerritsz for nine beavers. Thus he, Hendrick Gerritsz, assigns over to said Van Nes, the said nine beavers due from the same Arent *de timmerman*, which he, Arent Jansz, not only hereby accepts, and promises to pay the same nine beavers within six months after this date, but he also pledges for it as a special mortgage and collateral the aforesaid lot with the domicile standing thereupon; and moreover, he generally pledges his person and estate without exception subject to all laws and judges to recoup, if necessary, the payment without any cost or damage. And for as much as Hendrick Gerritsz furthermore remains indebted to Van Nes, being *per reste* the sum of thirty-seven guilders in beavers, he promises to honestly and properly satisfy the same within the time of six months after this date, as well, under pledge of his person and estate without exception, subject as before. Done in Albany, dated as above.

Hindrick Geritsen
Arent Jansz
R. V. Rensselaer
Teunis Cornelisz
In my presence,
D. V. Schelluijne, secretary 1667.

[*In the margin was written*:] By quittance of Cornelis van Nes it appeared to me that Arent Jansz *timmerman* has paid the nine beavers mentioned herein on the 24th of July 1668. Therefore this mortgage is canceled.

[SALE OF A HOUSE AND LOT BY GERARD SWART, ATTORNEY FOR PIETER HARTGERS, TO HENDRICK CUIJLER]

We, the undersigned magistrates of Albany, colony of Rensselaerswijck and Schanechtade attest and declare that [**666**] before us appeared *Sr.* Gerard Swart, *schout* of this court, both for himself and substituting and acting for Captain Abraham Staes, magistrate of the same court, together in capacity of attorneys for *Sr.* Pieter Hartgers, and declared in that capacity to hereby cede, convey and make over in true, rightful and free ownership to and for the benefit of Hendrick Cuijler, said Hartgers' domicile and lot standing and located here in Albany, and this in consequence and by virtue of the bill of sale thereof dated the 27th of February 1664, as, according to the tenor of the same bill of sale, to which here is referred, the same domicile and lot is standing at the hill within its fence, enclosure and boundaries; without the grantor, in his aforesaid capacity, having the least claim upon it anymore, acknowledging to have been fully satisfied and paid for it through the hands of the said Hendrick Cuijler, the last penny with the first; giving therefore *plenam actionem cessam* and full power to the said Cuijler, his heirs and descendants, or those who hereafter may acquire his title, to dispose of the same as he might do with his other patrimonial effects, promising in his said capacity to protect and free the said domicile and lot from all actions, trouble and claims of each and every person as is right, and moreover, nevermore to do or to let anything be done against the same, either with or without law, in any way, under pledge of his person and estate, without exception, subject to all laws and judges. Done in Albany the 24th of April/ 4th of May 1667.

G. Swartt
Philip Pietersz Schuijler
Teunes Cornelisz

In my presence,
D. V. Schelluijne, secretary 1667.

[ACKNOWLEDGMENT OF DEBT BY HENDRICK CUIJLER]

[**667**] Notwithstanding the above standing conveyance passed for the benefit of Hendrick Cuijler, he, Cuijler, acknowledges to still be justly indebted for the last two payments of purchase money for the above standing house and lot, together amounting to the sum of five hundred and sixty-six guilders, to be paid in good whole beavers, which sum he, Cuijler, promises to pay for the said attorney on the first occasion, if requested, pledging therefore as a special mortgage and collateral the said house and lot to, if necessary, recover its payment without cost and damage, and, moreover, under pledge of his person and estate without exception, subject to all laws and judges. Done in Albany, dated as above.

Hendrick Cuijler
In my presence,
D. V. Schelluijne, secretary 1667.

[SALE OF A STRIP OF A LOT WITH A GARDEN BY JEREMIAS VAN RENSSELAER TO JAN EVERTSZ]

We, the undersigned magistrates of Albany, colony of Rensselaerswijck and Schanechtade attest and declare that on date underwritten the lord Jeremias van Rensselaer, director of the said colony, hereby cedes and conveys in rightful, true and free ownership to and for the benefit of Jan Evertsz *schoenmaecker* a small strip of a lot with a small garden behind it, upon which the horse mill and mill house have stood, in such manner as he acquired the same lot by purchase and conveyance from Willem Bout, according to the deed thereof, dated the 18th of November 1662, located here in Albany next to the house and lot conveyed to him, Jan Evertsz by Theunis Cornelisz; [**668**] without the grantor making the least claim upon the same anymore, acknowledging to have been fully satisfied and paid for it, promising nevermore to do or to let anything be done against the same in any way, under pledge according to law. Done in Albany the 25th of April/5th of May 1667.

J. V. Rensselaer
R. V. Rensselaer
Teunis Cornelisz
In my presence,
D. V. Schelluijne, secretary 1667.

[SALE OF A HOUSE AND LOT BY PHILIP PIETERSZ SCHUIJLER AND DIRCK VAN SCHELLUIJNE AS ADMINISTRATORS OF THE ESTATE OF CORNELIS BOGAERDUS TO JAN VINHAGEN]

Appeared before us, undersigned magistrates of Albany, Colony of Rensselaerswijck and Schanechtade, Phillip Pietersz Schuijler and Dirck van Schelluijne in the capacity of administrators of the estate of the late Cornelis Bogaerdus, who declared to hereby cede, convey and make over to and for the benefit of Jan Vinhagen the said Bogaerdus' domicile and lot standing and located here in Albany, presently occupied by him, Vinhagen, and this by virtue and in consequence of a bill of sale of the 5th/15th of September 1666, and further evidences thereof, without they, grantors in their aforesaid capacity, making the least claim upon it anymore, acknowledging to have been fully satisfied and paid for it, (a portion of which payment was made to the said Jan Jansz Bleecker, and further, this should be done to said Jan Jansz Bleecker according to the purport and contents of the said bill of sale, as he, Jan Jansz Bleecker, according to sentence, is preferred); giving therefore *plenam actionem cessam* and complete power to the said Vinhaegen, his heirs and descendants or those who hereafter may acquire his title, to **[669]** use and possess said domicile and lot in full ownership, as he might do with his own patrimonial effects; promising on their behalf to protect and free the said domicile and lot from all actions, trouble and claims, as is right, and moreover, nevermore to do or to let anything be done against the same in any way, under pledge of their respective persons and estates, in their said capacity. Done in Albany the 27th of April/ 7th of May 1667.

Philip Pietersz Schuijler
D. V. Schelluijne
R. V. Rensselaer
A. Van Curler
In my presence,
G: Swartt, schout at Albany.

Pursuant to the aforesaid conveyance and bill of sale Jan Vinhagen acknowledges to be indebted *per resto* the quantity of fifty beavers or their value, according to the contents of said bill of sale, promising to pay the same sum at the set time as is mentioned in the bill of sale, pledging therefore as a special mortgage and collateral the aforesaid domicile and lot, and further, generally his person and estate without exception subject to all laws and judges, to recover, if necessary, the payment without cost and damage. Done in Albany, dated as above.

Jan Vinhaeghen
Acknowledged by me,
G: Swartt, schout at Albany, etc.

[SALE OF A LOT BY CARSTEN CARSTENSZ *NOORMAN* TO CLAES THEUNISZ]

[670] Appeared before us, undersigned magistrates of Albany, Colony of Rensselaerswijck and Schanechtade, Carsten Carstensz *Noorman* who hereby declared that he has ceded, conveyed and made over in true, rightful and free ownership to and for the benefit of Claes Theunisz a garden plot located behind Fort Albany; to the west of the said Claes Theunisz long six rods, to the south wide three rods, to the east an empty lot long six rods, towards the road wide three rods, according to the survey bill of the surveyor Jan Roeloffs thereof, as the aforesaid has possessed the same lot for many years in ownership by permission of the lords magistrates, but apparently it was not formally registered, as it was not to be found in the protocol, without them, grantors, making the least claim upon it anymore, acknowledging to have been fully satisfied and paid for it through the hands of him, Claes Theunissen, the last penny with the first; giving therefore *plenam actionem cessam* and complete power to the said Claes Theunisz, his heirs and descendants or those who hereafter may receive his title, to dispose of it as he might do with his patrimonial effects, promising to protect and free the said lot from all actions, trouble and claims of each and every person as is right, and moreover, nevermore to do or to let anything be done against the same, either with or without law, in any way; under pledge according to law. Done in Albany the 27th of April/7th of May 1667.

This mark  is made by Carsten Carstensz *Noorman.*
R. V. Rensselaer
Teunis Cornelisz
In my presence,
D.V. Schelluijne, secretary 1667.

[DONATION BY SANDER LEENDERTSZ GLEN TO HIS SONS JACOB, SANDER AND JOHANNES]

[**671**] We, the undersigned magistrates of Albany, colony of Rensselaerswijck and Schanechtade attest and declare that on date underwritten appeared before us the honorable Sander Leendertsz Glen, dwelling at Schanechtade, who declared to hereby cede, convey and make over deliberately by donation *intervivos* and free gift among the living, to and for the benefit of his three sons named Jacob, Sander, and Johannes Sandertsz Glen, a certain parcel of land located between the lake and the river, across from the village at Schanechtade, fifty morgens in size, according to the patent thereof of date [*blank*]; [together with a mare and increase to each; namely: Jacob a mare named Volck with a filly; Sander a mare named [*blank*] with two colts, and Johannes Sandertsz],[†] renouncing and giving up therefore the same forever for the benefit as mentioned before, and this for good reasons, and because of good services rendered by them to him, appearer;

† The text between brackets was crossed out in the original.

promising nevermore to do or to let anything be done against the same, either with or without law, in any way; under pledge of his person and estate, without exception, subject to all laws and justices. Done in Albany the 11th/21st of May 1667.
Sander Lenrsen Glen
A. van Curler
R. V. Rensselaer

[*In the margin*:] This donation was canceled on this 9th of March 1669.

[ACKNOWLEDGMENT OF DEBT BY JAQUES CORNELISZ VAN SLIJCK TO JAN HENDRICXSZ VAN BAEL]

[672] We, the undersigned magistrates of Albany, colony of Rensselaerswijck and Schanechtade attest and declare that on date underwritten appeared before us Jaques Cornelisz van Slijck, dwelling at Schanechtade, who acknowledged to be honestly and truly indebted to *Sr.* Jan Hendricxsz van Bael, former magistrate, for the sum of four hundred fifty-five guilders and six stuivers, stemming from goods received to his content; according to promissory note passed by him, appearer, on the 3rd of January 1666, to be paid in beavers figured at eight guilders apiece; which aforesaid sum of *f*455:6 he, appearer, with the consent of him, Van Baele, shall pay within the time of four consecutive years, and that with its interest at ten to the hundred a year, commencing on this date and running until the full payment, without, however, under the pretext of payment of interest, being allowed to keep the capital sum any longer than the aforesaid time of four years as will please Van Bael or the lawful bearer of this paper. Therefore he, appearer, pledges as a special mortgage and collateral his farm located at said Schanechtade as he, appearer, presently owns it, and moreover, his person and estate, moveable and immoveable, present and future without exception, subject to all laws and justices, to recover payment if necessary without costs and damage. Done in Albany the 6th/16th of July 1667.

ACKES
R.V. Rensselaer

Abram Staas
Acknowledged by me,
D. V. Schelluijne, secretary 1667.

[SALE OF TWO GARDENS BY JEREMIAS VAN RENSSELAER AS ADMINISTRATOR OF THE ESTATE OF JAN BASTIAENSZ VAN GUTSENHOVEN TO JAN HENDRICK BRUIJNS]

[**673**] There appeared before us, the undersigned magistrates of Albany, colony of Rensselaerswijck and Schanechtade the lord Jeremias van Rensselaer in capacity of administrator of the estate of the late Jan Bastiaensz van Gutsenhoven, who hereby declared to cede, convey and make over in rightful, true and free ownership to and for the benefit of *Sr.* Jan Hendrick Bruijns certain two attached gardens, lying within its fence behind fort Albany, and this in accordance with, and by virtue of a deed of conveyance passed by Sander Leendertsz Glen for the benefit of said Gutsenhoven on the 25th of October 1662 before the former lord vice director and commissary La Montagne in the presence of two magistrates, without he, grantor in his said capacity, having any claim upon the same anymore, as it appears that he, Gutsenhoven, was already fully paid for it by him, Bruijns, with the sum of *f*120 on the 14th of December 1665. giving therefore *plenam actionem cessam* and full power to him, Bruijns, his heirs and descendants or those who hereafter may acquire his title, to dispose of the same two gardens as he might do with his own patrimonial lands and effects; promising in his said capacity, to protect and free the said gardens from all actions, trouble and claims of each and every person as is right, and nevermore to do or to let anything be done against the same, either with or without law, in any way; under pledge of his [**674**] of his person and estate without exception, subject to all laws and justices. Done in Albany the 6th /16th of July 1667.

Jeremias van Rensselaer
Abram Staas
R. V. Rensselaer

In my presence,
D.V. Schelluijne, secretary 1667.

[SALE OF A HOUSE AND LOT BY THE HEIRS OF ANNEKE BOGARDUS TO DIRCK WESSELSZ]

Appeared before us, the undersigned magistrates of Albany, colony of Rensselaerswijck and Schanechtade *Srs.* Pieter Bogardus and Jonas Bogardus, both for themselves and as attorneys for *Sr.* Johannes van Brugh, Pieter Hartgers, Sara Roeloffs, widow of the late Mr. Hans Kierstede, in his life *chirurgijn*, Jan Roeloffs, Willem Bogaerdus and on account of the widow of Cornelis Bogaerdus, deceased; all children and heirs of their late mother Anneke Bogardus, who declared, pursuant to a bill of sale dated the 21st of June 1663 passed before the clerk Johannes Provoost and certain witnesses, and by virtue of patents, first granted by director general and councilors of New Netherland on the 23rd of April 1652, and now, on the 10th of this month of July by the right honorable lord governor general Richard Nicolls, to hereby cede, convey and make over in rightful, true and free ownership to and for the benefit of Dirck Wessels, a certain domicile and lot of the said late Anneke Bogaerdus, standing and located here in Albany, occupied by him, Dirck Wessels, being bounded, built upon, enclosed and in width and length according to purport and contents of the aforesaid bill of sale to which here is referred; without they, grantors, having any claim thereto anymore, **[675]** acknowledging to have been fully satisfied and paid for it through the hands of him, Dirck Wessels, the last penny with the first; giving therefore *plenam actionem cessam* and full power to said Dirck Wessels, his heirs and descendants, or those who hereafter may acquire his title, to dispose of the said domicile and lot and to do with it as he might do with his patrimonial effects; promising to protect and free the same from all actions, trouble and claims of each and every person as is right, and moreover, nevermore to do or to let anything be done against the same, either with or without law, in any way; under pledge of their persons and estates without exception, subject to all law and justices. Done in Albany the 17th/27th of July 1667.

Pieter Bogardus
Jonas Bogardus
Tuenus Cornelisen
Abram Staas
In my presence,
D. V. Schelluijne, secretary 1667.

[DECLARATION BY DIRCK HESSELINGH AND YTIE HENDRICXSDR. REGARDING THE RELEASE OF A LOST AND FOUND SISTER]

Appeared before us, the undersigned magistrates of Albany, colony of Rensselaerswijck and Schanechtade the honorable Dirck Hesselingh and Ytie Hendricxsdr., newlyweds, dwelling here at Albany, **[676]** who, in the presence of Jan Coster van Aecken (former guardian of said Ytie Hendricxs since the year 1655—the time that she, together with her three sisters was taken prisoner by the Indian barbarians on the land of Van der Donck on the east side of the North River—until her state of marriage) declared that they had hereby appointed and fully empowered *Sr.* Samuel van Goedenhuijsen, merchant at New Haven in New England, especially to demand and claim from *Mr.* Ling, also merchant there, a daughter named Albrechie Hendricxs, sister of the aforesaid Ytie Hendricxs, about 17 or 18 years old, who, together with her and her said two other sisters was taken prisoner by the said Indians, as well, and she, Albrechie was kept there for a long time after their release, and finally, through God's mercy, had arrived under the Christians at New Haven, as they, appearers with certainty have been notified. Accordingly, upon having presently received the aforesaid Aelbrechie Hendricxs from her aforesaid *Mr.*, she will be sent up to the Manhatans or New York as soon as possible by the bearer of this, Claes Lock, so that the same can as soon as possible reach her said sister Ytie Hendricxs here in Albany. And in case of unwillingness (which is not hoped for), to make the case known to the judge there, and to solicit and request the full effect hereof, and further, to do **[677]** everything in this matter that is necessary and that he may deem advisable. Promising at all times to be grateful with all their hearts and to accept everything that by virtue of this paper will be done and performed in this matter by the said *Mr.* Goedenhuijsen without any objections, on pledge according to law. Done in Albany the 28th of October/ 7th of November 1667.

Dirck Hesselingh
IJtie Hendericks
Jan Koster
R. V. Rensselaer
J. de Hinsse
In my presence,
D. V. Schelluijne, secretary 1667.

[ACKNOWLEDGMENT OF DEBT BY ANDRIES TELLER TO JURRIAEN THEUNISSEN]

Appeared before us, undersigned magistrates of Albany, colony of Rensselaerswijck and Schanechtade *Sr.* Andries Tailler, merchant here, who acknowledged that he is honestly and truly indebted to Jurriaen Theunissen *glaesemaecker* for the quantity of ninety good merchantable beavers figured at eight guilders apiece, stemming from the matter of the last installment of purchase and mortgage money for a certain house and lot bought from him by the appearer according to the bill of sale thereof, dated 7/17th of August last, which aforesaid sum of ninety beavers he, appearer, according to its purport and contents **[678]** promises to pay punctually on the next coming 7th /17th of August 1668, especially pledging therefor this said house and lot and moreover, generally his person and estate, moveable and immoveable, present and future without exception, subject to all laws and judges, done in Albany, the 12th /22nd of November 1667.

A. Teller
Philip Pietersz Schuijler
J. Dehinsse
Acknowledged by me,
D. V. Schelluijne, secretary 1667.

[SALE OF A LOT, HOUSE AND OTHER BUILDINGS BY JURRIAEN THEUNISSEN TO ANDRIES TAILLER]

Appeared before us, undersigned magistrates of Albany, colony of Rensselaerswijck and Schanechtade, Jurriaen Theunissen *glasemaecker* who declared to hereby cede, convey and make over in rightful, true and free ownership to and for the benefit of Andries Tailler, merchant here, his heirs and descendants, or his assigns a certain lot of the grantor with the domicile and other buildings built upon it, standing and located here in Albany (presently in possession of said Tailler), and this by virtue of a conveyance passed by Andries de Vos for his benefit on the 18th/28th of April last, the survey bill thereof by the surveyor, and according to said patent granted to him, appearer, by the right honorable lord general on the 24th day of April, old style, and further, in consequence of the bill of sale of the said domicile and lot passed on the 7th/17th of August last; all of which are hereby delivered to said Tailler. And regarding the boundaries, length and width of the said [**679**] domicile and lot, the grantor refers to the said evidences delivered, acknowledging to have been fully satisfied and paid for said domicile and lot through the hands of him, Tailler, namely, with the sum of ninety beavers received by him to his content, and with a mortgage of a similar sum according to the purport of the said bill of sale, without him, appearer, having the least claim upon it anymore, giving therefore *plenam actionem cessam* and full power to him, Tailler and his said heirs to dispose of the same as he might do with his patrimonial effects; promising to protect and free the said house and lot from all actions, trouble and claims of each and every person as is right, and moreover, nevermore to do or to let anything be done against the same, either with or without law, in any way; under pledge according to law. Done in Albany the 12th /22nd of November 1667.

Jure Jan Tunsen
Philip Pietersz Schuijler
J. Dehinsse
Acknowledged by me,
D. V. Schelluijne, secretary 1667.

[SALE OF A LOT BY LUDOVICUS COBES TO JAN CLUTE]

[**680**] Appeared before us, undersigned magistrates of Albany, colony of Rensselaerswijck and Schanechtade, Ludovicus Cobes, court messenger of the board of said magistrates, who hereby declares to cede, convey and make over in true, rightful, and free possession to and for the benefit of *Sr.* Jan Clute his certain lot, granted to him by the said lords magistrates, being according to the drawing of lots no. 4; wide in front on the street thirty-six and a half feet, long six rods westward, located here in Albany at the hill; adjoins to the south the lot of Geertruijd Vosburch, being no. 3, and to the north the lot of Willem Bout, being no. 5, and further east the public street, and to the west public works as well. And this by virtue of the said license and the patent

of the right honorable lord general dated the 6th of September last, together with such rights and immunities, and easements as he, grantor, acquired those, as mentioned before. He, grantor, acknowledging to have been fully satisfied and paid for it by the exchange of a house and lot also located here in Albany, for the said lot, by the aforesaid Jan Clute likewise passed to him, grantor on this date; giving therefore *plenam actionem cessam* and full power to the said Jan Clute, his heirs and descendants or those who hereafter may acquire his title, to dispose of the same as he might do with his own patrimonial effects; promising, moreover, to protect and free the said lot from all **[681]** actions, trouble and claims of each and every person as is right, and nevermore to do or to let anything be done against the same, either with or without law, in any way; pledging his person and estate, moveable and immoveable without exception, subject to all laws and judges. Done in Albany the 23rd of November/3rd of December 1667.

Ludovicus Cobes
Goosen Gerretsen
R. V. Rensselaer
Acknowledged by me,
D. V. Schelluijne, secretary 1667.

[SALE OF A HOUSE AND LOT BY JAN CLUTE TO LUDOVICUS COBES]

Appeared before us, undersigned magistrates of Albany, colony of Rensselaerswijck and Schanhechtade, *Sr.* Jan Clute, merchant here, who declared to hereby cede, convey and make over in true, rightful, and free possession to and for the benefit of Ludovicus Cobes, court messenger, his certain domicile and lot standing and located here in Albany, in length, width and boundaries as he acquired it by conveyance from Willem Bout on date the 27th of August/8th of September 1666, to which here is referred, and according to patent thereof of the right honorable lord general dated the 1st of April 1666 **[682]**, he, grantor, acknowledging that he has been fully satisfied and paid for it through the hands of him, Ludovicus Cobes, with a lot conveyed to him today, located here in Albany at the hill, being no. 4, according to the conveyance thereof; giving therefore *plenam actionem cessam* and full power to the said Ludovicus Cobes, his heirs and descendants or those, who hereafter may acquire his title to dispose of it as he might do with his patrimonial effects; promising to protect and free the said domicile and lot from all actions, trouble and claims of each and every person as is right, and further, nevermore to do or to let anything be done against the same, either with or without law, in any way; pledging his person and estate without exception, subject to all laws and judges. Done in Albany the 23rd of November/3rd of December 1667.

Johannes Clute
Goosen Gerretsen
R. V. Rensselaer
Acknowledged by me,
D. V. Schelluijne, secretary 1667.

[SALE OF A LOT BY THE MAGISTRATES
TO JAN COSTER VAN AECKEN]

[683] We, the magistrates of Albany, colony of Rensselaerswijck and Schanechtade hereby declare to cede, convey and make over in true, rightful, and free possession to and for the benefit of Jan Coster van Aecken a certain lot located here in Albany at the hill; adjoins to the east the lot of Jan Thomasz, to the south the public street, to the west the common fence, and to the north the lot of Captain Backer, the lot being wide in front on the street on the aforesaid south side forty feet, without our making any claim upon the same anymore, acknowledging that we have been fully satisfied and paid for it through the hands of said Van Aecken according to the bill of sale thereof, dated the 16th /26th of July last; giving therefore *plenam actionem cessam* and full power to the said Van Aecken, his heirs and descendants or those, who may receive title from him to dispose of it as he might do with his own patrimonial effects, but together with his neighbors remaining subject to the public burdens; promising to protect and free the said lot from all actions of each and every person as is right, and further, nevermore to do or to let anything be done against the same. Done at the meeting of the lords magistrates in Albany the 28th of November/8th of December 1667.

R. V. Rensselaer
Philip Pietersz Schuijler

Acknowledged by me,
D. V. Schelluijne, secretary 1667.

[ACKNOWLEDGMENT OF DEBT BY HENDRICK JOCHEMSZ TO ABRAHAM WESSELS]

[**684**] Copy promissory note and mortgage, registered at the request of the lord J.V. Rensselaer.

Appeared before us, Jacob Burhans and Hendrick Aertsen, magistrates of the village of Wildwijck, the honorable Hendrick Jochemsz, who acknowledges that he is well and truly indebted to *Sr.* Abraham Wessels or his order, for the sum of two hundred and twenty-one guilders six stuivers in beavers, growing out of merchandise received from *Sr.* Jan Bastiaensz, and the appearer promises to pay the said sum of *f*221–6– in beavers in the next fall of this year 1668, for which the appearer pledges as a special mortgage his house and lot with the declaration that the same is free and unencumbered; which house and lot are standing and located at Fort Orange across from the church, south of Jan Rinchout and to the north Philip Pietersz; moreover, pledging his person and further estate, present and future, subject to all laws and judges. For the record the appearer has, together with Jacob Burhans and Hendrick Aertsz, signed this with his own hands in the village of Wildwijck this 19th /29th of February 1668. Below stood: Agrees with the original. Was signed, Wil. Beeckman, schout in the Esopus in absence of the secretary.

After collation with the authentic [copy] of date and subscription as above, this is found to agree therewith.
In Albany, the 5th/15th of March 1667/8.

By me,
D. V. Schelluijne, secretary 1667/8.

[CONVEYANCE OF A HOUSE AND LOT BY GERRIT LANSINGH TO JAN BRICKER]

Appeared before us, undersigned magistrates of Albany, colony of Rensselaerswijck and Schanechtade, the honorable Gerrit Lansingh, who declared to cede, convey and make over in true, rightful, and free possession to and for the benefit of Jan Bricker, his certain **[685]** domicile and lot as he, Bricker, has bought the same from him and occupies it, and as the grantor has acquired the same by conveyance and delivery from *Sr.* Jan van Bael, on date the $15^{th}/25^{th}$ of April 1667. Standing and located here in Albany, built upon, fenced, enclosed and bounded according to purport and contents of the aforesaid conveyance, and this by virtue of the same and of the patent and further evidences thereof to which here is referred, which have been delivered to him, Bricker, together with this transaction; without the grantor making the least claim upon said domicile and lot anymore, acknowledging that he has been fully satisfied and paid for it by hand of him, Bricker, the last penny with the first; giving therefore *plenam actionem cessam* and full power to him, Bricker, his heirs and descendants or those, who may receive title from him, to dispose of the said domicile and lot as he might do with his own patrimonial effects; promising to protect and free the said domicile and lot from all actions, trouble and claims of each and every person as is right, and moreover, nevermore to do or to let anything be done against the same, either with law or without in any manner. Upon pledge of his person and estate, moveable and immoveable without exception, subject to all laws and judges. Done in Albany the 6th /16th of March 1667/8.

Gerrit Lansinck
Goosen Gerretsen
J. Dehinsse
Acknowledged by me,
D. V. Schelluijne, secretary 1667/8.

[686][*blank*]

[CONDITIONS AND TERMS UPON WHICH ULDERICK KLEIN ACCEPTS THE COW HERDERSHIP]

[687] Conditions and terms upon which some burghers of Albany intend to contract a cow herder for their cattle.

First, the herder shall be obliged to tend the cattle at his own expense, also to keep a suitable youngster with him to look after the cattle; and he shall begin to drive them out on the 20th of April 1667, new style, and not leave off before the 16th of November.

Second, the herder shall blow the horn three times every morning before or at sunrise, and then with the youngster and the cattle go out to where the cattle best can get food, or to where the masters (named below) shall order him to go; and about a quarter of an hour before sunset he shall bring back the cattle near the church.

Third, if one or more animals shall happen to die through neglect of the herder, the herder shall be obliged to make (according to the appraisal) full recompense for the animal or animals.

Fourth, if the herder be found drinking in any tavern, he shall forfeit ten guilders in sewant every time.

If one or more animals happen to die or if they are led away within half of said time, no more than half of the herder's wages shall be paid therefor, and that punctually at that time.

Similarly, all those who join and deliver their cattle to be herded shall be obliged as soon as half of said time of herding shall have expired, to pay half of the stipulated herder's wages to the herder without any delay.

On these above-written conditions Ulderick Kleijn accepts the contract and for his pains he shall receive twenty guilders in sewant for each full-grown animal or two heifers in place of one full-grown animal, and he shall acknowledge and obey as his masters and principals **[688]** the honorable Jurriaen Teunisz and Aernout Cornelisz.

Below, all those (who have their cattle herded) pledge their cattle, and the herder pledges his person and estate, without exception, both present and future, under obligation according to all laws and judges, and for the confirmation of the same they have signed this, without craft or guile, with their own hands on the 2nd/12th of April 1667.

Ulderijck Klein
Jure Jan Tunsen
Arnout Cornelisz

1668. On this 31st of March/10th of April Uldrick Cleijn has accepted the said cow herdership according to the said conditions (except the price of last year), but he has now agreed to sixteen guilders in sewant for each full-grown animal, or for two heifers as much as for one full-grown animal, and therefore he shall be obliged to go out next Friday the 3rd/13th of April of this year, and shall not leave off before the 6th/16th of November, and he shall acknowledge and obey as his masters and principals the honorable Jan Clute and Mr. Cornelis van Dijck. In acknowledgment of the truth the aforesaid herder and the said masters have signed with their own hands. In Albany, dated as above.

Ulderijck Klein
Johan Clute
Cornelis van Dijck

[**689**] On the said conditions of the year 1668 the said Uldrick Cleijn has accepted it again provided that he shall begin to go out with the cattle on the 13th/23rd of April 1669, and not leave off until the 6th/16th of November of this year, and that he shall receive for each full-grown animal fourteen guilders in sewant, or for two heifers as much as for one animal; and he will acknowledge and obey as his masters and principals the honorable Dirck Wesselsz and Heijndrick Brisz. Done in Albany, this 5th/15th of April 1669.

Ulderick Klein
Dierck Wesselsz
Hendrick Bries

[SACHARIAS SICKLES ACCEPTS COWHERDERSHIP]

On this 5th of April Sacharias Sickles has accepted the said cowherdership on said and read conditions, provided that he and his boys and the cattle shall begin to go out on the 12th of this month, and shall not leave off until the 6th of November, old style; and he shall receive for his pains seventeen guilders in sewant, and he shall acknowledge and obey as his masters and principals the honorable Jan Vinhaghen and Heyndrick Kuijler. Done in Albany, dated as above.

Sacharias Seickels
Jan Vinhaeghen
Hendrick Cuijler

[690]*

[*Endorsed*:] Contract for the cowherdership.†

1671, the 27th of March promises to herd	
Harmen Gansevoort for	*f*23–:–
Sacharias Sickles for	*f*20–:–
Harmen Gansevoort	*f*19–:–
Sacharias Sickles	*f*18–:–
Jacob Gerritsen van Vost	*f*17–:–
Sacharias Sickles	*f*16–:–
1672, the 28th of March	
Jurriaen Jansz Groenewout in sewant	*f*25–:–
Jacob Tijsz vander Heijden sewant	*f*19–:–

* This document carries an endorsement for [**589**] and the following account inverted at the bottom of the page.

† Documents 687–690 appear to have been loose pages before being bound in the present volume. It was folded in the middle with this endorsement on the verso.

Jan Mangelsz	*f*18–:–
Sacharias Sickels	*f*17–:–

[PROMISSORY NOTE OF WILLEM TAILLER]

[691] ...to recover payment under subjection and authority as above. Done in Albany, the 14th/24th of August 1667.†

Willem Teller
Present with the orphan masters
Phillip Pietersz Schuijler
Goossen Gerritsz and
the officer Gerard Swart
Acknowledged by me,
D. V. Schelluijne, secretary, 1667.

The above promissory note having been read to Willem Tailler, he answers that he can not understand that he shall sign it, but he offers the orphan masters that they choose from his effects that, from which they think the payment for the minor children could be recovered according to the sentence; concerning the grown-up children he says that he has also assented to their portion, namely, that he, Tailler, would pass a promissory note to the two grown-up children, and that he would pay Helena at the first opportunity, which discourse and conversation between him and Andries Tailler and Pieter van Alen took place in the presence of the orphan masters, and concerning Helena's portion, he says that he has to cut that back by what, according to account, comes to him, with the exception of what had been annulled by the said sentence. He also says that the orphan masters could stand surety as they demand from him. I will provide payment provided that I receive the interest of it at 10 percent per year until the minor children will have come of age. [Item that it is not the intent of the sentence that the 85 beavers on account of Helena should be paid without reducing what she has

† Page starts at the end of a document, indicating that a preceding page has been lost. See [**695**], which has same date and witnesses.

received.]† The orphan masters, on the contrary, maintain that he, Tailler, is obliged to sign the above promissory note, by which the disagreement was returned and referred to the honorable lord general, requesting his honor's decision in this matter. Done in Albany the 23rd of July/2nd of August 1667. Present, the orphan masters, Willem Tailler and his wife.

[**692**] On date the 23rd of July/2nd of August 1667 I, court messenger, together with the lord schout have found myself at the house and dwelling of Willem Teller and asked him for the third time whether he would or would not sign the promissory note shown to him, or else, that with the honorable court's authorization there shall be proceeded to execution. Willem Teller answers that he can not see that the promissory note is according to sentence, but that he is willing, as said before, to provide security and instruction of his estate according to the sentence granted by the court of assizes, again requesting his honor's decision in this matter.

By me,
G: Swart, schout
Ludovicus Cobes, court messenger of Albany

[*In the margin*:] This information was mistakenly provided, and was therefore completely canceled.

On date as above the lord officer has reported to Willem Teller that he, Teller, should satisfy his daughter Helena and pay her according to sentence of the court of Assizes, provided that that which he should have [received] by settlement will be reduced. Concerning the minor children, that he provide instructions about the estate to the satisfaction of the same, according to sentence, as above.

Willem Teller answers that he never had anything against this, but that he is satisfied to follow up the same, if it please them, according to the sentence of the honorable court.

---

† The sentence between brackets was crossed out in the original.

By me, G: Swart, schout
Ludovicus Cobes, court messenger.

[693] On date as before, the officer, by order of the magistrates, has in my, the secretary's, presence, requested and asked Willem Tailler whether he would be willing to sign the above promissory note according to the agreement made with Andries Tailler and Pieter van Alen, and whether he would pay the eighty-five beavers to Helena Taillers according to sentence, upon which he answered as in the above first statement of the schout and messenger, and concerning Helena, that, if the lord general would understand that he is not allowed to reduce that which he, Tailler should receive according to account (except for the account that has been canceled by the sentence of the court of Assize), he shall pay the entire sum for or on behalf of Helena. *Adij ut supra.*

By me, G. Swartt, schout
D. V. Schelluijne, secretary 1667.

[694] Today, the 24th of July/3rd of August 1667 Willem Tailler acknowledged that he is well and truly indebted to his adult son Andries Tailler, and to Pieter van Aelen, husband and guardian of Maria Tailler, each the sum of eighty-five beavers, according to the sentence of the honorable court of Assize at New York, pronounced on the 1st of October *anno* 1666, reducing the value of twenty beavers received by Pieter van Alen's wife, namely, a long woman's gown and a red cloth skirt, being of her late mother's clothes; promising to pay the said respective sums according to purport and contents of the said sentence, pledging thereto his person and estate, moveable and immoveable, present and future without exception, under obligation according to all laws and judges. Done in Albany, dated as above.

Willem Teller
Present one magistrate Philip Pietersz Schuijler

And said two orphan masters Jan Verbeeck
Evert Jansz Wendel

In my presence,
D. V. Schelluijne, secretary 1667.

[695] In accordance with the order of the lord general dated the 30th of July past, Willem Tailler has signed the above promissory note for the benefit of his four minor children on the 14th/24th of August, 1667 with promise also to pay his daughter Helena her portion of eighty-five beavers.

Present the orphan masters and magistrates Phillip Pietersz Schuijler and Goossen Gerritsz, together with schout G. Swart.†

Copy.

I, the undersigned Helena Tailler, acknowledge that I have received of my father, Willem Tailler the quantity of eighty-five good beavers, as was assigned to me by the honorable court of Assize at New York on the first of October, 1666, and I release him from all claims. In witness of the truth I have written and signed this with my own hand in Albany on the 7$^{th/}$17th of September, 1667. Was signed, Helenar Teller, widow of Cornelis Bogardus and (in my presence) D. V. Schelluijne, secretary, besides (as administrators) Phillip Pietersz and D. V. Schelluijne.

[696–706] [*blank*]

---

† See document [**692**] which has the same date and witnesses.

[FRAGMENT OF SALE OF A LOT TO HELMER OTTEN AT PUBLIC AUCTION]†

[**707**] ... according to the survey and regulation of the surveyor dated the 25th of April/5th of May past, which lot the aforesaid Helmer Otten has bought and paid for at public auction according to conditions, and this free and unencumbered (except for the lord's right). Therefore giving full power to said Helmert Otten, his heirs and descendants or those who hereafter may acquire his title, to dispose thereof as he might do with his own patrimonial effects, and therefore he is allowed to request a patent of the said lot of the right honorable lord general. Done in Albany the 29th of May/8th of June 1668.

R. V. Rensselaer
Acknowledged by me,
D. V. Schelluijne, secretary 1668.

[CONVEYANCE OF A LOT BY THE MAGISTRATES TO JAN CLUTE]

The magistrates of Albany, colony of Rensselaerswijck and Schanechtade hereby declare that they cede, convey and make over in true, rightful and free ownership to and for the benefit of Jan Clute the lot no. 11, located at the hill here in Albany; wide in front two rods nine feet, in the rear two rods eleven feet, long on the west side two rods ten feet four inches, on the east side two rods eleven feet and nine inches; adjoins on the west Helmert Otten, on the north the public street, on the east Jan Clute himself, and on the south Jacob Loockermans, according to measurement and regulation of the surveyors on the 25th of April/5th of May past. Which lot the said Jan Clute has bought and paid for according to conditions at public auction, and this free [**708**] and unencumbered, except for the lord's right. giving therefor full power to said Jan Clute, his heirs and descendants or those who may receive title from him, to dispose thereof as he might do with his own patrimonial effects, and therefore he is allowed to request a patent for the same lot of

---

† In the margin in another handwriting: Transports May 1668 to May 1670.

the right honorable lord general. Done in Albany the 29th of May/8th of June 1668.

R. V. Rensselaer
Acknowledged by me,
D. V. Schelluijne, secretary 1668.

[CONVEYANCE OF A LOT BY THE MAGISTRATES TO GOOSSEN GERRITSZ]†

The magistrates of Albany, colony of Rensselaerswijck and Schanechtade hereby declare that they cede, convey and make over in true, rightful and free ownership to *Sr.* Goossen Gerritsz, for the benefit of his son-in-law Henderick Coster, a lot no. 12, located at the hill here in Albany; wide in front two rods seven feet and two inches, in the rear two rods five and a half feet, long on the west side four rods and four feet, on the east side three rods eleven feet; adjoins on the east Barent Reijnderts, on the south and west the public streets, and on the north Do. Schaets, according to measurement and regulation of the surveyors of date the 25th of April/5th of May past. Which said lot the said Goossen Gerritsen has bought and paid for according to conditions at public auction, and this free and unencumbered, except for the lord's right. giving therefore full power to said Goossen Gerritsz, for the benefit as above, his heirs and [**841**] descendants, or those who hereafter may acquire title from him, to do with and dispose of the said house and lot as he, Hendrick Coster, might do with his own patrimonial effects, and therefore is allowed to request a patent from the right honorable lord general. Done in Albany, the 29th of May/8th of June 1668.

R. V. Rensselaer

---

† This document is continued on the first page of a group of documents [**841–843**] displaced toward the end of the volume. They have been placed back in their proper order between [**708**] and [**709**].

Acknowledged by me,
D. V. Schelluijne, secretary 1668.

[*In the margin was written*:] Transports by Schelluijne and L. Cobus began 9th of June 1668 to 6th April 1670.

[CONVEYANCE OF A LOT BY THE MAGISTRATES TO BARENT REYNDERTSZ]

The magistrates of Albany, colony of Rensselaerswijck and Schanhechtade hereby declare that they cede, convey and make over in true, rightful and free ownership to Barent Reijndertsz *smith*, a lot no. 13, located at the hill here in Albany; wide in front two rods five feet, in the rear two rods and nine inches, long on the east side three rods seven feet, on the west side three rods and eleven feet; adjoins on the west Goossen Gerritsz, on the east Willem Bout, on the south the public street, and on the north Do. Schaets, according to measurement and survey of the surveyors thereof of date the 25th of April/5th of May past. Which said lot the said Barent Reijndertsz has bought and paid for according to conditions at public auction, and this free and unencumbered (except for the lord's right), giving therefor full power to said Barent Reijndertsz, his heirs and descendants, or those who hereafter may acquire his title, to do with and dispose of the said house and lot as he might do with his own patrimonial effects, and therefore he is allowed to request a patent for the said lot from the right honorable lord general. Done in Albany, the 29th of May/8th of June 1668.

R. V. Rensselaer
Acknowledged by me,
D. V. Schelluijne, secretary 1668.

[CONVEYANCE OF A LOT BY THE MAGISTRATES TO DOMINE GIDEON SCHAETS]

[**842**] The magistrates of Albany, colony of Rensselaerswijck and Schaenhechtade hereby declare that they permit, grant, and allow in true, rightful and free ownership to the minister, Do. Gideon Schaets, a lot no. 14, located here in Albany at the hill; wide in front and back twenty-five feet, long on the south side four rods six feet three inches, on the north side four rods, three feet, three inches; adjoins on the east side Claes van Rotterdam, on the south side Barent Reijndertsz *smith*, on the west side and north side the public road and grounds, according to the measurement and survey thereof of by the surveyors on date the 25th of April/5th of May past; and this free and unencumbered (except for the lord's right), giving therefor full power to said Do. Schaets, his heirs and descendants, or those who hereafter may acquire his title, to dispose thereof as he might do with his own patrimonial effects, and therefore [he] is allowed to request a patent for the said lot from the right honorable lord general. Done in Albany, the 29th of May/8th of June 1668.

R. V. Rensselaer
Acknowledged by me,
D. V. Schelluijne, secretary 1668.

[POWER OF ATTORNEY BY TIJS EVERTSZ *DE GOIJER* TO JACOB SCHERMERHOORN]

[**843**] Today, the 3rd/13th of July 1668, Tijs Evertsz *de Goijer*, dwelling in the colony of Rensselaerswijck, declares that he hereby appoints and fully empowers *Sr.* Jacob Schermerhoorn, intending to depart for Holland, to especially claim, collect, demand and receive from his brother Evert Evertsz *de Goijer*, master carpenter, at Amsterdam in Holland, the payment of the sum of one hundred and eighty guilders with the accrued interest thereof, which his mother the late Grietie Jansz, widow of the late Evert Tijsz, his late father (deceased at Naerden), has left him as his hereditary portion according to his said brother's writing dated the 23rd of September 1663 and the 5th of April,

1666, for which the appointer on the 17th of June 1664 has given his brother a power of attorney; together with what was bequeathed to him by his said father, deceased; therefore to issue quittance of the receipt of the said capital and accrued interest, together with whatever is found to be coming to him from his late father, *ex testamento vel ab intestato*, to his said brother or whoever has the direction thereof, and further to do, transact and perform everything that he deems necessary and appropriate; promising at all times, without any gainsaying to accept everything that the said attorney shall do and perform in the said matter, under obligation as provided for it according to law, provided that the attorney shall be obliged, if requested, to properly justify his said transactions and receipts. Done in Albany in America, dated as above in the presence of Cornelis Cornelisz van Voorhout and Barent Albertsz as witnesses.

Thijs Evertsen
This mark was made  by Cornelis Cornelisz van Voorhout.
This mark was made  by said Barent Albertsz
In my presence,
D. V. Schelluijne, secretary 1668.

[ACKNOWLEDGMENT OF DEBT BY JAN LOWIES *SOLDAET* TO JURRIAEN JANSZ GROENEWOUT]

[**709**] Appeared before me Ludovicus Cobes, secretary of Albany, colony of Rensselaerswijck and Schaenhechtade in the presence of the honorable lords magistrates of the same court, Monsr. Ryckart van Rensselaer and Mr. Jan Verbeeck, Jan Lowies *soldaet* in the service of his Royal Majesty of England, who acknowledges that he is well and truly indebted to Jurriaen Jansz Groenewout for the quantity of one hundred and two whole good and merchantable beaver skins figured at eight guilders apiece, growing out of a matter of three remaining installments for the purchase and mortgage money of a certain house and lot, bought by him, appearer, according to the bill of sale dated the 8th of February *anno* 1669; which aforesaid sum of one hundred and two beaver skins the appearer promises to pay according to the purport and contents of the same in three installments, each time a third part of the

said sum; the first on the first of August next, 1670; the second and third each time a year later, especially pledging for it the said house and lot, and moreover, generally his person and estate, moveable and immoveable, present and future without exception, subject to all the lord's laws and judges, to recover (if necessary) the payment without costs and damage. Done in Albany in the 22nd year of his Majesty's government, the 9th of February *Anno Domini* 1669.

John Lewis
R. V. Rensselaer
Jan Verbeeck
In my presence,
Ludovicus Cobes, secretary.

[CONVEYANCE OF A LOT WITH PART OF A HOUSE, GARDEN, AND ORCHARD BY PIETER ADRIAENSZ TO HIS SON PITER PIETERSE]

[710] Appeared before me Ludovicus Cobes, secretary of Albany, colony of Rensselaerswijck and Schaenhechtade in the presence of the honorable lords magistrates of the same court, *Mr*. Jan Verbeeck and *Sr*. Philip Pietersz Schuijler, Piter Adriaensz, who declared to hereby cede, convey and make over in true, rightful and free ownership to his son Piter Pieterse his heirs and descendants or assigns, a certain lot with a dilapidated part of a [house], garden, and fruit trees, standing and located at Lubberde land in the colony of Rensselaerswijck, and according to the written title thereof; extending along and adjoining next to the lot of Barent Pitersz as the same in length and width is lying within its fence; and this free and unencumbered, without any claim standing or issuing against the same, except for the right of the lord patroon of this colony; without him, grantor, making the least claim upon the same anymore, acknowledging that he is fully satisfied and paid for the same, the last penny with the first, giving therefor plenam actionem cessam and full power to the aforesaid Piter Pitersz, his son, his heirs and descendants, or those who hereafter may acquire title from him, to do with and dispose of the same as he might do with his patrimonial estate and effects; promising to protect and free the said lot with a part of a [house], garden, and fruit trees against all persons from all trouble, claims and charges as is right, and moreover, never again to do or allow anything to be done against the same, either with or without law, in any manner whatsoever, under obligation according to law. Done in Albany the 11th of February 1669.

Pieter Aedriaensz
Philip Pietersz
Jan Verbeeck
In my presence,
Ludovicus Cobes, secretary.

N.B. This conveyance is made on condition that the grantor shall receive half of the stones lying near the house, and annually two *schepels* of apples from the fruit trees.

[CONVEYANCE OF AN ISLAND BY PITER VAN OLINDA TO JAN CLUTE]

[711] Appeared before me Ludovicus Cobes, secretary of Albany, colony of Rensselaerswijck and Schaenhechtede in the presence of the honorable lords magistrates of the same court, *Mr*. Jan Verbeeck and *Sr*. Philip Pietersz Schuijler, Piter van Olinda, inhabitant of Schaenhechtede, who declared to hereby cede, convey and make over in true, rightful and free ownership to and for the benefit of *Mr*. Jan Clute, his heirs and descendants or assigns, a certain the grantor's large island located in the Maquaeskil at Canastagioene, given to his wife Hilleken Cornelis by the chief of the Maquaasen, the lawful owners, on date of the 11th of June 1667, with such title as the grantor has thereto; located and bounded as the patent thereof shows, which [patent] was granted to him, grantor, by the right honorable lord governor general of New York, Richard Nicolls, on date of the 8th of May 1668, to which here is referred; and this, free and unencumbered, without any claim standing or issuing against the same, except for the lord's right; without him, grantor, making the least claim upon the same anymore, acknowledging that he is fully satisfied and paid for the same, the last penny with the first, giving therefore *plenam actionem cessam* and full power to the aforesaid *Hr.* Jan Clute, his heirs and descendants, or those who

hereafter may acquire title from him, to do with and dispose of the same as he might do with his patrimonial estate and effects; promising to protect and free the said island and the title thereof against all persons from all trouble, claims and charges as is right, and further, never again to do nor allow anything to be done against the same, either with or without the law, in any manner whatsoever, under obligation according to law. Done in Albany the 4th of March 1669.

Pieter Daniels van Olinda
Jan Verbeeck
Philip Pietersz
In my presence,
Ludovicus Cobes, secretary.

[CONVEYANCE OF A PARCEL OF LAND BY SANDER LEENDERTSZ GLEN TO HIS SONS JACOB, SANDER, AND JOHANNES SANDERSZ GLEN]

[712] Appeared before me Ludovicus Cobes, secretary of Albany, colony of Rensselaerswijck and Schaenhechtade in the presence of the honorable lords magistrates of the same court, *Sr.* Rijckart van Rensselaer and Mr. Jan Verbeeck, Sander Leendertsz Glen, dwelling at Schaenhechtede, who declared to hereby cede, convey and make over in true, rightful and free ownership to and for the benefit of his three sons named Jacob, Sander, and Johannes Sandersz Glen, a certain parcel of land located between the lake and the river across from the village at Schaenhechtede, fifty morgens in size, according to the patent thereof from he right honorable lord governor general Richard Nicolls, dated the 3rd of November 1665, to which here is referred; and this, free and unencumbered, without any claim standing or issuing against the same, except for the lord's right; without the grantor making the least claim upon the same anymore, acknowledging that he is fully satisfied and paid for the same, the last penny with the first, and that, through the hands of his three sons, shown by a sound account; giving therefore *plenam actionem cessam* and full power to his aforesaid three sons, their heirs and descendants, or those who hereafter may acquire their title and claims, to do with and dispose of the same as they might do with their

patrimonial estates and effects; promising to protect and free the said land against all persons from all trouble, claims and charges as is right, and further, never to do nor allow anything to be done against the same, either with or without law, in any manner, under obligation according to law. Done in Albany the 9th of March 1669.

Sander Lenrsen Glen
R. V. Rensselaer
Jan Verbeeck
In my presence,
Ludovicus Cobes, secretary.

[POWER OF ATTORNEY FROM CORNELIS THEUNISZ VAN VECHTEN AND HIS WIFE SARA SALOMONS TO MIJNDERT FREDERICKSEN]

[713] Appeared before us, undersigned magistrates of Albany, colony of Rensselaerswijck and Schanechtade in America the honorable Cornelis Theunisz van Vechten, farmer, in the aforesaid colony, and Sara Salomons, his wife, daughter of Salomon Abelsz, deceased, in his lifetime carpenter here in this country, born in Amsterdam in Holland, who make known that she, Sara Salomons and her four brothers and sister, named Phillip, Jacob, Jan, David, and Lijsbet Salomons (of whom, here in this country are still alive besides her, Sara, the said Jacob, Jan and Lijsbet Salomons), by will of their uncle Poppe Abels, deceased (deceased at said Amsterdam), each have inherited the sum of one hundred guilders capital; which capital was put out at interest there, and the interest of the same has accumulated to at least fifty guilders, to wit, of each of the said hundred guilders capital, and of which their guardians named Cornelis Brantsz and Benningh Weijman, dwelling at said Amsterdam, keep the administration and the management. And as they, appearers, acknowledge to have received to their content and satisfaction here in said Albany the value of the said one hundred and fifty guilders Holland money in various goods and commodities out of the hands of Mijndert Fredericksz *smit*, they, appearers, hereby declare that they cede, convey and make over in true, rightful and free ownership to and for the benefit of the said Mijndert Fredericxsz, or his attorney, the lawful bearer of this, whom in Holland he will authorize

and fully empower to collect, demand and receive as his free, own estate the [**714**] said hundred guilders capital and its interest from the aforesaid guardians, or where it is appropriate, their just and hereditary portion in the said inherited inheritance *ex testamento* of their uncle Poppen Abels, deceased, at the sum of one hundred guilders capital mentioned above with its aforesaid interest (accumulating to the full and complete payment thereof); without they, appearers, making the least claim upon the same anymore, acknowledging that they are contented and satisfied for the same to their great delight, renouncing and waiving all their right and title to the aforesaid inheritance for the benefit as above; therefore they, appearers, promise never to do nor allow anything to be done against the same, either with or without law, in any manner whatsoever, pledging their persons and estates without exception, under an obligation according to all laws and judges. Done in Albany the 27th of June/7th of July 1668.

Cornelus Theunisen
This mark  is made by said Sara Salomons.
Philip Pietersz Schuijler
J Dehinsse
Acknowledged by me,
D. V. Schelluijne, secretary 1668.

[CONVEYANCE OF A HOUSE AND LOT BY GERRIT SLICHTENHORST TO HENDRICK BRIES]

[**715**] Appeared before us, undersigned magistrates of Albany, colony of Rensselaerswijck and Schanechtade *Sr.* Gerrit Slichtenhorst, who declared to hereby cede, convey and make over in true, rightful and free ownership to and for the benefit of Hendrick Bries a lot, wide twenty-three feet, length and boundaries according to the bill of sale dated the 19th/29th of September 1666, located here in Albany, and this by virtue of a patent for a larger lot, granted to the grantor by the right honorable lord general Richard Nicolls, dated the 27th of April 1667; giving therefore full *actionem cessam* and power to the aforesaid Bries, his heirs and descendants, or those who hereafter may acquire title from him, to dispose of the same as he might do with his own patrimonial

effects; without he, grantor, having the least claim upon the same anymore, acknowledging that he has been fully satisfied and paid for the same through the hands of said Bries; promising therefore to protect and free the said lot against all persons from all trouble and claims as is right, and further, nevermore to do nor allow anything to be done against the same, either with or without law, in any manner, pledging his person and estate, without exception, subject to all laws and judges. Done in Albany the 2nd/12th of July 1668.

Gerrit Slichtenhorst
Philip Pietersz Schuijler
Goosen Gerretsen
In my presence,
D. V. Schelluijne, secretary 1668.

[CONVEYANCE OF A LOT BY GERRIT SLICHTENHORST TO FRANS JANSZ PRUIJN]

[716] Appeared before us, undersigned magistrates of Albany, colony of Rensselaerswijck and Schanechtade *Sr.* Gerrit Slichtenhorst who declared to hereby cede, convey and make over in true, rightful and free ownership to and for the benefit of Frans Jansz Pruijn a certain lot situated here in Albany, being wide, long and bounded according to purport and contents of the bill of sale thereof dated the 19th/29th of September 1666, and this by virtue of a patent for a larger lot, granted to him by the right honorable lord general Richard Nicolls, dated the 27th of April 1667; giving therefor full power to the aforesaid Frans Jansz Pruijn, his heirs and descendants, or those who hereafter may acquire title from him, to dispose of the said lot as he might do with his own patrimonial effects; acknowledging that he has been fully satisfied and paid for the same through the hands of said Frans Jansz Pruijn; promising thereof to protect and free the said lot against all persons from all trouble and claims as is right, and further, nevermore to do nor allow anything to be done against the same, either with or without law, in any manner, pledging his person and estate, without exception, subject to all laws and judges. Done in Albany, dated as above.

Gerrit Slichtenhorst
Philip Pietersz Schuijler
Goosen Gerretsen
In my presence,
D. V. Schelluijne, secretary 1668.

[CONVEYANCE OF A LOT BY GERRIT SLICHTENHORST TO GERRIT LANSINGH]

[717] Appeared before us, magistrates of Albany, colony of Rensselaerswijck and Schaenhechtade *Sr.* Gerrit Slichtenhorst, who declared to hereby cede, convey and make over in true, rightful and free ownership to and for the benefit of Gerrit Lansingh a certain lot situated here in Albany, wide twenty-five feet, long to the lot of Robbert Sandertsz; adjoins on the east side Henderick Bries, on the south side the public street, on the west side the grantor, and on the north the aforesaid Robbert Sandertsz, and this by virtue of a patent for a lot dated the 27th of April 1667, granted to him by the right honorable lord general Richard Nicolls; giving therefore *plenam actionem cessam* and full power to the aforesaid Gerrit Lansingh, his heirs and descendants, or those who hereafter may acquire title from him, to dispose of the said lot as he might do with his patrimonial effects; acknowledging that he has been fully satisfied and paid for the same by the hands of said Gerrit Lansingh; promising therefore to protect and free the said lot against all persons from all trouble and claims as is right, and further, nevermore to do nor allow anything to be done against the same, either with or without law, in any manner, pledging his person and estate, without exception, subject to all laws and judges. Done in Albany, the 2nd/12th of July 1668.

Gerrit Slichtenhorst
Philip Pietersz Schuijler
Goosen Gerretsen
In my presence,
D. V. Schelluijne, secretary 1668.

[CONVEYANCE OF THE ABOVE LOT BY GERRIT LANSINGH
TO BARENT ALBERTSZ]

[**718**] By virtue and in consequence of the conveyance passed today by *Sr.* Slichtenhorst for the benefit of Gerrit Lansingh, of a lot located here in Albany, wide and long according to purport and contents of the same, he, Gerrit Lansingh, declared that, accordingly, he has ceded, conveyed and made over in true, rightful, free ownership to and for the benefit of Barent Albertsz, his heirs and descendants or those who hereafter may acquire title from him, the same lot with upon it the domicile and other buildings; acknowledging that he has been fully satisfied and paid for the same by the hands of him, Barent Albertsz, giving and conveying to him, Barent Albertsz, the aforesaid lot with such right as he has received it from Gerrit Slichtenhorst; acknowledging also that he has been fully satisfied and paid by him, Barent Albertsz, for the domicile and other buildings standing thereupon; promising to nevermore do nor allow anything to be done against the same, either with or without law, in any manner, pledging his person and estate, without exception, subject to all laws and judges. Done in Albany, the $2^{nd}/12^{th}$ of July 1668.

Gerret Lansinck
Philip Pietersz Schuijler
Goosen Gerretsen
In my presence,
D. V. Schelluijne, secretary 1668.

[CONVEYANCE OF A GARDEN BY ADRIAEN GERRITSZ
TO CARSTEN FREDERICKSZ]

[**719**] Appeared before us, undersigned magistrates of Albany, colony of Rensselaerswijck and Schanechtade *Sr.* Adriaen Gerritsz, burgher and inhabitant here in Albany, who declared to hereby cede, convey and make over in true, rightful and free ownership to and for the benefit of Carsten Fredericksz, master smith, a garden, by the drawing of lots no. 5, located in Albany as the same lies within its fence and boundaries; adjoins on the east side the lord dr. Jeremias van Rensselaer, on the south side the church yard, on the west side the public street, and on the

north side *Mr.* Abraham Staets; and this by virtue and in consequence of a deed of conveyance dated the 28th of October *anno* 1656, passed by Adriaen Jansz van Ilpendam for his benefit; giving therefore *plenam actionem cessam* and full power to the aforesaid Carsten Fredericksz *smith*, his heirs and descendants, or those who hereafter may acquire title from him, to dispose of the same as he might do with his own patrimonial effects, acknowledging that he has been fully satisfied and paid for the same; promising to protect and free the said garden against all persons from all trouble and claims as is right, and further, nevermore to do nor allow anything to be done against the same, either with or without law, in any manner, under pledge of his person and estate, without exception, subject to all laws and judges. Done in Albany the $3^{rd}/13^{th}$ of July 1668.

Adriaen Gerretsen
Goosen GerretsenPhilip Pietersz Schuijler
In my presence,
D. V. Schelluijne, secretary 1668.

[CONVEYANCE OF A LOT FOR A GARDEN BY MIJNDERT AND CARSTEN FREDERICKSZ TO JAN CLUTE]

[720] Appeared before us, undersigned magistrates of Albany, colony of Rensselaerswijck and Schanechtade Mijndert and Carsten Fredericksz, brothers, dwelling here in Albany, who declare to hereby cede, convey and make over in true, rightful, free ownership to and for the benefit of Jan Clute a lot for a garden, located here in Albany, wide four and a half rods, long seven and a half rods; adjoins to the south Thomas Sandertsz, to the east Jacob Clomp, to the north the road, to the west an empty plain; and this by virtue and in consequence of a deed of conveyance passed to their benefit on the 30th of July 1655 by Cornelis Steenwijck as attorney for Gabriel Leendertsz; giving therefore *plenam actionem cessam* and full power to the aforesaid Jan Clute, his heirs and descendants, or those who hereafter may acquire title from him, to dispose of the said lot as he might do with his own patrimonial effects; acknowledging that they have been fully satisfied and paid for the same; promising therefore to protect and free the said lot against all persons from all trouble and claims as is right, and further, nevermore to do nor allow anything to be done against the same, either with or without law, in any manner, upon pledge of their persons and estates, without exception, subject to all laws and judges. Done in Albany the 3rd/13th of July 1668.

This  mark is made by said Mijndert Fredericxsz.
Carsten Frederikes
Philip Pietersz Schuijler
Goosen Gerretsen
In my presence,
D. V. Schelluijne, secretary 1668.

[POWER OF ATTORNEY FROM PHILIP PIETERSZ SCHUIJLER AND MARGARITA SLICHTENHORST TO JOHAN BAPTIST VAN RENSSELAER]

[721] Appeared before us undersigned magistrates of Albany, the colony of Rensselaerswijck and Schanechtade, *Sr.* Philip Pietersz Schuijler, our fellow councilor, and *Juffr.* Margarita Slichtenhorst, his wife, dwelling here at Albany in America, who declared that they hereby appoint and fully empower the lord Johan Baptist van Rensselaer, merchant at Amsterdam in Holland, especially, together with his brother-in-law, *Sr.* Gerrit Slichtenhorst (who intends to depart for Holland) to demand condition and inventory of the estate, or copy of the will, as it may have been made by the lord Brant van Slichtenhorst, deceased father of the said Margrita and Gerrit Slichtenhorst, (deceased at Nijkerk in Gelderland); and accordingly to collect, demand and receive their, appearers' contingent and hereditary portion in the aforesaid inheritance, to pass quittance for the receipts; if necessary and if the matter requires it, together with his said brother-in-law to check or to approve of the condition and inventory of the estate, or to examine the same; to compromise, agree and arrange a compromise about the immoveable estate of land, houses and lots, as also to sell the furniture which may have come to the appearers as part of their hereditary portion; to establish and inherit the purchasers in the said real estate, and to disestablish and disinherit the appearers from the same; to receive the

stipulated purchase moneys; also to give quittance of the receipts, and, if necessary (which is not to be hoped) to collect, demand and receive their said right and title in the said inheritance by means and [722] ways of justice from him, who has the care of it. For this purpose to observe all terms of justice until sentence, including its extreme execution, with power to appoint one or two substitutes in his place with similar or limited power, and moreover, to do, transact and perform everything either with law or without, that he thinks necessary and advisable; promising at all times, without any gainsaying to accept everything that the said attorney and his substitute shall have done in this matter, under obligation provided for it according to law, provided that the attorney (if requested) shall be obliged to properly justify his transactions and receipts. Done in Albany the 3rd/13th of July 1668.

Philip Pietersz Schuijler
Margrita van Slichtenhorst
Goosen Gerretsen
Jan Thomasz
In my presence,
D. V. Schelluijne, secretary 1668.

[CONVEYANCE OF A HOUSE, LOT AND GARDEN BY ANTHONIJ JANSZ TO JAN HENDRICK BRUIJNS]

[723] Appeared before us, undersigned magistrates of Albany, Colony of Rensselaerswijck and Schanechtade, *Sr.* Goossen Gerritsen and Jan Coster van Aecken as attorneys for Anthonij Jansz, who, in that capacity declared to hereby cede, convey and make over to and for the benefit of *Sr.* Jan Hendrick Bruijns a certain domicile, lot, and garden, presently occupied by Jurriaen Theunisz *glaesemaecker,* and belonging to him, Anthonij Jansz as he has bought the same from him, Jurriaen Theunisz, and as it was delivered and conveyed to him by the same according to the evidences thereof, hereby delivered to said Bruijns, as the said domicile, lot, and garden are built upon, fenced and enclosed, standing and located here in Albany according to purport and contents of the bill of sale and further evidences to which is referred here. And this pursuant to the conditions upon which the same were offered at public sale and

maintained to the final offer, namely, that he, Bruijns shall receive the rent of the said house, lot and garden for which Jurriaen Theunisz lives in it, to be counted from the date of auction until the end of the lease without anything more; without they, grantors in their aforesaid capacity making the least claim thereupon anymore, acknowledging to have been fully satisfied and paid for it by bill of exchange in Holland for the value of *f*695 in beavers; except that (which is not to be hoped), if the bill of exchange will not be paid in Holland, we, grantors, will maintain their right and title especially to the said house, lot and garden, and moreover, generally to his person and estate; giving therefore *plenam actionem cessam* and complete power to the said Jan Henderick Bruijns, his heirs and descendants or those, who may receive title from him, to dispose of said domicile, lot and garden as he might do with his own patrimonial effects; promising therefore to protect and free the same against all persons from all trouble and claims, and moreover, nevermore to do or to let anything be done against the same, either with law or without in any way, under pledge of their persons and estates, without exception, subject to all laws and judges. Done in Albany the $5^{th}/15^{th}$ of July1668.

Jan Koster
Goosen Gerretsen
Philip Pietersz Schuijler
Jan Thomasz
In my presence,
D. V. Schelluijne, secretary 1668.

[POWER OF ATTORNEY FROM CORNELIS VAN NES AND MARITIE DAEMEN TO LIJSBET DIRCX VAN EPS]

[**724**] Appeared before us, undersigned schout, magistrates of Albany, the colony of Rensselaerswijck and Schaenechtade in America, the honorable Cornelis van Nes, former magistrate and Maritie Daemen, last widow of Henderick Andriesz, deceased, now his wife, dwelling here in Albany, who declare that they hereby appoint and fully empower Lijsbet Dircx van Eps, daughter of her, Maritie Daemen, wife of Gerrit Bancken, intending to depart for Holland; first, he, Cornelis van Nes,

especially, according to the copy of the enclosed account, to collect, demand and receive from Joost Aertsz vanden Burchgraeff, his cousin dwelling at Gorinchem in Holland, or from him, who has it in use, the annual rent of three morgens of land located at Laeckervelt, due since the 1st of May *anno* 1661 until now, annually amounting to the sum of forty-eight guilders; to give quittance for the receipt of the same. Secondly, in the name of and on behalf of the said Maritie Daemen to demand of and receive out of the hands of J. S. Sijbingh, merchant at Amsterdam in Holland, a certain letter sealed with the mark  which she left in his hands at said Amsterdam on the 23rd of August 1662, according to the manuscript thereof of said Sijbingh; of which hereby the original is placed in the hands of said Lysbet Dircx van Eps to deliver to him, Sijbingh, together with the delivery of the said sealed letter, with the commission to then acquit him, Sijbingh, of all claims for it. Having received the same sealed letter, [725] to open it, and pursuant to the contents of the same to demand, claim, and receive the capital sum of *f*3500 with the accrued interest on the same according to the purport of the said sealed letter due until now; to issue quittance of the same from Jor. Schaep, or, if deceased, from his heirs or those, who are his administrators, dwelling at Doesburch; but if Jor. Schaep or his heirs wish to retain the said capital, this may be done provided that sufficient security will be offered and that the appointers will receive an authentic copy in their hands. Otherwise, to take and receive the same capital with the said due interest; and to deposit it in the General Treasury in Holland or at Amsterdam, or elsewhere, to bring along, or to send over evidence of the same, and to use the interest already due for such goods and merchandise as the attorney will be ordered by them, appointers, and to bring those here, or to send them over. And in case of any unwillingness in either case, to require the respective right and title on behalf of the appointers by means of justice; for this purpose to observe all terms of justice until sentence, including its extreme execution, with power to appoint one or two substitutes in her place with similar or limited power, and moreover, to do, transact and perform everything that she deems necessary and advisable, either with law or without; [726] promising at all times, without any gainsaying to accept everything that her appointed daughter Lijsbet or her substitute, by virtue of this shall have done and performed in this matter, under obligation provided thereto according to law, provided that the attorney, if requested, shall be obliged to properly justify her said transactions and receipts. Done in Albany the 5th/15th of July 1668.

Cornelis van Nes
Maerrien Daemen
As witness G. Swartt schout
Goosen Gerretsen
Philip Pietersz Schuijler
In my presence,
D. V. Schelluijne, secretary, 1668.

[CONVEYANCE OF A LOT BY JAN COSTER VAN AECKEN TO WILLEM TELLER]

Appeared before us, undersigned magistrates of Albany, Colony of Rensselaerswijck and Schanechtade, Jan Coster van Aecken, who declared to hereby cede, convey and make over to and for the benefit of Willem Teller a lot, located here in Albany at the hill; wide in front on the street 21 feet, long until the lot of Captain Backer, and wide in the rear 20 feet Rhineland measure; together with an alley on the west side of his, Van Aecken's house of three feet wide, which shall remain a common alley included within the said width of 21 feet, and length as far as the alley runs; adjoins to the east the grantor, to the south the said street, to the west Jan van Bael, and to the north said Captain Backer, and this, by virtue of a conveyance dated the 28th November/8th of December 1667, by the lords magistrates passed for his benefit; giving therefor full power to the said Willem Teller, his heirs and descendants or those who hereafter may receive title from him, to dispose thereof as he might do with his own patrimonial effects [727]; without him, grantor, making the least claim upon the same anymore, acknowledging to have been fully satisfied and paid for it through the hands of said Willem Teller; promising therefore to protect and free the said lot against all persons from all trouble and claims as is right, and moreover, nevermore to do or to let anything be done against the same either with or without law, in any way, under pledge of his person and estate, without exception, subject to all laws and judges. Done in Albany the 6th/16th of July 1668.

Jan Koster
Teunis Cornelisz
Goosen Gerretsen
In my presence,
D. V. Schelluijne, secretary 1668.

[POWER OF ATTORNEY FROM ANTHONIA SLACHBOOM TO GERRIT SLICHTENHORST]

Appeared before us, undersigned magistrates of Albany, Colony of Rensselaerswijck and Schanechtade *Joffr.* Anthonia Slachboom, widow of the late lord Arent van Curlar, in his lifetime magistrate of the colony of Rensselaerswijck and our late fellow councilor, who declares that she hereby appoints and fully empowers *Sr.* Gerrit Slichtenhorst, who intends to depart for Holland, especially to collect, demand and receive out of the property and immoveable goods of Huselmans's estate in the jurisdiction of Nijkerck (in Gelderland), located in the hamlet of Nautena, the right and title thereof, which is a freed estate of the abbot of Paterborn, as it comes to her, the appointer, by virtue of the certificate of usufruct as her late husband and she, appearer, have insured each other on the 30th of September 1646 before the lords Diderick van der Sande and Everard Everwijn, magistrates of the town of Arnhem; which original certificate for this purpose was hereby handed over to the attorney, [**728**] as her late husband during his lifetime already had alienated and sold the other lands and effects mentioned therein; after the receipt of her overdue claims to agree with the other heirs of said Huselmans, or those who have the management thereof, to arrange for a full redemption and acquittance of the further rights she has therein, and nevermore at any time lay any claim to it; therefore in her name and on her behalf to fully desist and give up the same and all her actions and claims with respect thereto, and to issue quittance of the aforesaid matter; and all of this to recover the sum of *f*1159 according to promissory note dated the 9th of October 1655, passed by said Curlar, deceased, for the benefit of the honorable Brant van Slichtenhorst, deceased, late father of said Gerrit van Slichtenhorst, and also by account the sum of *f*27 for merchandise received from him, attorney; everything to be received in current silver money; and, moreover, in the said matter to do, transact and perform everything that he deems necessary and advisable; promising at all times, without any gainsaying to accept everything that the attorney shall do and perform in the said matter, under an obligation according to law. Done in Albany the 6th/16th of July 1668.

This mark was  made by said *Juffr.* Anthonia Slachtboom.
Goosen Gerretsen
Richard van Rensselaer

In my presence,
D. V. Schelluijne, secretary 1668.

[POWER OF ATTORNEY FROM WILLEM JANSZ SCHUT
TO STOFFEL JANSZ ABEEL]

Appeared before us, undersigned magistrates of Albany, colony of Rensselaerswijck and Schanechtade Willem Jansz Schut, also known as *Dommelaer*, dwelling **[729]** in the said colony, who declared to hereby appoint and fully empower Stoffel Jansz Abeel, master carpenter, here, intending to depart for Holland, together with his cousin named Eyttie Meijndertse, dwelling at Amsterdam in Holland, according to her writing of the 12th of April 1666, especially to collect, demand and receive from Sijmon Janssen, his uncle dwelling at Wieringen, everything that he inherited after the death of his grandmother, with its accrued interest, deposited with his said uncle; to issue quittance for the receipts, and moreover, to do, transact and perform what they deem necessary and advisable; promising at all times to accept everything that the said attorneys shall do and perform in the said matter, without any gainsaying, under obligation provided for it according to law, provided that the attorneys shall be obliged to properly justify their said transactions and receipts. Done in Albany the 6th/16th of July 1668.

Willem Jansen Schut
Goosen Gerretsen
Richard van Rensselaer

In my presence,
D. V. Schelluijne, secretary 1668.

[POWER OF ATTORNEY FROM JAN VINHAGEN TO HERMAN VEDDER]

Appeared before us, undersigned magistrates of Albany, colony of Rensselaerswijck and Schanechtade in America, the honorable Jan Vinhagen, master tailor, here in Albany, born in Geemen in the bishopric of Munster, who declared to **[730]** hereby appoint and fully empower *Sr.* Herman Vedder, merchant, here, intending to depart for Holland, especially to collect, demand and receive from his brother Wilhelm Vinhaegen, dwelling at said Geemen, what was inherited by him, Wilhelm and Anthonij Vinhagen, his youngest brother, by the death and decease of their father Dirck Vinhagen, deceased *anno* 1659, and their mother deceased, Aeltie der A., deceased before that date at said Geemen, [which is] deposited with his said brother Wilhelm Vinhagen; to demand condition and inventory of the estate or the will, if one was made; once the appointer's just portion of the said inheritance has been received, to issue quittance thereof; also, by buying out or otherwise, to have power to compromise, and in case of any unwillingness (which is not to be hoped), to demand his said portion by means and ways of justice; to that end to observe all terms of law, including sentence and extreme execution of the same; also with power to appoint one or more substitutes in his place with similar or less power; and moreover, to do, transact and perform everything that he deems necessary and advisable; promising at all times, without any gainsaying to accept everything that the said attorney, or his substitute shall do and perform in the said matter, provided that the attorney shall be obliged, if requested, to properly justify his said transactions and receipts. Done in Albany the 6th/16th of July 1668.

Jan Vinhaeghen
Goosen Gerretsen
Richard van Rensselaer

In my presence,
D. V. Schelluijne, secretary 1668.

[CONVEYANCE OF A BRICK KILN BY ADRIAEN VAN ILPENDAM TO PIETER QUACKEBOS]

[**731**] Appeared before us, undersigned magistrates of Albany, colony of Rensselaerswijck and Schanechtade *Mr.* Adriaen van Ilpendam, who declared that he has ceded, conveyed, and made over in true, rightful and free ownership to Pieter Quackebos the brick kiln according to the boundary markers placed for it, located here in the colony, and in use by him, Pieter Quackebos; according to the right and ownership of the ground as he has bought and paid for it to the *Joffr.*, widow of the late Johan de Hulter, now wife of Jeronimus Ebbinck, according to receipt dated the 20th of August 1664, provided that he, Quackebos, annually shall pay a rent of two Carolus guilders to the lord director of the colony according to purport of the bill of sale thereof dated the 11th of November 1657, to which here is referred. giving therefor full power to him, Quackebos, his heirs and descendants, or those who hereafter may acquire title from him, to dispose of the same as he might do with his own patrimonial effects, acknowledging to have been fully satisfied and paid for the same; promising therefore to protect and free the said brick kiln from all trouble and claims as is right, and nevermore to do or allow anything to be done against the same, in any manner, subject to all laws and judges. Done in Albany the 11th/21st of July 1668.

Adriaen van Ilpendam
Goosen Gerretsen
Philip Pietersz Schuijler
In my presence,
D. V. Schelluijne, secretary 1668.

[MORTGAGE OF A HOUSE AND LOT BY ARENT JANSZ]

[732] Appeared before us, undersigned magistrates of Albany, colony of Rensselaerswijck and Schanechtade, Arent Jansz, master carpenter, here, intending to depart for Holland, who declared that, in consequence of the sentence of a court minute by the honorable court here, of the 18th/28th of June and 25th of June/5th of July of this year, he places as special mortgage and bond his house and lot standing and located here in Albany, as he acquired the lot by conveyance from Henderick Gerritsz Vermeulen on the 23rd of April/3rd of May 1667, and this free and unencumbered except for the lord's right; together with everything that he has inherited upon the decease of his godmother Lijsbet Willems, which is held by his brother Willem Jansz, mason, at Amsterdam in Holland, and, moreover, generally his person and estate, moveable and immoveable without any exception, subject to all laws and judges, in order to recover [payment] without cost and damage if it is found in Amsterdam that he, appearer, will be obliged to pay out the two hundred and three hundred guilders mentioned in the sentence, along with its interest to the estate of the father of Gerritie Gerritse, wife of Aernout Cornelisz, also dwelling here. And if the contrary would appear according to the reasons by the appearer alleged before the court according to purport of the said sentence and minute, then this certificate of mortgage shall be void and of no effect. Done in Albany on the 13th/23rd of July 1668.

Arent Jansen
J Dehinsse
Goosen Gerretsen
In my presence,
D. V. Schelluijne, secretary 1668.

[CONVEYANCE OF A LOT BY THE MAGISTRATES TO STOFFEL JANSZ ABEEL]

[733] The magistrates of Albany, Colony of Rensselaerswijck and Schanechtade hereby declare that they hereby cede, convey and make over in true, rightful and free ownership to and for the benefit of Stoffel

Jansz, master carpenter, here, a lot located here at the hill; wide thirty-two Rhineland feet long until the back of the lot of Captain Abraham Staes; adjoins on the east side the powder cellar, on the south side ditto Captn. Staes, on the west side David Schuijler, and to the north the street; and this free and unencumbered, except for the lord's right; which lot he, Stoffel Jansz has bought and paid for. Therefore giving full power to him, his heirs and descendants or those, who may receive title from him, to dispose thereof as he might do with his own patrimonial effects, and therefore he is allowed to request a patent for the same lot of the right honorable lord general. Done in Albany the 13th/23rd of July 1668.

Philip Pietersz Schuijler
Acknowledged by me,
D. V. Schelluijne, secretary 1668.

[POWER OF ATTORNEY FROM CORNELIS THEUNISZ VAN SLIJCK TO JOHANNES VANDEN BOGAERT VAN BREUCKELEN]

[734] Appeared before us, undersigned magistrates of Albany, colony of Rensselaerswijck and Schanechtade, Cornelis Theunisz van Slijck, born near Breuckelen in the bishopric of Utrecht, former council member of the said colony, making known that he has with certainty been informed that his brother Cors Theunisz van Slijck, who in his lifetime dwelled in said Breuckelen in the brewery of the *Vijffhoeck*, is deceased, and as since four or five years he has received no news from his said brother and his other friends and relatives, he, appearer, declares to hereby appoint and fully empower the honorable Johannes vanden Bogaert, [ ] of said Breuckele and its dependencies or, in case of his honor's decease, whoever may have succeeded to his place, especially in his name and on his behalf to find out what he may have inherited by the death of his said brother and other friends *ex testamento vel ab intestato*, to collect and receive his rights and title in this matter, both in moveable and immoveable estate, actions and credits; to administer those to his advantage, issue quittance of the receipt, and in case of unwillingness of the trustees in the said matter (which is not to be hoped) to proceed by means and ways of justice, with

power to substitute someone in his place, having similar or limited power, and further, to do, transact and perform everything that he deems necessary and advisable; promising at all times, [735] to accept everything that the said attorney, or his substitute shall do and perform in the said matter without any gainsaying, under obligation according to law, provided that the attorney shall be obliged, if requested, to properly justify his said transactions and receipts. Done in Albany the $21^{st}/31^{st}$ of July 1668.

Cornelis van Slick
Philip Pietersz Schuijler
R. V. Rensselaer
In my presence,
D. V. Schelluijne, secretary 1668.

[CONVEYANCE OF A HOUSE AND LOT BY JACOB TEIJSEN VANDER HEIJDEN TO JOHN CONELL AND FROM JOHN CONELL TO JACOB TEIJSEN VANDER HEIJDEN]

Appeared before us, undersigned magistrates of Albany, colony of Rensselaerswijck and Schanechtade, Jacob Tijsz vander Heijde and John Coneall who declare that by exchange with each other they hereby cede, convey and make over in true, rightful and free ownership, namely, Jacob Tijsz vander Heijden to him, Coneall, his house and lot standing and located here in Albany, by virtue of a deed of conveyance thereof dated the $10^{th}/20^{th}$ of October 1665, as the same is standing within its fence and boundaries, except that a small a strip of the lot is taken off of the ground lying without the fence for an alley; adjoins according to the purport and contents of the said conveyance. And John Coneall hereby conveys and makes over [736] to and for the benefit of said Vander Heijde his house and lot also standing and located here in Albany at the hill; wide in front on the street twenty-two feet, and long six rods, and this by virtue of a patent and bill of sale dated the 21st of January 1667, as the lot came to him by purchase from Sergeant Percker. And this respectively, the one to the other, free and unencumbered, without any charge standing or issuing against the same, except for the lord's right, without either party making the least claim upon the other anymore concerning the said case, acknowledging that they mutually have been fully satisfied and paid for it by each other, the last penny with the first; giving therefore *plenam actionem cessam* and complete power, the one to the other respectively, to their heirs and descendants or those who hereafter may receive their title, to each dispose of his [property] as they respectively might do with their own patrimonial effects; the one promising to the other as before, to protect and free the said houses and lots from all trouble and claims, as is right, and moreover, nevermore to do nor to let anything be done against the same in any way, upon pledge of their respective persons and estates, without exception, subject to all laws and judges. Done in Albany the 29th of July/8th of August *anno* 1668.

Jacob Teijsen
John Conell
R. V. Rensselaer
Philip Pietersz Schuijler
In my presence,
D. V. Schelluijne, secretary 1668.

[PAYMENT BY JOHANNES PROVOOST
TO HARMEN VEDDER]

[737] Appeared before us, undersigned magistrates of Albany, colony of Rensselaerswijck and Schanechtade, *Sr.* Johannes Provoost, dwelling here in Albany, who declares to hereby cede, convey and make over to Harmen Vedder, his brother-in-law who intends to depart for Holland, such a sum of eight hundred and thirty guilders, 15 stuivers and 12 pennies, as is coming to him *per resto* from an account *anno* 1664 of the honorable lords directors of the Chartered West India Company, chamber of Amsterdam in Holland, earned here in this country in the capacity of assistant in their honor's service, according to the purport and contents of the same account, of which the original was hereby given into the hands of the assignee, acknowledging that he has been fully satisfied and paid for it with goods received to his satisfaction; giving therefor full power to his said brother-in-law Harmen Vedder or the lawful bearer of this, to request, collect and receive the payment of

the said sum of *f*830–15–12 from the said lords directors, to issue quittance of the receipt, which shall be valid as if it were granted by the appearer himself; moreover, to do and perform everything to receive the said sum, which the appearer could or might do if he were present himself, even if the case would demand greater or more special authority than herein is expressed; promising at all times to accept whatever will be done by virtue hereof, under an obligation according to law. Done in Albany in America the 30th of July/9th of August 1668.

Johannes Provoost
Philip Pietersz Schuijler
Goosen Gerretsen
In my presence,
D. V. Schelluijne, secretary 1668.

[**738**] [*blank*]

[SALE OF A HOUSE AND LOT WITH A GARDEN BY PHILIP PIETERSZ SCHUIJLER TO ABRAHAM STAETS]

[**739**] Appeared before us, undersigned magistrates of Albany, colony of Rensselaerswijck and Schaenhechtede, Philip Pietersz Schuijler, who declared that he hereby cedes, conveys and makes over in true, rightful and free ownership to and for the benefit of *Mr*. Abraham Staets a house and lot with a garden across the back street, by virtue of a patent thereof and a conveyance dated the 24th of April 1667 and 9/19th of June 1666 respectively; also according to a bill of sale dated the 10th/20th of February of the year 1666; the lot extending in front along the street wide thirty wood feet; in length to the back of the fence of Herman Rutgers' brewery, where the width is the same, including the small alley that runs to the garden; such as the said portion of the lot, house, and garden are located here in Albany; adjoins according to the purport and contents of the bill of sale to which here is referred, which came to him, grantor, from Volkert Jansz, attorney for Hendrick Jocchims; without he, grantor having the least claim upon the same anymore, acknowledging to have been fully satisfied and paid for it through the hands of said *Mr*. Abraham Staats, the last penny with the first; giving therefor to the said *Mr*. Abraham, his heirs and descendants, or those who may receive title from him *plenam actionem cessam* and full power

to do with and to dispose thereof as he might do with his patrimonial estate and effects, promising to protect and free the said house, lot and garden from all trouble, claims and charges as is right, and moreover, nevermore to [**740**] do nor to let anything be done against the same, either with or without law, in any way, under obligation according to law. Done in Albany the 5th/15th of September 1668.

Philip Pietersz Schuijler
R. V. Rensselaer
J. Dehinsse
In my presence,
Ludovicus Cobes, secretary.

[ACKNOWLEDGMENT OF DEBT BY CLAES FREDERICXS VAN PETTEN AND CORNELIS CORNELISZ VIELEN TO MARTEN CORNELISZ]

Appeared before us, undersigned magistrates of Albany, colony of Rensselaerswijck and Schaenhechtede, Claes Fredericxs van Petten and Cornelis Cornelisz Veilen farmers dwelling at Schaenhechtede, who acknowledge that they are well and truly indebted to Martten Cornelisz for the quantity of two hundred and twenty beavers figured at eight guilders apiece, growing out of the matter of two remaining installments of purchase and mortgage money of a certain farm with dwelling, barn, and three hay barracks, with four horses, five milch cows, eight hogs, wagon, plough and harrow, bought by the appearers from him according to the bill of sale thereof, dated 4/14th of July 1667, which aforesaid sum of two hundred and twenty beavers they, appearers, promise to pay according to the purport and contents of the same; namely, one hundred and ten beavers in the month of February 1669, and the remaining one hundred and ten beavers in the month of February 1670, each time punctually, especially pledging therefor the aforesaid farm and effects, and further, generally their persons and estates, moveable and immoveable, present and future, without exception, subject to all laws. Done in Albany the 23rd of October 1668.

Claes Frericksen
Cornelis Cornelisz Vielen
R. V. Rensselaer
Abram Staas

Concerning the payment of Cornelis Cornelisz Vile this mortgage has been satisfied, but of Claes van Petten not yet. Albany, 17 February 1670.

[SALE OF A FARM BY MARTEN CORNELISZ TO CLAES FREDERICXSZ AND CORNELIS CORNELISZ VIELEN]

[741] Appeared before us, undersigned magistrates of Albany, colony of Rensselaerswijck and Schaenechtede, Martten Cornelisz, farmer, who declared that he hereby cedes, conveys and makes over in true, rightful and free ownership to and for the benefit of Claes Fredericxsz van Petten and Cornelis Cornelisz Veilen, farmers, at Schaenhechtede, their heirs and descendants or their assigns, a certain the grantor's farm with dwelling, barn, three hay barracks, four horses, five milch-cows, eight hogs, wagon, plough, and harrow, standing and located in Schaenechtede, presently in possession of them, Claes Fredericxsz and Cornelis Cornelisz; and this according to the patent granted to him, appearer, by the right honorable lord general dated the 13th of April 1668, and moreover, in consequence of the bill of sale of the said farm and effects passed on the 4th/14th of July 1667, all of which are hereby delivered to the said Claes Fredericxsz and Cornelis Cornelisz; and concerning the boundaries, length and width of the said farm, the appearer refers to the said four evidences delivered, acknowledging to have been fully satisfied and paid for the said farm and effects through the hands of them, Claes Fredericxsz and Cornelis Cornelisz, namely with the sum of one hundred and ten beavers by him received to his content, and with a mortgage for two hundred and twenty beavers according to the purport of the said bill of sale, without he, grantor hereafter having the least claim upon it anymore, giving therefore *plenam actionem cessam* and full power to them, Claes Fredericxsz and Cornelis Cornelissen and their said heirs, to dispose of the same as they might do with their patrimonial effects, promising to protect and free the

said farm and effects against each and every person from all actions, trouble, and claims as is right, and moreover, nevermore to [742] do nor let anything be done against the same, either with or without law, in any way, under an obligation according to law. Done in Albany the 23rd of October 1668.

The mark of Martten  Cornelisz, made with his own hand.
R. V. Rensselaer
Abram Staas
In my presence,
Ludovicus Cobes.

[ACKNOWLEDGMENT OF DEBT BY RHIJNIER VANDER COELEN TO LUYCAS ANDRIESZ AND JAN JOOSTEN]

Appeared before us, undersigned magistrates of Albany, colony of Rensselaerswijck and Schaenhechtede, Rhijnier vander Coelen, dwelling in the Esopus, presently here in Albany, who acknowledged that he is well and truly indebted to the skippers Luijcas Andriesz and Jan Joosten dwelling at New York for the sum of three hundred and forty-one guilders and eighteen stuivers in good strung sewant, growing out of the matter of freights earned and goods received at various times since the year 1666, received from them to his content, which aforesaid sum of three hundred and forty-one guilders and eighteen stuivers he, Vander Coelen, promises to pay at the latest in the beginning of the coming month of November, exactly when they, creditors, or the lawful holders of this promissory note will have arrived in the Esopus; especially pledging therefor his distilling kettle, helmet and worm which he will now bring from here to the Esopus, and moreover, generally his person and estate without exception, under obligation of all laws and judges, to recover the said sum without costs and damage, and [743] for the greater security of the said special pledge for the said sum, the same shall, if need be, be registered by the secretary in the Esopus. Done in Albany the 24th of September 1668.

Reijnier vander Coele
J. Dehinsse

Jan Verbeeck
In my presence,
Ludovicus Cobes, secretary.

[ACKNOWLEDGMENT OF DEBT BY WILLEM MARTENSZ HUIS TO ELDERT GERBERTSEN CRUIJFF]

Appeared before us, undersigned magistrates of Albany, colony of Rensselaerswijck and Schaenhechtede, Willem Martensz Huis, sailor, presently here in Albany, who acknowledged that he is well and truly indebted to Eldert Gerbertsen Cruijff for the sum of seven hundred guilders in good sewant, growing out of the matter of a large barge with sail and rigging, anchor, and rope, bought from him in the year 1658, along with some other wares received to his full content; which aforesaid sum of seven hundred guilders in sewant he, Willem Martensz, promises to pay as follows: when he will now come down to New York one hundred guilders in sewant to Aeltie van Breemen, and when he will come up again in the fall, another hundred guilders in sewant; and the remaining five hundred guilders in next April or half way May of the year 1669; especially pledging for it his half scow or his share, which he has in company with Evert Luijcas, and, moreover, generally his person and estate without exception, under obligation [744] according to all laws and judges to recover the payment of said sum without any cost or damage. Done in Albany the 29th of September *anno* 1668.

Willem Maartensz Hues
J. Dehinsse
Jan Thomasz
In my presence,
Ludovicus Cobes, secretary.

[*In the margin was written*:] This is canceled and annuled in the presence of Volckert Jansz and Jan Bruijn on the 27th of May 1669.

[SALE OF HALF A YACHT BY DAVID PIETERSZ SCHUIJLER TO CLAES LOCK]

Appeared before us, undersigned magistrates of Albany, colony of Rensselaerswijck and Schaenhechtede, Davidt Pietersz Schuijler, who declared that he has ceded, conveyed and made over in true, rightful and free ownership to and for the benefit of Claes Locq, his heirs and descendants, or his assigns, the grantor's certain half yacht which he has acquired together with said Lock, and which presently is in possession of the same, and this by virtue of a bill of sale thereof; acknowledging that he has been fully satisfied and paid for the said half yacht through the hands of him, Claes Locq, the last penny wit the first, without he, appearer, having the least claim upon it anymore; giving therefor plenam actionem cessam and full power to Claes Lock and his heirs, to dispose of it as he might do with his patrimonial effects, promising to protect and free the said half yacht from all actions, trouble, and claims of each and every person as is right, and moreover, nevermore to do nor to let anything be done against the same, either with or without law, in any way, under an obligation according to law. Done in Albany the 29th of October 1668.

Davijet Schuijler
R. V. Rensselaer
Abram Staas.

[EXCHANGE OF A HOUSE AND LOT BETWEEN JAN CORNEEL TO JOHANNES *DE WANDELAER*]

[**745**] Appeared before us, undersigned magistrates of Albany, colony of Rensselaerswijck and Schaenhechtede, John Corneel and Johannes *de Wandelaer*, who declare that they hereby, by exchange, the one to the other, have ceded, conveyed and made over in true, rightful and free ownership, namely, Jan Corneel to him, *Wandelaer*, his house and lot standing and located here in Albany by virtue of a deed of conveyance thereof dated the 10/20th of October 1665, as the same is standing within its fence and boundaries, of which a small strip of the lot for an alley is taken off of the ground situated outside of the fence; adjoins according

to the purport and contents of the said conveyance. And Johannes *de Wandelaer* hereby conveys and makes over to and for the benefit of the said John Corneel his house and lot also standing and located here in Albany at the hill; wide in front on the street eighteen and a half wood feet, and in length according to what is shown in the auction book, being the just half, which was bought in company with Omy la Grand; and this respectively the one to the other, free and unencumbered without any charges standing or issuing against the same, except for the lord's right; without either party making the least claim upon the said matter anymore, acknowledging to mutually have been fully satisfied and paid for it. But Johannes de Wandelaer in the said exchange shall be obliged to contribute twenty-two whole good and merchantable beaver skins, to be paid on the first of July *anno* 1669, of which a mortgage shall be passed; giving therefore, the one to the other respectively, *plenam actionem cessam* and full power to their heirs and descendants or those, who hereafter may acquire their title, to each dispose of his [house and lot] as they respectively might do with their own patrimonial effects, promising, the one to the other as before, to protect and free the said houses and lots from all trouble and claims, as is right, and moreover, nevermore to do nor to let anything be done against the same in any way, under obligation of their respective persons and estates, with no exception, subject to all laws and judges. Done in Albany the 3rd of December 1668.

John Conell
Johannes de Wandelaer
Abram Staas
R. V. Rensselaer.
In my presence,
Ludovicus Cobes, secretary.

[ACKNOWLEDGMENT OF DEBT BY JOHANNES *DE WANDELAER* TO JAN CORNEEL]

[746] Appeared before us, undersigned magistrates of Albany, colony of Rensselaerswijck and Schaenhechtede, Johannes *de Wandelaer*, young man, dwelling here in Albany, who acknowledges that he is well and truly indebted to Jan Corneel for the quantity of twenty-two whole and merchantable beaver skins figured at eight guilders apiece, stemming from the matter of a remaining installment for the purchase and mortgage money of a certain domicile and lot, bought, or exchanged by him, appearer; which aforesaid sum of 22 whole beavers the appearer promises to pay on the first of July of the year 1669 punctually, pledging therefore the said domicile and lot, and, moreover, generally his person and estate, moveable and immoveable, present and future with no exception, subject to all the lord's laws and judges, to recover (if necessary) the payment thereof without any cost and damage. Done in Albany, this 3rd of December 1668.

Johannes *de Wandelaer*
Abram Staas
R. V. Rensselaer
In my presence,
Ludovicus Cobes, secretary.

[CONVEYANCE OF A HOUSE, LOT, BARN, GARDEN, AND FRUIT TREES BY FRANS JANSZ PRUIJN FOR AQUE CORNELISZ TO JAN LABATIE]

Appeared before us, undersigned magistrates of Albany, colony of Rensselaerswijck and Schaenhechtede, Frans Jansz Pruijn, acting on behalf of Aques Cornelisz, who declared that he hereby cedes, conveys and makes over in true, rightful and free ownership to and for the benefit of Jan Labatie, his heirs and descendants or his assigns, the grantor's house, lot, hay barrack barn, garden and fruit trees, standing and located in the colony of Rensselaerswijck, and this according to evidence of the auction book of the said colony, dated the 16th of January 1664; extending and [747] adjoining on the westerly side the lord patroon of the colony, northerly Corst Bouts, easterly and southerly the public road, as the same lies in length and breadth within its fence; free and unencumbered without any charges standing or issuing against the same, except for the right of the lord patroon of the colony, according to the purport and contents of the conditions and stipulations of the said auction book, and by virtue of a conveyance dated the 5th of May new style 1666, passed in the Esopus, to which here reference is made, and which came to him, grantor, from Hendrick Jochimsz; without he, grantor making the least claim upon the same anymore, acknowledging that he is fully satisfied and paid for the same, the last penny with the first, giving therefore *plenam actionem cessam* and full power to the aforesaid Jan Labate, his heirs and descendants, or those who hereafter may acquire his right and title, to do with and dispose of the same as he might do with his patrimonial estate and effects; promising to protect and free the said house, lot, hay barrack barn, garden and fruit trees against all persons from all trouble, claims and charges as is right, and further, nevermore to do nor allow anything to be done against the same, either with law or without, in any manner, under a pledge according to law. Done in Albany the 7th of January 1668/9.

Frans Jansen Pruen
Jan Verbeeck
Jan Thomasz
In my presence,
Ludovicus Cobes, secretary.

[CONVEYANCE OF A HOUSE, LOT, BARN, GARDEN AND FRUIT TREES BY JAN LABATIE TO BARENT PIETERSZ]

[**748**] Appeared before me, Ludovicus Cobes, secretary of Albany, colony of Rensselaerswijck and Schaenhechtede, in the presence of the honorable lords magistrates of the same court *Mr*. Jacob de Hinsse and *Mr*. Jan Verbeeck, Jan Labate, who declared that he hereby cedes, conveys and makes over in true, rightful and free ownership to and for the benefit of Barent Pitersz, his heirs and descendants or his assigns, a certain the grantor's house, lot, hay barrack barn, garden and fruit trees, standing and located in the colony of Rensselaerswijck, and this according to evidence of the auction book of the said colony, bid on by him, Labatie at public auction on the 16th of January 1664; extending and adjoining on the westerly side the lord patroon of the colony, northerly Corst Bouts, easterly and southerly the public road, as the same in length and breadth lies within its fence; free and unencumbered

without any charges standing or issuing against the same, except for the right of the lord patroon of the colony, according to the purport and contents of the conditions and stipulations of the said book of auctions, and by virtue of a conveyance dated the 5th of May new style 1666 passed in the Esopus, to which reference is made here, and which came to him, grantor, from Frans Janssen and Aques Cornelisz; without the grantor making the least claim upon the same anymore, acknowledging that he is fully satisfied and paid for the same, the last penny with the first, giving therefore *plenam actionem cessam* and full power to the aforesaid Barent Pietersz, his heirs and descendants, or those who hereafter may acquire his right and title, to do with and dispose of it as he might do with his patrimonial estate and effects; promising to protect and free the said house, lot, hay barrack barn, garden and fruit trees against all persons from all trouble, claims and charges as is right, and further, nevermore to do nor allow anything to be done against the same, either with or without law, in any manner, under obligation according to law. Done in Albany the 12th of January 1668/9.

Jean Labatie
J Dehinsse
Jan Verbeeck
In my presence,
Ludovicus Cobes, secretary.

[SALE OF A PARCEL OF LAND WITH A LOT FOR A FARM BY JAN BRONCK, ATTORNEY FOR HILLETIE BRONCX, TO MARTTEN GERRITSEN VIA THE ADMINISTRATORS OF THE ESTATE OF JAN ANDRIESSEN]

[749] Appeared before me, Ludovicus Cobes, secretary of Albany, colony of Rensselaerswijck and Schaenhechtede, in the presence of the honorable lords magistrates of the same court *Mr.* Jacob de Hinsse and *Mr.* Jan Verbeeck, Jan Bronck, in capacity of attorney for his mother Hilletie Broncx, who declared that he hereby cedes, conveys and makes over in true, rightful and free ownership to and for the benefit of Johannes Provoost, auctioneer and trustee for the estate of the late Jan Andriesz the Irishman, assisted by the lord officer Gerrart Swart (who,

in turn, transfers this conveyance to Martten Gerritsen, his heirs and descendants or his assigns) a certain parcel of land of about 69 morgens, sold to him, Jan Andriesz, deceased, with a lot for a farm stead, wide 20 rods and long 30 rods, adjoining according to the descriptions of the patent to which hereby is referred; they, grantors, Jan Bronck as well as Provoost, acknowledging that they have been fully paid and satisfied for the said land, the first penny with the last, without the grantors making the least claim upon the same anymore; giving therefore *plenam actionem cessam* and full power to him, Martten Gerritsz and his heirs, to dispose of the same as he might do with his patrimonial effects; promising to protect and free the said piece or parcel of land against all persons from all trouble, actions and claims as is right, and further, nevermore to do nor allow anything to be done against the same, either with or without law, in any manner, under obligation according to law. Done in Albany the 8th of March 1669.

Jan Pietersen Bronck
Johannes Provoost
G. Swart, schout
J. Dehinsse
Jan Verbeeck
In my presence,
Ludovicus Cobes, secretary.

[ACKNOWLEDGMENT OF DEBT BY DIRCKIE HERMS TO JEREMIAS VAN RENSSELAER AND JACOB SANDERSEN GLEN, ATTORNEYS FOR *SRS.* MOMMAES]

[**750**] Appeared before me, Ludovicus Cobes, secretary of Albany, colony of Rensselaerswijck and Schaenhechtede, in the presence of the honorable lords magistrates of the same court the lord Rijckert van Rensselaer and *Mr*. Jacob de Hinsse, Dirckie Herms, wife of Jan Martensen, who acknowledged that she is well and truly indebted to the lord Jeremias van Rensselaer and Jacob Sandersz Glen, attorneys for the *Srs*. Mommaes, merchants at Amsterdam, for the sum of [*blank*] in beavers, according to a promissory note passed in the year 1661 on date of [*blank*], which aforesaid sum of [*blank*] in beavers she, appearer,

promises to pay to the mentioned *Sr*. Rensselaer and Jacob Sandersz or their order, namely, twenty beavers each following year until the full payment has been made; pledging thereto her person and estate, moveable and immoveable, present and future, and especially three horses, to wit, an old mare and two young mare colts in their second year, also three little oxen of two years old, also three little oxen of one year, and a heifer of one year; also a milch cow of three years which is a good one, to recover payment, if necessary, without cost and damage. The milch cow of 3 years must be delivered in the coming month of May. Done in Albany, the 13th of March 1668/9.

Derckien Hermes.

[ACKNOWLEDGMENT OF DEBT BY SWEER THEUNISZ TO GEERTRUIJT BARENTS]

[751] Appeared before me, Ludovicus Cobes, secretary of Albany, colony of Rensselaerswijck and Schaenhechtede, in the presence of the honorable lords magistrates of the same court the lord Rychart van Rensselaer and *Mr*. Jacob de Hinsse, Sweer Theunisz, farmer, dwelling in the colony of Rensselaerswijck, who acknowledged that he is well and truly indebted to Geertruijt Barents, wife of Jacob Heven, for the number of 14 whole and merchantable beaver skins for money advanced and merchandise received to his full content, according to promissory notes thereof; which said beavers he, appearer, promises to pay with their interest from the receipt thereof until the full satisfaction; especially pledging therefore his two lots located at *Lubberde Landt*, in use by Jacob Heven, and generally his person and estate, moveable and immoveable, present and future, without exception, to recover payment thereof if need be, without cost or damage. Done in Albany the 27th of May 1669.

Sweer Thoonussen
R. V. Rensselaer

[CONVEYANCE OF A LOT BY JOHANNA EBBINCK TO SWEER THEUNISZ]

Appeared before me, Ludovicus Cobes, secretary of Albany, colony of Rensselaerswijck and Schaenhechtede, in the presence of the honorable lords magistrates of the same court the *Monsr.* Rijchart van Rensselaer and Mr. Jacob de Hinsse, *Juffr.* Johanna Ebbinck, attorney for and commissioned by her husband *Sr.* Jeronimus Ebbinck, who declared that she hereby cedes, conveys and makes over in true, rightful and free ownership to and for the benefit of Sweer Theunisz, his heirs and descendants or his assigns a certain, the grantor's lot located to the west of the river between Hendrick Reur and him, Sweer Theunisz, at *Lubberde Landt* in the colony of Rensselaerswijck, according to the description thereof in the bill of sale with his predecessor Jan Barentsz Wemp, deceased; and this in such length and breadth as the buyer has taken the same in possession, and this free and unencumbered without any charges standing or issuing against the same, except for the right of the lord patroon of the colony; without [**752**] she, grantor, making the least claim upon the same anymore, acknowledging that she is fully satisfied and paid for it, the last penny with the first, giving therefore *plenam actionem cessam* and full power to the aforesaid Sweer Theunisz, his heirs and descendants, or those who may acquire his right and title, to do with and dispose of the same as he might do with his patrimonial estate and effects; promising to protect and free the said lot against all persons from all trouble, claims and charges as is right, and further, nevermore to do nor allow anything to be done against the same, either with or without law, in any manner, under obligation according to law. Done in Albany the 13th of June 1669.

Johanna Ebbinck
R. V. Rensselaer
J Dehinsse.

[CONVEYANCE OF A CERTAIN HOUSE AND LOT BY VOLCKERT JANSZ, ATTORNEY FOR HENDRICK JOCHIMSZ TO ABRAHAM STAETS]

Appeared before me, Ludovicus Cobes, secretary of Albany, colony of Rensselaerswijck and Schanechtede, in the presence of the honorable lords magistrates of the same court *Mr*. Jan Verbeeck and *Mr*. Jacob de Hinsse, Volckert Jansz, attorney for Hendrick Jocchumsz, who declared that he hereby cedes, conveys and makes over in true, rightful and free ownership to and for the benefit of *Mr*. Abraham Staas, his heirs and descendants or his assigns a certain domicile and lot standing and located in Albany, being the lot extending as far as the brewery of the grantor, in length [*blank*] and width [*blank*], adjoining to the south said *Mr*. Abraham, to the north Jan Rinckhout, to the west the street, to the east the brewery; and this by virtue of a **[753]** patent dated the 23rd of April 1652, to which is referred here, and which came to him from from Hendrick Westerkamp; without the grantor making the least claim upon the same anymore, acknowledging that he is fully satisfied and paid for the same through the hands of the said *Mr*. Abraham Staas, the last penny with the first, giving therefore *plenam actionem cessam* and full power to the aforesaid *Mr*. Abraham, his heirs and descendants, or those who may acquire his right and title, to do with and dispose of the same as he might do with his patrimonial estate and effects; promising to protect and free the said house and lot against all persons from all trouble, claims and charges as is right, and further, nevermore to do nor allow anything to be done against the same, either with or without law, in any manner, under obligation according to law. Done in Albany the 12th of July 1669.

Volckart Jansz

[CONVEYANCE OF A HOUSE AND LOT BY JOHANNES DE WANDELAER TO WILLIAM PATERSON]

[754] Appeared before me, Ludovicus Cobes, secretary of Albany, colony of Rensselaerswijck and Schaenhechtede, in the presence of the honorable lords magistrates of the same court the *Mr*. Jan Verbeeck and

Mr. Jacob de Hinsse, Johannes *de Wandelaer*, who declared that he hereby cedes, conveys and makes over in true, rightful and free ownership to and for the benefit of *Mr*. William Paterson, his heirs and descendants or his assigns, a certain domicile and lot standing and located here in Albany, in consequence of the deed of conveyance dated the 3rd of December 1668, received by the grantee from Jan Corneel by way of exchange, and this, as the same is standing within its fence and boundaries to which is referred here; without the grantor making the least claim upon the same anymore, acknowledging that he is fully satisfied and paid for the same, the last penny with the first, through the hands of the said *Mr*. William Paterson, giving therefore *plenam actionem cessam* and full power to the aforesaid *Mr*. William Paterson, his heirs and descendants, or those who may acquire his right and title, to do with and dispose of the same as he might do with his patrimonial estate and effects; promising to protect and free the said house and lot against all persons from all trouble, claims and charges as is right, and further, nevermore to do nor allow anything to be done against the same, either with or without law, in any manner, under an obligation according to law. Done in Albany the 21st of July 1669.

Johannus de Wandelaer
Jan Verbeeck
J Dehinsse
In my presence,
Ludovicus Cobes, secretary.

[ACKNOWLEDGMENT OF DEBT BY JACOB JANSZ FLODDER TO ELDERT GERBERTSEN CRUIJFF]

[755] Appeared before me, Ludovicus Cobes, secretary of Albany, colony of Rensselaerswijck and Schaenhechtede, in the presence of the honorable lords magistrates of the same court *Mr*. Jan Verbeeck and *Mr*. Jacob de Hinsse, Jacob Jansz Flodder, who acknowledged that he is well and truly indebted and in arrears to Eldert Gerbertsen Cruijff for the sum of one hundred and fourteen guilders in beavers, on account of Lambert Albertsz van Neck, taken over by him; and this for merchandise received to his full content; which aforesaid sum of *f* 114 in beavers the

appearer promises to pay to Eldert Gerbertsz or the lawful bearer of this in boards, twenty-three per beaver, and this punctually on the first of November next; especially pledging therefor his Negro boy named *Bockie*, and moreover, generally his person and estate nothing excepted, subject to all laws, to recover the payment of said sum without cost or damage. Done in Albany the 4th of August anno 1669.

Jacob Jansen Gerdenijer
Jan Verbeeck
J. Dehinsse

In my presence,
Ludovicus Cobes, secretary.

[ACKNOWLEDGMENT OF DEBT BY JACOB JANSZ FLODDER TO JEREMIAS VAN RENSSELAER AND JACOB SANDERSZ GLEN, ATTORNEYS FOR THE *SRS.* MOMMAES]

[756] Appeared before me, Ludovicus Cobes, secretary of Albany, colony of Rensselaerswijck and Schaenhechtede, in the presence of the honorable lords magistrates of the same court *Monsr*. R. V. Rensselaer and *Mr*. Jan Verbeeck, Jacob Jansz Gardenier, who acknowledged that he is well indebted to the lord Jeremias van Rensselaer and Jacob Sandersz Glen, attorneys for the *Srs*. Mommaes concerning the estate of the late Jan Bastiaensz van Gutsenhoven, for the sum of two hundred and twenty-five guilders and seventeen stuivers in beavers, for merchandise and wares received to his full content, which aforesaid sum of *f*225–17 in beavers the appearer promises to pay to the said *Srs*. or the lawful bearer of this instrument, in the month of June 1670 punctually and without any further delay, especially pledging therefor his mills and effects located on the kil, his farm, horses and cattle at Kinderhoeck, the Negress with a Negro boy named Christiaen, and moreover, generally his person and estate, present and future without exception, subject to all the lord's laws and justices, to recover, if necessary, the payment thereof without cost or damage. Done in Albany the 5th of August 1669.

Jacob Jansen Gerdenijer
R. V. Rensselaer
In my presence,
Ludovicus Cobes, secretary.

[CONVEYANCE OF A LOT BY JACOB LOOCKERMANS TO HANS HENDRICXSZ AND HELMER OTTEN]

[757] Appeared before me, Ludovicus Cobes, secretary of Albany, colony of Rensselaerswijck and Schaenhechtede, in the presence of the honorable lords magistrates of the same court *Monsr.* R. V. Rensselaer and *Mr.* Jacob de Hinsse, Jacob Loockermans, who declared that he hereby cedes, conveys and makes over in true, rightful and free ownership to and for the benefit of Hans Hendricxsz and Helmer Otten, their heirs and descendants or their assigns, a certain, the grantor's lot, located at the hill here in Albany; wide in front two rods eleven inches, in the back two rods; long on the south side six rods, one foot and nine inches, on the north side five rods, ten feet and eight inches; adjoins on the north side Helmer Otten and Jan Clute, on the east side Geertruijt Vosburch, on the south side Omy La Grand, on the west side the public street; which he, grantor, received from the lords magistrates of Albany, and by virtue of a conveyance dated the 29th of May/8th of June of the year 1668, to which hereby reference is made; and this free and unencumbered without any charges standing or issuing against the same, except for the lord's right; giving therefore *plenam actionem cessam* and full power to the aforesaid Hans Hendricxsz and Helmer Otten, their heirs and descendants, or those who hereafter may acquire their right and title, to dispose of the same as they might do with their own patrimonial effects; promising to protect and free the said lot against all persons from all trouble, claims and charges as is right, and further, nevermore to do nor allow anything to be done against the same, either with or without law, in any manner, under a pledge according to law. Done in Albany the 15th of August 1669.

Jacob Lokermans
R. V. Rensselaer
J. Dehinsse

In my presence,
Ludovicus Cobes, secretary.

[CONVEYANCE OF A HOUSE AND LOT BY JAN LABATIE TO PIETER JACOBSZ BORSBOOM]

[**758**] Appeared before me, Ludovicus Cobes, secretary of Albany, colony of Rensselaerswijck and Schaenhechtede, in the presence of the honorable lords magistrates of the same court *Mr*. Jan Verbeeck and *Mr*. Jacob de Hinsse, Jan Labatie, who declared that he hereby cedes, conveys and makes over in true, rightful and free ownership to and for the benefit of Piter Jacobsz Borsboom, his heirs and descendants or his assigns, a certain, the grantor's house and lot located here in Albany; wide in front on the street forty wood feet and 3½ inches, and in the rear on the end of Jacob Joosten's lot wide thirty wood feet, and in the rear on the beach wide twenty-eight wood feet, and long as far as the beach; which said house and lot are bounded to the north of the king's house and to the south of the house of Jacob Joosten; and this by virtue of a patent deposited with *Mr*. Jacob de Hinsse, dated the 3rd of May 1667, to which hereby is referred; provided that the grantor has bought another few feet of a lot from Sander Leenderts, which are also being conveyed, and which extend as far as the king's house; and also a garden behind the fort, adjoining on the one side Herman Vedder, and on the other side *Mr*. Willet; and this free and unencumbered without any charges standing or issuing against the same, except for the lord's right; giving therefore *plenam actionem cessam* and full power to the aforesaid Piter Jacob Borsboom, his heirs and descendants, or those who hereafter may acquire his right and title, to dispose thereof as he might do with his own patrimonial effects; promising to protect and free the said house and lot against all persons from all trouble, claims and charges as is right, and further, nevermore to do nor allow anything to be done against the same, either with or without law, in any manner, under an obligation according to law. Done in Albany the 17th of September 1669.

Jan Labatie
Jan Verbeeck
J Dehinsse

[CONVEYANCE OF A PARCEL OF LAND BY PITER JACOBSZ BORSBOOM TO JAN LABATIE]

[**759**] Appeared before me, Ludovicus Cobes, secretary of Albany, colony of Rensselaerswijck and Schaenhechtede, in the presence of the honorable lords magistrates of the same court *Mr*. Jan Verbeeck and *Mr*. Jacob de Hinsse, Piter Jacobsz Borsboom, who declared that he hereby cedes, conveys and makes over in true, rightful and free ownership to and for the benefit of Jan Labatie, his heirs and descendants or his assigns, a certain, the grantor's front parcel of land located at Schaenhechtede, adjoining next to the land of Gerrit Bancken and the land of Claes van Petten; in size eleven morgens and two hundred sixty-three rods, and this by virtue of a patent from the right honorable lord general Richard Nicolls, dated the 9th of May 1668, to which hereby is referred; and this free and unencumbered without any charges standing or issuing against the same, except for the lord's right; giving therefore *plenam actionem cessam* and full power to the aforesaid Jan Labatie, his heirs and descendants, or those who hereafter may acquire his right and title, to dispose of the same as he might do with his own patrimonial effects; promising to protect and free the said lot of land against all persons from all trouble, claims and charges as is right, and further, nevermore to do nor allow anything to be done against the same, either with or without law, in any manner, under an obligation according to law. Done in Albany the 17th of September 1669.

Pieter Yacopsen Borsboom
Jan Verbeeck
J. Dehinsse

[ACKNOWLEDGMENT OF DEBT BY RHIJNIER VANDER KOELEN TO HELMER OTTEN]

[**760**] Appeared before me, Ludovicus Cobes, secretary of Albany, colony of Rensselaerswijck and Schaenhechtede, in the presence of the honorable lords *Mr*. Jan Verbeeck and *Mr*. Jacob de Hinsse, magistrates of the same court, Rhijnier vander Koelen, dwelling in the Esopus, who acknowledged that he is well and truly indebted and in arrears to *Sr*.

Helmer Otten for the quantity of one hundred and ninety whole and merchantable beaver skins to be paid in two installments, for a house and lot purchased from him, according to the contract thereof, and which is located here in Albany, which aforesaid money the appearer promises to pay punctually at the stipulated time, especially pledging therefor the said house and lot and generally his person and estate without exception, subject to all laws and justices to recover, if necessary, the said sum without cost or damage. Done in Albany the 6th of October 1669.

Reijnier Vandaer Coele
Jan Verbeeck
J. Dehinsse
In my presence,
Ludovicus Cobes, secretary.

[ACKNOWLEDGMENT OF DEBT BY CAPTAIN THOMAS WILLET TO PHILIP PIETERSZ SCHUIJLER]

Appeared before me, Ludovicus Cobes, secretary of Albany, colony of Rensselaerswijck and Schaenhechtede, in the presence of the honorable lords magistrates *Mr.* Jan Verbeeck and *Mr.* Jacob de Hinsse, Capt. Thomas Willet, who acknowledged that he is well and truly indebted and in arrears to *Sr.* Philip Pietersz Schuijler, for the quantity of four hundred ells of the best English *dosijnties* on account of beavers received therefore in payment to his full content; which said four hundred ells of *dosijnties* the appearer promises to pay to *Sr.* Philip Pietersz Schuijler or his order at the latest in the coming month of May in the year 1670, and this half blue and half red, like these samples included, **[761]** especially pledging therefor his house and lot located here in Albany, and generally his person and estate, without exception, subject to all laws and justices, to recover, if necessary, the said four hundred ells of *dosijnties* without cost or damage. Done in Albany the 7th of October 1669.

Tho. Willett
Jan Verbeeck

J. Dehinsse
In my presence,
Ludovicus Cobes, secretary.

[CONVEYANCE OF A PART OF A LOT BY HENDRICK KOSTER TO ROBBERT SANDERSZ]

Appeared before me, Ludovicus Cobes, secretary of Albany, colony of Rensselaerswijck and Schaenhechtede, in the presence of the honorable lords magistrates of the same court Jan Verbeeck and *Mr*. Jacob de Hinsse, *Mr*. Hendrick Koster, who hereby declares that he hereby cedes, conveys and makes over in true, rightful and free ownership to *Mr*. Robbert Sandersz a portion of a lot of No. 12, located at the hill here in Albany; wide in front on the street fourteen feet and one inch, and in the back twelve feet and three inches Rhineland measure; long three rods eleven feet, which has come to him, grantor, from the lords magistrates, as the same is adjoining and located according to the description in the patent thereof from the right honorable governor general Francis Lovelace, dated the 24th of May *anno* 1669, to which hereby is referred; and this free and unencumbered without any charges standing or issuing against the same, except for the lord's right; without the grantor making the least claim upon the same anymore, acknowledging that he is fully satisfied and paid therefor, the last penny with the first, through the hands of said Robbert Sandersz; giving therefore *plenam actionem cessam* and full power to the aforesaid Robbert Sandersz, his heirs and descendants, or those who may acquire his right and title, to do with and dispose of the same as he might do with his patrimonial estate and effects; promising to **[762]** protect and free the said portion of the lot against all persons from all trouble, claims and charges as is right, and further, nevermore to do nor allow anything to be done against the same, either with or without law, in any manner, under an obligation according to law. Done in Albany the 11th of October 1669.

Hendereck Koster
Jan Verbeeck
J. Dehinsse

In my presence,
Ludovicus Cobes, secretary.

[CONVEYANCE OF SOME PARCELS OF LAND AT THE ESOPUS BY PHILIP PIETERSEN SCHUIJLER TO THOMAS DE LAVALL]

Appeared before me, Ludovicus Cobes, secretary of Albany, colony of Rensselaerswijck and Schaenhechtede, in the presence of the honorable lords magistrates *Mr*. Jan Verbeeck and *Mr*. Rychart van Rensselaer, *Sr*. Philip Pitersen Schuijler, who declared that he hereby cedes, conveys and makes over in true, rightful and free ownership to and for the benefit of my lord Thomas de Lavall, merchant, dwelling at New York, certain parcels of land located in the Esopus, adjoining according to the description in the patent thereof from the right honorable governor general Richard Nicolls, dated the 23rd of April 1667, to which hereby is referred; and this free and unencumbered without any charges standing or issuing against the same, except for the lord's right; without the grantor making the least claim upon the same anymore, acknowledging that he is fully satisfied and paid for the same, the last penny with the first, through the hands of said lord De Lavall; giving therefore *plenam actionem cessam* and full power to the aforesaid mylord De Lavall, his heirs and descendants, or those who hereafter may acquire his right and title, to do with and dispose of the same as he might do with his patrimonial estate and effects; promising to protect and free the said parcels of land against all persons from all trouble, claims and charges as is right, and further, nevermore to do nor allow anything to be done against the same, either with or without law, in any manner, under obligation according to law. Done in Albany the 2nd of November 1669.

Philip Pietersz Schuijler
Jan Verbeeck
R. V. Rensselaer
In my presence,
Ludovicus Cobes, secretary.

[CONVEYANCE OF SOME PARCELS OF LAND AT THE ESOPUS BY GOOSSEN GERRITSZ TO THOMAS DE LAVALL]

[**763**] Appeared before me, Ludovicus Cobes, secretary of Albany, colony of Rensselaerswijck and Schaenhechtede, in the presence of the honorable lords magistrates *Mr*. Jan Verbeeck and *Mr*. Philip Pitersz Schuijler, Goossen Gerritsz, merchant, who declares that he hereby cedes, conveys and makes over in true, rightful and free ownership to Mister Thomas de Laval, merchant, dwelling at New York, certain parcels of land located in the Esopus, adjoining according to the description in the patent thereof from the right honorable governor general Richard Nicolls, dated the 25th of April 1667, to which hereby is referred; and this free and unencumbered without any charges standing or issuing against the same, except for the lord's right; without the grantor making the least claim upon the same anymore, acknowledging that he is fully satisfied and paid for the same, the last penny with the first, through the hands of said lord De Lavall; giving therefore *plenam actionem cessam* and full power to the aforesaid mister De Lavall, his heirs and descendants, or those who may acquire his right and title, to do with and dispose of the same as he might do with his patrimonial estate and effects; promising to protect and free the said parcels of land against all persons from all trouble, claims and charges as is right, and further, nevermore to do nor allow anything to be done against the same, either with or without law, in any manner, under obligation according to law. Done in Albany the 5th of November *anno* 1669.

Note that the above conveyance is made with this reservation: As Goossen Gerritsen has sold the said land to Claes Theunisz for three hundred and fifty schepels of wheat, which purchase begins now, and said Claes Theunisz has to pay the said 350 schepels of grain within the time of four years, each time a fourth part, the first installment next year, and so on, every year until the actual satisfaction; which payment shall be made to the lord De Lavall; and failing to make payment, he, Claes Theunisz, shall be deprived of the purchase of the land. Dated as above.

Goosen Gerretsen
Jan Verbeeck
Philip Pietersz Schuijler

In my presence,
Ludovicus Cobes, secretary.

[CONVEYANCE OF HALF A FARM AND LAND AT THE HALVE MAEN BY GOOSSEN GERRITSEN TO PHILIP PIETERSEN SCHUIJLER]

[**764**] Appeared before me, Ludovicus Cobes, secretary of Albany, colony of Rensselaerswijck and Schaenhechtede, in the presence of the honorable lords magistrates *Monsr*. Rychart van Rensselaer and Jan Verbeeck, *Sr*. Goossen Gerritsz, merchant, dwelling here in Albany, who declares that he hereby cedes, conveys and makes over in true, rightful and free ownership to *Sr*. Philip Pietersen Schuijler, also merchant dwelling here, half of his farm with all appurtenances, both lands as well as cattle and horses, to which he, in company with said *Sr*. Schuijler, lawfully has a right; together with the lands located at Half Moon, set forth in three patents thereof held by said Schuijler, to which hereby is referred; and this free and unencumbered without any charges standing or issuing against the same, except for the lord's right; without the grantor making the least claim upon the same anymore, acknowledging that he is fully satisfied and paid for it by a bill of exchange of fifteen hundred guilders Holland money, through the hands of said *Sr*. Schuijler; giving therefore *plenam actionem cessam* and full power to the aforesaid Philip Schuijler, his heirs and descendants, or those who hereafter may acquire his right and title, to do with and dispose of the same as he might do with his patrimonial estate and effects; promising to protect and free the said half of the farm and its appurtenances against all persons from all trouble, claims and charges as is right, and further, nevermore to do nor allow anything to be done against the same in any manner, either with or without law, under obligation as is provided for it according to law. Done in Albany the 23rd of November, 1669.

Goosen Gerretsen
R. V. Rensselaer
Jan Verbeeck
In my presence,
Ludovicus Cobes, secretary.

[*In the margin was written*:] This conveyance was canceled on this 8th of March 1669.

[ACKNOWLEDGMENT OF DEBT BY PHILIP PIETERSZ SCHUIJLER TO GOOSSEN GERRITSEN]

[**765**] Appeared before me, Ludovicus Cobes, secretary of Albany, colony of Rensselaerswijck and Schaenhechtede, in the presence of the honorable lords magistrates *Mr*. Rychart van Rensselaer and *Mr*. Jan Verbeeck, *Sr*. Philip Pitersz Schuijler, merchant and magistrate of Albany, who acknowledged that he is well and truly indebted and in arrears to *Sr*. Goossen Gerritsen for the sum of fifteen hundred Carolus guilders, to be paid in Holland by bill of exchange in the month of November of the coming year 1670; growing out of the matter of purchase and mortgage money of one half of a farm and lands with their appurtenances, purchased from him by the appearer according to descriptions of three patents thereof; which *f* 1500 Holland money the appearer promises to pay to said *Sr*. Goossen Gerritsz by bill of exchange, according to the purport and tenor hereof, especially pledging there for the said half of the farm and its appurtenances, and further, generally his person and estate, moveable and immoveable, present and future without exception, subject to all laws, to recover, if need be, the payment without cost or damage. Done in Albany the 23rd of November 1669.

Philip Pietersz Schuijler
R. V. Rensselaer
Jan Verbeeck
In my presence,
Ludovicus Cobes, secretary.

[*In the margin was written*:] This mortgage was canceled on this 8th of March 1669.

[ACKNOWLEDGMENT OF DEBT BY JAN JANSZ BLEECKER TO JAN CLUTE]

[**766**] Appeared before me, Ludovicus Cobes, secretary of Albany, colony of Rensselaerswijck and Schaenhechtede, in the presence of the honorable lords magistrates of the same court *Monsr.* Rychart van Rensselaer and *Sr.* Philip Pitersz Schuijler, Jan Jansz Bleecker, burgher and inhabitant here, dwelling in Albany, who acknowledged that he is well and truly indebted and in arrears to *Sr.* Jan Clute for the quantity of eighty-five whole and good merchantable beaver skins figured at *f*8 apiece, growing out of the matter of two remaining installments on the purchase and mortgage money of a certain domicile and lot bought from him by the appearer, according to the bill of sale thereof dated the 5th of January 1669; which said sum of 85 whole beavers the appearer promises to pay according to the purport and contents of the same in two installments, each time half, in the years 1670 and 1671, on the first of July punctually; especially pledging to that end the said house and lot, and further, generally his person and estate, moveable and immoveable, present and future without exception, subject to all laws and judges, to recover, if need be, the payment without cost or damage. Done in Albany the 5th of January 1669.

Jan Jansz Bleecker
R. V. Rensselaer
Philip Pietersz Schuijler
In my presence,
Ludovicus Cobes, secretary.

[CONVEYANCE OF A HOUSE AND LOT BY JURRIAEN JANSZ GROENEWOUT TO JAN CONNEEL]

[**767**] Appeared before me, Ludovicus Cobes, secretary of Albany, colony of Rensselaerswijck and Schaenhechtede, in the presence of the honorable lords magistrates of the same court *Monsr.* Rychart van Rensselaer and *Mr.* Jan Verbeeck, Juriaen Jansz Groenewout, who declares that he hereby cedes, conveys and makes over in true, rightful and free ownership to Jan Conneel, a certain house and lot located here

in Albany with everything that is attached by earth and nail, and in breadth and length as it is lying within its fence; adjoining north of the *dwarshuijs*,† and south of the house of Paulus Martensen provided that the *dwarshuijs* will keep one foot of the lot at the northeast corner, and then, subsequently, straight, and a free drop between him and Paulus Martensz; and this, by virtue of a patent from the right honorable lord general Richard Nicolls, dated the 11th of May 1667, to which is here referred; and this free and unencumbered without any charges standing or issuing against the same, except for the lord's right; without the grantor making the least claim upon the same anymore, acknowledging that he has received a mortgage through the hands of him, Jan Conneel, for the sum of sixty-five beavers, to be paid in two installments; giving therefore *plenam actionem cessam* and full power to the aforesaid Jan Conneel, his heirs and descendants, or those who hereafter may acquire his right and title, to do with and dispose of the same as he might do with his patrimonial estate and effects; promising to protect and free the said house and lot against all persons from all trouble, claims and charges as is right, and further, nevermore to do nor allow anything to be done against the same, either with or without law in any manner, under obligation as provided for it according to law. Done in Albany the 8th of February 1669.

The mark  of Juriaen Jansz Groenewout,
made with his own hand.
R. V. Rensselaer
Jan Verbeeck
In my presence,
Ludovicus Cobes, secretary.

[*In the margin was written*:] Today, the 31st of December 1670 in Albany I, subscriber, acknowledge to have been fully satisfied on account of the mortgage, mentioned alongside.

This is  the mark of Jurian Janse Groenwout made with his own hand. In my presence, Ro: Livingston, secretary.

† A house in the shape of a T with the top on the T running parallel to the street. It can also be a house with the gable ends running perpendicular to the street, thus a T-house without the leg of the T.

[ACKNOWLEDGMENT OF DEBT BY JAN CONNEEL
TO JURIAEN JANSZ GROENEWOUT]

[768] Appeared before me, Ludovicus Cobes, secretary of Albany, colony of Rensselaerswijck and Schaenhechtede, in the presence of the honorable lords magistrates of the same court *Monsr*. Rychart van Rensselaer and *Sr*. Jan Verbeeck, Jan Conneel, burgher here in Albany, who acknowledges that he is well and truly indebted to Juriaen Jansz Groenewout for the quantity of sixty-five whole, good and merchantable beaver skins, growing out of the matter of two remaining installments on the purchase and mortgage money of a certain house and lot bought from him by the appearer; which said sum of sixty-five whole and good merchantable beaver skins the appearer promises to pay in two installments according to the purport and contents of the same, to wit, thirty beavers on the last of July of this coming year 1670, and thirty-five beavers the following year; especially pledging to this end the said house and lot, and further, generally his person and estate, moveable and immoveable, present and future without exception, subject to all laws, to recover, if need be, the payment without cost or damage. Done in Albany the 8th of February 1669.

John Conell
R. V. Rensselaer
Jan Verbeeck
In my presence,
Ludovicus Cobes, secretary.

[CONVEYANCE OF A BARN, HAY BARRACK, GARDEN, AND SOME
LAND AT SCHAENHECHTEDE BY PIETER ADRIAENSEN
TO HELMER OTTEN]

[769] Appeared before me, Ludovicus Cobes, secretary of Albany, colony of Rensselaerswijck and Schaenhechtede, in the presence of the honorable lords magistrates of the same court *Mr*. Abraham Staas and *Mr*. Jan Verbeeck, Pieter Adriaensz, who declared that he hereby cedes, conveys and makes over in true, rightful and free ownership to and for the benefit of Helmer Otten, a barn and a hay barrack, located in

Schaenhechtede, and a garden in an empty lot; together with twenty-six morgens of land and one hundred and sixty-four rods in two allotments bounding and adjoining according to the description in the patent thereof from the right honorable Lord general Nicolls, dated the 5th of June 1667, to which here is referred; and this free and unencumbered without any charges standing or issuing against the same, except for the lord's right; without the grantor making the least claim upon it anymore, acknowledging that he has been fully satisfied and paid for it with a mortgage for the sum of 35 beavers; giving therefore *plenam actionem cessam* and full power to the aforesaid Helmer Otten, his heirs and descendants, or those who hereafter may acquire his right and title, to do with and dispose of the said barn, hay barrack, garden and allotments of land as he might do with his patrimonial estate and effects; promising to protect and free the same against all persons from all trouble, claims and charges as is right, and further, nevermore **[770]** to do nor allow anything to be done against the same, either with or without law in any manner, under obligation as provided for it according to law. Done in Albany the 13th of August 1670.

Pieter Adriaensz
In my presence,
Ludovicus Cobes, secretary.

[CONVEYANCE OF A HOUSE AND LOT BY DOMINE GIDEON SCHAETS TO THOMAS DE LAVAL]

On the date underwritten appeared before me, Ludovicus Cobes, secretary of Albany, colony of Rensselaerswijck and Schaenhechtede, in the presence of the honorable lords magistrates of the same court *Mr.* Abraham Staas and *Mr.* Jan Verbeeck, Domine Gideon Schaets, minister here, who declared that he hereby cedes, conveys and makes over in true, rightful and free ownership to and for the benefit of the honorable lord Thomas de Laval his house and lot located here in Albany at the hill, with everything that is attached by earth and nail; and the lot is wide in front and back twenty-five feet, long on the south side four rods six feet and three inches, on the north side four rods, three feet, three inches; adjoins on the east side Claes van Rotterdam, on the south side Barent Rhijndertsz, smith, on the west and north side the public road and grounds, according to measurement and survey of the surveyors on date the 5th of May 1668, and by virtue of a conveyance granted to him, grantor, to which here is referred; and this free and unencumbered without any charges standing or issuing against the same, except for the lord's right; without the grantor making the least claim upon the same anymore, acknowledging that he is fully satisfied and paid for the same, the first penny with the last; [**771**] giving therefore *plenam actionem cessam* and full power to the aforesaid my lord D. Laval, his heirs and descendants, or those who hereafter may acquire his right and title, to do with and dispose of the said house and lot as he might do with his own patrimonial estate and effects; promising to protect and free the same lot against all persons from all trouble, claims and charges, as is right, and further, nevermore to do nor allow anything to be done against the same, either with or without law, in any manner, under obligation as provided for it according to law. Done in Albany the 17th of August 1670.

This conveyance is made with the restriction that the honorable lord De Laval shall furnish surety and security for the remaining installment to secure, according to the condition of the auction, satisfaction to Domine Schaets or his order.

Gideon Schaets, P[astor] in N. Albany
Abram Staas
Jan Verbeeck
In my presence,
Ludovicus Cobes, secretary.

[CONVEYANCE OF A HOUSE AND LOT BY THOMAS DE LAVAL TO JAN CONEEL]

By virtue of the conveyance by Domine Schaets passed for the benefit of the honorable lord De Laval of a house and lot located at the hill here in Albany, in breadth and length and boundaries according to the purport and contents of the same, my lord Thomas de Laval declares that he hereby cedes, conveys and makes over the same house and lot in true, rightful and free ownership to Jan Coneel, burgher, dwelling here, his heirs and descendants, or his those who may receive title from him; acknowledging that he has been [772] satisfied therefor through the hands of said Jan Conneel with half of the promised purchase money, and with a mortgage for the other half; giving therefore *plenam actionem cessam* and full power to the aforesaid Jan Conneel, or those who hereafter may acquire his right, to do with and dispose of the said house and lot as he might do with his patrimonial estate and effects; promising to protect and free the said lot against all persons from all trouble, claims and charges as is right, and further, nevermore to do nor allow anything to be done against the same, either with or without law in any manner, under obligation as provided for it according to law. Done in Albany the 17th of August 1670.

Tho. DeLavall
Abram Staas
Jan Verbeeck
In my presence,
Ludovicus Cobes, secretary.

[ACKNOWLEDGMENT OF DEBT BY JAN CONNEEL
TO MY LORD DE LAVAL]

Appeared before me, Ludovicus Cobes, secretary of Albany, colony of Rensselaerswijck and Schaenhechtede, in the presence of the honorable lords magistrates of the same court the *Mr*. Jan Verbeeck and *Mr*. Abraham Staas, Jan Conneel, burgher here, who acknowledged that he is well and truly indebted to the honorable lord de Laval, for the sum of *f*207 in whole, good and merchantable beaver skins stemming from the remaining installment of purchase and mortgage money for a certain house and lot bought by him, appearer from him, according to the [773] purport and contents of the conditions and stipulations thereof; which said sum of *f*207 in whole, good and merchantable beaver skins the appearer promises to pay on the set day of payment; especially pledging for this purpose the said house and lot, and generally his person and estate, moveable and immoveable without exception, submitting the same to the lord's laws and justices, to recover (if necessary), the payment without cost or damage. Done in Albany the 17th of August 1670.

John Conele
Abram Staas
Jan Verbeeck
In my presence,
Ludovicus Cobes, secretary.

[CONVEYANCE OF A SHED AND A LOT BY JAN CONNEEL TO JOHN STUART]

On the date written below appeared before me, Ludovicus Cobes, secretary of Albany, colony of Rensselaerswijck and Schaenhechtede, in the presence of the honorable lords magistrates of the same court *Mr.* Jan Verbeeck and *Mr.* Abraham Staas, Jan Conneel, who declared that he hereby cedes, conveys and makes over in true, rightful and free ownership to and for the benefit of *Mr.* John Stuart a shed with its lot, located at the hill between Evert Jansz and Wijnant Gerritsen; and the lot is wide 12 feet 7½ inches Rhineland measure, and long backward six rods and five feet; free and unencumbered without any charges standing or issuing against the same, except for the lord's right; without the grantor making **[774]** the least claim upon the same anymore, acknowledging that he is fully satisfied and paid for the same, the first penny with the last through the hands of said Stuart; giving therefore *plenam actionem cessam* and full power to *Mr.* Stuart, his heirs and descendants, or those who hereafter may acquire his right and title, to do with and dispose of the said shed and lot as he might do with his patrimonial estate and effects; promising to protect and free the same against all persons from all trouble, claims and charges as is right, and further, nevermore to do nor allow anything to be done against the same, either with or without law, in any manner, under obligation as provided for it according to law. Done in Albany the 20th of August 1670.

John Conell
Abram Staas
Jan Verbeeck

In my presence,
Ludovicus Cobes, secretary.

[CONVEYANCE OF LAND CALLED *STEENICH ARABIEN* BY HERMAN VEDDER TO ROBBERT SANDERSZ]

[775] Appeared before me, Ludovicus Cobes, secretary of Albany, colony of Rensselaerswijck and Schaenhechtede, in the presence of the honorable lords magistrates of the same court *Mr*. Jan Verbeeck and *Mr*. Abraham Staas, Herman Vedder, who declared that he hereby cedes, conveys and makes over in true, rightful and free ownership to and for the benefit of Robbert Sandersz half of the land named *Steenich Arabien* [Stony Arabia], with all his rights thereto; and this free and unencumbered without any charges standing or issuing against the same, except for the lord's right; without the grantor making the least claim upon the same anymore, acknowledging that he is fully satisfied and paid for the same, the first penny with the last, through the hands of Robbert Sandersz; giving therefore *plenam actionem cessam* and full power to said Robbert Sandersz, his heirs and descendants, or those who hereafter may acquire his right and title, to do with and dispose of the said land, or portion, as he might do with his patrimonial estate and effects; promising to protect and free the same against all persons from all trouble, claims and charges as is right, and further, nevermore to do nor allow anything to be done against the same, either with or without law, in any manner, under obligation as provided for it according to law. Done in Albany the 21st of August 1670.

Harmen Vedder
Abram Staas
Jan Verbeeck
In my presence,
Ludovicus Cobes, secretary.

[CONVEYANCE OF LAND BY JURRIAEN THEUNISZ TO ABRAHAM STAAS AND JOHANNES PROVOOST]

[**776**] Appeared before me, Ludovicus Cobes, secretary of Albany, colony of Rensselaerswijck and Schaenhechtede, in the presence of the honorable lords magistrates of the same court *Mr*. Jan Verbeeck and *Mr*. Philip Pietersz Schuijler, *Mr*. Jurriaen Theunisz Tappen, who declared that he hereby cedes, conveys and makes over in true, rightful and free ownership to and for the benefit of *Mr*. Abraham Staas and *Mr*. Johannes Provoost his just third portion of land, belonging to him in partnership with Jan Bruijns and Jan Clute, with the barn and the rights that he has to it, according to the bill of sale thereof and by virtue of a patent thereof granted by the right honorable lord general Nicolls, in the custody of Jan Bruijns, to which hereby is referred; and this free and unencumbered without any charges standing or issuing against the same, except for the lord's right; without the grantor making the least claim upon the same anymore, acknowledging that he is fully satisfied and paid for the same, the first penny with the last through the hands of the said *Mr*. Abraham Staes and Johannes Provoost; giving therefore *plenam actionem cessam* and full power to the said *Mr*. Abraham Staas and Johannes Provoost, their heirs and descendants, or those who hereafter may acquire their right and title, to do with and dispose of the said third portion of land, barn and appurtenances of the same, as they might do with their patrimonial [**777**] estate and effects; promising to protect and free the said third portion of the land, barn and its appurtenances against all persons from all trouble, claims and charges as is right, and further, nevermore to do nor allow anything to be done against the same, either with or without law, in any manner, under obligation as provided for it according to law. Done in Albany the 24th of August 1670.

Jure Jan Tunsen
Jan Verbeeck
Philip Pietersz Schuijler
In my presence,
Ludovicus Cobes, secretary.

[CONVEYANCE OF A HOUSE, BARN, THREE HAY BARRACKS, GARDEN AND LAND AT SCHAENHECHTEDE BY CORNELIS CORNELISZ VIELE TO JURRIAEN THEUNISZ]

Appeared before me, Ludovicus Cobes, secretary of Albany, colony of Rensselaerswijck and Schaenhechtede, in the presence of the honorable lords magistrates of the same court *Mr*. Jan Verbeeck and *Mr*. Abraham Staes, Cornelis Cornelisz Viele, who declared that he hereby cedes, conveys and makes over in true, rightful and free ownership to and for the benefit of Jurriaen Theunisz a house and a barn with two hay barracks, and another on the land, with a garden behind the house; together with twelve morgens and one hundred and thirty rods of land located at Schaenhechtede, being no. 9, bounding and adjoining according to the description in the patent thereof, to which here is referred; and this free and unencumbered without any charges standing or issuing against the same, except for the lord's right; without him, grantor, making the least claim upon the same anymore, acknowledging that he is [778] fully satisfied and paid for the same, the first penny with the last through the hands of the said Juriaen Theunisz; giving therefore *plenam actionem cessam* and full power to said Jurriaen Theunisz, his heirs and descendants, or those who hereafter may acquire his right and title, to do with and dispose of the said house, lot, garden, hay barracks and land as he might do with his patrimonial estates and effects; promising to protect and free the same against all persons from all trouble, claims and charges as is right, and further, nevermore to do nor allow anything to be done against the same, either with or without law, in any manner, under obligation as provided for it according to law. Done in Albany the 25th of August 1670.

Cornelis Cornelissen Viele
Abram Staas
Jan Verbeeck
In my presence,
Ludovicus Cobes, secretary.

[CONVEYANCE OF A HOUSE AND LOT BY JURRIAEN THEUNISZ TAPPEN TO CORNELIS CORNELISZ VIELE]

Appeared before me, Ludovicus Cobes, secretary of Albany, colony of Rensselaerswijck and Schaenhechtede, in the presence of the honorable lords magistrates of the same court *Mr*. Jan Verbeeck and *Mr*. Abraham Staes, Jurriaen Theunisz Tappen, who declared that he hereby cedes, conveys and makes over in true, rightful and free ownership to and for the benefit of Cornelis Cornelisz Viele a house and lot located here in Albany on the south side of Pieter Hartgras, to the west the First Kil, on the north side the large street; in breadth in front on the street one rod, three feet and eleven inches, and in the rear on the kil one rod, one foot and four inches, long on the east side five rods, one foot and ten inches, on the west side five rods, five feet and two inches, Rhineland measure; by **[779]** virtue of the patent thereof from the right honorable lord general Nicolls, dated the 2nd of May 1668, to which hereby is referred; and this free and unencumbered without any charges standing or issuing against the same, except for the lord's right; without him, grantor, making the least claim upon the same anymore, acknowledging that he is fully satisfied and paid for the same, the first penny with the last; giving therefore *plenam actionem cessam* and full power to said Cornelis Cornelisz Viele, his heirs and descendants, or those who hereafter may acquire his right and title, to do with and dispose of the said house and lot as he might do with his other patrimonial estates and effects; promising to protect and free the same against all persons from all trouble, claims and charges as is right, and further, nevermore to do nor allow anything to be done against the same, either with or without law, in any manner, under obligation as provided for it according to law. Done in Albany the 26th of August 1670.

Jure Jan Tunsen
Abram Staas
Jan Verbeeck
In my presence,
Ludovicus Cobes, secretary.

[CONVEYANCE OF A GARDEN BY CAPT. THOMAS WILLET TO JAN BIJVANCK]

[**780**] Appeared before me, Ludovicus Cobes, secretary of Albany, colony of Rensselaerswijck and Schaenhechtede, in the presence of the honorable lords magistrates of the same court *Mr*. Rijckart van Rensselaer and *Mr*. Jan Verbeeck, Capt. Thomas Willet, merchant, who declared that he hereby cedes, conveys and makes over in true, rightful and free ownership to and for the benefit of Jan Bijvanck a garden located behind Fort Albany, before this belonging to Gerrit de Kuijper, and this as it presently lies in fence, between the garden of Jan Hermensz *backer* and Pieter Jacobsz Borsboom; and this free and unencumbered without any charges standing or issuing against the same, except for the lord's right; without him, grantor, making the least claim upon the same anymore, acknowledging that he is fully satisfied and paid for the same, the first penny with the last through the hands of Jan Bijvanck; giving therefore *plenam actionem cessam* and full power to said Jan Bijvanck, his heirs and descendants, or those who hereafter may acquire his right and title, to do with and dispose of the said garden as he might do with his patrimonial estates and effects; promising to protect and free the same against all persons from all trouble, claims and charges as is right, and further, nevermore to do nor allow anything to be done against the same, either with or without law, in any manner, under obligation as provided for it according to law. Done in Albany the 29th of August 1670.

Tho. Willet
Jan Verbeeck
R. V. Rensselaer
In my presence,
Ludovicus Cobes, secretary.

[ACKNOWLEDGMENT OF DEBT BY BARENT ALBERTSZ BRAT TO DANIEL HONDECOUTRE]

[**781**] Appeared before me, Ludovicus Cobes, secretary of Albany, colony of Rensselaerswijck and Schaenhechtede, in the presence of the

honorable lords magistrates of the same court *Mr*. Abraham Staes and *Mr*. Jan Verbeeck, Barent Aelbersz Brat, burgher here, who acknowledged that he is well and truly indebted and in arrears to *Sr*. Daniel Hondecoutre, for the sum of three hundred and seventy-eight guilders and nine stuivers in beavers, for merchandise received to his full content; which said *f*378–9 the appearer promises to pay to *Sr*. Hondecoutre or his order in good whole merchantable beaver skins figured at *f*8 apiece, in the month of June of the coming year 1671, and that with its interest at eight percent, but if he pays half of it he shall be free of interest; especially pledging there for his house and lot located here in Albany next to the house of Hendrick Bries, and moreover, generally his person and estate, moveable and immoveable, present and future, without exception, to recover (if need be), the payment in due time without cost or damage. Done in Albany the 6th of September 1670.

The mark of Barent  Aelbertsz Brat, made with his own hand

Abram Staas
Jan Verbeeck
In my presence,
Ludovicus Cobes, secretary.

[CONVEYANCE OF LAND AT COXSACKIE BY JAN CLUTE, JURRIAEN THEUNISZ AND MEIJNDERT FREDERICKSZ TO MARTEN GERRITSZ]

[**782**] Appeared before me, Ludovicus Cobes, secretary of Albany, colony of Rensselaerswijck and Schaenhechtede, in the presence of the honorable lords magistrates of the same court *Mr*. Jan Verbeeck and *Sr*. Philip Pietersz Schuijler, *Mr*. Jan Clute, Jurriaen Theunisz and Meijndert Fredericksz, who declared that they hereby cede, convey and make over in true, rightful and free ownership to and for the benefit of Marten Gerritsz a certain parcel of land located at Coxhaxki, adjoining to the south of the land of Hilleken Broncx and beginning at the Stone Kil south extending along the Catskil path as far as the fountain or the mountain, Stijffsinck, and east toward the river, and north again as far as the land of said Hilleken Broncx. [*canceled*]

[CONVEYANCE OF A HOUSE, LOT AND GARDEN BY JAN BRUIJNS TO HELMER OTTEN]

[**783**] On the date underwritten there appeared before me, Ludovicus Cobes, secretary of Albany, colony of Rensselaerswijck and Schaenhechtede, in the presence of the honorable lords magistrates of the same court *Mr*. Philip Schuijler and *Mr*. Jan van Bael, *Sr*. Jan Bruijns, who declared that he hereby cedes, conveys and makes over in true, rightful and free ownership to and for the benefit of *Mr*. Helmer Otten a certain domicile, lot and garden, presently occupied by Pieter Adriaensz, as the same is built upon, fenced and bounded, standing and located here in Albany; adjoins according to the purport and contents of the bill of sale, and further evidences to which here is referred; and this free and unencumbered without any charges standing or issuing against the same, except for the lord's right; without the grantor making the least claim upon the same anymore, acknowledging that he is fully satisfied and paid for the same with a promissory note and a mortgage through the hands of said Helmer Otten; giving therefore *plenam actionem cessam* and full power to said Helmer Otten, his heirs and descendants, or those who hereafter may acquire his right and title, to do with and dispose of the said house, lot and garden as he might do with his patrimonial estates and effects; promising to protect and free the same against all persons from all trouble, claims and charges as is right, and further, nevermore to do nor allow anything to be done against the same, either with or without law, in any manner, under obligation as provided for it according to law provided therefor. Done in Albany the 8th of October 1670.

Jan Henderck Bruijns
Philip Pietersz Schuijler
Jan Hendr. van Bael

In my presence,
Ludovicus Cobes, secretary.

[ACKNOWLEDGMENT OF DEBT BY HELMER OTTEN TO JAN BRUIJNS]

[**784**] Appeared before me, Ludovicus Cobes, secretary of Albany, colony of Rensselaerswijck and Schaenhechtede, in the presence of the witnesses mentioned hereafter *Mr*. Helmer Otten, who acknowledged that he is well and truly indebted and in arrears to *Sr*. Jan Bruijns for the quantity of one hundred whole good and merchantable beaver skins growing out of the purchase of a house, lot and garden, which said one hundred beavers the appearer promises to pay to said *Sr*. Bruijns, or the lawful bearer of this in this month of June 1671, and that with its proper interest at ten percent; pledging thereto his person and estate, moveable and immoveable, present and future, without exception, submitting the same to all the lord's laws and judges. In witness of the truth this was signed with his own hand on this 8th of October 1670 in Albany.

Helmerin Otten
In my presence,
Ludovicus Cobes, secretary.

Today, the 1st of April 1687, Reyer Jacobse Shermerhoorn has appeared before the secretary with an authentic copy of the said promissory note, and on the back of the same was written by Jan Hendr. Bruijns, Albany, the 22nd of July 1679, I acknowledge that I have received full satisfaction for this promissory note on the above date.

Was signed, Jan Hendrick Bruijns.
Quod attestor,
Robt. Livingston

[CONVEYANCE OF A HOUSE, LOT AND GARDEN BY HELMER OTTEN TO PIETER ADRIAENSZ]

[**785**] On the underwritten date there appeared before me, Ludovicus Cobes, secretary of Albany, colony of Rensselaerswijck and Schaenhechtede, in the presence of the honorable lords magistrates of the same court, *Mr*. Philip Schuijler and *Mr*. Jan Hendricxsz van Bael,

Helmer Otten, who declared that he hereby cedes, conveys and makes over in true, rightful and free ownership to and for the benefit of Pieter Adriaensz a certain domicile, lot and garden, as the same is built upon, fenced and bounded, standing and located here in Albany, which came to him, grantor, from Jan Bruijns; bounded according to the purport and contents of the bill of sale, and further evidences thereof to which here is referred; and this free and unencumbered without any charges standing or issuing against the same, except for the lord's right; without him, grantor, making the least claim upon the same anymore, acknowledging that he is fully satisfied and paid for the same, the first penny with the last through the hands of said Pieter Adriaensz; giving therefore *plenam actionem cessam* and full power to said Pieter Adriaensz, his heirs and descendants, or those who hereafter may acquire his right and title, to do with and dispose of the said house, lot and garden as he might do with his patrimonial estate and effects; promising to protect and free the same against all persons from all trouble, claims and charges as is right, and further, nevermore to do nor allow anything to be done against the same, either with or without law, in any manner, under obligation as provided for it according to law. Done in Albany the 12th of October 1670.

Helmerin Otten
Philip Pietersz Schuijler
Jan Hendr. van Bael
In my presence,
Ludovicus Cobes, secretary

[ACKNOWLEDGMENT OF DEBT BY HELMERICH OTTEN TO PIETER ADRIAENSZ]

[786] Appeared before me, Ludovicus Cobes, secretary of Albany, colony of Rensselaerswijck and Schaenechtede, in the presence of the witnesses mentioned hereafter Helmerich Otten, who acknowledged that he is well and truly indebted to Pieter Adriaensz, for the quantity of thirty-five whole good and merchantable beaver skins for the matter of exchange and extra gift on the house and lot conveyed to him today; which 35 beavers the appearer promises to pay to Piter Adriaensz, or his order on the date of expiration according to purport of the bill of sale;

pledging there for his person and estate, moveable and immoveable, present and future, without exception, submitting the same to all the lord's laws and judges. In witness of the truth this was signed with his own hand in the presence of *Mr.* Philip Schuijler as witness invited hereto on this 12th of October 1670 in Albany.

Helm Otten
Philip Pietersz Schuijler
In my presence,
Ludovicus Cobes, secretary.

[ACKNOWLEDGMENT OF DEBT BY CLAES BEVER TO JAN CORNELISZ ROOT]

[**787**] On the date underwritten there appeared before me, Ludovicus Cobes, secretary of Albany, colony of Rensselaerswijck and Schaenhechtede, in the presence of the honorable lords magistrates of the same court *Mr.* Philip Pietersz Schuijler and *Mr.* Jan van Bael, Claes Beever dwelling behind *Kinderhoeck*, who acknowledged that he is well and truly indebted and in arrears to Jan Cornelisz Root for the sum of one hundred and sixty guilders in good sewant and ten schepels of good winter wheat for the matter of a cow and a filly received by the appearer to his content; which said *ƒ*160 sewant and 10 schepels of wheat the appearer promises to pay to Jan Cornelis Root, or his order within the time of two months; especially pledging to this end the said cow and filly and generally his person and estate, moveable and immoveable, present and future, without exception, to recover, if necessary, the payment in due time without cost and damage; submitting the same to all the lord's laws and judges. Done in Albany the 15th of November 1670.

Claes Bever
Philip Pietersz Schuijler
Jan Hendricksz van Bael
In my presence,
Ludovicus Cobes, secretary.

[CONVEYANCE OF A LOT BY BASTIAEN DE WINTER
TO JAN LABATIE]

[788] On the date underwritten there appeared before me, Ludovicus Cobes, secretary of Albany, colony of Rensselaerswijck and Schaenhechtede, in the presence of the honorable lords magistrates of the same court *Mr*. Philip Schuijler and *Mr*. Jan Hendricxsz van Bael, Bastiaen de Winter, who declared that he hereby cedes, conveys and makes over in true, rightful and free ownership to and for the benefit of Jan Labatie a lot wide one hundred feet, or four or 5 feet more ground, as will appear by a just survey, located at Schaenhechtede; adjoins on the east side Pieter Olinda, on the south side Theunis Cornelisz, on the north side Joris Arisz, and on the west side the public road; by virtue of a patent thereof from the right honorable lord general Francis Lovelace, dated the 21st of October 1670, to which hereby is referred; and this free and unencumbered without any charges standing or issuing against the same, except for the lord's right; without the grantor making the least claim upon the same anymore, acknowledging that he is fully satisfied and paid for the same, the first penny with the last through the hands of said Labatie; giving therefore *plenam actionem cessam* and full power to said Jan Labatie, his heirs and descendants, to do with and dispose of the said lot as he might do with his patrimonial estate and effects; promising to protect and free the same against all persons from all trouble, claims and charges as is right, and further, nevermore to do nor allow anything to be done against the same, either with or without law, in any manner, under obligation as provided for it according to law. Done in Albany the 21st of November 1670.

Bastiaen de Winter
Philip Pietersz Schuijler
Jan Hendr. van Bael

In my presence,
Ludovicus Cobes, secretary.

[CONVEYANCE OF A PLANTATION BY BASTIAEN DE WINTER TO ELIAS VAN GIJSELINGEN AND PIETER CORNELISZ VIELE]

[**789**] Appeared before me, Ludovicus Cobes, secretary of Albany, colony of Rensselaerswijck and Schaenhechtede, in the presence of the honorable lords magistrates of the same court *Mr.* Philip Pietersz Schuijler and *Mr.* Jan van Bael, Bastiaen de Winter, who declared that he hereby cedes, conveys and makes over in true, rightful and free ownership to and for the benefit of Elias Gijselingh and Pieter Cornelisz Viele, a certain plantation located at Schaenhechtede, in width on the west side 350 rods and long on the north side 60 rods, located near the land of Willem Teller and Maritie Damen; by virtue of a patent thereof from the right honorable lord general Francis Lovelace, dated the 21st of October 1670, to which hereby is referred; and this free and unencumbered without any charges standing or issuing against the same, except for the lord's right; without the grantor making the least claim upon the same anymore, acknowledging that he is fully satisfied and paid for the same, the first penny with the last, through the hands of said Elias Gijselingh and Pieter Cornelisz Viele; giving therefore *plenam actionem cessam* and full power to said Elias Gijselingh and Pieter Cornelisz Viele, to do with and dispose of the said plantation as they might do with their patrimonial estates and effects; promising to protect and free the said plantation against all persons from all trouble, claims and charges as is right, and further, nevermore to do nor allow anything to be done against the same, either with or without law, in any manner, under obligation as provided for it according to law. Done in Albany the 22nd of November 1670.

Basteiaen de Winter
Philip Pietersz Schuijler
Jan Hend. van Bael

In my presence,
Ludovicus Cobes, secretary.

[CONVEYANCE OF A CELLAR DWELLING, HAY BARRACK BARN, AND LOT BY BASTIAEN DE WINTER TO JORISZ ARISZ]

[790] On the date underwritten there appeared before me, Ludovicus Cobes, secretary of Albany, colony of Rensselaerswijck and Schaenhechtede, in the presence of the honorable lords magistrates of the same court *Mr.* Philip Pietersz Schuijler and *Mr.* Jan van Bael, Bastiaen de Winter, who declared that he hereby cedes, conveys and makes over in true, rightful and free ownership to and for the benefit of Joris Arisz a cellar dwelling, hay barrack barn, and a lot, located at Schaenhechtede, the lot being wide one hundred feet and long two hundred feet; by virtue of a patent thereof from the right honorable lord general Lovelace, dated the 21st of October 1670, to which hereby is referred; and this free and unencumbered without any charges standing or issuing against the same, except for the lord's right; without the grantor making the least claim upon the same anymore, acknowledging that he is fully satisfied and paid for the same, the first penny with the last, through the hands of said Joris Arisz; giving therefore *plenam actionem cessam* and full power to said Joris Arisz, his heirs or descendants or those who hereafter may acquire his right and title, to do with and dispose of the said cellar dwelling, *schuerberch*, and lot as he might do with his patrimonial estates and effects; promising to protect and free the same against all persons from all trouble, claims and charges as is right, and further, nevermore to do nor allow anything to be done against the same, either with or without law, in any manner, under obligation as provided for it according to law. Done in Albany the 22nd of November 1670.

Basteiaen de Winter
Philip Pietersz Schuijler
Jan Hend. van Bael

In my presence,
Ludovicus Cobes, secretary.

[CONVEYANCE OF A GARDEN BY BASTIAEN DE WINTER TO GERRIT CLAESZ KULEMAN]

[791] On the date underwritten there appeared before me, Ludovicus Cobes, secretary of Albany, colony of Rensselaerswijck and Schaenhechtede, in the presence of the honorable lords magistrates of the same court *Mr.* Philip Pietersz Schuijler and *Mr.* Jan van Bael, Bastiaen de Winter, who declared that he hereby cedes, conveys and makes over in true, rightful and free ownership to and for the benefit of Gerrit Claesz Kuleman, a garden, located at Schaenhechtede, in length, width and boundaries according to purport and contents of the patent thereof to which hereby is referred; and this free and unencumbered without any charges standing or issuing against the same, except for the lord's right; without the grantor making the least claim upon the same anymore, acknowledging that he is fully satisfied and paid for it, the first penny with the last; giving therefore *plenam actionem cessam* and full power to the said Gerrit Claesz, his heirs or descendants or those who hereafter may acquire his right and title, to do with and dispose of the said garden, as he might do with his patrimonial estate and effects; promising to protect and free the same against all persons from all trouble, claims and charges as is right, and further, nevermore to do nor allow anything to be done against the same, either with or without law, in any manner, under obligation as provided for it according to law. Done in Albany the 24th of November 1670.

Basteiaen de Winter
Philip Pietersz Schuijler
Jan Hend. van Bael
In my presence,
Ludovicus Cobes, secretary.

[CONVEYANCE OF A PARCEL OF LAND BY VOLCKERT JANSZ AND JAN THOMASZ TO JAN LAURENSZ]

[792] On the date underwritten there appeared before me, Ludovicus Cobes, secretary of Albany, colony of Rensselaerswijck and Schaenhechtede, in the presence of the honorable lords magistrates of the same court, *Mr*. Philip Pietersz Schuijler and *Mr*. Jan Hendricksz van Bael, the honorable Volckert Jansz and Jan Thomasz, who declared that they hereby cede, convey and make over in true, rightful and free ownership to and for the benefit of Jan Laurensz a certain parcel of land or plantation as the same is lying within its fence, and was formerly used by Adriaen Dirricxsz de Vries, located on the mainland at Schotack with another strip outside of the fence, which was planted by the Indians before; and this free and unencumbered without any charges standing or issuing against the same, except for the lord's right; without the grantors making the least claim upon the same anymore, acknowledging that they are fully satisfied and paid for it, the first penny with the last; giving therefore *plenam actionem cessam* and full power to said Jan Laurensz, his heirs or descendants, or those who hereafter may acquire his right and title, to do with and dispose of the said land, as he might do with his patrimonial estate and effects; promising to protect and free the same against all persons from all trouble, claims and charges as is right, and further, nevermore to do nor allow anything to be done against the same, either with or without law, in any manner, under obligation as provided for it according to law. Done in Albany the 29th of December 1670.

Volckart Jansz
Jan Thomasz
Philip Pietersz Schuijler
Jan Hend. van Bael
In my presence,
Ludovicus Cobes, secretary.

[CONVEYANCE OF A LOT BY WILLIAM PARKER TO DIRCK AELBERTSZ BRATT]

[793] On the date underwritten there appeared before me, Ludovicus Cobes, secretary of Albany, colony of Rensselaerswijck and Schaenhechtede, in the presence of the honorable lords magistrates of the same court, *Mr*. Philip Pietersz Schuijler and Jan Hendricxsz van Bael, the honorable Sergeant William Parker, who declared that he hereby cedes, conveys and makes over in true, rightful and free

ownership to and for the benefit of Dirck Aelbertsz Bratt his certain lot located at the hill north of Rijck Claesz, in width 20 feet and long four rods; by virtue of a patent thereof dated the 2nd of June 1669, to which hereby is referred; and this free and unencumbered without any charges standing or issuing against the same, except for the lord's right; without the grantor making the least claim upon the same anymore, acknowledging that he is fully satisfied and paid for the same, the first penny with the last; giving therefore *plenam actionem cessam* and full power to said Dirck Aelbertsz, his heirs or descendants, or those who hereafter may acquire his right and title, to do with and dispose of the said land, as he might do with his patrimonial estate and effects; promising to protect and free the same against all persons from all trouble, claims and charges as is right, and further, nevermore to do nor allow anything to be done against the same, either with or without law, in any manner, under an obligation as is provided for it according to law. Done in Albany the 11th of February 1670/71.

Wm. Parker
Philip Pietersz Schuijler
Jan Hend. van Bael
In my presence,
Ludovicus Cobes, secretary.

[ACKNOWLEDGMENT OF DEBT BY DERCKIE HERMSZ, ATTORNEY FOR JAN MARTENSZ, TO GOOSSEN GERRITSZ]

[794] On the date underwritten there appeared before me, Ludovicus Cobes, secretary of Albany, colony of Rensselaerswijck and Schaenhechtede, in the presence of the honorable lords magistrates of the same court *Sr.* Philip Pietersz Schuijler and Theunis Cornelisz vander Poel, Derckie Hermsz, attorney for her husband Jan Martensz, who acknowledged that she is well and truly indebted and in arrears to *Sr.* Goossen Gerritsz for the sum of three hundred and eighteen guilders in good whole and merchantable beaver skins for the matter of wares and merchandise received by her to her full content; which said *f*318 in beavers she, appearer, promises to pay to said Goossen Gerritsen in the following manner: first, 25 schepels of winter wheat in this coming spring, or other wares at market and beaver price, and the remainder in three successive years, also in wheat and grains, and wares at beaver and market price; especially pledging there for her house, barn, hay barracks, cultivated and uncultivated land behind Kinderhoeck, together with all her horses and cattle, and generally her person and estate, moveable and immoveable, present and future, without exception, submitting the same to all the lord's laws and judges. Signed with own their hands in witness of the truth on the 21st of February 1670/71 in Albany.

The + mark of Jan Martensz, made with his own hand.
Derckien Hermens
Philip Pietersz Schuijler
Teunis Cornelisz
In my presence,
Ludovicus Cobes, secretary.

[CONVEYANCE OF A PIECE OF PASTURE LAND AT SCHAENHECHTEDE BY SYMON VOLCKERTSZ TO JORIS AERTSZ]

[795] On the date underwritten there appeared before me, Ludovicus Cobes, secretary of Albany, colony of Rensselaerswijck and Schaenhechtede, in the presence of the honorable lords magistrates of the same court *Mr.* Philip Pietersz Schuijler and Theunis Cornelisz vander Poel, Symon Volckerts, farmer, dwelling at Schaenhechtede, who declared that he hereby cedes, conveys and makes over in true, rightful and free ownership to and for the benefit of Joris Arisz, his certain piece of pasture located at Schaenhechtede, in length 75 rods, adjoins on the east Gerrit Bancken, on the north side the river, wide 15 rods, on the west side the common pasture, and on the east side the common woods' road; and this free and unencumbered without any charges standing or issuing against the same, except for the lord's right; without the grantor making the least claim upon the same anymore, acknowledging that he is fully satisfied and paid for the same, the first penny with the last, through the hands of the said Joris Arisz; giving therefore *plenam actionem cessam* and full power to said Arisz, his

heirs or descendants, or those who hereafter may acquire his right and title, to do with and dispose of the same as he might do with his patrimonial estate and effects; promising to protect and free the same against all persons from all trouble, claims and charges as is right, and further, nevermore to do nor allow anything to be done against the same, either with or without law, in any manner, under obligation as provided for it according to law. Done in Albany the 27th of February 1670/71.

The mark of  Symon Volckerts, made with his own hand.
Philip Pietersz
Theunis Cornelisz
In my presence,
Ludovicus Cobes, secretary.

[ACKNOWLEDGMENT OF DEBT BY DIRCK HESSELINGH TO JURRIAEN THEUNISZ TAPPEN]

[796] On the date underwritten there appeared before me, Ludovicus Cobes, secretary of Albany, colony of Rensselaerswijck and Schaenhechtede, in the presence of the honorable lords magistrates of the same court Theunis Cornelisz vander Poel and Pieter Meeusz Vroman, Dirck Hesselingh, who acknowledged that he is well and truly indebted to Jurriaen Theunisz Tappen for the quantity of one hundred and five good whole and merchantable beaver skins according to the conditions thereof passed on date the 21st of March, and this for the matter of a farm, house, barn, and hay barracks, located at Schaenhechtede, used and received to his content; which said 105 beavers the appearer promises to pay at the stipulated time, especially pledging there for his house and lot located here in Albany, and the aforesaid land, or farm with house, barn and hay barracks, and generally his person and estate, moveable and immoveable, present and future, to recover, if need be, the payment without cost and damage. Done in Albany the 21st of March 1670/1.

Dirck Hesselingh
Teunis Cornelissen
Pieter Meesz Vrooman

In my presence,
Ludovicus Cobes, secretary.

Jurriaen Theunisz acknowledges that he is well satisfied for this special mortgage. Albany, the 21st of October *anno* 1672.

Jure Jan Tunsen

[CONVEYANCE OF A HOUSE, BARN, HAY BARRACK, AND BUILDINGS AT *GREENEN BOSCH* BY JAN TIMMEL TO THEUNIS DIRRICX]

[797] On the underwritten date there appeared before me, Ludovicus Cobes, secretary of Albany, colony of Rensselaerswijck and Schaenhechtede, in the presence of the honorable lords magistrates of the same court *Srs*. Goossen Gerritsen and Jan Hendricx van Bael, Jan Timmel, who declared that he hereby cedes, conveys and makes over in true, rightful and free ownership to and for the benefit of Theunis Dirricx, his house, barn and hay barrack, and buildings standing in the *Greenen Bosch,* formerly belonging to Thomas Koningh, except for some boards, according to the conditions agreed on; and this free and unencumbered without any charges standing or issuing against the same, except for the right of the lord patroon of the colony; without him, grantor, making the least claim upon the same anymore, acknowledging that he is fully satisfied and paid for the same, the first penny with the last, through the hands of the said Theunis Dirricx; giving therefore *plenam actionem cessam* and full power to said Theunis Dirricx, his heirs or descendants, or those who hereafter may acquire his right and title, to do with and dispose of the said house, barn, hay barrack, and other buildings, as he might do with his patrimonial estate and effects; promising to protect and free the same against all persons from all trouble, claims and charges as is right, and further, nevermore to do nor allow anything to be done against the same, either with or without law, in any manner, [798] under obligation as provided for it according to law. Done in Albany the 30th of March 1670.

The mark of Jan  Timmel, made with his own hand.

Jan Hend. van Bael
Goosen Gerretsen
In my presence,
Ludovicus Cobes, secretary.

[CONVEYANCE OF A PARCEL OF LAND AT COXSACKIE BY JAN CLUTE, JURIAEN THEUNISZ AND MEIJNDERT FREDERICXSZ TO MARTTEN GERRITSZ]

On the date underwritten there appeared before me, Ludovicus Cobes, secretary of Albany, colony of Rensselaerswijck and Schaenhechtede, in the presence of the honorable lords magistrates of the same court *Sr*. Philip Pietersz Schuijler and Jan Hendricxsz van Bael, *Mr*. Jan Clute, Juriaen Theunisz, and Meijndert Fredericxsz, who declared that they hereby cede, convey and make over in true, rightful and free ownership to and for the benefit of Martten Gerretsz, a certain parcel of land located at Koxhaxki, adjoining to the south of the land of Hilleken Bronck, and beginning at the Stone Kil, extending south along the Catskil path as far as the fountain, or the mountain, *Stijffsinck*, and east toward the river, and north again as far as the land of Hilleken Bronck; and that by virtue of the patent thereof, to which here is referred; and this free and unencumbered, without any charges standing or issuing against the same, except for the lord's right; without them, grantors, making the least claim upon the same anymore, acknowledging that they are fully satisfied and paid for the same, the first penny with the last; giving therefore *plenam actionem cessam* and full **[799]** power to said Martten Gerritsz, his heirs or descendants, or those who hereafter may acquire his right and title, to do with and dispose of the said parcel of land, as he might do with his patrimonial estate and effects; promising to protect and free the same against all persons from all trouble, claims and charges as is right, and further, nevermore to do nor allow anything to be done against the same, either with or without law, in any manner, under obligation as is provided for it according to law. Done in Albany the 26th of April 1671.

Johanesz Clute
Jure Jan Tunsen

The mark of Meijndert  Fredericxsz, made with his own hand.
Philip Pietersz
Jan Hend. Van Bael
In my presence,
Ludovicus Cobes, secretary.

[ACKNOWLEDGMENT OF DEBT BY JOHN STUART TO GOOSEN GERRITSEN]

[800] Appeared before me, Ludovicus Cobes, secretary of Albany, colony of Rensselaerswijck and Schaenhechtede, in the presence of the honorable lords magistrates of the same court *Mr*. Philip Schuijler and Theunis Cornelisz vander Poel, *Mr*. John Stuart, who acknowledged that he is well and truly indebted and in arrears to *Sr*. Goossen Gerritsen, merchant, dwelling here, for the quantity of thirty whole and good beaver skins, each piece of which shall weigh 1½ pounds, for two pieces of duffel, received to his full content; in addition, another twenty-seven whole good and merchantable beaver skins for two pieces of blankets, also received to his, appearer's, content; which said beavers, both the heavy and the common, the appearer promises to pay to said *Sr*. Gerritsen, and this at the beginning of the coming trade [trading season], and further, according to opportunity, at the end of the same; especially pledging therefor his shed and its lot located at the hill, received by him from Jan Conneel according to a conveyance dated the 20th of August 1670, and moreover, generally his person and estate, moveable and immoveable, present and future, without exception, submitting the same to all the Lord's laws and judges, to recover (if necessary) the payment without cost and damage. Done in Albany the 27th of May 1671.

John Stewart
In my presence,
Ludovicus Cobes, secretary.

[ACKNOWLEDGMENT OF DEBT BY ADRIAEN APPEL TO PETRUS STUYVESANT]

Copia vera

[**801**] Appeared before me Nicolaes Baijard, admitted secretary of the honorable Mayor's court of the city of New York on the island of Manhattan, and in the presence of the afternamed witnesses, the honorable Adriaen Appel, inhabitant here in this city, being about to depart for Albany, who acknowledged that he is honestly and truly indebted to the lord Petrus Stuijvesant for a net sum of five hundred and fifteen guilders and eighteen stuivers in sewant, growing out of house rent due according to sentence of the honorable Mayor's court, dated the 2nd of March *anno* 1668/9.

Which aforesaid sum of *f*515–18 he, appearer, promises to pay to the said lord Stuijvesant or his lawful order, in good current strung sewant within the time of three successive years, each year one just third part of the said sum; for the recovery and the full payment of the said sum he, appearer, offers as a special mortgage and collateral his, appearer's domicile and lot standing and located in the said village of New Albany, to the north the domicile and lot of David Schuijler, and presently rented and used by Johannes Dijckman, and further, generally his person and estate, moveable and immoveable, submitting the same to all laws and judges, further requesting me, secretary, to pass hereof the deed *in communi forma*, so that the same can be registered in the protocol of the said village of Albany, to serve as is appropriate. In witness of the truth this was signed by the appearer and [**802**] undersigned witnesses with their own hands in New York, dated this 3rd of May *anno* 1671.

Was signed, A. Appel
Sijmon Romeijn
Cornelis vanden Burch
In my presence,
N. Bayard, secretary
Collated by me,
Ludovicus Cobes, secretary.

[CONVEYANCE OF A LOT BY ROBBERT ORTIERS AND JANNETIE DONCKERTS TO HENDRICK COENRAETS]

[**803**] Appeared before me, Ludovicus Cobes, secretary of Albany, colony of Rensselaerswijck and Schaenhechtede, in the presence of the honorable lords magistrates of the same court, *Mr.* Philip Pietersz Schuijler and Jan Hendricx van Bael, *Mr.* Robbert Ortiers, master hatmaker, and Jannetie Donckerts, widow of the late Thomas Paulus, deceased, who declared that they hereby cede, convey and make over in true, rightful and free ownership to and for the benefit of Hendrick Coenraets, a certain piece of a lot to the west of the kil behind the Kinderhoeck, extending on the eastside of a small interior creek [*binnen killetie*], and adjoins to the south Laurens van Alen; and this free and unencumbered, without any charges standing or issuing against the same, except for the lord's right; without them, grantors, making the least claim upon the same anymore, acknowledging that they are fully satisfied and paid for the same, the first penny with the last; giving therefore *plenam actionem cessam* and full power to said Hendrick Coenraets, his heirs or descendants, or those who hereafter may acquire his right and title, to do with and dispose of the said piece of a lot as he might do with his patrimonial estate and effects; promising to protect and free the same against all persons from all trouble, claims and charges as is right, and further, nevermore to do nor allow anything to be done against the same, either with or without law, in any manner, under obligation as is provided for it according to law. Done in Albany the 31st of May 1671.

Robert Orchard
The mark of Janneken X Donckers, made with her own hand.
Philip Pietersz
Jan Hend. van Bael

In my presence,
Ludovicus Cobes, secretary.

[CONVEYANCE OF A LOT AND LAND BY ROBBERT ORTIERS AND JANNEKEN DONCKERS TO LAURENS VAN ALEN]

[804] Appeared before me, Ludovicus Cobes, secretary of Albany, etc., in the presence of the honorable lords magistrates of the same court *Mr.* Philip Pietersz Schuijler and Jan Hendricx van Bael, *Mr.* Robbert Ortiers and Janneken Donckers, widow of the late Thomas Paulus, deceased, who declared that they hereby cede, convey and make over in true, rightful and free ownership to and for the benefit of Laurens van Alen, a certain piece of a lot and land located behind the Kinderhoeck to the west of the kil, to the south of Hendrick Coenraets, to the east of Jacob Jansz Flodder; and this free and unencumbered, without any charges standing or issuing against the same, except for the lord's right; without them, grantors, making the least claim upon the same anymore, acknowledging that they are fully satisfied and paid for the same, the first penny with the last; giving therefore *plenam actionem cessam* and full power to said Laurens van Alen, his heirs or descendants, or those who hereafter may acquire his right and title, to do with and dispose of the said piece of a lot and land as he might do with his patrimonial estate and effects; promising to protect and free the same against all persons from all trouble, claims and charges as is right, and further, nevermore to do nor allow anything to be done against the same, either with or without law, in any manner, under obligation as is provided for it according to law. Done in Albany the 31st of May 1671.

Robert Orchard
The mark of Janneken **X** Donckers, made with her own hand
Philip Pietersz
Jan Hend. van Bael
In my presence,
Ludovicus Cobes, secretary.

[CONVEYANCE OF A LOT AND LAND BY ROBBERT ORTIERS AND JANNEKEN DONCKERS TO JACOB MARTENSZ]

[805] Appeared before me, Ludovicus Cobes, secretary of Albany, colony of Rensselaerswijck and Schaenhechtede, in the presence of the honorable lords magistrates of the same court *Mr*. Philip Pietersz Schuijler and Jan Hendricsx van Bael, *Mr*. Robbert Ortiers and Janneken Donckerts, widow of the late Thomas Paulus, deceased, who declared that they hereby cede, convey and make over in true, rightful and free ownership to and for the benefit of Jacob Martensz, a certain lot located behind the Kinderhoeck to the west of the kil, wide on the kil 3 rods, on the road five rods; another parcel of land also there to the east of Jan Martensz, to the west of the kil; and this free and unencumbered, without any charges standing or issuing against the same, except for the lord's right; without them, grantors, making the least claim upon the same anymore, acknowledging that they are fully satisfied and paid for the same, the first penny with the last; giving therefore *plenam actionem cessam* and full power to said Jacob Martensz, his heirs or descendants, or those who hereafter may acquire his right and title, to do with and dispose of the same as he might do with his patrimonial estate and effects; promising to protect and free the same against all persons from all trouble, claims and charges as is right, and further, nevermore to do nor allow anything to be done against the same, either with or without law, in any manner, under obligation as is provided for it according to law. Done in Albany the 31st of May 1671.

Robert Orchard
The mark of Janneken X Donckerts, made with her own hand.
Philip Pietersz
Jan Hend. van Bael
In my presence,
Ludovicus Cobes, secretary.

[CONVEYANCE OF A LOT BY ROBBERT ORTIERS AND JANNEKEN DONCKERS TO DIRCK HENDRICX SWEED]

[806] Appeared before me, Ludovicus Cobes, secretary of Albany, colony of Rensselaerswijck and Schaenhechtede, in the presence of the honorable lords magistrates of the same court *Mr*. Philip Pietersz Schuijler and Jan Hendricsx van Bael, *Mr*. Robbert Ortiers and Janneken Donckerts, widow of the late Thomas Paulus, deceased, who declared that they hereby cede, convey and make over in true, rightful and free ownership to and for the benefit of Dirck Hendricx *Sweed*, a certain part of a lot located behind Kinderhoeck to the west of the kil, to the south of Jacob Martensz, to the east of Jan Martensz; and this free and unencumbered, without any charges standing or issuing against the same, except for the lord's right; without them, grantors, making the least claim upon the same anymore, acknowledging that they are fully satisfied and paid for the same, the first penny with the last; giving therefore *plenam actionem cessam* and full power to said Dirck Hendricxsz *Sweed*, his heirs and descendants, or those who hereafter may acquire his right and title, to do with and dispose of the said lot as he might do with his patrimonial estate and effects; promising to protect and free the same against all persons from all trouble, claims and charges as is right, and further, nevermore to do nor allow anything to be done against the same, either with or without law, in any manner, under obligation as is provided for it according to law. Done in Albany the 31st of May 1671.

Robert Orchard
The mark of Janneken X Donckerts, made with her own hand.
Philip Pietersz
Jan Hend. van Bael
In my presence,
Ludovicus Cobes, secretary.

[CONVEYANCE OF A PARCEL OF LAND BY ROBBERT ORTIERS AND JANNEKEN DONCKERS TO ANDRIESZ HANSZ]

[**807**] Appeared before me, Ludovicus Cobes, secretary of Albany, colony of Rensselaerswijck and Schaenhechtede, in the presence of the honorable lords magistrates of the same court *Mr*. Philip Pietersz Schuijler and Jan Hendricxsz van Bael, *Mr*. Robbert Ortiers and Janneken Donckerts, etc., who declared that they hereby cede, convey and make over in true, rightful and free ownership to and for the benefit of Andries Hansz a certain parcel of land located behind Kinderhoeck, separated by a small kil from the land of Jan Martensz; and this free and unencumbered, without any charges standing or issuing against the same, except for the lord's right; without them, grantors, making the

least claim upon the same anymore, acknowledging that they are fully satisfied and paid for the same with a mortgage for the sum of *f*64 in beavers and *f*7 in sewant; giving therefore *plenam actionem cessam* and full power to said Andries Hansz, his heirs and descendants, or those who hereafter may acquire his right and title, to do with and dispose of the said parcel of land as he might do with his patrimonial estate and effects; promising to protect and free the same against all persons from all trouble, claims and charges as is right, and further, nevermore to do nor allow anything to be done against the same, either with or without law, in any manner, under obligation as provided for it according to law. Done in Albany the 31st of May 1671.

Robert Orchard
The mark of Janneken X Donckerts, made with her own hand.
Philip Pietersz
Jan Hend. van Bael
In my presence,
Ludovicus Cobes, secretary.

[CONVEYANCE OF A PARCEL OF LAND BY ROBBERT ORTIERS AND JANNEKEN DONCKERS TO JAN MARTENSZ]

[808] Appeared before me, Ludovicus Cobes, secretary of Albany, etc., in the presence of the honorable lords magistrates of the same court Mr. Philip Schuijler and Jan Hendricxsz van Bael, Mr. Robbert Ortiers and Janneken Donckerts, who declared that they hereby cede, convey and make over in true, rightful and free ownership to and for the benefit of Jan Martensz a certain parcel of land located behind Kinderhoeck; adjoins to the south Dierck *de Sweed*, to the west Jacob Martensz and the kil, to the east of a little kil separating it from the land of Andries Hansz; and this free and unencumbered, without any charges standing or issuing against the same, except for the lord's right; without the grantors making the least claim upon the same anymore, acknowledging that they are fully satisfied and paid therefore with a mortgage for the sum of seventy whole good merchantable beaver skins as will follow hereafter; giving therefore *plenam actionem cessam* and full power to the said Jan Martensz, his heirs and descendants, or those who hereafter may acquire his right and title, to do with and dispose of the said parcel of land as he might do with his patrimonial estate and effects; promising to protect and free the same against all persons from all trouble, claims and charges as is right, and further, nevermore to do nor allow anything to be done against the same either with or without law, in any manner, under obligation as provided therefor according to law. Done in Albany the 31st of May 1671.

Robert Orchard
The mark of Janneken X Donckerts made, with her own hand.
Philip Pietersz
Jan Hend. van Bael
In my presence,
Ludovicus Cobes, secretary.

[ACKNOWLEDGMENT OF DEBT BY DIRCKIE HERMS, ATTORNEY FOR JAN MARTENSZ, TO JAN BRUIJNS]

[809] Appeared before me, Ludovicus Cobes, secretary of Albany, colony of Rensselaersw. and Schaenhechtede, in the presence of the honorable lords magistrates of the same court *Mr*. Philip Schuijler and Jan Hendricxsz van Bael, Dirckie Herms, attorney for her husband Jan Martensz, dwelling behind Kinderhoeck, who acknowledged that she is well and truly indebted and in arrears to *Mr*. Jan Bruijns for the quantity of seventy whole good and merchantable beaver skins stemming from the matter of purchase and mortgage money of a parcel of land, located behind Kinderhoeck, bought by her, appearer; which said 70 whole beavers she, appearer, promises to pay to the said *Mr*. Bruijns or his order, namely, thirty in the coming spring 1672, the remaining 40 beavers in the spring as well, and in default of payment of the 40 beavers, she promises to pay four beavers interest per year, but if she cannot make the payment in beavers, she promises to give good winter wheat at beaver's and market price; especially pledging therefor her land and farm behind Kinderhoeck, and generally her person and estate, moveable and immoveable, present and future, without exception, making the same subject to all laws and judges to recover (if necessary) the payment without cost and damage in due time. Done in Albany the 31st of May 1671.

Derckien Hermens
Philip Pietersz
Jan Hend van Bael
In my presence,
Ludovicus Cobes, secretary.

[ACKNOWLEDGMENT OF DEBT BY ELDERT GERBERTSEN CRUIJFF TO JAN HENDRICK BRUIJNS AND HANS HENDRIXSZ]

[**810**] Appeared before me, Ludovicus Cobes, secretary of Albany, colony of Rensselaersw. and Schaenhechtede, in the presence of the honorable lords magistrates of the same court *Mr.* Philip Pietersz Schuijler and Jan Hendricxsz van Bael, Eldert Gerbertsz Cruijff, who acknowledged that he is well and truly indebted and in arrears to the *Messieurs* Jan Hendrick Bruijns and Hans Hendricxsz for a net sum of *f*350 in beavers and *f*48 in sewant, together with 75 boards; stemming from a matter of security and having bound themselves for said Cruijff as principals in accordance with a certain sentence dated the 5th of January 1670/71; which said money the appearer promises to pay to the said Jan Hendrick Bruijns and Hans Hendricxsz within the time of six weeks exactly, and without any further delay; especially pledging therefor his distilling kettle with worm and helmet, his sawmill at Bethlehem, and all his lands at Catskil, together with all his rights to his house, brewery and lot, located here in Albany; likewise two cows here, four animals at Gerrit Theunisz's, two animals at Melgert Abrahamsz's at Schotack, three animals at Jan Helmsz's of which half belong to him, and three heifers and a bull at Henderick Maersz's, and further, generally his person and estate, moveable and immoveable, present and future, without exception, making the same subject to all the Lord's [**811**] laws and judges, to recover, if need be, the payment thereof in due time, without loss or cost. Done in Albany the 21st of June 1671.

Eldert Gerbertsz Cruijff
Philip Pietersz

Jan Hend van Bael
In my presence,
Ludovicus Cobes, secretary.

[CONVEYANCE OF A PLANTATION AT SCHAENHECHTEDE BY PAULUS JANSZ TO CHRISTIAEN CHRISTIAENSZ]

Appeared before me, Ludovicus Cobes, secretary of Albany, colony of Rensselaerswijck and Schaenhechtede, in the presence of the honorable lords magistrates of the same court *Mr*. Philip Pietersz Schuijler and Jan Hendricxsz van Bael, Paulus Jansz, who declared that he hereby cedes, conveys and makes over in true, rightful and free ownership to and for the benefit of Christiaen Christiaensz, dwelling at Schaenhechtede his plantation located there, one and a half morgen in size and bounded according to the patent thereof from the right honorable general of New York, Francis Lovelace, dated the 24th of May 1669, to which herein is referred; and this free and unencumbered, without any charges standing or issuing against the same, except for the lord's right; without the grantor making the least claim upon it anymore, acknowledging that he is fully satisfied and paid therefore, the first penny with the last; giving therefore *plenam actionem cessam* and full power to said Christiaen Christiaensz, his heirs and descendants, or those who hereafter might acquire his right and title, to **[812]** do with and dispose of the said plantation as he might do with his patrimonial estate and effects; promising to protect and free the same against all persons from all trouble, claims and charges as is right, and further, nevermore to do nor allow anything to be done against the same, either with or without law, in any manner, under obligation as is provided for it according to law. Done in Albany the 23rd of June 1671.

Poulijs Jansen
Philip Pietersz
Jan Hend. van Bael
In my presence,
Ludovicus Cobes, secretary.

[CONVEYANCE OF TWO GARDENS BY JAN BRUIJN TO HENDRICK GERRITSZ VERMEULEN]

Appeared before me, Ludovicus Cobes, secretary of Albany, colony of Rensselaerswijck and Schaenhechtede, in the presence of the honorable lords magistrates of the same court *Mr.* Philip Pietersz Schuijler and Jan Hendricxsz van Bael, *Mr.* Jan Bruijn, who hereby declared that he cedes, conveys and makes over in true, rightful and free ownership to and for the benefit of *Mr.* Hendrick Gerritsz Vermeulen, certain two gardens located near the others behind Fort Orange, and this by virtue of and in consequence of a deed of conveyance by the lord Jeremias van Rensselaer for the benefit of the grantor, dated the 6/16th of July 1667; without him, grantor, making the least claim upon the same anymore, acknowledging that he is fully satisfied and paid for the same, the first penny with the last; giving therefore *plenam actionem cessam* and full power to said Hendrick Gerritsz, his heirs and descendants, or those who hereafter may acquire his title, to [**813**] dispose of the same two gardens as he might do with his own patrimonial estate and effects; promising to protect and free the said gardens against all persons from all trouble, claims and charges as is right, and further, nevermore to do nor allow anything to be done against the same, either with or without law, in any manner, under obligation as provided for it according to law. Done in Albany the 18th of July 1671.

Jan Henderck Bruijns
Philip Pietersz
Jan Hend. van Bael

In my presence,
Ludovicus Cobes, secretary.

[*In the margin was written*:] In accordance with this said conveyance the two gardens are made over again to Herman Vedder.

[CONVEYANCE OF A SHED AND A LOT BY JAN BRUIJNS TO RUTH ARISZ]

Appeared before me, Ludovicus Cobes, secretary of Albany, etc., in the presence of the honorable lords magistrates of the same court *Mr*. Philip Pietersz Schuijler and Jan Hend van Bael, *Mr*. Jan Bruijns, who declared that he hereby cedes, conveys and makes over in true, rightful and free ownership to and for the benefit of Ruth Arisz, master shoemaker, a small shed and a lot, located here in Albany on the plain; to the east of the road long six rods, to the north the road wide three rods, to the west Thomas Paulis long six rods, to the south the plain wide three rods, by virtue of a patent thereof from the right honorable general Nicolls dated the 20th of April 1667, to which is here referred; and this free and unencumbered, without any charges standing or issuing against the same, except for the lord's right; without the grantor making the least claim upon the same anymore, acknowledging that he is fully satisfied and paid therefore, the first penny with the last; **[814]** giving therefore *plenam actionem cessam* and full power to said Ruth Arisz, his heirs and descendants, or those who hereafter may acquire his right and title, to do with and dispose of the said shed and lot as he might do with his other patrimonial estate and effects; promising to protect and free the same against all persons from all trouble, claims and charges as is right, and further, nevermore to do nor allow anything to be done against the same, either with or without law in any manner, under obligation as is provided for it according to law. Done in Albany the 18th of July 1671.

Jan Henderck Bruijns
Jan Hend. van Bael
Philip Pietersz

In my presence,
Ludovicus Cobes, secretary.

[CONVEYANCE OF A HOUSE AND LOT BY THOMAS WILLET TO PHILIP PIETERSZ SCHUIJLER]

Appeared before me, Ludovicus Cobes, secretary of Albany, colony of Rensselaersw. and Schaenhechtede, in the presence of the honorable lords magistrates of the same court and *Mrs*. Goossen Gerritsz and Jan Hendricx van Bael, Captn. Thomas Willet, who declared that he hereby cedes, conveys and makes over in true, rightful and free ownership to and for the benefit of *Sr*. Philip Pietersz Schuijler, a certain house and lot, located here in Albany, bounded and enclosed in accordance with a patent thereof from the right honorable lord general Richard Nicolls dated the 13th of August 1668; and this free and unencumbered, without any charges standing or issuing against the same **[815]** except for the lord's right; without the grantor making the least claim upon the same anymore, acknowledging that he is fully satisfied and paid for the same, the first penny with the last; giving therefore *plenam actionem cessam* and full power to the said Philip Schuijler, his heirs and descendants, or those who hereafter may acquire his right and title, to do with and dispose of the said house and lot as he might do with his patrimonial estate and effects; promising to protect and free the same against all persons from all trouble, claims and charges as is right, and further, nevermore to do nor allow anything to be done against the same, either with or without law in any manner, under obligation as provided for it according to law. Done in Albany the 2nd of September 1671.

Tho. Willet
Goosen Gerretsen
Jan Hend. van Bael
In my presence,
Ludovicus Cobes, secretary.

[CONVEYANCE OF A PARCEL OF A LOT BY HENDRICK KOSTER TO GERRIT REIJERSZ]

[816] Appeared before me, Ludovicus Cobes, secretary of Albany, etc., in the presence of the honorable lords magistrates of the same court *Mr*. Philip Schuijler and Jan Hendricxsz van Bael, Hendrick Koster, who declared that he hereby cedes, conveys and makes over in true, rightful and free ownership to and for the benefit of Gerrit Reijersz a certain parcel of a lot, located here at the hill, long to the south 15 feet and 8½ inches wood feet, to the north long 16 feet and one inch wood feet, and wide 15 feet Rhineland measure; by virtue of a patent granted to him, grantor; and this free and unencumbered, without any charges standing or issuing against the same except for the lord's right; without the grantor making the least claim upon the same anymore, acknowledging that he is fully satisfied and paid for the same, the first penny with the last; giving therefore *plenam actionem cessam* and full power to said Gerrit Reijersen, his heirs and descendants, or those who hereafter may acquire his right and title, to do with and dispose of the said lot as he might do with his patrimonial estate and effects; promising to protect and free the same against all persons from all trouble, claims and charges as is right, and further, nevermore to do nor allow anything to be done against the same, either with or without law, in any manner, under obligation as is provided for it according to law. Done in Albany the 13th of September 1671.

Hendereck Koster
Philip Pietersz
Jan Hend. van Bael

[CONVEYANCE OF A PARCEL OF A LOT BY ANDRIES DE VOS TO JAN ANDRIESEN]

[817] Appeared before me, Ludovicus Cobes, secretary of Albany, etc., in the presence of the honorable lords magistrates of the same court *Mrs.* Philip Schuijler and Jan Hend van Bael, Andries de Vos, who declared that he hereby cedes, conveys and makes over in true, rightful and free ownership to and for the benefit of Jan Andriesen a certain parcel of a lot, located here at the hill, adjoining on the north side the road, on the east side also a road, to the south the lot of Eduard Schot, to the west the lot of Jacob Thijsz; in breadth and length according to the boundary; and this free and unencumbered, without any charges standing or issuing against the same, except for the lord's right; without the grantor making the least claim upon the same anymore, acknowledging that he is fully satisfied and paid for the same, the first penny with the last; giving therefore *plenam actionem cessam* and full power to said Jan Andriesz, his heirs and descendants, or those who hereafter may acquire his right and title, to do with and dispose of the said lot as he might do with his patrimonial estate and effects; promising to protect and free the same against all persons from all trouble, claims and charges as is right, and further, nevermore to do nor allow anything to be done against the same, either with or without law, in any manner, **[818]** under obligation as provided for it according to law. Done in Albany the 13th of September 1671.

Andrijes de Vos
Philip Pietersz
Jan Hend. van Bael
In my presence,
Ludovicus Cobes, secretary.

[CONVEYANCE OF A HOUSE AND LOT BY JOHANNES *DE WANDELAER* TO EVERT JANSZ]

Appeared before me, Ludovicus Cobes, secretary of Albany, etc., in the presence of *Sr*. Philip Schuijler and Jan Hendricxsz van Bael, Johannes *de Wandelaer*, who declared that he hereby cedes, conveys and makes over in true, rightful and free ownership to and for the benefit of Evert Jansz his house and lot, located at the hill here in Albany; and the lot is wide in front 15 feet, and long six rods and five feet, in accordance with the patent thereof, held by Omij La Grand; and this free and unencumbered, without any charges standing or issuing against the same except for the lord's right; without the grantor making the least claim upon the same anymore, acknowledging that he is fully satisfied and paid for it, the first penny with the last; giving therefore *plenam actionem cessam* and full power to said Evert Jansz, his heirs and descendants, or those who hereafter may acquire his right and title, to do with and dispose of the said lot as he might do with his patrimonial estate and effects; promising to protect and free the same against all persons from all trouble, claims and charges as is right, and further, nevermore to do or allow anything to be done against the same, either with or without law, in any manner, under obligation as provided for it according to law. Albany the 22nd of September 1671.

Johannes de Wandelaer
Philip Pietersz
Jan Hend. van Bael
In my presence,
Ludovicus Cobes, secretary.

[CONVEYANCE OF A HOUSE AND LOT BY PIETER JACOBSZ BORSBOOM TO WILLIAM LOVERIDGE]

[**819**] Appeared before me, Ludovicus Cobes, secretary of Albany, colony of Rensselaersw. and Schaenh., in the presence of the honorable lords magistrates of the same court Philip Schuijler and Jan Hendricxsz van Bael, Pieter Jacobsz Borsboom, who declared that he hereby cedes, conveys and makes over in true, rightful and free ownership to and for the benefit of *Mr.* William Loveridge, his heirs and descendants a certain house and lot here in Albany, wide in front on the street 40 wood feet and 3½ inches, and in the rear at the end of Jacob Joosten's lot wide 30 wood feet, and in the rear on the beach wide 28 wood feet, and long as far as the beach; which said house and lot are bounded to the north of the king's house, and to the south of the house of Jacob Joosten; by virtue of a patent dated the 3rd of May 1667, held by the widow of the late *Mr.* Jacob de Hinsse, to which here is referred, provided that the grantor still has bought some feet of a lot from Sander Leendertsz, which are herein included as well, and which also extend as far as the king's house; everything free and unencumbered, without any charges standing or issuing against the same, except for the lord's right; without the grantor making the least claim upon the same anymore, acknowledging that he is fully satisfied and paid therefor with a sum of 19 beavers in merchandise, together with a mortgage on the same house and lot for the sum of thirty-five whole and [**820**] merchantable beaver skins; giving therefore *plenam actionem cessam* and full power to said *Mr.* William Loveridge, his heirs and descendants, or those who hereafter may acquire his right and title, to do with and dispose of the said house and lot as he might do with his patrimonial estate and effects;

promising to protect and free the same against all persons from all trouble, claims and charges as is right, and further, neither to do nor allow anything to be done against the same, either with or without law, in any manner, under obligation as is provided for it according to law. Done in Albany the 30th of September 1671.

Pieter Yacopse Borsboom
Jan Hend. van Bael
Philip Pietersz
In my presence,
Ludovicus Cobes, secretary.

[ACKNOWLEDGMENT OF DEBT BY WILLIAM LOVERIDGE TO PIETER JACOBSZ BORSBOOM]

Appeared before me, Ludovicus Cobes, secretary of Albany, in the presence of *Sr*. Philip Schuijler and Jan Hendricxsz van Bael, magistrates of the same court, *Mr*. William Loveridge, master hatmaker, who acknowledged that he is well and truly indebted and in arrears to Pieter Jacobsz Borsboom for the quantity of thirty-five whole good and merchantable beaver skins, stemming from the matter of purchase and mortgage money of a certain house and lot from him received; which said 35 beavers the appearer promises to pay to said **[821]** Pieter Jacobsz, or his order in two installments, each time half; the first in the coming trading season of 1673; the second the following year; especially pledging therefor the said house and lot, and generally his person and estate, moveable and immoveable, present and future, without exception; making the same subject to all the lord's laws and judges , to recover (if necessary), the payment without cost and damage. Done in Albany the 30th of September 1671.

William Loveridge
Jan Hend van Bael
Philip Pietersz
In my presence,
Ludovicus Cobes, secretary.

[CONVEYANCE OF A LOT BY WILLIAM PARKER TO RIJCK CLAESZ]

Appeared before me, Ludovicus Cobes, secretary of Albany, colony of Rensselaerswijck and Schaenhechtede, in the presence of the honorable lords magistrates of the same court *Srs*. Philip Pietersz Schuijler and Jan Hendricxsz van Bael, Sergeant William Parcker, who declared that he hereby cedes, conveys and makes over in true, rightful and free ownership to and for the benefit of Rijck Claesz, his certain lot located at the hill, wide 20 feet and long about 3½ rods; to the south of the lot of Dirck Aelbertsz Brat; by virtue of a patent thereof dated the 2nd of June 1669, to which here is referred; and this free and unencumbered, without any **[822]** charges standing or issuing against the same except for the lord's right; without the grantor making the least claim upon the same anymore, acknowledging that he is fully satisfied and paid for it, the first penny with the last; giving therefore *plenam actionem cessam* and full power to said Rijck Claesz, his heirs and descendants, or those who hereafter may acquire his right and title, to do with and dispose of the said lot as he might do with his patrimonial estate and effects; promising to protect and free the same against all persons from all trouble, claims and charges as is right, and further, nevermore to do nor allow anything to be done against the same, either with or without law, in any manner, under obligation as is provided for it according to law. Done in Albany the 13th of October 1671.

Wm. Parker
Philip Pietersz
Jan Hend. van Bael
In my presence,
Ludovicus Cobes, secretary.

[CONVEYANCE OF A HOUSE AND LOT BY ARIAENTIE CORNELIS VAN VELPEN, ATTORNEY FOR JACOB JOOSTEN, TO JAN CONNEEL]

[823] Appeared before me, Ludovicus Cobes, secretary of Albany, colony of Rensselaerswijck and Schaenhechtede, in the presence of the honorable lords magistrates of the same court *Srs*. Philip Pietersz Schuijler and Jan Hendricxsz van Bael, Adriaentie Cornelis van Velpen, wife and attorney of Jacob Joosten, who declared that she hereby cedes, conveys and makes over in true, rightful and free ownership to and for the benefit of Jan Conneel, her house and lot located here in Albany, in width, length and boundaries as is shown in the bill of sale thereof, to which here is referred; and this free and unencumbered, without any charge standing or issuing against the same, except for the lord's right; without the grantor making the least claim upon the same anymore, acknowledging that she is fully satisfied and paid for it the first penny with the last; giving therefore *plenam actionem cessam* and full power to said Jan Conneel, his heirs and descendants, or those who hereafter may acquire his right and title, to do with and dispose of the said house and lot as he might do with his patrimonial estate and effects; promising to protect and free the same against all persons from all trouble, claims and charges as is right, and further, nevermore to do nor allow anything to be done against the same, either with or without law, in any manner, under obligation as provided for it according to law. Done in Albany the 13th of October 1671.

Adriana Cornelis van Velpen
Philip Pietersz
Jan Hend. van Bael
In my presence,
Ludovicus Cobes, secretary.

[CONVEYANCE OF TWO HOUSES AND LOTS BY MARTTEN CREGIER TO JURRIAEN THEUNISZ TAPPEN]

[824] Appeared before me, Ludovicus Cobes, secretary of Albany, colony of Rensselaersw. and Schaenhechtede, in the presence of the honorable lords magistrates of the same court Jan Hendricxsz van Bael and G. van Slichtenhorst, *Mr*. Martten Cregier, who, at the discretion of and with a power of attorney from the right honorable lord general Francis Lovelace declared that he hereby cedes, conveys and makes over in true, rightful and free ownership to and for the benefit of Jurriaen Theunisz Tappen, two attached houses and their lots, formerly having belonged to Dirck Jansz Croon, standing and located here in Albany in such size and boundaries as the same are lying within their fence as far as the little kil; and this free and unencumbered, without any charges standing or issuing against the same except for the lord's right; without the grantor making the least claim upon the same anymore, acknowledging that he is fully satisfied and paid for it, the first penny with the last; giving therefore *plenam actionem cessam* and full power to said Juriaen Theunisz, his heirs and descendants, or those who hereafter may acquire his right and title to do with and dispose of the said two houses and lots as he might do with his patrimonial estate and effects; promising to protect and free the same against all persons from all trouble, claims and charges as is right, and further, nevermore to do nor allow anything to be done against the same, either with or without law, in any manner, **[825]** under obligation as provided for it according to law. Albany the 13th of September 1672.

M. Cregier Junior
Jan Hend. van Bael
Gerrit van Slichtenhorst
In my presence,
Ludovicus Cobes, secretary.

[*In the margin was written*:] *Nota Bene* that the lord de Lavall has received 70 beavers.

[ACKNOWLEDGMENT OF DEBT BY ELDERT GERBERTSZ CRUIJFF TO JEREMIAS VAN RENSSELAER]

Appeared before me, Ludovicus Cobes, secretary of Albany, colony of Rensselaersw. and Schaenhechtede, in the presence of the honorable lords magistrates of the same court Goossen Gerritsen and Jan Hendricxsz van Bael, Eldert Gerbertsz Cruijff, who acknowledged that he is well and truly indebted and in arrears to the lord Jeremias van Rensselaer, director of the colony of Rensselaerswijck, for a sum of two thousand six hundred and seventy guilders in grain; the wheat at ten guilders in beavers a *mudde*, and the oats at four guilders in beavers a *mudde*; together with another sum of two hundred and seventy-eight guilders in sewant, stemming from the lease of a water course and lands, etc.; of which sum the appearer makes over and conveys to the said lord

Rensselaer the quantity of fifty beavers to be received from Hendrick Maersz; which remaining sum in beavers and sewant the appearer promises to pay to said lord Rensselaer or his order in three installments, each time one-third; the first on the first of November 1672, the second in the month of August 1673, the third the following year; all punctually, or failing, interest on the same of 10 percent; especially pledging therefor his sawmill at Bethlehem and his house there, as well, together with his right and title to the lands at Catskill **[826]** and generally his person and estate, moveable and immoveable, present and future without exception, to recover, if need be, the payment without cost and damage. Done in Albany the 15th of November 1671.

Note: In this special contract is not included a certain promissory note chargeable to the appearer in favor of the lord Jan Baptist van Rensselaer.

Eldert Gerbertsz Cruijf
Jan Hend van Bael
Gerret van Slichtenhorst
In my presence,
Ludovicus Cobes, secretary.

[CONVEYANCE OF A LOT WITH A WELL BY SANDER LEENDERTSZ GLEN TO JURRIAEN THEUNISZ TAPPEN]

Appeared before me, Ludovicus Cobes, secretary of Albany, colony of Rensselaerswijck and Schaenhechtede, in the presence of the honorable lords magistrates of the same court Jan Hend. van Bael and Gerrit van Slichtenhorst, Sander Leendertsz Glen, who declared that he hereby cedes, conveys and makes over in true, rightful and free ownership to and for the benefit of *Mr*. Juriaen Theunisz Tappen, his certain lot with a well, located straight across from the king's house, formerly belonging to Jan Bastiaensz, deceased; being in width in front on the street as far as the town's fence, and in the back 24 feet wide; and in the back as far as as the hindmost post of the former town fence; and this free and unencumbered, without any charges standing or issuing against the same except for the lord's right; without the grantor making the least claim upon the same anymore, acknowledging that [**827**] he is fully satisfied and paid for it the first penny with the last; giving therefore *plenam actionem cessam* and full power to said Juriaen Theunisz, his heirs and descendants, or those who hereafter may acquire his right and title, to do with and dispose of the said lot and well as he might do with his patrimonial estate and effects; promising to protect and free the same against all persons from all trouble, claims and charges as is right, and further, nevermore to do nor allow anything to be done against the same, either with or without law, in any manner, under obligation as provided for it according to law. Done in Albany the 10th of January 1671/72.

Sander Lenrsen Glen
Jan Hend. van Bael
Gerrit van Slichtenhorst
In my presence,
Ludovicus Cobes, secretary.

[ACKNOWLEDGMENT OF DEBT BY PIETER PIETERSZ VAN WOGGELUM TO MEIJNDERT JANSZ WEMP]

[**828**] Appeared before me, Ludovicus Cobes, secretary of Albany, colony of Rensselaersw. and Schaenhechtede, in the presence of the honorable lords magistrates of the same court Jan Hendricxsz van Bael and Gerrart van Slichtenhorst, Pieter Pietersz van Woggelum, who acknowledged that he is well and truly indebted and in arrears to Meijndert Jansz Wemp for the quantity of two hundred and fifty whole good beaver skins to be paid in six installments in either wheat or sewant at beaver's price according to the market; and that in such time as is in accordance with the bill of sale thereof, dated the 15th of January 1671/72, stemming from the matter of a farm and lands bought from him; especially pledging therefore the said farm, lands, horses and cattle, and generally his person and estate, moveable and immoveable, present and future without exception, subject to all the lord's laws and judges to recover, if need be, the payment without cost and damage. Albany, the 15th of January 1671/72.

Pieter Pieterse
Jan Hend. van Bael
Gerrit van Slichtenhorst
In my presence,
Ludovicus Cobes, secretary.

[CONVEYANCE OF *SCHUTTERS* ISLAND BY VOLCKERT JANSZ TO BARENT PIETERSZ]

[**829**] Today, the 16th of April 1672 appeared before me, Ludovicus Cobes, secretary of Albany, etc., in the presence of the honorable lords magistrates of the same court *Mrs.* Gerrart van Slichtenhorst and Jacob Schermerhoren, Volckert Jansz, who declared that he hereby cedes, conveys and makes over in true, rightful and free ownership to and for the benefit of Barent Pietersz, his island named *Schutters* Island, located below *Beeren* Island in this river, by virtue of a patent thereof dated the 14th of August 1671, to which hereby is referred; and this free and unencumbered, without any charges standing or issuing against the same, except for the lord's right; without the grantor making the least claim upon the same anymore, acknowledging that he is fully satisfied and paid for it, the first penny with the last; giving therefore *plenam actionem cessam* and full power to said Barent Pietersz, his heirs and descendants, or those who hereafter may acquire his right and title, to do with and dispose of the said lot as he might do with his patrimonial estate and effects; promising to protect and free the same against all persons from all trouble, claims and charges as is right, and further, nevermore to do nor allow anything to be done against the same, either with or without law, in any manner, under obligation as provided for it according to law. Done in Albany.

Volckart Jansz
Gerrit van Slichtenh
Jacob Schermerhooren

In my presence,
Ludovicus Cobes, secretary.

[CONVEYANCE OF A LOT BY *MR*. SISTON TO PIETER ADRIAENSZ *SOO MACKELIJCK*]

[830] Today, the 14th of May 1672 appeared before me, Ludovicus Cobes, secretary of Albany etc., in the presence of the honorable lords magistrates of the same court *Srs*. Jan Hendricxsz van Bael and Gerrit van Slichtenhorst, *Mr*. Siston, who declared that he hereby cedes, conveys and makes over in true, rightful and free ownership to and for the benefit of Pieter Adriaensz *Soo Mackelijck* a certain lot located here in Albany at the hill, to the south of Wijnant Gerretse, to the north of Jocchum *Backer*; wide both in the rear as well as in the front 22½ feet, and long two rods and eleven feet, both south and north, everything Rhineland measure; and this free and unencumbered, without any charges standing or issuing against the same, except for the lord's right; without the grantor making the least claim upon the same anymore, acknowledging that he is fully satisfied and paid for it the first penny with the last; giving therefore *plenam actionem cessam* and full power to said Pieter Adriaensz, his heirs and descendants, or those who hereafter may acquire his right and title, to do with and dispose of the said lot as he might do with his patrimonial estate and effects; promising to protect and free the same against all persons from all trouble, claims and charges as is right, and further, nevermore to do nor allow anything to be done against the same, either with or without law, in any manner, under obligation as provided for it according to law. Done in Albany.

Mich Siston
Jan Hend van Bael
Gerrit van Slichtenhorst
In my presence,
Ludovicus Cobes, secretary.

[CONVEYANCE OF LOT NO. 1 BY ANDRIES DE VOS TO JAN CONNEEL]

[831] Today, the 18th of June 1672 appeared before me, Ludovicus Cobes, secretary of Albany, etc., in the presence of the honorable lords magistrates of the same court *Srs*. Jan Hendricxsz van Bael and Gerrit van Slichtenhorst, Andries de Vos, who declared that he hereby cedes, conveys and makes over in true, rightful and free ownership to and for the benefit of Jan Conneel a certain lot no. 1, located at the hill, adjoining westerly Jan Wardt, easterly the public road, northerly Pieter Winne; wide on the south side 4 rods, and westerly three rods and 6 feet; and this free and unencumbered, without any charges standing or issuing against the same, except for the lord's right; without the grantor making the least claim upon the same anymore, acknowledging that he is fully satisfied and paid for it the first penny with the last; giving therefore *plenam actionem cessam* and full power to said Jan Connel, his heirs and descendants, or those who hereafter may acquire his right and title, to do with and dispose of the said lot as he might do with his patrimonial estate and effects; promising to protect and free the same against all persons from all trouble, claims and charges as is right, and further, nevermore to do nor allow anything to be done against the same, either with or without law, in any manner, under obligation as provided for it according to law. Albany [ ]

Andrijes de Vos
Jan Hend van Bael
Gerrit van Slichtenhorst
In my presence,
Ludovicus Cobes, secretary.

[CONVEYANCE OF A HOUSE AND LOT BY JOCHIM WESSELSZ *BACKER* TO JACOB ABRAHAMSZ]

[832] Today, the 18th of June 1672 appeared before me, Ludovicus Cobes, secretary of Albany, Colony of Rensselaerswijck and Schaenhechtede, in the presence of the honorable lords magistrates of the same court *Srs.* Jan Hendricxsz van Bael and Gerrart van Slichtenhorst, Jocchim Wesselsz *Backer*, who declared that he hereby cedes, conveys and makes over in true, rightful and free ownership to and for the benefit of Jacob Abrahamsz his house and lot standing and located in the High Street in New York, adjoining between the premises of Abel Hardenbroeck and Adriaen van Laer, by virtue of a patent thereof to which hereby is referred; and this free and unencumbered, without any charges standing or issuing against the same, except for the lord's right; without the grantor making the least claim upon the same anymore, acknowledging that he is fully satisfied and paid for it, the first penny with the last; giving therefore *plenam actionem cessam* and full power to said Jacob Abrahamsz, his heirs and descendants, or those who hereafter may acquire his right and title, to do with and dispose of the said house and lot as he might do with his patrimonial estate and effects; promising to protect and free the same against all persons from all trouble, claims and charges as is right, and further, nevermore to do nor allow anything to be done against the same, either with or without law, in any manner, under obligation as provided for it according to law. Done in Albany.

Jochem *Backer*
Jan Hend van Bael
Gerrit van Slichtenhorst
In my presence,
Ludovicus Cobes, secretary.

[CONVEYANCE OF A HOUSE AND LOT BY PHILIP PIETERSZ SCHUIJLER TO JEREMIAS VAN RENSSELAER]

[**833**] Appeared before me, Ludovicus Cobes, secretary of Albany, colony of Rensselaerswijck and Schaenhechtede, in the presence of the honorable lords magistrates of the same court *Srs*. Jan Hendr van Bael and Gerrit van Slichtenhorst, *Sr*. Philip Pietersz Schuijler, who declared that he hereby cedes, conveys and makes over in true, rightful and free ownership to and for the benefit of the lord Jeremias van Rensselaer, director of the colony of Rensselaerswijck, a certain house and lot standing and located here in Albany, which he has received from Capt. Thomas Willet by virtue of a conveyance and a patent thereof to which here is referred; and this free and unencumbered, without any charges standing or issuing against the same, except for the lord's right; without the grantor making the least claim upon the same anymore, acknowledging that he is fully satisfied and paid for it the first penny with the last; giving therefore *plenam actionem cessam* and full power to the said lord Jeremias van Rensselaer, his heirs and descendants, or those who hereafter may acquire his right and title, to do with and

dispose of the said house and lot as he might do with his patrimonial estate and effects; promising to protect and free the same against all persons from all trouble, claims and charges as is right, and further, nevermore to do nor allow anything to be done against the same, either with or without law, in any manner, under obligation as provided for it according to law. Done in Albany the 3rd of July 1672.

Philip Schuijler
Jan Hend. van Bael
Gerrit van Slichtenhorst
In my presence,
Ludovicus Cobes, secretary.

[CONVEYANCE OF A HOUSE AND LOT BY JAN CONNEEL TO MARTEN HOFFMAN]

[**834**] Appeared before me, Ludovicus Cobes, secretary of Albany, in the presence of the honorable lords magistrates of the same court *Srs*. Jan Hend. van Bael and Gerrit van Slichtenhorst, Jan Conneel, who declared that he hereby cedes, conveys and makes over in true, rightful and free ownership to and for the benefit of Marten Hoffman, his house and lot, standing and located here in Albany, in breadth, length and boundaries according to the description of the bill of sale, which he acquired from Jacob Joosten, and by virtue of the conveyance thereof, to which here is referred; and this free and unencumbered, without any charges standing or issuing against the same except for the lord's right; without the grantor making the least claim upon the same anymore, acknowledging that he is fully satisfied and paid for it the first penny with the last; giving therefore *plenam actionem cessam* and full power to said Martten Hoffman, his heirs and descendants, or those who hereafter may acquire his right and title, to do with and dispose of the said lot as he might do with his patrimonial estate and effects; promising to protect and free the same against all persons from all trouble, claims and charges as is right, and further, nevermore to do nor allow anything to be done against the same, either with or without law, in any manner, under obligation as provided for it according to law. Done in Albany the 3rd of June 1672.

John Conell
Jan Hend. van Bael
Gerrit van Slichtenhorst
In my presence,
Ludovicus Cobes, secretary.

[ACKNOWLEDGMENT OF DEBT BY EVERT WENDEL
TO THE GUARDIANS OF ANNA THOMAS]

[835] Today, the 3rd of July there appeared before me, Ludovicus Cobes, secretary of Albany, colony of Rensselaersw. and Schaenhechtede, in the presence of the honorable lords magistrates of the same court Jan Hend van Bael and Gerrit van Slichtenhorst, *Mr*. Evert Wendel, who acknowledged that he is well and truly indebted and in arrears to *Mr*. Jan Verbeeck and Theunis Dirricxsz, in the capacity of guardians of Anna Thomas, young daughter of the late Thomas Jansz, the quantity of nineteen whole good and merchantable beaver skins, stemming from merchandise delivered, and received by him to his content; which aforesaid 19 beavers the appearer promises to pay to the said guardians or the lawful bearer of this paper, when the said little daughter shall have come to her lawful age or marriage stage, or sooner, with a proper interest of ten percent to be put aside annually; especially pledging therefore his house and lot here in Albany, and generally his person and estate, moveable and immoveable, present and future without exception, submitting the same to all the lord's laws and judges to recover, if need be, the payment in due time without cost and damage. Done in Albany the 3rd of July 1672.

Evert Wendel
Jan Hend. van Bael
Gerrit van Slichtenhorst
In my presence,
Ludovicus Cobes, secretary.

[CONVEYANCE OF A HOUSE AND LOT BY JOHANNA DE HULTER, ATTORNEY FOR JERONIMUS EBBINCK, TO PAULUS MARTENSZ]

[**836**] Today, the 12th of August 1672, there appeared before me, Ludovicus Cobes, secretary of Albany, colony of Rensselaersw. and Schaenhechtede, in the presence of the honorable lords magistrates of the same court, *Srs.* Jan Hendricxsz van Bael and Gerrart van Slichtenhorst, *Juffr.* Johanna de Hulter, attorney for her father, Jeronimus Ebbinck,[†] who declared that she hereby cedes, conveys and makes over in true, rightful and free ownership to and for the benefit of Paulus Martensz her certain [father's] domicile and lot standing and located here in Albany, adjoining on the east side the public street, on the south side the house of Hendrick *de backer*, on the west side the garden of Hendrick Andriesz and Lambert van Neck, and on the north side the house of Lambert van Neck; the lot being wide in front on the street 32 wood feet and four inches, and long 10 rods, as he acquired the said lot by conveyance from Tierck Claesz de Witt, by virtue of a patent and conveyance thereof; and this, with everything attached that is to and in it by earth and nail, and this free and unencumbered, without any charges standing or issuing against the same, except for the lord's right, acknowledging that he is fully satisfied and paid for it, the first penny with the last; giving therefore *plenam actionem cessam* and full power to said Paulus Martensz, his heirs and descendants, or those who hereafter may acquire his right and title, to do with and dispose of the said house and lot as he might do with his patrimonial estate and [**837**] effects; promising to protect and free the same against all persons from all trouble, claims and charges as is right, and further, nevermore to do nor allow anything to be done against the same, either with or without law, in any manner, under obligation as provided for it according to law. Done in Albany, dated as above.

Johanna de Hulter
Jan Hend. van Bael
Gerrit van Slichtenhorst

† Johanna de Hulter was the step-daughter of Jeronimus Ebbinck whom her mother, Johanna de Laet, married following the death of her first husband Johannes de Hulter around 1655.

In my presence,
Ludovicus Cobes, secretary.

[CONVEYANCE OF A HOUSE AND LOT BY PAULUS MAERTENSZ TO ARNHOUT CORNELISZ]

Today, the 12th of August 1672, there appeared before me, Ludovicus Cobes, secretary of Albany, etc., in the presence of the honorable lords magistrates of the same court, *Srs.* Jan Hendericxsz van Bael and Gerrart van Slichtenhorst, Paulus Maertensz, who declared that he hereby cedes, conveys and makes over in true, rightful and free ownership to and for the benefit of Arnhout Cornelisz a certain domicile and lot standing and located here in Albany, enclosed and bounded according to the patent and conveyance thereof, which came to him from *Sr.* Jeronimus Ebbinck; and this free and unencumbered, without any charges standing or issuing against the same except for the lord's right, without the grantor making the least claim upon the same anymore, acknowledging that he is fully satisfied and paid for it, the first penny with the last; giving therefore *plenam actionem cessam* and full power to said Aernhout Cornelisz, his heirs and descendants, or those who **[838]** hereafter might acquire his right and title, to do with and dispose of the said house and lot as he might do with his patrimonial estate and effects; promising to protect and free the same against all persons from all trouble, claims and charges as is right, and further, nevermore to do nor allow anything to be done against the same, either with or without law, in any manner, under obligation as provided for it according to law. Done in Albany, dated as above.

Poulis Marten
Jan Hend. van Bael
Gerrit van Slichtenhorst
In my presence,
Ludovicus Cobes, secretary.

[CONVEYANCE OF A HOUSE AND LOT BY AERNHOUT CORNELISZ VIELEN TO JAN CORNELISZ VIJSELAER]

Today, the 13th of August 1672, there appeared before me, Ludovicus Cobes, secretary of Albany, etc., in the presence of the honorable lords magistrates of the same court, *Monsrs.* Jan Hendricx van Bael and Gerrart van Slichtenhorst, Aernhout Cornelisz Vielen, who declared that he hereby cedes, conveys and makes over in true, rightful and free ownership to and for the benefit of Jan Cornelisz Vijselaer a certain house and lot standing and located here in Albany, with everything that is attached by earth and nail, as it is lying within its square enclosure, which came to him from from Jan Koster; further by virtue of the patent and the bill of sale thereof dated the 9th of August 1670, to which here is referred; and this free and unencumbered, without any charge standing or issuing against the same, [**839**] except for the lord's right; without the grantor making the least claim upon the same anymore, acknowledging that he is fully satisfied and paid for it, the first penny with the last; giving therefore *plenam actionem cessam* and full power to said Jan Cornelisz Vijselaer, his heirs and descendants, or those who hereafter may acquire his right and title, to do with and dispose of the said house and lot as he might do with his patrimonial estate and effects; promising to protect and free the same against all persons from all trouble, claims and charges as is right, and further, nevermore to do nor allow anything to be done against the same, either with or without law, in any manner, under obligation as provided for it according to law. Albany, dated as above.

Arnout Cor: Vielen
Jan Hend. van Bael
Gerrit van Slichtenhorst

In my presence,
Ludovicus Cobes, secretary.

[CONVEYANCE OF A HOUSE AND LOT BY GIJSBERT GERRITSZ, ATTORNEY FOR MARIJ GOOSSENS, TO BARENT PIETERSZ *MOLENAER*]

Today, the 23rd of August 1672, there appeared before me, Ludovicus Cobes, secretary of Albany, etc., in the presence of the honorable lords magistrates of the same court, *Monsr.* Jan Hendricxsz van Bael and Gerrart van Slichtenhorst, Gijsbert Gerritsz, attorney for Marij Goossens, who declared that he hereby cedes, conveys and makes over in true, rightful and free ownership to and for the benefit of Barent Pietersz *molenaer* a certain house and lot, as the same is lying within its fence, with everything that is attached by earth and nail, located in the **[840]** colony of Rensselaerswijck next to the premises of said Barent Pietersz; and this free and unencumbered, without any charges standing or issuing against the same, except for the lord's right; without the grantor making the least claim upon the same anymore, acknowledging that he is fully satisfied and paid for it, the first penny with the last; giving therefore *plenam actionem cessam* and full power to said Barent Pietersz, his heirs and descendants, or those who hereafter may acquire his right and title, to do with and dispose of the said house and lot as he might do with his patrimonial estate and effects; promising to protect and free the same against all persons from all trouble, claims and charges as is right, and further, nevermore to do nor allow anything to be done against the same, either with or without law, in any manner, under obligation as provided for it according to law. Albany, dated as above.

The mark of Gijsbert Gerritsz, made with his own hand.
Jan Hend. van Bael
Gerrit van Slichtenhorst

In my presence,
Ludovicus Cobes, secretary.

[844-846] [*blank*][†]

[CONVEYANCE OF A LOT BY CAPTAIN BACKER TO WIJNANT GERRITSZ VAN DER POEL]

[847] Appeared before me, Ludovicus Cobes, secretary of Albany, colony of Rensselaersw. and Schaenhechtede, in the presence of the honorable lords magistrates of the same court, *Monsr*. Rijckart van Rensselaer and *Mr*. Jan Verbeeck, Capt. Backer, who declared that he hereby cedes, conveys and makes over in true, rightful and free ownership to and for the benefit of Wijnant Gerritsz vander Poel a lot no. 6, located at the hill here in Albany; wide in front two rods five inches, in the rear two rods, long on the south six rods eleven feet, to the north six rods and eight feet; adjoins to the north Gerrit Hardenberch, to the east the grantor himself, to the south Jacob Schermerhorn, Van Bael, and Jan Tomasz, and to the west the public street, according to the measurement and survey thereof by the surveyors dated the 5th of May 1668; and this free and unencumbered without any charges standing or issuing against the same, except for the lord's right; without the grantor making the least claim upon the same anymore, acknowledging that he is fully satisfied and paid for it, the first penny with the last; giving therefore *plenam actionem cessam* and full power to said Wijnant Gerritsz, his heirs and descendants, or those who hereafter may acquire his right and title, to do with and dispose of the same as he might do with his patrimonial estate and effects; promising to protect and free the said lot against all persons from all trouble, claims and charges as is right, and further, nevermore to do nor allow anything to be done against the same, either with or without law, in any manner, under obligation as provided for it according to law. Done in Albany, the 16th of March 1669.

---

† Documents [841–843] have been moved to their correct location on pages 437, 438, and 439.

John Baker
RV Rensselaer
Jan Verbeeck

[ACKNOWLEDGMENT OF DEBT BY HENDRICK MEEUS VROOMAN TO TRIJNTIE CLAES]

[**848**] Appeared before me, Ludovicus Cobes, secretary of Albany, colony of Rensselaersw. and Schaenhechtede, in the presence of the honorable lords magistrates of the same court, *Mr.* Jan Verbeeck and *Mr.* Philip Schuijler, Hendrick Meeus Vrooman, farmer, dwelling on the land behind Kinderhoeck, who acknowledged that he is well and truly indebted and in arrears to Trijntie Claesz for the quantity of one hundred and twenty-five schepels of good winter wheat or in sewant, *f*25: for every six schepels to the full sum and its supplement, and on top of that another *f*3 in sewant for goods received to his full content and satisfaction; which aforesaid sums the appearer promises to pay in the manner described hereafter; first, in the coming month of May, three beavers, each of which shall be worth nine guilders; and in the following month of June *f*100: in sewant, and in the following fall one of his largest oxen, to be estimated by impartial persons; especially pledging therefor five roaming hogs and a wagon, and generally his person and estate, moveable and immoveable, present and future, without exception, submitting the same to all laws and judges to recover (if necessary) the payment without cost and damage in due time. Done in Albany the 6th of April 1670.

Heinderick Meessen
Jan Verbeeck
Philip Pietersz Schuijler

In my presence,
Ludovicus Cobes, secretary.

[CONVEYANCE OF SOME PARCELS OF LAND AT THE ESOPUS BY JAN THOMASZ TO THOMAS DE LAVALL]

[849] On the underwritten date appeared before me, Ludovicus Cobes, secretary of Albany, colony of Rensselaerswijck and Schaenechtede, in the presence of the honorable lords magistrates of the same court, *Mr.* Jan Verbeeck and Philip Pietersz Schuijler, Jan Thomasz, former magistrate, who declared that he hereby cedes, conveys and makes over in true, rightful and free ownership to and for the benefit of mister Thomas de Lavall, merchant, his certain claim upon some parcels of land located in the Esopus according to the bill of sale and the patent thereof, to which hereby is referred; and this free and unencumbered without any charges standing or issuing against the same, except for the lord's right; without the grantor making the least claim upon the same anymore, acknowledging that he is fully satisfied and paid for the same, the first penny with the last, through the hands of said lord Lavall; giving therefore *plenam actionem cessam* and full power to said mister Lavall, his heirs and descendants, or those who hereafter may acquire his right and title, to do with the said bill of sale, claim, and patent with its appurtenances thereof, as he might do with his patrimonial estate and effects; promising to defend and warrant the same against whatever may be brought against it, as is right, and further, nevermore to do nor allow anything to be done against the same, either with or without law, in any manner, under obligation according to law. Done in Albany the 30th of April 1670.

Jan Thomasz
Jan Verbeeck
Philip Pietersz Schuijler
In my presence,
Ludovicus Cobes, secretary.

[CONVEYANCE OF SOME PARCELS OF LAND AND BUILDINGS AT THE ESOPUS BY VOLCKERT JANSZ TO THOMAS DE LAVALL]

[850] Appeared before me, Ludovicus Cobes, secretary of Albany, colony of Rensselaerswijck and Schaenechtede, in the presence of the honorable lords magistrates of the same court *Mr.* Jan Verbeeck and Philip Pietersz Schuijler, Volckert Jansz, burgher and inhabitant here, who declared that he hereby cedes, conveys and makes over in true, rightful and free ownership to and for the benefit of mister Thomas de Lavall, merchant at New York, his certain claim upon some parcels of land and the buildings standing thereupon, located at the Esopus according to the patent thereof, granted to the grantor by the right honorable lord governor general Richard Nicolls, to which hereby is referred; and this free and unencumbered without any charges standing or issuing against the same, except for the lord's right; without the grantor making the least claim upon the same anymore, acknowledging that he is fully satisfied and paid for it, the first penny with the last, through the hands of said lord De Lavall; giving therefore *plenam actionem cessam* and full power to said my lord Lavall, his heirs and descendants, or those who hereafter may acquire his right and title, to do with and dispose of the said title to the land, patent and appendances and dependences thereof as he might do with his patrimonial estate and effects; promising to protect and free the same against all persons from all trouble, claims and charges as is right, and further, nevermore to do nor allow anything to be done against the same, either with or without law, in any manner, under obligation according to law. Done in Albany the 3rd of May 1670.

Volckart Jansz

This conveyance is made with the reservation that the grantor shall pay the carpenters, according to the contract, but the food and drink used by the carpenters after the date of this conveyance shall be at the expense of the honorable lord de Laval.

Jan Verbeeck
Philip Pietersz Schuijler
In my presence,
Ludovicus Cobes, secretary.

[851] With the aforesaid conveyance Volckert Jansz promises to deliver to the honorable lord de Laval the materials brought there by the grantor, such as wagon, plows, harrows, and everything he has there. Albany, the 3rd of May 1670.

[GRANT OF A PARCEL OF LAND AT LUBBERDE LANDT BY THE MAGISTRATES TO DIRCK HESSELINGH]

The honorable lords magistrates of Albany, colony of Rensselaersw. and Schaenhechtede, having granted a warrant on two sentences, the one of date the 17th of January 1664, and the other of the 16/26th of January, 1667/8 against Dirck van Schelluijne, former secretary here, and in favor of Jacobus Vis, the same executions as those that have been brought into effect by the sale of a parcel of land located at *Lubberde landt* in the colony of Rensselaerswijck, which belonged to Dirck van Schelluijne; and this at public auction to the highest bidder on date the 26th of October 1668 according to the evidences of the conditions and stipulations thereof, held by *Mr.* Provoost, auctioneer, according to which conditions the buyer was promised letters of decree; and Dirck Hesselingh remained the final bidder and buyer of the said piece of land for the sum of *f*120 in beavers. And as the said Vis, victor, had ordered to pay the said money to *Mr.* Withart or his servant Jan Jansz Bleecker, the said Hesselingh, after the payment was made, requests the said and promised decree, for which their honors grant their warrant and letters of decree and inheritance of the said parcel of land, as they hereby decree and grant him the hereditary rights to said land, in order to do with and dispose of it as he might do with his patrimonial estate and effects *et tanquam actor et procurator in rem suam ac propriam*, promising to free the same from all claims and charges as is right, **[852]** and further, nevermore to do nor allow anything to be done against the same, either with or without law. Given in Albany the 17th of June 1670.

Abram Staas
Jan Verbeeck
In my presence,
Ludovicus Cobes, secretary

[CONVEYANCE OF A LOT BY ROELOF SWARTWOUT TO RYCKIE DARETH]

Appeared before me, Ludovicus Cobes, secretary of Albany, colony of Rensselaerswijck and Schaenhechtede, in the presence of the honorable lords magistrates of the same court, *Mr.* Abraham Staes and *Mr.* Jan Verbeeck, *Mr.* Roeloff Swartwout, dwelling in the Esopus, who declared that he hereby cedes, conveys and makes over in true, rightful and free ownership to and for the benefit of Ryckie Dareth, widow of the late Jan Dareth, dwelling here in Albany, a lot located on the road to the south and to the east of the house of Volckert Jansz, according to the abstract of the conditions of the auction thereof in length and width as the same is lying within its fence, and at present is owned by Sturm vander Zee; and this free and unencumbered without any charges standing or issuing against the same, except for the lord's right; without the grantor making the least claim upon the same anymore, acknowledging that he is fully satisfied and paid for the same, the first penny with the last, through the hands of said Ryckie Dareth; giving therefore *plenam actionem cessam* and full power to said Ryckie Dareth, her heirs and descendants, to do with and dispose of it as she might do with her patrimonial estate and effects; promising to protect and free the same against all persons....[*Remainder of document missing.*]

[CONVEYANCE OF A HOUSE AND LOT BY JAN CLUTE
TO GABRIEL THOMASZ]

[853] Appeared before me, Ludovicus Cobes, secretary of Albany, colony of Rensselaersw. and Schaenhechtede, in the presence of the honorable lords magistrates of the same court, *Mr.* Jan Verbeeck and *Mr.* Abraham Staas, Jan Clute, burgher and inhabitant here, who declared that he hereby cedes, conveys and makes over in true, rightful and free ownership to and for the benefit of *Sr.* Gabriel Thomasz a certain domicile and lot standing here in Albany; and the lot is long on the east side of Evert Luycas five rods seven feet and two inches, on the south side the public road, wide two rods and one foot, on the north side wide two rods, and on the west side Ruth Arentsz, long five rods, one foot and two inches, Rhineland measure; and this by virtue of a patent thereof granted by the right honorable former lord general Nicolls on date of the 24th of May 1667, to which here is referred, except that fifteen feet, which were sold by the grantor to Meijndert Fredericsz, will be taken off of the lot, and which is taken out of the patent; and the same house and lot shall be delivered to him, Gabriel Thomasz, free and unencumbered without any charges standing or issuing against the same, except for the lord's right; without the grantor making the least claim upon the same anymore, acknowledging that he is fully satisfied and paid for the same, the first penny with the last, through the hands of said Gabriel Thomasz; giving therefore *plenam actionem cessam* and full power to said Gabriel Thomasz, his heirs and descendants, or those who hereafter may acquire his right and title, to do with and dispose of the said domicile and lot as he might do with his own patrimonial estate and effects; promising to protect and free the same against all persons... [*remainder missing*]

[FRAGMENT OF A CONVEYANCE FROM ROBERT SANDERS TO POULUS MARTENSZ]

[854] ...and this free and unencumbered without any charges standing or issuing against the same, except for the lord's right; without the grantor making the least claim upon the same anymore, acknowledging that he is fully satisfied and paid for the same, the first penny with the last, through the hands of said Paulus Martensz, giving therefore *plenam actionem cessam* and full power to said Poulus Martensz, his heirs and descendants, or those who hereafter may acquire his right and title, to dispose of the same as he might do with his patrimonial estate and effects; promising to protect and free the said domicile and lot against all persons and to free it from all trouble, claims and charges as is right, and further, nevermore to do nor allow anything to be done against the same either with law or without, in any manner, under obligation as provided for it according to law. Done in Albany the 25th of July 1670.

Robbert Sandersz
Jan Verbeeck
Abram Staas
In my presence,
Ludovicus Cobes secretary

[CONVEYANCE OF A HOUSE, BARN, HAY BARRACK, ORCHARD, AND LAND FROM PIETER MEEUSZ VROMAN TO PHILIP PIETERSZ SCHUIJLER]

[**855**] Today, on date the 25th of August, there appeared before me, Ludovicus Cobes, secretary of Albany, colony of Rensselaersw. and Schaenhechtede, in the presence of the honorable lords magistrates of the same court, *Monsrs*. Jan Hendricxsz van Bael and Gerrart van Slichtenhorst, Pieter Meeusz Vroman, who declared that he hereby cedes, conveys and makes over in true, rightful and free ownership to and for the benefit of *Monsr*. Philip Pietersz Schuijler a certain house, barn and hay barrack, orchard, and three morgens of land as the same is lying within its fence (except for the stone pile); such, standing and located in the colony of Rensselaerswijck by virtue of the bill of sale thereof dated the 22nd of January 1671/72, and the conveyance given to the appearer by *Juffr*. Ebbingh on the 28th of June 1661, to which here is referred, and this free and unencumbered without any charges standing or issuing against the same, except for the lord's right; without the grantor making the least claim upon it anymore, acknowledging that he has been fully satisfied and paid for it the first penny with the last; giving therefore *plenam actionem cessam* and full power to the aforesaid *Monsr*. Philip Schuijler, his heirs and descendants, or those who hereafter may acquire his right and title, to do with and dispose of the said house, barn, hay barrack, orchard, and land as he might do with his patrimonial estate and effects; promising to protect and free the same against all persons from all trouble, claims and charges as is right, and further, nevermore to do nor allow anything to be done against the same, either with or without law, in any manner, under obligation as provided for it according to law. Albany.

Pieter Meesen Vrooman
Jan Hend van Bael
Gerrit van Slichtenhorst
In my presence,
Ludovicus Cobes, secretary.

[CONVEYANCE OF A HOUSE AND LOT FROM HENDRICK KOSTER TO JAN CLUTE]

[856] Today, the 9th of September 1672, there appeared before me, Ludovicus Cobes, secretary of Albany, colony of Rensselaersw. and Schaenhechtede, in the presence of the honorable lords magistrates of the same court, *Monsrs.* Jan Hendricxsz van Bael and Gerrart van Slichtenhorst, Hendrick Koster, who declared that he hereby cedes, conveys and makes over in true, rightful and free ownership to and for the benefit of *Mr.* Jan Clute his house and lot located at the hill here in Albany, to the north Hendrick Rooseboom, to the south the widow of Hendrick Andriessen, east and west the public highway, wide five rods, and long eighteen rods, such as the same has been sold at public auction (on the date of the 7th of September 1672), by virtue of the patent and conveyance thereof, to which is referred here, and this free and unencumbered without any charges standing or issuing against the same, except for the lord's right; without the grantor making the least claim upon it anymore, acknowledging that he has been fully satisfied and paid for it, the first penny with the last; giving therefore *plenam actionem cessam* and full power to the aforesaid *Mr.* Clute, his heirs and descendants, or those who hereafter may acquire his right and title, to do with and dispose of it as he might do with his patrimonial estate and effects; promising to protect and free the same against all persons from all trouble, claims and charges as is right, and further, nevermore to do nor allow anything to be done against the same, either with or without law, in any manner, under obligation as provided for it according to law. Albany, dated as above.

Henderick Koster
Jan Hend van Bael
Gerrit van Slichtenhorst

In my presence,
Ludovicus Cobes, secretary.

[FRAGMENT OF A CONVEYANCE MADE BY GEERTRUIJT VOSBURCH]

[**857**] […..] effects; promising to protect and free the said part of the lot against all persons from all trouble, claims and charges as is right, and further, nevermore to do nor allow anything to be done against the same, either with or without law, in any manner, under obligation as provided for it according to law. Done in Albany, the 11th of August 1670.

The mark of + Geertruijt Vosburch, made with her own hand.
Jan Verbeeck
Philip Pietersz Schuijler
Acknowledged before me,
Ludovicus Cobes, secretary.

[ACKNOWLEDGMENT OF DEBT SANDER LEENDERTSZ GLEN TO ABRAHAM STAES]

On the underwritten date there appeared before me, Ludovicus Cobes, secretary of Albany, colony of Rensselaersw. and Schaenhechtede, in the presence of the honorable lords magistrates of the same court, Sander Leendertsz Glen, former magistrate, dwelling at Schaenhechtede, who acknowledged that he is well and truly indebted to Mr. Abraham Staes for the sum of two hundred and eighty-eight guilders in beavers for the matter of wares and merchandise received to his full content, which aforesaid *f*288 in beavers the appearer promises to pay to *Mr*. Abraham Staas or his order within the time of two years, especially pledging therefor his farm with land, house, barn, and hay barracks located at Schaenhechtede, and moreover, generally his person and estate, moveable and immoveable, present and future, without exception, to recover (if need be), the payment without cost [**858**] or damage. Done in Schaenhechtede the 12th of August 1670.

Sander Lenrsen Glen
Jan Verbeeck
Philip Pietersz Schuijler
In my presence,
Ludovicus Cobes, secretary.

[*In the margin was written*:] Today, the 5th of July, 1687 Maj. Abraham Staas has appeared at the town clerk's office and declared that he has received out of the hands of Catharina, widow of the late Jacob Sanderse Glen, oldest son of [Sander] Leendertse Glen, [full] payment and satisfaction for the ACKNOWLEDGMENT of debt written [on the] opposite [page], which was passed for the benefit of the subscriber on the 12th of August 1670, and therefore he releases all heirs and descendants of said Sander Leendertsz Glenn from all trouble and claims. For the confirmation of which I have hereto set my hand and seal in Albany, dated as above.

Abram Staas
Acknowledged by me, [*seal*]

[ACKNOWLEDGMENT OF DEBT BY SANDER LEENDERTSZ GLEN TO JEREMIAS VAN RENSSELAER AND JACOB SANDERSZ GLEN, ATTORNEYS FOR THE LATE JAN BASTIAENSZ]

[**858**] On the underwritten date there appeared before me, Ludovicus Cobes, secretary of Albany, colony of Rensselaersw. and Schaenhechtede, in the presence of the honorable lords magistrates of the same court, *Mr.* Abraham Staas and Phi[lip Schuijler], Sander Leendertsz Glen, former magistrate, dwelling at Schaenhechtede, who acknowledged that he is well and truly indebted and in arrears to the lord Jeremias van Rensselaer and Jacob Sandersz Glen, attorneys for the masters of the late Jan Bastiaensz, for the sum of *f*6000 in beavers for the matter of wares and merchandise received to his full content, as appears in a promissory note thereof. Which sum of *f*6000 in beavers the appearer promises to pay to the said attorneys or their order, especially pledging thereto his farm, land, house, barn and hay barracks, horses and cattle there, located at Schaenhechtede, and generally his person and estate, moveable and immoveable, present and future, without exception, to recover, (if need be) the payment in due time without cost or damage. Done at Schaenhechtede, the 13th of August 1670.

Sander Lenrsen Glen
In my presence,
Ludovicus Cobes, secretary.

[CONVEYANCE OF A HOUSE AND LOT BY JAN CLUTE TO JAN JANSZ BLEECKER]

[**859**] Today, the 9th of September 1672 there appeared before me, Ludovicus Cobes, secretary of Albany, etc., in the presence of the honorable lords magistrates of the same court, *Monsr.* Jan Hendericx van Bael and Gerrart van Slichtenhorst, *Mr.* Jan Clute, who declared that he hereby cedes, conveys and makes over in true, rightful and free ownership to and for the benefit of Jan Jansz Bleecker his house and lot standing and located here in Albany at the hill, on the west side Helmer Otten the same is long two rods, ten feet and three inches, in front on the public road one rod and 10 feet and 9 inches, wide in the rear one rod and 10 feet and 6 inches, long on the east side three rods, everything Rhineland measure; also a small corner of a lot that adjoins the same lot in the rear, which is wide one rod, 10 feet and 6 inches, and the south end one rod, 9 feet and 2 inches, long east and west 6 feet minus three inches, also Rhineland measure. And this free and unencumbered without any charges standing or issuing against the same, except for the lord's right; without the grantor making the least claim upon it anymore, acknowledging that he is fully satisfied and paid therefor, the first penny with the last, giving therefore *plenam actionem cessam* and full power to said Jan Jansz Bleecker, his heirs and descendants, or those who hereafter may acquire his right and title, to do with and dispose of the said house and lot as he might do with his patrimonial estate and effects; promising to protect and free the same against all persons as is right and further, nevermore to do nor allow anything to be done against the same, either with law or without, under obligation as provided for it according to law. Albany dated as above.

Johanesz Clute
Jan Hend van Bael
Gerrit van Slichtenhorst

[CONVEYANCE OF A LOT BY JAN CLUTE TO HENDRICK LANSINCK AND LUYCAS GERRITSZ]

[860] Today, the 9th of September 1672, there appeared before me, Ludovicus Cobes, secretary of Albany, etc. in the presence of the honorable lords magistrates of the same court, *Monsr.* Jan Hendricxsz van Bael and Gerrart van Slichtenhorst, *Mr.* Jan Clute, who declared that he hereby cedes, conveys and makes over in true, rightful and free ownership to and for the benefit of Hendrick Lansinck and Luijcas Gerritsz a certain lot located at the hill, and the same is wide in front on the street three rods and 1½foot, and in the rear on the east side the same, and on the west two rods and 11 feet, everything Rhineland measure, and this free and unencumbered without any charges standing or issuing against the same, except for the lord's right; without the grantor making the least claim upon the same anymore, acknowledging that he is fully satisfied and paid for the same, the first penny with the last, giving therefore *plenam actionem cessam* and full power to said Hendrick Lansinck and Luijcas Gerritsz, their heirs and descendants, or those who hereafter may acquire their right and title, to do with and dispose of the said lot as they might do with their patrimonial estate and effects; promising to protect and free the same against all persons from all trouble, claims and charges as is right, and further nevermore to do nor allow anything to be done against the same, either with law or without, under obligation as provided for it according to law. Albany dated as above.

Johanes Clute
Jan Hend van Bael
Gerrit van Slichtenhorst

[CONVEYANCE OF A LOT BY JAN CLUTE TO JAN BIJVANCK]

[861] Today, the 9th of September 1672, there appeared before me, Ludovicus Cobes, secretary of Albany, etc. in the presence of the honorable lords magistrates of the same court, *Monsr.* Jan Hendricxsz van Bael and Gerrart van Slichtenhorst, *Mr.* Jan Clute, who declared that he hereby cedes, conveys and makes over in true, rightful and free ownership to and for the benefit of Jan Bijvanck a certain lot located at the hill; is long on the east side next to Hendrick Lansinck two rods and eleven feet, in front on the street 21 feet and 7 inches, in the rear two rods minus half a foot, long on the west side next to Gerret Hardenberch, 34 feet and one inch, everything Rhineland measure; and this free and unencumbered without any charges standing or issuing against the same, except for the lord's right; without the grantor making the least claim upon the same anymore, acknowledging that he is fully satisfied and paid for the same, the first penny with the last, giving therefore *plenam actionem cessam* and full power to said Jan Bijvanck, his heirs and descendants, or those who hereafter may acquire his right and title, to do with and dispose of the said lot as he might do with his patrimonial estate and effects; promising to protect and free the same against all persons from all trouble, claims and charges as is right and further, nevermore to do nor allow anything to be done against the same, either with law or without, in any manner, under obligation as provided for it according to law. Albany, dated as above.

Johanes Clute
Jan Hend van Bael
Gerrit van Slichtenhorst

[CONVEYANCE OF A LOT BY JAN CLUTE TO GERRIT HARDENBERCH]

[862] Today, the 9th of September 1672, there appeared before me, Ludovicus Cobes, secretary of Albany, etc. in the presence of the honorable lords magistrates of the same court, *Mrs*. Jan Hendricxsz van Bael and Gerrart van Slichtenhorst, *Mr*. Jan Clute, who declared that he hereby cedes, conveys and makes over in true, rightful and free ownership to and for the benefit of Gerrit Hardenberch a certain lot located at the hill; long on the east side next to Jan Bijvanck 3[4] feet and one inch Rhineland measure, and wide in front as well as in the back 24 wood feet, on the west side next to Jan Bleecker 32 feet and eight inches Rhineland measure; with another small corner of a lot in the back, the very far end, wide, in front as well as in the back 10 feet

$3\frac{1}{6}$ inch, on the east side long 2 rods, on the west side two rods and two inches; and this free and unencumbered without any charges standing or issuing against the same, except for the lord's right; without the grantor making the least claim upon the same anymore, acknowledging that he is fully satisfied and paid for the same, the first penny with the last, giving therefore *plenam actionem cessam* and full power to said Gerrit Hardenberch, his heirs and descendants, or those who hereafter may acquire his right and title, to do with and dispose of the said lot as he might do with his patrimonial estate and effects; promising to protect and free the same against all persons from all trouble, claims and charges as is right, and further, nevermore to do nor allow anything to be done against the same, either with law or without in any manner, under obligation as provided for it according to law. Albany, dated as above.

Johanes Clute
Jan Hend van Bael
Gerrit van Slichtenhorst

[CONVEYANCE OF A HOUSE AND LOT BY CLAES RIPSEN TO GERRIT THEUNISZ]

[863] Today, the 19th of September 1672, there appeared before me, Ludovicus Cobes, secretary of Albany, etc. in the presence of the honorable lords magistrates of the same court, *Srs*. Jan Hendricxsz van Bael and Gerrart van Slichtenhorst, Claes Ripsen, who declared that he hereby cedes, conveys and makes over in true, rightful and free ownership to and for the benefit of Gerrit Theunisz his certain domicile and lot as it has come to him by conveyance from Marcelis Jansz and Cornelis Wijnkoop, and by virtue of the patent thereof, of date the 6th of June 1667 to which hereby is referred, and this free and unencumbered without any charges standing or issuing against the same, except for the lord's right; without the grantor making the least claim upon the same anymore, acknowledging that he is fully satisfied and paid for it, the first penny with the last, giving therefore *plenam actionem cessam* and full power to said Gerrit Theunisse, his heirs and descendants, or those who hereafter may acquire his right and title, to do with and dispose of the said house and lot as he might do with his patrimonial estate and effects; promising to protect and free the same against all persons from all trouble, claims and charges as is right, and further, nevermore to do nor allow anything to be done against the same, either with law or without in any way, under obligation as provided for it according to law. Albany dated as above.

Claes Ripsen van Dam
Jan Hend van Bael
Gerrit van Slichtenhorst
Acknowledged by me,
Ludovicus Cobes, secretary.

[CONVEYANCE OF A HOUSE AND LOT BY GERRIT THEUNISSEN TO RICCHARD SHISAIR]

[864] Today, the 19th of September 1672, there appeared before me, Ludovicus Cobes, secretary of Albany, etc. in the presence of the honorable lords magistrates of the same court, *Monsr.* Jan Hendricxsz van Bael and Gerrart van Slichtenhorst, Gerrit Teunissen, who declared that he hereby cedes, conveys and makes over in true, rightful and free ownership to and for the benefit of Ricchard Sensair his certain house and lot, which has come to him from Claes Ripsen, and by virtue of the patent thereof to which hereby is referred; and this free and unencumbered without any charges standing or issuing against the same, except for the lord's right; without the grantor making the least claim upon the same anymore, acknowledging that he is fully satisfied and paid for the same, the first penny with the last, giving therefore *plenam actionem cessam* and full power to said Ricchard Sensair, his heirs and descendants, or those who hereafter may acquire his right and title, to do with and dispose of the said house and lot as he might do with his patrimonial estate and effects; promising to protect and free the same against all persons from all trouble, claims and charges as is right, and further, nevermore to do nor allow anything to be done against the same, either with or without law in any manner, under obligation as provided for it according to law. Albany, dated as above.

The mark of Gerrit  Theunisz, made with his own hand.
Jan Hend van Bael
Gerrit van Slichtenhorst
Acknowledged by me,
Ludovicus Cobes, secretary.

[865] [*blank*]

[CONVEYANCE OF A HOUSE, BARN, HAY BARRACKS, GARDEN AND LAND AT SCHAENHECHTEDE BY JURIAEN THEUNISZ TAPPEN TO HERMEN VEDDER]

[866] Today, the 17th of December 1672, there appeared before me, Ludovicus Cobes, secretary of Albany, etc. in the presence of the honorable lords magistrates of the same court, *Monsrs*. Anderies Teller and Adriaen Gerretsen, Juriaen Theunisz Tappen, who declared that he hereby cedes, conveys and makes over in true, rightful and free ownership to and for the benefit of Hermen Vedder a house, barn and hay barracks, and a garden on the land in the rear, together with 12 morgens and 130 rods of land located at Schaenhechtede, being no: 8, bounding and adjoining according to the description of the patent thereof to which here is referred; and this free and unencumbered without any charges standing or issuing against the same, except for the lord's right; without the grantor making the least claim upon the same anymore, acknowledging that he is fully satisfied and paid for the same, the first penny with the last, through the hands of said Hermen Vedder, giving therefore *plenam actionem cessam* and full power to Herman Vedder, his heirs and descendants, or those who hereafter may acquire his right and title, to do with and dispose of the said house, lot, garden and lands as he might do with his patrimonial estate and effects; promising to protect and free the same against all persons from all trouble, claims and charges as is right and further, nevermore to do nor allow anything to be done against the same, either with law or without in any manner, under obligation as provided for it according to law. Albany, dated as above.

Jure Jan Tunsen Tappen
Adriaen Gerretsen
A. Teller
Acknowledged by me,
Ludovicus Cobes, secretary.

[867] [*Endorsement*:] Conveyance for Harme Vedder's farm.

[CONVEYANCE OF A LOT BY PIETER JANSE LOKERMANS
TO JAN ANDRIESE *DE CUIJPER*]

[868] Appeared before me, Ro: Livingston, secretary of Albany, colony of Rensselaerswijck and Schaenhechtede in the presence of the honorable lords *Mr.* Dirck Wessels and *Mr.* Corn. Van Dijck, magistrates of the same court, Pieter Janse Lokermans, who declared that he hereby cedes, conveys and makes over in true, rightful and free ownership to and for the benefit of Jan Andriese *de Cuijper* a certain lot located here in Albany upon which the same Jan Andriese's house is standing; adjoining to the south the lot of Wijnant Gerritse van der Poel, to the north the house of him, grantor, Pr. Lokermans, to the east the public road, and to the west the wagon road; is wide in front on the street twenty wood feet and six inches, and in the rear twenty wood feet; is long to the south and north seven and a half rods, which he, grantor, does by virtue of a patent received from the former governor Richard Nicolls of date the 14th of May 1667, to which here is referred. And this free and unencumbered without any charges standing or issuing against the same, except for the lord's right; without the grantor making the least claim upon the same anymore, acknowledging that he is fully satisfied and paid for the same, the first penny with the last, giving therefore *plenam actionem cessam* and full power to do with and dispose of the same as he might do with his own patrimonial estate and effects; promising nevermore to do nor allow anything to be done against the same, either with law or without, in any way, under obligation as provided for it according to law. Done in Albany, the 3[?] of March 1679.†

Pieter Loockermans
Acknowledged by me,
Rot. Livingston, secretary.

[CONVEYANCE BY RYCKIE STAES TO PIETER SCHUIJLER OF A HOUSE, LOT, AND BARN]

[869] Appeared before me, Ro: Livingston, secretary of Albany, Colony of Rensselaerswijck and Schaenhechtede in the presence of Arnout Corn: Viele and William Parker, Ryckie Staes, wife of Jacob Staes, who declared that she has sold, and [that] Pieter Schuijler has bought her, seller's [house] lot with the barn and everything that is attached by earth and nail, standing and located here in Albany, adjoining to the [north?] the first little kil and Jochem Wessels, to the west the public street, to the south the domicile of Wm. Loveridge, hat maker, and to the east the river; is wide in front on the street nine rods and four rods and nine feet [in the back]; length on the south side thirteen rods, and to the north seventeen rods; from which lot forty feet in width in front on the street has to be deducted for the public street, and twenty feet in the rear; with everything that appertains thereto according to the patent thereof from Gov. R. Nicolls of the year 1667 (except for the lord's right). In addition, the buyer is obliged and promises to pay to said Rijkje Staes or her order, or those who hereafter may acquire his title, the quantity of [one] hundred and fifty good whole merchantable beaver skins, to be paid in two installments, namely, the first installment in next July, a just half, being seventy-five beavers, and the second installment in July 1680 the remaining half; the buyer shall be allowed immediately to accept, possess, and use the said house and lot. The conveyance will

† The gap in dates from 1672 to 1679 is caused by the addition of loose document pages at the end of this volume.

take place at the full satisfaction; in witness of which, they, appearers, have subscribed this in the presence of the aforesaid witnesses. Done in Albany the ... [*not executed*]

Appendix A

Over the years translators of the descriptions of house lots in the Fort Orange Records have been often confronted with the problem of more than one possible interpretation. Different backgrounds of Beverwijck's/ Albany's inhabitants and the confusion resulting from that may have been one of the reasons for some inconsistent use of the terminology—whether people were aware of it or not. Many sellers or buyers, when describing their properties to the recording secretary, probably spoke, or at least were influenced by their own native language or dialect, which easily could have resulted in a description, different from the actual situation.

In [166], for example, the description in the original ...*een tuyn gelegen inde durpe Beverwijck achter de fort Orange belenden ten oosten de tuyn van Pieter Loockermans benoorden de tuyn van Rem Janssen bewesten en besuyden de weg...* places the garden on the west side of the garden of Pieter Loockermans, since the verb *belenden* usually appears with the preposition *aan*. In [356], however unusual, the verb also appears with the preposition *van*, which creates an opposite meaning (*belent ten oosten van Barent van Marle*, meaning: adjoining to the east of Barent van Marle). The words *bewesten* [ ] *de wegh* place the garden on the west side of the road (meaning that both Pieter Loockerman's garden and the road are on the east side). A similar conflict exists in document [670] ...*een tuyn erff gelegen achter tfort Albany bewesten den voorn: Claes Theunisz lanck ses roeden ten suyden breet drye roeden ten oosten een leech erff lanck...* suggesting that the garden is located to the west of Claes Theunisz as well as to the west of an empty lot, but if the preposition *van* would be placed between *oosten* and *erff*, it would be east of the empty lot.

In [232] the description *een huys en erff gelegen inde durpe Beverwijck besuyden Claes Janssen benoorden den transportant beoosten de rievierkant bewesten de gemeene wegh...* could at first sight very well be correct, but knowing that Beverwijck was located on the west side of the river, it would be impossible for the lot concerned to be located *beoosten de rievierkant*, meaning to the east of the river's edge. This may indicate that the other directions should be interpreted differently as well. Examples like these may warn the reader that also elsewhere the words *benoorden*, *besuijden*, *bewesten*, and *beoosten* may not carry the meaning of "to the north of …" or "on the north side" as it is given in the *WNT*. That the secretary was aware of the difference between *besuijden* and *ten suijden* may be shown in document [608]: Of the text …*belent ten noorden Pieter Adriaensz nu Phillip Pietersz Schuyler, ten suyden Adriaen Jansz van Leijden ende oost ende west s'Heeren straete*…the *be*- in both *benoorden* and *besuijden* has been crossed out and replaced with *ten*. It may, however, also have been changed because of the fact that Philip Pietersz Schuijler then was at the lot where previously Pieter Adriaensz was.

Document [422] …*een tuyn gelegen inde voorn: durpe ten westen de rivierkom ten oosten de straet ten suyden Pieter Bronck benoorden meede de straet*… caused an additional problem. Not only does it place both Pieter Bronck and the street to the south of the garden, but it also literally places the river to the west side of it, and suggests that the secretary omitted the preposition *van*, thus making the meaning opposite of what one would understand initially. The same interpretation could count for documents [216b], [341], and [852].

Extracts of those documents with a possibility for more than one interpretation have been placed in the following appendix:

[166] …*een tuyn gelegen inde durpe Beverwijck achter de fort Orange belenden ten oosten de tuyn van Pieter Loockermans benoorden de tuyn van Rem Janssen bewesten en besuyden de weg*…

[194] …*een huys ende erff gelegen inde voorn: durpe belenden benoorden Matthewes Abrahamsen besuyden Wouter de Ramaecker beoosten en bewesten de straet*…

[197] …*een huys ende erff gelegen inde durpe van Beverwijck besuyden den transportant benoorden Pieter Bronck ten westen het geberghte ten oosten de straet*…

[198] …*belendende besuyden Jacob Tyssen vander Heyden en benoorder lambert Albertsen van Neck, oost en west de straet*…

[216a] …*een erf gelegen inde colonie Rencelaerswijck benoorden Henderick Reur besuyden Roelof Swartwout*…

[216b] *...sijn huys gelegen inde fort Orange ten oosten Arent vanden Bergh ten westen Teunis Spitsbergen...*

[219] *...een erff tot een tuyn gelegen ontrent de fort Orange besuyden Luycas Pietersen benoorden een pleyn beoosten de wagenwegh, bewesten d'pleyn...*

[225] *...een huys en erff gelegen inde durpe Beverwijck, voorn: besuyden de derde kil beoosten Jan Martensen benoorden de straet...*

[227] *...een huys en erff gelegen inde durpe Beverwijck besuyden de derde kill beoosten Jan Martensen benoorden de straet...*

[229] *...een tuyn gelegen inde durpe Beverwijck beoosten de wegh ten westen do. Schaets besuyden Annetie Bogardus...*

[230] *...een huys en erff gelegen inde durpe Beverwijck oost west ende noordt een straet, besuyden Gillis Pietersen...*

[231] *...een huys en erff gelegen inde durpe Beverwijck benoorden den transportant besuyden Henderick Gerritsen beoosten de straet bewesten Jacob de brouwer...*

[232] *...een huys en erff gelegen inde durpe Beverwijck besuyden Claes Janssen benoorden den transportant beoosten de rievierkant bewesten de gemeene wegh...*

[233] *...een huys en erff gelegen inde durpe Beverwijck besuyden Claes Janssen benoorden Leendert Philipsen beoosten de rievierkant bewesten de gemeene straet...*

[327] *... belendende besuyden het huijs van Mr Abraham, benoorden het huijs van Claes van Rotterdam..*

[558] *...een stuck claer bouwlant leggende inde Esopus belendende benoorden juffrouw Ebbinghs ende besuyden Jurriaen Westvael...*

[341] *...sijn brouwhuys en voor het woonhuys met het moolenhuys en de paerdestal mitsgaders de waterputt met de erve daerbij gelegen inden*

gemelten durpe van Beverwijck is breet voor aende straet drie roeden een voet en ses duym ten suyden het blockhuys lanck elff roeden acht voeten ten noorden van Leendert Philipsen lanck elf roeden acht voeten…

[397] *...belent besuyden Evert Janssen Wendel noort en west de straet...*

[422] *…een tuyn gelegen inde voorn: durpe ten westen de rivierkom ten oosten de straet ten suyden Pieter Bronck benoorden meede de straet…*

[454] *…een erff tot een tuyn gelegen aende fort Orange voorn: belent ten westen het erff van Jeremias van Renselaer benoorden het erff vanden acceptant…*

[473] *…een huijs en erve gelegen inde durpe Beverwijck benoorden belent David Schuijler ende besuijden Wouter de rademaker …*

[488] *...een huijs ende erff gelegen inden durpe Beverwijck belent benoorden Jan Dareth ende besuyden Pieter Loockemans...*

[489] *…een huys ende erff gelegen inden durpe van Beverwijck, belendt oost ende west ende besuyden sHeeren wegh benoorden het huys van Gillis Pietersz…*

[493] *…een tuyn gelegen inden durpe Beverwijck, ontrent de fortresse Orange, belent achter de heer Renselaer ten suyden vande erffgenamen van Annetie Bogardus ten oosten vande wegh ende ten noorden den acceptant…*

[504] *…een huys ende erff gelegen inden durpe van Beverwijck aent geberghte belent benoorden Henderick Rosenboom besuyden de weduwe van Henderick Anderissen, oost ende west s'Heeren wegh…*

[506] *…sijn aenpart vant huys en erff…gelegen inden dorpe Beverwijck voornt: aent geberghte belent benoorden Henderick Roosenboom ende besuyden de weduwe van Henderick Anderiessen, oost ende west s'Heeren wegh…*

[511] *...een huys ende erff gelegen inden dorpe Albany aent geberghte palen*[*de*] *besuyden Jacob Schermerhoorn, benoorden ende beoosten de wegh bewesten het geberghte...*

[608] *...belent ten noorden Pieter Adriaensz nu Phillip Pietersz Schuyler, ten suyden Adriaen Jansz van Leyden ende oost ende west s'Heeren straete...*

[610] *...seecker erff tot een thuyn bij lotinge No 18 paelende besuyden Pieter Hartgers benoorden en beoosten s'Heeren wech ende bewesten Jacob de brouwer...*

[611] *...seeckere des transportants huysinge ende erve soo hem aengecomen is van Andries Herbertsz Constapel (sijnde t huys opt erff bij den transportant selffs doen timmeren) staende ende gelegen alhier in Albany streckende vande voorsz constapels poort aff tot de heyning van Trijn Claesz ende voorts soot selve in sijn heyninge en bepaelinge is...*

[650] *...beneden de wech twee roe acht voet en een halff, beoosten de wech drye roe, besuijden een roe elff voet, en bewesten twee roe seven voet...*

[670] *...een tuyn erff gelegen achter tfort Albany bewesten den voorn: Claes Theunisz lanck ses roeden ten suyden breet drye roeden ten oosten een leech erff lanck...*

[751] *...erve gelegen bewesten de rivier tusschen Hendrick Reur ende hem, Sweer Theunisz...*

[758] *...welck* [voorsz] *huys ende erve belent is benoorden het conincx huys ende besuyden het huys van Jacob Joosten...*

[767] *...seecker huys ende erve...belendende benoorden het dwarshuys, ende besuyden het huys van Paulus Martensen...*

[778] *...een huys ende erve gelegen alhier in Albany aende suydtsijde van Pieter Hartgras ten westen de eerst kil, aende noortsijde de groote straet...*

[782], [798] *...belendende besuijden het lant van Hilleken Broncx ende sijn begin neemende vande steenen kil streckende suijden lancx het Katskilsche pat...*

[805] *...seecker erff gelegen achter de Kinderhoeck bewesten de kil....*[ ] *noch een parcel lants mede aldaer beoosten Jan Martens, bewesten de kil...*

[806] *...seecker lot erff* [...] *bewesten de kil besuijden Jacob Martensz, beoosten Jan Martensz....*

[808] *...seeckere parceele landts gelegen achter Kinderhoeck belent ten suyden Dierck de Sweed ten westen Jacob Martensz ende kil, beoosten een kleyn killetie scheydende met het landt van Andries Hansz...*

[819] *...welck voorsz huys ende erve belent is benoorden het conincx huys, ende besuyden het huys van Jacob Joosten...*

830] *...een seeckere erve besuijden Wijnant Gerretse benoorden Jochum Backer...*

[852] *...een erff gelegen aenden wech ten suijden ende beoosten het huijs van Volckert Jansz...*

Glossary

backer	baker
barquier	skipper of a bark— a two-masted, single-decked, round-sterned, vessel having no superstructures, ranging in size from 12 to 100 tons, rigged with two or more square sails. The largest barks often carried a third mast rigged with a lateen mizzen sail. Noted for its practicality and versatility, skillful skippers were able to sail barks in inland waterways, coastal channels and open seas.
beaver	used as a monetary standard equal to 8 guiders
bijeenwoninge	literally a 'living together'; a village or community
boer	farmer
bouwman	farmer
broer	brother
brouwer	brewer
burgher	a class of citizenship in the community
chirurgijn	surgeon; the profession involved more rigorous training, (usually four years) than a *barbier*
cleermaker	tailor
colony	Rensselaerswijck, usually called the colony or colonie
commissary	a position appointed by the colonial council on Manhattan to oversee the WIC trading operations at posts such as Fort Orange and to serve as a commander of the garrison
constapel	non–commissioned officer in charge of ordnance

Croaet/Crawaet	Croatian: name develops into cravat (necktie) after the uniform neckgear of Croatian soldiers in the Thirty Years' War
cuyper	cooper
daelder	equivalent of one and a half guilders
de Paep	the pope
Dolle	mad
Dominee	minister of the Reformed Church.
Dommelaer	drowsy
dosijnties	a kind of woolen cloth or kersey
–dr.	daughter of, or the feminine equivalent (*dochter*) of the masculine marker *–sz* (son of); although the masculine is commonly used for both genders
glaesemaecker	glazier
Goyer	likely a settler from *Het Gooi*, a district along the southern coast of the *Ijsselmeer* in the province of Utrecht
Greenen Bosch	pine woods; misinterpreted by the English in several placenames as Green Bush
guilder	monetary unit of the Netherlands, consisting of twenty *stuivers*
guyt	rogue
Halve Maen	*Half Moon*; the name of the East India Company's ship and shoreline in the shape of a crescent just north of Beverwijck on the west side of the Hudson River
herbergier	tavernkeeper

Hr.	abbreviation for *Heer* or lord; a title of high respect
Iersman	Irishman
Juffr.	*Juffrouw*, meaning madam or lady
karreman	cartman or carter
kistemaker	cabinetmaker
kleermaker	tailor
kleijn	little, small
klootdraeyer	bowl turner
kuyper/kuijper	*see* ***cuyper***
la[de]macker	gunstock maker
looper	runner; courier for the court
maecker	maker; someone who works with or shapes metal
mael boer	crazy farmer; also spelled *malle*
magistrate	local official of the court with executive, legislative and judicial authority; selected by the director general and council on Manhattan from a double list submitted by the sitting magistrates
met de baert	with the beard; nick name, also used by the bearded man's wife
metselaer	mason
molenaer	miller
Monsieur	mister; French title of respect (not as strong as *Heer*) often reduced to *Sieur* or *Sr.*, and *Monsr.*
Mr.	*meester*, a title of respect for a *schoolmeester* (schoolmaster) or short for *heelmeester* (barber-surgeon)

Noorman Norseman or Norwegian

pannebacker pantile maker

patria Latin for fatherland which the Dutch use frequently when referring to the homeland

ra[e]demaeker wheelwright; also spelled *ramaker*

roothaer red head

Scheel/Scheelighe squinty-eyed

schepen *see* **magistrate**

schoenmacker shoemaker

Schornsteen [*veger*] chimney sweep

schout an appointed law enforcement officer acting as both sheriff and prosecuting attorney

seyllemaker sail maker

Sinneken used by the Dutch to identify any of the four Iroquois tribes west of the Mohawks

smit blacksmith

snijder tailor

Sogemaecklijk nice and easy

Sr. *see* ***Monsieur***

stuivers *see* guilders

Sweed Swede

timmerman carpenter

Wandelaer walker or stroller

Index

FORT ORANGE RECORDS, 1654–1679

was composed in Times Roman on a Pentium D
by New Netherland Project;
printed by sheet-fed offset on 50-pound, acid-free House Natural Smooth
and Smyth-sewn and bound over binder's boards in Arrestox B
by Sheridan Books, Inc.;
and published by

SYRACUSE UNIVERSITY PRESS
SYRACUSE, NEW YORK 13244-5160